Perception
and
Experience

PERCEPTION AND PERCEPTUAL DEVELOPMENT
A Critical Review Series

Series Editors:
Herbert L. Pick, Jr.
University of Minnesota, Minneapolis, Minnesota
and
Richard D. Walk
George Washington University, Washington, D.C.

Volume 1   **Perception and Experience**
Edited by Richard D. Walk and Herbert L. Pick, Jr.

A Continuation Order Plan is available for this series. A continuation order will bring delivery of each new volume immediately upon publication. Volumes are billed only upon actual shipment. For further information please contact the publisher.

Perception and Experience

Edited by
RICHARD D. WALK
George Washington University
Washington, D.C.

and
HERBERT L. PICK, JR.
University of Minnesota
Minneapolis, Minnesota

Plenum Press · **New York and London**

Library of Congress Cataloging in Publication Data

Main entry under title:

Perception and experience.

(Perception and perceptual development; v. 1)
Includes bibliographies and index.
1. Perception. 2. Experience. I. Walk, Richard D. II. Pick, Herbert L. III. Series.
[DNLM: 1. Perception. W1 PE78GM v. 1/BF311 P428]
BF311.P349   153.7   77-19129
ISBN 0-306-34381-9

10-04-78

© 1978 Plenum Press, New York
A Division of Plenum Publishing Corporation
227 West 17th Street, New York, N.Y. 10011

Printed in the United States of America

Contributors

Edward P. Berlá, Special Education Unit, School of Education, University of Louisville, Louisville, Kentucky

William Bevan, Department of Psychology, Duke University, Durham, North Carolina

Peter D. Eimas, Walter S. Hunter Laboratory of Psychology, Brown University, Providence, Rhode Island

Emerson Foulke, Perceptual Alternatives Laboratory, University of Louisville, Louisville, Kentucky

Susan Gaylord, Department of Psychology, Duke University, Durham, North Carolina

Margaret A. Hagen, Department of Psychology, Boston University, Boston, Massachusetts

I. P. Howard, Department of Psychology, York University, Toronto, Ontario, Canada

James J. Jenkins, Center for Research in Human Learning, University of Minnesota, Minneapolis, Minnesota

Richard Johnson, U.S. Army Research Institute for the Behavioral and Social Sciences, Alexandria, Virginia

Rebecca K. Jones, Department of Psychology, University of Edinburgh, Edinburgh, Scotland

Masakazu Konishi, Division of Biology, California Institute of Technology, Pasadena, California

Joanne L. Miller, Department of Psychology, Northeastern University, Boston, Massachusetts

Donald E. Mitchell, Psychology Department, Dalhousie University, Halifax, Nova Scotia, Canada

Herbert L. Pick, Jr., Center for Research in Human Learning, University of Minnesota, Minneapolis, Minnesota

H. N. Reynolds, Department of Psychology, Gallaudet College, Washington, D.C.

Lawrence A. Rothblat, Department of Psychology, George Washington University, Washington, D.C.

Michael L. Schwartz, Department of Psychology, George Washington University, Washington, D.C.

Winifred Strange, Center for Research in Human Learning, University of Minnesota, Minneapolis, Minnesota

Louise S. Tighe, Department of Psychology, Dartmouth College, Hanover, New Hampshire

Thomas J. Tighe, Department of Psychology, Dartmouth College, Hanover, New Hampshire

John Uhlarik, Department of Psychology, Kansas State University, Manhattan, Kansas

Richard D. Walk, Department of Psychology, George Washington University, Washington, D.C.

Preface

In recent years, significant, indeed dramatic, advances have occurred in the study of perception. These have been made possible by, and, in fact, include methodological advances such as the development of signal detection theory and the application of linear systems analysis to auditory and visual perception. They are reflected in an interest in the study of ecologically valid perceptual problems, e.g., control of locomotion, speech perception, reading, perceptual-motor coordination, and perception of events. At the same time, exciting new insights have been gained to some of the classical problems of perception—stereoscopic vision, color vision, attention, position constancy, to mention a few. A broad, comparative approach to perception has also been taken. This approach, which includes the detailed study of human infant perception as well as cross-cultural and cross-species investigations, has given us a very broad perspective of the perceptual process.

In this context, the present volume inaugurates a new series entitled "Perception and Perceptual Development: A Critical Review Series." The editors are particularly gratified by the enthusiastic support for their ideas by Seymour Weingarten of Plenum Press. He and the editorial staff of Plenum Press have been of immense help in initiating the series as well as helping with the details of this first volume.

Grateful acknowledgment is also due to Kathleen Casey of the Center for Research in Human Learning of the University of Minnesota for secretarial help, to David Walk for editorial assistance, and to David Miller, Jacqueline Samuel, and Michael Schwartz of the Psychology Department of George Washington University. Preparation of this book was supported by grants from the National Institute of Child Health and Human Development (HD–01136) and the National Science Foundation (BNS 75–03816) to the Center for Research in Human Learning, and from the National Institute of Mental Health (MH–25864) to George Washington University.

R.D.W.
H.L.P.

Contents

3 · Depth Perception and Experience
Richard D. Walk

4 · Auditory Environment and Vocal Development in Birds
Masakazu Konishi

PART II · Effects of Prolonged Experience on Human Perception

5 · Role of Linguistic Experience in the Perception of Speech
Winifred Strange and James J. Jenkins

6 · Cultural Effects on Pictorial Perception: How Many Words Is One Picture Really Worth?
Margaret A. Hagen and Rebecca K. Jónes

7 · Visual Impairment and the Development of Perceptual Ability
Emerson Foulke and Edward P. Berlá

8 · Perceptual Effects of Deafness
H. N. Reynolds

11 · Development of Form Perception in Repeated Brief Exposures to Visual Stimuli
John Uhlarik and Richard Johnson

12 · Stimuli, the Perceiver, and Perception
William Bevan and Susan Gaylord

13 · A Perceptual View of Conceptual Development
Thomas J. Tighe and Louise S. Tighe

Introduction

Psychology has always been interested in the effects of experience on behavior. In relation to perception, this interest was manifest in the classical positions of Locke and Berkeley and Mr. Molyneux's problem (see Chapter 2 by Mitchell) as well as in Helmholtz's empiricist point of view. In recent years this long-standing interest has led to exciting research on the effects of experience on perception. Among the people very influential in bringing these developments to a head were Donald Hebb and Eleanor and James Gibson. Hebb's book, *The Organization of Behavior* (1949), helped show that the old dichotomy of nature vs. nurture should yield to the notion that there might be a little of both. Our own indebtedness is particularly to the Gibsons and their role in defining the field of perceptual learning. Let us begin by commenting briefly on these two general contributions.

In 1955 James and Eleanor Gibson published their seminal paper, "Perceptual Learning: Differentiation or Enrichment" (Gibson and Gibson, 1955a). They argued that perceptual learning was not a process of traditional associative learning. Instead, they took the position that perceptual learning was a process of differentiation of the stimulus, a process whereby the organism learned to make finer and finer discriminations with respect to the stimulus, and not what they termed "enrichment" or a process of acquiring richer and richer associations to the stimulus. For their own position, they wrote, the organism differentiates more and more properties of the stimulus (later they would term these the "distinctive features" and "invariant properties" of the stimulus). They felt that the other, the associationistic position, ignored the stimulus and emphasized the associations that were formed with it.

A lively controversy arose between Postman (1955) and the Gibsons (1955b). The details of this exchange need not be described. Postman summed up his argument by writing, "The case for the associationistic position has been reaffirmed, and the adequacy of the specificity formulation has been questioned" (Postman, 1955, p. 446). The Gibsons wrote, "He says the organism has perceived the meaning of a stimulus 'when it has learned to make the appropriate response' (p. 445). We would say *when it has learned to identify the stimulus relative to all possible stimuli"* (Gibson and Gibson, 1955*b*, p. 450). For the Postman position the stimulus seems relatively unimportant, and the focus is on the response to it; for the Gibsons the focus is always on the stimulus.

What has happened in the more than 20 years since this exchange? Perceptual learning has carved out a field that is relatively independent of traditional associationistic learning. By its research the field has shown that it should not be considered part of the traditional study of learning. (Chapter 13 by T. J. and L. S. Tighe represents one example of research on perceptual learning tracing its roots back to the issues raised by the Gibsons and Postman.)

Much of the basic research on perceptual learning has been performed by Eleanor Gibson and her colleagues. The most influential book on the topic is Eleanor Gibson's *Principles of Perceptual Learning and Development* (1969). Here she summarizes her own theoretical position and the other major theoretical positions in perceptual learning. She also reviews the research in perceptual learning to that date, an impressive mine of information that is well written and superbly organized. It should be read by anyone interested in an overview of the field. A more recent book, *The Psychology of Reading* by Eleanor Gibson and Harry Levin, published in 1975, is an intensive treatment of the topic of reading with a heavy emphasis on perceptual learning. It is too soon to gauge its influence, but we would predict that it will be an indispensable source for psychologists and educationalists interested in reading.

The modern approach to the "nature-nurture" issue for perception was begun by Donald Hebb. In his book, *The Organization of Behavior* (1949), Hebb examined a considerable amount of research, especially comparative research, bearing on the effects of early experience on perception. He also reviewed a number of clinical cases reported by von Senden (1932, 1960). These were cases of individuals, blind from birth, who had vision partially restored by removal of cataracts. Hebb concluded that some aspects of perception were innate while others were learned. He felt in particular that figure-ground organization was unlearned while form or pattern perception was learned. Hebb's book helped to trigger a vast increase in research on perceptual development and learning with both humans and animals. The "either-or" aspect of the nature-nurture controversy was defused, but the heredity-environment issue and offshoots from it still dominate much of the research on perceptual learning.

The current view is that perception is partly innate and partly learned. This seems like a simple, safe position, but the determination of what is learned, what is innate, and how the two interact is very difficult. Maturation is entwined with learning. For example, is Hebb's statement that figure-ground perception is unlearned and pattern perception learned tenable today? Salapatek (1975), in an extensive chapter on form perception of infants, relates changes in pattern perception to age. But are these due to learning or to maturation? Salapatek concludes, in particular, that after 2 months of age the human infant pays attention to features of the visual pattern that might be called "form." But whether maturation or learning is responsible for this shift cannot be ascertained.

The present volume has a number of chapters relevant to the nature-nurture issue. All the chapters of Part I are relevant. Part I contains chapters on the effects of early environment on the brain and visual behavior by Rothblat and Schwartz, on the development of perceptual abilities by Mitchell, on the role of experience in depth perception by Walk, and on birdsong learning by Konishi. Later chapters on language by Strange and Jenkins and on picture perception by Hagen and Jones are also relevant to the nature-nurture issue. Anyone who reads these chapters will approach this issue with a new sophistication, but a simple answer to the question of what is learned and what is innate will not be forthcoming.

Does a psychological interest in the nature-nurture issue as related to perception have any consequences? Or is it a point for scholars to argue, most appropriate for what William James called the language of the den, good for polite conversation after dinner over coffee and sherry? Actually, in investigating what is learned and what is innate we are also investigating plasticity, the extent to which the organism adapts to the environment, the most appropriate period for plasticity, if there is any, and its permanence. The consequences of the study of early perceptual learning reach from the nursery into the school and thence to later life.

The notion of sensitive or critical period refers to the most appropriate period of time for plasticity. Is there a specific time when a particular kind of experience is necessary for the development of some behavior? How broad or narrow is this window of time? The existence and nature of such periods constitute a general question that applies to many of the chapters in this volume. The importance of early experience, or experience at a particular time in the life history of the organism, is well documented for birdsongs (see Chapter 4 by Konishi) and for binocular vision (see Chapter 1 by Rothblat and Schwartz and Chapter 2 by Mitchell). For example, in order to produce normal songs, some birds must hear the appropriate model for their species at a particular time well before they actually produce birdsongs themselves. Another example is that a cat is likely to have deficient binocular vision if it is subjected to abnormal visual stimulation to one eye (such as having the eyelids sewn shut) for even brief periods during a sensitive period in the first 4–14 weeks of life. As Mitchell points out, a similar sensitive period also exists for human visual development, although the time constraints are different.

The concept of sensitive period is particularly relevant for language learning (see Chapter 5 by Strange and Jenkins), and in a general way it may fit some of the data discussed by Hagen and Jones (Chapter 6) on cross-cultural studies of picture perception. The critical period does not seem to be very applicable in understanding the results of cross-cultural studies of susceptibility to visual illusions (Pick and Pick, in press). Similarly, the study of depth perception finds influences of experience on the discrimination of depth but little evidence, at least as yet, that these differences are dependent on a particular period in early life.

Can we be more precise about the nature of a critical or sensitive period? What exactly does this concept refer to? It means a time in the life of the organism when stimulation of a particular type is needed. Without that stimulation, the organism lacks behavior appropriate for its species. The term is particularly applicable to "imprinting," the time when a precocial bird, such as a chick or a duck, must be exposed to a motherlike object. Unless exposed during the first few days of life, the bird does not follow its mother and hence is exposed to danger and to starvation. There may also be consequences to later development of social behavior. To determine whether there really is a sensitive period requires appropriate experimental controls. For example, kittens with eyes sutured during the second month of life have to be compared to kittens whose eyes were sutured shut at other comparable time periods, say the sixth or seventh month of life. Since the abnormal behavior is present only in the early-sutured kitten, we may conclude that that period is particularly important, that it is a sensitive or critical period. Much of the research on early experience, e.g., on depth perception, has not looked at sensitive periods; the research has demonstrated an influence of experience without showing the time constraints on such experience. The reader who is interested in early or sensitive periods must make sure that the research is adequately controlled to demonstrate such periods.

Are all sensitive or critical periods the same? Most assuredly not. They may differ in time of occurrence across species. Thus the sensitive periods for binocular vision are different for kitten, monkey, and man (see Chapter 2 by Mitchell). They may differ between sense modalities within a species or for different functions within the same modality. On the other hand, Rothblat and Schwartz (Chapter 1) describe a critical period of 4–14 weeks in the development of both binocularity and sensitivity to lines of specific orientation.

Given that experience does have an effect on perception with or without a critical period, what biological function is being served? Why should there be plasticity or perceptual learning at all? One general answer might point to the survival value of having the organism adapt to the environment. The usefulness of this answer, which one presumes is generally true, is limited because species differ in perceptual learning and a given species appears to be susceptible to perceptual learning for some aspects of the environment and not for others. The chick that must follow its mother within the first 48 hr after birth does not have a sensitive binocular system like the kitten does, and the vocal behavior of the chick is not dependent on stimulation from its own species, as is that of the song sparrow. Thus the general answer of survival value must be carefully related to the environmental demands on and the capabilities of each species. The reader may wish to keep this issue in mind in reading the chapters of this volume.

A second hypothesis related to biological function is that the "higher" organism is more capable of perceptual learning than is the lower organism. By this hypothesis, the superiority of perceptual learning in man is just one more manifestation of man's more complex brain with its capacity for learning. This hypothesis can perhaps be traced to work on limb and muscle transplants where amphibians were found to be unable to recoordinate new connections while humans could (Weiss, 1941). For perception, the early research most relevant to the hypothesis is the work on adaptation to distorted visual stimulation. Humans adapt to prismatic displacement almost immediately while originally it was thought that chicks adapt very little. The demonstration that the chick is capable of some perceptual learning to prismatic displacement (Rossi, 1968) weakens the data base of this hypothesis, but one might still entertain it, stating that humans are *relatively* more plastic than chicks. In order to be viable this hypothesis of differences in relative plasticity in higher and lower organisms will have to be much more systematically studied. Although very general, it does have the virtue of trying to make some sense out of differences in plasticity.

To understand the meaning of plasticity and perceptual learning, to answer the question "why" we need to look at broader aspects of behavior than is customary for psychologists to do, requires considerations that are more in the ethological than in the psychological vein. In the long run we must look also at the role of perceptual learning in the life history of the organism. This will enrich our research and make it more ecologically relevant.

A final general issue that is raised by the chapters in this volume concerns the similarity of short- and long-term experience. One would like to be able to model the effects of long-term experience with experimental manipulations of short-term experience. But to what extent is it possible to equate the differences in perception dependent on experience in a one-hour (or even a one-week) laboratory session with differences that appear to depend on the life history of the organism? This is a difficult question to answer, but let us at least try to raise some relevant points.

First of all there is a traditional aspect that concerns the relation between duration of experience and time of occurrence of experience. Life history experiences described in a number of the chapters in this volume tend to be prolonged. However, this is not necessary. As noted above, some important life history experiences must occur during relatively early critical periods. On the other hand, the short-term experimental experiences typically provided to human subjects can be extended, but their effects generally reach asymptotic levels quite quickly. These manipulations are usually conducted with adults, and it is possible that similar experiments conducted with children or babies would show more flexibility and more persistence. This in fact might be the essential difference between some of the rearing experiments discussed in the chapters by Rothblat and Schwartz and by Mitchell and some of the experiments on selective adaptation in the chapter by Eimas and Miller. In the rearing experiments, kittens were raised in environments consisting only of stripes of a particular orientation while in the selective adaptation experiments adult humans were exposed for several minutes to lines of a specific orientation.

The aspect of persistence is closely tied to that of reversibility. Are the effects of life history experiences more persistent and less reversible than the effects of short-term experience? The general results would suggest yes. For example, the reader of Strange and Jenkins's chapter will learn that people raised in one linguistic environment find it almost impossible to learn to perceive certain kinds of phonetic distinctions used in other languages. Conversely, Eimas and Miller indicate that many selective adaptation effects are short-lasting. However, these general results are not without exceptions. On the one hand, linguists do learn to hear distinctions not phonetically relevant in their own language. (Are there individual differences which account for this ability, or are there particular types of training?) On the other hand, Eimas and Miller point out that some of the selective adaptation effects are very persistent (although so far none has been reported as irreversible).

Finally the type of experience itself varies in studies of short- and long-term experience on *human* perception. The long-term experience variable tends to be of a very general nature—linguistic environment (Strange and Jenkins), presence or absence of exposure to pictures (Hagen and Jones), presence or absence of visual stimulation (Foulke and Berlá), presence or absence of auditory stimulation (Reynolds). The studies of short-term experience are very specific—selective adaptation to very particular stimulation (Eimas and Miller), exposure to brief repetitions of a specific stimulus (Uhlarik and Johnson). With respect to the type of experiential variable involved, the long-term experience studies with animals are a better analogue to the short-term human experiments than are the long-term experience studies with humans.

Many interesting areas for perception and experience must, of necessity, be omitted from this book. We would have liked to have had a description of some of the research on visual illusions and a discussion of the perceptual factors related to a skill like reading. The child develops skills in understanding music from experience, a topic now beginning to be explored in research (see *The Journal of Research in Music Education*). Psychologists have rediscovered the area of motor skills—think of the long-term perceptual effects on the child who studies ballet, tennis, or horseback riding from an early age. Taste is another interesting topic. Cultural taste preferences must have some pervasive effects and the indiscriminate junk-food addict and the fastidious gourmet surely must have something to tell us of perceptual experience. Some readers may remember that a chocolate malted milk that used to taste like nectar now is sickly sweet enough to turn the stomach. What is responsible for such changes? Is it only bodily needs or is it some other kind of perceptual learning?

This book is divided into three parts, one on comparative studies of perception and experience, a second on the effects of prolonged experience on human perception, and a third on the effects of short-term experience on human perception.

In Part I on comparative studies, research, primarily research with animals, is presented, but it includes some human research that is directly related to the animal research. Rothblat and Schwartz (Chapter 1) discuss the effects of special environments on the brain and visual behavior. Their discussion is concerned primarily with kittens and with rats. In Chapter 2, Mitchell carries on the theme from the first chapter with a consideration of special environmental conditions for early animal and human experience. The effects of the blocking of vision by suturing the eyes or experimental surgical strabismus with cats, for example, are related to human findings where one eye was temporarily shut, through injury, or where deviating eyes were corrected at various intervals after birth. In Chapter 3, Walk discusses the nature-nurture question and the role of experience in depth perception. Konishi, in Chapter 4, shows that some species of birds cannot develop normal birdsongs without an appropriate early auditory environment.

Part II on prolonged experience related to human perception discusses natural long-term environmental modifications. Strange and Jenkins (Chapter 5) show that the early language environment can alter the perception of speech sounds. Hagen and Jones (Chapter 6) discuss, by reviewing cross-cultural research, the controversy over whether one learns to see pictures or sees them without special training. Researchers have found individuals in other cultures with little exposure to Western pictures. How well can they interpret our pictures? Two special naturally deprived human populations are the blind and the deaf. Foulke and Berlá (Chapter 7) describe the effects of the lack of visual experience on perception by the blind, and Reynolds (Chapter 8) discusses the perceptual effects of deafness.

Part III focuses on more experimentally controlled short-term experience on perception. Howard (Chapter 9) describes some issues concerning the effects of optical distortions on perception. Eimas and Miller (Chapter 10) describe ways in which the use of the selective adaptation experiment can yield information about the basic organization of auditory and visual perception. The microgenesis of perception, the way perception develops for the normal adult when the stimulus is presented for brief, repeated exposures, is explored by Uhlarik and Johnson in Chapter 11. In their chapter on the relation of the stimulus, the perceiver, and perception, Bevan and Gaylord (Chapter 12) describe the contributions of adaptation-level theory to the study of perception. In the last chapter, Chapter 13, Thomas and Louise Tighe describe their research on discrimination learning with children and show the relation between perceptual experience and how the stimulus in a learning situation is analyzed.

These chapters, as we mentioned previously, describe but a small portion of a very active field. We think that they are a good representative sample of the research on perception and experience, and we hope our reader will experience as much excitement with these contributions as we have. We introduce each part with a discussion of some of the pertinent issues.

References

Cohen, L. B., and Salapatek, P. (Eds.) *Infant perception: From sensation to cognition.* 2 vols. New York: Academic Press, 1975.

Gibson, E. J. *Principles of perceptual learning and development.* New York: Appleton-Century-Crofts, 1969.

Gibson, E. J., and Levin, H. *The psychology of reading.* Cambridge, Mass.: MIT Press, 1975.

Gibson, J. J., and Gibson, E. J. Perceptual learning: Differentiation or enrichment? *Psychological Review*, 1955a, *62*, 32–41.

Gibson, J. J., and Gibson, E. J. What is learned in perceptual learning? A reply to Professor Postman. *Psychological Review*, 1955b, *62*, 447–450.

Hebb, D. O. *The organization of behavior.* New York: Wiley, 1949.

Pick, A. D., and Pick, H. L., Jr. Culture and perception. In E. C. Carterette and M. P. Friedman (Eds.), *Handbook of perception.* New York: Academic Press, in press.

Postman, L. Association theory and perceptual learning. *Psychological Review*, 1955, *62*, 438–446.

Rossi, P. J. Adaptation and negative aftereffect to lateral optical displacement in newly hatched chicks. *Science*, 1968, *160*, 430–432.

Salapatek, P. Pattern perception in early infancy. In L. B. Cohen and P. Salapatek (Eds.), *Infant perception: From sensation to cognition.* Vol. 1: *Basic visual processes.* New York: Academic Press, 1975, pp. 133–248.

von Senden, M. *Raum- und Gestaltauffassung bei operierten Blindgeborenen vor und nach der Operation.* Leipzig: Barth, 1932.

von Senden, M. *Space and sight: The perception of space and shape in the cogenitally blind before and after operation.* Translated by P. Heath. London: Methuen, 1960.

Weiss, P. Self differentiation of the basic patterns of coordination. *Comparative Psychology Monographs*, 1941, *17*, No. 4.

PART I

Comparative Studies of Effects of Experience on Perception

Introduction

The emphasis of this part of the book is on the relation of studies with animals to problems of perceptual modification. Each individual chapter has its own focus. Both the chapter by Rothblat and Schwartz and the one by Mitchell concentrate on the effect of early experience on the visual system. Rothblat and Schwartz deal exclusively with animal studies and describe the exciting research initiated by Hubel and Wiesel in which "feature detectors" that seemed to be congruent with properties of the visual environment were discovered in the visual cortex of kittens. The Hubel and Wiesel research and the research that followed it have implications for many topics of perception and experience: the nature-nurture question, the importance of the method of deprivation for studying the role of experience in perception, and the existence of sensitive and critical periods for perception. This chapter is a good starting point for those interested in understanding modern advances in the physiology of the visual system and in the relation between the physiological findings and behavior. While Mitchell's chapter first concentrates on animal studies, it quickly shifts to human studies. The research on "sensitive periods" with cats which found that interference with binocular vision can have harmful effects helped to inspire investigations with humans. The goal was to determine both the sensitive periods and the severity of effects for abnormalities of the visual system during childhood. Such abnormalities include early childhood strabismus and astigmatism. The findings of these studies have many parallels with the research on kittens.

The focus of the chapter by Konishi is on the effect of early experience on auditory development of birds. The reader should question the extent of similarity between the effects of early auditory and early visual experience on perceptual development as well as the extent of similarity of effects on different species. The chapter by Walk examines the importance of experience for depth perception. While he concludes that visual depth perception appears to be unlearned or innate for all species investigated so far, he also shows that experience is important for depth perception.

The following topics form a common thread for the chapters in this part: deprivation effects, sensitive and critical periods, species differences in plasticity, the theoretical importance of the influence of early experience on perception, and the function of perceptual modifications.

All the authors deal with the effects of deprivation on perception, all discuss critical or sensitive periods, and, in marked contrast to other chapters in this volume, all describe animal studies. This does not mean that human studies are excluded. Mitchell's chapter is essentially about human research related to the animal research, and Walk's chapter examines problems of depth perception with human infants that are similar to those investigated with animals.

Deprivation means depriving the subject of selected aspects of normal experience. This set of chapters shows many ways in which deprivation is useful to the psychologist in studying the effects of experience on perception:

1. Preventing normal binocular experience by monocular exposure to the visual environment (Rothblat and Schwartz, Mitchell). The animals may be allowed to use only one eye, or an occluder may be placed first on one eye and then on the other so that the animal sees out of each but never from both at the same time.
2. Binocular deprivation by suturing both eyes closed (Rothblat and Schwartz, Mitchell) or by raising the animal in the dark until it is to be tested (Walk).
3. Deprivation of visuomotor experience. The animal may scan the environment visually but it cannot locomote through it (Walk).
4. Deprivation of normal patterned experience but exposure to lines in only one orientation (Rothblat and Schwartz, Mitchell).
5. Deprivation of auditory feedback from the bird's own vocal production by deafening (Konishi).
6. Deprivation of normal song environment by rearing birds in isolation. It can hear its own song but not those of any other birds (Konishi).
7. Deprivation of auditory stimulation from the animal's (bird) own species. It can hear only the songs of other species (Konishi).

These are all examples of the method of deprivation. The ways in which investigators have used the method to investigate selected problems are described in the chapters indicated. We are all perceptually deprived in the sense of some of the effects explored by these and other chapters. We all hear mainly our own language from birth and are deprived of the full richness of auditory experience, somewhat like the birds described in studies by Konishi. We all grow up in our own cultural environment. For Westerners this may be a special visual environment which includes lots of pictures, TV displays, and carpentered artifacts. Perhaps this is only quantitatively different from the special environments of animals reared with lines of only one orientation.

All of the authors in this part also discuss sensitive or critical periods in perceptual development. Rothblat and Schwartz describe the period from 3 to 14 weeks of age when occlusion of vision to one eye of the kitten will affect normal binocular functioning. The same period appears to be important in environmental modification of the orientation specificity of cortical cells. Mitchell's chapter refers to species differences in sensitive periods—different for cat, monkey, and man. Konishi reports critical periods for the development of birdsongs. But research on experiential modifications of depth perception has produced little evidence of sensitive periods, except, perhaps, for the chick. There are usually multiple cues for depth perception, and perhaps additional research will find sensitive periods for these cues treated separately. For example, stereopsis and motion parallax may have different sensitive periods.

Differences in plasticity among species are illustrated particularly by Konishi's chapter and Walk's chapter. Konishi describes some species, such as the chicken and turkey, where the variations in the auditory environment have no effect on vocal development. Even species that are affected by the auditory environment differ in plasticity. The white-crowned sparrow cannot produce a normal song without the correct model, while the song sparrow can.

Konishi encompasses a number of the phenomena relevant to the development of birdsongs with the concept of a template. This hypothetical construct refers to a neural mechanism that apparently encodes the perceptual and motor essence of a particular birdsong. Some species of birds must have heard the song of their own species to produce it when mature; others do not require this. Auditory feedback while singing is apparently important for appropriate song production by mature birds of several species. They must match their current production to the template. Are there any other examples of such templatelike behavior in the perception literature? Perhaps some aspects of human infant imitation of facial expression come close. Young human infants imitate facial movements like tongue protrusion and older infants imitate more complex facial expressions without the opportunity of visual feedback of their productions. The imitations are like the species-specific birdsongs in that the eliciting stimuli and the productions are so much alike and in that they do not seem to require long exposure to the appropriate stimuli. Exploration of such a mechanism requires phenomena with very discrete patterns of motor behavior. Most of the research on perception and experience does not involve such phenomena.

The chapter authors are not always in agreement. Both Rothblat and Schwartz and Mitchell comment on the dramatic findings of Hirsch and Spinelli (1970) and Blakemore and Cooper (1970), where the orientation specificity of cortical cells of animals was modified by selected exposure to horizontal and vertical lines. The conditions under which these results are obtained are a matter of some dispute since Stryker and Sherk (1975) failed to replicate the findings of Blakemore and Cooper (1970) where free-moving animals were allowed selective exposure to a striped environment (see Fig. 11 in Chapter 1 by Rothblat and Schwartz). They did replicate the results of the more constricting Hirsch and Spinelli (1970) study, in which animals could see the stripes through a fitted mask (see Fig. 10 in Chapter 1 by Rothblat and Schwartz). Mitchell acknowledges the controversial nature of these environmental modification studies but supports them. Rothblat and Schwartz are more cautious and remark on the small behavioral effects observed in such experiments.

What is the importance of these results and of this controversy? The question concerns the extent to which the visual/perceptual system of the organism is influenced by the visual environment. We live in what has been termed a "carpentered" visual environment (Segall, Campbell, and Herskovits, 1966). We do not sleep in the open on a flat plain or in small thatched huts in the middle of a tropical rainforest. We live in houses where the walls are vertical, the floors and ceilings are horizontal, and the joining corners are rectangular. Does such an environment change the visual system when we are infants so that we always see the world through the limits of our early experience? Do you and I see the world slightly differently because your mother exposed you to Calder's mobiles and colorful Picasso prints while my mother let me sleep in a drab subdued room with no clinking, tinkling movable objects? Does the Bushman see a different world than the city man sees? Are there individual and cultural differences in perception based on our early visual environment?

In truth, the evidence is that you, I, and the Bushman see the world in much the same way and the differences are small and minor. But if this is comforting, turn to auditory perception (see the chapter by Strange and Jenkins) and you will find experimental confirmation for the "tower of Babel" mentioned in the Bible. We not only cannot understand another person's language, the experimental evidence is that after a certain amount of selective auditory experience we cannot even perceive some of the distinctions of the other tongue.

This contrast of vision and audition helps show why psychologists are interested in the relation of experience to perception. Are we selectively tuned to the environment because (1) we develop and change through experience, sharpening and developing from a neutral tabula rasa, or (2) does our experience maintain what is already there with some aspects lost through attrition when experience furnishes no appropriate stimulation? By the first view we develop complexity from a neutral base; by the second one we are given everything but lose what we do not need.

What is the function of the perceptual modifications? This topic was discussed in the Introduction and it has particular relevance to the chapters in this part. Both the chapter by Rothblat and Schwartz and the one by Mitchell describe cortical changes that result from occlusion of one eye. One way to look at these results is to note the fragility of the developing binocular system. Mitchell cites research which shows that an eyepatch placed for a limited period of time over the eye of a child during a sensitive period may have profound visual effects. One may ask: is this a characteristic of all binocular systems? We might look, for example, at the visual development of an altricial species like the hunting hawks to test for the generality of fragility across species. Or we might ask: is there a function for the changes that occur? A cat with an occluded eye quickly develops cortical preference for that eye alone while the normal cat has few cortical cells driven by one eye alone. Evidently the special experience has changed the distribution of the cells, preventing binocularity and strengthening monocularity. If so, we would expect that the monocular kitten, when full grown, would have some advantages over a cat that had lost one eye as an adult. To use an example: perhaps the monocular cat would not catch as many mice as the normal binocular cat, but the cat that had lost an eye when it was a kitten should catch more mice than the cat that did not lose an eye until it was fully grown. This is because the visual cortex of the young deprived kitten has changed to concentrate on the one good eye, while the older cat has a crystallized cortex, carrying around binocular cells that can no longer function as efficiently. A functional analysis also asks what it is in the environment of the various species of birds that makes apparently similar species differ in plasticity—one presumes that each system has some survival gain related to the individual species' ecological environment. Similar speculations would hold for the individual species differences in plasticity of depth perception.

References

Blakemore, C., and Cooper, G. F. Development of the brain depends on the visual environment. *Nature,* 1970, *228,* 477–478.

Hirsch, H. V. B., and Spinelli, D. N. Visual experience modifies distribution of horizontally and vertically oriented receptive fields in cats. *Science,* 1970, *168,* 869–871.

Segall, M. H., Campbell, D. T., and Herskovits, M. J. *The influence of culture on visual perception.* Indianapolis: Bobbs-Merrill, 1966.

Stryker, M. P., and Sherk, H. Modification of cortical orientation selectivity in the cat by restricted visual experience: A re-examination. *Science,* 1975, *190,* 904–906.

Altered Early Environment: Effects on the Brain and Visual Behavior

LAWRENCE A. ROTHBLAT AND
MICHAEL L. SCHWARTZ

1. Advantages of Visual System Analysis

During postnatal ontogeny the brain is actively undergoing major morphological change, and much work has focused on the maturation of behavior contingent on this structural development. Although genetic factors seem to be primarily involved in the initial proliferation of axons and dendrites, there is now sufficient evidence to indicate that early sensory experience can influence neuronal organization. A generally accepted distinction has been made between macroneurons, whose structure and function are constrained genetically, and microneurons, which develop with little genetic control in terms of their connectivity (Altman and Das, 1967). It is the microneuron that is thought to be responsive to exogenous stimulation, providing the organism with the plasticity for experiential modification.

The field of developmental neuropsychology is new in that it has been only within the past several years that a multidisciplinary approach has been emphasized toward an understanding of the ontological changes that occur within the nervous system. Behavioral and functional changes correlated with morphological alterations of the developing nervous system are now being widely investigated. The visual system in particular lends itself to such inves-

LAWRENCE A. ROTHBLAT AND MICHAEL L. SCHWARTZ • Department of Psychology, George Washington University, Washington, D.C. 20052. The preparation of this chapter and the experimental work described from the authors' laboratory were supported by NIMH Grant R01-MH-27424.

tigation, as much information is already available regarding its normal morphology and function. In addition, a great variety of behavioral measures are accessible to investigation. One question seems particularly promising for research: in what way does postnatal visual experience modify the development of the brain, and how is this expressed in behavioral change? This question is the main concern of the present chapter.

2. Feature Detectors: A Model of Visual Processing

2.1. Detectors in the Adult

The development of techniques for recording electrical activity from individual neurons of the intact brain has provided what seem to be exciting breakthroughs in the understanding of how the visual system functions in the detection and recognition of shapes. In addition to providing an understanding of how pattern perception is accomplished by a hierarchy of feature detectors, these findings have served as a useful model for the study of early environmental influences on the development of the brain.

In an elegant series of studies Hubel and Wiesel (1959, 1961,1962, 1965a, 1968) demonstrated that single cells in the visual system function in a highly organized manner, detecting specific features of the environment such as circles, lines, edges, and angles. Cells throughout the visual system were described by the pattern of retinal stimulation with which they could best be activated. This was referred to as the cell's "receptive field." Cells in the lateral geniculate, like retinal ganglion cells (Kuffler, 1953), were found to have concentric fields with an antagonistic center-surround organization. Cortical cells were categorized into several classes (see Fig. 1). One type, called "simple cells," was recognized by its response to stationary bars or contours of a particular size, position, and orientation. Two other types were termed "complex" or "hypercomplex" depending on the selectivity of their response. The importance of stimulus position and the distinctiveness of the excitatory and inhibitory areas within the receptive field were used to define these categories. In all cases, cells fired maximally to a preferred orientation. It was hypothesized that at each level in the visual system cells would respond to specific stimulus elements and that at each successive level these elements were synthesized and combined, creating a progressive increase in the complexity of the features which could be detected. Hypercomplex receptive fields were thought to be determined by a combination of inputs from complex cells, complex receptive fields from simple cells, and simple receptive fields from lateral geniculate cells.

Nearby cells in the visual cortex were found to have superimposed or overlapping receptive fields. Moreover, it was determined that neurons were ar-

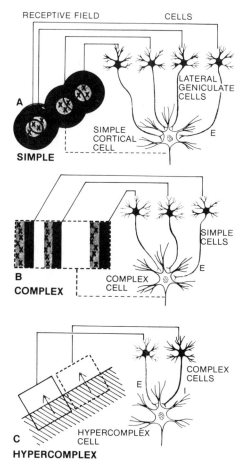

Fig. 1. Synthesis of receptive fields. Hypothesis devised by Hubel and Wiesel (1962, 1965a) to explain the synthesis of simple, complex, and hypercomplex receptive fields. In each case, lower-order cells converge to form receptive fields of higher order neurons. A: Fields of simple cells are elaborated by the convergence of many geniculate neurons with concentric fields (only four appear in the sketch). They must be arranged in a straight line on the retina according to the axis orientation of simple receptive fields. B: Simple cells responding best to a vertically oriented edge of slightly different positions could bring about the behavior of a complex cell which responds well to a vertically oriented edge situated anywhere within its field. C: Each of the two complex cells responds best to an obliquely oriented edge. But one cell is excitatory and the other is inhibitory to the hypercomplex cell. Hence an edge that covers both fields, as in the sketch, is ineffective, while a corner restricted to the left field would excite. Reproduced from Kuffler and Nicholls (1976, p. 53).

ranged in columns, all neurons within a column displaying functional similarities, such as responding to a particular orientation. In addition, nearly 80% of the cells in the adult cat's visual cortex could be activated binocularly. By assessing eye preference, Hubel and Wiesel (1962) grouped cortical cells into seven categories based on the degree to which a cell was influenced by each eye. The resulting ocular dominance distribution from a normal adult cat is shown in Fig. 2A. Cells which responded binocularly (groups 2–6) had receptive fields in closely corresponding parts of the two retinas. These receptive fields were of the same size and type (e.g., simple, complex), as well as axis orientation.

The existence of such an intricate system has been demonstrated in the cat (Hubel and Wiesel, 1962), monkey (Hubel and Wiesel, 1968), and man (Marg, Adams, and Rutkin, 1968), but different arrangements have been discovered in other species. Most notable has been the work with frogs (Lettvin, Maturana, McCulloch, and Pitts, 1959), pigeons (Maturana and Frenk, 1963), squirrels (Michael, 1968), and rabbits (Barlow and Hill, 1963; Levick, 1967). It has been found that in these species, as compared to cats and monkeys, more complex processing occurs in the retina and optic tectum. Retinal ganglion cells of the rabbit, for example, seem to perform functions similar to those of cortical cells in cat and monkey, firing selectively to stimulus direction and orientation.

2.2. Detectors in the Newborn

Attempts to determine whether these characteristics of adult visual cortex, i.e., (1) orientation selectivity, (2) columns (functional architecture), and (3) binocularity, are both present and fixed at birth have rested on findings from studies using a variety of experimental preparations. One of the first questions asked was whether the organization seen in the adult visual system was present in the newborn. The demonstration of such "adultlike" properties would obviously point strongly to the importance of genetic factors in determining neural organization. In one of the first studies, Hubel and Wiesel (1963) recorded

Fig. 2. Ocular dominance distributions reproduced from studies by Hubel and Wiesel. In each graph, group 1 cells were driven only by the contralateral eye, group 4 cells were driven equally by either eye, and group 7 cells were driven exclusively by the ipsilateral eye. Groups 2 and 3 and 5 and 6 showed gradations in dominance by the contralateral and ipsilateral eyes, respectively. A: Ocular dominance distribution from several normal adult cats. B: Distribution from two kittens with no visual experience (shaded portion) and one 20-day-old normal kitten (unshaded portion). C: Ocular dominance distribution from five monocularly deprived kittens. D: Distribution from four binocularly deprived kittens. Both C and D also contain information on response properties of the cells recorded; shading indicates normal response properties, absence of shading indicates lack of orientation specificity, and the interrupted lines indicate cells unresponsive to either eye. Adapted from Hubel and Wiesel (1962, 1963) and Wiesel and Hubel (1965a).

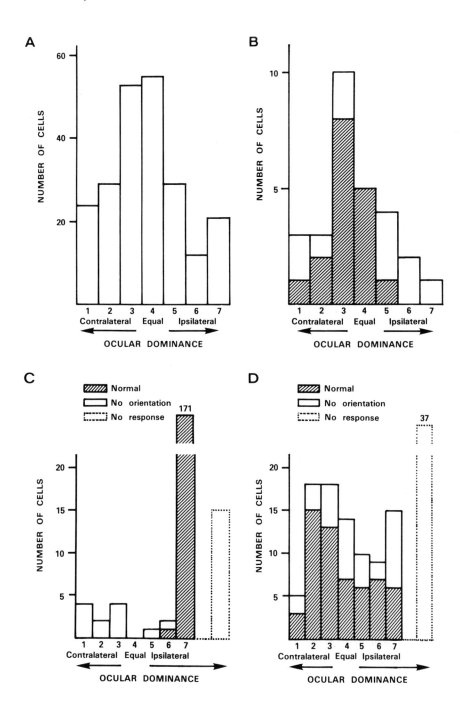

from neurons of four young kittens between the ages of 8 and 20 days. Two had no patterned light experience, one had 10 days of monocular stimulation, while the fourth had 11 days of normal stimulation in both eyes. Although the cells in these young animals were generally less responsive, the authors concluded that receptive field organization (orientation specificity), binocularity (Fig. 2B), and functional architecture were all similar to those of the adult cortex. When they recorded from the cortex of very young monkeys (3–4 weeks of age) which had been deprived of visual experience from birth (one was delivered by Caesarian section) or shortly thereafter, the results were similar (Wiesel and Hubel, 1974). Highly organized orientation-specific columns were already present, thus strengthening the belief that this system is innately determined.

Although Hubel and Wiesel's findings on binocularity have been generally supported (Barlow and Pettigrew, 1971; Pettigrew, 1974; Imbert and Buisseret, 1975; Sherk and Stryker, 1976), some investigators remain unconvinced that visual neurons of the newborn display the same degree of orientation specificity as those of the mature animal (Barlow and Pettigrew, 1971; Pettigrew, 1974; Imbert and Buisseret, 1975). One difficulty in resolving this issue is the fact that the cortex of the young animal is more difficult to excite and is easily fatigued. Because visual cortical neurons are particularly responsive to movement, moving rather than stationary stimuli are often used to map the young cells, which complicates the disassociation of direction from orientation specificity. Although Pettigrew (1974) claims that neurons in the young kitten display directional but not orientation selectivity, Sherk and Stryker (1976) have convincing evidence that both properties can be demonstrated.

3. Altered Early Environments: A Means of Assessing Innate vs. Experiential Factors

3.1. Monocular and Binocular Deprivation

Because of the inherent difficulties in working with very young animals, many investigators have turned to the procedure of sensory deprivation. By suturing the eyelids, using opaque or translucent contact occluders, or rearing in darkness, visual exposure can be reduced or totally eliminated and the role visual experience plays in the development of the system can be further assessed. Total sensory deprivation, however, is known to produce widespread morphological, neurochemical, and behavioral change, making the effects on visual function, *per se,* difficult to evaluate (see Riesen, 1966, 1975). Some of these problems can be overcome by restricting vision in one eye while allowing normal experience with the other.

Wiesel and Hubel (1963b), utilizing this technique, eliminated or reduced stimulation in one eye of kittens from birth to 3 months of age. After such a period of monocular deprivation, almost all cells in the cortex can be driven only by the experienced eye (Fig. 2C). The few cells which can be activated through the deprived eye have grossly abnormal receptive fields.

Under the assumption that the inability of the unused eye to activate cortical neurons resulted from the disruption of innately determined geniculocortical connections, it was expected that in kittens deprived of all stimulation, most cells of the visual cortex would be abnormal. Surprisingly, unit activity from the cortex of animals reared with both eyes closed was more similar to that of normals than to monocularly deprived animals (Wiesel and Hubel, 1965a). Compared to monocular deprivation, the cortex was more responsive, more cells could be driven binocularly (Fig. 2D), and of those cells which did respond over half had normal receptive fields.

These findings suggested that the effects of sensory deprivation, at least at the cortical level, cannot be accounted for solely in terms of deterioration of innate connections resulting from disuse. In short, the effect of closure of one eye on visual cortex depends on the state of the other eye. With these results in mind, Wiesel and Hubel (1963b) proposed a model of "binocular competition," where axons from cells in the lateral geniculate nucleus "compete" for cortical synaptic sites.

The notion of binocular competition is consistent with the organization of the cat's lateral geniculate. As can be seen in Fig. 3, that portion of the geniculate which corresponds to the binocular part of the visual field is laminated, with alternate layers receiving optic tract fibers from the retina on the same (A1) or opposite side (A). There appears to be little binocular interaction at the level of the geniculate; i.e., there are few, if any, cells that can be activated by stimulation of either eye. However, this laminated portion is referred to as the "binocular segment," because cells at corresponding areas of alternate layers represent the same point in the binocular portion of the visual field and give a binocular input to single cortical neurons (Guillery and Stelzner, 1970). A small unlaminated monocular crescent of the geniculate receives only a monocular input from the contralateral eye. This in turn projects to the monocular segment of visual cortex.

The organization of the geniculate is particularly useful for studying the effects of monocular deprivation, as one layer of each geniculate receives input from the deprived eye and one layer from the experienced eye. Wiesel and Hubel (1963a) have found a 30–40% reduction in size of cells in the deprived lamina, whereas cells in the lamina receiving input from the experienced eye appear normal. Because geniculate cells are thought to compete for cortical synaptic sites, lack of visual stimulation places the cells in the deprived lamina at a disadvantage, allowing axons from cells in the normal layers to occupy additional space and control the cortical neurons.

The most direct tests of the binocular competition model have been conducted by Guillery and his colleagues (Guillery and Stelzner, 1970; Guillery,

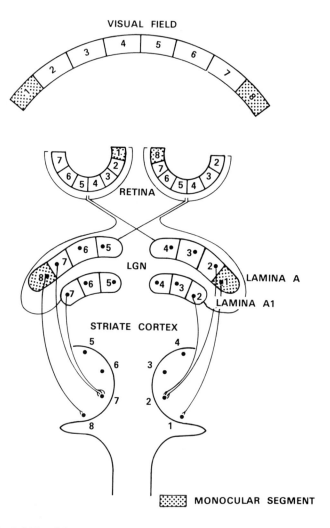

Fig. 3. Visual field and its topographic representation on the retina, lateral geniculate nucleus (LGN), and visual cortex in the cat. Shading shows monocular portion of the visual field and corresponding segments of retina and LGN. The nasal hemifield of each retina (which includes the monocular segment of the visual field) projects contralaterally to lamina A of the LGN, while the temporal hemifield of each retina projects ipsilaterally to A1. Although there appears to be little binocular interaction in the LGN (see text), the laminated (unshaded) portion is referred to as the binocular segment since a point in the visual field (e.g., 6) has a representation in both lamina A and A1, and this point is topographically positioned in the LGN along a line of projection through both lamina. Cells along a projection line (e.g., 2 and 7) can thus give a binocular input to single cells in striate cortex. The monocular segments of the LGN (1 and 8 of lamina A) receive input only from the contralateral eye and project to the monocular portion of the visual cortex. For simplicity, laminae other than A and A1 have not been represented. For detailed maps, see Sanderson (1971).

1972, 1973). They argue that if competition results in a disadvantage for cells in the geniculate layers receiving input from the deprived eye, this should occur only in the binocular segment of the nucleus. Cells in the monocular portion, even though they receive fibers from only the inexperienced eye, should not be placed at a competitive disadvantage. Guillery and Stelzner (1970) found that, after 3 months of monocular deprivation, cell atrophy is found only in the binocular segment of the deprived lamina, whereas cells in the monocular crescent appear normal.

It should not be assumed that binocular deprivation spares visual function. Even though suturing of both eyes produces less drastic effects than monocular closure, Wiesel and Hubel (1965a) reported that 32% of the cells recorded from kittens binocularly deprived were abnormal. Assuming that the newborn does possess neurons with adultlike characteristics, a mechanism other than binocular competition is required to account for these binocular effects. Buisseret and Imbert (1976) found that kittens reared in the dark for the first 12–17 days had the same percentage of cells with specific receptive field characteristics (23%, direction and orientation selective) as animals reared in a normal environment for the same period. The percentage of specific cells decreased dramatically (from 23% to 2%) in kittens dark-reared up to 42 days, while it increased (from 23% to 76%) in normal age–mate controls. These results indicate that visual experience is necessary to maintain as well as further develop the specificity already present in the very young animal. A similar conclusion can be drawn from morphological analyses. Although it was originally claimed that bilateral lid-suture had no effect on geniculate cell size (Guillery, 1973), more recent reports have suggested that, in addition to a competitive mechanism, deprivation itself can cause cell atrophy (Kalil, 1975; Hickey, Spear, and Kratz, 1977).

Regardless of whether one or both eyes are deprived, it is generally agreed that the major effects of abnormal stimulation are confined, in the kitten, to a period extending from 3 weeks to 3 months postnatally. Periods of monocular deprivation for up to 1 year in the adult cat produce no detrimental effects (Hubel and Wiesel, 1970). Within the sensitive period, as little as 2½ days of monocular closure has been found to cause dramatic shifts in ocular dominance (Olson and Freeman, 1975). Interestingly, these short-term deprivation effects do not seem related to the animals' prior visual experience. The ocular dominance shifts were as pronounced for animals which were allowed normal use of both eyes during the period preceding monocular closure as they were for animals which were dark-reared.

Despite the impressive evidence of morphological and physiological modification due to early visual deprivation, progress in relating these alterations to systematic changes in behavior has been limited. If the orientation-selective coding system delineated by Hubel and Wiesel serves in the detection and recognition of contour, we might assume that conditions producing abnormal cortical activity would result in congruent aberrant behavior. On the basis of electrophysiological findings it could be predicted that visual impairments following binocular deprivation would be less severe than those found after monocular closure. Both forms of deprivation were originally thought to produce behavioral blindness, and it was believed that the animals' capacity to recover, "whether measured behaviorally, morphologically, or in terms of single cell cortical physiology, is severely limited, even for recovery periods of over a year" (Wiesel and Hubel, 1965b).

Although the permanency of the morphological and physiological alterations has been substantially confirmed (Wiesel and Hubel, 1965b), a surprising degree of behavioral recovery has been demonstrated. Formal techniques, particularly tests of visuomotor behavior, visual acuity, and visual pattern discrimination, have been utilized for behavioral assessment, but the extent to which each of these functions is disturbed is still unclear. Binocular lid-suture has been shown to produce lasting deficits in discriminating visual patterns such as cross vs. disk (Chow and Stewart, 1972) and upright vs. inverted triangles (Ganz, Hirsch, and Tieman, 1972). Monocular closure has been found to produce similar deficiencies (Chow and Stewart, 1972; Ganz et al., 1972), although evaluation of the degree of impairment has been somewhat confounded by the finding that forced usage of the deprived eye facilitates recovery (Ganz and Fitch, 1968; Dews and Wiesel, 1970). After a period of early closure, the deprived eye shows better behavioral recovery if the normal eye is closed than if both eyes are allowed to remain open, although the deprived eye is unable to drive more cells in the visual cortex (Wiesel and Hubel, 1965b). Even when tested under conditions of reverse suture, lasting impairments in visual discrimination performance are still reported (Ganz and Fitch, 1968; Dews and Wiesel, 1970; Rizzolatti and Tradardi, 1971; Ganz and Haffner, 1974).

The fact that a high degree of discriminative capacity can be demonstrated with the deprived eye has been attributed by some investigators to the animals' use of extraneous cues (Rizzolati and Tradardi, 1971; Ganz and Haffner, 1974). Using a series of training and transfer tasks, Ganz and Haffner (1974) were able to show that monocularly deprived cats demonstrate a strong reliance on local flux rather than form cues when learning pattern discriminations with the deprived eye and concluded that "normal form perception, which is characterized by a certain degree of abstractness from the particulars of any individual stimulus, is rendered permanently impossible for an eye that can activate only a population of less selective receptive fields." In disagreement with this conclusion, however, van Hof-van Duin (1976) reports normal pattern discrimination in cats monocularly deprived from birth to 8–10 months. The normal discriminative capacity in this instance is attributed to the type of apparatus in which the animals were tested, one which minimized visuomotor requirements. This was believed to be particularly important as deficits in visually guided reaching, visual cliff behavior, obstacle avoidance, tracking, jumping, and visual eye blink could still be detected 2 years after reverse suture. In addition, permanent impairment following monocular deprivation of young kittens has been found on tests of visual acuity (Dews and Wiesel, 1970; see Mitchell, this volume). A similar impairment in acuity, without recovery, is produced by monocular suture during the first 4 weeks of life in the monkey (von Noorden, Dowling, and Ferguson, 1970).

Many of the inconsistencies arising from these behavioral studies may eventually be resolved by the findings of Sherman and his colleagues (Sherman, 1973, 1974; Sherman, Guillery, Kaas, and Sanderson, 1974). They have recently shown that monocular and binocular deprivation each produce "blindness" in a specific portion of the visual field (see Section 3.3). Thus, an animal's performance on any task may well reflect its ability to compensate by using that part of the visual field which remains intact.

Although there have been many studies dealing with visual deprivation in the rat, most have dealt with the effects of dark-rearing (see Riesen and Zilbert, 1975, for review). Rats dark-reared until 90 days of age show deficits on the visual cliff (Walk and Bond, 1968) and on complex visual discriminations (Tees, 1968). As an experimental preparation, monocular deprivation in the rat offers

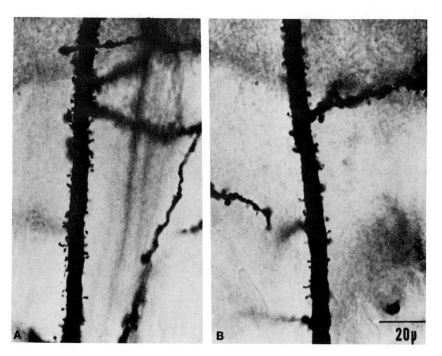

Fig. 4. Shafts of apical dendrites of layer V pyramids, photographed in layer IV, of the visual cortex connected with the normal eye (A) and the deprived eye (B). From Fifkova (1970).

some interesting possibilities. Because the visual system of the rat is nearly 93% crossed, it is possible to consider the visual cortex contralateral to the deprived eye as being a "deprived" cortex and similarly the cortex contralateral to the experienced eye as "normal" cortex. The two hemispheres can be directly compared to assess the effects of visual experience on cortical morphology. Monocular deprivation in the rat has been shown to produce a severe loss of visually responsive neurons in the deprived cortex (Shaw, Yinon, and Auerbach, 1974). In addition, pyramidal cells in layer V of the deprived cortex show a reduction in spines on their apical dendrites (Fifkova, 1970) (see Fig. 4). The dendrite spines on the apical shafts of pyramidal cells are believed to be the site of geniculocortical synapses, either directly (Globus and Scheibel, 1967) or through intermediary stellate cells (Garey and Powell, 1971).

Monocular deprivation in the rat also disturbs visual behavior (Schwartz and Rothblat, 1976; Rothblat and Schwartz, in preparation). When rats are monocularly deprived from the time of eye opening (approximately 15 days) until 45 days of age, reverse-sutured, and then tested with the deprived eye, they are severely impaired in discriminating between columns and rows of ¼-inch squares, although they are able to discriminate differences in flux normally. Deprivation from time of eye opening to 30 days of age (15–30) or from 30 to 45 days of age produces no significant effect on discrimination behavior. Just how the change in visual behavior following 30 days of monocular closure relates to alterations in cortical morphology, such as dendritic spine dysgenesis, remains to be determined.

3.2. X, Y, and W Afferents: An Addition to the Model

To this point, we have assumed that visual information is processed in a serial, hierarchical manner, as was originally proposed by Hubel and Wiesel. The results of recent studies, however, have led some investigators to suggest an alternate or adjunct form of processing which occurs via parallel and functionally distinct channels (Stone, 1972). This conceptualization is illustrated in Fig. 5.

Enroth-Cugell and Robson (1966) first reported the existence of at least two electrophysiologically distinct classes of retinal ganglion cells in the cat, which they called X and Y cells. It was noted that X cells summed the influences of the center and surround portion of the receptive field in a linear manner, whereas Y cells summed these influences nonlinearly. Subsequent work (Fukuda, 1971; Cleland et al., 1971) has shown that these cell classes can be further differentiated by a number of other response properties. Specifically, Y cells have larger receptive fields than X cells, have faster axonal conduction velocities, and respond better to rapidly moving grating patterns. In addition, Y cells are rarely found in the area centralis but increase in number with greater retinal eccentricity. The converse is true for X cells.

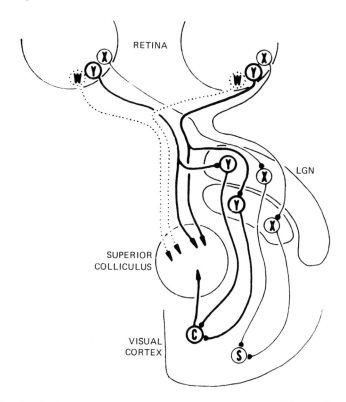

Fig. 5. Functionally distinct pathways to the lateral geniculate nucleus (LGN), superior colliculus, and visual cortex in the cat. It is stressed that this diagram is partially speculative. Both eyes contribute to all pathways. Afferents to the LGN and visual cortex: (1) the retinal X cells synapse onto LGN X cells which in turn project to cortical simple cells, and (2) the retinal Y cells synapse onto LGN Y cells which project to cortical complex cells. Pathways to the superior colliculus: (1) the W-direct originating from retinal W cells, (2) the Y-direct originating from retinal Y cells, and (3) the Y-indirect originating from retinal Y cells and relayed through the LGN Y cells and cortical complex cells. Adapted from Hoffman and Sherman (1974).

Still more recently, a third class of retinal ganglion cells has been recognized; these have been called W cells (Stone and Hoffman, 1972). W cells can have a variety of different receptive field properties which may include phasic or tonic, suppressed by contrast, on-off center direction selective, or on center direction selective responding (Stone and Fukuda, 1974). W cells have the slowest conducting axons, have receptive fields similar in size to Y cells, and yet have a retinal distribution similar to X cells (Stone and Fukuda, 1974; Fukuda and Stone, 1974).

As can be seen in Fig. 5, these cell types can also be differentiated according to the locus of their axonal projections. X cells project exclusively to X relay cells of the lateral geniculate. Retinal Y cells send axons to Y relay cells of the geniculate, and may in addition send a collateral branch to the superior colliculus. W cells project almost exclusively to the colliculus, although it has been reported that some W cells may send axons to specific portions of the geniculate as well (Wilson and Stone, 1975). The relay cells of the lateral geniculate are characterized by their input from retinal ganglion cells and have receptive field properties similar to their retinal counterparts. For example, Y geniculate relay cells have larger receptive fields, faster-conducting axons, and so on (Hoffmann, Stone, and Sherman, 1972).

The maintenance of parallel channels has also been suggested at the cortical level. Although still a matter of some controversy, Hoffmann and Stone (1971) have presented evidence that simple and hypercomplex cells may be activated by X geniculate cells, whereas complex cells may be driven by Y-type relay cells. Stone (1972) has further suggested that the properties of the receptive fields of simple, complex, and hypercomplex cells are consistent with what might be predicted based on the characteristics of X and Y relay cells.

In addition to this work with the cat, there is now growing evidence that similar pathways exist in a number of other species. X- and Y-like systems have been demonstrated for the rat (Fukuda and Sugitani, 1974), the tree shrew (Sherman, Norton, and Casagrande, 1975), and the owl monkey (Sherman, Wilson, Kaas, and Webb, 1976).

3.3. Effect of Visual Deprivation on X, Y, and W Cells

An important distinction between X, Y, and W cells appears to be their individual susceptibility to the effects of early visual deprivation. Although neither monocular nor binocular deprivation has a significant effect on the X or W cell systems, both have been shown to produce a profound reduction in the proportion of Y cells in the lateral geniculate (Sherman, Hoffmann, and Stone, 1972). Following monocular closure there is a decrease in Y cells in the binocular but not the monocular segment of the geniculate. Binocular deprivation, on the other hand, results in a loss of Y cells throughout; the loss is less severe in the binocular segment than with monocular deprivation.

The effects of deprivation on Y cells are primarily restricted to the geniculocortical segment of the system. This has been clearly illustrated by studies attempting to assess the effects of deprivation on superior colliculus responsiveness (Hoffmann and Sherman, 1974, 1975). The superior colliculus is known to receive input from three distinct pathways (Hoffmann, 1973) (see Figs. 5 and 6A). Two of these represent direct retinotectal connections composed of axons from W retinal ganglion cells (W-direct pathway) and from collateral Y retinal ganglion cells (Y-direct pathway). The third input is from the Y-indirect pathway which originates from Y retinal ganglion cells and is transmitted via Y relay cells, to cortical cells, then to the colliculus. As can be seen

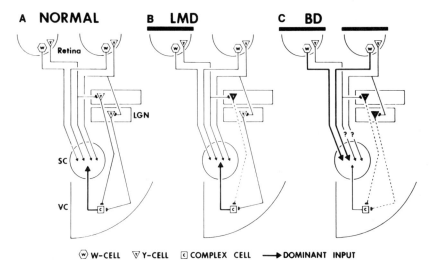

Fig. 6. Summary showing afferents to the superior colliculus (SC) in a normal (A), a left monocularly deprived (B), and a binocularly deprived (C) cat. These diagrams are hypothetical explanations of many data from this and related studies. W cells, Y cells, and complex cells are shown as indicated. Unrecordable Y cells in the lateral geniculate nucleus (LGN) are shown as black. X cells and cortical simple cells are omitted since they play no major or obvious role in collicular afferentation. A: Pathways to the SC in a normal cat. Each eye provides W-direct and Y-direct retinotectal input plus Y-indirect corticotectal input. The last involves Y cells from retina and the LGN plus complex cells from visual cortex (VC). The Y-indirect input seems to dominate many neuronal properties in the SC. B: Pathways to the SC in a left monocularly deprived cat. All three inputs (W- and Y-direct plus Y-indirect) are evident from the nondeprived (right) eye, and the retinotectal inputs (W- and Y-direct) are normal from the deprived (left) eye. However, the deprived eye provides no Y-indirect input because Y cells are no longer available in the LGN. Although not illustrated, this deficit is limited to the binocular segment of the LGN. As in the normal cat, the Y-indirect input (from only the nondeprived eye in the binocular segment) is dominant among afferents to the SC. C: Pathways to the SC in a binocularly deprived cat. From each eye, the W-direct input is normal, the Y-direct input is probably reduced, and the Y-indirect input is completely missing. The Y-indirect input loss is due to a loss of recordable Y cells throughout binocular and monocular segments of the LGN. However, unlike normal and monocularly deprived cats, the W-direct pathway dominates among afferents to the SC. From Hoffmann and Sherman (1975).

in Fig. 6B, monocular deprivation results in a dramatic loss of input via the binocular segment of the Y-indirect pathway associated with the deprived eye (Hoffmann and Sherman, 1974). The W- and Y-direct pathways from the deprived eye as well as the three pathways associated with the nondeprived eye are unaffected. Following binocular deprivation (Fig. 6C), both the monocular and binocular segments of the Y-indirect pathway from the deprived eye are lost and the Y-direct pathway appears to be weakened (Hoffmann and Sherman, 1975).

The relationship between deprivation effects on these neuronal pathways and the behavior of cats has been systematically investigated by Sherman and his colleagues (Sherman, 1973, 1974; Sherman *et al.*, 1974). Using a test for visual field perimetry (see Figs. 7 and 8), Sherman (1973) has found a pattern of impaired behavioral orienting to stimuli presented in specific portions of the visual field of deprived cats. Animals reared with monocular closure demonstrate an inability to respond to stimuli in the binocular portion of the visual field (45° contralateral–45° ipsilateral) when forced to use only the deprived eye. Binocularly deprived animals appeared to be able to respond to stimuli presented only within the ipsilateral hemifield of the eye tested. This pattern of behavior led Sherman to suggest that "each MD cat seemed to behave as if guided by normal development of the monocular segment of the visual cortex (and perhaps also the superior colliculus) whereas each BD cat seemed to behave as if guided by normal development of only contralateral retinotectal pathways." Indeed, this suggestion agrees well with what might be hypothesized based on the specific effect of monocular and binocular deprivation on the Y cell system. However, many questions remain unanswered. The X cell system is presumably spared from the effects of deprivation, yet, thus far, there is no evidence of remaining visual function in the affected portion of the visual field. This is particularly relevant in light of the proposed dichotomy of function between X and Y cells. It has been suggested that the response properties of X cells may implicate them as necessary for pattern or form vision, while the characteristics of Y cells make them suited for motion detection and visuomotor

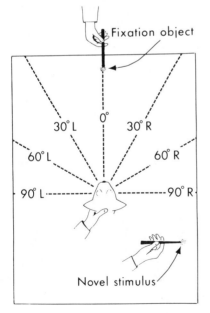

Fig. 7. Method for perimetry testing. The cat is restrained with its lateral canthi aligned along the 90° guidelines and its nose pointed along the 0° guideline to the fixation object (a piece of food in forceps). For tests of specific visual responses, the novel stimulus (food in forceps or a painted ball at the end of a stiff wire) is introduced along one of the guidelines after which the cat is freed from restraint and its behavior noted. For control tests of nonspecific responses, the novel stimulus either is not introduced or is introduced at approximately 120° lateral (out of the cat's visual field); before the cat is freed. From Sherman (1973).

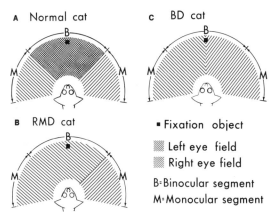

A Normal cat

c BD cat

B RMD cat

- Fixation object

▨ Left eye field
▨ Right eye field

B = Binocular segment
M = Monocular segment

Fig. 8. Summary of idealized visual field perimetry testing of cats, after correction for eccentric fixation. This figure does not include response levels. It is assumed here that each cat has both visual axes aligned on the fixation object. A: Normal cat. The binocular field extends between about 100° on either side. The monocular fields each extend from about ipsilateral 100° to contralateral 45°, which delineates the binocular segment of visual field as bounded bilaterally by about 45° on either side and the monocular segment on each side as extending from about 45° to about 100°. B: MD cat. The binocular field has a normal extent as in A. Also, the nondeprived eye monocular field is normal but the deprived eye monocular field includes only the monocular segment. C: BD cat. The binocular field has a normal extent as in A, but each monocular field includes only the ipsilateral hemifield. From Sherman (1973).

orientation (Stone and Fukuda, 1974). Although X cells seem not to be lost following deprivation, it is possible that their response properties are significantly modified (Maffei and Fiorentini, 1976), so that they are unable to subserve their intended function. Nonetheless, the finding that early deprivation can produce a loss of selected portions of the visual field has important implications which future behavioral investigations will have to consider.

3.4. Alternating Monocular Occlusion and Surgically Induced Squint

While deprivation studies have been useful in showing that early pattern vision is essential for normal receptive field organization, the use of more subtle alterations of early visual experience has pointed to the importance of congruent input between the two eyes for development of cortical binocularity. Rearing kittens under conditions of alternating monocular occlusion, where one eye is covered each day, on a day-to-day basis, leads to a significant reduction in the number of binocularly activated cortical neurons (Hubel and Wiesel, 1965b). In contrast to these changes in ocular dominance, other receptive field properties, e.g., orientation selectivity, appear normal. It has also been shown that rearing kittens (Hubel and Wiesel, 1965b; Gordon and Gummow, 1975;

Yinon, Auerbach, Blank, and Friesenhausen, 1975), or monkeys (Baker, Grigg, and von Noorden, 1974; Hubel and Wiesel, 1974; von Noorden and Middleditch, 1975) with artificial squint (strabismus) produces similar changes in ocular dominance, although differences resulting from the two procedures have been noted.

For example, with alternating monocular occlusion both eyes drive an equal number of cortical neurons (Blake and Hirsch, 1975), while in the strabismic animal the squinting eye is deficient in this capacity (Baker *et al.*, 1974; Yinon, 1976). It has also been reported that cells activated through the squinting eye have poorly organized receptive fields (Yinon *et al.*, 1975). It should be noted that the effects of squint on cortical binocularity and the ability of the squinting eye to drive cells are dependent on the form of strabismus (Fig. 9). Convergent squint (esotropia) has been found to produce a more severe effect on cortical function than has divergent squint (exotropia). In addition to these cortical changes, Gordon and Gummow (1975) have reported that the squinting eye activates fewer cells in the superior colliculus and that the proportion of colliculus cells with a directional preference for vertical movement is increased.

Many of the binocular cells found in the visual cortex of the normal adult cat seem to detect retinal disparity. To activate these cells optimally, disparate areas of the two retinas must be stimulated. Thus, it is believed that these

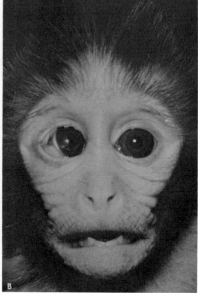

Fig. 9. A: Monkey with surgically induced divergent squint (exotropia). B: Monkey with surgically induced convergent squint (esotropia). From von Noorden and Dowling (1970).

disparity-detecting neurons underlie stereoscopic vision (Barlow, Blakemore, and Pettigrew, 1967). To test this assumption, Blake and Hirsch (1975) reared cats from the time of eye opening to 6 months of age with alternating occlusion. These cats were then trained at 1½–2 years of age to (1) resolve vertical gratings and (2) detect the depth of vertical rods using one or both eyes. As might be expected from the electrophysiological findings, following alternating occlusion, cats showed no deficit in visual acuity but were impaired when required to determine the depth of rods when using both eyes. For normal animals, performance on the depth task was better when the display was viewed binocularly than when viewed monocularly. The fact that animals reared with alternating occlusion performed like monocular normals, regardless of whether they used one or both eyes, suggests that they failed to use stereopsis. These results have been essentially confirmed by Packwood and Gordon (1975), who tested alternating occluded cats for stereoscopic vision using a shadow-casting technique which eliminates all depth cues with the exception of retinal disparity. The cautious conclusion of these investigators, however, is worth reiterating: "These results imply that animals without binocular cells in area 17 do not have stereoscopic vision, but do not determine if disparity-selective cells in the visual cortex are responsible for stereopsis."

Following surgically induced squint, the behavioral picture is somewhat more complicated. In rhesus monkeys with esotropia, the acuity of the squinting eye is severely reduced, yet the squinting eye of exotropic monkeys shows no loss of acuity (von Noorden and Dowling, 1970; von Noorden and Middleditch, 1975). The difference in acuity between monkeys with convergent and divergent squint agrees well with what is seen in humans with these forms of strabismus (see Mitchell, this volume).

Hubel and Wiesel (1965b) reported no effects of squint on the perceptual capacities of their cats, but these animals had divergent squint and were not systematically tested. Franklin, Ikeda, Jacobson, and McDonald (1975) have shown that cats reared with a surgically induced convergent squint show a 70% reduction in acuity with the squinting eye. In support of these behavioral results, Ikeda and Wright (1976) have reported that X cells of the lateral geniculate have a reduced resolution for high spatial frequency gratings if they receive their input from the squinting eye. This effect of convergent squint on X cells appears to be confined to the central retina and is not evident in the periphery. This result is consistent with the notion that X cells are involved in form detection and acuity and may explain the acuity impairments described above. Although it is only one of several models proposed, Ikeda and Wright (1976) suggest that the effects of strabismus result from the inability to focus both eyes clearly on a viewed object. In normal animals, the mechanisms involved in accommodation and fixation assure both eyes of clearly focused images, but in animals with convergent squint the normal eye is often exposed to a defocused image. As a result, X cells of the retina and lateral geniculate do not become finely tuned during development, producing decreased acuity which can be measured both behaviorally and electrophysiologically. With divergent squint the two eyes seldom fixate a mutual object and so the animal tends to alternate fixations between the two eyes (this effect would be similar to that found following alternating monocular occlusion). The result is that both eyes receive sharply focused images and therefore develop normal receptive field properties. As such, it would not be surprising to find normal acuity for the squinting eye of animals reared with divergent squint.

The behavioral evidence from monkeys and humans seems to be handled well with this model. As yet it is not clear whether the data from cats are equally supportive. The results of Franklin *et al.* (1975) with convergent squint are in agreement, but the lack of more sophisticated testing of cats with divergent squint leave this proposal open for further investigation.

3.5. Early Selective Visual Experience

Another important extension of the experimental work on postnatal deprivation is the procedure of limiting an animal's early experience to lines and edges of a single contour. Hirsch and Spinelli (1970) raised kittens from birth to 3 months of age with specialized goggles (see Fig. 10) so that one eye viewed only vertical and the other eye only horizontal lines. Electrical recordings taken at 12 weeks indicated that the cells of the visual cortex would respond only to the particular orientation to which they had been exposed. No oblique fields were found and all cells were monocular. Blakemore and Cooper (1970) found similar effects in kittens which had been raised for 5 months (3 hr a day) in cylinders containing either vertical or horizontal stripes (Fig. 11). Unit analysis revealed that the cortical neurons were essentially normal except for the distribution of preferred orientations. Optimal orientation for all cells centered around the vertical or horizontal position, depending on the experience during rearing. Virtually no neurons had a preferred orientation within 45° of the inappropriate axis. It was thought that this neural modification was not merely passive degeneration of certain cortical neurons because of underactivity, for Blakemore and Cooper did not notice any large regions of "silent" cortex corresponding to missing columns. They felt, instead, that the visual cortex adjusts itself during maturation to the nature of its visual experience. It has also been found that when kittens are reared in environments lacking visual contour, cortical units respond only to spots of light (Pettigrew and Freeman, 1973). Two features of visual system organization were thought to be related to this neuronal plasticity: (1) the complexity of retinal processing and (2) the amount of binocular interaction (Mize and Murphy, 1973). Receptive field characteristics in the rabbit, for example, which has more complex retinal processing than the cat and a limited binocular field, are not changed by early visual exposure which is limited to horizontal and vertical lines (Mize and Murphy, 1973).

Fig. 10. Kitten wearing one of the masks used to provide selective visual exposure. Stimulus patterns are mounted on the inside surface of the black plastic sheet: one pattern in front of the left eye, a second in front of the right eye. A lens is mounted in the mask in front of each eye so that the patterns are located at the focal plane of the lens. When the kitten's eye is relaxed, the patterns should thus be in focus on the retina. Light entering through the white diffusing plastic illuminates the patterns. Adapted from Hirsch and Jacobson (1975).

Fig. 11. Apparatus for exposure to vertical stripes. Adapted from Blakemore (1974).

At present, however, these cylinder-induced changes are an issue of some controversy. For in a recent study, carefully designed to control cell sampling and experimenter bias, Blakemore and Cooper's stripe-rearing effects were not confirmed (Stryker and Sherk, 1975). Whether this contradiction can eventually be resolved by consideration of subtle differences in rearing variables such as the animal's alertness, head orientation, or motivational level remains to be determined.

Stryker and Sherk (1975) were able, however, to reproduce the findings of Hirsch and Spinelli (1970) when kittens were raised with horizontal/vertical goggles. Here, as in the original study, approximately half of the cells sampled were unresponsive or nonselective in their response to visual stimuli. Although Blakemore and Cooper's (1970) suggestion that visual cortical neurons have the plasticity to match their early visual input is most exciting, it has, in fact, received relatively little support. At present, a more congruous interpretation would be that exposure to a particular orientation is necessary to maintain and sharpen the innately determined response pattern of a given neuron, while cells which are not properly activated become nonfunctional.

Regardless of the mechanism, the time frame in which selective modification can occur is fixed. As with binocularity, there is a critical period for environmental modification of orientation selectivity. In the kitten, experience must occur between 3 and 14 weeks of age for the system to function normally (Blakemore, 1974). However, within this sensitive period, modification of orientation selectivity of cortical cells is reported to occur with as little as 1 hr of visual exposure (Blakemore and Mitchell, 1973). Similarly, 6 hr of exposure to vertically oriented stripes moving in one direction is sufficient to bias directional selectivity (Tretter, Cynader, and Singer, 1975).

With selective visual experience, behavior is altered as well, but the nature and extent of this alteration are far from clear. Blakemore and Cooper (1970) administered simple behavioral tests (e.g., moving a horizontally or vertically oriented stick toward the animal) to the kittens they had exposed to single contours. They reported that rearing with selective experience produced virtual "blindness" for lines orthogonal to those experienced. Although the neurophysiological changes were permanent, the blindness disappeared in several weeks. Long-term behavioral impairments resulting from selective exposure have proved to be surprisingly mild.

Hirsch (1972) was able to revive goggle-reared kittens that had been used for electrophysiological study (Hirsch and Spinelli, 1970) and test them on a variety of behavioral tasks. These included response to horizontal and vertical lines, discrimination of flux, line orientation, and mirror images. Interocular transfer of these discriminations was also assessed. The findings are exemplified by the threshold tests of line orientation. Cats were initially trained to discriminate 45° orientation differences. Threshold measures were then obtained by reducing the orientation differences between the positive and negative stimuli. It was predicted that when using the eye which had been exposed to vertical lines the animal would perform well on a vertical orientation test (vertical vs. 135°), since all cortical neurons driven through this eye had vertically oriented receptive fields. When this eye was tested on a horizontal orientation test (horizontal vs. 45°), however, performance should have been grossly impaired. The opposite results were expected when the cat was tested with the horizontally exposed eye. Although slight differences were found in the expected direction, the animals performed surprisingly well on both tests, with either eye. In addition, Hirsch reexamined the receptive field properties of cortical neurons and found that orientation selectivity had not changed. Cells with vertical receptive fields could only be activated through the vertically exposed eye, while those with horizontal receptive fields were driven exclusively by the eye which had been exposed to horizontals. These results led Hirsch to conclude "that an animal's ability to make pattern discrimination is not rigidly determined by the shape and orientation of its receptive fields" (Hirsch, 1972).

In a related study, Muir and Mitchell (1973) reared three kittens for 5 hr a day in environments similar to those used by Blakemore and Cooper (1970). The kittens were exposed to either vertical or horizontal stripes from 20 days until 5 months of age. When tested at 6 months, it was found that the ability to resolve either vertical or horizontal gratings was normal for animals which had experienced those orientations. However, the cats showed small but significant deficits when required to resolve contours to which they had never been exposed, and this impairment was not reduced even after animals were allowed normal exposure for over 1 year. Muir and Mitchell (1973) concluded that "the longstanding consequences of early selective visual deprivation is not blindness for contours of the orientation orthogonal to those present in the early visual environment, but only a slight reduction in acuity."

4. Conclusions

We have summarized much evidence showing that developing neurons can change their functional properties as a result of altered early environment, but the implications of this research must be clarified by further and more detailed studies. Many of the attempts to uncover the neurological and behavioral effects of various types of early experience have used rather gross alteration of the developmental milieu by total visual deprivation. Thus it is not surprising that these treatments produce widespread physiological effects which have been difficult to relate to behavior. Using a somewhat opposite approach, i.e., rearing animals in "enriched" environments (involving more social contact and sensory stimulation), has led to similar difficulties. For example, in addition to having heavier brains and greater whole brain acetylcholinesterase (Bennett, Diamond, Krech, and Rosenzweig, 1964), rats reared in enriched conditions have heavier adrenal glands, higher activities of the corticosteroid-inducible liver enzymes tyrosine and tryptophan aminotransferase, and more brain norepinephrine than isolated controls (Geller and Yuwiler, 1968; Geller, Yuwiler, and Zolman, 1965). The nonspecificity of enriched rearing effects is perhaps best illustrated by the finding that although enrichment affects striate cortex more than other regions, visual stimulation is not totally responsible. Significant differences in the striate cortex of animals raised in complex or isolated environments still exist even when the rats are reared blind (Rosenzweig, Krech, Bennett, and Diamond, 1968). Specific behavioral change has been difficult to demonstrate as most workers have concentrated their study on investigations of problem-solving ability and the task most frequently used has been the Rabinovitch and Rosvold (1951) modification of the closed field test (see Meyers, 1971). Problem solving is a behavior with a nebulous definition, and it has been difficult to determine what abilities are measured by the Hebb-Williams maze.

An important extension in experimental work on postnatal environmental alteration includes the procedures of monocular deprivation, alternating monocular occlusion, and surgically induced strabismus. Each has been found to produce drastic changes in cortical physiology. Studies with alternating occlusion and squint have proven to be particularly useful in elucidating neural mechanisms underlying stereoscopic vision and visual acuity, but the behavioral capacity of an animal using an inexperienced eye remains unclear. It appears, however, that further study of the functional significance of the X and Y cell systems, especially knowledge of how this relates to simple, complex, and hypercomplex cell organization, holds much promise for eventually resolving this important issue.

The procedure of limiting an animal's early experience to lines and edges of a single contour has provided what may be the most dramatic electrophysiological changes, but again the impairments in visual behavior seem surprisingly mild. Hubel and Wiesel's notion of sensory processing by hierarchically organized feature detectors has proven to be very appealing, and has gained widespread acceptance by researchers in a variety of diverse areas (see Eimas, this volume). Yet, how well it serves the purpose for which it was intended—i.e., to provide an understanding of visual pattern perception—is still open to question. The behavioral evidence from the studies reviewed here is less than overwhelming. Whether the fault lies with the model, as presently conceived, or with the behavioral techniques used for its assessment remains to be determined.

ACKNOWLEDGMENTS

We thank M. Snyder and P. Kasdan for reading the manuscript and offering helpful suggestions. We also thank G. K. von Noorden, H. V. B. Hirsch, and C. Blakemore for providing the photographs used in Figures 9, 10, and 11, respectively.

5. References

Altman, J., and Das, G. D. Postnatal neurogenesis in the guinea pig. *Nature*, 1967, *214*, 1098–1101.

Baker, F. H., Grigg, P., and von Noorden, G. K. Effects of visual deprivation and strabismus on the response of neurons in the visual cortex of the monkey, including studies on the striate and prestriate cortex in the normal animal. *Brain Research*, 1974, *66*, 185–208.

Barlow, H. B., and Hill, R. M. Selective sensitivity to direction of movement in ganglion cells of the rabbit retina. *Science*, 1963, *139*, 412–414.

Barlow, H. B., and Pettigrew, J. D. Lack of specificity of neurons in the visual cortex of young kittens. *Journal of Physiology*, 1971, *218*, 98–100.

Barlow, H. B., Blakemore, C., and Pettigrew, J. D. The neural mechanism of binocular depth discrimination. *Journal of Physiology*, 1967, *193*, 327–342.

Bennett, E. L., Diamond, M. C., Krech, D., and Rosenzweig, M. R. Chemical and anatomical plasticity of the brain. *Science*, 1964, *146*, 610–619.

Blake, R., and Hirsch, H. V. B. Deficits in binocular depth perception in cats after alternating monocular deprivation. *Science*, 1975, *190*, 1114–1116.

Blakemore, C. Developmental factors in the formation of feature extracting neurons. In F. O. Schmitt and F. C. Worden (Eds.), *The neurosciences: Third study program*. Cambridge, Mass.: MIT Press, 1974, pp. 105–113.

Blakemore, C., and Cooper, G. F. Development of the brain depends on the visual environment. *Nature*, 1970, *228*, 477–478.

Blakemore, C., and Mitchell, D. E. Environmental modification of the visual cortex and the neural basis of learning and memory. *Nature*, 1973, *241*, 467–468.

Buisseret, P., and Imbert, M. Visual cortical cells: Their developmental properties in normal and dark reared kittens. *Journal of Physiology*, 1976, *255*, 511–525.

Chow, K. L., and Stewart, D. L. Reversal of structural and functional effects of long-term deprivation in cats. *Experimental Neurology*, 1972, *34*, 409–433.

Cleland, B. G., Dubin, M. W., and Levick, W. R. Sustained and transient neurons in the cat's retina and lateral geniculate nucleus. *Journal of Physiology*, 1971, *217*, 473–496.

Dews, P. B., and Wiesel, T. N. Consequences of monocular deprivation on visual behavior in kittens. *Journal of Physiology*, 1970, *206*, 437–455.

Enroth-Cugell, C., and Robson, J. G. The contrast sensitivity of retinal ganglion cells of the cat. *Journal of Physiology*, 1966, *187*, 517–552.

Fifkova, E. The effect of unilateral deprivation on visual centers in rats. *Journal of Comparative Neurology*, 1970, *140*, 431–438.

Franklin, K. B. J., Ikeda, H., Jacobson, S. G., and McDonald, W. I. Visual acuity in cats raised with surgically produced squint. *Journal of Physiology*, 1975, *256*, 114–115.

Fukuda, Y. Receptive field organization of cat optic nerve fibers with special reference to conduction velocity. *Vision Research*, 1971, *11*, 209–226.

Fukuda, Y., and Stone, J. Retinal distribution and central projections of Y-, X-, and W- cells of the cat's retina. *Journal of Neurophysiology*, 1974, *37*, 749–772.

Fukuda, Y., and Sugitani, M. Cortical projections of two types of principal cells of the rat lateral geniculate body. *Brain Research*, 1974, *67*, 157–161.

Ganz, L., and Fitch, M. The effect of visual deprivation on perceptual behavior. *Experimental Neurology*, 1968, *22*, 638–660.

Ganz, L., and Haffner, M. E. Permanent perceptual and neurophysiological effects on visual deprivation in the cat. *Experimental Brain Research*, 1974, *20*, 67–87.

Ganz, L., Hirsch, H. V. B., and Tieman, S. B. The nature of perceptual deficits in visually deprived cats. *Brain Research*, 1972, *44*, 527–546.

Garey, L. J., and Powell, T. P. S. An experimental study of the termination of the lateral geniculo-cortical pathway in the cat and monkey. *Proceedings of the Royal Society Series B*, 1971, *179*, 41–63.

Geller, E., and Yuwiler, A. Environmental effects on the biochemistry of developing rat brain. In L. Jilek and S. Trojan (Eds.), *Ontogenesis of the brain*. Prague: Charles University Press, 1968, pp. 277–284.

Geller, E., Yuwiler, A., and Zolman, J. Effects of environmental complexity on constituents of brain and liver. *Journal of Neurochemistry*, 1965, *12*, 949–955.

Globus, A., and Scheibel, A. B. Synaptic loci on visual cortical neurons of the rabbit: The specific afferent radiation. *Experimental Neurology*, 1967, *18*, 116–131.

Gordon, B., and Gummow, L. Effects of extraocular muscle section on receptive fields in cat superior colliculus. *Vision Research*, 1975, *15*, 1011–1019.

Guillery, R. W. Binocular competition in the control of geniculate cell growth. *Journal of Comparative Neurology*, 1972, *144*, 117–127.

Guillery, R. W. The effect of lid suture upon the growth of cells in the dorsal lateral geniculate nucleus of kittens. *Journal of Comparative Neurology*, 1973, *148*, 417–422.

Guillery, R. W., and Stelzner, D. J. The differential effects of unilateral lid closure upon the monocular and binocular segments of the dorsal lateral geniculate nucleus in the cat. *Journal of Comparative Neurology*, 1970, *139*, 413–422.

Hickey, T. L., Spear, P. D., and Kratz, K. E. Quantitative studies of cell size in the cat's lateral geniculate nucleus following visual deprivation. *Journal of Comparative Neurology*, in press.

Hirsch, H. V. B. Visual perception in cats after environmental surgery. *Experimental Brain Research*, 1972, *15*, 405–423.

Hirsch, H. V. B., and Jacobson, M. The perfectible brain: Principles of neuronal development. In M. S. Gazzaniga and C. Blakemore (Eds.), *Handbook of psychobiology*. New York: Academic Press, 1975.

Hirsch, H. V. B., and Spinelli, D. N. Visual experience modifies distribution of horizontally and vertically oriented receptive fields in cats. *Science*, 1970, *168*, 869–871.

Hoffmann, K. P. Conduction velocity in pathways from retina to superior colliculus in the cat: A correlation with receptive-field properties. *Journal of Neurophysiology*, 1973, *36*, 409–424.

Hoffmann, K. P., and Sherman, S. M. Effects of early monocular deprivation on visual input to cat superior colliculus. *Journal of Neurophysiology*, 1974, *37(6)*, 1276–1286.

Hoffmann, K. P., and Sherman, S. M. Effects of early binocular deprivation on visual input to cat superior colliculus. *Journal of Neurophysiology*, 1975, *38*, 1049–1059.

Hoffmann, K. P., and Stone, J. Conduction velocity of afferents to cat visual cortex: A correlation with cortical receptive field properties. *Brain Research*, 1971, *32*, 460–466.

Hoffmann, K. P., Stone, J., and Sherman, S. M. Relay of receptive-field properties in dorsal lateral geniculate nucleus of the cat. *Journal of Neurophysiology*, 1972, *35*, 518–531.

Hubel, D. H., and Wiesel, T. N. Receptive fields of single neurons in the cat's striate cortex. *Journal of Physiology*, 1959, *148*, 574–591.

Hubel, D. H., and Wiesel, T. N. Integrative action in the cat's lateral geniculate body. *Journal of Physiology*, 1961, *155*, 385–598.

Hubel, D. H., and Wiesel, T. N. Receptive fields, binocular interaction and functional architecture of the cat's visual cortex. *Journal of Physiology*, 1962, *160*, 106–154.

Hubel, D. H., and Wiesel, T. N. Receptive fields of cells in striate cortex of very young, visually inexperienced kittens. *Journal of Neurophysiology*, 1963, *26*, 994–1002.

Hubel, D. H., and Wiesel, T. N. Receptive fields and functional architecture in two non-striate visual areas (18 and 19) of the cat. *Journal of Neurophysiology*, 1965a, *28*, 229–289.

Hubel, D. H., and Wiesel, T. N. Binocular interaction in striate cortex of kittens reared with artificial squint. *Journal of Neurophysiology*, 1965b, *28*, 1041–1059.

Hubel, D. H., and Wiesel, T. N. Receptive fields and functional architecture of monkey striate cortex. *Journal of Physiology*, 1968, *195*, 215–243.

Hubel, D. H., and Wiesel, T. N. The period of susceptibility to the physiological effects of unilateral eye closure in kittens. *Journal of Physiology*, London, 1970, *206*, 419–436.

Hubel, D. H., and Wiesel, T. N. Sequence regularity and geometry of orientation columns in the monkey striate cortex. *Journal of Comparative Neurology*, 1974, *158*, 267–294.

Ikeda, H., and Wright, M. J. Properties of LGN cells in kittens reared with convergent squint: A neurophysiological demonstration of amblyopia. *Experimental Brain Research*, 1976, *25*, 63–77.

Imbert, M., and Buisseret, P. Receptive field characteristics and plastic properties of visual cortical cells in kittens reared with or without visual experience. *Experimental Brain Research*, 1975, *22*, 25–36.

Kalil, R. E. Effects of dark rearing on the growth of lateral geniculate cells in the kitten. *Anatomical Record*, 1975, *181*, 535.

Kuffler, S. W. Discharge patterns and functional organization of mammalian retina. *Journal of Neurophysiology*, 1953, *16*, 37–68.

Kuffler, S. W., and Nicholls, J. G. *From neuron to brain*. Sunderland, Mass.: Sinauer Associates, 1976.

Lettvin, J. Y., Maturana, H. R., McCulloch, W. S., and Pitts, W. H. What the frog's eye tells the frog's brain. *Proceedings of the Institute of Radio Engineers*, 1959, *47*, 1940–1951.

Levick, W. R. Receptive fields and trigger features of ganglion cells in the visual streak of the rabbit's retina. *Journal of Physiology*, 1967, *188*, 285–307.

Maffei, L., and Fiorentini, A. Monocular deprivation in kittens impairs the spatial resolution of geniculate neurons. *Nature*, 1976, *264*, 754–755.

Marg, E., Adams, J. E., and Rutkin, B. Receptive fields of cells in the human visual cortex. *Experientia*, 1968, *24*, 348–350.

Maturana, H. R., and Frenk, S. Directional movement and horizontal edge detectors in the pigeon retina. *Science*, 1963, *149*, 1115–1116.

Meyers, B. Early experience and problem-solving behavior. In H. Moltz (Ed.), *The ontogeny of vertebrate behavior*. New York: Academic Press, 1971, pp. 57–94.

Michael, C. R. Receptive fields of single optic nerve fibers in a mammal with an all-cone retina. II. Directionally selective units. *Journal of Neurophysiology*, 1968, *31*, 257–267.

Mize, R. R., and Murphy, E. H. Selective visual experience fails to modify receptive field properties of rabbit striate cortex neurons. *Science*, 1973, *180*, 320–322.

Muir, D. W., and Mitchell, D. E. Visual resolution and experience: Acuity deficits in cats following early selective visual deprivation. *Science*, 1973, *180*, 420–422.

Olson, C. R., and Freeman, R. D. Progressive changes in kitten striate cortex during monocular vision. *Journal of Neurophysiology*, 1975, *38*(6), 26–32.

Packwood J., and Gordon, B. Stereopsis in normal domestic cat, Siamese cat, and cat raised with alternating monocular occlusion. *Journal of Neurophysiology*, 1975, *38*, 1485–1499.

Pettigrew, J. D. The effect of visual experience on the development of stimulus specificity by kitten cortical neurons. *Journal of Physiology*, 1974, *237*, 49–74.

Pettigrew, J. D., and Freeman, R. D. Visual experience without lines: Effect on developing cortical neurons. *Science*, 1973, *182*, 599–601.

Rabinovitch, M. S., and Rosvold, H. E. A closed-field intelligence test for rats. *Canadian Journal of Psychology*, 1951, *5*, 122–128.

Riesen, A. H. Sensory deprivation. In E. Stellar and J. M. Sprague (Eds.), *Progress in physiological psychology*. Vol. 1. New York: Academic Press, 1966, pp. 117–147.

Riesen, A. H. Electrophysiological changes after sensory deprivation. In A. H. Riesen (Ed.), *The developmental neuropsychology of sensory deprivation*. New York: Academic Press, 1975, pp. 153–164.

Riesen, A. H., and Zilbert, D. E. Behavioral consequences of variations in early sensory environments. In A. H. Riesen (Ed.), *The developmental neuropsychology of sensory deprivation*. New York: Academic Press, 1975, pp. 211–246.

Rizzolatti, G., and Tradardi, V. Pattern discrimination in monocularly reared cats. *Experimental Neurology*, 1971, *33*, 181–194.

Rosenzweig, M. R., Krech, D., Bennett, E. L., and Diamond, M. C. Modifying brain chemistry and anatomy by enrichment or impoverishment of experience. In G. Newton and S. Levine (Eds.), *Early experience and behavior: The psychobiology of development*. Springfield, Ill.: Thomas, 1968, pp. 258–298.

Rothblat, L. A., and Schwartz, M. L. The effect of monocular deprivation in the rat on the discrimination of pattern: Search for a sensitive period. In preparation.

Sanderson, K. J. The projection of the visual field to lateral geniculate and medial inter-laminar nuclei in the cat. *Journal of Comparative Neurology*, 1971, *143*, 101–118.

Schwartz, M. L., and Rothblat, L. A. Effect of monocular deprivation on visual behavior in rats. Presented at the sixth annual meeting of the Society for Neuroscience, Toronto, November, 1976.

Schwartz, M. L., and Rothblat, L. A. The effect of monocular and binocular deprivation on pattern discrimination in the rat. In preparation.

Shaw, C., Yinon, U., and Auerbach, E. Diminution of evoked neuronal activity in the visual cortex of pattern deprived rats. *Experimental Neurology*, 1974, *45*, 42–49.

Sherk, H., and Stryker, M. P. Quantitative study of cortical orientation selectivity in visually inexperienced kitten. *Journal of Neurophysiology,* 1976, *39(1),* 63–70.

Sherman, S. M. Visual field defects in monocularly and binocularly deprived cats. *Brain Research,* 1973, *49,* 25–45.

Sherman, S. M. Permanence of visual perimetry deficits in monocularly and binocularly deprived cats. *Brain Research,* 1974, *73,* 491–501.

Sherman, S. M., Hoffmann, K. P., and Stone, J. Loss of a specific cell type from dorsal lateral geniculate nucleus in visually deprived cats. *Journal of Neurophysiology,* 1972, *35,* 532–541.

Sherman, S. M., Guillery, R. W., Kaas, J. H., and Sanderson, K. J. Behavioral, electrophysiological and morphological studies of binocular competition in the development of the geniculo-cortical pathways of cats. *Journal of Comparative Neurology,* 1974, *158,* 1–18.

Sherman, S. M., Norton, T. T., and Casagrande, V. A. X- and Y- cells in the dorsal lateral geniculate nucleus of the tree shrew (*Tupaia glis*). *Brain Research,* 1975, *93,* 152–157.

Sherman, S. M., Wilson, J. R., Kaas, J. H., and Webb, S. V. X- and Y- cells in the dorsal lateral geniculate nucleus of the owl monkey (*Aotus trivirgatus*). *Science,* 1976, *192,* 475–477.

Stone, J. Morphology and physiology of the geniculocortical synapse in the cat: The question of parallel input to the striate cortex. *Investigative Ophthalmology,* 1972, *11,* 338–344.

Stone, J., and Fukuda, Y. Properties of cat retinal ganglion cells: A comparison W-cells with X- and Y- cells. *Journal of Neurophysiology,* 1974, *37,* 722–748.

Stone, J., and Hoffmann, K. P. Very slow conducting ganglion cells in the cat's retina: A major, new functional type? *Brain Research,* 1972, *43,* 610–616.

Stryker, M. P., and Sherk, H. Modification of cortical orientation selectivity in the cat by restricted visual experience: A reexamination. *Science,* 1975, *190,* 904–906.

Tees, R. C. Effect of early restriction on later form discrimination in the rat. *Canadian Journal of Psychology,* 1968, *22,* 294–301.

Tretter, F., Cynader, M., and Singer, W. Modification of direction selectivity of neurons in the visual cortex of kittens. *Brain Research,* 1975, *84,* 143–149.

Van Hof-Van Duin, J. Early and permanent effects of monocular deprivation on pattern discrimination and visuomotor behavior in cats. *Brain Research,* 1976, *111,* 261–276.

von Noorden, G. K., and Dowling, J. E. II. Behavioral studies in strabismic amblyopia. *Archives of Ophthalmology,* 1970, *84,* 215–220.

von Noorden, G. K., and Middleditch, P. R. Histology of the monkey lateral geniculate nucleus after unilateral lid closure and experimental strabismus: Further observation. *Investigative Ophthalmology,* 1975, *14,* 674–683.

von Noorden, G. K., Dowling, J. E., and Ferguson, D. C. Experimental amblyopia in monkeys. I. Behavioral studies of stimulus deprivation amblyopia. *Archives of Ophthalmology,* 1970, *84,* 206–214.

Walk, R. D., and Bond, E. K. Deficit in depth perception of 90-day-old dark-reared rats. *Psychonomic Science,* 1968, *10(11),* 383–384.

Wiesel, T. N., and Hubel, D. H. Effects of visual deprivation on morphology and physiology of cells in the cat's lateral geniculate body. *Journal of Neurophysiology,* 1963a, *26,* 978–993.

Wiesel, T. N., and Hubel, D. H. Single-cell responses in striate cortex of kittens deprived of vision in one eye. *Journal of Neurophysiology,* 1963b, *26,* 1003–10017.

Wiesel, T. N., and Hubel, D. H. Comparison of the effects of unilateral and bilateral eye closure on cortical unit responses in kittens. *Journal of Neurophysiology,* 1965a, *28,* 1029–1040.

Wiesel, T. N., and Hubel, D. H. Extent of recovery from the effects of visual deprivation in kittens. *Journal of Neurophysiology,* 1965b, *28,* 1060–1072.

Wiesel, T. N., and Hubel, D. H. Ordered arrangement of orientation columns in monkeys lacking visual experience. *Journal of Comparative Neurology,* 1974, *158,* 307–318.

Wilson, P. D., and Stone, J. Evidence of W-cell input to the cat's visual cortex via the C laminae of the lateral geniculate nucleus. *Brain Research,* 1975, *92,* 472–478.

Yinon, U. Age dependence of the effect of squint on cells in kittens' visual cortex. *Experimental Brain Research*, 1976, *26*, 151–157.

Yinon, U., Auerbach, E., Blank, M., and Friesenhausen, J. The ocular dominance of cortical neurons in cats developed with divergent and convergent squint. *Vision Research*, 1975, *15*, 1251–1256.

2

Effect of Early Visual Experience on the Development of Certain Perceptual Abilities in Animals and Man

DONALD E. MITCHELL

1. Historical Perspective

In 1694, the English philosopher John Locke published a letter that he had received from William Molyneux in which the latter posed the following problem:

> Suppose a man *born* blind, and now adult, and taught by his *touch* to distinguish between a cube and a sphere of the same metal, and nighly of the same bigness, so as to tell, when he felt one and the other, which is the cube, which the sphere. Suppose then the cube and sphere placed on a table, and the blind man be made to see: *query,* whether *by his sight, before he touched them* he could now distinguish and tell which is the globe, and which the cube? (cited by Pastore, 1971, p. 66)

Ever since this question was posed (which is frequently referred to as Molyneux's problem), philosophers and psychologists have engaged themselves in a vigorous debate concerning the manner by which we attain our ability to perceive the visual world. Over the years, attempts to answer this question have been derived from three major sources: (1) studies of the perceptual abilities of the neonate, (2) studies of the perceptual abilities of people who have had sight restored after having been deprived of vision early in their lives, and (3) studies of the adaptability of the adult to distorted visual input. Until recently, data from the first of these were difficult to obtain so that much of the

---

DONALD E. MITCHELL • Psychology Department, Dalhousie University, Halifax, Nova Scotia, Canada. The preparation of this chapter was aided by grants from the National (AP-7660) and Medical (MA-5027) Research Councils of Canada.

fuel for the debate over the relative role that genetics and environment play in determining our perceptual abilities has been derived from the latter two sources, in particular from patients with restored sight. It was thought that subjects such as these could tell us what an infant sees, the argument being that vision did not either deteriorate or improve during the period of prolonged visual deprivation beyond the level it had achieved when the deprivation was imposed.

In 1934 von Senden published a book that documented many cases of this sort, but, despite the large number of cases, the results have not always been clear-cut. Most subjects regain only rudimentary sight after removal of some peripheral obstruction to vision that had been present from birth, such as a cataract (an opaque crystalline lens) or an opaque cornea. Typically they suffer great visual confusion following the image-restoring operation (von Senden, 1960), but under controlled experimental conditions a certain degree of structure can be found to their visual perceptions (Valvo, 1971). Nevertheless, there is a great deal of variability with respect to postoperative visual rehabilitation after congenital blindness. In contrast to the general picture, other patients seem to attain quite good vision. The equivocal nature of the data from such cases is well illustrated by the results of two recently published cases of this sort. Gregory and Wallace (1963) describe an amazing degree of recovery in a man who had extensive corneal scarring from the age of 10 months that prevented the formation of any patterned images on the two retinas. He was a highly intelligent man who led a very active life while blind. At the age of 52, a corneal graft operation was performed. Within a few days he could maneuver himself around without recourse to other senses, could name objects using sight alone, and was even able to tell the time from a large clock on the wall. Nevertheless, he still had difficulty judging distances and often was unable to name objects until he touched them.

The second case (Ackroyd, Humphrey, and Warrington, 1974) was of a young woman who had been blinded by a corneal opacity following the contraction of smallpox at 3 years of age. When she was 27 a successful corneal graft was performed on her left eye. Despite the fact that the eye's optics were now clear, no significant recovery of vision occurred in the first 22 weeks following the operation. Detailed tests revealed that the retina was functionally intact, since she demonstrated normal dark adaptation curves and her electroretinogram was of normal amplitude and form. Nevertheless, her vision was very poor and she suffered a form of reactive depression similar to that of several of von Senden's and Valvo's cases and of the subject of Gregory and Wallace (1963). Moving objects were seen best, and, in fact, she felt that her most vivid visual impressions occurred while being driven around in a car. She had great difficulty in judging colors and never showed any convincing evidence of being able to recognize objects by shape. On formal tests of form discrimination she would scan each stimulus with her eyes very close to the pattern, suggesting that she might have attempted to solve these form discriminations by converting them to temporal brightness discriminations. Thus, despite the fact that she had possessed good vision until 3 years of age, she was unable to recognize colors and shapes of objects. On the other hand, Gregory and Wallace's subject, who began to lose vision at 10 months of age, immediately had these abilities following restoration of retinal images.

These two cases point out the variability associated with studies of "restored sight." Part of the variability may be due to individual differences in the amount of normal or partial vision early in life or in the length of deprivation (Valvo, 1971; Jeannerod, 1975). Many of these clinical conditions develop slowly, so that it is possible that many subjects may have been partially sighted for a much longer period than supposed. The deficit following partial deprivation, which permits luminous perception prior to operation, tends to be far less severe than following a more total deprivation, which may cause atrophy of retinal ganglion cells. With most clinical cases, knowledge of the exact nature of the early visual input is poor, so that subjects with possibly quite different visual histories are often judged equivalent.

Until comparatively recently, data from all three of the sources mentioned earlier failed to provide an answer to the debate over the origin of human perceptual abilities. This was not solely due to the variability of the data derived from subjects with restored sight, since it was also possible to argue on purely logical grounds that such data do not necessarily provide a clue to the state of the visual system near birth. It is not necessarily true that a peripheral obstruction to vision results in nothing more than a simple arrest of visual development; indeed, the later evidence, derived from animal work that is discussed below, suggests that in many cases the visual system may, in fact, deteriorate under certain conditions of early visual deprivation. Furthermore, the demonstration of a certain degree of adaptability in adult human perception does not necessarily argue that the development of the visual system was initially "molded" by its early visual input.

2. New Evidence

Since the early 1960s evidence from an entirely new source has emerged that not only goes a long way toward permitting a resolution of the nature-nurture controversy in visual perception but also provides a rubric for understanding earlier clinical data. This new line of evidence stems from studies of the properties of neurons in the visual cortex of cats and monkeys.

In their pioneering study of the properties of neurons in the cat visual cortex, Hubel and Wiesel (1962) noted that, in contrast to neurons at lower levels in the visual pathway, cortical neurons only responded to quite complex visual features. Typically, they responded best to linear contours (straight edges or bars) of a certain orientation that often needed to be moved in a certain direction (thus demonstrating directional selectivity). Binocular cells, which constitute 80% of cat cortical neurons, tend to be highly specific for retinal disparity, so that they respond best to a stimulus at a certain distance from the eyes (Barlow, Blakemore, and Pettigrew, 1967; Nikara, Bishop, and Pettigrew, 1968). This particular feature is particularly evident in cells in area 18 of the monkey (Hubel and Wiesel, 1970a). They are thus thought to provide the neural basis for stereopsis in these animals (Fox and Blake, 1971; Cowey, Parkinson, and Warnick, 1975).

These discoveries made a tremendous impact on psychology, since it was thought that studies of the properties of these cortical cells could lead to an understanding of perception itself. Shortly after their first description of these cortical cells, Hubel and Wiesel published two papers (Hubel and Wiesel, 1963; Wiesel and Hubel, 1963) that have been seminal for studies that investigate the relative role of genetics and experience in perception. Having demonstrated the rather complicated nature of cortical cells, they then turned their attention to experiments which, they hoped, would lead to an understanding of how these complex properties arose. Did they develop through experience or were they genetically specified? Hubel and Wiesel approached this problem in two ways, identical, in fact, to the first two traditional approaches that were outlined at the beginning of this chapter for studying the origins of human perception: (1) study of the properties of cortical cells in the neonate prior to visual experience, and (2) studies of cortical cells in animals that had undergone various forms of early visual deprivation.

2.1. Properties of Visual Cortical Cells in the Neonate

In 1963 Hubel and Wiesel reported that "much of the richness of visual physiology in the cortex of the adult cat—the receptive field organization, binocular interaction, and functional architecture—is present in very young kittens without visual experience" (p. 999). While some features of this general conclusion have been disputed (Barlow and Pettigrew, 1971; Pettigrew, 1974; Buisseret and Imbert, 1976; Blakemore and van Sluyters, 1975), there is a general agreement that certain properties of cortical neurons are innately specified. Not only is the normal topographic representation of the cortex present at birth, but also many of the properties of binocular neurons, such as their ocular dominance, appear similar to those in the visually experienced animal and many cells appear to be directionally selective. The largest disagreement concerns estimates of the proportion of cells with orientation specificity comparable to that observed in the adult. These estimates range from as low as 0% (Pettigrew, 1974) to as high as 92% (Sherk and Stryker, 1976); the other groups arrive at figures intermediate between these extremes. There is no doubt, however, that cortical neurons are incompletely specified at birth. Hubel and Wiesel (1963) themselves comment on the general lack of responsiveness of cells and a tendency for rapid habituation; most cells were also broadly tuned for orientation. In addition to confirming these observations, later work (Pettigrew, 1974) has established that cortical cells in the neonatal kitten are extremely broadly tuned for retinal disparity, and achieve their normal tight tuning only after 2 months of normal visual experience. These findings are not surprising in view of Cragg's (1972) discovery that only 1.5% of the adult number of synapses per cortical cell are present 8 days after birth, at the time of normal eye-opening.

In contrast to the kitten, which shows very poor visual behavior in the first 3 weeks after birth and has cloudy optic media, the infant monkey shows good visual behavior and has clear optics. Not surprisingly, then, the visual response characteristics of cortical cells in the newborn monkey appear to resemble those seen in the adult more closely than they do in the kitten. Furthermore, the visual cortex of the newborn monkey appears to possess a rudimentary form of the columnar organization that is such a striking feature of the adult cortex (Wiesel and Hubel, 1974). Recent anatomical demonstrations indicate that although the initial segregation of cortical cells into right and left ocular dominance columns (regions of cortex where one eye dominates the responses of all cells) begins well before birth (Rakic, 1976), this organization is still far from complete 7 days after birth (Hubel, Wiesel, and LeVay, 1976). Thus it is not unreasonable to assume that cortical cells in the monkey, like those in the cat, are incompletely specified at birth and require normal visual input in order to achieve the tight spatial tuning that is characteristic of cells in the adult.

2.2. Effects of Selective Visual Deprivation

Although many physiological properties of cortical neurons are genetically determined, visual experience during the first few postnatal months appears to be necessary in order to maintain the neural connections that subserve these properties. Cortical neurons in kittens or monkeys reared in total darkness tend to lose the specificity that was present at birth (Wiesel and Hubel, 1965, 1974; Buisseret and Imbert, 1976; Blakemore and van Sluyters, 1975). In addition to this rather passive role of early visual experience, there is now much evidence, some of it controversial, that the early visual input may, in many instances, influence the development of the visual response characteristics of these neurons. Again, the first and most repeatably reliable demonstration of this constructive role of visual experience was made by Wiesel and Hubel (1963), who covered one eye of each of several kittens, soon after birth, for up to 2 or 3 months, after which the kittens were found to have extremely defective vision in the deprived eye. Recordings from the visual cortex of these animals revealed that the great majority of cortical neurons could be excited only through the non-deprived eye. Later work has established that there is only a brief period in the animal's life, a critical period, during which cortical neurons are susceptible to monocular deprivation (Wiesel and Hubel, 1963, 1965; Hubel and Wiesel, 1970b; Blakemore and van Sluyters, 1974a). The result that first led to this conclusion are summarized in Fig. 1, which shows the ocular dominance distribution of a sample of cortical neurons recorded from animals that had undergone periods of monocular deprivation during the times shown. A cell with an ocular dominance of either 1 or 7 can only be monocularly driven, through either the eye contralateral or that ipsilateral to the recording electrode, respectively. All other cells are binocular; cells in ocular dominance group 4 are influenced equally through the two eyes, while cells in the other groups are influenced to a greater degree by one eye than the other. A typical distribution of ocular dominance among a sample of cells recorded from a normal animal is shown in Fig. 2A. This is virtually identical to the pattern observed in Fig. 1F in an animal deprived for 3 months at 4 months of age. It can be seen that monocular suture prior to the fourth week or after the 12th week has little effect, but monocular closure for a period as brief as 3 days in the fourth week can exert a profound change on the ocular dominance distribution.

An analogous effect can be observed in the monkey both behaviorally (von Noorden, Dowling, and Ferguson, 1970; von Noorden, 1973) and physiologically (Baker, Grigg, and von Noorden, 1974). Here, however, the critical period for the effects of monocular deprivation may last much longer than in the cat, extending perhaps to 18 months of age (Wiesel, 1975).

Later work has shown that the proportion of binocular cortical cells can also be diminished by manipulations that are perhaps more subtle than monocular deprivation. As can be seen from Fig. 2, conditions that result in noncongruent images in the two eyes, such as alternate monocular occlusion (where occlusion is switched from right eye to left on a daily basis), or surgically induced strabismus in which case the two eyes point in different directions and therefore usually receive different images,[1] lead to a reduction in the proportion of cells that can be influenced through the two eyes (Hubel and Wiesel, 1965; Blakemore and van Sluyters, 1974b; Pettigrew, Olson, and Hirsch, 1973).

While there is no dispute concerning these observations on the modifiability of binocular connections, some controversy surrounds the question of whether or not other properties of cortical neurons can be affected by early visual experience. In 1970, two groups, using different procedures, reported that the orientation specificity of cortical neurons could be altered by abnormal visual input. Both groups reared kittens in such a way that each eye saw contours

---

[1] Parenthetically, it should be noted that Maffei and Bisti (1976) have offered an alternative explanation for the loss of binocular cells in strabismic kittens. Rather than owing its origin to the discordant nature of the visual *input*, they suggest that the reduced binocularity was due to an asymmetry in eye movements. The basis for this suggestion was their observation that kittens made artificially strabismic by section of one of the extraocular eye muscles lost binocularity even if they were reared in total darkness.

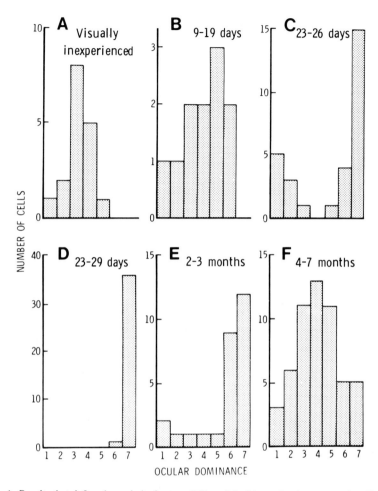

Fig. 1. Results that define the period of susceptibility of the kitten visual cortex to the effects of monocular deprivation. Each histogram depicts the number of cells with various degrees of ocular dominance recorded from the left hemisphere of kittens that had had their right eye occluded for the periods shown. Ocular dominance groups are as defined by Hubel and Wiesel (1962). In this recording situation, group 1 and 7 cells were activated by only the right and left eyes, respectively. Group 2 cells showed a much stronger response for the right eye than for the left, while group 3 cells showed only slightly stronger responses for the right eye. Group 4 cells were influenced equally by the two eyes. Cells in groups 5 and 6 were dominated by the left eye, markedly in the case of the former but only marginally so for cells in the latter group. The histogram depicted in F for a cat deprived for 3 months from the age of 4 months is almost identical to the results that would be obtained from a normal animal (see Fig. 2). Redrawn from Hubel and Wiesel (1963, 1970b).

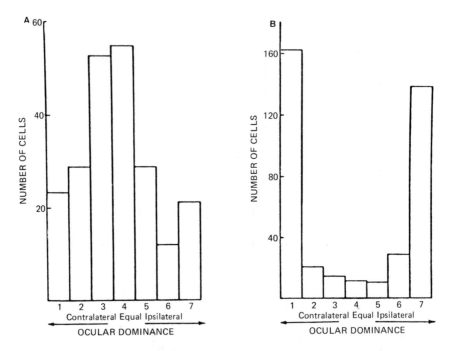

Fig. 2. A: Ocular dominance of a sample of 223 cells recorded from a number of normal animals. B: Ocular dominance of a sample of 384 cells recorded from four kittens that had had their right medial rectus severed at the time of normal eye opening in order to produce a divergent strabismus. Note the reduction in the number of binocular cells in this group of animals; instead of 80% of the cells being binocular as in the normal animals (A), only 20% could be driven by the two eyes. Reproduced from Hubel and Wiesel (1965).

of only a single orientation, either vertical or horizontal. Hirsch and Spinelli's (1970) kittens wore goggles for a few hours each day, so that one eye saw three vertical bars while the other viewed three bars that were horizontal. On the other hand, Blakemore and Cooper's (1970) animals were reared in a manner similar to that shown in Fig. 3 so that their visual input was confined to the patterns of stripes posted on the inside wall of the cylinder. When Hirsch and Spinelli (1970) recorded from their animals they found very few binocular cells (consistent with the discordant nature of their early visual input) and a large proportion of nonoriented cells, but the others all had elongated receptive fields with an orientation similar to those experienced by that particular eye in early life. Blakemore and Cooper (1970) reported an even more dramatic result. Not only did they report a normal complement of specified cells, but they also found that nearly all neurons were optimally excited by contours with an orientation similar to the stripes to which the animal had been exposed early in its life. They found no cells at all that were optimally stimulated by contours

Fig. 3. Photograph of a kitten in a cylinder similar to that employed by Blakemore and Cooper (1970) and Muir and Mitchell (1973) to restrict visual input to contours of a single orientation (in this case, vertical).

perpendicular to the stripes they saw as kittens. Because they encountered no regions of the cortex that were silent, Blakemore and Cooper suggested that the orientation specificity of some cortical cells might actually have been modified to match the orientation of the contours in the animal's early visual environment. However, certain of these observations have been disputed by Stryker and Sherk (1975).[2] Although they carefully duplicated the rearing procedures of Blakemore and Cooper (1970), they were unable to replicate the dramatic orientation bias reported by these authors. However, they did observe a strong tendency for the cortical cells of cats reared in the fashion of Hirsch and Spinelli (1970) to be optimally excited by contours with orientations similar to those to which the eyes had been exposed as kittens. Like Hirsch and Spinelli (1970), they encountered many cells that were not orientation selective at all. On this basis they argued that the orientation bias that they observed in their animals was the result of an atrophy, rather than a recruitment, of the cells that were genetically predisposed to be selective for contours with orientations that were very different from that of the bars which the animals saw when wearing their goggles as kittens.

More recently, there have been a number of demonstrations which suggest that it may be possible to bias other visual response characteristics of cortical neurons, such as their directional selectivity (Tretter, Cynader, and Singer,

[2] Ignoring species differences, such as in studies using rabbits (Mize and Murphy, 1973), the only investigators who have failed to replicate the original phenomenon reported by Hirsch and Spinelli (1970) and Blakemore and Cooper (1970) were Stryker and Sherk (1975). The only differences between the studies were procedural; Stryker and Sherk recorded without knowledge of the animal's rearing history, advanced the electrode in steps of 100 μm so as to sample large areas of cortex, and plotted most receptive fields by use of a computer. It is unlikely that these procedural modifications (important as they were) could account for the discrepancy in the results since Blasdel, Mitchell, Muir, and Pettigrew (1977) were able to replicate the original findings of Blakemore and Cooper (1970) even when these precautions were taken. Other groups have also reported a substantial bias in the distribution of preferred orientations of cortical cells, following exposure to contours of one orientation (Blakemore and Mitchell, 1973; Freeman and Pettigrew, 1973; Pettigrew and Garey, 1974; Turkel, Gijsbers, and Pritchard, 1975). Most likely the discrepancy arises from the nature of the rearing procedure itself, since Stryker and Sherk (1975) were able to replicate the results of Hirsch and Spinelli (1970), who used goggles to ensure that the visual input was confined to contours of a single orientation. While this may also be achieved with the rearing procedure of Blakemore and Cooper, there is far greater possibility for active animals to receive inappropriate stimulation by tilting their heads, thus increasing the likelihood for variability in the results. Recent results of Blakemore (1977) fully support this position. Using a single-blind procedure and a sampling technique similar to that employed by Stryker and Sherk (1975) on cats reared in cylinders, convincing results (a distribution of preferred orientations decidedly skewed toward the orientation of the stripes in the cylinders) were observed in only four of six cats. The results were unconvincing in one cat and were even quite negative in the other. However, in three cats that were monocularly exposed to stripes in goggles, the preferred orientations of cortical cells were tightly skewed toward the experienced orientation. As with previous reports in which goggles had been employed to restrict the early visual input, the general responsiveness of neurons was poorer than that observed in either normally reared animals or kittens reared in cylinders.

1975; Cynader, Berman, and Hein, 1975; Daw and Wyatt, 1976) and disparity specificity (Shlaer, 1971) by suitable manipulation of the animal's early visual input. Thus, for example, recordings from animals exposed to stimuli moving in only one direction in early life reveal many more cortical neurons that are directionally selective for stimuli moving in this particular direction than are selective for motion in the opposite direction. But just as with the earlier demonstrations, it is unclear how the various biases in the stimulus specificity of cortical neurons that are observed in selectively visually deprived animals are produced.

The evidence from these various studies suggests very strongly that, despite the fact that the neural connections that subserve many of the visual response characteristics of cortical neurons are present at birth and therefore to a certain extent genetically determined (Hubel and Wiesel, 1963; Wiesel and Hubel, 1974; Blakemore and van Sluyters, 1975), they can nevertheless be influenced by the animal's early visual experience. Kittens and monkeys that receive grossly anomalous early visual input develop cortical neurons with abnormal properties. However, the manner in which the early visual input influences the properties of cortical neurons is a source of considerable debate and controversy. Perhaps the issue that is most contentious is the extent to which the various visual response characteristics of a given neuron can be altered by the animal's early visual input. Some investigations even suggest that cortical connections are sufficiently malleable in early life to permit the production of visual response characteristics unlike those encountered in the normal animal! Among these are studies which suggest that it is possible to produce cortical cells which respond better to spots of light than to lines or edges by rearing animals in a planetarium-like environment devoid of lines (Pettigrew and Freeman, 1973; van Sluyters and Blakemore, 1973). By contrast, other investigators (e.g., Stryker and Sherk, 1975) suggest that the cortical connections that subserve certain visual response characteristics of cortical cells are far less malleable and that the biases observed in the response characteristics of populations of neurons recorded from certain selectively deprived animals are due to a loss of specificity or atrophy of certain cells. However, at this point there is insufficient evidence to decide the extent to which either of these extreme positions is correct for any given response characteristic of cortical neurons.

3. Implications for Perception

3.1. Modification of Vision in Animals by Abnormal Early Visual Input

Irrespective of the mechanism by which they arise, the changes that are observed in cortical physiology in selectively deprived animals hold important implications for perception. If the early visual experience can influence connections in the animal's visual cortex, then surely it should influence its ability to perceive the visual world. Thus it would be expected that the changes that occur in the visual response characteristics of cortical cells after early selected visual deprivation would be reflected by concordant changes in the animal's visual behavior. There is good evidence that this is in fact so (for recent extensive reviews, see Ganz, 1975; Riesen and Zilbert, 1975; Rothblat and Schwartz, this volume). Two measures of perceptual capability that have provided an important insight in this regard have been tests of visual acuity, which examine the animal's ability to discriminate fine spatial detail, and tests of stereopsis, which measure the animal's ability to discriminate depth by use of retinal disparity cues alone. Rather than exhaustively review all of the studies that have examined change in these and other perceptual capabilities after selected visual deprivation, I shall concentrate on just a few studies, including some recent ones from my own laboratory, on the effects of monocular or alternate monocular deprivation that illustrate best the connection between the changes that are observed in cortical physiology and the alterations that occur in the animal's visual behavior.

We have recently developed a simple procedure for testing the visual acuity of young kittens that permits the tracking of changes in perception during development or following various forms of early visual deprivation and will in the future permit study of the factors that influence the development of form vision (Mitchell, Giffin, Wilkinson, Anderson, and Smith, 1976; Mitchell, Giffin, and Timney, 1977). The principle of the procedure is illustrated in Fig. 4; the cat is prompted to leap from the pedestal P onto the grating placed on top of

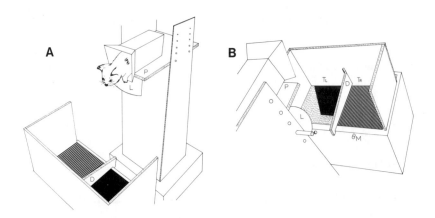

Fig. 4. Jumping stand employed for measurement of visual resolution in young kittens. A: Shows the situation confronting the cat before it leaps. B: The consequences of an incorrect leap onto the gray uniform field. The trapdoor beneath it (T_L) opens and the kitten falls to the floor. Reproduced from Mitchell et al. (1976).

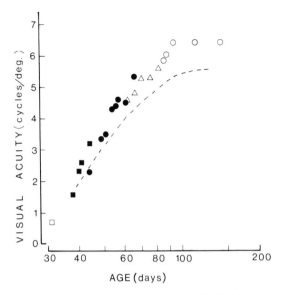

Fig. 5. Development of visual acuity in young kittens measured in the jumping stand of Fig. 4. The acuity is defined as the spatial frequency of the grating to which the animal jumped correctly on 70% of trials. The space average luminance of the stimuli was 170 cd/m². The different symbols refer to results obtained from several different animals. The dashed line shows the average values for acuity obtained in an earlier study (Mitchell *et al.*, 1976) which employed stimuli of lower luminance (35 cd/m²).

one of the two trapdoors T_L and T_R. If it does so, it is rewarded by petting and a piece of food. If it jumps instead to the other stimulus, a uniform field matched in luminance to the grating (so that from a distance the two fields appear identical), the trapdoor beneath it opens and the kitten falls 18 inches to the floor. An estimate of the acuity can be made very simply by progressively increasing the spatial frequency of the grating (the number of periods or cycles of the grating per degree of visual angle) until the animal can no longer make the discrimination. We define as threshold the spatial frequency of the grating for which the animal performs correctly on 70% of the trials.

Figure 5 illustrates the way in which acuity develops in kittens from 31 days of age, the age of the youngest kitten that could be run in this way. Perhaps reflecting the infantile state of development of the eye and of the visual cortex (Donovan, 1966), acuity is poor at first and develops slowly, reaching adult values of 6 cycles/deg or better (only about one-eighth of typical values for human visual acuity) at around 3 months of age. During this time various manipulations of the visual input, such as monocular deprivation, can result in substantial reductions in acuity.

Monocular deprivation, particularly if prolonged throughout the first 3 months of life, can have extremely dramatic effects on vision (e.g., Dews and

Wiesel, 1970; Ganz and Fitch, 1968), although some recovery of vision may occur over a long period of time. Figure 6 illustrates the effect of either 23 or 25 days of monocular occlusion, imposed during the times shown, on the acuity of three kittens. If imposed early in the critical period, even a brief period of monocular occlusion can lead to temporary blindness for a week, following which considerable recovery occurs. When the period of deprivation is imposed progressively later in life, the initial deficit in acuity becomes smaller so that in the case of the third kitten, deprived from 84 to 109 days of age, the acuity in the deprived eye was initially reduced by only about 30% to 4 cycles/deg.

As mentioned earlier, alternate monocular occlusion reduces the proportion of binocular neurons without affecting the number of neurons driven by each eye (Hubel and Wiesel, 1965). The perceptual deficit that follows this form of deprivation is not a reduction in the animal's visual acuity, which is normal in the two eyes; instead, there is a tenfold reduction in the ability of the animal to perceive depth (Blake and Hirsch, 1975; Packwood and Gordon, 1975). By use of anaglyphs, Packwood and Gordon (1975) were able to show that animals reared in this way had completely lost stereopsis; they were totally unable to utilize the cue to depth provided by retinal disparity. This result, incidentally, provides further support for the widely held opinion that implicates binocular neurons as the neural substrate for stereopsis (Barlow et al., 1967).

Studies with monkeys are less numerous but the few that have been performed support the findings from studies with cats. For example, monocular deprivation for periods as brief as 2–4 weeks during the first 2 months of life has an equally profound effect on the vision of monkeys (Von Noorden et al., 1970; von Noorden, 1973).

3.2. Modification of Vision in Humans by Abnormal Early Visual Input

a. Vision in Newborn Infants. With the advent of techniques that enable measurements to be made of the visual capacities of human infants, it has been possible to show that human spatial resolution is extremely poor during the first 2 months of life (Atkinson, Braddick, and Braddick, 1974; Teller, Morse, Borton, and Regal, 1974; Banks and Salapatek, 1976). Figure 7 shows the average results of measurements of spatial resolution in five 2-month-old infants made by a method which utilizes the well-known tendency of young infants to stare at contoured surfaces in preference to nonstructured or featureless regions of their visual field. The infants were placed before a large uniform screen that filled nearly all their visual field. In the center of the screen was a small light upon which the infant would usually gaze because of the absence of any other object in its field of view. Two observers viewed the infant's eyes through a mirror that also prevented them from seeing the screen. When they were satisfied that the baby was looking at the light, a large sinusoidal grating was

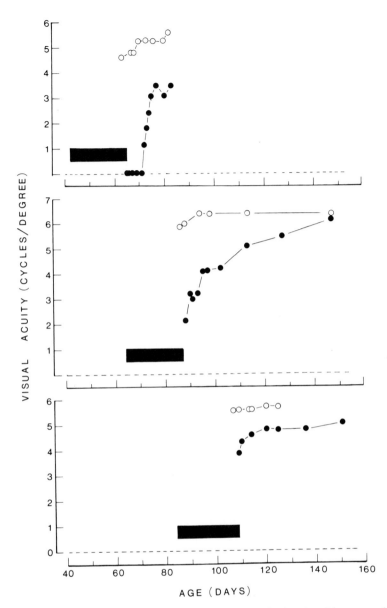

Fig. 6. Effects of brief periods of monocular occlusion on the visual acuity of three young kittens. The right eye was occluded during the period indicated by the black bars; at the end of this time the eye was opened and separate acuity measurements were made in the two eyes. A large opaque contact lens occluder was used to cover one eye for these measurements. Open and closed symbols depict the acuity (defined in Fig. 5) of the normal (left) and deprived (right) eyes, respectively. An acuity of zero indicates that the animal was unable to distinguish between an open and a closed trapdoor on the jumping stand. Note that the deprived eye initially showed reduced acuity, the impairment becoming progressively smaller as the deprivation was imposed increasingly later in life. Notice also the substantial recovery of vision afterward.

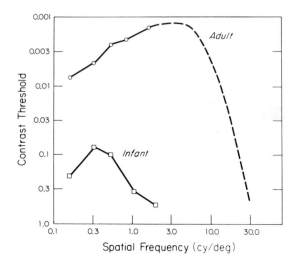

Fig. 7. Spatial resolution of 2-month-old human infants compared to that of an adult observer. The average contrast thresholds for sinusoidal gratings of five 2-month-old infants are plotted as a function of the spatial frequency of the gratings. Typical data for an adult observer are shown for comparison. Note how poor infant resolution is in relation to that of the adult. Reproduced by permission from Banks and Salapatek (1976).

flashed immediately to one side of the light and a uniform field of the same size and luminance was simultaneously flashed on the other. At the same instant the fields were presented, the fixation light was extinguished. The observers watched the baby's eyes to determine which field the baby fixated first. With gratings of low spatial frequency and of high contrast the baby invariably looked first at the grating, but when gratings of higher spatial frequencies or of lower contrast were presented no such fixation preference was apparent. For gratings of any given spatial frequency it was possible to determine the minimum contrast that was necessary for a fixation preference to emerge. The reciprocals of the threshold contrasts (the contrast sensitivities), as defined in this way, were determined for gratings of several different spatial frequencies on all five subjects. The mean results of these measurements are depicted by the open squares in Fig. 7. Typical results from an adult observer under comparable conditions are shown for comparison.[3] As is readily apparent, it is unlikely that a

[3] The reader is referred to a standard text such as Cornsweet (1970) for detailed description of how these measurements of contrast thresholds are typically made. Briefly, the subject views a grating with a sinusoidal luminance profile whose contrast [defined as $(I_{max} - I_{min})/(I_{max} + I_{min})$ where I_{max} and I_{min} are, respectively, the highest and lowest intensities of the pattern] is slowly elevated until the subject can just detect the presence of a grating. The reciprocal of this threshold contrast, the contrast sensitivity, is measured for gratings of many different spatial frequencies; the function that is generated when these contrast sensitivities are plotted against the spatial frequency of the grating is the frequency response function (sometimes referred to as the "contrast sensitivity function").

2-month-old infant can resolve gratings with spatial frequencies higher than about 2.5 cycles/degree. However, recent measurements suggest that human vision improves rapidly over the next few months and approaches adult levels by the age of 6 months (Marg, Freeman, Pheltzman, and Goldstein, 1976; Harris, Atkinson, and Braddick, 1976). Nevertheless, there is considerable evidence that the visual system is susceptible to modification by abnormal visual exposure for months and possibly years afterward.

b. Effects of Abnormal Early Visual Experience. The key to revealing the effects of abnormal early visual experience on both cortical physiology and perception in animals was to impose a certain restricted visual input in early life. Of course, this approach cannot be used in humans since we cannot alter or restrict the visual environment of a baby in this way. However, there are a number of people born with naturally occurring clinical conditions which, to some degree, result in unusual visual inputs similar to those employed in animal studies. Just as we have learned a great deal about color vision from studies of people born with defective color vision, so we have learned about the influence exerted by the early visual input on the developing visual system from subjects with other kinds of visual defects, such as astigmatism or strabismus, whose early visual input was unusual. When examined later in life, after the original defect had been either optically or surgically corrected, these subjects often show residual perceptual deficits that are sometimes large and on other occasions subtle but always consistent with the nature of the early visual input. The ability to perceive form, as indicated by tests of visual acuity, as well as certain binocular functions which require cooperation between the two eyes (such as stereopsis) have both been shown to be strongly influenced by abnormal early visual input.

Ophthalmologists and optometrists have long suspected that the condition of "amblyopia," a term used to denote lowered vision in one eye (or occasionally both eyes) in the absence of any obvious optical error or organic lesion, may arise from some anomalous early visual input, since it is nearly always associated with conditions that produce noncongruent imagery in the two eyes, such as unequal refractive errors (a condition referred to as anisometropia), unilateral cataracts or corneal opacities, and strabismus (Duke-Elder and Wybar, 1973). Occasionally amblyopia is observed bilaterally after some particularly severe peripheral obstruction to vision in both eyes (such as bilateral cataracts) that was present from birth. From studies of cases such as these, it has become clear that the amblyopia is irreversible unless the obstruction to congruent binocular vision is removed early in life; conversely, amblyopia does not develop when the strabismus (or other obstruction) occurs in late childhood.

c. Effects of Early Monocular Visual Deprivation (Amblyopia ex Anopsia). The term "amblyopia ex anopsia" has recently been employed to describe lowered vision associated with "disuse" due to lack of formation of a patterned retinal image early in life arising, for example, from unilateral medial opacities or ptosis (drooping) of an eyelid (von Noorden and Maumenee, 1968). These conditions are fortunately rare, but there have been a sufficient number of documented cases of this sort to indicate that the consequences of even a very brief period of monocular occlusion early in life can be extremely severe. Von Noorden (1973) describes two such subjects; one of these had sustained a scratch on the right cornea at 2 months of age which was treated by suitable antibiotics and patching of the eye for only 1 month. When tested at 6 years of age the acuity of the right eye was reduced to about one-third that of the left. An interesting series of similar cases from Japan were reported by Awaya, Miyake, Imaizumi, Shiose, Kandu, and Komura (1973), who describe 15 patients who had undergone unilateral occlusion for only 1 week following lid surgery during the first year of life. All of these subsequently had extremely poor vision in that eye. Unfortunately, it is not entirely clear whether the reduction in acuity could be entirely attributed to the occlusion, since all of the subjects developed a strabismus which itself may have contributed to the amblyopia. Nevertheless, it is clear that a very brief period of monocular occlusion early in life can have dramatic consequences, both to vision and to the oculomotor system. Longer periods of deprivation resulting from unilateral dense opacities of the optic media or even occlusion for treatment of eye disease and strabismus can certainly lead to profound deficits in acuity unless the cause of the deprivation is removed early, a practice that is becoming increasingly common (von Noorden, 1973; Enoch and Rabinowicz, 1976).

   d. *Effects of Early Astigmatism (Meridional Amblyopia)*. Astigmatism is an optical defect in which one or more of the optical surfaces of the eye (but particularly the cornea) have an unusual shape. Instead of having the normal spherical shape, in which case the curvature of the surface is the same in every meridian, the surfaces have a toroidal shape (rather like the shape of a lemon) so that the curvature is not identical in every meridian. Just as a lemon has its greatest curvature around its equator and is flattest around its poles, so can an astigmatic surface be described by the curvatures of the meridians of maximum and minimum curvature, which are mutually perpendicular and are referred to as the "axes" of the astigmatism. As a consequence of its shape, an astigmatic optical surface does not image a distant point of light as a point but instead images it as two lines parallel to the axes of astigmatism. This is illustrated in Fig. 8, which shows how an astigmatic, or cylindrical, convex lens whose axes are vertical and horizontal, images a distant point object. This particular lens has its greatest curvature, and hence light-bending power, in the vertical meridian so that vertical wavefronts converge to focus at F_V, forming there a horizontal focal line. Likewise, horizontal wavefronts are imaged as a vertical focal line at F_H. Figures 9B, C illustrate the appearance of the corridor scene of Fig. 9A to a subject with astigmatism similar to that of Fig. 8 where the axes are vertical and horizontal. Figure 9B shows the appearance of the corridor when the retina coincides with the position of the vertical focal line, while Fig.

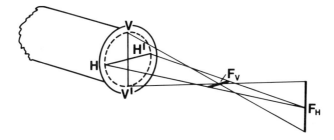

Fig. 8. Image formation by an astigmatic convex lens with axes (the meridians of maximum and minimum curvature or power) horizontal and vertical. A distant point object is imaged not as a point but as two focal lines at F_V and F_H parallel to the axes of the astigmatism. Reproduced from Mitchell *et al.* (1973).

9C shows how the scene would appear if the horizontal focal line and the retina were congruent. Notice that contours parallel to the focal line that coincides with the retina are sharp while orthogonal edges are blurred. Thus, for example, in Fig. 9C the vertical contours, such as the doors, are blurred while horizontal ones such as the light housing are sharp. Note that in both cases oblique contours are blurred.

It is apparent from Fig. 9 that a person born with high astigmatism would receive a biased early visual input; a person having astigmatism of the type depicted in Fig. 9C, for example, could be regarded as being systematically deprived of clear images of vertical contours. To some extent, people with this affliction could be regarded as having a milder version of the biased visual input Blakemore and Cooper (1970) imposed upon their two kittens.

Clinical data suggest that in cases of astigmatism of moderate amounts the condition is present from birth and changes very little thereafter (Duke-Elder, 1969) so that it is likely that many astigmats suffer a biased visual input throughout infancy, until, in fact, they first receive spectacles. As long ago as 1890, Georges Martin, a French ophthalmologist, reported that many of his astigmatic patients could never be provided with lenses which enabled them to see contours of certain orientations as clearly as others. In every case of this sort the impairment was always for contours that were habitually seen blurred prior to correction of the refractive error. This is exactly what would be expected if the visual system of these patients had been modified by their abnormal early visual input so that they developed a greater capacity to resolve contours that were imaged sharply early in life than contours that were frequently defocused in infancy.

A few years ago I examined this possibility further in collaboration with Drs. Ralph Freeman, at Berkeley, and Michel Millodot, who was then at Montreal (Mitchell, Freeman, Millodot, and Haegerstrom, 1973). We examined 38 astigmats for their ability to resolve gratings of different orientations

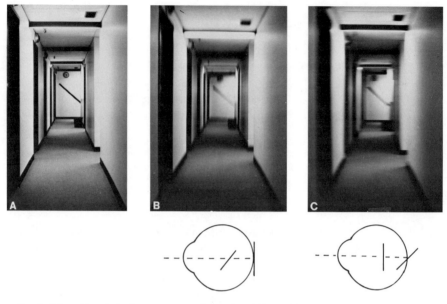

Fig. 9. Attempt to mimic the appearance of a corridor (A) to subjects with astigmatism similar to that of Fig. 8 where the axes are vertical and horizontal. B: Appearance of the corridor when the retina coincides with the position of the vertical focal line. C. Appearance if the horizontal focal line was imaged on the retina.

after their optical error was fully corrected so that we knew that gratings of all orientations were imaged equally clearly on their retinas. For all but two of these subjects the axes of the astigmatism were horizontal and vertical so that contours of one of these orientations are seen clearest of all while contours of the other orientation are seen least well by the unaided eye. Normal (nonastigmatic) subjects typically see vertical and horizontal gratings equally well but oblique stimuli are not seen quite as clearly. This is the so-called oblique effect which manifests itself as a slight reduction in the visual acuity for oblique gratings (Fig. 11). An autodemonstration of this rather small but robust effect is presented in Fig. 10.

By way of contrast, many, but not all, of the astigmats we examined showed a reduced acuity for either vertical or horizontal gratings even when wearing the best spectacle correction. Figure 12 illustrates representative results from two groups of astigmats; for group A the acuity for vertical gratings was depressed while group B exhibited reduced acuity for gratings that were horizontal. Comparison with Fig. 11 shows that these subjects achieved normal or near-normal acuity for vertical (B) or horizontal gratings (A) but the acuity for gratings perpendicular to these was severely depressed. This difference between the acuities for vertical and horizontal gratings can be as large as a factor of 2

Fig. 10. Autodemonstration of the "oblique effect." While holding the book at a comfortable reading distance, count how many gratings can be resolved in each row. Readers who possess the classical "oblique effect" will be able to see further along the row of vertical and horizontal gratings than along either of the two rows of oblique gratings. The period of each grating differs from its immediate neighbors in the row by one-fourth of an octave, where an octave represents a difference of a factor of 2.

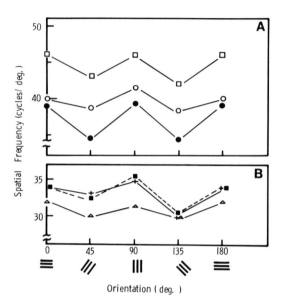

Fig. 11. Measurement of the oblique effect on six observers. A: Acuity of three subjects for square wave gratings having a mean luminance of 50 cd/m² of four different orientations. B: Results of similar measurements made on three more subjects with sinusoidal gratings having a mean luminance of 10 cd/m². Notice that the acuity for vertical and horizontal gratings are almost identical and higher than the acuity for either of the two oblique gratings. Reproduced from Mitchell *et al.* (1973).

in some subjects. Just as Martin (1890) reported, in every astigmat who manifested a meridional deficit in acuity (a meridional amblyopia), the deficit was for the stimulus orientation that the subjects saw least clearly when not wearing his spectacles (see figure caption). This is also illustrated by the results of A. M. in Fig. 13, where measurements of acuity were made every 15°. The open and filled arrows depict the orientation of distant contours that are most defocused when the two eyes are optically uncorrected. As can be seen, these coincide almost exactly with the orientations that are resolved worst *after* correction of the refractive error.

The acuity loss in these subjects was certainly neural in origin, since the measurements were made with the optical error corrected. Additional measurements made with gratings generated by interference within the eye itself, thereby bypassing any small residual errors of focus of the eye that may have remained, confirmed this view, since the pattern of change of acuity with orientation was just as pronounced when measured in this way (Mitchell *et al.*, 1973; Mitchell and Wilkinson, 1974).

Although simple measurements of visual acuity are useful, measurements of the full frequency response function which describes the contrast sensitivity of the observer for sine wave gratings of many different spatial frequencies can provide a more complete picture of the deficit in these subjects.[4] Figures 14 and 15 show frequency response functions measured in three astigmats and one normal observer. In the case of the normal observer (Fig. 14A) measurements were made with gratings of four orientations (vertical, horizontal, and oblique). Measurements were made with gratings of only two orientations on two of the astigmats corresponding to the meridians of the astigmatism. In the case of N. I. and A. M. (Figs. 14B, C) these were vertical and horizontal (or nearly so). The subject of Fig. 15, described by Freeman and Thibos (1975), was one of those rare astigmats whose axes are oblique. In this particular individual the maximum acuity (and indeed the minimum as well) was for an oblique grating, rather than one that was either vertical and horizontal, as is the usual case. In addition to data obtained with vertical and horizontal gratings, measurements on this particular subject (Fig. 15) were made with the two oblique gratings that were resolved respectively, best (65°) and worst (155°) coinciding with the axes of her astigmatism.

The normal observer of Fig. 14 resolved vertical and horizontal gratings (filled and open circles, respectively) better than oblique gratings at all spatial frequencies above about 5 cycles/deg, the difference becoming progressively greater with increasing spatial frequency. In contrast to this, the meridional amblyopia for gratings of one orientation, shown by two of the astigmats, horizontal in the case of A. M. (Fig. 14C) and oblique at 155° for the subject of Fig. 15, existed with gratings of 1 cycle/deg, the lowest spatial frequency tested in most cases. The deficit for vertical gratings exhibited by N. I., the subject of Fig. 14B, first appeared at 5 cycles/deg. Thus in many cases of astigmatism the meridional amblyopia extends to very low spatial frequencies, well below the spatial frequency for which the oblique effect begins to emerge in normal observers.

These results illustrate well the close link that is seen in many astigmats between the deficits in vision after correction of the refractive error and the vision with the unaided eye. Even after optical correction the visual system of these observers failed to resolve contours that were habitually seen blurred as well as contours that were seen clearly. As can be seen from Figs. 14 and 15, this seems to be true no matter what the axis of the astigmatism. This strongly suggests that the visual system of these subjects had been modified by their asymmetrical early visual input. However, these results tell us neither what has been modified nor the level(s) in the visual pathway where the changes have occurred. It could be that the changes are similar to those observed after more stringent, but comparable, deprivation in cats (Blakemore and Cooper, 1970; Hirsch and Spinelli, 1970), but they could be far more subtle, such as an anisotropy in the spatial resolution of cortical cells.

[4] See footnote 3.

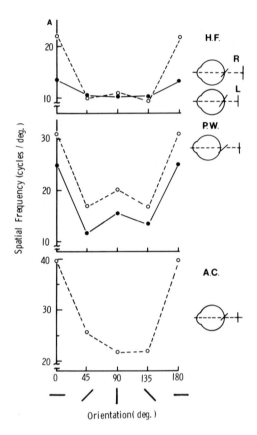

Fig. 12. Visual acuity for gratings of four different orientations measured on a number of astigmats *after full correction of the optical error*. The disposition of the focal lines with respect to the retina when the eye is *uncorrected* and looking into the distance are drawn beside the curves for each subject. Open symbols connected by dotted lines depict the acuities of the left eye, while the filled symbols and solid lines show the data from the right eye. The conditions for these measurements were identical to those of Fig. 11. A: Results for three astigmats who show a severe impairment in their ability to resolve vertical gratings. Notice that in every case the vertical focal line lies farthest

As previously mentioned, not all astigmats exhibit a meridional amblyopia. One likely reason for this is that these subjects did not receive a biased early visual input. Although recent work with astigmatic infants indicates that they do receive an asymmetrical visual input (Gwiazda, Brill, and Held, 1976; Gaston and Teller, 1976), it is possible that this may not always be the case. Many astigmats can alter the state of accommodation of their eyes in order to sharply image contours of any orientation, although at any one time only one orientation can be in sharp focus. By continually adjusting the state of accom-

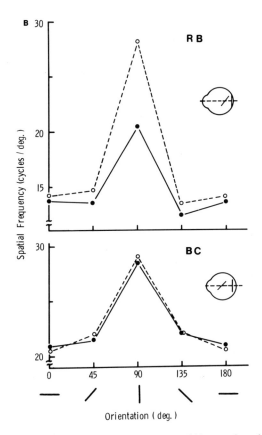

from the retina so that prior to correction vertical contours would be seen less clearly than horizontal detail. B: Results of similar measurements made on two astigmats who show a severe impairment in their ability to resolve horizontal gratings. On these subjects the focal line that lies farthest from the retina is the horizontal one so that horizontal contours would have habitually been seen blurred prior to correction of the optical error with spectacles. Reproduced from Mitchell *et al.* (1973).

modation in this way, some astigmats could prevent a biased early visual input and thereby prevent the development of a meridional amblyopia.

    e. The Oblique Effect. It could be argued that the oblique effect itself might develop as a consequence of a small bias in the early visual input of infants brought up in an urban environment since in such an environment vertical and horizontal contours may be encountered more frequently than oblique features. In favor of this view is evidence which suggests that the oblique effect may indeed be culturally determined. Annis and Frost (1973) examined a group of

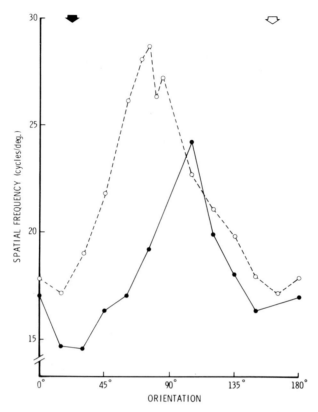

Fig. 13. Orientation differences in visual resolution for sinusoidal gratings exhibited by an astig-mat, A. M. Open and filled circles depict the results for the right and left eyes, respectively. The gratings had a mean luminance of 170 cd/m² and were viewed through 3-mm artificial pupils with the subject wearing his best optical correction. The open and filled arrows indicate the orientation of distant contours that are most defocused by the astigmatic right and left eyes, respectively. Reproduced from Mitchell and Wilkinson (1974).

Fig. 14. Contrast sensitivity as a function of spatial frequency for sinusoidal gratings of several dif-ferent orientations measured on one normal observer (A) and two optically corrected astigmats (B and C). The stimuli had a luminance of 170 cd/m². Measurements were made with gratings of four different orientations [● vertical, ○ horizontal, ▲ oblique (45°), and oblique (135°)] on the nor-mal observer. Note that the contrast sensitivities for vertical and horizontal gratings are nearly iden-tical, and for spatial frequencies above 5 c/deg were always better than those for oblique gratings. This particular observer was able to resolve oblique gratings at 45° somewhat better than those at 135°. B: Results of similar measurements made on a second astigmat, N. I., with vertical (●) and horizontal (○) gratings. C: Results of measurements made on the right eye of A. M. (Fig. 13) with gratings having orientations of 75° (●) and 165° (○). Notice that the difference in the sen-sitivities for vertical and horizontal gratings extended to very low spatial frequencies in the case of A. M. but was evident only above 5 c/deg for N. I. The data in A and C were redrawn from Mitchell and Wilkinson (1974).

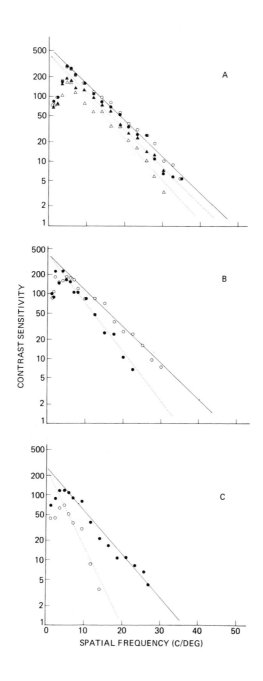

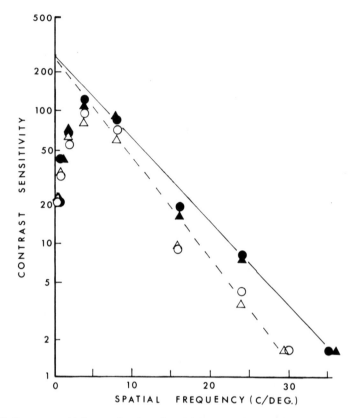

Fig. 15. Contrast sensitivity as a function of spatial frequency for sinusoidal gratings of four different orientations measured on a subject with oblique axis astigmatism after correction of the optical error. Measurements were made with gratings having a luminance somewhat lower (22 cd/m²)
than those employed for the measurements of Fig. 14. The contrast sensitivities for gratings parallel
to the axes of the astigmatism, which were at 65° and 155°, are depicted by filled and open triangles, respectively. Data obtained with vertical (●) and horizontal (○) gratings are presented for
comparison. Notice that the peak sensitivity of this observer was for an oblique grating at 65°. The
minimum sensitivity was for the oblique grating orthogonal to this (155°) which corresponded to
the focal line that is most defocused when the astigmatism is uncorrected. Redrawn from Freeman
and Thibos (1975).

Cree Indians who were perhaps the last to be brought up in a traditional manner
in dwellings that lack the preponderance of vertical and horizontal contours encountered in an urban environment. As a group, these Indians failed to exhibit
any oblique effect. Although this result argues for an environmental origin for
the effect, later findings argue against this theory. Population surveys now
suggest that the oblique effect itself may not be nearly so common as hitherto
thought. A recent examination of 100 students at Queens University in Ontario
who had all been reared in an urban environment revealed that the phenomenon

was far from universal (Timney and Muir, 1976). Many individuals failed to show the effect at all, and some even exhibited the effect in reverse, showing better acuity for oblique gratings than for gratings of any other orientation. The same investigators also examined a smaller group of Chinese students who had spent their early years in Hong Kong. As a whole, these students, who had also been reared in an urban setting, showed a considerably smaller oblique effect than the Caucasian students, suggesting that the effect might be genetically determined.

This notion receives further support from studies of infants. Using a preferential looking technique modified from the procedure employed by Teller *et al.* (1974), Leehey, Moskowitz-Cook, Brill, and Held (1975) obtained some evidence to indicate that the oblique effect was present in babies as young as 6 weeks of age. When confronted with identical gratings, one vertical (or horizontal) and the other oblique, in a preferential looking paradigm, most infants preferentially looked at the vertical or horizontal grating, suggesting that it might be easier for them to see. However, other investigators who employed a slightly different procedure obtained no evidence for an oblique effect in infants up to 6 months of age (Teller *et al.*, 1974). Thus at present the weight of available evidence would suggest that the oblique effect does not arise as a consequence of a biased early visual input, but rather is genetically determined and may even be present shortly after birth.

f. Modification of Binocular Functions. Since Wheatstone's (1838) experiments with his stereoscope, it has been known that, in order to perceive depth in stereograms, the brain has to be able to detect small differences between the positions of the images of corresponding features in the two eyes. The sensation of depth provided by this retinal disparity is extremely vivid and is referred to as "stereopsis." Since disparities of only 5″ of arc can be detected, it represents the most sensitive cue to depth available. Unfortunately, some people are stereoblind, and therefore they have to rely on monocular cues in order to perceive depth. It has long been noted that people who have suffered embarrassment to concordant binocular vision early in life (such as a strabismus or anisometropia) are likely to be stereoblind (Richards, 1970; Julesz, 1971; Duke-Elder and Wybar, 1973). From neurophysiological experiments described earlier, it is known that similar early deprivation in animals results in a reduction in the proportion of binocular neurons, the very neurons that are thought to be necessary for stereopsis. It is not, therefore, unreasonable to suppose that the stereoblindness observed in humans with early embarrassment to binocular vision arises from a comparable reduction in the number of neurons that receive binocular connections. This view receives strong support from a measurement of the extent of interocular transfer of various aftereffects in these subjects.

There are a number of well-known aftereffects, such as the motion or tilt aftereffects, that are briefly observed after looking for a period of time at certain stimuli. An example of one of these, the well-known tilt aftereffect, is il-

Fig. 16. Demonstration of the tilt aftereffect. Stare at the horizontal line between the two gratings on the right for a minute, allowing the eyes to wander along the line. Then quickly transfer fixation to the line between the two left-hand gratings. Instead of appearing vertical, they will briefly appear to be tilted in opposite directions to each other.

lustrated in Fig. 16. After one has looked at the horizontal line between the two
adapting gratings on the right for a minute or so, the truly vertical gratings on the
left no longer appear upright but will appear tilted in opposite directions to
each other. After one has stared at an adapting grating tilted 10° clockwise, a
vertical grating will appear tilted as much as 5° anticlockwise. In common with
most aftereffects, the tilt aftereffect exhibits partial interocular transfer, so that
after adapting only one eye the test grating will appear tilted when viewed by
the other, but by a smaller amount than it does to the adapted eye. Aftereffects
in general have long been attributed to fatigue of cortical neurons as a result of
prolonged stimulation, and in fact it has been demonstrated that cortical
neurons in the cat do fatigue in this way (Maffei, Fiorentini, and Bisti, 1973).
Since the aftereffect exhibits interocular transfer, many of the neurons that are
fatigued must receive connections from the two eyes. Now, if stereoblind subjects possess few or no binocular neurons, then interocular transfer may be impossible since the physiological substrate for it is absent. Just such a result has
been demonstrated with the tilt and motion aftereffects (Movshon, Chambers,
and Blakemore, 1972; Mitchell and Ware, 1974; Mitchell, Reardon, and Muir,
1975).

Figure 17 shows typical results of measurements of the tilt aftereffects
in the adapted and nonadapted eyes of two normal observers (A) and two

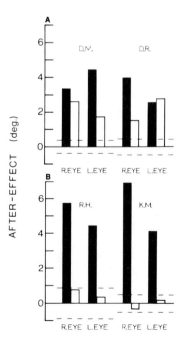

Fig. 17. Histograms showing the magnitude of the tilt
aftereffect in the two eyes of two normal (A) and two
stereoblind (B) observers. Conditions for these measurements were similar to those of Fig. 15; the data
show the average aftereffect that was obtained on a
vertical test grating following adaptation to gratings
tilted 10° clockwise and 10° anticlockwise from vertical. Filled and open bars show the size of the aftereffect in the adapted and nonadapted eye, respectively.
The eye in which the aftereffect was measured is
shown below each pair of histograms. The horizontal
dashed lines show the 95% confidence limits for significant deviation from the settings made prior to adaptation. Whereas the two normal observers show about
70% interocular transfer, the two subjects without
stereopsis failed to exhibit any whatsoever. Redrawn
from Mitchell and Ware (1974).

stereoblind subjects (B). The conditions for this experiment were identical to those illustrated in Fig. 16; namely, the adapting grating was tilted 10° from vertical and the subject indicated the apparent tilt of a vertical test grating by setting a line viewed in peripheral vision parallel to it (Mitchell and Ware, 1974). The filled and open bars show the size of the aftereffect in the adapted and nonadapted eyes, respectively; the eye in which the effect was measured is shown below each pair of histograms. With the adapted eye the test grating appeared tilted by between 3° and 7° depending on the observer. In the nonadapted eye of the two normal subjects D. M. and D. R., the mean aftereffect was only 70% of that measured in the eye that was adapted. By way of contrast, the stereoblind subjects showed no interocular transfer whatsoever.

This finding provides strong support for the idea that stereoblind subjects possess a reduced complement of binocular neurons as a consequence of the discordant nature of early visual input to the two eyes. Two groups have used

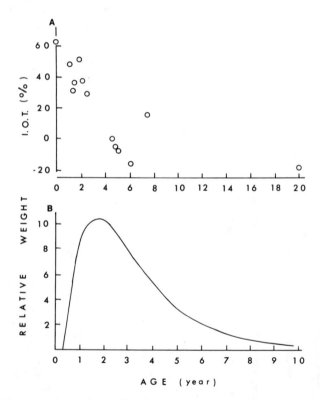

Fig. 18. A: Percentage interocular transfer (I.O.T.) of the tilt aftereffect exhibited by 12 surgically corrected congenital esotropes, plotted as a function of the age at which the strabismus was surgically corrected. The data of a normal observer are plotted at zero years. B: Curve derived from the data of A that defines the critical period for the development of binocularity in humans. Redrawn from Banks, Aslin, and Letson (1975).

the measure of binocularity afforded by measurement of interocular transfer to ascertain the sensitive period for the development of binocular vision (Hohman and Creutzfeldt, 1975; Banks, Aslin, and Letson, 1975). The latter group (Banks *et al.*, 1975) examined 12 subjects with surgically corrected congenital strabismus so that the dates of both onset and correction of the abnormal input were known precisely. As can be seen from Fig. 18A, subjects who had been surgically corrected in the first year of life had nearly normal interocular transfer while those corrected later had reduced transfer. Subjects corrected after 4 years of age showed no transfer at all, suggesting that the normal experience after that time was insufficient to reestablish binocular connections. From these findings these authors were able to generate a curve (Fig. 18B) that described the sensitive period of the human visual system for the development of binocularity. They conclude that the sensitive period begins several months after birth and peaks at 2 years of age, following which there is a gradual decline. This picture of the sensitive period is by and large supported by the results of Hohman and Creutzfeldt (1975).

While the results of measurements of the tilt and motion aftereffect, as well as other measures (Williams, 1974) on stereoblind observers, could be used to prove that they suffer from a complete loss of binocular neurons, recent measurements with other aftereffects indicate that these same subjects still retain some binocular neurons, since they exhibit a small but nevertheless significant amount of interocular transfer of the threshold elevation that follows adaptation to drifting gratings. After one has stared at a high-contrast grating that drifts in one direction, say to the right, the threshold contrast required to detect a grating of similar spatial frequency drifting in the same direction is markedly elevated. Once again this aftereffect exhibits interocular transfer in normal observers, but even stereoblind observers who exhibit no transfer of the suprathreshold aftereffects still exhibit a very small degree of interocular transfer (Anderson and Mitchell, in preparation). From this it must be concluded that these observers still retain a few binocular neurons which, however, are insufficient to mediate stereopsis or interocular transfer of a number of other aftereffects.

4. Conclusions

The nature of the perceptual defects exhibited by humans with abnormal early visual experience strongly suggests that the visual cortex of man is modified by this anomalous experience in much the same way as that of the cat and monkey. Electrophysiological studies of animals reveal that the visual response characteristics of visual cortical neurons are only partially specified at birth and that they can be influenced by the nature of the animal's early visual experience. There is very good evidence that the ocular dominance of cortical cells can be markedly influenced by disruptions to concordant binocular vision in

early life, and there are good indications that other visual response characteristics of cortical cells, such as their preference for orientation, direction of
movement, and disparity, may also be affected by biased early visual exposure.
However, although demonstrations of early enviornmental modification of the
properties of cortical neurons in animals are becoming increasingly numerous,
the nature of the process underlying these changes is not yet well understood.
At present the major unanswered question concerns the extent to which the
genetically determined but crude specificity that is observed in cortical neurons
at birth can be altered by the animal's early visual experience. Can the op-
timum stimulus for a given cell, such as its preference for orientation or direction of movement of a stimulus, be actually altered, or can the early visual experience only refine or degrade the tuning of the cell about its genetically
determined preference?

Possibly reflecting the state of the visual cortex, but also the state of development of the eye itself (Donovan, 1966; Duke-Elder and Cook, 1973), cats
(Mitchell *et al.*, 1976), monkeys (Gaston and Teller, 1976), and humans (Teller *et al.*, 1974) all begin life with poor spatial resolution. Vision improves
markedly in the next few months so that by the age of 6 months, when the retina has achieved its adultlike form (Duke-Elder and Cook, 1973), human spatial resolution has also reached adultlike levels. But just as with cats and
monkeys, human spatial resolution and other capacities such as stereopsis are
dependent on the nature of the early visual input.

One major difference that seems to have emerged between animals and
man is the length of time during which the visual system is susceptible to modification by abnormal visual input. In the cat this period has ceased by 4 months
of age, while in the monkey it may extend to 1½ years of age (Wiesel, 1975).
The evidence of Fig. 18, together with much older clinical evidence (Worth,
1903; Juler, 1921; Flom, 1970; Duke-Elder and Wybar, 1973), suggests that
the human visual system may be modifiable for a much longer period of time,
perhaps to 6 years of age, although in common with animals there is a progressive decline in susceptibility with age. Unfortunately, data on susceptible
periods in animals as well as man are sparse at present, but already there is
reason for caution in extrapolating from data obtained from one class of early
environmental manipulation to others, since the critical periods for modifiability of some properties of cortical neurons may be different from that for others.
Already there is evidence that this is true for the cat, since the critical period for
modifiability of directional selectivity seems to occur earlier than that for the
effects of monocular deprivation (Daw and Wyatt, 1976). By analogy, it may
very well be true that in man the period of susceptibility to the effects of astigmatism may be different from that indicated in Fig. 18 for binocularity. It is
obviously important to establish the period(s) of susceptibility of the human visual system to environmental modification very exactly since this knowledge
can be of immense clinical benefit.

Why is the visual system modifiable? This is an important question, since it would be thought that whatever benefit is gained from possessing a modifiable visual system must be great indeed since the damage produced by accidental abnormal early input can be very large. One clue is provided by the observation that environmental modification appears to be most pronounced in animals with frontal eyes. The cortex of animals with panoramic vision, such as the rabbit, does not appear to be dramatically influenced by abnormal visual input even in the region of binocular overlap of the two visual fields (van Sluyters and Stewart, 1974; Mize and Murphy, 1973). This has led to speculation that early neural plasticity may be linked to the possession of stereopsis, a function that is possible only when the eyes are frontal, thereby permitting considerable overlap of the visual fields. Blakemore (1974) and Blakemore and van Sluyters (1975) have argued that the biological function of environmental modification is to ensure that the preference of binocular neurons becomes closely matched in the two eyes, a possible necessary prerequisite for the detection of the disparity required for stereoscopic vision. It is also apparent that any binocular function, including fusion, would require that binocular neurons be tuned to take account of the range of disparities that occur in normal life. It is very unlikely that this could be achieved by genetic means since any imbalance in growth or position of the two eyes could disrupt binocular vision entirely. However, if cortical neurons in the infant were to some extent modifiable by visual experience, then any imbalance of this sort that could arise during periods of rapid growth could be readily compensated for. This hypothesis can also account for the longer critical period in man than in the cat or even monkey, since the human head continues to grow (thereby increasing the risk of imbalance between the two eyes) for a much longer period of time than does that of either the cat or the monkey.

ACKNOWLEDGMENT

I would like to thank Nancy Beattie for her patience and skill in typing various drafts of this chapter.

5. References

Ackroyd, C., Humphrey, N. K., and Warrington, E. K. Lasting effects of early blindness: A case study. *Quarterly Journal of Experimental Psychology,* 1974, *26,* 114–124.

Annis, R. C., and Frost, B. Human visual ecology and orientation anisotropies in acuity. *Science (N.Y.),* 1973, *182,* 729–731.

Atkinson, J., Braddick, O., and Braddick, F. Acuity and contrast sensitivity of infant vision. *Nature,* 1974, *247,* 403–404.

Awaya, S., Miyake, Y., Imaizumi, Y., Shiose, Y., Kandu, T., and Komuro, K. Amblyopia in man, suggestive of stimulus deprivation amblyopia. *Japanese Journal of Ophthalmology,* 1973, *17,* 69–82.

72   Donald E. Mitchell

Baker, F. H., Grigg, P., and von Noorden, G. K. Effects of visual deprivation and strabismus on the response of neurons in the visual cortex of the monkey, including studies on the striate and prestriate cortex in the normal animal. *Brain Research*, 1974, *66*, 185–208.

Banks, M. S., and Salapatek, P. Contrast sensitivity function of the infant visual system. *Vision Research*, 1976, *8*, 867–869.

Banks, M. S., Aslin, R. N., and Letson, R. D. Sensitive period for the development of human binocular vision. *Science (N.Y.)*, 1975, *190*, 675–677.

Barlow, H. B., and Pettigrew, J. D. Lack of specificity of neurons in the visual cortex of young kittens. *Journal of Physiology*, 1971, *218*, 98–100p.

Barlow, H. B., Blakemore, C., and Pettigrew, J. D. The neural mechanism of binocular depth discrimination. *Journal of Physiology*, 1967, *193*, 327–342.

Blake, R., and Hirsch, H. V. B. Deficits in binocular depth perception in cats after alternating monocular deprivation. *Science (N.Y.)*, 1975, *190*, 1114–1116.

Blakemore, C. Developmental factors in the formation of feature extracting neuro   in F. O. Schmitt and F. G. Worden (Eds.), *The neurosciences: Third study program.*   ambridge, Mass.: MIT Press, 1974, pp. 105–113.

Blakemore, C. Genetic instruction and developmental plasticity in the kitten's visual   tex. *Philosophical Transactions of the Royal Society (London), Series B*, 1977, *278*, 425–)4.

Blakemore, C., and Cooper, G. F. Development of the brain depends on the visual   nvironment. *Nature*, 1970, *228*, 477–478.

Blakemore, C., and Mitchell, D. E. Environmental modification of the visual cortex and the neural basis of learning and memory. *Nature*, 1973, *241*, 467–468.

Blakemore, C., and van Sluyters, R. C. Reversal of the physiological effects of monocular deprivation in kittens: Further evidence for a critical period. *Journal of Physiology*, 1974a, *237*, 195–216.

Blakemore, C., and van Sluyters, R. C. Experimental analysis of amblyopia and strabismus. *British Journal of Ophthalmology*, 1974b, *58*, 176–182.

Blakemore, C., and van Sluyters, R. C. Innate and environmental factors in the development of the kitten's visual cortex. *Journal of Physiology*, 1975, *248*, 663–716.

Blasdel, G. G., Mitchell, D. E., Muir, D. W., and Pettigrew, J. D. A combined physiological and behavioural study of the effect of early visual experience with contours of a single orientation. *Journal of Physiology*, 1977, *265*, 615–636.

Buisseret, P., and Imbert, M. Visual cortical cells: Their developmental properties in normal and dark reared kittens. *Journal Physiology*, 1976, *255*, 511–525.

Cornsweet, T. N. *Visual perception.* New York: Academic Press, 1970.

Cowey, A. Parkinson, A. M., and Warnick, L. Global stereopsis in rhesus monkeys. *Quarterly Journal of Experimental Psychology*, 1975, *27*, 93–109.

Cragg, B. G. The development of synapses in cat visual cortex. *Investigative Ophthalmology*, 1972, *11*, 377–385.

Cynader, M., Berman, N., and Hein, A. Cats raised in a one-directional world: Effects on receptive fields in visual cortex and superior colliculus. *Experimental Brain Research*, 1975, *22*, 267–280.

Daw, N. W., and Wyatt, H. J. Kittens reared in a unidirectional environment: Evidence for a critical period. *Journal of Physiology*, 1976, *257*, 155–170.

Dews, P. B., and Wiesel, T. N. Consequences of monocular deprivation on visual behaviour in kittens. *Journal of Physiology*, 1970, *206*, 437–455.

Donovan, A. The postnatal development of the cat retina. *Experimental Eye Research*, 1966, *5*, 249–254.

Duke-Elder, W. S. *The practice of refraction.* St. Louis: Mosby, 1969.

Duke-Elder, W. S., and Cook, C. Normal and abnormal development. Part I. Embryology. In W. S. Duke-Elder (Ed.), *System of ophthalmology.* Vol. III. London: Henry Kimpton, 1973.

Duke-Elder, W. S., and Wybar, K. C. Ocular motility and strabismus. In W. S. Duke-Elder (Ed.), *System of ophthalmology.* Vol. VI. London: Henry Kimpton, 1973.

Enoch, J. M., and Rabinowicz, I. M. Early surgery and visual correction of an infant born with unilateral eye lens opacity. *Documenta Ophthalmologica,* 1976, *41,* 371–382.

Flom, M. C. Early experience in the development of visual coordination. In F. Young and D. E. Lindsley (Eds.), *Early experience and visual information processing in perceptual and reading disorders.* Washington, D.C.: National Academy of Sciences, 1970.

Fox, R., and Blake, R. R. Stereoscopic vision in the cat. *Nature,* 1971, *233,* 55–56.

Freeman, R. D., and Pettigrew, J. D. Alteration of visual cortex from environmental asymmetries. *Nature,* 1973, *246,* 359–360.

Freeman, R. D., and Thibos, L. N. Contrast sensitivity in humans with abnormal visual experience. *Journal of Physiology,* 1975, *247,* 687–710.

Ganz, L. Orientation in visual space by neonates and its modification by visual deprivation. In A. H. Riesen (Ed.), *The developmental neuropsychology of sensory deprivation.* New York: Academic Press, 1975.

Ganz, L., and Fitch, M. The effect of visual deprivation on visual behavior. *Experimental Neurology,* 1968, *22,* 638–660.

Gaston, J. A., and Teller, D. Y. Astigmatism and acuity in two primate infants. Talk presented at the Association for Research in Vision and Ophthalmology meeting, Sarasota, Fla., April 27, 1976.

Gregory, R. L., and Wallace, J. G. Recovery from early blindness: A case study. *Experimental Psychology Society Monograph, No. 2,* Cambridge, 1963.

Gwiazda, J., Brill, S., and Held, R. Meridional acuity in infant astigmats. Talk presented at the Association for Research in Vision and Ophthalmology meeting, Sarasota, Fla., April 27, 1976.

Harris, L., Atkinson, J., and Braddick, O. Visual contrast sensitivity of a 6-month-old infant measured by the evoked potential. *Nature,* 1976, *264,* 570–571.

Hirsch, H. V. B., and Spinelli, D. N. Visual experience modifies distribution of horizontally and vertically oriented receptive fields in cats. *Science (N.Y.),* 1970, *168,* 869–871.

Hohman, A., and Creutzfeldt, O. D. Squint and the development of binocularity in humans. *Nature,* 1975, *254,* 613–614.

Hubel, D. H., and Wiesel, T. N. Receptive fields, binocular interaction and functional architecture in the cat's visual cortex. *Journal of Physiology,* 1962, *160,* 106–154.

Hubel, D. H., and Wiesel, T. N. Receptive fields of cells in striate cortex of very young, visually inexperienced kittens. *Journal of Neurophysiology,* 1963, *26,* 994–1002.

Hubel, D. H., and Wiesel, T. N. Binocular interaction in striate cortex of kittens reared with artificial squint. *Journal of Neurophysiology,* 1965, *28,* 1041–1059.

Hubel, D. H., and Wiesel, T. N. Cells sensitive to binocular depth in area 18 of the macaque monkey cortex. *Nature,* 1970a, *225,* 41–42.

Hubel, D. H., and Wiesel, T. N. The period of susceptibility to the physiological effects of unilateral eye closure in kittens. *Journal of Physiology,* 1970b, *206,* 419–436.

Hubel, D. H., Wiesel, T. N., and LeVay, S. Functional architecture of area 17 in normal and monocularly deprived macaque monkey. *Cold Spring Harbor Symposia on Quantitative Biology,* 1976, *40,* 581–589.

Jeannerod, M. Déficit visual persistant chez les aveugles-nés opérés données cliniques et expérimentales. *Année Psychologie,* 1975, *75,* 169–196.

Juler, F. Amblyopia from disuse: Visual acuity after traumatic cataract in children. *Transactions of the Ophthalmological Society of the United Kingdom,* 1921, *41,* 129–139.

Julesz, B. *Foundations of cyclopean perception.* Chicago: University of Chicago Press, 1971, p. 187.

Leehey, S. C., Moskowitz-Cook, A., Brill, S., and Held, R. Orientational anistropy in infant vision. *Science (N.Y.),* 1975, *190,* 900–902.

Maffei, L., and Bisti, S. Binocular interaction in strabismic kittens deprived of vision. *Science (N.Y.)*, 1976, *191*, 579–580.

Maffei, L., Fiorentini, A., and Bisti, S. Neural correlate of perceptual adaptation to gratings. *Science (N.Y.)*, 1973, *182*, 1036–1038.

Marg, E., Freeman, D. N., Pheltzman, P., and Goldstein, P. J. Visual acuity development in human infants: Evoked potential estimates. *Investigative Ophthalmology*, 1976, *15*, 150–153.

Martin, G. Théorie et clinique de l'amblyopie astigmatique. *Annales d'Oculistique*, 1890, *104*, 101–138.

Mitchell, D. E., and Ware, C. Interocular transfer of a visual after-effect in normal and stereoblind humans. *Journal of Physiology*, 1974, *236*, 707–721.

Mitchell, D. E., and Wilkinson, F. The effect of early astigmatism on the visual resolution of gratings. *Journal of Physiology*, 1974, *243*, 739–756.

Mitchell, D. E., Freeman, R. D., Millodot, M., and Haegerstrom, G. Meridional amblyopia: Evidence for modification of the human visual system by early visual experience. *Vision Research*, 1973, *13*, 535–558.

Mitchell, D. E., Reardon, J., and Muir, D. W. Interocular transfer of the motion after-effect in normal and stereoblind observers. *Experimental Brain Research*, 1975, *22*, 163–173.

Mitchell, D. E., Giffin, F., Wilkinson, F., Anderson, P., and Smith, M. L. Visual resolution in young kittens. *Vision Research*, 1976, *16*, 363–366.

Mitchell, D. E., Griffin, F., and Timney, B. A behavioural technique for the rapid assessment of the visual capabilities of kittens. *Perception*, 1977, *6*, 181–193.

Mize, R. R., and Murphy, E. H. Selective visual experience fails to modify receptive field properties of rabbit striate cortex neurons. *Science (N.Y.)*, 1973, *180*, 320–323.

Movshon, J. A., Chambers, B. E. I., and Blakemore, C. Interocular transfer in normal humans and those who lack stereopsis. *Perception*, 1972, *1*, 483–490.

Muir, D. W., and Mitchell, D. E. Visual resolution and experience: Acuity deficits in cats following early selective visual deprivation. *Science (N.Y.)*, 1973, *180*, 420–422.

Nikara, T., Bishop, P. O., and Pettigrew, J. D. Analysis of retinal correspondence by studying receptive fields of binocular single units in cat striate cortex. *Experimental Brain Research*, 1968, *6*, 353–372.

Packwood, J., and Gordon, B. Stereopsis in normal domestic cat, Siamese cat, and cat raised with alternating monocular occlusion. *Journal of Neurophysiology*, 1975, *38*, 1485–1499.

Pastore, N. *Selective history of theories of visual perception: 1650–1950*. New York: Oxford University Press, 1971.

Pettigrew, J. D. The effect of visual experience on the development of stimulus specificity by kitten cortical neurones. *Journal of Physiology*, 1974, *237*, 49–74.

Pettigrew, J. D., and Freeman, R. D. Visual experience without lines: Effects on developing cortical neurons. *Science (N.Y.)*, 1973, *182*, 599–601.

Pettigrew, J. D., and Garey, L. J. Selective modification of single neuron properties in the visual cortex of kittens. *Brain Research*, 1974, *66*, 160–164.

Pettigrew, J. D., Olson, C., and Hirsch, H. V. B. Cortical effect of selective visual experience: Degeneration or reorganization? *Brain Research*, 1973, *51*, 345–351.

Rakic, P. Prenatal genesis of connections subserving ocular dominance in rhesus monkey. *Nature*, 1976, *261*, 467–471.

Richards, W. Stereopsis and stereoblindness. *Experimental Brain Research*, 1970, *10*, 380–388.

Riesen, A. H., and Zilbert, D. E. Behavioral consequences of variations in early sensory environments. In A. H. Riesen (Ed.), *The developmental neuropsychology of sensory deprivation*. New York: Academic Press, 1975.

Sherk, H., and Stryker, M. P. Quantitative study of cortical orientation selectivity in visually inexperienced kittens. *Journal of Neurophysiology*, 1976, *39*, 63–70.

Shlaer, S. Shift in binocular disparity causes compensatory change in the cortical structure of kittens. *Science (N.Y.)*, 1971, *173*, 638–641.

Stryker, M. P., and Sherk, M. Modification of cortical orientation selectivity in the cat by restricted visual experience: A reexamination. *Science (N.Y.)*, 1975, *190*, 904–906.

Teller, D. Y., Morse, R., Borton, R., and Regal, D. Visual acuity for vertical and diagonal gratings in human infants. *Vision Research*, 1974, *14*, 1433–1439.

Timney, B. N., and Muir, D. W. Orientation anisotropy: Incidence and magnitude in Caucasian and Chinese subjects. *Science (N.Y.)*, 1976, *193*, 699–701.

Tretter, F., Cynader, M., and Singer, W. Modification of direction selectivity of neurons in the visual cortex of kittens. *Brain Research*, 1975, *84*, 143–149.

Turkel, J., Gijsbers, K., and Pritchard, R. Environmental modification of oculomotor and neural function in cats. Paper presented at Association for Research in Vision and Ophthalmology meeting, Sarasota, Fla., 1975.

Valvo, A. In L. L. Clark and Z. Z. Jastrzembska (Eds.), *Sight restoration after long-term blindness: The problem and behavior patterns of visual rehabilitation*. New York: American Foundation for the Blind, 1971.

van Sluyters, R. C., and Blakemore, C. Experimental creation of unusual neuronal properties in visual cortex of kittens. *Nature*, 1973, *246*, 506–508.

van Sluyters, R. C., and Stewart, D. L. Binocular neurons of the rabbit's visual cortex: Effects of monocular sensory deprivation. *Experimental Brain Research*, 1974, *19*, 196–204.

von Noorden, G. K. Experimental amblyopia in monkeys: Further behavioral observation and clinical correlations. *Investigative Ophthalmology*, 1973, *12*, 721–726.

von Noorden, G. K., and Maumenee, A. E. Clinical observations on stimulus-deprivation amblyopia (amblyopia ex anopsia). *American Journal of Ophthalmology*, 1968, *65*, 220–224.

von Noorden, G. K., Dowling, J. E., and Ferguson, D. C. Experimental amblyopia in monkeys. I. Behavioral studies of stimulus deprivation amblyopia. *American Medical Association Archives of Ophthalmology*, 1970, *84*, 206–214.

von Senden, M. *Space and sight*. Translated by P. Heath. London: Methuen, 1960.

Wheatstone, C. Contributions to the physiology of vision. I. On some remarkable and hitherto unobserved phenomena of binocular vision. *Philosophical Transactions of the Royal Society*, 1838, *II*, 371–394.

Wiesel, T. N. Monkey visual cortex. II. Modification induced by visual deprivation. Friedenwald lecture delivered at the Association for Research in Vision and Ophthalmology meeting, Sarasota, Fla., May 1, 1975.

Wiesel, T. N., and Hubel, D. H. Single-cell responses in striate cortex of kittens deprived of vision in one eye. *Journal of Neurophysiology*, 1963, *26*, 1003–1017.

Wiesel, T. N., and Hubel, D. H. Comparison of the effects of unilateral and bilateral eye closure on cortical unit responses in kittens. *Journal of Neurophysiology*, 1965, *28*, 1029–1040.

Wiesel, T. N., and Hubel, D. H. Ordered arrangements of orientation columns in monkeys lacking visual experience. *Journal of Comparative Neurology*, 1974, *158*, 307–318.

Williams, R. The effect of strabismus on dichoptic summation of form information. *Vision Research*, 1974, *14*, 307–309.

Worth, C. A. *Squint: Its causes, pathology and treatment*. Philadelphia: Blakiston, 1903.

3

Depth Perception and Experience

RICHARD D. WALK

1. Introduction

I get out of bed in the morning and go into the bathroom to shave, shower, etc. Then I get dressed and come downstairs, eager for my breakfast and impatient to get on with my plans for the day. This simple, overlearned sequence of behavior is very similar to that performed by millions of other adults, but it does require me to avoid obstacles, to gauge depths, and to reach accurately for objects. In a few brief minutes in the morning we all demonstrate a series of highly skilled perceptual-motor acts.

Is vision necessary for this behavior? Obviously, a blind individual might behave almost like the sighted, particularly in a very familiar environment. What about the role of experience? For an adult, the importance of prior experience for this particular perceptual-motor behavior is very difficult to assess.

This chapter will review the role of experience in depth perception. Generally, the approach will be an ecological one. By that is meant the primary focus on depth perception will be on the interaction of the organism with the environment for behavior related to depth. If we assume that the function of such behavior is to react appropriately to depth, this means that the particular sense modality involved is not so important as is appropriate overall behavior. If the behavior is (or is not) appropriate, we might then ask: Why? What function is served by reacting appropriately to depth? What function is served by what may seem an inappropriate reaction to depth? The reaction to depth is part of the mechanism for survival of the organism; the reaction to depth is subsidiary to

RICHARD D. WALK • Department of Psychology, George Washington University, Washington, D.C. 20052. The preparation of this chapter was supported in part by Grant MH-25864 from the National Institute of Mental Health.

the overall plan of the organism. We might assume that since depths are a threat to survival, every organism will be best served by always reacting appropriately to depth. But an organism at a particular stage of development or an organism in a particular environment may, or may not, best be served in an overall sense by reacting appropriately to depth.

Consider the human infant. The human infant crawls at around 6–9 months of age. Every mother knows, or should know, that the human infant is not to be trusted in a depth situation. The child will crawl off beds or chairs; it is so awkward or careless that it might fall off a precipice, not necessarily by directly crawling over the cliff but by stumbling. To protect their infants from the consequences of the environment, mothers (or caretakers) keep their children close to them. Suppose the infant of 9 months could be trusted to be infallible in avoiding depths. Then, one might speculate, mothers would not keep the child close to them. But the *in*competent infant is gaining something else: by staying close to the mother and the primary group the child learns language and that whole complex of behavior for group survival that has placed man in the ecological niche he now occupies. The incompetence of the infant—in reaction to depth and in much other behavior—serves a higher survival value.

Surely, one may hold, this is speculation. Indeed it is. But, to return to the task at hand, that of reaction to depth, the incompetence of the infant for depths is just as important as is the competence. From an experimental point of view we must plumb for weaknesses and try to understand them just as much as we must try to find strengths for, in this case, reactions to depth. One measure may not be enough. We need many measures under a host of conditions to understand the behavior. The point was made that an appropriate reaction to depth need not be visual, and indeed it may not, but in order to understand the behavior relatively completely we also need to understand whether the behavior is controlled primarily by vision, or which modality or modalities do control it.

To reiterate. Depth perception in this chapter means the *discrimination* of depth. Any means by which depth is discriminated is of interest.

The human infant is a good starting point to understand depth perception as related to experience. More questions will be raised than will be answered. The animal research generally permits better experimental control than does the human infant research and it will follow the human infant discussion.

2. The Human Infant

The human infant can discriminate visual depth soon after birth. The infant will draw away from an approaching object, a reaction to visual looming. The infant will also demonstrate stereoscopic vision by reaching for an intangible object, formed by fusion of two images, when wearing polaroid glasses. This research, and other research that shows early spatial perception, has been reviewed by Bower (1974), who is responsible for much of the research with prelocomotor infants, and also by Walk (1976), as part of an extensive review of the development of space perception. The focus of the present discussion is with older, crawling infants, tested with the visual cliff. The visual cliff research both demonstrates the importance of multiple measures to understand depth perception and raises a few questions relevant to the importance of experience for depth perception.

As soon as the infant begins to crawl, around the age of 6–9 months, the child can discriminate depth on the visual cliff. The visual cliff apparatus is illustrated schematically in Figs. 1 and 2. The child is placed on a glass-topped table with a pattern directly under the heavy glass on one side (the "shallow" side) and a pattern some distance below the glass on the other side (the "deep" side). Figure 1 shows an infant being called to the mother from the deep side. As long as the visual depth is great enough (about 3 ft or more), less than 10% of the infants cross the glass of the deep side to the mother (Walk and Gibson, 1961), while they will readily crawl to her on the side where a visual pattern is directly beneath the glass. When the pattern is brought closer to the glass of the deep side, more and more infants crawl across the deep side to the mother—at 10 inches of visual depth 38% crawl to her there as compared to 8% at 40 inches.

But, if the infant is called by the mother from the end of a narrowing center board that almost forces the child off of the center board to get to the mother, over 90% "choose" to get to the mother over the shallow side at a visual depth of 10 inches (Walk, 1969). This is shown in Fig. 2 and is called the "bisection" condition.

The two different methods each show depth discrimination, but the method of coaxing the child toward the deep side shows a weakness in depth perception that is not revealed with the bisection method. Neither method is more "true" or better than the other. One might hold that for the mother to coax an infant over an apparent abyss is not representative of mother behavior and this voids our concern for "ecological validity." But infants are attracted to interesting parts of the environment and a reasonable supposition would be that this is similar to being coaxed toward the deep side by the mother.

The glass controls for nonvisual cues, so the infant's response must be based on vision, but the glass also serves another function. It protects the infant. But for the glass many infants would fall, because they often throw a leg or half of the body over the deep side while being tested, even though they will not be coaxed to the deep side. The human infant is awkward.

Further analysis of the difference between the two methods reveals an age difference. The number of infants coaxed across the deep side by the mother is no different for visual depths of 20 and 40 inches. But with 10 inches of visual depth 65% of the infants 7-9 months of age are coaxed across the deep side while only 21% of the 10- to 13-month-old crawling infants are coaxed there

Fig. 1. Mother calls her infant from the deep side of the visual cliff. The checks toward the observer are covered with heavy glass. Heavy glass also covers the deep side, and a checked pattern, not visible here, is placed some distance below the glass. The glass protects the infant from falling and ensures that the choice is based on vision. Drawing by Ruth Ansel.

(Walk, 1969). Since the difference between the younger and older groups occurs at the "threshold" depth of 10 inches, it is a reasonable supposition that the younger infants have a motion parallax weakness. This is adequate for most depth discrimination situations but inadequate for those near threshold. It also squares with the reports of mothers that their child will crawl off low places, like beds, when they are younger, and that they later become more cautious.

Several studies have shown that older infants are more fearful of visual depth than are younger infants. Schwartz, Campos, and Baisel (1973) placed infants successively on the deep and shallow sides of the visual cliff. The heart rate of 5-month-old, prelocomotor infants decelerated on the deep side while the heart rate of 9-month-olds accelerated. Schwartz *et al.* interpreted the heart rate change of the younger infants as indicative of attention and that of the older children as representing fear. Scarr and Salapatek (1970) studied the fear of infants on the visual cliff and found a linear relation to age, that while 25% of the infants less than 7 months old showed fear, 100% were fearful by the age of 13 months. We placed locomotor (7- to 13-month-old) infants successively on the deep and shallow sides of the visual cliff and had the mothers call to them to come to her (Walk, 1963). Infants over 10 months of age were more likely than the younger infants to "freeze" on the deep side and not crawl to

Fig. 2. Mother calls her infant from the end of a narrowing center board. The infant leaves the center board and crawls over the glass-covered shallow side, to the right, or over the glass-covered deep side, to the left. Note the checks below the glass on the deep side to the left of the infant. Drawing by Ruth Ansel.

the mother at all. The locomotor freezing was usually accompanied by intense, loud distress.

The age of the infant was also related to the discrimination of ambiguous, unpatterned stimuli. The younger crawling infants were more likely to be coaxed across the deep side when a homogeneous gray was on the deep side than were the older ones. This may indicate less visual acuity for the younger infants, or it might mean that the younger child will crawl forward in the face of uncertainty while the other infant is more cautious.

The amount of crawling experience is also important for depth discrimination. "Late" crawlers, infants who did not start to crawl until they were 9–11 months of age, were less cautious on the visual cliff than were similarly aged infants who had started to crawl at 6–8 months of age (Walk, 1966). Both groups were over 10 months of age when tested but the "late" crawlers were not so cautious as the early crawlers; the late crawlers acted like 7- to 9-month-old infants, usually less cautious, not like the usual cautious 10- to 13-month-old. This might point to a perceptual-motor experience factor in depth discrimination.

Related data related to age and crawling were secured when infants were allowed the use of only one eye (Walk, 1968 a). The method of testing was the "bisection" method because the infants would not keep the eye patch on long enough for another method of testing. With the bisection method one only need observe on which side of the center board the child crawls. With this method 93% of the choices were to the shallow side for visual depths of 10 inches or more. At a depth of 5 inches the monocular infants went 67% shallow as compared to 84% of the binocular infants. The infants 8½ months of age and younger tended to crawl toward the uncovered eye and early crawlers behaved more appropriately than late crawlers. Again, a weakness is revealed that depends on a threshold, since only at the depth of 5 inches was an age-related weakness revealed for monocular infants.

The human infant research reveals weakness related to age. Older human infants have had more perceptual experience than younger ones but the older infant is also more mature. The differences may be due to maturity and not due to visual experience at all. Amount of crawling experience is similarly flawed: an infant who crawls late is also maturing late and amount of crawling experience *per se* may not be important. This does not mean that the human infant results should be summarily dismissed; it only means that they must be accepted with caution. On the other hand, Bower (1974) and others have shown space perception present in infants almost from birth and almost a year later the infants are still improving in the discrimination of a visual dropoff. From an overall ecological point of view even the year-old child does not seem to have finished perceptual development for depth.

The study of animals permits more controlled observations. From animal studies one can get a better fix on whether experience is needed for the development of space perception. The precocial species will be discussed first, then the altricial species.

3. The Unlearned Nature of Depth Perception

3.1. Precocial Species

Precocial species are capable of independent locomotion soon after birth and visual depth perception seems to be present at the time. The first recorded observations are those of Spalding (1872), who kept chicks "in a state of blindness, from one to three days . . ." and observed that within a few minutes of the time they were placed in the light they followed moving objects (crawling insects) by vision, avoided obstacles in their path, and pecked at objects "showing not merely an instinctive perception of distance, but an original ability to measure distance with something like infallible accuracy" (Spalding, 1872, p. 485). Spalding also observed a day-old duckling catch a fly on the wing and a piglet, blindfolded at birth, accurately judge depth when placed on a chair, since it knelt and leapt down (Spalding, 1875).

Recent observations have confirmed Spalding's conclusions. Day-old chicks normally hatched discriminate depth on the visual cliff (Walk and Gibson, 1961), and day-old chicks kept in the dark until tested on the visual cliff also discriminate depth (Shinkman, 1963; Walk, 1965). Kear (1967) and Walk (1972) studied very young ducklings and observed good discrimination of visual depth. Nyström and Hansson (1974) kept eider ducklings in the dark until tested at 1–3 days of age. They found that all chose the shallow side of the visual cliff.

Walk and Gibson (1961) observed very young pigs, lambs, and goats on the visual cliff and found flawless performance. Lemmon (cited in Hahn, 1972) found that goats discriminated visual depth as soon as they could stand.

Precocial species discriminate depth at birth. While few of all possible precocial species have been studied, and only the chick and the duck have been observed under the most rigorous conditions (kept in the dark until tested), the conclusion is inescapable that precocial animals can discriminate visual depth without prior visual experience. Recent research confirms Spalding's original conclusions.

3.2. Altricial Species

Altricial animals are not capable of independent locomotion at birth. Mammals like the kitten, the dog, and the rat are born with their eyes closed (the human infant, also altricial, has eyes open from birth). The eyes of the kitten open in about 10 days; it is about 2 weeks later before locomotion is adequate and visual depth perception can reliably be demonstrated.

The rat can be reared in the dark for over 3 months and still discriminate depth with a jumping stand technique (Lashley and Russell, 1934) or with the visual cliff (Walk, Gibson, and Tighe, 1957). This shows that at least some altricial species have depth discrimination with no opportunity for learning.

The kitten at first seemed to be an exception to this rule. Kittens reared in the dark for 4 weeks did not discriminate depth on the visual cliff (Walk and Gibson, 1961). Held and Hein (1963) reared kittens in the dark for 8 weeks and then passively exposed some of them to a visual environment (they could see the environment, but not their own limbs and they could not locomote); other kittens were allowed to move actively through the visual environment. Only the active kittens discriminated depth on the visual cliff. Held and Hein concluded that active motion in the light was necessary for the development of visual depth perception. Miller and Walk (1977) reared some kittens in the dark for 4 weeks while littermates started active or passive light exposure for several hours a day at 18 days of age. Normal controls and dark-reared groups were also part of this experiment. All groups, even the dark-reared, showed some depth discrimination at 4 weeks of age. On one test, animals were called by the experimenter from the deep or shallow sides of the visual cliff. Animals from all groups were slower to descend toward the deep side than the shallow side. In addition, some animals were reared in the dark for 8 weeks, similar to the Held and Hein (1963) experiment, and depth perception was lacking on all measures in the passively exposed and the dark-reared animals but not for the active kittens. The second experiment confirmed Held and Hein's results, but the first one also showed that some depth perception was present with no opportunity for active locomotion in the light.

The kitten and the rat have been the most extensively studied of the altricial species. From them one may conclude that visual depth perception appears without an opportunity for practice in the light. The animals may be relatively helpless at birth and not capable of independent locomotion until several weeks of age. Nevertheless, the animals still show depth discrimination after being kept in the dark while locomotor ability matures.

The Syrian hamster appears to be a very similar to the rat in that it can be reared in the dark for at least 60 days and still show excellent depth discrimination (Schiffman, 1971). The albino rabbit displays similar tendencies. When kept in the dark for 4 weeks, most animals are relatively immobile and refuse to descend from the center board of the visual cliff. Those that do move around show a strong tendency toward unlearned depth discrimination, but the difficulty of testing these animals after a prolonged period of dark-rearing makes this conclusion only tentative (Walk, 1966).

Spalding (1875) tested altricial birds by keeping them from practicing flying. He confined swallows in a small box that was too small for them to extend their wings and the parents fed the young through wire mesh. The birds were released from the box when they were fully fledged. They flew a little awkwardly at first, but within a few minutes were indistinguishable from other swallows. Spalding repeated the experiment with titmice, tomtits, and wrens, and, although he gave no details, the results were similar.

We tested a few ring doves on the visual cliff when they were 14–15 days old, soon after the young ring dove begins to be active (10–12 days of age) and long before the birds are weaned (20–25 days of age). They were awkward and difficult to test, but all responses (only nine responses were secured from a total of three birds) were toward the shallow side (Walk, 1966). This agrees with Spalding.

Altricial animals are more difficult to test than precocial ones because, for the best control, they must be kept in the dark to prevent visual experience until they can be tested. Nevertheless, the species tested can discriminate visual depth.

The conclusion from the research with altricial and precocial species is that visual depth perception is unlearned. This does not mean that visual experience is unimportant for depth perception. Indeed, it is very important, as the next series of studies will show.

4. Studies of Experience with Animals

4.1. Genetic Ecological Experience

Not all species respond to depth in the same way. As Yerkes (1904) pointed out long ago, aquatic and terrestrial turtles respond differently to depth; in his study aquatic turtles fell off a board into a net while terrestrial turtles usually remained on the platform. We found that aquatic turtles were the most careless of all animals tested on the visual cliff (Walk and Gibson, 1961). Routtenberg and Glickman (1964) tested land and aquatic turtles on the visual cliff and replicated Yerkes's findings since more aquatic than land turtles went to the deep side. Routtenberg and Glickman (1964) also observed that the snow leopard, a mountain dweller, has much better depth perception on the visual cliff than the tiger which lives in flat country. The duckling, an aquatic bird, discriminates depth but is much more careless in the presence of visual depth than is the chick (Walk, 1972). But Kear (1967) found that newly hatched ground-nesting ducklings avoided the deep side more than those whose nests were in holes above the ground, a tendency she ascribed to the necessity of jumping from the nesting hole to the ground soon after the bird hatched. Horner (1954) tested a number of species of deer mice (*Peromyscus*) on a platform raised above the ground. The animals from the prairie desert, sandhill, or beach country tended to fall off the platform, while the semiarboreal species stayed on it. All deer mice had been reared in the laboratory for several generations so the only "experience," that of the ordinary laboratory cage, was similar for all animals.

Observations on various species of gulls constitute probably the strongest demonstration of the interaction of environment and heredity for the discrimination of depth.

Cullen (1957) first observed the way the Kittiwake gull had adapted to cliff nesting in her studies on the Farne Islands off the Northhumberland coast of England. She described a number of changes in the Kittiwake that reflect the environment of the cliff as compared to the ground and also the relaxation of the pressure from predators in the cliff site. The cliff environment has led to changes in fighting methods, copulation, the response of the young to attack, how long the young stay in the nest or whether they face toward or huddle close to a wall, the nesting sites, and the method of nest building. Even the claws of cliff nesters are stronger and better adapted for grasping than are the claws of ground nesters. Because predators are rarer, the Kittiwake seldom gives alarm calls or responds to predators and the clutch size is smaller than for ground nesters. Cullen (p. 299) concludes, "I know of no other case where one relatively simple change can be shown to have been responsible for so many alterations."

Cullen's research shows that depth reactions of a species are part of its overall adaptation to its ecological niche. Subsequent research, particularly by Emlen (1963), Smith (1966), and McLannahan (1973), has extended her observations.

Smith (1966) studied the adaptations of a number of cliff-nesting gulls in the Arctic and compared them to ground nesters. He found that cliff nesters build deeper nests than do ground nesters. Two species of cliff nesters have different adaptations for egg laying. Thayer's gull (*Larus thayeri*) lays long eggs that roll in tight circles in the wind, while the Iceland gull (*L. glaucoides*) lays rounder eggs that are more vulnerable to the wind. The Iceland gulls lose more eggs in the first few days after hatching but lay replacement eggs easily, while Thayer's gulls lose fewer eggs but are also less likely to lay replacement eggs. Smith also found, as did Cullen (1957), that cliff nesters are fed from the parent's throat while ground nesters give a feeding call and the young come to the food. Even the recognition of chicks is affected by the environment. Ground nesters, whose chicks often must disperse, recognize their own chicks when the chicks are a few days old, while cliff nesters, whose young must remain in the nest, do not recognize a foreign chick in the nest until the chicks are at least 28 days old.

In his review of habitat, Smith (1966) found that, in his environment, the Herring gull (*L. argentatus*) always nested on the ground, while three species—the Glaucous gull (*L. hyperboreus*), the Iceland gull, and Thayer's gull—were mainly cliff nesters, and the Kittiwake (*L. rissa tridactyla*) nested only on tiny ledges on steep cliffs. He extensively tested four species: the Herring gull, Glaucous gull, Iceland gull, and Thayer's gull. For the last three species he was able to study gull chicks raised on the ground as well as chicks raised in a cliff environment.

The test consisted of an approach of two men to within 5 m of the nest. The chicks' reactions were scored in three categories: (1) jumped or ran from the nest, (2) moved to the edge of the nest but remained in it, (3) remained motionless.

The results are shown in Table 1. The cliff nesters, Iceland gulls and Thayer's gulls, seldom jumped from the nest, while Glaucous chicks, although cliff nesters, tended to jump or move to the edge of the nest. When the Glaucous gull, Iceland gull, and Thayer's gull were reared on the ground, the species reacted differently. Thayer's gull chicks behaved as if they were still in the cliff environment in that few moved at all. The Iceland gull chicks, on the other hand, switched completely, since they acted like Herring gull chicks in that many fled the nest and few remained motionless. Glaucous gull chicks also had a greater tendency to flee in the ground environment, but they were jumpers in the cliff environment, so the change was not as marked.

Prior to this study, Emlen (1963) had shown that Herring gull chicks from Kent Island, New Brunswick, where the Herring gull nests both on open

Table 1. Reaction to Approach of the Nest for Four Species of Gull Chicks from Different Environments [a]

Species	Environment			N	Reaction to approach		
	Eggs	Raised	Tested		Jumped (%)	Moved to edge (%)	Motionless (%)
Thayer's gull	Cliff	Cliff	Cliff	570	1	22	77
	Ground	Ground	Ground	155	1	24	75
Iceland gull	Cliff	Cliff	Cliff	630	3	40	57
	Ground	Ground	Ground	205	43	52	5
Glaucous gull	Cliff	Cliff	Cliff	335	32	48	20
	Ground	Ground	Ground	95	42	58	—
Herring gull	Ground	Ground	Ground	470	41	51	8

[a] From Smith (1966).

ground and on cliffs, performed on a raised platform appropriately for the environment in which they were raised. The cliff nesters were more cautious in behavioral tests than were the ground nesters.

These experiments may have shown that gulls are influenced by the environment in which they are reared. Ground nesters are more careless of visual depth than are cliff nesters, and species which use both types of nesting environment tend to adapt to the environment where they are reared. An exception is Thayer's gull. Thayer's chicks behave like cliff nesters no matter where they are raised.

The experimental flaw so far is that ground nesters and cliff nesters, even though of the same species, could be of different genetic stock. This requires cross-rearing, taking the eggs from one environment and raising the chicks in another. Even the testing environment, whether the chicks were tested on the ground or at the cliff, might be an influence. This is an experimental modification of depth discrimination and the studies so far could be an experimental modification of depth discrimination or they could be genetic differences. This is a separate topic and, for continuity, the studies with gulls will be discussed first.

4.2. Reared in "Flat," "Cliff," or "Enriched" Environments, or over Visual Depths

Emlen (1963) cross-fostered Herring gull eggs. Eggs from the cliff colony were taken to ground nesters and *vice versa*. The fostered chicks behaved appropriately to the environment in which they were raised. Herring gull chicks reared on the plateau, even though the eggs came from the cliff sites, tended to

Table 2. Reaction to Nest Approach of Four Species of Gull Chicks When Testing and Rearing Environments Are Changed [a]

	Environment				Reaction to approach		
Species	Eggs	Raised	Tested	N	Jumped (%)	Moved to edge (%)	Motionless (%)
Thayer's gull	Ground	Ground	Cliff	75	—	20	80
Iceland gull	Ground	Ground	Cliff	125	46	32	22
	Ground	Cliff	Cliff	75	3	45	52
	Cliff	Cliff	Ground	90	11	66	23
Glaucous gull	Ground	Ground	Cliff	90	54	33	12
Herring gull	Ground	Ground	Cliff	275	54	35	11
	Ground	Cliff	Cliff	295	13	54	33
	Ground	Cliff	Ground	130	11	52	38

[a] From Smith (1966).

jump from a platform, while those reared in the cliff environment, even if they were from plateau eggs, were cautious on the platform.

    Smith (1966) also modified the environment, and the experimental manipulations are shown in Table 2. An examination of Table 2 shows that he changed the place where the chicks were raised, that some eggs from the ground-hatched chicks were raised on the cliff. He also tested the chicks in the opposite environment from the one where they were raised. One might hold that a chick tested on the ground would act like a ground nester simply because of the testing environment. An examination of Table 2 compared to Table 1 shows that the important factor is the environment in which the chick is raised. Those reared on the ground act like ground nesters, no matter where they are tested; likewise, those raised on the cliff act like cliff nesters when tested on the ground. The site of the eggs is also not a factor in that chicks from ground eggs raised on the cliff act like cliff nesters and are slow to react to the approach of an intruder. Smith found that the appropriate reactions were acquired in the first 8 days after hatching.

    Table 2 strengthens the conclusions drawn from Table 1 and confirms the observations of Emlen (1963) on Herring gulls (Smith did not find any cliff-nesting Herring gulls). The four species seem to form a continuum: Thayer's gull is the least modifiable, a cliff inhabitant in any environment. The Glaucous gull is somewhat modifiable by the environment, but the tendency is to act like a ground nester even if reared on the cliffs. The Herring gull is fairly adaptable in that it is much less apt to move from the nest if raised on the cliff, but the 11–13% which jump in that situation, while far fewer than the 40–50% for the ground nesters, are far more than the 1–3% for Thayer's gull or the Iceland gull. The Iceland gull would appear to be the most adaptable in that few jump from the nest in the cliff situation while those raised on the ground have the same tendency to flee the nest as Herring gulls or Iceland gulls.

The Kittiwake was compared to the Herring gull by McLannahan (1973) in observations on islands off the coast of England. The Kittiwake, it will be recalled, was mentioned by Smith (1966) as a species that nests only on high cliffs. McLannahan made a number of observations of the two species of gulls related to survival, such as the tendency of the chicks to snuggle close to a wall, and she also reared chicks in special environments: on the ground, in cliff boxes, or over transparent Perspex. Generally, as might be expected from the previous discussion, she found the Kittiwake almost unmodifiable, while the Herring gull did adapt to the environments. No Kittiwakes reacted inappropriately to the visual cliff; they always, even at 1 day of age, withdrew rapidly from the visual edge. But Herring gulls were cautious if reared in a cliff box. The Perspex-reared were the least cautious, while the ground-reared were intermediate. McLannahan did get a slight experience effect with ground-reared Kittiwake gulls. The day-old ground-reared Kittiwake chicks did not avoid a tactile edge (the edge was a real one and the experiment was carried out in darkness) since on the first day all but one chick fell. Performance on the tactile edge was perfect after the first day. The cliff-reared, on the other hand, behaved perfectly. Needless to say, Herring gulls, from whatever environment, generally fell from the tactile edge.

The gull studies are a good case study of experience and genetic factors in depth discrimination. A variety of measures agree: cliff nesters are cautious on platforms and visual cliffs, and they do not jump from the nest when intruders approach. For some species, such as the Kittiwake or Thayer's gull, the response is so genetic that even different rearing conditions have a minimal effect; for others, such as the Iceland gull or the Herring gull, the environment can modify the reaction to depth situations. We are discussing serious consequences—a gull chick in the wrong environment for its background would not survive. But all gulls are flying species and the long-term differences in perceptual abilities are probably minimal. Rather, we seem to have situational-developmental determinants of perceptual behavior.

Studies of "cliff" or "enriched" environments have been carried out with gerbils and rats. Thiessen, Lindzey, and Collins (1969) raised Mongolian gerbils for 52 days in three different environments. Two groups were raised in an environment with a physical cliff where they could go from the high to the low side by way of a ramp. One group had the environment painted gray while the second group had a patterned environment of black and white squares. A third group had a flat environment that was painted gray. The group raised with a patterned cliff environment was the best in terms of accuracy on the visual cliff and latency of choice: they responded quickly and their descents were almost exclusively to the shallow side. The unpatterned cliff group was slower in latency and significantly worse in discrimination since all animals went to the deep side at least once. The animals raised in the unpatterned flat environment discriminated depth well but latencies were high, slower than any other group.

Bradley and Shea (1977) extended the Thiessen *et al.* (1969) study by beginning to test for depth discrimination soon after the eyes of the gerbils opened at 20 days of age. They raised Mongolian gerbils in either a cliff environment or a flat environment and began testing on the 21st day. The cliff-reared group rapidly discriminated depth on the visual cliff while the flat-reared animals did not. But at 60 days of age both cliff-reared and flat-reared animals discriminated visual depth equally well. Thus, the cliff environment appeared to accelerate the acquisition of visual depth discrimination.

A subtle effect from rearing in an enriched environment as compared to a normal laboratory cage environment was shown by Eichengren, Coren, and Nachmias (1966). Hooded rats were reared from the age of 10 days (shortly before the eyes open) until tested at 21 days of age in either a normal cage environment or a larger cage with climbing platforms. When tested binocularly on the visual cliff at 21 days of age, both normal cage-reared and enriched environment animals discriminated depth on the visual cliff. Of animals rendered monocular by the application of collodion, however, only the "enriched" animals discriminated visual depth. Lore, Kam, and Newby (1967) repeated the experiment and varied the height of the center board. When the center board was the same height as that used by Eichengren *et al.* (1.8 inches), monocular animals did not discriminate depth on the visual cliff; when the center board height was raised slightly, to 2.25 inches, the monocular animals significantly preferred the shallow side. This means that some depth discrimination still remained for animals reared in a normal environment provided that the center board was raised high enough so that animals were forced to use visual cues. The Eichengren *et al.* (1966) experiment showed a weakness, similar to weaknesses observed with human infants. The extent of the weakness and how long it would last have not been extensively probed.

This section thus shows that experimental rearing in the presence of "cliffs" or varied depths makes the animal (gulls, gerbils, rats) more responsive to depth while rearing in a flat environment leads to less responsiveness to depth.

One method of experimental modification is to rear an animal over the deep side of the visual cliff. This is not an ecologically representative environment since, so far as is known, no species raises its young on a glass plate over an apparent abyss. Still, interesting results have been secured with this method.

Tallarico and Farrell (1964) raised baby chicks for about 35 hr after birth on glass with a pattern either directly below the glass or some distance below it. The shallow-reared animals had a definite preference for the shallow side, while the deep-reared chicks had only a slight preference for the deep side, essentially a chance preference. Similar results were secured by Zeier (1970) with 45 hr of exposure. The shallow-reared chicks chose the shallow side and the chicks reared on the deep side had no preference for either side.

Seitz, Seitz, and Kaufman (1973) used chicks to study the effect of "primacy" and "recency" of experience when chicks were raised on the deep side of the visual cliff. The chicks were raised for 4 days in an environment that simulated the deep or the shallow side of the visual cliff and then half of each group was shifted to the opposite environment. The predominant choice was to the side that represented the environment of initial rearing (whether deep or shallow) and the 4 days in the other environment did not affect the choices. This is the only study of an early or "critical" period for animals reared on the deep side of the visual cliff. Kaufman (1976) continued these studies to determine the length of time required to reverse the preference for the shallow side. With groups raised for 22, 46, 70, 94, or 118 hr on the deep side, she found that after 70 hr on the deep side the first descent was more likely to be toward the deep side than the shallow side. But when the chicks were tested informally with a visual cliff without a glass floor the chicks did not step off onto the deep side.

Eider ducks were raised in the dark for various periods of time and then exposed for 6–24 hr to a simulated deep or shallow side of the visual cliff by Nyström and Hansson (1974). When tested on the visual cliff, all shallow-exposed ducks chose the shallow side. The deep-exposed animals chose the deep side as a function of length of exposure and age. The optimal length of exposure for deep choices was 12 hr or more on the deep side with the animal 55 hr or more old. The ducklings were in the dark except when they were being exposed to the environment or tested.

McLannahan (1973) reared a few Herring gull and Kittiwake chicks with floors of transparent Perspex. The environment had minimal effects for the Kittiwake chicks, although they did seem more disturbed in avoiding a cliff edge than other Kittiwake chicks. The Perspex-reared Herring gull chicks were the most deliberate and less disturbed, but no differences were significant. In contrast to other studies, McLannahan's experiments emphasize genetic differences in modifiability.

Two experiments have used rats. Kaess and Wilson (1964) raised hooded rats in cages with floors like the shallow or deep sides of the visual cliff from just prior to eye opening until 2 weeks after the eyes opened. When the rats were tested at 28–30 days of age, those reared on a shallowlike environment chose the shallow side and those reared with a deep environment predominantly chose the deep side. In second experiment, Carr and McGuigan (1965) reared albino rats in wire mesh cages over a checked oilcloth that was either close to the cage floor ("shallow") or with the checked pattern 12 inches below the mesh floor ("deep"). The shallow-reared subjects chose the shallow side while those reared over the deeplike pattern had no preference for either side. When the rats were placed on a board with visual depth on both sides (both sides "deep"), the shallow-reared animals generally remained on the center board while the deep-reared subjects descended from it.

While animals raised in a "cliff" environment become more responsive to depth, those raised on glass over a depth seem to have the responsiveness weakened. They become relatively indifferent to depth as represented by the large number of deep descents on the visual cliff. These are short-term experiments, and the generality of such effects needs to be investigated.

4.3. Visual Deprivation

Visual deprivation is experience, but it is a special kind of experience—the lack of an opportunity to use visual cues for guidance through the environment. Prolonged deprivation can produce physiological side effects but this possibility will be generally ignored to concentrate on behavior.

Extended visual deprivation will eventually abolish visually guided behavior, but, with exposure to patterned light, the behavior will return. Long exposure to homogeneous unpatterned light produces results similar to complete darkness.

A long period of visual deprivation abolishes visually guided behavior, but the rate of loss seems to depend on the species. Nealey and Riley (1963) first showed that extensive deprivation (for 10 months) eliminates visual depth discrimination for the rat. They also showed that the behavior would return if the animals were left in the light. Whereas rats can be left in the dark for 3 months or more without visual depth discrimination being abolished, their ability to discriminate fine visual depths deteriorates (Walk and Bond, 1968). They choose the shallow side for a visual depth of 10 inches but not for one of 4 inches. This study was followed by those of Walk and Walters (1973) and by Tees (1974). Walk and Walters (1973) found some impairment in the discrimination of fine depths after as little as 30 days in the dark. Tees (1974) found impairment for fine depths but not until 60–80 days in the dark. After 2 weeks in the light, rats reared in the dark for 60 days did not recover the discrimination of 4 inch depths in the Walk and Walters (1973) study. But Tees (1976) was able to secure complete recovery to discriminate 4-inch depths by animals reared for 90 days in the dark after they had been in the light for 50–70 days.

Van Hof-Van Duin (1976) studied kittens that were visually deprived for either 4 or 7 months. Deficits were relatively mild for the 4-month-old kittens but quite prolonged for the 7-month-old animals. The behavior that was recovered was obstacle avoidance, visual tracking, optokinetic nystagmus, visual placing, visual cliff behavior, and jumping from a pedestal. The last behavior to be acquired was visually guided reaching (6–8 weeks), visual cliff discrimination (7–8 weeks), and practiced jumping from a 2-foot-high step chair (6–10 weeks). No irreversible effects were found from such prolonged deprivation, although one might expect from neurophysiological research (see chapters by Rothblat and Schwartz and by Mitchell) that visual deprivation past the 4-month-old critical period might produce irreversible deficits.

Baxter (1966) varied the type of experience after deprivation by keeping some cats in their cages and others in the home. The recovery period for visual placing, jumping from a pedestal, visual following, the eye blink to an approaching object, and avoidance was about 10 days for two kittens taken home and over 30 days for two animals left in laboratory cages. The type of "therapy" is an influence on recovery, a finding similar to that of Eichengren *et al.* (1966) with rats where those in an enriched environment recovered more rapidly than those in a deprived one.

The influence of visual deprivation on the visually guided behavior of rhesus monkeys has been studied by Fantz (1965) and also Wilson and Riesen (1966). Fantz (1965) deprived monkeys for 3 days to 20 weeks. The younger monkeys traversed through an obstacle field and discriminated depth on the visual cliff very quickly, but the animals deprived for 5 weeks or more were very adversely affected. No animals deprived for 11 weeks or more discriminated depth on the visual cliff, but some vision must have remained because all animals were able to get through the obstacle field without touching the posts. The monkey is often emotional and difficult to test, and prolonged deprivation would not help the testing program.

Wilson and Riesen (1966) deprived rhesus monkeys of patterned light for 20 or 60 days. They were kept in the dark except for 2.5 hr of diffused light a day through translucent occluders. While the monkeys initially lacked such behavior as visual tracking, visual placing, and visual cliff discrimination, these all appeared eventually. Visual cliff behavior was the most adversely affected. While it is present in normal monkeys a day or 2 after birth, it did not appear until a median of 16 days (range 14–21 days) in those deprived 20 days and a median of 20 days (range 11–34 days) in the 60-day group.

Very prolonged periods of visual deprivation may produce permanent deficits. Riesen (1950) kept chimpanzees in the dark for about 1½ years, two from shortly after birth and one starting at the age of 7 months. All three animals essentially seemed to lose their ability to function visually.

The deprivation studies show that visual experience in the sense of exposure to patterned light is necessary to maintain visually guided behavior. The effects of several months' visual deprivation are surprisingly long lasting, but the animals appear to recover if left in the light long enough, except, perhaps, for very prolonged deprivation. Methods of expediting recovery have not been extensively investigated, but the optimal method seems to be one that exposes the animal to a wide variety of patterns and depths.

4.4. Visuomotor Experience

The importance of visuomotor experience for depth perception has been stressed by Richard Held and Alan Hein (Held and Hein, 1963; Hein, 1972). Their first experiment with kittens has been mentioned earlier. The kittens raised in the dark until 8–12 weeks of age were divided into pairs, and one member of the pair actively locomoted in an enclosed circular environment, pulling another kitten around a hub as it walked. The second kitten was in a small box; it could see the general environment but not its limbs. In a sense, the second kitten received the same visual information as the first, but visuomotor experience dependent on its own actions was limited. When tested on the visual cliff, the first kitten discriminated depth, the second did not. Subsequent experiments are summarized by Hein (1972). For example, the authors tested whether more experience in the gondola would help develop depth discrimination. It did not. In fact, the gondola environment was somewhat disruptive of the acquisition of visually guided behavior. Kittens reared in holders where they could not see their limbs were able to acquire visually guided behavior more rapidly than kittens reared for an equivalent amount of time in the gondola (Hein, 1972). In a demonstration of the specificity of experience, kittens were raised with "passive" exposure to one eye and "active" exposure to the other. They acquired guided visuomotor experience with the active eye and not with the passive eye (Hein, Held, and Gower, 1970). Another instance of specificity was shown when kittens wore plastic "ruffs" that permitted them to walk around yet prevented them from viewing their limbs. These kittens developed discrimination of depth on the visual cliff, but they did not develop "visually guided reaching" (Hein and Held, 1967). Visually guided reaching means that a kitten brought toward a surface with prongs that extend out will reach specifically toward one of the prongs and hit it. The kittens reached out (visual placing) but their reach toward the irregularly placed prongs was not accurate.

The Held and Hein research shows the importance of visuomotor activity and also the extreme specificity of some types of plasticity. Our own research (Miller and Walk, 1977) has replicated the deleterious effects of passive visual exposure as long as the animals are kept in the dark long enough prior to exposure to the light. While the kitten may have some depth perception without active locomotion (Miller and Walk, 1977), its continuance depends on interaction with the environment.

4.5. "Mothering"

"Mothering" has been shown to have a brief influence on depth discrimination. Lemmon and Patterson (1964) separated twin lambs at birth, leaving one twin with the mother while the other twin was kept in a pen with the other lambs. Both twins were placed on the visual cliff once an hour until they exhibited avoidance of the deep side. The "mothered" twins avoided the deep side about 3–4 hr after birth, while the "unmothered" twins did not consistently avoid the deep side until 6–7 hr after birth. In every pair the "mothered" twin was ahead of the "unmothered" twin. This experience effect was a brief one, within the first 24 hr after birth. The same experiment carried out with goats, however, showed no influence of mothering. The kid goats all passed the visual cliff test as soon as they could stand up, shortly after birth (W. Lemmon, unpublished, reported in Hahn, 1972). Even in this brief period after birth an interaction of species behavior and experience was shown. The sheep, a grazing and generally flatlands ungulate, shows some effect of experience. The goat, more accustomed to mountainous terrain, avoids depth within a few minutes after birth.

4.6. Improvement and Experience

Does depth perception improve through experience when experience is not confounded with maturation? This is a very difficult question to answer. The human infant improves in the sense that older infants behave more precisely than younger ones, but the improvement could be through either maturation or experience. Developmental studies with animals have the same problem. The results with young kittens and rabbits of improved visual cliff discrimination with age (Walk, 1966) could be maturation or experience. Placing an animal in the dark allows the animal to develop without visual experience, but an animal like the kitten shows chance choices on the visual cliff after only 4 weeks in the dark.

Two methods seem appropriate to investigate this topic. One method is to keep an animal like the rat that is relatively unaffected by visual deprivation in the dark while it matures. A second method is to give experience to one group.

The first method is illustrated by a study by Tees (1974). He seemed to show some improvement for the light-reared that was not reflected in the dark-reared. But Tees plotted a line of 75% discrimination, and his raw data, also included in the article, were much less definite. The raw data were always well above chance and often just missed the 75% point. Walk and Walters (1973) found no improvement with age in the discrimination of fine depth differences. This may seem like a disagreement with the Tees (1974) study, but it is not. This is because the Tees raw data show the animals well above chance; the Tees (1974) and the Walk and Walters (1973) studies are not significantly different from each other.

Future research with the rat may show some improvement that is unequivocably related to experience—or it may not. But the Tees (1974) and the Walk and Walters (1973) studies are so much in agreement that one may hazard a guess that the *percent of improvement* from experience found in any future studies is bound to be slight.

The second method, extra experience during normal development, was mentioned previously in the study by Bradley and Shea (1977). The final levels of performance for cliff-reared and flat-environment-reared gerbils did not differ, but the cliff-reared animals had a high level of visual cliff avoidance by the age of 30 days while the flat-reared subjects were still essentially at a chance level. Yet by 60 days of age all subjects showed a high level of depth discrimination.

A number of studies have shown that depth discrimination develops gradually in altricial mammals (the rat, Bauer, 1973; the cat, Karmel, Miller, Dettweiler, and Anderson, 1970; Van Hof-Van Duin, 1976; Walk, 1966; the rabbit, Karmel *et al.*, 1970; Walk, 1966; the dog, Fox, 1971; Walk, 1968*b*). The Bradley and Shea (1977) study needs to be followed by other similar studies that permit an assessment of the influence of experience on development. Prenatal as well as postnatal experience may be important (Gottlieb, 1976).

5. Discussion and Conclusion

This chapter shows that experience influences depth perception in many ways. Initial depth perception appears to be unlearned, but subsequent experience modifies the initial behavior. Experience in a special environment, especially one that gives experience with depths as a cliff environment does, will lead to better depth discrimination. Conversely, a flat environment is not conducive to good depth perception. Experimental studies and genetic influences agree. Species from cliff environments have better depth discrimination (e.g., goats, deer mice, leopards, Thayer's gulls, Kittiwake gulls) and experimental rearing in a cliff environment or one with varied depths also makes for more sensitivity to visual depths (e.g., studies with gerbils, rats, and Iceland gulls).

Visual deprivation will abolish depth discrimination but an extended period in the light will restore it. Sensorimotor experience in the light is necessary to maintain depth discrimination; an animal may be exposed to the light, but depth discrimination is not maintained unless the animal locomotes through the visual environment.

Extended experience in the light may be required for the full development of depth discrimination in some species, but the evidence is not conclusive. Human infants appear to develop fear of visual depths and better motion parallax with increased age.

Prolonged exposure to visual depths without consequences as in the studies where the animal is raised on the deep side of the visual cliff seems to extinguish some aspects of the response to visual depth. The result of being reared in perceptual midair is similar in some ways to being reared in a flat environment. Many years ago, when I first began to test infants at George Washington University, a mother called up to volunteer an infant with unusual past experience for my study. She said that she was interested in the visual cliff study because she had a glass-topped coffee table and her child crawled all over it. A few days later, she called to cancel the appointment. The child had fallen out of its crib and received a concussion. This anecdote reveals possible broader effects of learning to ignore the visual cues to depth than do the laboratory studies here.

What are the lessons to be learned from the study of experience and depth discrimination? What are the questions that future research should answer?

5.1. Adaptation and Ecology

In the beginning, the importance of the function of perceptual experience was stressed. The most obvious function of experience is that of adaptation. For some species, however, perceptual adaptation may mean too high a cost in terms of survival. The goat and the Kittiwake, for example, may inhabit environments where the cost of a misstep is too high, and the species have lost their plasticity. Should the environment change—if, by some magic, all cliffs disappeared—the Kittiwake also might disappear. Other gulls, such as the Herring gull, may not be so adapted to cliff situations, but they are better adapted to flee from the predators that are common in a flatter environment. The nimble mountain goat may also be at a disadvantage on flat ground. Looking at functions gets us beyond depth perception *per se*. Cullen's (1957) analysis of ground-nesting and cliff-nesting gulls is a classic in its demonstration of the pervasiveness of the effects of adaptation to a cliff environment. To understand depth perception, we must understand where depth perception fits into the total ecology of the organism.

5.2. Psychology and Ethology

The impression one gets in reading some papers by psychologists is that of great precision and little concern for ecological validity. The papers by ethologists are much more ecologically valid, but they are not quite so laboratory precise. The ethological papers also represent much more patient work, often several years in the field, to make the total picture very impressive. The psychological papers tend to be much more short-term. Despite the different approaches, however, the overall agreement on the effect of environment on the depth discrimination of a number of species is somewhat surprising.

5.3. Measures of Depth Perception

One obvious lesson from prior research is the need for a great many measures that are interrelated. Threshold studies are very useful because they help to probe weaknesses. Even now, one occasionally reads studies that seem to regard depth perception as something that either "is" or "is not." Depth perception (or, more neutrally, depth discrimination) appears as a function of different testing conditions. If one gets better depth discrimination with one method than with another, this does not mean that one method is necessarily more valid than another. We must be as patient as the ethologists in trying to understand the meaning of the behavior.

An example of the use of different testing conditions is the use of platforms that vary in real or visual height to supplement the visual cliff measures. Another example is to bring the deep side of the visual cliff gradually toward the shallow side until the animal has no preference for either side. Obstacle avoidance is a measure of depth or distance ahead and more might be done with it. Many measures of visual space perception are either confined to a few species or have not been developed with a wider range of species: the visual placing response, visually guided reaching, the eye blink to an approaching object which can be studied in pure form by an expanding shadow or "visual looming," pecking at objects (confined to birds). Other methods require extensive training (e.g., precise measures of stereopsis), and they either take too long if one is studying development or recovery from deprivation or may not be applicable to all species.

The most natural methods of testing depth discrimination are obstacle avoidance (distance ahead) or an avoidance of or response to depths (visual cliff, platforms). These involve no extensive pretraining, take very little time, and apply to a wide variety of species. But we need to develop more measures, particularly a "natural" way to measure stereopsis.

5.4. The Perceptual Response

One can get into a very sticky argument over what is being modified in many of the studies where experience influences depth discrimination. How "real" are the effects? Can the organism avoid obstacles? Catch prey? Avoid real cliffs? We do not really know. But my own initial skepticism (Walk, 1966, p. 86) has changed to a conviction that all of the studies of the influence of experience on depth perception are important. The data fit together too well even if many parameters need to be worked out.

5.5. Sensorimotor Effects

William James (1890) noted a case cited by Schopenhauer of an Estonian girl, Eva Lauk, who was born without arms or legs, yet whose intellect developed as rapidly as that of her brothers and sisters and who also judged the size and distance of objects as well as they did (James, 1890, II, p. 214). James believed that even if a person's eyeballs were fixed and unable to move the individual would develop visual depth perception. James argued that the movement of objects across the retina would reveal not only two-dimensional perception but three-dimensional perception as well. The method seems somewhat similar to the demonstration of the kinetic depth effect by Wallach (Wallach and O'Connell, 1953), or of the invariant properties of objects as shown by perspective transformations by Gibson (1957). The kinetic depth effect demonstrates that the shadow of an object projected on a screen is two-dimensional until it rotates and then three-dimensional properties are revealed in the two-dimensional shadow. The perspective transformations projected as moving shdows on a screen have revealed, as examples, precise estimates of slant, rigid and nonrigid motion, surfaces moving in depth in different planes, and a "looming" that may make an observer duck when the expanding shadow fills the screen. James seemed to conceptualize using the eye as a two-dimensional screen.

But the living eye could not be so restricted, and discriminate visual space. First, if the eyeballs were fixed, immovable, the retinal image would disappear since an image stablized on the retina disappears quickly (Pritchard, 1961). Second, even if the eyes were allowed to move, some motion of the observer would be required to maintain depth perception. It is true that the observer in the Wallach and Gibson studies is passive as he observes a moving shadow on a two-dimensional screen that reveals the three-dimensional object. But such passive motion is not enough to maintain depth perception; active interaction with the visual world is necessary. Modern research, then, would agree that Eva Lauk would perceive the three-dimensional world accurately, but it would stress that, despite her lack of arms and legs, she could still interact with the environment. Researchers may disagree on the actual form the interaction would have to take, but they would agree that such interaction is necessary.

5.6. Plasticity and Pervasiveness

The perception of depth is modified by experience, but we know little of the pervasiveness of its effects. Depth perception as measured by choices on the visual cliff may be altered, but we do not know, unless we test, whether any other aspects of spatial perception have been changed. Pervasive changes were observed in gulls reared in special environments, but most studies use only one measure. As has been indicated, more measures and more sensitive measures, as with thresholds, are needed.

The length of time that experience lasts is another example of the pervasiveness of effects. Many studies use one measure at one point in time. Effects that are brief may have some theoretical interest, but they are not so impressive as long-term effects. We should be able to plot the time the experience lasts as well as its initial extent.

Critical periods for the influence of experience on depth perception have not been investigated. The closest to the study of a critical period is the one by Seitz *et al.* (1973) with chicks. That study demonstrated that the 4 days of initial experience was more important than the 4 days of later experience and found, incidentally, that the initial experience effects lasted at least 4 days, although the length of time the experience lasted after that (or, indeed, if it ever extinguished) was not investigated. One cannot conclude that all or part of the first 4 days after hatching is the critical period because chicks kept in the dark for 4 days might be equally susceptible when first exposed to the visual environment.

5.7. Plasticity and Phylogeny

The plasticity of chicks that was shown in studies where they were reared over the deep side of the visual cliff (Seitz *et al.*, 1973; Kaufman, 1976) is to be contrasted with the relative lack of plasticity observed for chicks when they were fitted with a prism that displaced the image to one side (Hess, 1956). Hess's original conclusion on the relative lack of plasticity of the chick must be modified by Rossi's (1968) demonstration of some plasticity after wearing prisms, but the amount of plasticity was not great. Gregory (1966) generalized from the Hess (1956) studies to assert that animals lower on the phylogenetic scale are not so adaptable as are higher species, such as humans and monkeys. But the studies cited here of gulls as well as chicks show a degree of plasticity in "lower" species that belies such a generalization. The gull studies found that plasticity seems to be related to habitat. In any event, conclusions as to the reasons for the plasticity or lack of plasticity of a species are premature until much more research with a greater variety of measures has been performed.

The individual differences in species modifiability observed with the gulls are related to studies of birdsongs. The depth perception of some species of gulls is fairly plastic and that of others is not; similarly, the birdsongs of some species are modified by experience while the birdsongs of closely related species may not be (see chapter by Konishi).

Animals used in laboratory studies, such as rats, cats, chicks, hamsters, and gerbils, are readily available from suppliers, but they do not permit the understanding of plasticity that would come from a number of different species that are closely related. The laboratory mouse is available in many inbred species, but the indivdual differences in depth perception have seldom been investigated. The deermouse studies (Horner, 1954) show that the deermouse is a possible candidate for the study of genetic differences in plasticity. More studies of gulls, particularly studies like those of McLannahan (1973) that combine the field approach with the laboratory one, would be desirable.

Plasticity may have intersensory effects. The visual and the motor systems are closely linked and one need not expect only visual or visuomotor experience to influence depth perception. Eggs must be turned frequently to hatch both in the laboratory and in nature. The prenatal mammal experiences the effects of movement and gravity as the mother moves about.

The research by Gottlieb (1976) shows many effects of prenatal auditory experience. We have no reason to doubt that prenatal influences may also affect depth perception.

6. References

Bauer, J. H. Development of visual cliff discrimination by infant hooded rats. *Journal of Comparative and Physiological Psychology*, 1973, *84*, 380–385.

Baxter, B. L. Effect of visual deprivation during postnatal maturation on the electroencephalogram of the cat. *Experimental Neurology*, 1966, *14*, 224–237.

Bower, T. G. R. *Development in infancy*. San Francisco: W. H. Freeman, 1974.

Bradley, D. R., and Shea, S. L. The effect of environment on visual cliff performance in the Mongolian gerbil. *Perception and Psychophysics*, 1977, *21*, 171–179.

Carr, W. J., and McGuigan, D. I. The stimulus basis and modification of visual cliff performance in the rat. *Animal Behaviour*, 1965, *13*, 25–29.

Cullen, E. Adaptations in the kittiwake to cliff-nesting. *Ibis*, 1957, *99*, 272–302.

Eichengren, J. M., Coren, S., and Nachmias, J. Visual cliff preference by infant rats: Effects of rearing and test conditions. *Science*, 1966, *151*, 830–831.

Emlen, J. T., Jr. Determinants of cliff edge and escape responses in herring gull chicks in nature. *Behaviour*, 1963, *22*, 1–16.

Fantz, ʼR. L. Ontogeny of perception. In A. M. Schrier, H. F. Harlow, and F. Stollnitz (eds.), *Behavior of nonhuman primates*. Vol. II. New York: Academic Press, 1965, pp. 365–403.

Fox, M. W. *Integrative development of brain and behavior in the dog*. Chicago: University of Chicago Press, 1971.

Gibson, J. J. Optical motions and transformations as stimuli for visual perception. *Psychological Review*, 1957, *64*, 288–295.

Gottlieb, G. Conceptions of prenatal development: Behavioral embryology. *Psychological Review*, 1976, *83*, 215–234.

Gregory, R. L. *Eye and brain: The psychology of seeing*. World University Library. New York: McGraw-Hill, 1966.

Hahn, E. *On the side of the apes*. New York: Arena Books, 1972.

Hein, A. Acquiring components of visually guided behavior. In Pick, A. D. (Ed.), *Minnesota symposia on child psychology*. Vol. 6. Minneapolis: University of Minnesota Press, 1972, pp. 53–68.

Hein, A., and Held, R. Dissociation of the visual placing response into elicited and guided components. *Science*, 1967, *158*, 390–392.

Hein, A., Held, R., and Gower, E. C. Development and segmentation of visually-controlled movement by selective exposure during rearing. *Journal of Comparative and Physiological Psychology*, 1970, *73*, 181–187.

Held, R., and Hein, A. Movement-produced stimulation in the development of visually-guided behavior. *Journal of Comparative and Physiological Psychology*, 1963, *56*, 872–876.

Hess, E. H. Space perception in the chick. *Scientific American*, 1956, *195(1)*, 71–80.

Horner, B. E. Arboreal adaptations of *Peromyscus*, with special reference to use of the tail. *Contributions from the Laboratory of Vertebrate Biology (University of Michigan)*, 1954, *61*, 1–84.

James, W. *The principles of psychology*. Vol. II. New York: Holt, 1890.

Kaess, D. W., and Wilson, J. P. Modification of the rat's avoidance of visual depth. *Journal of Comparative and Physiological Psychology*, 1964, *58*, 151–152.

Karmel, B. Z., Miller, P. N., Dettweiler, L., and Anderson, G. Texture density and normal development of visual depth avoidance. *Developmental Psychobiology*, 1970, *3*, 73–90.

Kaufman, L. W. Duration of early visual experience and visual cliff behavior of chicks. *Developmental Psychobiology*, 1976, *9*, 1–4.

Kear, J. Experiments with young nidifugous birds on a visual cliff. *Wildfowl Trust 18th Annual Report*, 1967, pp. 122–124.

Lashley, K. S., and Russell, J. T. The mechanism of vision. XI. A preliminary test of innate organization. *Journal of Genetic Psychology,* 1934, *45,* 136–144.

Lemmon, W. B., and Patterson, G. H. Depth perception in sheep: Effects of interrupting the mother-neonate bond. *Science,* 1964, *145,* 835–836.

Lore, R., Kam, B, and Newby, V. Visual and nonvisual depth avoidance in young and adult rats. *Journal of Comparative and Physiological Psychology,* 1967, *64,* 525–528.

McLannahan, H. M. C. Some aspects of the ontogeny of cliff nesting behaviour in the kittiwake (*Rissa trydactyla*) and the herring gull (*Larus argentatus*). *Behaviour,* 1973, *44,* 36–88.

Miller, D. R., and Walk, R. D. Visual motor experience and visual depth discrimination in kittens. Unpublished paper, 1977.

Nealey, S. M., and Riley, D. A. Loss and recovery of visual depth in dark-reared rats. *American Journal of Psychology,* 1963, *76,* 329–332.

Nyström, M., and Hansson, S. B. Interaction between early experience and depth avoidance in young eider ducks (*Somateria mollissima* L.). *Behaviour,* 1974, *48,* 303–314.

Pritchard, R. M. Stabilized images on the retina. *Scientific American,* 1961, *204*(6), 72–78.

Riesen, A. H. Arrested vision. *Scientific American,* 1950, *183*(*1*), 16–19.

Rossi, P. J. Adaptation and negative aftereffect to lateral optical displacement in newly hatched chicks. *Science,* 1968, *160,* 430–432.

Routtenberg, A., and Glickman, S. E. Visual cliff behavior in undomesticated rodents, land and aquatic turtles, and cats (*Panthera*). *Journal of Comparative and Physiological Psychology,* 1964, *58,* 143–146.

Scarr, S., and Salapatek, P. Patterns of fear development during infancy. *Merrill-Palmer Quarterly,* 1970, *16,* 53–90.

Schiffman, H. R. Depth perception of the Syrian hamster as a function of age and photic conditions of rearing. *Journal of Comparative and Physiological Psychology,* 1971, *76,* 491–495.

Schwartz, A. N., Campos, J. J., and Baisel, E. J., Jr. The visual cliff: Cardiac and behavioral responses on the deep and shallow sides at five and nine months of age. *Journal of Experimental Child Psychology,* 1973, *15,* 86–89.

Seitz, V., Seitz, T., and Kaufman, L. Loss of depth avoidance in chicks as a function of early environmental influences. *Journal of Comparative and Physiological Psychology,* 1973, *85,* 139–143.

Shinkman, P. G. Visual depth discrimination in day-old chicks. *Journal of Comparative and Physiological Psychology,* 1963, *56,* 410–414.

Smith, N. G. Adaptations to cliff-nesting in some Arctic gulls (*Larus*). *Ibis,* 1966, *108,* 68–83.

Spalding, D. A. On instinct. *Nature,* 1872, *6,* 485–486.

Spalding, D. A. Instinct and acquisition. *Nature,* 1875, *12,* 507–508.

Tallarico, R. B., and Farrell, W. M. Studies of visual depth perception: An effect of early experience on chicks on a visual cliff. *Journal of Comparative and Physiological Psychology,* 1964, *57,* 94–96.

Tees, R. C. Effect of visual deprivation on development of depth perception in the rat. *Journal of Comparative and Physiological Psychology,* 1974, *86,* 300–308.

Tees, R. C. Depth perception after infant and adult visual neocortical lesions in light- and dark-reared rats. *Developmental Psychobiology,* 1976, *9,* 223–235.

Thiessen, D. D., Lindzey, G., and Collins, A. Early experience and visual cliff behavior in the Mongolian gerbil (*Meriones unguiculatus*). II. *Psychonomic Science,* 1969, *16,* 240–241.

Van Hof-Van Duin, J. Development of visuomotor behavior in normal and dark-reared cats. *Brain Research,* 1976, *104,* 233–241.

Walk, R. D. Chronological age as a determinant of responsiveness to visual depth in human infants. *American Psychologist,* 1963, *18,* 424.

Walk, R. D. The study of visual depth and distance perception in animals. In D. S. Lehrman, R. A. Hinde, and E. Shaw (Eds.), *Advances in the study of behavior.* Vol. 1. New York: Academic Press, 1965, pp. 99–153.

Walk, R. D. The development of depth perception in animals and human infants. *Child Development Monograph*, 1966, *31(107)*, 82–108.

Walk, R. D. Monocular compared to binocular depth perception in human infants. *Science*, 1968a, *162*, 473–475.

Walk, R. D. The influence of level of illumination and size of pattern on the depth perception of the kitten and the puppy. *Psychonomic Science,* 1968b, *12,* 199–200.

Walk, R. D. Two types of depth discrimination by the human infant with five inches of visual depth. *Psychonomic Science*, 1969, *14,* 253–254.

Walk, R. D. Visual depth preferences of the domestic duckling. *Journal of Comparative and Physiological Psychology*, 1972, *78,* 14–21.

Walk, R. D. Development of spatial perception. In V. Hamilton and M. D. Vernon (Eds.), *The development of cognitive processes*. London: Academic Press, 1976, pp. 237–275.

Walk, R. D., and Bond, E. K. Deficit in depth perception of 90-day-old dark-reared rats. *Psychonomic Science,* 1968, *10,* 383–384.

Walk, R. D., and Gibson, E. J. A comparative and analytical study of visual depth perception. *Psychological Monographs,* 1961, *75(15)*, Whole No. 519.

Walk, R. D., and Walters, C. P. Effect of visual deprivation on depth discrimination of hooded rats. *Journal of Comparative and Physiological Psychology*, 1973, *85,* 559–563.

Walk, R. D., Gibson, E. J., and Tighe, T. J. Behavior of light- and dark-reared rats on a visual cliff. *Science*, 1957, *126,* 80–81.

Wallach, H., and O'Connell, D. N. The kinetic depth effect. *Journal of Experimental Psychology*, 1953, *45,* 205–217.

Wilson, P. D., and Riesen, A. H. Visual development in rhesus monkeys neonatally deprived of patterned light. *Journal of Comparative and Physiological Psychology*, 1966, *61,* 87–95.

Yerkes, R. M. Space perception of tortoises. *Journal of Comparative Neurology and Psychology*, 1904, *4,* 17–26.

Zeier, H. Lack of eye to eye transfer of an early response modification in birds. *Nature*, 1970, *225,* 708–709.

4

Auditory Environment and Vocal Development in Birds

MASAKAZU KONISHI

1. Introduction

Bird voice, a seemingly esoteric topic for scientific inquiry, is known to exhibit some of the most interesting phenomena of behavioral development such as the effects of sensory exposure, deprivation, and isolation, inborn perceptual preference, and critical impressionable period. Sexual imprinting in birds shares some of these attributes (Immelman, 1972a,b). The development of response properties in the cat visual cortex is another example (Wiesel and Hubel, 1965; Barlow, 1975; see also Mitchell, this volume). The perception of speech sounds in human infants seems to show some similarities to song development in birds (Eimas, 1975; see also Strange and Jenkins, this volume). The study of developmental plasticity in avian vocalizations has been greatly facilitated both by the objective means of describing voice and by the ease with which auditory environment can be manipulated. The results suggest that bird song can be a useful model to obtain deeper insights into the general principles of behavioral development. The main aim of this chapter is to discuss the ontogeny of bird voice as it relates to these principles rather than to present a descriptive review of the field, which is already available (Konishi and Nottebohm, 1969; Marler and Mundinger, 1971).

MASAKAZU KONISHI • Division of Biology, California Institute of Technology, Pasadena, California 91125. Supported by NSF Grant BNS 76–81840.

2. Vocal Development Independent of Auditory Environment

Comparative studies of different species show that the course of vocal development is inflexible in some birds and plastic in others. The auditory environment of developing birds has no influence on the former and has distinct effects on the latter. The domestic chicken, turkey, and ring dove belong to the former group (Konishi, 1963; Nottebohm and Nottebohm, 1971; Schleidt, 1964).

The domestic chicken produces about 30 different calls (Bäumer, 1962). Schjelderup-Ebbe (1923) was the first to make an attempt to answer the question whether young chickens must learn their calls from adults. Chickens hatched in an incubator and raised in isolation developed normal species-specific vocalizations as judged by unaided ears.

The calls of roosters deafened immediately after hatching appear normal on audiospectrograms so far as their basic patterns are concerned (Konishi,

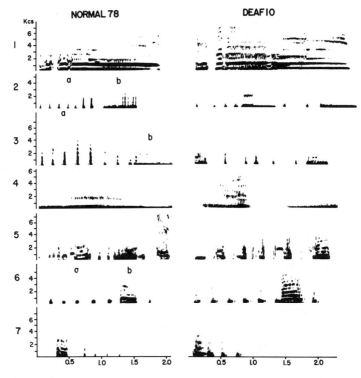

Fig. 1. Seven different calls of a normal and a deaf domestic chicken. 1. Crowing; 2. aggressive call; 3. food call; 4. aerial alarm call; 5. distress calls and cries; 6. ground enemy alarm; 7. mild alerting call. So far as their basic patterns are concerned, these calls can develop in the absence of both tutor and auditory feedback of the bird's own voice.

1963) (Fig. 1). However, the finer aspects of the calls show considerable variation among normal as well as among deaf roosters, which makes it hard to detect small differences between normal and deaf birds. It is interesting to note that the calls of deaf roosters are not only structurally but also functionally normal. For example, a deaf rooster can attract normal hens by producing the food call which is used to entice females.

3. Birdsong

Because of its developmental plasticity, birdsong has occupied the central position in the study of avian vocal ontogeny. Songbirds have both songs and

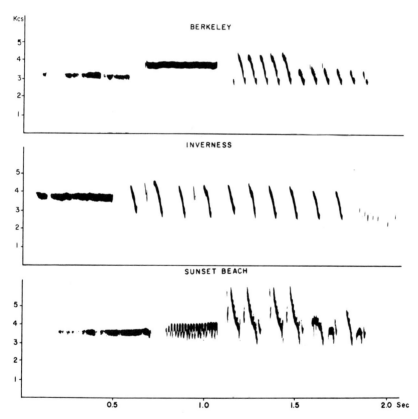

Fig. 2. Song dialects in the white-crowned sparrow. There are acoustic properties common to all dialects such as the introductory whistle shown as a thick horizontal bar on the sound spectrogram. Different dialects vary most in the fine structure of the notes in the trill section which appears as a series of vertically slanted bars. Dialects are maintained from generation to generation through learning of adult song by young birds. Berkeley, Inverness, and Sunset Beach are coastal locations in Northern California.

calls, but little is known about the development of calls. Although crowing of a rooster and cooing of a dove are perhaps equivalent to singing of a songbird, the term "song" has been generally reserved for songbirds.

Song is distinguished from calls by several criteria. In many songbirds only the sexually mature male sings during the breeding season, whereas most calls are produced by both sexes all year around. In most species song is the most elaborate vocalization. The delivery of song is usually highly periodic and spontaneous, while calls may be produced at irregular intervals often in response to specific stimuli such as predators. Highly stereotyped postures and movements accompany singing. Most calls are produced without such conspicuous bodily involvement.

Song is species specific; i.e., each species has a unique song (Marler, 1957). Playback of song in the field shows that male birds defending their territories during the breeding season respond exclusively to the song of their own species. The study of song variation indicates that song has characters both common and unique to different individuals. Some of the common properties are used for species recognition, and individual differences in song facilitate the identification of individuals (Marler, 1960). In some species song varies conspicuously from one geographic area to another, while it is unusually homogeneous in each area (Marler and Tamura, 1962; Lemon, 1966; Thielcke, 1969). This phenomenon is known as "song dialect," exemplified here by the white-crowned sparrow (Fig. 2).

How do such attributes as species specificity and individual and populational differences in song develop during ontogeny? The answer to this question is no longer simply either instinct or learning but involves intricate relationships between the genetic and environmental determinants, which call for a much more analytical way of looking at the old nature-nurture concept than before.

4. Effects of Auditory Isolation on Song Development

The structural attributes of song may be maintained from generation to generation through learning by young birds of adult song. This notion can be easily tested by rearing young birds in acoustic isolation.

The effects of isolation on song development vary from species to species among passerine birds. Most of the birds studied so far developed abnormal songs in isolation (e.g., Thorpe, 1958a,b; Lanyon, 1957; Lemon and Scott, 1966). These songs depart from the normal song in a number of ways. They may lack some of the species characteristics and/or have features that are outside the normal range of individual variation. For example, white-crowned sparrows which had never been exposed to the song of their own species developed abnormal songs, as shown in Fig. 3A,B.

Since the development of complex behavior may require integration of various environmental and organismic factors, abnormal songs may be due to

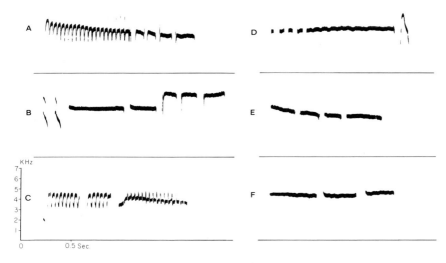

Fig. 3. Songs of white-crowned sparrows raised in isolation or unsuccessfully tutored. Birds raised from the egg without exposure to the song of the species (A, B) and birds caught as nestlings (C–F) failed to learn tutor songs. Note the individual differences in these songs.

any number of causes. For example, the absence of nonauditory social stimuli might cause abnormal vocal development. Besides the conditions for the maintenance of the bird's normal health the only requirement for normal song development is exposure to the conspecific song. When young white-crowned sparrows are exposed to playback of their species' song on tape, they develop normal songs later in life (Marler, 1970). Similar results were obtained in other species (e.g., Thorpe, 1958a,b).

5. Predisposition to Learn Conspecific Song

Each animal species has a unique perceptual world and response repertoire, as early ethologists pointed out (von Uexküll, 1909). In nature a young bird is exposed to the songs of many species living in the same environment, yet it learns the song of its own species. The bird must pay attention to a particular feature of its auditory environment. Thorpe (1961) in his early work with the chaffinch developed the idea that a naive bird has a blueprint of its species song to help select the correct song to copy. The white-crowned sparrow learns its species song to the exclusion of alien songs. If a young bird is exposed to an alien song alone, the bird does not copy it but develops an abnormal song as if it had been raised in total auditory isolation (Marler, 1970).

In both the chaffinch and early white-crown work, the young birds had spent the first few days of life in the wild before they were isolated. Therefore, the preference for the species song might have been due to early exposure to it.

In addition to this reservation, there is another basic problem in interpreting the available data pertaining to the concept of a song blueprint. That is, whether the selective learning of song is due to perceptual preference or motor constraints. A bird may appear to have rejected a song as a model to copy because it cannot sing it. Learning of a song model can be assessed only when the bird sings it. Immelmann (1965, 1967, 1969) provided evidence that is least subject to the above reservations. When male zebra finch nestlings were hatched and raised by Bengalese finch parents, they learned the song of the foster father even if they could hear the conspecific song in the same room. However, if young zebra finches heard both Bengalese finches and conspecifics sing while they were reared by two silent female Bengalese finches, they copied the zebra finch song. Since the zebra finch can produce the vocal motor pattern of the Bengalese finch, its preference for the conspecific song is less likely due to motor constraints than to an inborn perceptual bias.

6. Cues for Song Recognition

How do young birds recognize the song of their own species? As mentioned above, young zebra finches learn the song of the Bengalese foster father, indicating that social relationships may play a crucial role in the selection of song. However, when there is no father to copy, the young birds prefer the conspecific song to alien song. In this case the birds must be using some acoustic cues in the song to distinguish the conspecific from alien songs.

Young white-crowned sparrows reject the song of the song sparrow and copy the conspecific song in a choice situation. There is no preference for the bird's own home dialect. Any young white-crowned sparrow can copy any of the song dialects tested so far (Marler and Tamura, 1964; Marler, 1970). This suggests that different dialects contain common properties, some of which must be used by the bird to recognize the species song. All dialects begin with a whistle which may be followed by another one or a buzz. Another property in common is a trill after the whistle or buzz section. The trill notes are frequency-modulated sounds in which frequency always sweeps from high to low (Baptista, 1975; see also Fig. 2).

However, neither this basic whistle-trill composition nor the elaborate patterns of timing and frequency modulation of the wild-type song are necessary for the acceptance of a song as a model to learn because an isolate song that lacked them turned out to be acceptable. The isolate song does contain properties which trained listeners can recognize as those of the white-crown. The identification of the cues will require very careful analysis of the time-varying spectral distribution of each note and testing all combinations of acoustic parameters.

Although tutoring with various forms of natural song and its modified versions could provide some useful information on the cues for song recognition, a much more precise control of acoustic parameters is needed to conduct finer analysis of the clues. For this reason we have synthesized songs on a digital computer which enables us to generate any sound to the exact specifications set by the composer.

We use a computer music program called Music 4 which is written in For-

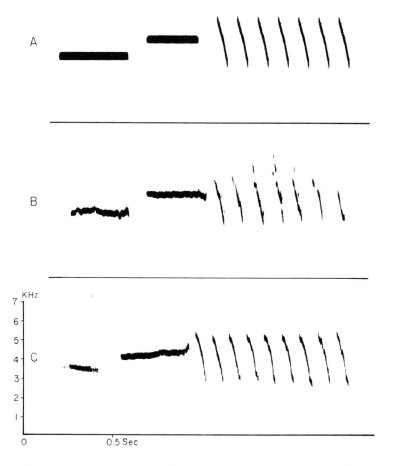

Fig. 4. A computer-synthesized song and its copy. A: A computer song consisting of an introductory pure tone note of 3450 Hz and 400 msec in duration, a silent interval of 100 msec, a second pure tone note of 4300 Hz and 300 msec in duration, another 100 msec pause, and a trill composed of seven identical frequency-modulated notes each 65 msec in duration and silent intervals of 50 msec. B: An early copy of A, singing induced by testosterone injection. Note that the range, duration, rate of frequency modulation, and the number of trill notes are either identical or similar to those of the model. C: The same bird produced a more stable song later but the number of trill notes increased and the intervals between them shortened. Nevertheless, the general pattern of song still clearly resembles the model.

tran. The greatest merit of this method lies in the fact that a song can be defined by a set of numbers. If the white-crowned sparrow copies a computer-synthesized song, it can be systematically modified by changing the numbers until we produce a song that is no longer acceptable to the bird. It is then possible to define the acoustic cues necessary for learning.

The results obtained so far indicate that young white-crowned sparrows seem to use a rather simple set of acoustic cues to recognize the conspecific song. A song consisting of two pure tone notes followed by a trill made up of seven identical frequency-modulated notes is acceptable as a model (Fig. 4). This song may be regarded as an idealized song devoid of all elaborate sound patterns that occur in the natural song. The synthetic song uses two pure tone notes (3450 Hz and 4300 Hz) in place of the natural whistles, which are narrow-band noises. To the human ear, pure tones do not sound like bird whistles. The natural trill notes have elaborate structures which usually distinguish different dialects from one another. They can be replaced by simpler notes in which frequency sweeps once from 5500 Hz to 3000 Hz in 65 msec.

The bird's copy of the computer song, especially its whistle section, sounded different from the model, even though they look alike in the sound spectrogram. The pure tone notes of the synthetic song lacked the quality of the bird whistle without distribution of sound energy in a narrow band around the center frequency, which the natural song has. However, the center frequencies of the bird's whistles were close to 3450 Hz and 4300 Hz. The trill section of the copy and original sounded remarkably alike because the important features of the model such as the frequency range, rate of frequency modulation, durations of note, and silent intervals were closely copied by the bird.

7. Critical Period of Song Learning

In some of the species studied so far, auditory exposure has effects on subsequent song development only during a particular period in a bird's life. The duration and nature of the period seem to vary from species to species. Normal song development in the chaffinch requires exposure to conspecific song both during the first few weeks of life in spring and during the early phase of singing. Young zebra finches memorize all the component notes of their father's song within 45 days after hatching. They do not sing themselves during this period. The duration of song and the sequence of the notes are copied later as the birds start singing. In the white-crowned sparrow the results reported so far show that the bird must memorize the model song between 14 and 50 days after hatching. This period ends before the bird starts singing.

Song development in birds with normal auditory experience is characterized by a series of progressive changes consisting of the nestling stage, juvenile and adult subsong, plastic song, and final full song stages. The transition from one stage to the next is gradual; elements of nestling calls may be found in early subsong, which gradually becomes more stereotyped, louder, and recurrent during transformation to plastic song. This is unstable but contains some of the basic features of the species song. It finally develops into a highly stereotyped and discrete full song. This process of song development was called "crystallization" because patterns or forms emerge from amorphous substrates. In most species studied so far it occurs in the bird's first singing season. Song remains unchanged and unaffected by any auditory exposure after crystallization and for the rest of the bird's life. This may be called absolute irreversibility in song learning.

Song development and crystallization do not seem to depend strictly on the bird's age in some species. Many song birds develop song and sing under the influence of androgen. If young male chaffinches are prevented from developing song in their first singing season by castration, they can copy a new song pattern in their second year as they are induced to sing by the hormone (Nottebohm, 1969). Thus, in this case, the end of the critical period is not directly dependent on the bird's age. The process of crystalization itself might terminate the period.

Song learning may be reversible before the crystallization stage. The reversibility not only varies among different species but also seems to depend on the nature of the early auditory experience. Chaffinches with experience of having heard the conspecific song in their youth will not later learn artificially modified chaffinch songs which naive birds readily learn (Thorpe, 1958a,b). There are interesting parallels between song learning and sexual imprinting in birds. The study of one may facilitate the understanding of the other.

According to Immelmann (1972a,b), when young male zebra finches are raised by Bengalese foster parents, they become sexually imprinted on the foster mother; i.e., when sexually mature they choose their mates among Bengalese females. However, if zebra finches are first raised by their natural parents and transferred to Bengalese foster parents, they no longer imprint on the foster mother. This example shows that (1) sexual imprinting is reversible within the critical period, (2) some objects are more preferable than others, (3) exposure to a better model makes the bird refractory to a less acceptable model, and (4) the nature of exposure affects the length of the critical period. There are some indications suggesting that these rules may also apply to song learning. The nature of early auditory exposure also affects song crystallization; it takes a longer time if birds are either tutored with an unacceptable model or raised in isolation (Marler, 1970). This could be explained in terms of the template theory as mentioned later.

8. Role of Auditory Feedback

A white crowned sparrow can vocally reproduce the model song to which it was exposed earlier without hearing the song again from any external source.

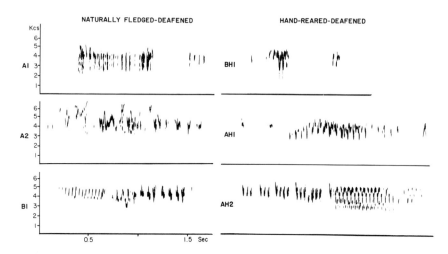

Fig. 5. Songs of six white-crowned sparrows deafened before the onset of singing. Left column: Birds had been exposed to a wild white-crown song during the critical period and then lost hearing before being able to reproduce the model song. Right column: Birds had been acoustically isolated before deafening.

The bird must use the memory of the song to reproduce it. There are two obvious ways in which the song memory can be used; one is to link it directly with the central vocal motor mechanism and the other is to utilize it as the reference for controlling vocal output by auditory feedback. It was possible to decide between these alternatives by deafening white-crowned sparrows before the onset of singing but after they had memorized a model song (Konishi, 1965b). These birds could not vocally reproduce the model song. After deafening, both birds isolated as 5-day-old nestlings and those which had spent their critical period in the field produced extremely abnormal songs of a similar nature (Fig. 5). These results indicate that deafening renders the song memory unavailable for the vocal reproduction of the model song. The song memory does not directly affect the central vocal motor control system but must be used via auditory feedback.

Although the songs of deaf white-crowns resemble bursts of noises, the birds assume the normal posture during singing and deliver song at the normal interval. In a normal bird, song is highly stereotyped, i.e., all its structural details are repeated precisely from song to song. In a deaf bird the structural details of song fluctuate from delivery to delivery, although the song as a whole maintains its identity to the extent that different birds can be recognized by their songs year after year. Similar results were obtained in other species (Konishi, 1964, 1965a; Mulligan, 1966; Nottebohm, 1968).

The type of instability in song mentioned above does not occur if a bird is deafened after it has completed song crystallization. The song can be maintained without auditory feedback for many months in the white-crowned sparrow. Chaffinches deafened earlier during song ontogeny develop more abnormal songs than those deafened later (Nottebohm, 1968).

9. Concept of a Song Template

The song memory is used like a template. The bird adjusts its vocal output until it matches with the song memory established earlier (Fig. 6A). The amor-

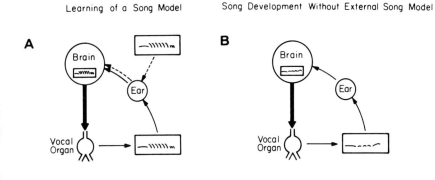

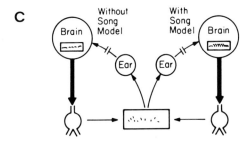

Fig. 6. Role of auditory feedback in song development. A: Song learning in the white-crowned sparrow consists of two stages. The bird memorizes the model song without singing it in the first stage. The vocal reproduction of the model occurs in the second stage. The song memory is used like a template with which the bird matches its vocal output. B: An internal or innate song template may be used to guide song development in the absence of an acceptable external model. The innate template seems crude in the white-crown. C: Whether an acquired or innate song template is involved, it cannot be used without auditory feedback. The vocal motor system as indicated by the thick arrow going to the vocal organ cannot produce patterned sounds without auditory feedback.

phous song of the deaf white-crowned sparrow indicates that its vocal motor system alone has no intrinsic pattern generating mechanism. Central motor systems which depend so much on sensory feedback for pattern generation as the above case seem rare.

A white-crowned sparrow which has never heard conspecific song develops a sound pattern different both from the deaf bird's song and from the wild-type song. Where does this pattern come from? It is conceivable that the bird has an innate song template. This becomes modified when the bird is exposed to an appropriate model. The bird refers to the unmodified innate model in the absence of an acceptable external model (Fig. 6B). However, the wide range of individual variation among the isolate songs suggests that the innate song template of the white-crown only crudely defines a small number of song attributes. Individual differences among the songs of isolates and unsuccessfully tutored birds may be due to "improvisation," a phenomenon which has already been described in other species (Marler, Kreith, and Tamura, 1962). The bird wanders from one vocal pattern to another during improvisation, which may be responsible for the slow rate of crystallization in the absence of an acquired song template as a result of having failed to hear an acceptable model.

A young white-crowned sparrow produces various sounds including calls and subsong before the onset of full song. The bird's hearing its own voice might bias its auditory perception which in turn influences song development later on. Superficially, this process would not require any song template to guide song development (Nottebohm, 1968). However, it must presume that the naive bird knows among its various sounds which ones to remember and which to ignore for future reference. Therefore, in the final analysis, the above idea cannot dispense with the concept of an innate template. Whether the template is innate or modified by auditory exposure, it cannot be used without auditory feedback; the bird fails to produce the patterned vocal output defined by the template (Fig. 6C).

In the white-crown the innate song template is insufficient to produce wild-type song. The song sparrow, on the other hand, seems to have an innate template sufficient for the development of normal song. Three song sparrows that are raised by canary foster parents from the egg were said to have produced basically normal songs without ever hearing conspecifics sing, whereas one deaf individual produced a very abnormal song (Mulligan, 1966). However, when Kroodsma (1977) repeated the above experiment some birds developed abnormal as well as normal songs. Nevertheless, it is significant that these birds could produce normal songs. The song sparrow sings much more complex songs than the white-crowned sparrow, so that the differences between the species is not due to one species having a more complex song than the other. This example is by far the best evidence for the concept of an innate song template.

10. Concluding Remarks

For the student of perceptual development, song learning presents a unique case in which an early sensory experience manifests itself as a motor pattern later in life. Song can serve as a window to the auditory perceptual world of the bird.

The most recent development in this field is the discovery of the neural substrate for song (Nottebohm, Stokes, and Leonard, 1976). This corresponds to the hypothetical vocal motor system in the diagrams of Fig. 6. Song of the oscine passerine is controlled not by a diffuse system of neurons but by a discrete chain of nuclei and fiber tracts. This system seems to be associated with song learning. The most striking thing about it is developmental plasticity. It is bilaterally present, but the left side is responsible for generating a majority of' the song notes. This hemispheric dominance is developmentally labile. If one of the principal nuclei in the left vocal control system is damaged before song is crystallized, the right side can take over the role of generating most of the notes. This discovery opened up an important new avenue to the study of neural mechanism of song learning.

11. References

Baptista, L. F. Song dialects and demes in sedentary populations of the white-crowned sparrow (*Zonotrichia leucophyrys nuttali*). *University of California Publications in Zoology*, 1975, *105*, 1–52.

Barlow, H. B. Visual experience and cortical development. *Nature*, 1975, *258*, 199–204.

Bäumer, E. Lebensart des Haushuhns, III—Über seine Laute und allgemeine Ergänzungen. *Zeitschrift für Tierpsychologie*, 1962, *19*, 394–416.

Eimas, P. D. Speech perception in early infancy. In L. B. Cohen and P. Salapatek (Eds.), *Perception*. New York: Academic Press, 1975.

Immelmann, K. Prägungserscheinungen in der Gesangsentwicklung junger Zebrafinken. *Naturwissenschaften*, 1965, *52*, 169–170.

Immelmann, K. Zur ontogenetischen Gesangsentwicklung bei Prachtfinken. *Verhandlungen der deutschen Zoologischen Gesellschaft, Göttingen*, 1967, *1966*, 320–332.

Immelmann, K. Song development in the zebra finch and other estrildid finches. In R. A. Hinde (Ed.), *Bird vocalizations*. London: Cambridge University Press, 1969.

Immelmann, K. The influence of early experience upon the development of social behaviour in estrildine finches. *Proceedings of the XVth International Ornithological Congress*, 1972a, pp. 316–338.

Immelmann, K. Sexual and other long-term aspects of imprinting in birds and other species. *Advances in the Study of Behaviour,* 1972b, *4*, 147–174.

Konishi, M. The role of auditory feedback in the vocal behavior of the domestic fowl. *Zeitschrift für Tierpsychologie,* 1963, *20*, 349–367.

Konishi, M. Effects of deafening on song development in two species of juncos. *Condor*, 1964, *66*, 85–102.

Konishi, M. Effects of deafening on song development in American robins and black-headed grosbeaks. *Zeitschrift für Tierpsychologie*, 1965a, *22*, 584–599.

Konishi, M. The role of auditory feedback in the control of vocalization in the white-crowned sparrow. *Zeitschrift für Tierpsychologie*, 1965b, *22*, 770–783.

Konishi, M., and Nottebohm, F. Experimental studies in the ontogeny of avian vocalizations. In R. A. Hinde (Ed.), *Bird vocalizations*. London: Cambridge University Press, 1969.

Kroodsma, D. E. Re-evaluation of song development in the song sparrow. *Animal Behaviour*, 1977, *25*, 390–399.

Lanyon, W. E. The comparative biology of the meadowlarks (*Sturnella*) in Wisconsin. *Publication of the Nuttall Ornithological Club*, 1957, *1*, 1–67.

Lemon, R. E. Geographical variation in the song of cardinals. *Canadian Journal of Zoology*, 1966, *44*, 413–428.

Lemon, R. E., and Scott, D. M. On the development of song in young cardinals. *Canadian Journal of Zoology*, 1966, *44*, 191–197.

Marler, P. Species distinctiveness in the communication signals of birds. *Behaviour*, 1957, *11*, 13–29.

Marler, P. Bird songs and mate selection. In W. E. Lanyon and W. N. Tavolga (Eds.), *Animal sounds and communication*. Washington, D.C.: American Institute of Biological Sciences, 1960, pp. 348–367.

Marler, P. A comparative approach to vocal learning: Song development in white-crowned sparrows. *Journal of Comparative and Physiological Psychology Monograph*, 1970, *71*(2), Part 2, 1–25.

Marler, P., and Mundinger, P. Vocal learning in birds. In H. Moltz (Ed.), *The ontogeny of vertebrate behavior*. New York: Academic Press, 1971.

Marler, P., and Tamura, M. Culturally transmitted patterns of vocal behavior in sparrows. *Science*, 1964, *146*, 1483–1486.

Marler, P., and Tamura, M. Song "dialects" in three populations of white-crowned sparrows. *Condor*, 1962, *64*, 363–399.

Marler, P., Kreith, M., and Tamura, M. Song development in hand-raised Oregon juncos. *Auk*, 1962, *79*, 12–30.

Mulligan, J. A. Singing behavior and its development in the song sparrow *Melospiza melodia*. *University of California Publications in Zoology*, 1966, *81*, 1–73.

Nottebohm, F. Auditory experience and song development in the chaffinch (*Fringilla coelebs*). *Ibis*, 1968, *110*, 549–568.

Nottebohm, F. The "critical period" for song learning in birds. *Ibis*, 1969, *3*, 386–387.

Nottebohm, F., and Nottebohm, M. E. Vocalizations and breeding behaviour of surgically deafened ring doves (*Streptopelia risonia*). *Animal Behaviour*, 1971, *19*, 313–327.

Nottebohm, F., Stokes, T. M., and Leonard, C. M. Central control of song in the canary, *Serinus canarius*. *Journal of Comparative Neurology*, 1976, *165*, 457–486.

Schjelderup-Ebbe, T. Weitere Beiträge zur Sozial -und Individuel-Psychologie des Haushuhns. *Zeitschrift für Psychologie*, 1923, *92*, 60–87.

Schleidt, W. M. Über die Spontaneität von Erbkoordinationen. *Zeitschrift für Tierpsychologie*, 1964, *21*, 235–256.

Thielcke, G. Geographic variation in bird vocalizations. In R. A. Hinde (Ed.), *Bird vocalizations*. London: Cambridge University Press, 1969.

Thorpe, W. H. The learning of song patterns by birds, with especial reference to the song of the chaffinch, *Fringilla coelebs*. *Ibis*, 1958a, *100*, 535–570.

Thorpe, W. H. Further studies on the process of song learning in the chaffinch (*Fringilla coelebs gengleri*). *Nature*, 1958b, *182*, 554–557.

Thorpe, W. H. *Bird-song*. London: Cambridge University Press, 1961.

von Uexküll, J. *Umwelt und Innenleben der Tiere*. Berlin, 1909.

Wiesel, T. N., and Hubel, D. H. Comparison of the effects of unilateral and bilateral eye closure on cortical unit responses in kittens. *Journal of Neurophysiology*, 1965, *28*, 1029–1040.

PART **II**

Effects of Prolonged Experience on Human Perception

Introduction

What variations in experience will produce differences in human perception? In first asking this question, it is natural to examine the consequences of gross long-term variations in experience. When these consequences are identified, they will provide direction for the investigation of more subtle experiences and their consequences. But where do the perceptually relevant gross and long-term variations in human experience occur? In general, we cannot ethically produce such variations experimentally. We must look for them to occur naturally. There are two main types. One is cultural variation—persons of different cultures are selectively exposed to specific kinds of stimulation from their man-made environments.[1] The other is the variation of perceptual experience which is defined by sensory handicap. In this part of the book, examples of both these types of perceptually relevant experience will be considered.

The examples of cultural variation are provided by Strange and Jenkins's chapter on linguistic experience and speech perception, and Hagen and Jones's chapter on pictorial perception. The perceptual variation produced by sensory handicap is generally that of deprivation of specific types of experience, although sensory distortion is possible. (Indeed, some of the visual anomalies discussed by Mitchell in Chapter 2 might be considered examples of distortion rather than deprivation.) In this part, two examples of sensory deprivation will be considered: Foulke and Berla discuss perceptual development in the blind, and Reynolds discusses the perceptual development in the deaf.

Certain issues are common to many investigations of the effects of pro-

---

[1] Variation in physical ecology might constitute an additional type of perceptually relevant difference in human experience. However, no one has convincingly shown that such variations make a difference in perception.

119

longed experience on perception. One is the nature of the relevant experience. In the naturally occurring variations of experience under consideration here, the investigators have little control over the experience of their subjects. This difficulty is of two types. First, subjects selected for the presence or absence of particular kinds of experience may not be ideal cases. For example, in considering the effects of lack of exposure to Western art on picture perception, it is often unclear exactly how little exposure particular groups have had. Second, it is often unclear, if differences in perception are found, what the critical variation in experience is. In cross-cultural studies, the problem is immense. Cultures differ on so many variables that one can rarely be confident that the particular variable that the researcher focuses on is the one actually responsible for the difference in perception. The problem also exists in great measure for studies of sensory handicap. As a concrete example, Foulke and Berlá point out that the development of the object concept is delayed in the blind, but is this due specifically to the lack of visual experience or is it due to a generally decreased interaction of the infant with his environment? The answer has important practical consequences. Thus Bower (1977) has reported that a blind infant wearing an echolocation device kept up with his sighted peers in concept development. The description of the experiment suggests that the active interaction of the baby in maintaining contact with the objects in the environment is the crucial aspect of the experience.

Bower's observation leads to a second general issue relevant to the effects of prolonged experiential variation in perception. What is the mechanism by which differences in experience produce differences in perception? Bower's observation implicates action in perception. In the case of the blind, one of the difficulties noted by Foulke and Berlá in reading by listening is the lack of active control by the "reader" over the rate and quality of information input. Again, with speech perception, many have believed there is a close tie between production and perception. Strange and Jenkins summarize some developmental studies which suggest that deviant perception and production often go together in children. However, they also describe a study of some Japanese subjects correctly differentiating between r's and l's in their production but being unable to perceive the distinction in either their own production or productions by Americans. Thus the status of action as a mechanism mediating between perception and experience is currently ambiguous.

In fact, there are only hints in the data of these chapters as to the underlying mechanisms for the effects of experience in perception. With speech perception some categorical distinctions are present at birth but disappear in the adult speaker, while in other cases some categorical distinctions can be made by the adult speaker but are not made by the infant. In the first case there appears to be unlearning or suppression while in the other cases there appears to be learning of a new distinction. With picture perception, Hagen and Jones hint that one problem for pictorially naive viewers in seeing depth in pictures is that they tend not to separate the pictorial space from the contextual space in which the picture rests. With the deaf, Reynolds points out that disruption of normal intersensory processes might lead to deficits in some modalities other than audition. Congruent with this idea, a higher incidence of visual refractive errors is found among the deaf than among the hearing. However, it is not obvious what intersensory process would account for this relationship. On the other side, it is possible that the particular techniques of the handicapped can lead to improved perception in other modalities. Reynolds describes examples of deaf subjects performing better than hearing subjects in perception of sequentially presented letters. This may be due to considerable practice in reading sequentially occurring signs in normal communication.

The extent of the plasticity of perception and possible critical periods for relevant experience is a third issue which occurs in all of the chapters in this part. Evidence for a critical period is clearest in speech perception, where even the most arduous training was shown to have limited success in getting mature "speaker-listeners" of English to make phonemic perceptual distinctions not used in English. In considering the cultural effects on picture perception, the evidence is not nearly so striking, but Hagen and Jones do report a number of cases where older subjects (often above 40 years of age) have more difficulty with pictures than do younger subjects. These difficulties occur in identifying outline drawings, recognizing dynamic events, and perceiving depth information.

The notion of critical period implies a period of time in an organism's life when a particular kind of experience is *necessary* for normal perceptual functioning. Related to this is the idea that there may be a period of time when some specific experience is *sufficient* for normal perceptual development. Foulke and Berla note that many of the deleterious effects normally occurring with the blind are reduced or eliminated if the onset of blindness is late or if the blindness is not total. In particular, the delays in object concept development do not typically occur in legally blind children who have some residual vision. Furthermore, older blind people who have learned to read before the onset of blindness are able to do so with vision so limited as to preclude initially learning to read. With the deaf, deficits in language abilities occur very early. However, it has also been observed that the babbling of deaf infants is normal until about the age of 3–6 months (Lenneberg, 1967). One wonders whether remedial constructive stimulation that was started very early, such as Bower is attempting with blind babies, might not also be effective with the deaf. On the other side, the end of plasticity itself raises interesting questions. First, are there any operations which could maintain plasticity, e.g., in speech perception? For example, if second language learning were started relatively early, would plasticity be maintained so as to facilitate learning a third language? Second, is there any biological function served by an end to plasticity? In the case of speech perception (and production), it is possible to hypothesize that an initial period of plasticity serves to make possible for all the young to learn the language of a given community and the relatively early end of plasticity protects the community from easy infiltration by foreigners. Of course, it is also possible that the end of plasticity is simply a side effect of high degree of mastery of a given system. This seems at least as plausible as the community isolation hypothesis since adults do learn foreign languages and can function quite well with them. It appears difficult to get over an accent in speech production and that does mark one as a foreigner. However, the perceptual differences between a native speaker and a foreigner are quite subtle and probably are of little practical impact in language functioning.

In addition to the above issues which the four chapters have in common, there are several more specific issues which deserve comment. Categorical perception is a central concept in the chapter on speech perception and experience by Strange and Jenkins. As they describe in detail, "categorical perception" refers to the fact that stimuli within a class or category are not discriminated from each other, although the differences among them may be as great as or greater than the difference between stimuli in two different categories. Put another way, discrimination is no better than identification in categorical perception, although with most psychophysical dimensions we can discriminate differences among stimuli to a much finer degree than we can identify stimuli. As Strange and Jenkins point out, some stimuli are perceived categorically by young infants. Other speech stimuli seem to be perceived categorically only after experience with a language. Interestingly, certain musical features are also perceived categorically, but by skilled musicians and not by musically inexperienced subjects. Can this observation be integrated with those of Bever and Chiarello (1974) suggesting that music perception is localized in the left cortical hemisphere for trained musicians, but not for musically untrained persons?

Hagen and Jones discovered in some of their own research a fact which may bring some of the cultural differences in art styles closer together. Some observers have suggested that linear perspective is a culturally conventional technique of representation in art, pointing to examples of Oriental art which do not use our form of converging linear perspective. Hagen and Jones argue convincingly against this suggestion of the arbitrariness of linear perspective as a cue. Linear perspective exists in images projected to the eye from the real world. However, they do find in their own research that even adult Western viewers prefer pictorial representations where the degree of convergence is very small. Such pictures are judged as more realistic and natural. Western children, on the other hand, prefer greater convergence under some conditions (Hagen and Jones, in press). The preference for less convergence, i.e., more nearly parallel projection, may be a function of experience, that things go toward what we know them to be, a constancy explanation.

An area of some interest in the cross-cultural study of perception closely related to pictorial perception is that of susceptibility to geometric illusions. Such illusions are typically presented by means of figures on paper. Indeed, a very popular interpretation of illusions such as the Müller-Lyer and the horizontal-vertical illusions is based on the idea that the figures are taken to be projections from three-dimensional objects or spaces (see, for instance, Segall, Campbell, and Herskovits, 1966; Gregory, 1972). Segall *et al.,* for example, argue that the oblique angles of the Müller-Lyer figure are taken as projections of right-angled corners because of our very great experience with carpentered objects in our environment. In support of this argument, they showed, across a number of cultures, that the extent of the Müller-Lyer illusion is significantly correlated with degree of carpentering in the environment. However, there are also a variety of other factors which partially covary with extent of carpentering and hence are correlated with susceptibility to the Müller-Lyer illusion, e.g., educational level in general and experience with pictures in particular, and amount of ocular pigmentation. Details of various explanations of cross-cultural differences in susceptibility to illusions have been discussed by Pick and Pick (in press). A completely satisfactory explanation is lacking at present. However, it would be attractive to unite the cross-cultural differences in picture perception and in susceptibility to illusions.

An important concern with respect to sensory handicap is how to overcome deleterious effects. This, of course, would depend on just what aspects of the handicap produced the effects. So, for example, Foulke and Berlá point out that blind subjects do not obtain certain kinds of experience such as perception of clouds or snowflakes which are silent and ungraspable. When they are able to substitute haptic stimulation for visual, the form of stimulation is often different. Haptic perception is much less simultaneous or parallel; information must often be sequentially processed. This, no doubt, imposes unusual short-term memory problems in information processing. It suggests perhaps a different question in the development of compensatory devices and techniques. Can the parallel processing capacity of vision be captured in tactual sensitivity? One promising approach has been developed by Bach-y-rita and his colleagues (White, Saunders, Scadden, Bach-y-rita, and Collins, 1970). They have devised a vibratory tactual matrix that is applied to a subject's chest or back. The vibrators are differentially driven by the bright and dark areas of a TV picture and hence convert a visual pattern into a tactual pattern. The TV camera can be manipulated by a sightless subject. Ideally the camera is head-mounted. Subjects can learn to identify small sets of objects on the basis of these "tactual pictures" in relatively short periods of time. The most dramatic result reported so far, however, was one subject's response to an expanding visual display which occurred when the TV camera lens was accidentally zoomed. After having had only limited experience with the device, he reacted as if the display were looming toward him. Such sensitivity, if confirmed, would imply that a complex pattern of transformation on the skin was an effective stimulus for change of distance just as a similar pattern of transformation has been found to be for visual perception. It is unlikely that such sensitivity would be learned in a paired associationistic way with just a brief period of experience. It is more likely that this tactual display capitalizes on sensitivity to a higher-order amodal invariant of stimulation.

It is interesting in this regard, as Reynolds points out, that the arbitrary associationistic techniques of transducing language to skin vibration for the deaf have not been very successful. He notes that the most successful technique is the Tadoma method, where the deaf "listener" feels the mouth and throat configurations and vibrations of the speaker. Reynolds suggests that this tactual-haptic stimulation is most likely to capture the complex invariants of speech.

One final point in relation to the perceptual effects of sensory handicap is methodological. In the case of blindness there are numerous analogue studies using visual deprivation with animals. It is interesting, though, that these studies have focused primarily on the effects of *visual* deprivation on subsequent *visual* performance. Very few studies have examined the effects of visual deprivation on subsequent nonvisual perceptual behavior. In the case of deafness, there are few analogue studies with animals at all. The major exception has been in investigation of development of birdsongs such as discussed by Konishi in Chapter 4. But there the focus, by definition, has not been on understanding nonauditory perceptual development. One would think that for animals which depend on audition for communication and other functions, such as orienting, auditory deprivation might have substantial effects on nonauditory perception. Studies of the effects of sensory handicap in one modality on perceptual development in other modalities might prove very fruitful.

References

Bever, T. G., and Chiarello, R. J. Cerebral dominance in musicians and nonmusicians. *Science*, 1974, *185*, 537–539.

Bower, T. G. R. Blind babies see with their ears. *New Scientist*, February 3, 1977.

Gregory, R. L. *Eye and brain.* New York: McGraw-Hill, 1972.

Hagen, M. A., and Jones, R. K. Differential patterns of preference for modified linear perspective in children and adults. *Journal of Experimental Child Psychology*, in press.

Lenneberg, E. H. *Biological foundations of language.* New York: Wiley, 1967.

Pick, A. D., and Pick, H. L., Jr. Culture and perception. In E. C. Carterette and M. P. Friedman (Eds.), *Handbook of perception*. Vol. IX. New York: Academic Press, in press.

Segall, M. H., Campbell, D. T., and Herskovits, M. J. *The influence of culture on visual perception.* Indianapolis: Bobbs-Merrill, 1966.

White, B. W., Saunders, F. H., Scadden, L., Bach-y-rita, P., and Collins, C. C. Seeing with the skin. *Perception and Psychophysics*, 1970, *7*, 23–27.

5

Role of Linguistic Experience in the Perception of Speech

WINIFRED STRANGE AND JAMES J. JENKINS

1. Introduction

Although the linguistic and psycholinguistic theories of the 1960s emphasized the predispositional and maturational aspects of language acquisition, no one denies that experiential variables have profound effects on all aspects of the development of language functions. The knowledge of a language possessed by a normal adult is a product of many years of exposure to a specific language environment. Both receptive and expressive modes of language behavior are molded by the speaker-hearer's interaction with the linguistic community. In literate societies, the perceptual aspects of receptive language function include both vision (reading) and audition (speech perception), but, obviously, the latter is the primary mode by which language is learned and used by all normal humans. (For a comparison and contrast of the visual and auditory modes, see Kavanagh and Mattingly, 1972.)

This chapter is concerned with the effects of linguistic experience on *phonetic perception*—that is, the identification and discrimination of phonetic categories that are distinguished in the languages of the world. As a focus for our discussion, we have chosen the phenomenon known as *categorical perception*.[1] Section 3 of the chapter provides a brief review of the research on the

---

[1] Of necessity, we must omit other sources of data which bear on questions of the malleability of language systems by environmental influence. It is well known that languages change systematically over time. While the causes for such change are likely to be environmentally mediated,

---

WINIFRED STRANGE AND JAMES J. JENKINS • Center for Research in Human Learning, University of Minnesota, Minneapolis, Minnesota 55455.

categorical perception phenomenon. In section 4, we deal with some of the recent research that arose from questions concerning the etiology of the phenomenon. Section 5 takes up the major topic of the chapter: how phonetic perception is molded and modified by differing linguistic experiences. We review experimental findings of cross-language studies with monolinguals and bilinguals and laboratory training studies of perceptual learning. In Section 6, we consider the development of phonetic perception in the individual. Finally, in Section 7, we summarize the state of the field as we see it today, pointing out promising areas for future research. Before taking up the research on categorical perception, however, a few introductory comments on the nature of the speech signal as it relates to the phonetic message are offered to set the stage for the subsequent discussion.

2. The Speech Code

The distinctive "speech sounds" that make up the syllables of a language are called *phonemes*. Phonemes are the smallest functional segments of language; they are meaningless in themselves, but in combinations they serve to differentiate the lexical items of a language. Thus, for example, the words "bit" and "pit" are distinguished by their initial phonemes /b/ and /p/; "bit" and "bet" by their second phonemes /ɪ/ and /ɛ/; and "bit" and "bin" by their final phonemes /t/ and /n/.

The phonemes in every language can be described by a relatively small set of *phonetic features*. As linguistic entities, phonetic features can be considered to be subphonemic aspects that describe similarities and differences among phonemes. In traditional phonetics, features have usually been characterized in terms of articulatory parameters such as *manner* of articulation, *place of articulation, voicing,* and *nasality.* Thus, American English phonemes are categorized into the major manner classes: *stops, approximants,* [2] *fricatives,* and *vowels.* For example, the members of the stop class, /b, d, g, p, t, k, m, n, ŋ/,

---

the phenomenon is not well understood. It is also well known that languages in contact influence one another with respect to many levels of language; i.e., the languages "borrow" from one another some aspects of sound structure, some aspects of syntax, and so on. These are clear environmental influences that result in appreciable change in the language system over time and that affect the perceptions of individuals. We will only be able to touch on this topic as it arises in certain studies of bilinguals. In a very different realm there are many studies concerning the perception of nonlinguistic aspects of speech: judging the emotional state, the personal traits, the social level, class or race of the speaker; judging the truth or falsity of the speaker's utterances, and so on. Undoubtedly, many aspects of such perceptual judgments are learned through many kinds of experience, but we will not attempt to deal with this literature here. We have deliberately restricted ourselves to laboratory studies and to perception of language at the level of phoneme.

[2] The term "approximant," as used by Ladefoged (1975), refers to the class of phonemes /r/, /l/ (often called liquids) /w/, /y/ (sometimes called glides or semivowels), and /h/.

Table 1. Phonetic Features Contrasting Stop
Consonants

	Place of articulation		
	Labial	Apical	Velar
Voiceless oral	p (pin)	t (tin)	k (kin)
Voiced oral	b (bib)	d (did)	g (dig)
Voiced nasal	m (ram)	n (ran)	ŋ (rang)

can be contrasted with members of other classes by the fact that all of them in-volve complete closure of the oral cavity in their production. Within this broad category, phonemes are further contrasted by other articulatory features, as il-lustrated in Table 1. The stop consonants can be differentiated in terms of three places of articulation: *labial* /b/, /p/, and /m/; *apical* /d/, /t/, and /n/; and *velar* /g/, /k/, and /ŋ/. The voicing feature contrasts *voiceless* /p/, /t/, and /k/ with the remaining six *voiced* stops. The phonemes /m/, /n/, and /ŋ/ are *nasal,* while the other six are *oral.* It is readily apparent that phonemes are systematically re-lated; feature specifications attempt to capture the dimensions of the system.[3]

Theories of speech perception are concerned with how the listener re-covers the phonemic message from the speech signal. This involves a twofold question: What are the acoustic parameters that differentiate the phonemes, or perhaps, more specifically, the subphonemic features? and What perceptual processes are involved in the detection and recognition of these parameters?

The speech signal is a complexly structured, continuously varying acoustic pattern. Much research over the past 40–50 years has been devoted to the description of this complex signal as it relates to the linguistic message per-ceived by the listener. From what is currently known, the acoustic patterns ap-pear to be a "code" on the phonemic message (Liberman, Cooper, Shankwei-ler, and Studdert-Kennedy, 1967; Liberman, 1970). That is, there is no simple one-to-one correspondence between temporal segments in the speech signal and phonemic segments in the linguistic utterance. Rather, the acoustic specifica-tion of a phonemic segment is distributed over the temporal course of signals at least syllabic in length. Further, the acoustic instantiation of a particular pho-neme varies drastically as a function of the preceding and following phonetic context. There is a multiple mapping from phoneme to sound and from sound to phoneme.

In their attempts to "crack the speech code," investigators have been as-sisted by the development of two devices, the sound spectrograph and the

[3] If the reader is unfamiliar with phonetic feature characterizations of phonemes, Denes and Pinson (1963) and Ladefoged (1975) are good introductory sources. For an advanced discussion of pho-netic feature characterization of phonological aspects of language, see Chomsky and Halle(1968).

speech synthesizer. The sound spectrograph is a device that analyzes the speech signal into a frequency-by-time visual display (see Potter, Kopp, and Green, 1947). It records the amount of energy in a particular frequency region at a particular time interval. This instrument disclosed almost immediately that speech information was importantly related to concentrations of energy in broad frequency bands that were modulated rapidly over time as a function of the changing resonances of the moving vocal tract. These bands of energy are called *formants*. They are numbered from low to high frequency (i.e., F1, F2, F3) as in Fig. 1, which shows the spectrographic analysis of the word "bib."

Speech synthesizers were constructed to produce signals that had acoustic properties suggested by the spectrographic analysis. A very useful synthesizer, Pattern Playback II (Cooper, 1950), was, in fact, specifically designed to convert modified spectrograms back into auditory signals. Working back and forth between analysis (spectrograms) and synthesis (speech synthesizers), researchers isolated a variety of acoustic "cues" that served to distinguish phonemes in minimal pairs. This research revealed systematic patterns of relations that corresponded roughly to phonetic features. Some examples are shown in the schematic spectrograms of Fig. 2. The simple vowel /a/ can be represented by steady-state formants. Consonants are added through various discontinuities. The modifications of patterns which produce the various phonemes begin to emerge from a study of the chart. For example, when one discovers the difference between the voiced labial, /ba/, and the voiceless labial, /pa/, namely,

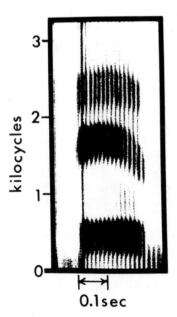

Fig. 1. Spectrographic representation of the syllable "bib." The spectrogram shows concentrations of energy (dark tracings) at spectral frequencies (ordinate) as they change over time (abscissa). The speech formants are numbered from low frequency to high frequency.

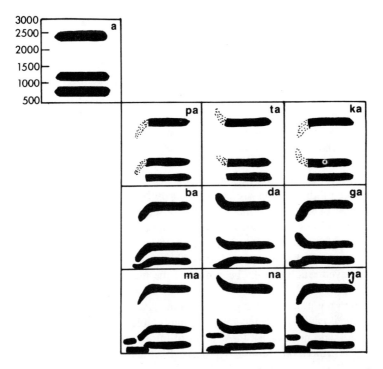

Fig. 2. Schematic spectrographic representations of speech sounds. Solid bars represent formants during voiced portions of the syllables. Dotted areas represent voiceless noisy portions.

the delay in the onset of the first formant, one can also see how to change the voiced apical, /da/, to the voiceless apical, /ta/, and how to change the voiced velar, /ga/, to the voiceless velar, /ka/. Further, one can see that the relation between the voiced labial, /ba/, and the voiced apical, /da/, is parallel to the relation between the voiceless labial, /pa/, and the voiceless apical, /ta/. The parallels with the nasal series are likewise apparent.

This research (which is, of course, vastly oversimplified here) led to the following generalizations:

1. Formants carry much of the important information for phoneme identification. The change in frequency of formants over time characterizes much of the speech signal. Also important for phoneme identification is the presence of noisiness in particular frequency locations.
2. Consonants are associated with discontinuities in the acoustic signal (specifically, changes in frequency of the formants, called transitions, and brief bursts of noise) whereas vowels can be simulated by relatively unchanging or *steady-state* configurations of the first two or three speech formants.

3. Differences in manner-of-articulation are often cued by the rate of change in formant transitions. Stop consonants show very rapid transitions (about 40 msec); approximants show more gradual transitions (about 100 msec).
4. Fricatives can be identified by the presence of noisiness (called frication noise) within specific frequency ranges. They also show formant transitions.
5. Differences in place-of-articulation in consonants are cued by the direction and extent of transitions of the second and third formants. The frequency location of the noise bursts also provides information about place-of-articulation in stop consonants.
6. Voicing distinctions are cued primarily by the temporal relation of the onset of the first formant and the onset of higher formants; this relationship has been called *voice onset time* (VOT). In English, the first formant in voiced phonemes begins prior to or simultaneous with the onset of higher formants. For voiceless consonants, the first formant is delayed relative to the beginning of the higher formants.

We hasten to point out that the generalizations given here characterize only one set of minimal cues for the generation of intelligible synthetic speech syllables. They certainly do not exhaust the sources of information that are found in natural speech. Furthermore, stimuli synthesized in this way are sometimes highly "unnatural." For example, steady-state vowels rarely occur in natural speech spoken at normal conversational rates. In addition, the rules for synthesis of phonemes are highly context-conditioned. The construction of a consonant-vowel syllable depends on more than the identity of that consonant and vowel. Constraints from preceding and following segments as far removed as three phonemes and prosodic factors such as stress, intonation, and speaking rate all affect the final acoustic form of the syllable.

Given these limitations, the synthetic speech used in the studies reported below might best be considered as a first approximation to natural speech stimuli. As we shall see, the results and conclusions drawn from the research are sometimes affected in important ways by considerations of the quality and naturalness of the synthetic materials used.

3. The Categorical Perception Phenomenon

Having isolated some of the important acoustic dimensions along which phonemes are differentiated, research on the nature of the perception of these dimensions progressed by the use of synthetic stimuli that allowed for the precise control of the stimulus parameters under study. An early experiment by Liberman, Harris, Hoffman, and Griffith (1957) serves as a paradigmatic example of the research technique with which we will be primarily concerned in this chapter.

Thirteen two-formant synthetic consonant-vowel (CV) syllables were constructed that differed only in the direction and extent of the initial second-formant (F2) transition into the vowel (i.e., a "cue" for place-of-articulation).

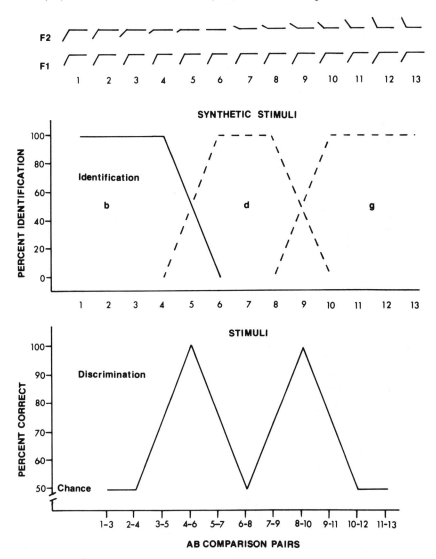

Fig. 3. Categorical perception of consonants. Schematic representation of synthetic consonant-vowel series (top) and idealized results of identification tests (middle) and discrimination tests (bottom).

The starting frequency of F2 differed in equal frequency intervals over a range sufficient for the perception of the stop consonants: /b/, /d/, and /g/. (See the top portion of Fig. 3 for a schematic representation of the stimuli.)

When one hears these syllables played in order, the impression is that the changes from "ba" to "da" to "ga" are abrupt: i.e., across this continuously varying physical series, there are perceptual discontinuities. Typically, only one or two stimuli at the boundaries sound ambiguous; the other stimuli are clear cases of one syllable or another. This impression is confirmed by the labeling of the items when they are presented in random orders, and by the inability of subjects to discriminate one stimulus from another when they are both drawn from the same phoneme category, even though they readily discriminate pairs of stimuli drawn from separate phoneme categories. This is the essence of the categorical perception phenomenon.

The empirical examination of the phenomenon has been accomplished in the following way. Two types of perceptual tests are required: an *identification test*, in which listeners assign a phonemic label to each syllable presented singly, and a *discrimination test*, in which listeners hear triads of syllables in an ABX design. In the discrimination task, listeners must choose whether the third syllable (X) is identical with the first (A) or second (B) syllable.

The Liberman *et al.* study tested identification for each syllable and then tested discrimination with AB pairs that differed by a fixed interval along the acoustic dimension. Thus, the relative discriminability of pairs, differing by the same acoustic interval along the F2 stimulus dimension, could be compared. Figure 3 shows (in idealized form) the interesting relationship that these investigators discovered between phoneme identification and the discrimination of the acoustic dimension that differentiated the phonemes. The identification functions were characterized by highly consistent labeling within phoneme categories and steep slopes (indicating an abrupt change) at the category boundaries. These changes correspond to the impression of perceptual discontinuities.

The most impressive illustration of the perceptual discontinuity, however, was found in the results of the discrimination test. Not surprisingly, discrimination was highly accurate for pairs whose members were drawn from *across* a phoneme boundary. In contrast, however, discrimination of pairs differing by the same amount acoustically but drawn from *within* a phoneme category was only slightly better than chance. That is, discrimination of acoustic differences was only as good as could be predicted from performance on a phoneme labeling task. Acoustic differences that were phonetically irrelevant were not clearly perceived as different, but acoustic differences of the same magnitude that were phonetically relevant were very clearly perceived.

This result is surprising because identification and discrimination are rarely so closely yoked. In the case of pitch perception, for example, the average individual can only *identify* a small number of tones that are well separated; he can *discriminate* thousands of values of pitch, however, when two tones are played consecutively. The same holds true for color. The average person can identify only a small set of colors, well separated in the color space, but he can success-fully discriminate thousands of hues when they are presented side by side (see Miller, 1956; Pollack, 1952). The speech case, then, appeared to be especially interesting as a violation of a general principle of the relation between iden-tification and discrimination. (See Eimas, 1963, for specific comparisons of identification and discrimination of noise bursts, shades of gray, vowels, and consonants.)

Categorical perception as it has been defined empirically is characterized by the following three criteria that relate performance on a (relative) discrimi-nation test and a phoneme identification test. Discrimination functions must show (1) "peaks" of highly accurate discrimination, (2) "troughs" of discrim-ination near chance, and (3) a correspondence between the peaks and troughs and identification functions, with peaks occurring for comparison pairs whose members are drawn from different phoneme categories (cross-boundary com-parisons) and troughs occurring for comparison pairs whose members are drawn from within a single phoneme category (within-category comparisons).

The categorical perception phenomenon has been observed in many stud-ies. Mattingly, Liberman, Syrdal, and Halwes (1971) also showed categorical perception of /ba, da, ga/. They employed stimuli that differed on the initial F2 transition dimension in two-formant CV stimulus and used an oddity discrimi-nation task.[4] Pisoni (1973) reported categorical results for /ba, da, ga/ using three-formant stimuli in which both the F2 transition and the F3 transition varied in appropriate ways to cue place-of-articulation.

Studies of acoustic dimensions that provide information about *voicing* in stop consonants, for example, /d/ vs. /t/, and /b/ vs. /p/, have also shown the categorical perception phenomenon (Liberman, Harris, Kinney, and Lane, 1961a; Abramson and Lisker, 1970; Liberman, Harris, Eimas, Lisker, and Bas-tian, 1961b). For all these studies, discrimination of intracategory comparisons was only slightly better than could be predicted from absolute identification. This was true for almost all individual subjects, as well as for data averaged across groups of individuals.

In contrast to the findings for dimensions underlying stop consonantal fea-tures, dimensions that distinguish place-of-articulation in steady-state vowels were found *not* to be perceived categorically. For example, Fry, Abramson, Eimas, and Liberman (1962) investigated the identification and discrimination of a series of two-formant stimuli that ranged from /ɪ/ to /ɛ/ to /æ/. These vowels can be differentiated acoustically by their characteristic first and second formant frequencies. The stimulus series was generated by interpolating be-tween these characteristic frequencies in equal frequency steps to create a 13-stimulus series.

---

[4] Oddity discrimination presents three stimuli, one of which is different from the other two. The subject is required to state which syllable is "odd." It differs from the ABX procedure in having a chance level of 33% rather than 50%.

Figure 4 presents an idealized version of the results typically obtained in studies with steady-state vowels. Note first that the identification categories show more gradual slopes than those obtained for the stop consonants. That is, subjects are inconsistent in assigning phoneme labels to several of the intermediate stimuli. Phenomenologically these stimuli are heard as ambiguous tokens of the phoneme categories.

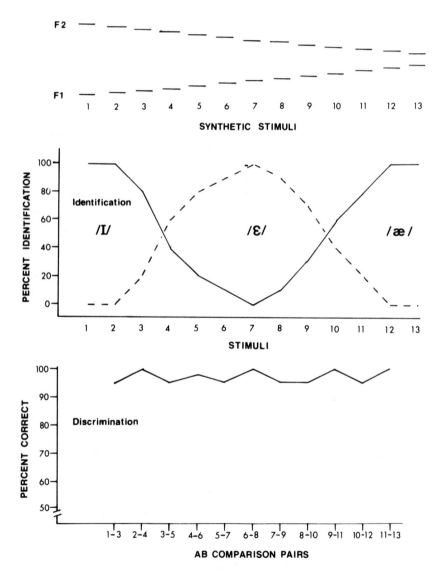

Fig. 4. Continuous perception of vowels. Schematic representation of synthetic vowel series (top) and idealized results of identification tests (middle) and discrimination tests (bottom).

As indicated in the bottom part of the figure, discrimination tests for vowel stimuli yield strikingly different results from those obtained for the stop consonant dimensions. Performance is more uniform across the series than for the stops, and discrimination is typically very accurate for both within-category pairs and cross-boundary pairs. That is, discrimination of intraphonemic differences is far above chance; indeed, it is nearly as good as interphonemic discrimination. This result has been called *continuous* perception, and is more typical of discrimination of simple nonspeech acoustic dimensions.

Other studies of steady-state vowels have confirmed the continuous perception results. Pisoni (1971) replicated the Fry *et al.* results with three-formant stimuli. Stevens, Liberman, Studdert-Kennedy, and Öhman (1969) reported continuous perception by both Swedish and American listeners of an *unrounded* vowel series (/i/-/ɪ/-/ɛ/ in English) and a *rounded* vowel series (/i/-/y/-/ʉ/ in Swedish).

It is apparent that the results for the stop consonantal dimensions and those for steady-state vowel dimensions show distinctly different kinds of discrimination performance. In the former, subjects' ability to differentiate acoustic variants appears to be highly constrained by the phonetic identity of the stimuli; discrimination is little better than absolute identification. In the case of vowels, discrimination of acoustic differences appears not to be restricted by phoneme identity. As with many nonspeech dimensions, physical differences among tokens of the same identification category are readily discriminated.

It is important to note in this respect that steady-state vowels, such as those used in the experiments reported above, are rarely realized in ongoing natural speech. Especially in rapidly articulated speech, both consonants and vowels are acoustically realized as dynamic changes in formant values (transitions) over the entire temporal course of the syllable. In this sense, then, steady-state vowels are "unnatural" as speech stimuli.

A study by Stevens (1968) compared the identification and discrimination of synthetic vowels generated in a fixed consonantal context, /b/-vowel-/l/, with the same tests for comparable steady-state vowels. Vowels in CVC syllables were perceived more categorically; i.e., intraphonemic discrimination was much poorer than interphonemic discrimination. This suggests that the more "natural" the syllable becomes, the more categorical will be the perception of the vowel; but this suggestion awaits further research.

The perception of acoustic dimensions underlying features of other classes of phonemes has been investigated more recently. Miyawaki, Strange, Verbrugge, Liberman, Jenkins, and Fujimura (1975) found that a series of syllables differing in initial steady state and transition of F3 (which differentiates the place difference in /ra/ vs. /la/) was perceived categorically by American listeners. McGovern and Strange (1977) replicated this finding with both syllable-initial and syllable-final /r/ and /l/ in combination with the vowel /i/ (i.e., /ri/ vs. /li/ and /ir/ vs. /il/).

An early study of the identification and discrimination of nasal stops (Garcia, 1967*a,b*) yielded ambiguous results with respect to categorical perception. This outcome seems to be attributable to the poor quality of the synthetic stimuli, as shown by the fact that the identification functions were irregular within subjects and highly variable from subject to subject. A more recent study by Larkey, Wald, and Strange (1978) with better stimuli has shown that systematic variation of the F2–F3 transitions, which provides the major cues for place-of-articulation in nasal stops (/m/, /n/, /ŋ/), is perceived categorically in both syllable-initial and syllable-final position. Miller and Eimas (1977) also found nearly categorical discrimination of place-of-articulation differences in nasals, /m/ vs. /n/, although subjects' discrimination performance was superior to that predicted from their identification functions.

Miller and Eimas (1977) also tested identification and discrimination of an acoustic dimension that distinguishes nasal stops from oral stops (e.g., /m/ from /b/). The nasality distinction was cued by variations in the duration of the nasal resonance and the starting frequency of the first oral formant. Results of identification tests showed more gradual slopes between phoneme categories than for the place-of-articulation dimension within nasal stops and lower peaks of discrimination of cross-category comparison pairs. However, discrimination of intracategory comparisons was inferior to cross-category discrimination, as would be predicted for categorically perceived dimensions.

The difference between /ʃ/ as in "shop" and /tʃ/ as in "chop" (fricative vs. affricate) can be produced by varying the duration from onset to full amplitude (rise time) of the syllable (Gerstman, 1957). Thus a syllable with short rise time may be heard as /tʃa/ while one with longer rise time may be heard as /ʃa/. Cutting and Rosner (1974) showed that identification and discrimination tests of stimuli along a dimension from short to long rise time yielded categorical perception. While identification of the syllables was not as consistent as for stop consonant dimensions, the discrimination observed was the same as that which was predicted from the identification functions, thus qualifying as categorical perception.

The above studies supply ample evidence for categorical perception of many different acoustic dimensions that differentiate phonemes. Dimensions cueing place-of-articulation in oral and nasal stops and approximants, voicing in stops,[5] manner-of-articulation in affricates and fricatives, and, to a lesser extent, nasality, have all been shown to display the phenomenon.

---

[5] However, Raphael (1972) found evidence for continuous perception of the voicing distinction in word-final consonants cued acoustically by preceding vowel duration. Identification functions showed gradual slopes for some consonant comparisons (e.g., /f/ vs. /v/) and steep slopes for others (e.g., /p/ vs. /b/). Discrimination of pairs that were drawn from across the identification boundaries was not consistently better than discrimination of those taken from within a phoneme category. The stimuli tested in this experiment were synthesized on the Pattern Playback, an early synthesizer at Haskins Laboratories. It is possible that the stimuli sounded highly "unnatural." The study should be replicated with new materials.

In response to early methodological criticisms of the categorical perception research, several techniques in addition to the oddity or ABX tasks have been employed to test subjects' ability to discriminate stimuli along relevant acoustic dimensions (Vinegrad, 1972; Strange, 1972; Dorman, 1974; Pisoni, 1971). These studies have demonstrated discontinuities in discriminability of consonantal dimensions under a variety of different methods, ranging from direct magnitude estimation to auditory evoked response.[6] We can conclude that the discrimination by adult listeners of many phonetically relevant acoustic dimensions appears to be rather strictly determined by the linguistic significance of the differences along those dimensions. It would seem that the perception of these types of signals involves processes that are different in some respects from those serving the perception of many (simple) nonspeech acoustic dimensions.

4. Some Recent Research on Categorical Perception

Early theoretical explanations of the categorical perception phenomenon by Liberman and others (Liberman *et al.*, 1967; Studdert-Kennedy, Liberman, Harris, and Cooper, 1970; Stevens, 1960; Stevens and Halle, 1967) stressed the special nature of the perception of acoustic parameters underlying phonetic distinctions in relation to their production. According to these "motor theory" accounts, the speech signal was "decoded" by processes that were also involved in speech production at some level. Categorical perception (as well as other phenomena of speech perception) was thus thought to be a function of special processes that were unique to the processing of speech and (perhaps) part of the species-specific, innate capacity for language possessed by human organisms. (See Stevens and House, 1972, for further discussion of analysis-by-synthesis models and motor theories of speech perception.)

This general conception of the perceptual processes for speech has generated several lines of research in the last 10 years: (1) Research on the perception of nonspeech dimensions was pursued in response to the claim that categorical perception is a function of special processes used only for the perception of speech sounds. (2) Investigations of the perception of speech by nonhuman species were undertaken to determine whether categorical perception is mediated by species-specific mechanisms. (3) Related research with young infants was initiated to determine whether the processes responsible for categorical perception are, at least in part, "built-in" predispositions of human organisms.

---

[6] Under certain conditions, subjects can demonstrate intracategory discrimination significantly above a chance level. See Pisoni and Tash (1974) for a study of reaction times to stimuli differing in Voice Onset Time and Barclay (1972) for a study of differential labeling of stimuli differing in F2 transitions.

In this section we will restrict ourselves to a presentation of some of the most recent experimental results in the first two lines of research. The infant research has been reviewed extensively elsewhere (Eimas, 1975a, in press; Morse, 1974; Butterfield and Cairns, 1974; Kuhl, in press), and we will not attempt to review it here.[7]

4.1. Is Categorical Perception Unique to Speech?

The claim that categorical perception is unique to the perception of speech sounds was supported by results of discrimination tests of several "nonspeech" stimulus series that were used as control conditions for synthetic dimensions (Liberman et al., 1961a; Studdert-Kennedy, et al., 1970; Mattingly et al., 1971; Cutting, 1974; Miyawaki et al., 1975). In these studies the nonspeech series contained the same acoustic variations in components that were perceived categorically when they were embedded in speech syllables. However, these components were presented either in isolation or in an altered acoustic context in such a way that the resulting patterns were not linguistically informative (i.e., they were not identifiable as phonetic entities). Results of these studies produced continuous functions in which acoustic variations that corresponded to "intraphonemic" comparisons (in the speech context) were discriminated nearly as well as "interphonemic" comparisons; i.e., the acoustic differences were perceived continuously when they were presented in isolation or embedded in a nonspeech context. Liberman and others interpreted these results as evidence for two "modes" of auditory perception. According to this interpretation, perception in the "speech mode" was qualitatively different from perception of nonspeech auditory signals presumed to be processed in a "general auditory" mode.

Recent studies with adults have investigated other acoustic dimensions related to those known to be important in phonetic contrasts. Miller, Wier, Pastore, Kelly, and Dooling (1976) studied the perception of relative onset of a noise to a buzz (analogous to the VOT cue for voicing in initial stop conso-

---

[7] To summarize briefly, however, infants as young as 1 month of age show categorical discrimination of acoustic dimensions for voicing (Eimas, Siqueland, Jusczyk, and Vigorito, 1971) and place-of-articulation in stops (Morse, 1972; Eimas, 1974) and liquids (Eimas, 1975b). That is, differences that are phonetically relevant for adult listeners are discriminated while differences of the same magnitude that constitute intraphonemic variation are not. Experiments which explore whether infants' perception of these stimuli is phonetic (in the same sense as for adults) have only recently been attempted (Fodor, Garrett, and Brill, 1975) and no strong conclusions can yet be made. It can be concluded, however, that human infants are able to differentiate at a very early age exactly those sounds that are used in languages to make phonetic distinctions. We will return to the question of the nature of infants' discrimination of speech (and nonspeech) sounds in a later section.

nants) in an oddity discrimination task with feedback. Subjects were highly experienced listeners who typically made superior scores on auditory discrimination tasks. Discrimination functions for the group as a whole showed categorical peaks and troughs (for inter- and intracategory comparisons, respectively) that were comparable to results by Abramson and Lisker (1970) for VOT in speech stimuli. (However, there was a good deal of subject variability; some subjects showed rather poor discrimination for all comparison pairs.)

Pisoni conducted a similar experiment with a stimulus dimension that varied the relative onset time of two tones such that the lower tone preceded, was simultaneous with, or lagged after the higher tone. After considerable training, most subjects were able to identify stimuli as belonging to one of two categories with an abrupt boundary between categories. Subsequent ABX discrimination tests showed categorical peaks of relatively accurate discrimination for comparison pairs drawn from different identification categories and troughs of poor discrimination for intracategory comparisons.

Cutting and Rosner (1974) investigated the perception of the rapidity of onset (rise time) of musiclike stimuli, pure-tone stimuli, and speech sounds. The musiclike stimuli were characterized as varying along a dimension from a "plucked" sound (rapid onset) to a "bowed" sound (gradual onset). This is comparable acoustically to the distinction in manner between the affricate /tʃ/ and fricative /ʃ/ in syllable-initial position. For both musiclike and speech dimensions, discrimination was significantly better for pairs of stimuli drawn from different identification categories; within-category comparisons were discriminated quite poorly. For the pure-tone dimensions, the location of the discrimination peak could also be predicted from identification performance. However, the overall identification functions showed a gradual slope with considerable inconsistency in labeling the gradual-onset stimuli, and discrimination for cross-boundary comparisons was below the level predicted from identification functions (i.e., overall discrimination scores for all comparison pairs were below 70% accuracy).

Locke and Kellar (1973) investigated the perception of musical chords by experienced musicians and nonmusicians. They required subjects to discriminate pairs of triadic chords in which the middle component varied in 2 Hz steps over a range from a "tempered A major" to an "A minor" chord. Subjects were also asked to categorize these stimuli as compared to a "standard." (This was similar to an identification test, except that no linguistic labels were used.)

Results of the categorization test by experienced musicians showed an abrupt crossover between the two categories and the musicians' discrimination functions showed peaks of relatively greater accuracy for pairs that straddled the categorization boundary. Discrimination of intracategory pairs was somewhat greater than was predicted from categorization, however. The inexperienced listeners produced very different results. Categorization was very inconsistent and discrimination showed no systematic peaks. The authors concluded that musical intervals are perceived categorically by experienced musicians, but not by inexperienced listeners.

Burns and Ward (1973, 1975) investigated the perception of melodic musical intervals (frequency ratios) by trained musicians. They varied their stimuli by equal increments along the logarithmic frequency scale defining musical pitch. Subjects identified intervals as intervals of the chromatic scale (e.g., a fourth or a fifth). In discrimination, subjects were presented with pairs of intervals and asked to indicate which interval was wider. Most subjects showed categorical perception of the intervals; i.e., their discrimination was largely predictable from their ability to identify the intervals differentially. Using standard psychophysical techniques, Burns and Ward then determined just-noticeable-differences (JNDs) for interval width. In initial judgments, they found that JNDs were considerably smaller at the boundaries than within the identification categories, as would be predicted for categorical perception. With training, JNDs became smaller, finally achieving a relatively flat distribution across the range of intervals being tested, implying that the subjects had been trained to perceive the intervals continuously. When the subjects were retested with the discrimination test, however, they still showed categorical perception. Nonmusicians tested on the discrimination task showed essentially continuous perception and their overall performance level was much poorer than that of the musicians.

Siegel and Siegel (1977) investigated the perception of tonal intervals that varied from a musically accurate fourth, through an augmented fourth or tritone, to an accurate fifth. An identification test and a magnitude estimation task (in which subjects judged each tonal interval of the series against a "standard" tritone) both showed categorical-like perception by the extremely highly trained musicians tested.

These studies offer evidence that categorical perception is not unique to speech. The phenomenon appears to be a function of processes of the human auditory system that can be used to differentiate some kinds of nonspeech acoustic dimensions as well. It is interesting to point out in this respect that the studies reported here all tested discrimination of relatively complex relational aspects of acoustic patterns, rather than simple psychophysical dimensions such as frequency and intensity.

An interesting observation with respect to the topic of this chapter is the relationship suggested by these studies between the categorical nature of perception and the listeners' experience with the (complex) dimensions. With the exception of Cutting and Rosner (1974), who tested untrained listeners, these experiments demonstrated the categorical phenomenon with listeners who were highly experienced with the stimulus dimensions being tested, or who were in some way experts at the kinds of tasks required (as in Miller et al., 1976) or trained specifically with the experimental materials (as in Pisoni, 1977).

4.2. Is Categorical Perception of Speech Unique to Humans?

Recent studies have attempted to discover whether some nonhuman organisms perceive phonetically relevant acoustic dimensions in a categorical manner. Morse and Snowdon (1975) used a paradigm that monitors changes in heart rate with rhesus monkeys to measure their discrimination of the F2–F3 cues for place-of-articulation. Significant differences were observed to both within-category and cross-boundary changes (relative to a no-change control condition). However, they observed that the cross-boundary change was significantly larger than was the within-category change. Morse (in press) concludes that monkeys' discrimination of phonetic and nonphonetic acoustic contrasts shows differences that are similar to those produced by human infants (Miller and Morse, 1975) and comparable to behavioral results for adults. However, unlike human infants and adults, monkeys do not seem to be as closely constrained by the phonetic identity of the stimuli; intraphonemic differences are also discriminable according to the heart rate measure.

Waters and Wilson (1976) also tested rhesus monkeys, using a shock avoidance paradigm to measure discrimination of the VOT cue for voicing. The animals were trained to respond differentially to several sets of reference end points on the labial dimension (heard as /ba/ and /pa/ by human listeners). They were then tested for generalization to intermediate labial stimuli and to stimuli with comparable VOT values from the velar series (heard as /g/ and /k/ by humans). Most monkeys did separate the stimuli into two categories that were roughly comparable to those produced by human subjects. However, the data for the monkeys show very gradually sloping boundaries and strong anchoring effects as a function of the particular reference stimuli presented. (No such anchoring effects occur in human performance.) Further, the shift in VOT boundary location from labial to velar stimuli is opposite that found for adult human listeners (Abramson and Lisker, 1970).

Kuhl and Miller (1975a,b) tested the ability of chinchillas to differentiate stimuli along a VOT dimension that distinguished /da/ from /ta/ for humans. A shock avoidance paradigm was used in which the animal was required to cross a barrier from one compartment to another to avoid shock when the "negative" stimulus (e.g., /da/) was presented. When the positive stimulus (e.g., /ta/) was presented, the animal could remain in the home compartment and drink from a free water supply. Thirsty animals were trained to criterion with reference stimuli from the ends of the VOT dimensions. They were then given generalization trials on intermediate stimuli (with no shock administered on any trials). The "identification" functions for chinchillas showed boundaries in the same location as humans; i.e., the animals avoided only those tokens that were identified (by humans) as the same phoneme as the negative stimulus. Furthermore, generalization tests to labial and velar stimuli (/ba/-/pa/ and /ga/-/ka/ dimensions) showed boundary locations similar to those produced by human listeners (Kuhl and Miller, 1975*b*). The boundary crossovers for chinchillas were slightly less steep than crossovers typically produced by adult human listeners, although they were within the range shown by some individual adult subjects and that obtained for very young children (Zlatin and Koenigsknecht, 1975).

These rather surprising results of tests of monkeys and chinchillas suggest that some animals may be able to discriminate some phonetically relevant acoustic dimensions in a categorical manner. However, the research involves very complex methodologies and the data often show a great deal of variability that makes interpretation difficult. The most promising results—those with chinchillas—offer the interesting possibility that categorical perception, at least for VOT dimensions, may be due in part to auditory processes common to man and chinchilla. We must await the outcome of further studies with these and other species and with other stimulus dimensions to see to what extent categorical perception, as it is manifested in humans, is determined by perceptual processes that are present in subhuman animals.

5. Categorical Perception and Linguistic Experience

The results of the studies reviewed above (as well as other types of research in speech perception) raise important questions about the explanation of the categorical perception phenomenon. While there is currently no consensus among researchers in the field, some preliminary models have been offered to account for the empirical findings on phonetic perception, including categorical phenomena (Fujisaki and Kawashima, 1969, 1970; Studdert-Kennedy, 1976; Pisoni and Sawusch, 1975; Cutting and Pisoni, in press). These models, many of which are described within an information processing framework, emphasize the multiplicity of the processes involved in decoding the phonetic message from the speech signal.

Questions of the development of these processes and their short-term modification have been addressed, in part, by the feature detector models proposed by Eimas and others (Cutting and Eimas, 1975; Eimas and Miller, this volume). However, several other lines of research regarding the influence of various kinds of experience, especially linguistic experience, on the categorical perception of acoustic dimensions have not been given as much attention. It is to these research efforts that the next section of this chapter is devoted. Research dealing with linguistic experience includes cross-language studies of monolinguals and bilinguals, within-language studies of familiar feature distinctions in unfamiliar phonetic contexts, and studies of the effects of laboratory training on phonetic perception.

5.1. Cross-Language Studies of Voice Onset Time

As stated in the introduction, each language uses a small set of phonetic features to differentiate the phonemes or functionally distinctive sounds of that language. Different languages utilize different subsets and combinations of phonetic features. Thus, a contrast that is phonemic in one language may not be in another. The variation in the latter language (if it occurs at all) is considered an intraphonemic difference. Thus, for instance, in English the approximants /r/ and /1/ are contrasted, in terms of place of articulation. In Japanese, however, these sounds do not occur as distinct phonemes.

This fact about the phonemic structure of different languages provides speech perception researchers a natural way to ask questions about the influence of linguistic experience (i.e., phonemic usage) on the perception of phonetically relevant acoustic dimensions. The general paradigm used is one in which two groups of listeners who speak different languages are tested on an acoustic dimension of interest. For one group of subjects the contrast cued by the dimension is phonemic; for the other group it is not. A difference in the ability to discriminate the acoustic dimension can thus be attributed to the linguistic use of the distinction.

Much of the research of this type has investigated voicing distinctions in stop consonants. Abramson and Lisker studied the VOT dimension along which initial consonants are differentiated in many languages. Acoustic analyses of 11 languages (Lisker and Abramson, 1964) indicated that initial stops, contrasted in terms of voicing and aspiration, were distributed along the VOT dimension in three major clusters: (1) prevoiced stops, (2) stops in which voicing was simultaneous or lagged only briefly, and (3) postvoiced stops in which there was a long voicing lag. Languages contrasted simultaneous VOT tokens or examplars either with prevoiced tokens (as in Spanish and French unaspirated [p] versus prevoiced [b]), with long-lag tokens (as in English unaspirated [p] vs. aspirated [pʰ]), or with both (as in Thai, which contrasts prevoiced [b], unaspirated [p], and postvoiced aspirated [pʰ]). Figure 5 illustrates the distributions of VOT values in words spoken by four language groups. Prevoicing, where the onset of the first formant precedes onset of higher formants, is indicated by minus (−) values (in msec) along the dimensions, while postvoicing, where onset of the first formant is delayed, is shown by plus (+) values. Note that the phoneme /b/ in English is highly similar acoustically to the phoneme /p/ as spoken in Spanish and French and the unaspirated [p] spoken in Thai.

Identification and oddity discrimination tests were conducted with speakers of different languages to determine the effects of linguistic usage on the perception of the VOT dimension. In a study that compared speakers of Thai and American English (Abramson and Lisker, 1970), Thai listeners separated the labial VOT series into three distinct categories on the identification task (with boundaries at about −20 VOT and +40 VOT), and produced two categorical peaks in discrimination corresponding to these two identification boundaries. In contrast, American subjects produced a single categorical peak on pairs that contrasted the short-lag tokens identified as the phoneme "b" with the long-lag tokens identified as "p." They showed no indication of better discrimination for pairs that crossed the Thai −20 VOT boundary than for within-category

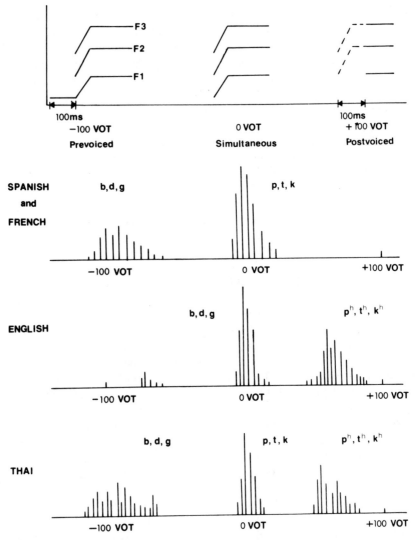

Fig. 5. Schematic spectrographic patterns that vary in Voice Onset Time (VOT) in the top diagram. Distribution of VOT values for words spoken in four languages. Redrawn from Lisker and Abramson (1964).

comparisons. Figure 6 shows the idealized pattern of results for these groups of subjects.

The differential pattern of results for Thai and American listeners was replicated with the apical VOT series which is also divided into three phoneme categories by Thai subjects (d-t-tʰ) and two categories (d-t) by Americans

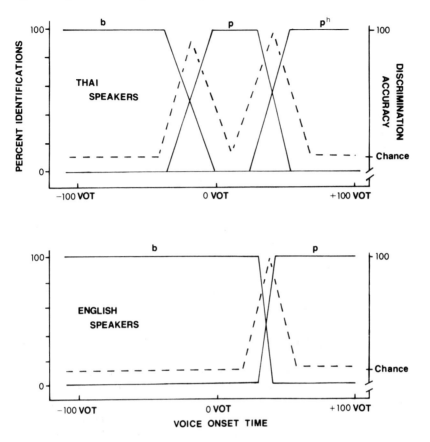

Fig. 6. Idealized version of results of identification and discrimination tests by speakers of Thai (upper) and English (lower). Identification is shown by solid lines; discrimination functions are superimposed using dashed lines.

(Abramson and Lisker, 1970). Again, the Thais showed two categorical peaks, while the Americans showed only one.

Abramson and Lisker (1973) and Williams (1974) tested speakers of Spanish, for whom a single contrast between prevoiced and short-lag tokens is phonemic. While the study by Abramson and Lisker produced somewhat ambiguous results, the identification and discrimination functions for eight Spanish monolinguals reported by Williams (experiment 1) showed clear differences from those produced by American subjects. As indicated in Fig. 7, the peak of most accurate discrimination for the Spanish subjects occurred at the identification boundary located just slightly to the prevoiced side of simultaneity (−4 VOT). In comparison, the English-speaking subjects were accurate in discrimination only at their boundary, which is to the postvoiced side of simultaneity

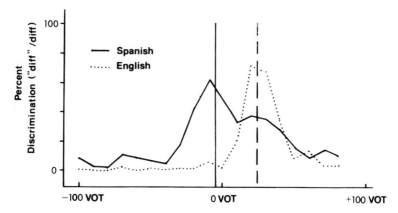

Fig. 7. Discrimination functions for Spanish and English monolinguals. Vertical lines represent the 50% crossover in identification functions for the same groups of subjects. Redrawn from Williams (1974).

(+25 VOT). Note that the Spanish monolinguals also discriminated pairs at the English boundary appreciably better than chance, although not as well as did the American subjects.

Studies with bilinguals have asked whether listeners adopt a double standard in perceiving an acoustic dimension that is separated differently by the two languages. Williams (1974, experiment II) tested Spanish-English bilinguals on VOT in two sessions in which the language of presentation differed. While she found no effects of language of presentation, she did find differences among subjects' discrimination results. None of the subjects adopted Spanish identification boundaries; however, three of the eight subjects showed broad peaks in discrimination for pairs within a range that included both Spanish and English monolingual identification boundaries (−5 VOT to +25 VOT). The remaining five subjects produced discrimination functions typical of those shown by English monolinguals. Williams points out that the VOT synthetic series does not contain secondary acoustic characteristics that bilinguals may use to distinguish naturally spoken consonants in Spanish.

A study of Caramazza, Yeni-Komshian, Zurif, and Carbone (1973) with bilinguals and monolinguals of Canadian-English and French also indicated that the VOT dimension provides a strong cue for the perception of the English distinction, but not for the French distinction. These investigators reported identification data for three groups of subjects: French monolinguals, English monolinguals, and bilinguals under both French and English testing conditions. The English monolingual functions showed sharp boundaries in the postvoiced region for the labial, apical, and velar VOT series. The French monolingual results showed an identification boundary that was more toward the prevoiced end of the dimension, as would be expected. However, the slope of the boundary was very gradual and nonmonotonic, indicating considerable ambiguity in listeners' phonemic judgments. The bilinguals' identification boundaries fell between the two monolingual functions; there were no differences due to the language used during the test sessions. No discrimination tests were given in this experiment.

Taken as a group, the cross-language and bilingual studies provide convincing evidence that linguistic experience exerts a major influence on the perception (by adults) of the VOT dimension. The monolingual studies indicate that highly accurate discrimination of small differences in VOT is restricted in large part to just those values that constitute phonemic differences for the listeners. However, there is evidence that discrimination of VOT differences in the region of short-lag values is quite accurate even for subjects whose languages do not contrast these values. The bilingual data also suggest that VOT differences in the region of the English boundary are in some way more salient than differences on the prevoiced side of simultaneity. In part, this may be due to factors involved in the synthesis of these stimuli, i.e., to how well the synthetic syllables have incorporated the acoustic variables present in natural speech that control the perception of phonetic contrasts by speakers of these languages. We will return to these concerns in a later section.

5.2. Cross-Language Studies of Place of Articulation

Cross-language research on acoustic dimensions other than VOT has been less extensive. Miyawaki *et al.* (1975) compared the discrimination of the F3 cue for place-of-articulation in syllable-initial liquids by adult Japanese and American listeners. (Recall that in Japanese liquids are not contrasted phonemically.) In addition to testing subjects on discrimination of the speech stimuli, a comparable nonspeech series, consisting of the F3 formants in isolation, was presented to both language groups.

As indicated in Fig. 8, Japanese subjects showed no peak of accurate discrimination for speech comparison pairs that straddled the English phoneme boundary comparable to that produced by the Americans. For 18 of the 21 Japanese, discrimination of speech stimuli was uniformly poor across the entire F3 dimension. (The three exceptional subjects are discussed below.) However, for the nonspeech stimuli, both Japanese and American listeners discriminated all comparison pairs with far greater than chance accuracy, and there were no differences between Japanese and American functions.

Stevens *et al.* (1969) tested the discrimination of place-of-articulation in two series of steady-state vowels by speakers of English and Swedish. One set of vowels—the unrounded vowels—was phonemic for both language groups. The series were identified as consisting of three phoneme categories: /i/, /e/, /ä/ in Swedish and /i/, /ɪ/, /ɛ/ in English. The vowels in the other set were also contrasted in place-of-articulation, but consisted of the Swedish rounded front

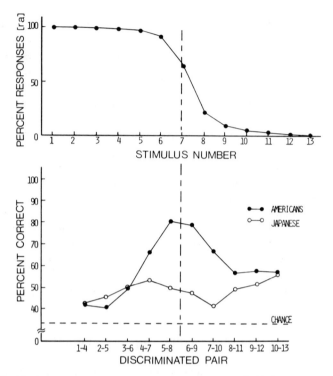

Fig. 8. Identification (upper) and discrimination (lower) of the /ra/-/la/ synthetic series. From Miyawaki *et al.* (1975).

vowels /i/, /y/, /ʉ/ that do not occur in English. (Rounding is a redundant feature in English that occurs only in back vowels.)

Results of identification and discrimination tests for Swedish and American listeners indicated that the acoustic dimensions were perceived in a continuous manner by both groups. Identification boundaries were characterized by gradual slopes, and discrimination along the entire place dimension was significantly better than chance for both rounded and unrounded series. Furthermore, there were no differences between American and Swedish listeners' discrimination of either series.

Two aspects of this study deserve mention. First, note that the acoustic dimension under study (i.e., F1, F2, F3 frequency differences) cued contrasts in place-of-articulation among vowels. Thus, although front rounded vowels as a class are not phonemic for American listeners, the distinction in place-of-articulation *among* the rounded vowels is one which is familiar to English-speaking subjects. Second, this study was conducted using steady-state vowels. As previously mentioned, these are rather artificial stimuli in that naturally occurring vowels contain transitions into and out of the adjacent consonants.

We can conclude from these cross-language studies that categorical perception of at least some phonetically relevant acoustic dimensions is strongly affected by the specific linguistic experience of the listeners. For some voicing and place distinctions in consonants, subjects' ability to discriminate acoustic differences appears to be constrained by their phonemic use of those differences. Potential contrasts that are not utilized in the language of the listener are, in many cases, not discriminated much better than differences that are nonphonemic in all languages.

5.3. Within-Language Studies

Another way to study the effects of linguistic usage on categorical perception involves testing speakers of a single language which uses a particular phonetic contrast in one context, but not in another. For example, as we described before, Thai initial stop consonants with labial and apical place-of-articulation are contrasted in both voicing and aspiration (i.e., [b]-[p]-[pʰ] and [d]-[t]-[tʰ]). However, for stops with velar place-of-articulation, only aspiration is contrasted phonemically (i.e., [k]-[kʰ]); prevoiced [g] does not occur. Thus there is a "hole in the pattern" of possible feature combinations that are actually used to make phonemic distinctions.

This kind of configuration provides an opportunity to ask about the effects of specific linguistic experience on categorical perception. Do listeners who are familiar with a particular phonetic contrast in one context perceive the contrast categorically in an unfamiliar context?

The study by Abramson and Lisker (1970) with Thai subjects reported results of discrimination tests on a velar VOT series that was comparable to the labial and apical series on which the subjects produced two peaks of accurate discrimination. Neither of the two subjects tested produced a peak of accurate discrimination for pairs with VOT values comparable to the prevoiced-voiceless unaspirated boundary in the labial and apical series. Their discrimination of the velar series showed a single categorical peak at the (phonemic) voiceless unaspirated-aspirated boundary. That is, categorical perception was specific to just those feature combinations that were phonemic in the language.

A study of the discrimination of place-of-articulation in nasal stop consonants by Americans investigated whether categorical perception was specific to the syllabic context in which the contrast is phonemic. In English, nasal consonants with labial, apical, and velar place-of-articulation occur in syllable-final position. However, only labial and apical nasals occur initially; the velar nasal /ŋ/ is not phonemic in syllable-initial position.

Larkey et al. (1978) tested the identification and discrimination of the F2–F3 acoustic dimension that cues place-of-articulation for both syllable-initial and syllable-final nasal consonants. They found significant differences in subjects' perception of the /n/-/ŋ/ contrast in the two syllabic contexts. Stimuli in the final nasal series were identified as three distinct categories and discrimination tests showed two categorical peaks at the phoneme boundaries. For the initial nasal series, identification functions showed more gradual slopes for the boundary between /n/ and /ŋ/ and discrimination was not as accurate for pairs that straddled this boundary as for pairs at the syllable-initial /m/-/n/ boundary or for syllable-final /n/-/ŋ/ pairs.

These studies suggest that the specificity of the categorical perception phenomenon may extend in some cases to particular phonemic and syllabic contexts actually used in the language of the subjects. We need more studies of this kind in order to draw firm conclusions, but these initial attempts point out that linguistic experience with particular combinations of phonetic features can play a large part in determining the relative salience of acoustic parameters for adult perceivers. We may conclude tentatively that considerable perceptual learning takes place as a function of exposure to a particular language environment that results in a modification of the way in which these dimensions are differentiated by adult listeners. The studies to be reviewed in the next section deal with questions of the nature of this perceptual learning and the success of various kinds of laboratory training techniques in modifying adults' perception of speech-relevant dimensions.

5.4. Laboratory Training Studies

The first efforts to modify phonetic perception by laboratory training methods came in response to an early critical review of the motor theory of speech perception. Lane (1965) argued that categorical perception of speech was a function of "conditioning" by the language community, and thus could be explained solely in terms of the learning theoretical concepts of discrimination training and response differentiation. He claimed further that categorical discrimination of nonspeech acoustic dimensions "could be obtained quickly in the laboratory after a few minutes of conditioning . . ." (1967, p. 86) as evidenced by results of his training studies that used spectrally inverted synthetic speech patterns (Lane and Schneider, 1963) and visual dimensions (Cross, Lane, and Sheppard, 1965).

In reply to Lane's review, Studdert-Kennedy et al. (1970) pointed out that a critical fact of categorical perception of speech was that intraphonemic differences were not discriminated. (Recall the criteria set forth in Section 3.) While Lane's data showed that it was possible to enhance the discrimination of certain stimulus dimensions at category boundaries by identification training, within-category discrimination still remained high. Thus, categorical perception was not demonstrated for these dimensions.

Pisoni (1971) attempted to train subjects to identify two categories of isolated second formants (which in speech contexts usually cue differences in place-of-articulation) in order to test the effects of this training on discrimi-

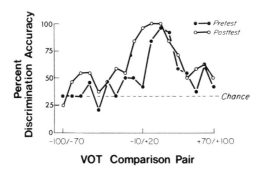

Fig. 9. Pretest and posttest discrimination of the VOT labial series by subjects trained in discrimination. From Strange (1972).

nation. The six subjects produced extremely variable results; identification boundaries were inconsistant and none of the subjects produced peaks in post-training discrimination that could be predicted from their identification functions. Pisoni concluded that the process by which categorical perception of speech is shaped by linguistic experience must involve a kind of learning very different from that resulting from the "quick and easy" training procedures suggested by Lane.

Other studies have been concerned more directly with the modification of the perception of speech dimensions by laboratory training methods. One of the present authors (Strange, 1972) undertook a series of studies with American college-age students that asked whether adults could be trained to discriminate syllables whose initial consonants differed in VOT over a range that did not represent a phonemic contrast in English. Specifically, she attempted to train subjects to differentiate VOT differences in the region of the Thai prevoiced-voiced unaspirated boundary.

In the first study, four subjects were given specific practice with feedback in the oddity discrimination task. They were told about the Thai distinction and were presented good instances of prevoiced and voiced tokens, but were given no formal instruction in the production of the contrast. Figure 9 shows that 5 hr of training over the course of several sessions did produce changes in subjects' discrimination of the labial VOT dimension. All four subjects showed improved discrimination of pairs to the prevoiced side of their original discrimination peak. The greatest improvement occurred for pairs that straddled the Spanish prevoiced-voiced boundary (−4 VOT according to Williams's data). No significant improvement occurred for pairs in the region of the Thai identification boundary (−20 VOT). Subsequent identification tests showed small shifts in the boundary locations toward the prevoicing end of the dimension.

In a second study, three subjects were given practice in categorizing an abbreviated apical VOT series (−100 VOT to +10 VOT) into two distinct "phoneme" classes. (Prior to the training, all these stimuli were identified as "d" and discrimination was not above chance.) After 7 hr of practice in which subjects were shown only the results of their performance after each block of trials, all three subjects could classify the dimension into two categories consistently, although the slope of the boundary for one subject was quite gradual. Subsequent discrimination tests showed a consistent categorical peak for one subject, a somewhat lower peak for the second subject, and erratic performance for the third subject, whose identification boundary was most gradual. Tests of identification and discrimination of comparable labial VOT series showed no generalization of improvement in the perception of the same VOT differences in another phonemic context.

A third study used a direct-magnitude scaling technique similar to that of Vinegrad (1972) in which the subjects rated each stimulus by placing it on a scale between endpoint reference stimuli. Eight hours of practice was completed on an abbreviated VOT series (-100 to $+10$ VOT). Posttests on the full VOT series (-100 to $+100$ VOT) showed a change in perception for some subjects; their scaling functions showed more continuous perception compared to pretest results. However, only one subject showed a tendency toward a categorical function for the stimuli between -100 and $+10$ VOT. Results of posttraining tests of oddity discrimination produced mixed results. Only two subjects showed overall improvement in discrimination of the abbreviated dimensions; neither produced categorical peaks. Here, too, there were no systematic transfer effects to VOT dimensions other than those used in training.

The results of these three studies show that, in general, changing the perception of VOT dimensions by adult English speakers is not easily accomplished by techniques that involved several hours of practice spread over several sessions. Although performance on each of the kinds of tests did change somewhat with experience, only the identification training task (which involved practice with general feedback only) produced categorical results approaching those found for native speakers of Thai. Even in this case, only two of the three subjects succeeded in distinguishing sharply between prevoiced and voiceless, unaspirated stop consonants.

Lisker (1970) conducted a training study with adult Russian speakers on labial VOT stimuli with values from $+10$ to $+60$ VOT. All these stimuli fall within a single phoneme category in Russian, a voiceless unaspirated stop that is contrasted with a prevoiced stop, as in Spanish. Fifteen subjects were given repeated trials differentially labeling the endpoints ($+10$ VOT and $+60$ VOT) and were then tested on the identification of intermediate values. The overall identification function (averaged over subjects) showed a very gradual slope between the end points that reflected a great deal of inter- and intrasubject variability. That is, the Russians produced rather continuous identification functions, very different from those of English-speaking subjects, for whom the voiced-voiceless boundary falls at $+20$ VOT. Discrimination tests were not given to the Russian subjects.

Carney, Widin, and Viemeister (1977) used a different method to train subjects on the discrimination of VOT differences in labial stop consonants. They obtained psychometric functions for each of three subjects using each stimulus from a 21-stimulus series as a "standard" in successive blocks of an AX ("same-different") test. They then undertook training trials with immediate feedback using five different "standard" stimuli. Posttraining tests using the same standards (in which no feedback was given) showed considerable improvement in intraphonemic discrimination for all subjects. Indeed, one subject produced 100% correct performance for all stimuli when contrasted with the +20 VOT and +80 VOT standards! Subsequent oddity discrimination tests also showed intraphonemic discrimination far above the chance level for both subjects. These researchers are currently extending this training to new subjects and new acoustic dimensions in order to test the generality of their findings. On the basis of their preliminary results, however, this technique appears to be by far the most successful for inducing a change in perception of acoustic dimensions underlying phonetic distinctions.

The training studies reviewed here all attempted to change the perception of the VOT dimension. We are not aware of studies that have used other acoustic dimensions in a training paradigm. Much more research is needed in this area before we will be able to make any generalizations about the ability of adults to modify their perception of phonetic contrasts by laboratory training methods.

The research to date suggests that significant modification of phonetic perception is not easily obtained by simple laboratory training techniques. While changes did occur in some cases, the modification seemed to be rather narrowly restricted to just the dimensions on which the listeners were trained. There was little, if any, generalization of change to new stimulus materials and only limited generalization to new perceptual tasks.

6. Development of Phonetic Perception

The results of cross-language and within-language studies indicate that adults' ability to discriminate along linguistically relevant acoustic dimensions is highly constrained by many years of experience in a specific language environment. The training studies suggest that phonetic perception, once shaped by this specific experience, is not easily modified by limited practice on single dimensions. We might be tempted to conclude that categorical perception is a product of highly overlearned "habits" of categorization. However, research with infants reveals discontinuities in the perception of some acoustic dimensions even for 1-month-olds who have had very little exposure to language and no productive experience with phonetic contrasts. Studies of infants from different language environments provide additional evidence about the role of linguistic experience in phonetic perception. These studies address the question of whether or not it is necessary for an infant to have at least minimal receptive experience with a particular phonetic contrast before it can be discriminated.

Studies of infant perception are methodologically complex and sometimes unreliable. Most techniques depend on an habituation-dishabituation procedure. A sound is presented repeatedly until its effect on some dependent measure (such as heart rate deceleration or frequency of nonnutritive sucking) is minimized; then the sound is changed. If the dependent measure changes abruptly at this point (relative to a control group for which the sound is not changed), it is taken as evidence that the infant has detected the difference in the signals. If the dependent measure does not change, it is viewed as negative evidence concerning the importance, salience, or detectability of the stimulus difference.

6.1. Cross-Language Studies with Infants

Eimas (1975a) reports that 2- to 3-month-old infants from English-speaking environments discriminated VOT differences in the prevoicing region (-100 VOT/-40 VOT and -70 VOT/$+10$ VOT) that English-speaking adults do not differentiate. However, as Eimas points out, prevoiced stops are produced in English as allophonic variations, so it is possible that the infants had been exposed to these sounds.

The results of a study by Lasky, Syrdal-Lasky, and Klein (1975) are even more interesting with respect to the question of linguistic exposure. Using a heart rate measure, these investigators tested infants from Spanish-speaking environments on three VOT contrasts: -60 VOT/-20 VOT, -20 VOT/$+20$ VOT, and $+20$ VOT/$+60$ VOT. (Recall that only the $-20/+20$ contrast is phonemic in Spanish whereas only the $+20/+60$ contrast is phonemic in English.) Results indicated that Spanish infants discriminated both the $-60/-20$ difference and the $+20/+60$ difference, but not the $-20/+20$ contrast. This result is compatible with Eimas's data with infants from English-speaking environments obtained using a different methodology.

Streeter's research with Kikuyu infants (1974) also corroborates the results reported by Eimas (1975a) and Lasky et al. (1975). Using a contingent sucking rate measure, she found significant discrimination of labial VOT syllables with $+10$ VOT and $+40$ VOT values. Kikuyu uses a single prevoiced labial stop; thus the $+10/+40$ difference is not phonemic in this language and infants should not have been exposed to instances of either voiceless labial stop.

According to these studies, infants are able to discriminate differences in VOT across two "boundaries" that are located approximately at -50 VOT and $+30$ VOT for labial stops. Further, even infants from language environments in which neither of these differences is phonemic are able to discriminate them. These two boundaries correspond rather closely to the two boundaries found in Thai, but neither corresponds to the Spanish and Kikuyu voiced-voiceless unaspirated distinction. Studies with infants from language environments that do not make particular place contrasts (such as Japanese) are needed to determine if discrimination of other acoustic dimensions is categorical in the absence of any receptive experience.

We are left with a somewhat perplexing picture of the role of linguistic experience on the development of categorical perception. On the one hand, we see that categorical perception of at least some dimensions (or, more specifically, some values along some dimensions) is evidenced by infants who have had no experience with the distinctions. On the other hand, discrimination by adults of these and other acoustic dimensions reveals that a great deal of modification of these perceptual abilities takes place in the course of language development from infancy to adulthood. It is of primary importance to our understanding of this modification process to trace the development of phonetic perception during first-language learning as well as during second-language learning by children and adults. Unfortunately, this is an area in which our empirical base is most wanting.

6.2. Developmental Studies of Phonetic Perception

There have been relatively few developmental studies reported that have used carefully controlled stimuli in which the acoustic variations are well specified. Most of these studies have investigated voicing contrasts cued by the VOT dimension. In an early attempt, Winterkorn, MacNeilage, and Preston (1967) tested five English-speaking children from age 2:9 to 3:6 on identification of six apical VOT stimuli (-30 VOT, -5 VOT, $+20$ VOT, $+45$ VOT, $+70$ VOT, and $+100$ VOT). All but the youngest child consistently labeled the first three stimuli as /d/ and the remaining as /t/, in the same way as adult English speakers. No discrimination tests were given these subjects.

More recently, Zlatin and Koenigsknecht (1975) compared identification by 2-year-olds, 6-year-olds, and adults of several VOT series that contrasted labial, apical, and velar real-word pairs (bees/peas, bear/pear, dime/time, and goat/coat). Although all age groups showed highly similar boundary locations (for all but the velar series), there were developmentally related differences in the width of the boundaries. The youngest children showed wider boundaries than the 6-year-olds (for two of the series) and the adults (for all four series). These results suggest that while very young children are able to classify acoustically variable tokens into the same phonetic categories as do adults of their language community, the acoustic differences needed to differentiate categories may be greater for 2-year-olds than for older subjects. No pairwise discrimination tests were performed on these subjects, however.

Wolf (1973) tested the identification and discrimination of an abbreviated labial VOT dimension (-10 VOT to $+70$ VOT) by American children in kindergarten and second grade. Both age groups produced a sharp identification boundary located in the same place as the boundary for adult English speakers

*Table 2. VOT Value of 50% Crossover in
Identification Functions for Spanish-Speaking
Children Learning English* [a]

Age (yr)	Exposure to English		
	0–6 mo	1½–2 yr	3–3½ yr
8–10	+4.7	+7.5	+12.0
14–16	+2.0	+5.7	+8.7

[a] From Williams (1974).

(+25 VOT). AX discrimination functions showed peaks of accurate discrimination that could be predicted from identification functions. In a second experiment, Wolf replicated these findings with an apical VOT dimension (0 VOT to +80 VOT).

Menyuk and Anderson (1969) studied the identification of three dimensions that distinguish place-of-articulation in approximants (/w/ vs. /r/; /r/ vs. /l/; and /w/ vs. /l/) by 4- to 5-year-olds and by 10-year-olds. They found that the younger children were less consistent in their identification of the synthetic series than were the older children and adults given the same task. However, even the adults' identification functions showed inconsistency in labeling these stimulus series. The authors suggest that this could have been due either to the poor quality of the synthetic stimuli or to the fact that all *three* response alternatives were permitted on each condition in which only two intended phonemes were contrasted. Given the results for adults, it is difficult to draw any firm conclusions with respect to developmental trends in phonemic perception.

Williams (1974, experiment III) studied the perception of stimuli varying in VOT by Spanish-speaking children learning English as a second language. She tested six groups of children who differed in age (8–10 years vs. 14–16 years) and amount of exposure to English (0–6 months vs. 1½–2 years vs. 3–3½ years) on identification and discrimination of a labial VOT series. As Table 2 illustrates, boundaries differed primarily as a function of exposure to English. All groups showed crossovers somewhere between the adult monolingual Spanish boundary (−4 VOT) and the monolingual English boundary (+25 VOT). However, the crossover point was shifted more toward the English postvoiced location for the longer exposure groups. Further, for the same exposure duration, the younger children's boundaries were shifted more than were the older children's. That is, the shift from a Spanish to an English phoneme boundary appears to have taken place more rapidly for the younger children.

The results of AX discrimination tests for these groups were somewhat unusual in that the peaks of most accurate discrimination did not occur at the identification boundaries. The younger children in all exposure groups discriminated best the + 10 VOT/ + 30 VOT comparison pair, which fell within the /p/ identification category for all but the longest-exposure group. For the older children discrimination was again best for the + 10/ + 30 comparison, although pairs in the region of the Spanish monolingual boundary were also discriminated better than intraphonemic pairs.

Streeter and Landauer (1976) tested Kikuyu children of four ages (7½, 10, 13, and 15 years) on their perception of VOT differences in labial stop consonants. Kikuyu children begin to learn English as a second language in the second grade (about 8 years old). As stated previously, Kikuyu has but a single prevoiced labial stop, but it does distinguish between prevoiced and voiced stops with apical and velar place-of-articulation. Discrimination of three pairs of labial stimuli (− 30/0 VOT, + 10/ + 40 VOT, and + 50 / + 80 VOT) was tested using an oddity discrimination paradigm. While none of the age groups showed significant discrimination of the + 50/ + 80 pair, all groups showed above chance discrimination of the other two comparisons. However, as Fig. 10 shows, the greatest accuracy in discrimination was for the + 10/ + 40 VOT pair; discrimination improved markedly with age (and exposure to English) for this comparison. However, there was also some improvement with age and exposure in discrimination of the − 30/0 VOT pair that is not contrasted in English, nor in Kikuyu in labial stops.

From these limited data on but a few acoustic dimensions it is not possible to draw any firm conclusions about the effects of linguistic experience on the development of phonetic perception. The studies reviewed here, however,

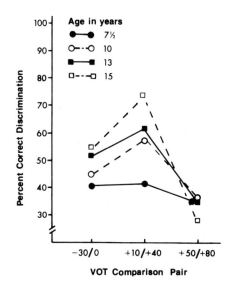

Fig. 10. Discrimination of labial VOT comparison pairs by Kikuyu children learning English as a second language. Redrawn from Streeter and Landauer (1976).

suggest that interaction of at least two factors is at work in the course of development. The perception of some acoustic differences that cue phonetic distinctions appears to change rather gradually as a function of linguistic exposure, while the perception of other dimensions (or values along specific dimensions) appears to be more a result of "built-in" capacities. More research is needed on the perception of dimensions other than VOT by children from different linguistic environments to determine the exact nature of the interaction.

It is of interest to ask two additional questions about the role of linguistic experience in the development of phonetic perception: (1) Are there *critical periods* during which exposure to a particular linguistic environment has maximal effects on perceptual development? and (2) What is the relationship between articulatory development and the development of phonetic perception?

6.3. Critical Periods in Perceptual Development

With respect to the first question, anecdotal evidence from second-language learning suggests that there are major differences in how children and adults learn a second language. Adults appear to have a great deal more difficulty than children do in learning to produce phonemic contrasts of a second language as a native speaker would (i.e., learning to speak without an accent). Less is known about possible differences in how adults and children differ in their facility for learning to perceive new phonemic contrasts.

It has been proposed that puberty marks the end of a critical period for language acquisition (Lenneberg, 1967). We might speculate therefore that linguistic exposure before puberty would be more influential in changing phonetic perception than exposure at a later age. Three studies offer some suggestions with respect to this question.

In the study of the discrimination of liquids by Japanese adults (Miyawaki *et al.*, 1975), three of the Japanese subjects were reported as exceptional in that they produced peaked discrimination functions for speech stimuli that were highly similar to the results for American listeners. Two of these three subjects had attended schools from the ages of 12 to 16 years in countries whose languages included the liquid distinction under study (English and German). While English is taught as a second language in Japan starting in the primary grades, this training stresses reading and writing; conversational English is not emphasized. All the other Japanese in this study had received English-language training of this sort.

Williams's (1974) data on 8- to 10-year-olds and 14- to 16-year-olds showed differences in the speed with which these children modified their phoneme identifications upon exposure to a second language. This may reflect a critical difference between the two ages, or it may indicate a gradual change with age. Longitudinal studies and more extensive cross-sectional investigations are needed to differentiate between the two possibilities.

Doty (1971) addressed the issue of critical periods in a training study with 10- and 11-year-olds. Using a technique similar to that used by Strange described above (Strange, 1972, experiment 1), Doty attempted to train five children to discriminate differences in the full labial VOT dimension (-150 VOT to $+150$ VOT). Results showed that improvement occurred primarily for pairs to the prevoiced side of the original English phoneme boundary, as was the case for college-age subjects reported by Strange. Posttraining discrimination by the children showed broad peaks of accurate discrimination for VOT differences around simultaneity, i.e., in the region of the Spanish and English monolingual phoneme boundaries. There was no systematic improvement in discrimination of prevoiced pairs straddling the Thai phoneme boundary, although two subjects showed more improvement in this region than did any of the adults. We can conclude that performance by the 10- and 11-year-olds was not qualitatively different from that shown by college-age subjects using this training procedure. Much more research is needed using other stimulus dimensions and improved training techniques such as those developed by Carney *et al.* (1977) in order to determine the potential importance of critical periods for phonetic perceptual development.

6.4. Relationship of Perception and Production

Related to the question of *when* linguistic experience has its greatest effect on the development of phonetic perception is the question of *what kinds* of experience are important in the modification of perceptual processes. In particular, we are interested in the relation between the development and modification of phonetic production (articulation) and phonetic perception. Here, too, there is scant empirical information (see Menyuk, 1974). However, results of the few studies that have been reported suggest some promising areas in which this relationship could be explored experimentally.

A study by Goto (1971) with adult Japanese-English bilinguals on the production and perception of liquids /l/ and /r/ yielded fascinating results. Goto recorded pairs of words which contrasted these phonemes spoken by both American and Japanese speakers, (e.g., "lead" and "read", "pray" and "play"). Several of the Japanese speakers produced tokens that American listeners could differentiate without error. In other words, some of the Japanese could produce the distinction appropriately. These subjects were then asked to discriminate recorded tokens of their own productions and those of American speakers. Results showed that they could not accurately discriminate the liquid phonemes even in their own productions! That is, these subjects were unable to discriminate the English phonemic distinction (in recorded words) even though they were able to produce the distinction appropriately, as judged by listening panels of native English speakers. This remarkable finding emphasizes the extreme difficulty adults apparently have learning to perceive auditorily a nonnative distinction. It also points to the importance of preprogramming or use of feedback other than auditory input (i.e., kinesthetic feedback) in controlling these subject's articulation.

It may be surmised that, for adults, production and (auditory) perception of phonemic distinctions not found in their native language are not necessarily closely related. But what about children learning their first or second language? Menyuk and Anderson (1969) noted that the ability of 4- to 5-year-olds to produce /w/, /l/, and /r/ in a repetition task was less accurate than their ability to identify these phonemes. They proposed that the developmental trend was as follows: (1) inability to either identify or reproduce specific phonemic differences, (2) ability to identify differences but the inability to reproduce them, and, finally, (3) the ability to identify and reproduce the phonemic differences.

Edwards (1974) tested English-speaking children ages 1:8 to 3:11 on their ability to perceive and produce phonemic distinctions in stops, fricatives, and approximants. She was interested in whether perception of particular distinctions preceded their accurate production and whether there was a systematic sequence of acquisition of phonemic distinctions. Perceptual tests employed a live-voice technique (Garnica, 1973) so that we cannot be sure on what acoustic basis the perception was determined. From extensive tests with 28 children, Edwards concluded that (1) phonemic perception develops in a gradual and patterned way; (2) perception of a particular phonemic difference generally precedes correct production of that difference; (3) order of acquisition tends to be uniform but the details vary greatly; and (4) the order of development in perception may not be identical with the order in production.

Studies of children who misarticulate particular sounds (Locke and Goldstein, 1971; Aungst and Frick, 1964; McReynolds, Kohn, and Williams, 1975; Chaney and Menyuk, 1975) have also indicated some perceptual deficits that appear to be closely related to production errors. Because of the wide variety of techniques used to test perception and production, however, it is not possible to draw any general conclusions about the relation of perception and production in the normal (or abnormal) acquisition of first-language phonology.

With respect to second-language learning by children, there are even fewer experimental data on the relation between perception and production. Williams (1974) notes that there was a shift in the production of both English and Spanish words by young learners of English accompanying the shift in perception, and that the shift was more rapid for the younger children. Thus, with exposure to English, native Spanish-speaking children showed both a decrease in their Spanish accent in the production of English words and an increase in interference from English in their production of words in Spanish.

6.5. Summary of the Developmental Research

Although work in the development of phonetic perception is mainly of recent origin and still very sparse, there is enough material to indicate a rich and interesting field. Infant studies suggest that prior to any extended linguistic experience, several "natural" phonetic boundaries may be observed. Such boundaries have been found even in linguistic environments where such distinctions are not utilized by the adult speakers. Yet, adult studies across languages show marked insensitivity to acoustic dimensions that do not have phonemic significance in the adult's language. Thus, it appears that appreciable modification of innate sensitivities takes place over the formative years while one acquires his native language.

Studies of the perception of speech by children during this developmental period are rare, but the data available at this time suggest that even very young children identify appropriate synthetic speech stimuli as adults do. There is also a suggestion, however, that they do not differentiate the speech categories as sharply as do adults. In spite of this possibility, categorical perception along the VOT continuum has been shown even in kindergarten children.

Studies of bilingual children suggest that perception of linguistic boundaries in the second language is a function of both years of exposure to that language and age of the child, with younger children showing more rapid and more complete boundary shifts than older children. There is some suggestion that there is a critical period in acquiring the sound system of a new language; it appears that, after adolescence, perceptual systems for speech are somewhat intractable.

There is little systematic knowledge concerning the relation between linguistic production and linguistic perception, but what there is suggests that production and perception are relatively independent in adults. Research with children suggests that perception of a phonemic distinction ordinarily precedes the ability to produce the distinction. Many promising studies of both normal and abnormal development of production and perception can be foreseen.

7. Conclusions and Directions for Future Research

In this chapter we have concentrated on the relatively narrow question of the role of experience in determining the perception of speech at the phonetic level. Within that domain, we have focused on a phenomenon that characterizes much of speech perception, namely, categorical perception. We reviewed the rudiments of this research and briefly summarized some of the most recent research concerning two questions: Is categorical perception unique to speech? and Is categorical perception of speech unique to humans? We then addressed the major concerns of this chapter: To what extent is categorical perception of speech determined by linguistic experience? and Is categorical perception a developmental function of particular language experiences of the child?

In regard to the question of whether categorical perception is unique to speech we concluded that the answer is no. Several sets of complex nonspeech stimuli (usually musical stimuli) have been shown to yield categorical results, at least by experienced or trained listeners for whom the acoustic dimension has some meaning.

As to the question of whether categorical perception of speech is unique to humans, we must give a guarded answer at this time. Animals may be sensitive to some of the dimensions important to phonetic discrimination (although there are major differences between their performance and that of humans). To this extent, the phenomena of speech perception may reflect general auditory capabilities common to many species rather than a species-specific, speech-specialized system unique to humans.

With regard to the question of whether categorical perception is influenced by linguistic experience, the answer is yes. Linguistic experience exerts influence on the discrimination of phonetically relevant acoustic dimensions. Many studies of the VOT dimension show that adults are most sensitive to differences in VOT at just those places along the dimension where their language places a phonemic boundary. The discrimination between /r/ and /l/ likewise appears to be language specific. In similar fashion there is scattered (but convincing) evidence that even within a particular language the perception of a phonetic distinction is highly accurate only in its familiar phonemic and syllabic context.

Although one new technique looks promising, laboratory training studies have had little effect on listeners' ability to discriminate distinctions not employed in the listeners' native language. Overall, it is apparent that linguistic experience does affect perception of variations in speech signals and, further, that differential sensitivities are quite resistant to change in adults.

Finally, with respect to the question of whether categorical perception of speech is a developmental function of the particular language experiences of the growing child, we have seen that a mixed answer is required. Infant studies suggest that some acoustic dimensions may be divided innately into natural categories by the child. On the other hand, there is abundant evidence that such categories may be modified, enhanced, and even suppressed by linguistic experience. Both age of the child and amount of exposure to particular linguistic distinctions appear to be important parameters in determining the rate and amount of change. Challenging research problems are readily evident in this area.

What general conclusion can be drawn from the research reviewed here? We start with the position that categorical perception of speech is a robust and pervasive phenomenon. For most of the phonetically relevant acoustic dimensions studied, discrimination by human listeners is restricted severely by the categorical identity of the variant speech sounds. Continuous perception of speech dimensions is relatively rare. In the case of steady-state vowels, which have been studied most extensively, we have noted that the artificiality of the stimuli may be responsible for the result. Research with vowels in syllable context offers supportive evidence for this contention.

It is possible to demonstrate noncategorical perception of consonantal dimensions by various experimental means (e.g., Barclay, 1972; Pisoni and Lazarus, 1974; Pisoni and Tash, 1974; Carney et al., 1977). While these results challenge the strongest claim of categorical perception—that listeners *cannot* discriminate phonetically irrelevant acoustic differences—we do not think they offer serious obstacles to a study of the major fact of interest here— that people *do not* discriminate acoustic differences that are phonetically irrelevant in a large variety of circumstances.

We turn then to a consideration of the factors that have been shown to influence phonetic perception by humans. The research reviewed here supports the view that categorical perception of speech dimensions is a function of a complex interaction involving both biologically determined tendencies and experiential factors. On the one hand, there is evidence that the human auditory system is especially attuned to some acoustic differences used to differentiate phonemes in many languages. In other words, there may be some "natural boundaries" in acoustic dimensions to which humans are particularly sensitive. We would expect that such boundaries would be exploited by the phonological systems of many languages. The boundary in VOT between simultaneous and postvoiced stop consonants (the "English" boundary) is a strong candidate for such a natural boundary (Stevens and Klatt, 1974). Chinchillas, human infants, and some adults for whom this distinction is not linguistically meaningful have shown relatively accurate discrimination of differences at this point on the VOT dimension. Further research with other dimensions might reveal other natural boundaries in temporal or spectral parameters to which the auditory system is especially attuned.

On the other hand, we see ample evidence that categorical perception of particular acoustic dimensions is strongly influenced by the subjects' linguistic experience. For adults, this shows up as a failure to differentiate differences that are phonemically irrelevant in their language, even though it can be shown that other adults for whom the distinction is phonemic discriminate the differences very accurately. A dramatic example of such a failure is given in the study of Russian speakers by Lisker (1970). Even with training, these subjects did not distinguish sharply between variations in VOT in the region of the "natural" English boundary. The failure of Japanese adults to distinguish between /r/ and /l/ is another example of perception having been modified by linguistic experience. (In both cases the acoustic differences are discriminated by infants but not by the specified adults.)

What is the process by which phonetic perception is modified by linguistic experience? Research of the kind necessary to answer this question is not available, but at least two possibilities must be entertained. First, as suggested by the above examples, the ability, present in infancy, to discriminate some differences appears to "drop out" through linguistic nonuse. In other words, "unlearning" occurs as a function of linguistic experience. Second, discrimination of some distinctions, not present at an early age, develops only for children learning languages that utilize the distinction. For instance, VOT differences that cue the Spanish voicing distinction are discriminated by Spanish adults but not by English speakers. We suspect that both processes go on during the course of phonological development. Cross-sectional studies of the sort initiated by Edwards, Williams, and others with a full range of acoustic dimensions are needed to determine the extent to which both of these processes occur. In addition, it would be fruitful to undertake longitudinal research on the development of phonetic perception from infancy to adulthood in order to get a firm grasp on the coordination of the changes that take place during first-language learning.

We can also look to the case of the abnormal development of language function. Specifically, research on the relationship between articulatory disorders and potential perceptual deficits seems most important, both to our understanding of the underlying processes of development and to the development of effective therapeutic techniques.

Another little-exploited area of research that we think would lead to important insights is that of phonetic perception and production in second-language learning. Again, the data reported in this chapter offer only intriguing hints about aspects of phonetic perception as a function of second-language exposure.

In the course of our treatment of the cross-language studies, it became apparent that a limitation on the interpretation of these studies concerns the question of the appropriateness of the synthetic stimuli. In many cases it appears that ambiguous or misleading results may be obtained because the acoustic dimensions under study fail to capture the information normally utilized by the listener in the perception of natural speech. This calls for a return to the basic questions introduced at the beginning of the chapter. What are the acoustic parameters that differentiate phonetic contrasts? We must expand our knowledge of these parameters for contrasts in several languages so that we can pursue with more confidence the question of the effects of linguistic exposure on perception.

8. References

Abramson, A. S., and Lisker, L. Discriminability along the voicing continuum: Cross-language tests. In *Proceedings of the Sixth International Congress of Phonetic Science*. Prague: Academia, 1970, pp. 569–573.

Abramson, A. S., and Lisker, L. Voice-timing perception in Spanish word-initial stops. *Journal of Phonetics*, 1973, *1*, 1–8.

Aungst, L. F., and Frick, J. V. Auditory discrimination ability and consistency of articulation of /r/, *Journal of Speech and Hearing Disorders*, 1964, *29*, 76–85.

Barclay, J. R. Noncategorical perception of a voiced stop: A replication. *Perception and Psychophysics*, 1972, *11*, 269–273.

Burdick, C. K., and Miller, J. D. Speech perception by the chinchilla: Discrimination of sustained /a/ and /i/. *Journal of the Acoustical Society of America*, 1975, *58*, 415–427.

Burns, E. M., and Ward, W. D. Categorical perception of musical intervals. *86th Meeting of the Acoustical Society of America*, 1973, JJ1,96(A).

Burns, E. M., and Ward, W. D. Further studies in musical interval perception. *Journal of the Acoustical Society of America*, 1975, *58*, Suppl. No. 1: S132(A).

Butterfield, E. C., and Cairns, G. F. Discussion summary: Infant reception research. In R. L. Schiefelbusch and L. L. Lloyd (Eds.), *Language perspectives: Acquisition, retardation and intervention*. Baltimore: University Park Press, 1974, pp. 75–102.

Caramazza, A., Yeni-Komshian, G., Zurif, E., and Carbone, E. The acquisition of a new phonological contrast: The case of stop consonants in French-English bilinguals. *Journal of the Acoustical Society of America*, 1973, *54*, 421–428.

Carney, A. E., Widin, G. P., and Viemeister, N. F. Noncategorical perception of stop consonants differing in VOT. *Journal of the Acoustical Society of America*, 1977, *62*, 961–970.

Chaney, C. F., and Menyuk, P. Production and identification of /w, r, 1, j/ in normal and articulation impaired children. Paper presented at the American Speech and Hearing Association Convention. Washington, D.C., 1975.

Chomsky, N., and Halle, M. *The sound pattern of English*. New York: Harper and Row, 1968.

Cooper, F. S. Research on reading machines for the blind. In P. A. Zahl (Ed.), *Blindness: Modern approaches to the unseen environment*. Princeton, N.J.: Princeton University Press, 1950, pp. 512–543.

Cross, D. V., Lane, H. L., and Sheppard, W. C. Identification and discrimination functions for a visual continuum and their relation to the motor theory of speech perception. *Journal of Experimental Psychology*, 1965, *70*, 63–74.

Cutting, J. E. Different speech-processing mechanisms can be reflected in the results of discrimination and dichotic listening tasks. *Brain and Language*, 1974, *1*, 363–373.

Cutting, J. E., and Eimas, P. D. Phonetic feature analyzers and the processing of speech in infants. In J. F. Kavanagh and J. E. Cutting (Eds.), *The role of speech in language*, Cambridge, Mass.: MIT Press, 1975, pp. 127–148.

Cutting, J. E., and Pisoni, D. B. An information-processing approach to speech perception. In J. F. Kavanagh and W. Strange (Eds.), *Speech and language in the laboratory, school, and clinic*. Cambridge, Mass.: MIT Press, in press.

Cutting, J., and Rosner, B. S. Categories and boundaries in speech and music. *Perception and Psychophysics*, 1974, *16*, 564–570.

Denes, P. B., and Pinson, E. N. *The speech chain*. New York: Bell Telephone Laboratories, 1963.

Dorman, M. F. Auditory evoked potential correlates of speech sound discrimination. *Perception and Psychophysics*, 1974, *15*, 215–220.

Doty, D. Training ten- and eleven-year-olds to discriminate within phoneme boundaries along the voicing continuum. Unpublished manuscript, 1971.

Edwards, M. L. Perception and production in child phonology: The testing of four hypotheses. *Journal of Child Language*, 1974, *1*, 205–219.

Eimas, P. D. The relation between identification and discrimination along speech and nonspeech continua. *Language and Speech*, 1963, *6*, 206–217.

Eimas, P. D. Auditory and linguistic processing of cues for place of articulation by infants. *Perception and Psychophysics*, 1974, *16*, 513–521.

Eimas, P. D. Speech perception in early infancy. In L. B. Cohen and P. Salapatek (Eds.), *Infant perception*. New York: Academic Press, 1975a, pp. 193–231.

Eimas, P. D. Auditory and phonetic coding of the cues for speech: Discrimination of the [r-l] distinction by young infants. *Perception and Psychophysics*, 1975b, *18*, 341–347.

Eimas, P. D. Developmental aspects of speech perception. In R. Held, H. Leibowitz, and H. L. Teuber (Eds.), *Handbook of sensory physiology: Perception*. New York: Springer-Verlag, in press.

Eimas, P. D., Siqueland, E. R., Jusczyk, P., and Vigorito, J. Speech perception in infants, *Science*, 1971, *171*, 303–306.

Fry, D. B., Abramson, A. S., Eimas, P. D., and Liberman, A. M. The identification and discrimination of synthetic vowels. *Language and Speech*, 1962, *5*, 171–189.

Fodor, J. A., Garrett, M. F., and Brill, S. L. Pi ka pu: The perception of speech sounds by prelinguistic infants. *Perception and Psychophysics*, 1975, *18*, 74–78.

Fujisaki, H., and Kawashima, T. On the modes and mechanisms of speech perception. *Annual Report of the Engineering Research Institute*. Vol. 28. Faculty of Engineering, University of Tokyo, Tokyo, 1969, pp. 67–73.

Fujisaki, H., and Kawashima, T. Some experiments on speech perception and a model for the perceptual mechanisms. *Annual Report of the Engineering Research Institute*, Tokyo, 1970, *29*, 207–214.

Garcia, E. Labeling of synthetic nasals. (II) *Haskins Laboratories: Status Report on Speech Research*, 1967a, SR-9.

Garcia, E. Discrimination of three-formant nasal-vowel syllables. (III) *Haskins Laboratories: Status Report on Speech Research*, 1967b, SR-12.

Garnica, O. K. The development of phonemic speech perception. In T. E. Moore (Ed.), *Cognitive development and the acquisition of language*. New York: Academic Press, 1973.

Gerstman, L. J. Perceptual dimensions for the friction portion of certain speech sounds. Unpublished doctoral dissertation. New York University, 1957.

Goto, H. Auditory perception by normal Japanese adults of the sounds "l" or "r". *Neuropsychologia*, 1971, *9*, 317–323.

Harris, K. S. Cues for the discrimination of American English fricatives in spoken syllables. *Language and Speech*, 1958, *1*, 1–17.

Kavanagh, J. F., and Mattingly, I. G. (Eds.) *Language by ear and by eye*. Cambridge, Mass.: MIT Press, 1972.

Kuhl, P. K. Predispositions for the perception of speech-sound categories: A species-specific phenomenon? In Proceedings of the Conference on "Early Behavioral Assessment of the Communicative and Cognitive Abilities of the Developmentally Disabled. Orcas Island, Wash., in press.

Kuhl, P. K., and Miller, J. D. Speech perception by the chinchilla: Voiced-voiceless distinction in alveolar plosive consonants. *Science*, 1975a, *190*, 69–72.

Kuhl, P. K., and Miller, J. D. Speech perception by the chinchilla: Phonetic boundaries for synthetic VOT stimuli. *Journal of the Acoustical Society of America*, 1975b, 57, Suppl. 1, S-49(A).

Ladefoged, P. *A course in phonetics*. New York: Harcourt Brace Jovanovich, 1975.

Lane, H. Motor theory of speech perception: A critical review. *Psychological Review*, 1965, *72*, 275–309.

Lane, H. L. A behavioral basis for the polarity principle in linguistics. *Language*, 1967, *43*, 494–511.

Lane, H. L., and Schneider, B. A. Discriminative control of concurrent responses by the intensity, duration, and relative onset time of auditory stimuli. Unpublished report, Behavior Analysis Laboratory, University of Michigan, 1963.

Larkey, L. S., Wald, J., and Strange, W. Perception and synthetic nasal consonants in initial and final syllable position. *Perception and Psychophysics*, in press.

Lasky, R. E., Syrdal-Lasky, A., and Klein, R. E. VOT discrimination by four to six and a half month old infants from Spanish environments. *Journal of Experimental Child Psychology*, 1975, *20*, 215–225.

Lenneberg, E. *Biological foundations of language*. New York: Wiley, 1967.

Liberman, A. M. The grammars of speech and language. *Cognitive Psychology*, 1970, *1*, 301–323.

Liberman, A. M., Harris, K. S., Hoffman, H. S., and Griffith, B. C. The discrimination of speech sounds within and across phoneme boundaries. *Journal of Experimental Psychology*, 1957, *54*, 358–368.

Liberman, A. M., Harris, K. S., Kinney, J. A., and Lane, H. The discrimination of relative onset time of the components of certain speech and nonspeech patterns. *Journal of Experimental Psychology*, 1961a, *61*, 379–388.

Liberman, A. M., Harris, K. S., Eimas, P. D., Lisker, L., and Bastian, J. An effect of learning on speech perception: The discrimination of durations of silence with and without phonetic significance. *Language and Speech*, 1961b, *4*, 175–195.

Liberman, A. M., Cooper, F. S., Shankweiler, D. P., and Studdert-Kennedy, M. Perception of the speech code. *Psychological Review*, 1967, *74*, 431–461.

Lisker, L. On learning a new contrast. *Haskins Laboratories: Status Report on Speech Research*, 1970, SR-24, 1–17.

Lisker, L., and Abramson, A. S. A cross-language study of voicing in initial stops: Acoustical measurements. *Word*, 1964, *20*, 384–422.

Lisker, L., and Abramson, A. S. The voicing dimension: Some experiments in comparative phonetics. In *Proceedings of the Sixth International Congress of Phonetic Science*, Prague: Academia, 1970, pp. 563–567.

Locke, J. L., and Goldstein, J. I. Children's identification and discrimination of phonemes. *British Journal of Disorders of Communication*, 1971, *6*, 107–112.

Locke, S., and Kellar, L. Categorical perception in a non-linguistic mode. *Cortex*, 1973, *9*, 355–369.

Mattingly, I. G., Liberman, A. M., Syrdal, A. K., and Halwes, T. Discrimination in speech and non-speech modes. *Cognitive Psychology*, 1971, *2*, 131–157.

McGovern, K., and Strange, W. The perception of /r/ and /l/ in syllable-initial and syllable-final position. *Perception and Psychophysics*, 1977, *21*, 162–170.

McReynolds, L. V., Kohn, J., and Williams, G. C. Articulatory-defective children's discrimination of their production errors. *Journal of Speech and Hearing Disorders*, 1975, *40*, 327–338.

Menyuk, P. Early development of perceptive language: From babbling to words. In R. L. Schiefelbusch and L. L. Lloyd (Eds.), *Language perspectives: Acquisition, retardation and intervention*. Baltimore: University Park Press, 1974, pp. 213–236.

Menyuk, P., and Anderson, S. Children's identification and reproduction of /w/, /r/ and /l/. *Journal of Speech and Hearing Research*, 1969, *12*, 39–52.

Miller, C. L., and Morse, P. A. The "heart" of categorical speech discrimination in young infants. *Infant Development Laboratory Research Status Report No. 1*. Madison, Wis.: Waisman Center on Mental Retardation in Human Development, University of Wisconsin, 1975, pp. 182–200.

Miller, J. D. Audibility curve of the chinchilla. *Journal of the Acoustical Society of America*, 1970, *48*, 513–523.

Miller, J. D., Wier, C. C., Pastore, R. E., Kelly, W. J., and Dooling, R. J. Discrimination and labeling of noise-buzz sequences with varying noise lead times: An example of categorical perception. *Journal of the Acoustical Society of America*, 1976, *60*, 410–417.

Miller, J. L., and Eimas, P. D. Studies on the perception of place and manner of articulation: A comparison of the labial-alveolar and nasal-stop distinctions. *Journal of the Acoustical Society of America*, 1977, *61*, 835–845.

Miller, G. A. The magical number seven, plus or minus two, or some limits on our capacity for processing information. *Psychological Review*, 1956, *63*, 81–96.

Miyawaki, K., Strange, W., Verbrugge, R. R., Liberman, A. M., Jenkins, J. J., and Fujimura, O. An effect of linguistic experience: The discrimination of [r] and [l] by native speakers of Japanese and English. *Perception and Psychophysics*, 1975, *18*, 331–340.

Morse, P. A. The discrimination of speech and nonspeech stimuli in early infancy. *Journal of Experimental Child Psychology*, 1972, *14*, 477–492.

Morse, P. A. Infant speech perception: A preliminary model and review of the literature. In R. L. Schiefelbusch and L. L. Lloyd (Eds.), *Language perspectives: Acquisition, retardation and intervention*. Baltimore: University Park Press, 1974, pp. 19–53.

Morse, P. A. Speech perception in the human infant and the rhesus monkey. Conference on Origins and Evolution of Language and Speech. *Annals of the New York Academy of Science*, in press.

Morse, P. A., and Snowdon, C. T. An investigation of categorical speech discrimination by rhesus monkeys. *Perception and Psychophysics*, 1975, *17*, 9–16.

Pisoni, D. B. On the nature of categorical perception of speech sounds. Ph.D. dissertation, University of Michigan, 1971.

Pisoni, D. B. Auditory and phonetic memory codes in the discrimination of consonants and vowels. *Perception and Psychophysics*, 1973, *13*, 253–260.

Pisoni, D. B. Identification and discrimination of the relative onset time of two component tones: Implications for voicing perception in stops. *Journal of the Acoustical Society of America*, 1977, *61*, 1352–1361.

Pisoni, D. B., and Lazarus, J. H. Categorical and noncategorical modes of speech perception along the voicing continuum. *Journal of the Acoustical Society of America*, 1974, *55*, 328–333.

Pisoni, D. B., and Sawusch, J. R. Some stages of processing in speech perception. In A. Cohen and S. Nooteboom (Eds.), *Structure and process in speech perception*. Heidelberg: Springer-Verlag, 1975.

Pisoni, D. B., and Tash, J. Reaction times to comparisons within and across phonetic categories. *Perception and Psychophysics*, 1974, *15*, 285–290.

Pollack, I. The information in elementary auditory displays. *Journal of the Acoustical Society of America*, 1952, *24*, 745–749.

Port, D. K., and Yeni-Komshian, G. H. Use of a scaling technique in the perception of stop consonants along a voicing continuum. Unpublished manuscript, 1971.

Potter, R. K., Kopp, G. A., and Green, H. C. *Visible speech*. New York: Van Nostrand, 1947.

Raphael, L. J. Preceding vowel duration as a cue to the perception of the voicing characteristic of word-final consonants in American English. *Journal of the Acoustical Society of America*, 1972, *51*, 1296–1303.

Siegel, J. A., and Siegel, W. Categorical perception of tonal intervals: Musicians can't tell *sharp* from *flat*. *Perception and Psychophysics*, 1977, *21*, 399–407.

Stevens, K. N. Toward a model for speech recognition. *Journal of the Acoustical Society of America*, 1960, *32*, 47–55.

Stevens, K. N. On the relations between speech movements and speech perception. *Zeitschrift für Phonetik, Sprachwissenschaft und Kommunikations Forschung*, 1968, *21*, 102–106.

Stevens, K. N., and Halle, M. Remarks on analysis by synthesis and distinctive features. In W. Wathen-Dunn (Ed.), *Models for the perception of speech and visual form*. Cambridge, Mass.: MIT Press, 1967, pp. 88–102.

Stevens, K. N., and House, A. S. Speech perception. In J. Tobias (Ed.), *Foundations of modern auditory theory*, Vol. 2. New York: Academic Press, 1972, pp. 3–62.

Stevens, K. N., and Klatt, D. H. Role of formant transitions in the voiced-voiceless distinction for stops. *Journal of the Acoustical Society of America*, 1974, *55*, 653–659.

Stevens, K. N., Liberman, A. M., Studdert-Kennedy, M., and Ohman, S. Cross-language study of vowel perception. *Language and Speech*, 1969, *12*, 1–23.

Strange, W. The effects of training on the perception of synthetic speech sounds: Voice onset time. Unpublished doctoral dissertation, University of Minnesota, 1972.

Streeter, L. A. The effects of linguistic experience on phonetic perception. Unpublished dissertation, Columbia University, New York, 1974.

Streeter, L. A., and Landauer, T. K. Effects of learning English as a second language on the acquisition of a new phonemic contrast. *Journal of the Acoustical Society of America*, 1976, *59*, 448–451.

Studdert-Kennedy, M. The perception of speech. In T. A. Sebeok (Ed.), *Current trends in linguistics*. Vol. XII. The Hague: Mouton, 1974.

Studdert-Kennedy, M. Speech perception. In N. J. Lass (Ed.), *Contemporary issues in experimental phonetics*. New York: Academic Press, 1976, pp. 243 293.

Studdert-Kennedy, M., Liberman, A. M., Harris, K. S., and Cooper, F. S. Motor theory of speech perception: A reply to Lane's critical review. *Psychological Review*, 1970, 77, 234–249.

Vinegrad, M. D. A direct magnitude scaling method to investigate categorical vs. continuous modes of speech perception. *Language and Speech*, 1972, 15, 114–121.

Waters, R. S., and Wilson, W. A., Jr. Speech perception by rhesus monkeys: The voicing distinction in synthesized labial and velar stop consonants. *Perception and Psychophysics*, 1976, 19, 285–289.

Williams, L. Speech perception and production as a function of exposure to a second language. Unpublished doctoral dissertation, Harvard University, Cambridge, Mass., 1974.

Winterkorn, J. M. S., MacNeilage, R. F., and Preston, M. S. Perception of voiced and voiceless stop consonants in three-year-old children. *Haskins Laboratories: Status Report on Speech Research*, 1967, SR-11.

Wolf, C. G. The perception of stop consonants by children. *Journal of Experimental Child Psychology*, 1973, 16, 318–331.

Zlatin, M. A., and Koenigsknecht, R. A. Development of the voicing contrast: Perception of stop consonants. *Journal of Speech and Hearing Research*, 1975, 18, 541–553.

6

Cultural Effects on Pictorial Perception: How Many Words Is One Picture Really Worth?

MARGARET A. HAGEN AND REBECCA K. JONES

1. Introduction

Why would anyone study pictorial perception cross-culturally? Two reasons are given in the literature. The first is to identify group differences among cultures in their understanding of pictorial materials. This reason is pragmatic. Pictures are ubiquitous in urban, industrialized cultures and we rely on their information-carrying value in teaching, testing, transportation, communications, industry, etc. In the past, the unspoken assumption has been that specific experience with pictures was not a necessary prerequisite to understanding them since it was commonly held that a picture was indeed worth at least a thousand words. However, this unspoken assumption was not always supported by the experiences of people in nonurban/industrialized cultures. Reports began to appear on the general inadequacy of pictorial materials as universal and culture-independent instruments of communication and the cross-cultural picture work was begun. The aim of the work is to identify groups failing to perceive in the previously expected manner and to isolate the causes of that failure, e.g., absence of Western schooling.

The second reason for studying picture perception cross-culturally is less

MARGARET A. HAGEN • Department of Psychology, Boston University, Boston, Massachusetts 02215.   REBECCA K. JONES • Department of Psychology, University of Edinburgh, Edinburgh, Scotland. The research and writing of this chapter were supported in part by a grant to the first author from the National Institute of Mental Health, No. 1R01MH27947-0.

immediately pragmatic and more general in scope. The aim is to understand pictorial perception *per se,* to specify the nature of depiction itself and the perceptual processes involved in its comprehension. This endeavor addresses the problem of the relationship between picture and pictured reality and the question of the special character of pictorial perception within a larger characterization of the perceptual process in general.

We would like to argue that one cannot adequately identify and describe group differences in pictorial perception without a careful specification of the nature of the depiction employed in the determination of those differences. Further, in order to adequately specify the nature of the depiction used, one must know where the picture fits into a systematic, theoretical analysis of pictures and pictorial perception in general. The field offers a range of such analyses, the two extremes of which are represented by the positions occupied by Gibson (1950, 1966, 1971) and Goodman (1968). Gibson argues that there is a physical resemblance of some order between a picture and its subject. The information contained in the delimited optic array coming from a picture is the same kind of information as that found in the optic array of the ordinary environment, according to Gibson. Thus, such pictorial components as size, linear, texture and aerial perspective, overlapping, shadows, and projective height all bear a specifiable geometric relationship to the scene generating them. Work on the specification of such monocular information for size, distance, slant, etc. was begun by Gibson and has been continued by his students, e.g., Purdy (1960), Sedgwick (1973), and Kennedy (1974). That such monocular information can function as well in pictures as in real scenes is evident from the success of *trompe-l'oeil* art wherein pictures are often mistaken for their models. That is, observers can not tell the picture from the "real thing."

In diametric opposition to Gibson's position is that of Goodman (1968), who rejects absolutely and explicitly any notion of resemblance between pictures and the world they represent. A picture as a representation is an instance of a system of arbitrarily assigned pictorial labels. It is only through understanding of the pictorial label system that pictures are given meaning and informative function. Goodman rejects any attempt to root pictorial labels in an objective analysis of the structure of the visible world. For him, realism, and thus resemblance, is relative, determined solely by the system of the pictorial labels standard for a given culture or person at a given time. All pictures must be read according to a culturally standardized system. We read pictures painted in ordinary perspective and normal color almost effortlessly because practice has made our pictorial symbol system so automatic that we have lost awareness of its order-giving functions. We can see no other alternatives and the ease of interpretation of a picture depends only on how stereotyped the mode of representation has become. According to Goodman, realism is a matter of habit and that a picture looks like nature often means only that it looks the way nature is usually painted.

Support for Goodman's position comes from the observation that artists and photographers often violate the laws of geometry, principally perspective, in order to produce natural-looking pictures. Similarly, most ordinary pictures appear to be substantially removed from *trompe-l'oeil* or laboratory situations. Many pictures are modified or impoverished in a variety of ways and often contain components completely absent from the ordinary visual environment. Thus, one may agree with Gibson that fully colored and textured, geometrically accurate pictures contain the same kind of information as that found in the non-pictorial world, and still question the informational equivalence and perceptual effectiveness of impoverished or modified pictures. Gibson (1971) is willing to extend the principle of formal equivalence between picture and subject even to caricature, but the question of perceptual equivalence must be explored empirically.

The field of cross-cultural picture perception is clearly an excellent arena for the contestants in this debate. The testing of subjects from relatively pictureless environments will allow us to address the questions of informational equivalence, impoverishment, and modification as well as the informational content of artistic options in style cross-culturally and historically. To this end, we will undertake a review of the literature in terms of the information contained in, deleted from, and modified by the pictorial materials used in cross-cultural investigation, while addressing at the same time general problems of pictorial perception attendant upon the use of any such materials.

2. Trivial Projective Ambiguity: Fully Colored and Detailed Pictures

The problem which we are calling "trivial projective ambiguity" arises in pictures because any single, static projection of a real object or scene is infinitely ambiguous geometrically. This problem has been treated in endless detail for centuries and need not be elaborated here. Suffice it to say that any single two-dimensional projection, on retina, paper, canvas, or screen, could be a geometrically correct projection from an infinite number of three-dimensional models. How then is the observer ever to decide which three-dimensional object or scene serves as model for the present projection? Gibson (1950, 1966), Purdy (1960), Kennedy (1974), and Hagen (1974) have all argued that there is sufficient information in such single views provided by color, texture, edges, and shadow information to completely rewrite the projective ambiguity question from the days of Berkeley's (1709) argument that distance is presented two-dimensionally only as a point. (A good presentation of the different treatments of the projective ambiguity issue is presented in Bower 1974.) It is clear that a two-dimensional projection can contain far more information about the size, shape, distance, and location of three-dimensional objects than was suggested before Gibson's reformulation of the problem in 1950. But even Gibson (1966) recognized the persistence of geometric projective ambiguity despite the richness of the newly specified sources of information. He argued that only motion perspective, the systematic motion-generated changes in perspective view occasioned by observer movements, is sufficient, strictly speaking, to provide unambiguous, unequivocal information for the layout of surfaces in the environment. We think that whereas this is true logically and geometrically, it may not be true perceptually. To take an example, let us suppose that the observer is presented with a single static view of an ordinary scene filled with ordinary objects, for instance, a field with three cows, a man, and a pond. If the scene contains full color, texture, shadow and edge information, what alternative percepts are available to the observer? Our observer may see (1) a field, three cows, one man, etc., (2) a picture of a field, three cows, one man, etc., or (3) a real scene so ecologically unlikely that it would never occur to our naive observer. Thus we would like to argue that the problem of trivial projective ambiguity is indeed trivial, perceptually, and that the cross-cultural literature provides evidence for the lack of perceived ambiguity in full color, fully informative two-dimensional projections.

Unfortunately, despite the many years of existence of colored film—and, before film, paint and crayons—colored pictures are very seldom used in the work on cross-cultural picture perception, so the evidence we have to offer is somewhat limited. Segall, Campbell, and Herskovits (1966) write, "It is interesting that the experience of anthropologists shows that motion pictures are almost universally perceived without trouble and that colored prints are also—although here the naivete of the respondents may be questioned in more recent field experience" (p. 33). It is interesting to note that these authors also suggest that cut-out photographs done so that object and paper contours coincide, and line drawings, would be better perceived than ordinary photographs. These points will be discussed below. Deregowski (1976), one of the foremost researchers in the field, cites Lloyd (1904) on the immediate response of unsophisticated viewers to richly detailed photographic transparencies. Indeed, Deregowski goes so far as to say, "I shall not concern myself with pictures, such as the above transparency, which approximate to reality so closely as to be mistaken for it, but with pictures that depict reality showing sufficient clarity to be readily recognizable in one culture and yet present difficulties in another, since only such pictures can tell us what happens when we see a *picture* for the first time" (1976, p. 20). It is apparently this attitude on the part of researchers which accounts for the lack of work using colored pictures, but the only support for the attitude is from anecdote. (Since the Lloyd anecdote cited by Deregowski was from 1904 before the introduction of color film, it is difficult to understand his immediate acceptance of the evidence.) In any case, the only studies to look at the responses of naive subjects to colored, detailed pictures use such pictures as stimuli for reasons incidental to the central hypothesis.

Deregowski, Ellis, and Shepherd (1973) studied recognition memory for colored photographs of faces and cups with British adolescents and Rhodesian adults. The faces were Caucasian for the British subjects and Bantu for the Rhodesians. Cups and mugs were common in both cultures. The authors report that women in both cultures were better at recognizing cups than faces and that this difference was not present for men. They also report that the Africans scored significantly lower overall than the British. However, no direct analysis of number correct was performed. The mean number correct for Africans was as follows: cups, 7/10; faces, 6/10. For the British: cups, 8/10; faces, 8/10. It appears to us that these differences are trivial and indeed the authors dismiss them. As a brief methodological note we would like to point out that the differences between the two groups were not confined to race and culture. The British groups, on the average, had had twice as much schooling as the Africans and were half as old. Also, it is not reasonable to argue that the 5 years of schooling enjoyed by the black Rhodesians in Rhodesia 20 years previous to testing is in any significant way comparable to the 10 years of schooling experienced immediately prior to and during the testing by the White British subjects in Scotland. This type of lack of control is so common to so much of the cross-cultural work that we will refrain from belaboring the point unless we are forced to do so for purposes of clarification and interpretation.

In a study similar to the above, on recognition memory for colored photographs of faces, Shepherd, Deregowski, and Ellis (1974) found that Africans had superior recognition memory for African faces, and British subjects had superior memory for British faces. The makeup of the samples was similar to that described above and again British subjects showed a slight overall superiority. There was no difference in mean number correct among the groups, but there was a slight difference when scores were corrected for false alarms. As the authors themselves point out, the difference is not readily interpreted, since the two groups differed in race, culture, age, education, and experimental conditions. Lastly, in another follow-up study of colored photographs of black and white faces using Bantu and British male adolescents with about 11 years of schooling, Ellis, Deregowski, and Shepherd (1975) found that the verbal descriptions of the photographs given by the black and white samples differed. White subjects paid attention to features of white faces (hair, iris color) which black subjects largely ignored, and black subjects mentioned a greater number of discriminating facial features of black faces than those selected by white subjects from the same stimulus faces. Thus the authors are suggesting that past experience with the content of a photograph may determine the deployment of attention to different aspects of that content.

It is clear from this entire line of work that the recognition of fully colored and detailed photographs poses no particular problem for any of the cultural groups tested. It is true that the literature is very thin on this question, but there is no evidence whatsoever that the "trivial projective ambiguity" of such photographs is even detected perceptually. Indeed, what evidence there is suggests the opposite conclusion: that such pictures are too much like the "real thing" to create problems for members of different cultures. Differential response will most probably lie in the deployment of attention and the attribution of symbolic meaning to these pictures, but, in the absence of controlled work with unsophisticated observers, this conclusion is undoubtedly premature.

3. Conversion of Colored Pictures to Black and White

The conversion of colored pictures to varying degrees of black and white is most commonly the product of black and white photography, although shaded line drawings of sufficient detail are also included in this category. The obvious loss of information resulting from this transformation is the redundant surface information provided by color. While most of the naturally occurring surfaces in the ordinary environment are more or less homogeneously textured, a great many of these surfaces are also more or less homogeneously colored. That the rule is not as fast for color as for texture is obvious from a moment's contemplation of autumn leaves; however, there is still sufficient regularity of color across most surfaces to provide redundant information for changes in surfaces, for discontinuities between objects. It may be argued that such redundant information from color is responsible for the lack of difficulty in perceiving colored pictures encountered by unsophisticated picture observers. On the other hand, even with color removed, pictures such as ordinary black and white photographs still contain a great deal of information for size, shape, distance, and location given by edges, textures, and shadows. It may well be that information provided by these picture components is far more salient to the observer than color information, because they are more reliable sources of information in the ordinary environment. We must also confront here the question of conventionality, because the translation of different colors into various shades of black, white, and gray is, of course, a convention, primarily a by-product of photography. This type of optic array does not normally occur in the ordinary environment unless one wishes to argue the case from gray winter days, snowy landscapes, and twilight. It may be that all people have had at least some experience of naturally muted color, but the case for real achromaticity seems a little farfetched, particularly for people from tropical regions. However, let us see what answers, if any, are offered by the cross-cultural literature.

Black and white photographs were the most common types of pictures shown in early studies to people from relatively pictureless environments and early reports of their responses were primarily anecdotal. Deregowski (1976) cites an 1885 anecdote from Thomson illustrating what is commonly held to be the typical reaction of naive observers to black and white photographs. "To show them photos, and try to explain what I wanted only made them worse.

They imagined I was a magician trying to take possession of their souls, which once accomplished they would be entirely at my mercy" (p. 19). This seems to argue for an immediate recognition of photographic material by naive observers, but Kidd (1904) in *The Essential Kaffir* seems to find great individual differences. He writes: "The natives are frequently quite incapable of seeing pictures at first and wonder what the smudge on the paper is there for. When they see that it represents something they are very excited. Some see a picture instantly, while old men fail to see anything at all no matter how long and patiently one tries to explain the matter to them; occasionally they become irritable because others say they can see the picture" (pp. 282–283). E. S. Muldrow, in Deregowski, Muldrow, and Muldrow (1972), reports that people from a remote Ethiopian tribe when presented with a drawing of an animal would attend to the characteristics of the drawing paper but would ignore the picture. Although these pictures were drawings and not photographs, it is important to note the complete inattention of those subjects to the *content* of the representation while concentrating on the medium. This observation is similar not only to Kidd's but to Herskovits's often quoted anecdote about a Bushwoman presented for the first time with a photograph. He writes: "a Bush Negro woman turned a photograph of her own son this way and that, in attempting to make sense out of the shadings of greys on the piece of paper she held. It was only when the details of the photograph were pointed out to her that she was able to perceive the subject" (in Segall *et al.*, 1966, p. 32).

This line of research indicates that the critical variable in recognition of black and white photographs is again deployment of attention. Many naive subjects seem to experience an "Aha!" phenomenon as soon as their attention is directed to or caught by salient features of the depicted object. This conclusion is buttressed by some rather more systematic work by Deregowski. Deregowski (1968a) studied schoolboys and men from remote Zambia and found that both groups were above chance matching black and white photographs of familiar animals to models. Only the children were above chance matching with unfamiliar animals, but the author points out that the adults' failures cannot be due to detection errors, i.e., failure to see anything at all in the photograph, because no such responses were given and no such difficulty was experienced when the photographs were of familiar animals. In a second study of Zambian and Scottish schoolchildren, Deregowski and Serpell (1971) also found no evidence of detection errors. "Don't know" responses occurred as frequently to three-dimensional models as with colored and black and white photographs. Deregowski (1971a) replicated the finding of no detection errors in another study with illiterate adult females from Lusaka. He used black and white photographs and colored models. Each subject was required to match pictures to pictures, models to models, models to pictures, or pictures to models. Although the last two tasks were more difficult, the error rate never exceeded 13% in any group which certainly argues against detection errors. Nadel (1937) compared the picture perception of the Nupe, a people with imageless art, with the Yoruba, a people with art rich in images, using black and white photographs and found no failures of picture detection in either group, although identifications were frequently rather idiosyncratic or culture bound.

With respect to the black and white photograph work in general, there is no evidence that naive people have any difficulty in recognizing depiction in such photographs once attention is directed to or caught by the features of the content. It seems that the black and white transformation is very simple to learn and that there is sufficient information remaining in the pictures from edges, textures, and shadows to support perception. The extent of the accuracy of that perception in the naive observer is an open question. Children seem to be more successful than old people at picking up relevant information, and Deregowski and Serpell (1971) report that Scottish children sort photographs into finer categories than do Zambian children, but we are not very far forward in specifying the exact nature of these differences. We know, primarily, that they are not differences in the ability to detect the representational character of black and white photographs. Kidd's (1904) observation on the inability of old men to detect representational meaning is the only exception to this conclusion, as will be seen from a further discussion of Muldrow's work below. It is important to note, however, that the field has not looked at the pickup of information in photographed *scenes,* but has concentrated on single *objects.* Also, we lack systematic comparisons of the pickup of information for size, shape, distance, and location in colored photographs versus black and white photographs. We do not know if differences in perception between cultures and the possible detection errors in old men are due to the black and white transformation of the pictures, to the representational character *per se* of the pictures, or to extraneous variables like motivation. We also suggest, as does Miller (1973) in his extensive review of the field, that studies be designed along more psychophysical lines in order to pick up subtle differences among people which simply become lost in all-or-none response measures and categorizations of subjects.

4. Nontrivial Projective Ambiguity: Outline Drawings

This third category of pictures is the largest studied in the field and includes all the pictures known as outline drawings. Outline drawings considered here contain no information from color, texture, or shadows. All the information present is carried by lines depicting the edges of objects and surfaces. It can certainly be argued (e.g., Kennedy, 1974, 1975) that there is still adequate edge information in line drawings to support determinate perception even in naive observers despite the loss of redundant information from color, texture, and shadows. The removal of these latter forms of information does not generate arbitrarily conventional pictures, because the edge information remaining is still equivalent to edge information in the ordinary environment. Thus, response to outline drawings may be independent of culture. But, one may also argue that however equivalent the remaining information to that found in the ordinary environment, such pictures present naive observers with a very unnatural optic array. Objects are depicted as lacking in color and texture and are often floating in space unattached to surfaces. It would not be surprising if perception of the remaining information in these drawings required more substantial learning of a more significant order than the rather simple direction of attention. These are obviously the type of pictures characterized by Deregowski (1976) as pictures of interest to the field as stimuli because they are likely to provide difficulties for some people and not for others. Edge information is certainly present but is it sufficient alone to support perception? If not, what additional factors are required to afford detection of the depicted contents?

As noted above, the field is replete with examples of such pictures, but the review below will again reveal a certain lack of systematicity in task analysis and control. Line drawings have been used for a variety of purposes, not all of which are structured around theories of picture perception. For the sake of convenience, we will discuss the literature by grouping it into the following categories: (1) recognition of pictured objects, (2) Embedded Figures Tests, (3) pictorial depth perception. In each of these categories the only "real world" information preserved in the pictures is edge information.

5. Recognition of Pictured Objects in Line Drawings

The best-known and perhaps most interesting study of the recognition of pictured objects in line drawings was not conducted cross-culturally, but it nevertheless provides a baseline against which to compare the cross-cultural work. Hochberg and Brooks (1962) reared one of their own children until the age of 19 months with extremely restricted exposure to pictures and no exposure to picture-plus-naming experiences. At 19 months he was able to identify successfully simple and complex line drawings and photographs of familiar objects. The line drawings always (except on one presentation) preceded the photographs of the same object in the task. Concerning line drawings, the authors wrote:

> "Ghost shapes," as Gibson has called them, may be anemic, but they are by no means deceased . . . the complete absence of instruction in the present case . . . points to *some* irreducible minimum of native ability for pictorial recognition. If it is true also that there are cultures in which this ability is absent, such deficiency will require special explanation; we cannot assert that it is simply a matter of having not yet learned the 'language of pictures.' " (p. 628)

Whether or not there are cultures in which this ability is absent is still a subject of controversy. In a study of black South African infants between 18 and 36 months of age, Liddicoat and Koza (1963) found that for the number of correct identifications of pictured objects, the infants' performance was comparable to cited norms for American infants of the same age. The investigators noted that pictures were not at all common in the environment of these infants and that the babies responded to the pictures with a spontaneous curiosity and immediate interest. Similarly, Brimble (1963) studied perception of 58 "simple line drawings" in 937 women and 711 men from villages in Northern Rhodesia. The women, on the average, were correct 95% of the time, the men 98% of the time. Brimble says that most mistakes were made by the oldest subjects whom village headmen characterized as not too bright. There is, of course, no way of checking this statement and no further sample characteristics are presented, but the result is consistent with the results above. Some informal findings reported by Warburton (1951), however, are not consistent. Warburton administered ability tests to Gurkha army recruits. He wrote that he had to give up using pictorial tests because the subjects "often failed to recognize pictures even of those objects which they knew quite well" (p. 126). However, the interpretation of this finding is left open by a later comment by Warburton to the effect that "the most striking thing about the recruits was their lack of pep and slowness of movement." He also writes that "there was every indication that they were doing their best" and that the tests were given by Gurkha NCOs. We think it not unlikely that motivational variables greatly influenced the results in Warburton's study. This conclusion is supported by work by Kennedy and Ross (1975) with the Songe of Papua New Guinea, who have little or no indigenous pictorial art. They found that Songe subjects of both sexes of various ages with varying degrees of Western contact were able to identify a wide range of outline drawings depicting objects, animals and human forms. Schooled subjects 10–20 years old were 97% correct. Unschooled subjects 20–40 years old were 91% correct. Unschooled subjects over 40 were 68% correct. This last finding is similar to that of Brimble with his oldest subjects and certainly requires further investigation. The authors also note that in informal testing many of the 40+ Songe who understood outline drawings had trouble recognizing black and white photographs, unlike younger Songe who seemed to encounter no difficulty. This observation lends credence to the suggestion of Segall et. al. (1966) that outline drawings would present fewer difficulties than photographs to naive observers because of their clear contour depiction. It also suggests that contour is far more important than texture, at least for the recognition of single depicted objects. In sum, then, with Warburton aside and the question of older subjects' performance left open, the weight of the evidence supports the hypothesis that edge information alone, depicted by line, is sufficient to support the perception and recognition of objects in pictures by people from relatively pictureless environments. Systematic work comparing perception using line drawings, black and white photographs, and color photographs and caricatures, similar to the pioneer work of Ryan and Schwartz (1956) and

Smith, Smith, and Hubbard (1958) with Western subjects, remains to be done cross-culturally. We may well be surprised at the hierarchy of efficacy of information generated by such research.

6. Embedded Figures Tests

Given the task analysis nature of this review, it is somewhat difficult to explain the presence of Embedded Figures Tests within it, but they compose an ever-growing body of literature dealing with the perception of overlapped line drawings, if you will. So we will deal with them briefly. The purpose of the first study, by Schwitzgebel (1962), was simply to gather "perceptual and cognitive data from normal, young Zulu and Dutch-speaking adults" (p. 73). Among other tests, Schwitzgebel used the Gottshadt Embedded Figures Test and found that mean time to locate figures was 9 sec/figure for the Dutch South Africans and 45 sec/figure for the Zulus. While he also found that Zulus tended to underestimate time and size, the greatest difference between the two groups was on the Embedded Figures Test. Schwitzgebel concludes that "Regardless of the relative contribution of learned and genetic factors, certain visual capacities or potentials of the human being have been suppressed, constricted, lost, or diminished among young Zulus" (p. 76). We think this despondent conclusion is somewhat unwarranted since similar performance to the Zulus is obtained from women all over the world. Witkin (1966; Witkin, Lewis, Hartzman, Machover, Meissner, and Wapner, 1954) is the father of the concept of field dependence, often measured by performance on Embedded Figures Tests. The slower the search, the more field dependent the subject. Witkin (1966) reported that women are more field dependent than men in the United States, England, Holland, France, Italy, Israel, Hong Kong, and Sierra Leone, but that the size of these differences may be diminished by more permissive, independence-oriented childrearing. For example, Berry (1966) found no significant sex differences in field dependence among Eastern Eskimos because, he argues, these Eskimos girls are not reared to be dependent. MacArthur (1967) similarly found with Eskimos near-zero correlations between sex and performance on Embedded Figures Tests. Dawson (1967a, b) took this work to its logical extreme in Sierra Leone, West Africa, in a 4-year study of the Temne and the Mende tribes. Dawson was interested in isolating factors which contribute to field dependence as measured by slow performance on the Embedded Figures Test. He found support for the hypothesis that the following variables correlate with field dependence: strictness of upbringing, maternal dominance, intelligence, traditional attitudes, educational achievement, number of father's wives, sexual bias, and fat. In other words, the cluster of stereotyped feminine attributes leads to more field dependence. Dawson also reports that measures of field dependence can predict performance on three-dimensional picture perception tasks. In cultures where sex differences on Embedded Figures Tests or pictorial depth perception do not occur, the overriding variable is presumably more permissive childrearing practices, more independence training in girls.

For the purposes of this task analysis, this work is primarily important in alerting us to variables which may direct the deployment of attention or indicate the degree of subjects' comfort with a task. These are *not*, after all, studies of detection failures; they are studies of varying lengths of time to trace out overlapped figures in line drawings. We may be dealing with a single variable more properly labeled "self-confidence" than "femininity." In any case, people all over the world appear to treat the task as a relatively simple one. While we lack good descriptions of the samples in terms of experience with line drawings, a great many of the subjects have been illiterates from relatively pictureless environments, who nevertheless perform the task. Again, this provides evidence for the importance of information carried by depicted edges in line drawings, even for the unsophisticated observer.

7. Pictorial Depth Perception

So far we have dealt only with the depiction of isolated objects in outline drawings and have concluded that such drawings pose very few problems for naive observers. The perception of spatial relations, however—particularly depth—in outline drawings may well present the naive observer with problems of another order. Gibson (1950), Purdy (1960), and many others have argued that relative size, distance, and slant of objects and surfaces is given monocularly by gradient information—gradients of texture, height, width, density and compression, the gradient of size perspective, and the gradient of linear perspective. It is formally true as demonstrated by Purdy (1960) that all of these gradients are equivalent to one another and thus should equivalently specify the size, shape and slant of surfaces. However, formal mathematical equivalence may be one thing and perceptual equivalence another. That is, there may be considerable difference between perceiving relative distance in a picture showing the texture gradient from a receding cobblestone road and perceiving relative distance in a picture representing only the edges of that road receding to a vanishing point on the horizon. Similarly, in the ordinary environment, the horizon line marks the end of a continuously compressing gradient of texture stretching from one's feet out to the visual border with the textureless sky. Whether or not a single horizontal line drawn across a sheet of paper will function similarly as such a marker is an open question. Ideally we would like to report on a series of studies graded regularly from those using richly detailed geometrically correct and continuously textured drawings down to studies using very impoverished, minimal sketch drawings. Such a presentation would allow us to consider, for instance, whether depiction of a continuous gradient of texture was necessary to successful perception of a horizon line, but no such series of studies exists. We will start with geometrically inaccurate minimal sketches and effectively end with them. Thus this section should be more appropriately titled "Pictorial depth perception in geometrically inaccurate, texture-free outline drawings."

The original study in this field of work is that of Hudson (1960), who devised and published the Hudson Pictorial Depth Perception Test, which has since been used repeatedly by Hudson and many other investigators. The test consists of 12 pictures, six depicting horizontal space, five depicting vertical space, and one depicting horizontal space by a photograph of models. The test employs depth cues of relative size, overlap and linear perspective. Hudson tested 11 South African samples, white and black, schooled and unschooled, students, teachers, clerks, and laborers. Results are analyzed by depth cue. About 50% of the children in Standard 6 grade, whether white or black, perceive depth in pictures as measured by Hudson's criteria. Sometimes the percentage on a particular cue favors the black children, sometimes the white. Literate (primary school) laborers, white or black, who live isolated from the dominant community generally fail to report seeing depth in Hudson's pictures. Also, older school children, whether white or black, are categorized as three-dimensional perceivers more often than younger children. The older black children are categorized as three-dimensional perceivers more often then the older white children on the vertical set of pictures and the white children are more often categorized as three-dimensional perceivers on the horizontal pictures. With the photograph there is no difference. Both groups of older schoolchildren are more frequently categorized as three-dimensional perceivers than are the black teachers or clerks. Hudson notes:

> With all samples except high school pupils (black) and graduate teachers (black) responses whether 3D or 2D, were immediate. With the two samples specified hesitation in responding was noticeable and was particularly pronounced with the graduate teachers, some of whom took as long as one hour per picture to respond. . . . Candidates asked the tester for information on the mode of perception because there were to them two possibilities, viz., 2D or 3D, and they appealed for guidance in their perceptual choice (p. 203)

Such guidance was presumably not given since many of these subjects were classified as two-dimensional perceivers. It is not at all clear to us, however, how a person who can see a picture *both* as flat *and* in depth and *says* so can then be classified only as a two-dimensional picture perceiver. This is not reasonable. Nor is it reasonable to then take such data and argue for the importance of informal cultural training on pictorial depth perception. We said we would not belabor methodological points, but this study is taken far too often to demonstrate that black Africans do not see depth in pictures as often as white Africans, and there is no solid data basis for such a statement. Recall that neither white nor black literate laborers living in "cultural isolation" were categorized as three-dimensional perceivers. Hudson argues that such cultural isolation retards or prevents what he calls the process of pictorial depth perception, but it seems far more likely that cultural experience significantly affects one's attitude toward test-taking, whether it is the isolation experienced by the white and black laborers, or the occupational hazards experienced by black teachers and clerks in South Africa. It is also noteworthy that of the black clerks 70% were between 21 and 40 years of age and 25% were over 40. Mean age for the group is not given, but it seems likely that the schooling of these men took place at least 15 years prior to testing in South Africa.

A very full treatment of numerous methodological difficulties with Hudson's test can be found in Jahoda and McGurk (1974a), and a general treatment of further cross-cultural methodological points in Heron (1968). For the purpose of this analysis, however, we would like to discuss just two aspects of Hudson's work: (1) results on the photograph compared to results with the line drawings and (2) the adequacy of the information contained in the drawings and photograph. To create the photograph, the human figure, the elephant, and the antelope were modeled to scale and photographed to produce a scene somewhat similar to that depicted in the line drawing, P_1, which contained only size cues (see Fig. 1). Table 1 shows the results of the comparison of responses to these two pictures. The increase in three-dimensional responding with the photograph is striking, although for some reason Hudson does not discuss it. What can account for the dramatic increase in depth perception since the single depth cue of size was constant across both pictures? Observation of Fig. 1 may give us the

Table 1. Comparison of Percent of 3D Responders on Outline Drawings (P_1 and P_4) and Photograph

	Outline: size (P_1) (%)	Photo (%)	Percent difference P_1 vs. photo	Outline: perspective P_4 (%)	Percent difference P_4 vs. photo
White school age: standard 1, grade 1	26	72	46	29	43
White school age: standard 6, grade 1	47	85	38	57	28
Black school age: standard 6	50	76	26	53	23
Black teachers (graduate)	56	92	36	60	32
Black school age: standards 8 and 10	69	81	12	62	19
White school age: standards 5 and 6	75	100	25	81	19

Fig. 1. Outline drawing and photograph containing size cues from Hudson's pictorial depth perception test. From Hudson (1960).

answer. What information does the photograph provide which is lacking in the line drawing? Both pictures give us relative size cues, but only the photograph gives us a continuous texture gradient from hunter to horizon—information for a continuous surface receding in space. The line drawing depicts a bolder coplanar with the hunter topped by a bonsai tree and the world's smallest adult elephant. It is not at all surprising that with the additional distance information in the photograph more people responded "three-dimensionally." It is also useful to consider the comparison between the photograph and the line drawing containing central linear perspective, P_4 (see Fig. 2) (The percent of 3D responses to P_4 is very similar to that obtained with P_5 and P_6 also containing linear perspective.) The result of this comparison is also summarized in Table 1

Fig. 2. Outline drawing containing central linear perspective from Hudson's pictorial depth perception test (top) and projective extrapolation (bottom). Top figure from Hudson (1960); bottom figure courtesy of Lloyd Held.

and again we see very large increases in 3D responses for all groups. On the face of it, this is hard to understand because both pictures contain size information for depth and both contain gradients, a gradient of texture and a linear perspective gradient. Is it then the case that although these two gradients are formally equivalent (Purdy, 1960) they are not perceptually equivalent? This conclusion is tempting, but a further analysis of the pictures will not allow us to make it. The difficulty lies in the nature of the linear perspective information contained in the outline drawings, which information was apparently generated with a complete disregard for the laws of perspective. A projective extrapolation of the relative sizes of the objects contained in P_4 is presented in Fig. 2. The extrapolation was computed by maintaining a constant proportion of road occluded by the elephant at both near and far distances and a constant proportion of the tree above and below the horizon in accordance with the laws of projective geometry. As can be seen from Fig. 2, the resulting size relationships are very odd indeed, since the elephant is about the same size as the man and antelope. Now we are not trying to argue that a hunter may not be aiming at a baby elephant, nor that baby elephants may not be placed at varying distances from an observer. We are arguing that the successful perception of perspective information by the naive observer may well depend on a geometrically correct, nonconventional depiction rather than a hit-or-miss conventional approximation. This is particularly true with relative size depiction, which, in the absence of a series of identical objects receding in space, depends on knowledge or assumptions about the "real" relative size of the depicted objects coplanar in longitudinal space. In the photograph the visual angle occupied by the elephant is about one-third the visual angle occupied by the hunter from feet to top of spear; in the line drawing the visual angle of the elephant is about one-fifth that of the hunter—with no corresponding increase in distance information to make such compression understandable. It is therefore not at all surprising that far more 3D responses occurred to the photograph than to the line drawings. The photograph preserved nonconventional geometrically correct information equivalent to that in the ordinary environment. The line drawings employed geometrically inaccurate conventional approximation to such information. The responses of various cultural groups to *conventional* components of pictures is altogether a different issue from their response to ordinary environmental information contained in pictures. The question of conventional pictorial components will be discussed below.

In the light of the above discussion it does not seem necessary to exhaustively review the ever-growing number of Hudson replications and variations. However, in order to provide a well-rounded review of the literature in the field we will briefly summarize a number of such studies. (A more complete summary is in Jahoda and McGurk, 1974*a*.) Mundy-Castle and Nelson (1962) found that when groups of samples are ordered according to the percent of each sample consistently giving three-dimensional answers to Hudson's pictures, the order corresponds to grade level regardless of ethnic group. Mundy-Castle (1966), in a study of Hudson's pictures with Ghanaian children, found that 100% of the 5- to 8-year-old children and 96% of the 9- to 10-year-old children misidentified the horizon line; 61% of the 5- to 6-year-olds, 73% of the 7- to 8-year-olds, and 46% of the 9- to 10-year-olds misidentified the road. It is fairly clear that the spatial relations in these drawings are quite ambiguous even *with* correct identification of background features; *without* it, depth perception is extremely problematic. Kilbride, Robbins, and Freeman (1968) found that the relative amount of pictorial depth perception on Hudson's pictures among rural Baganda school children was directly related to amount of formal education. Similarly, Kilbride and Robbins (1968) found a direct relationship among the Baganda between formal education and correct identification of linear perspective cue as specifying a road, river, path, etc. Incorrect responses were hill, stone, ladder, letter "A," etc. Deregowski (1968*b*) found that a significant proportion of subjects, schoolboys and servants from Lusaka, classified as 2D by Hudson's test, nevertheless constructed three-dimensional models from line drawings depicting relative depth. He writes: "The frequency with which subjects who were 2D on Hudson's test made 3D responses to the construction test suggests that it is probably illegitimate to extrapolate from Hudson's findings to all types of pictorial material. A subject, it appears, cannot be classified as a 2D perceiver of all pictorial material merely because he is a 2D perceiver as far as Hudson's test is concerned" (p. 203). It is notable that Deregowski's samples were comparable to Hudson's.

   Omari and Cook (1972) tested lower-middle-class American, black, and Puerto Rican children and found very significant effects of varying the question asked of subjects: more 3D responding occurred to the question "which is/looks *farther* . . . rather than *nearer*." Hagen and Johnson (1977) testing white-middle-class American children found that results were significantly affected both by question ("aiming" vs. "nearer") and by story content of the pictures with depth cues constant, a hunting scene vs. a ball-playing scene. Similarly, Omari and MacGinitie (1974) found with Tanzanian children that percent of three-dimensional responding was increased by using familiar characters in neutral poses instead of Hudson's characters. Sinha and Shukla (1974) in a study contrasting Indian nurseryschool and orphanage children found that the absence of stimulation in orphanages had a general retarding influence on the development of pictorial depth perception. These authors, however, used their own pictorial depth perception test. Kennedy and Ross (1975) also used their own pictorial materials to study depth perception of the Songe of Papua, New Guinea. They found that 100% of the subjects 10–20 years old correctly perceived relative pictorial distance; 88% of the subjects 21–40 years old were correct, and 61% of the subjects over 40 were correct. Kennedy and Ross (1975) also looked at the perception of "kinetic" scenes, a fire and a river flowing, with the same subjects, and found that 100% of the 10–20 year age group correctly identified these scenes. Eighty-three percent of the 20- to 40-year-old subjects correctly identified the fire but only 50% identified the river. Very few of the subjects over 40 correctly identified either the fire or the river. Waldron and Gallimore (1973) also studied subjects from Papua New Guinea as well as white Australians, Torres Strait Islanders, and European and Part Aboriginal schoolchildren. All subjects had at least 7 years of education. Subjects of European extraction had higher mean scores on the Hudson test than all other groups. However, mean number of three-dimensional responses for the Europeans was only 4.7 out of 6 and 3.5 out of 6 for the non-Europeans. Further, the standard deviation of every group exceeded the mean difference between any two groups. Guthrie, Sinaiko, and Brislin (1971) administered the Hudson test to 18 Vietnamese and 18 American helicopter pilots and found that nine Vietnamese made no errors and nine made more than two errors. Fourteen Americans made no errors and only one made more than two. Littlejohn (1963) argues that Hudson's results are most probably due to the concepts of space held by his subjects; i.e., Hudson's black samples may have had a "physiognomic" concept of space rather than a "geometrical-technical" one. "I am not arguing here that Africans ordinarily perceive the actual world in 2D. It would be foolish to suggest so. They must inhabit the same 'objective space' which geometrical analysis has revealed to us; but for them 'objective space' is a not-explicitly apprehended background to the space in which they are conscious of living . . ." (p. 16). Similarly, DuToit (1966) suggests linguistic relativity as the explanation for intersample differences on Hudson's test, noting that Bantu languages may lack words for "background" and "foreground," thus diminishing the capacity of its speakers to perceive or conceive of relative distance. He writes: "Bantu 'inability' regarding pictorial depth perception might be caused by the fact that they do not automatically *look for* depth. They do not 'select out' depth because their language does not suggest or require them to think along those lines" (p. 59). The suggestions advanced by both Littlejohn and DuToit seem to us to be premature at best.

The study by Jahoda and McGurk (1974a) is the last Hudson-type study we will discuss. Basically their purpose was two fold: (1) to compare and critique the numerous replications and pseudo-replications of Hudson's work and (2) to compare results on Hudson's test with results on their new pictorial depth perception test, fully described in Jahoda and McGurk (1974b) and McGurk and Jahoda (1974). Their excellent review of Hudson-style work covers the following points: (1) questioning procedures, (2) scoring, (3) rapport with subjects, (4) response sets, (5) specific questions asked, (6) chance levels of response, and (7) the incomparability of results from diverse studies. On the basis of their review of the literature they noted as consistent findings that black African children lag behind their white counterparts in the acquisition of pictorial depth perception and that a majority of African primary schoolchildren fail to respond to depth cues in pictures. However, in the discussion of the results on their new test compared with results on Hudson's test, they conclude that both the Scottish and Ghanaian schoolchildren were significantly above chance (at least 3 times the standard error above chance) on the new test and that differences between the two groups were very small. Ghanaian performance on Hudson's test was largely two-dimensional and the difference between the cultural groups was great. They argue that these differing results are due to the decreased reliance on verbal instruction which their test offers and a concomitant decrease in task ambiguity.

Jahoda and McGurk's argument for performance measures rather than verbal measures is very persuasive and will, we hope, be accepted by workers in the field. However, there is one aspect of their performance test which we think deserves mention in light of the information-oriented nature of this review. Figure 3 shows an example of a stimulus picture from their new 3D test. It is described as depicting two adult women of the same height with the cues of elevation and texture gradient. This picture (and all others in the set) suffers from the same type of informational inaccuracy as those of Hudson. The picture was generated apparently without regard to the geometric rules of perspective and the far figure is depicted as considerably taller than the near figure. If the two figures were really the same height, the proportions of each above and below the horizon line would be constant with varying distance; however, they are not (see Sedgwick, 1973). So, once again, the information contained in these pictures is a conventional approximation to information geometrically

Fig. 3. Stimulus picture from Jahoda and McGurk's pictorial depth perception test. From Jahoda and McGurk (1974a).

equivalent to that found in the ordinary environment. What is perhaps most surprising is the *success* experienced by relatively naive groups in picking up these conventional approximations, and not their failures to do so.

Given the ubiquity of photographic equipment, the unwillingness of workers in the field of picture perception to use photography is very difficult to understand. Once a sharp photograph has been produced, it may be traced to produce line drawings if such pictures are desired. Further, the tracing may be shaded or elements deleted at will to vary amount of information present. They may even be conventionally modified if that is the will of the investigator, but the characteristics of such modification will then be specified and controlled. Hints on the inadequacy of information produced freehand have appeared in the literature since Hudson's first report in 1960. None of Hudson's groups, white or black, regardless of schooling ever consistently reached 100% three-dimensional responding. Why not? Jahoda and McGurk (1974a), tested Scottish adults on both Hudson's test and the new test and got maximum scores of 69% for the new test and 72% for the Hudson test. On neither of the tests did European adults uniformly attain the maximum score. Again, why not? There of course will always be some error scores simply due to not paying attention, lack of motivation, hostility, and other such factors, but surely not of this magnitude. We are willing to argue that any test of Western pictorial depth information which fails to generate nearly 100% three-dimensional responding in educated Western adults has faults of either design or procedure or both which leave its validity open to serious question. It seems to us very unlikely that some 30% of educated Scots are *incapable* of seeing depth in pictures stylistically indigenous to their culture. Their accuracy in judging size, distance, etc., is another question. Which cues function most informatively and how much informational impoverishment such subjects will tolerate are also questions for further research. It is clear that "all or none" categorizations of subjects as 2D or 3D will teach us very little. A carefully constructed informational analysis can teach us a great deal.

Similarly, if educated adults can see pictures as flat objects like any other objects and/or as scenes depicted in depth as noted by Hudson (1960), which conditions or instructions promote responding to the flat surface and which to the depth information? And can observers attend to both sources of information at the same time? What are the perceptual consequences of attending to one rather than another? The problem of coexisting flatness and depth information occurs in all pictures from fully colored and textured photographs to the most minimal line drawings. The problems it raises will be dealt with below.

8. Coexistence of Flatness and Depth Information in Pictures

All Western representational pictures of whatever detail provide the observer with two conflicting sources of information: information for flatness and information for depth. We know from the above review that this coexistence of information poses few problems even for naive observers when pictures represent only single solid objects. There is no evidence whatsoever that any group of people see pictures of faces, cups, hunters, antelopes, or elephants as flat "slices of life," as it were. Misperceptions of such objects in the many Hudson-style tests were restricted to identification errors, e.g., antelope was identified variously as goat, sheep, cow, dog, ass, horse, camel (Mundy-Castle, 1966). However, the situation is not as simple when we consider the depiction either of extended surfaces in space or of multiple objects in various spatial relations to each other and to the observer. We know from Mundy-Castle (1966) and from Kilbride and Robbins (1968) that the two straight converging lines in three of Hudson's pictures are insufficient to produce in all observers the perception of a road receding in space. With no systematic work on this question we do not know what additional information (geometrically correct or otherwise) must be added to the two lines to support the unambiguous specification of a road or roadlike object. If has been found, however, that many naive observers perceive the converging lines as rising vertically in space and not extending longitudinally toward the visual horizon (which, accordingly, is not perceived as such). Examples of vertical misidentifications are hill, stone, ladder, and tree. It would be simplest to conclude that observers who make such misidentifications perceive the pictures only as flat surfaces in which all objects are relatively equidistant. Indeed, Killbride and Robbins (1968) concluded that such subjects were incapable of using the linear perspective cue to pictorial depth perception. But, geometrically, the sides of a ladder or hill or tree converge in much the same manner vertically as they do longitudinally. In fact, it is quite possible to photograph while shooting *up* at a brick building and *out* at a brick walkway and produce identical texture and linear perspective gradients in the resulting photographs. So we cannot conclude that "vertical" perceivers are unable to perceive depictions of surfaces receding in depth. The remaining misidentifications of the road in Hudson's drawings fall into two categories: items uninterpretable without elaboration from the subjects, e.g., rubber gun, oven, and farm, and items which suggest that the observer saw the road lines essentially as a flat pattern, e.g., letter "A," triangle, sticks, and string. We cannot be sure of course without interviews with subjects that "flat" perception is truly implied by such identifications but it is at least indicated. These "flat layout perceivers" are subjects of great interest to the field of picture perception. These are the subjects for whom it would be most interesting to determine the additional information requisite to perceiving scenes as receding in depth. We have no way of telling just how consistently "two-dimensional" they would be. These may be the same subjects who "fail" to perceive three-dimensionally even on Jahoda and McGurk's performance test. What do they see when presented with a full color photograph of the road they walk on every day? What would they see with a similar black and white photograph? We don't know because systematic variation of pictorial information along these lines is not yet a characteristic of cross-cultural picture work.

What we do have is some fragmentary information on the role played by characteristics of the flat projection surface itself. After all, it may be argued that, no matter how much information one adds to the *content* of a picture, no differences in perception will ensue if the observer is not *attending* to the contents, but rather notices only the flat vehicle, canvas, paper, etc. It has been argued by some (E. J. Gibson, 1969; Yonas and Hagen, 1973) that sophisticated observers attend to the content, the depth information in pictures, and simply ignore the flat surface information. Others (Pirenne, 1970; Perkins, 1973; Hagen, 1976) have argued that attention to the flat surface information on some level of awareness is essential to the successful depth perception of most pictures viewed in the ordinary unrestrained manner. Researchers on both sides of this question agree, however, that at the proper station point for observation, at the geometric center of projection for the optical information contained in the picture, depth perception would be enhanced for all observers by the removal or minimization of flat surface information for the plane of projection. Yonas and Hagen (1973) found just such an effect for Western subjects, children and adults, when motion parallax information was removed from the viewing of back-projected transparencies. Deregowski and Byth (1970) attempted a similar manipulation in an apparatus known as "Pandora's box." They showed Hudson's pictures as back-projected transparencies with the apparatus described by Gregory (1966). The transparencies when displayed appeared as a network of black lines against a pale green luminous field. Essentially, the function of the apparatus is to reduce information from the flat background surface of the picture. The first two of Hudson's pictures were used: P_1 contains the size cues only, P_2 has size plus overlap information. View was monocular. Relative distances of hunter, elephant, and antelope were indicated by the subjects by adjusting a light until it appeared to be at the same distance from the observer as the specified object. Ten sophisticated Europeans and ten pictorially naive Zambian servants acted as subjects in the experiment. With P_1, size cues alone, 60% of the Europeans made responses indicative of depth perception, and 50% of the Zambians made such responses. With P_2, size and overlap cues, 80% of the Europeans and 30% of the Zambians made responses indicative of depth perception. Although Deregowski does not further analyze the Zambian data, it is clear from his tabulated results that for the Zambians the mean perceived distance of the elephant relative to the hunter was approximately 3 times as great as that of the antelope in P_1 and twice as great in P_2. These same subjects when run under the standard procedure were all classified as 2D. The European results with Pandora's box are quite similar to the Zambians', but a lack of consistency of patterning in the data rather casts doubt on the subjects' (both white and black) interpretation of the task requirements. However, the Pandora box procedure is very promising and merits further work with systematically varied pictorial materials. This is the only cross-cultural study we know of in which psychophysical rather than all-or-none procedures were employed to look at more subtle differences in depth perception.

Deregowski *et al.* (1972) also used an unusual background projection surface in their study of pictorial recognition in a remote Ethiopian population. As noted above, E. S. Muldrow, in prior work with the same population, discovered that "when a drawing of an animal, such as are common in children's coloring books, was presented to the subjects they would take the paper, feel, smell, taste, and listen to it whilst flexing it, but would ignore the picture" (p. 418). He suggested that the difficulty might simply be due to the subjects' unfamiliarity with paper, so the stimulus pictures were printed in black ink on coarse whitish cloth familiar to the subjects. There was no evidence of detection errors; most errors involved animal misnomers, e.g., "goat" instead of "buck." A comparison group who were presented with pictures printed on paper would have been most helpful, but these investigators bypassed the attention problem instead of studying it. These authors also noted a very interesting effect of vertical vs. horizontal presentation of a picture of a profiled standing buck. When the picture was presented lying flat on the ground, nine subjects reported that the buck was "lying down." Six of these subjects were then shown the picture vertically and all reported that the buck was then "standing up." This result is suggestive of similar findings with children by Benson and Yonas (1973) and Hagen (1976) which imply that there is a stage in the development of pictorial perception in which the space *behind* the picture plane is not completely separated from the space of the ordinary environment which *surrounds* the picture. For the sophisticated observer, a picture is not simply a window to the world; it is a window to a rigidly constructed tunnel which encloses a self-contained world independent of the surround. The simple window concept may well precede the tunnel concept. If so, spatial orientation of the pictorial materials will be a variable of critical importance in future cross-cultural work. Suggestions from the literature regarding differential cultural treatment of orientation and rotation are found in Nissen, Machover, and Kinder (1935), Shapiro (1960), McFie (1961), and Deregowski (1968c, 1971b).

Two studies, one by Dawson (1967a,b) and one by Duncan, Gourlay, and Hudson (1973), address the issue of teaching people who are apparently flat surface picture perceivers to attend to the depiction of depth information on that flat surface, using a simple window concept. Dawson studied two groups of West African mine workers, all of whom had been categorized as two-dimensional picture perceivers on Dawson's test (which was based on Hudson's). One group was given eight weekly 1-hr training sessions, and both groups were retested 3 months after the conclusion of the training. The training procedure consisted of teaching subjects to trace onto a window the main lines of outside scenery while sighting through a small aperture. Subjects were also required to sketch their window drawings onto paper and eventually to draw without using the window aid. Finally photographs of the outside scenery were shown to the subjects so they could become familiar with this medium. Three months later, not surprisingly, the training group showed far more 3D perception on Dawson's test than did the controls. Unfortunately, Dawson was not really concerned with picture perception *per se* so much as with field dependence, so no precise informational analysis of either test or training is given. The technique, however, seems most promising, and is nearly identical to that recommended by Duncan *et al.* (1973). The major differences are that Duncan *et al.* recommend a portable framed window which allows for the insertion of a piece of white cardboard behind the glass to familiarize subjects with the concept of projection onto an opaque surface. They also include a series of lesson plans for teaching various pictorial components which Duncan has implemented among Congolese adults with successful results. The suggested procedures are interesting, and may provide a means of looking more closely at the complex interrelationship between flatness and depth information in pictures.

9. Use of Conventional Symbols in Art

At this point in the analysis there still remains to be considered a third class of components of pictures besides the two classes comprised of flatness and depth information. This third class is the class of conventional symbols used in the art of any particular culture. Because most informational analyses of pictures are not theoretically based, the class of conventions is nearly always confused with the class of types of depth information. For instance, Miller (1973), in his review of the cross-cultural picture work, wrote: "It seems clear, then, that certain components of pictorial representations are not duplications of three-dimensional visual experiences but are rather conventions or techniques (e.g., superposition, linear perspective, shading, texture, etc.) used to represent such experiences" (p. 135).

We profoundly disagree with this statement. Superposition, linear perspective, shading, and texure are *not* conventions. They are present in the ambient optic array of the ordinary environment; they are present on the retina; they are present on the film plane of a pinhole camera. They are present by virtue of optical, logical, and geometric necessity, and *not* by virtue of arbitrary custom. To confuse these sources of ordinary environmental information with arbitrary symbols is to hopelessly entangle the multiple components of pictures beyond the reach of systematic analysis. We do not wish to argue that every culture *must* use these sources of information to depict spatial layout in its art; that would be clearly untrue. Nor do we wish to argue that there are not reasonable options available to cultures; indeed, the adoption of Western "snapshot" art as a custom may be regarded as a choice of convention by a particular culture.

But it does not follow that the components of such an art style are therefore conventional.

If we wish to move toward a clearer specification of cultural effects on picture perception, then we must avoid treating the various components of pictures as if they were all simply members of a large class called "cues" or "conventions." For example, Miller (1973) has argued that cultural differences in pictorial perception are essentially differences in response to cues or conventions as a function of past experience with such cues or conventions, and, further, that "experience in perceiving objects in the three-dimensional world is not sufficient to perceive those objects in pictorial representations . . . although such experience may well be of use in recognizing specific objects once flatness cues have been overcome." Not only do the data fail to support his argument, but also the logic is such that all picture components have essentially the same status. Similarly, types of pictures are distinguished not in terms of the types of information which they contain, e.g., textures and edges, but in terms of the techniques used in their generation, e.g., photographs vs. line drawings. This latter comparison *should* be of interest because of the varying amounts and salience of information preserved under each transformation and not simply because one or the other technique looks more or less like "a real three-dimensional image," which, according to Miller, does *not* contain superposition, linear perspective, texture, or shading (p. 135).

This same line of argument on the equal status of the multiple pictorial components is also pursued by Duncan *et al.* (1973) in their extended study of pictorial perception among Bantu and white primary schoolchildren in South Africa. These authors argue that we must expect that representational conventions in pictorial materials should raise problems with "unacculturated" groups. Accordingly, they tested children's perception of the following "conventions": object size, height on the picture plane, linear and aerial perspective, overlap, position in pictorial space, truncation of objects by bordering, shadows, artistic style, foreshortening, implied motion, and the zoom-lens principle. Each of these components is regarded as essentially of equal and identical status with all others such that the implied motion picture shown in the top panel of Fig. 4 should be of the same order of difficulty as the overlap picture shown in the bottom panel. Also, since all of these components are regarded as arbitrary conventions of Western art, no care was exercised to produce geometrically accurate pictures. Figure 5 shows a very surprising example of a "conventional" depiction of the relationship between the sun and shadows of illuminated objects. The authors write that in this picture "three items were shown with shadows angularly offset to a common illumination point." Perhaps so, but the common illumination point was not the sun. Yet children were asked to identify the circle in the drawing and the correct answer was "sun" or "moon." It is very interesting that about half the rural children failed to produce these answers. The rural children may well have been more aware of

Fig. 4. Pictures implying motion (top) and use of overlapping (bottom). Both figures from Duncan, Gourlay, and Hudson (1973).

the true relationship between sun and shadow and unwilling to accept such an ill-rendered approximation. Since systematic variation of degree of conventional modification was not a factor in the study, we are unable to come to any conclusions on the question.

It is perhaps a bit easier to understand this current state of the field if we consider briefly the origin of the present flood of work in South Africa on pictorial perception. Hudson's (1960) original work was motivated by the "unconventional" perception of Bantu factory workers of two pictures out of a set of 14 designed to obtain information on aspirational levels in an occupational situation. These two pictures, as described by Hudson, contained overlap information improperly interpreted by the factoryworkers. The pictures had not been designed with such problems in mind so very little attention was paid to their perceptual content. Hudson (1960) cites a similar difficulty in safety and health poster interpretation in Kenya reported by Holmes (1963). A particular health poster portrayed a "typical health assistant" and was captioned "This man is

Fig. 5. Depiction of light source and shadows. From Duncan, Gourlay, and Hudson (1973).

your friend." Some observers, however, responded to the poster thus: "Our health assistant wears brown socks, has a beard" (p. 195). Hudson describes this response as showing a lack of appreciation of the relationship between picture and reality, but it may, of course, be described in a diametrically opposite manner. The assumption of "prototypical" identity is necessarily a convention as are many of the components of such safety and health posters, e.g., pain stars, rain dashes, shock waves, speed lines, left-right sequencing, etc. These conventions might not be purely arbitrary, but they are not contained in the optic array of the ordinary environment and their interpretation may well be culturally determined. Winter (1963) shows some very interesting examples of Western ethnocentric poster depiction often misinterpreted by Bantu workers, e.g., the pain star in Fig. 6. It is quite obvious from this whole line of work that more careful attention to the various classes of pictorial components is critical not only to forwarding understanding of pictorial perception but also to successful utilization of pictorial materials as didactic aids. Systematic variation

Fig. 6. Safety poster containing misinterpreted "pain star." From Winter (1963).

of conventional components will allow us to specify more precisely their origin, nature, degree of universality, and conditions of interpretability.

10. Cultural and Historical Options in Depiction

We have argued throughout this chapter that the Western perspective tradition of depicting spatial relations in depth is by no means an arbitrary convention. We have argued that this style of depiction rests on the assumption that information equivalent to that found in the ordinary environment can be carried by a two-dimensional projection surface. Indeed, Western art essentially reduces to the principle of projection onto such a surface of the elements of a single static three-dimensional scene. Thus we have termed the style "snapshot" art because it contains only the information which can be captured in a single station point view of an object or scene. It is obvious, however, even from consideration of symbolic conventions like pain stars discussed above, that no artist or culture need restrict the contents of pictures to snapshot components. A culture may even reject *in toto* the assumption of snapshot art as a style. Various other options have been exercised historically and culturally, and a discussion of cultural effects on picture perception would not be complete without consideration of such optional styles from a perceptual point of view.

Thouless (1931a,b, 1933) was one of the first psychologists to consider the relationship between perception and the artistic style of a culture. Thouless studied the appearance of shapes of objects viewed obliquely and the sizes of objects viewed at different distances. He found that "what was seen was intermediate between what was given in peripheral stimulation and the 'real' character of the object. To this effect of the character of the 'real' object on the phenomenal character we may give the name 'phenomenal regression to the real object' " (1931a, p. 358). Thouless then computed for groups of Indian and British university students their respective indices of phenomenal regression for shape and size and found that Indian students have higher indices than their British counterparts, i.e., they show more phenomenal regression to the real object, more shape and size constancy. Thouless reasoned that certain features of Oriental art, particularly what he called the partial or total absence of perspective, were probably due to Orientals' great tendency to phenomenal regression. In a follow-up study, Beveridge (1935) found that West African natives also had a considerably higher index of phenomenal regression than Europeans. Later Beveridge (1940) again tested West African (Gold Coast) students to discover if the Africans' greater tendency to phenomenal regression affected their appreciation of pictorial art in line with Thouless's hypothesis. He presented African students with a set of 80 colored postcards, 40 of famous European pictures and 40 of Japanese, Indian, and Persian pictures. The pictures were paired roughly according to subject matter and approximately 100 students were asked to choose which picture of each pair was preferred. Not all subjects chose on every pair, but of 2827 choices the Western picture was preferred 86.5% of the time. Only two Oriental pictures were more popular than the corresponding European ones. "We must remember, however, that these subjects had been used to seeing European pictures from their earliest school days, whereas Oriental art was new to them. Had they been untouched by European influences the results might have been quite different" (p. 60). That is quite true. However, the relationship between phenomenal regression and artistic preference may well be a chicken-and-egg problem. That is, since the stimuli in phenomenal regression tests are two-dimensional pictorial objects and artistic preference must also be measured with flat pictorial objects, we have no way of telling whether artistic style influences perception or perception influences artistic style. Perhaps if we had a nonpictorial measure of phenomenal regression, we could begin to look at the relationship.

Various cultural art styles, notably that of Japan, certainly depict more "constant shape" for surfaces receding in the distance than does the Western perspective style (see Fig. 7). However, it is not correct, strictly speaking, to refer to such styles as lacking in perspective. The perspective in such pictures is parallel, or axonometric, and is the perspective obtained at an infinitely distant point of view. Functionally, this distance need not be infinite but simply sufficiently great that near-far compression is no longer detectable. Hagen and Elliott (1976), working with American subjects, have shown that a preference for more axonometric, nearly parallel, perspective is also evident in Western adults. Results indicate that Western adults accept a picture of an object as realistic and natural looking when it is painted, drawn, or photographed at a distance at least 10 times as great as the object is large. At such a distance, front to back convergence of a regular, symmetrical geometric object is about 10%. We do not yet know if such a preference also holds for background surfaces

Fig. 7. Parallel perspective typical of Japanese art. Detail of *Kibi's Adventures in China*. Courtesy of the Museum of Fine Arts, Boston.

Fig. 8. Split-style representation by the Northwest Coast American Indians. From Holm (1965).

like that depicted in Fig. 7. If it does, then careful cross-cultural work may show that differences between Western and Oriental subjects in terms of perceptual preference may not be nearly so great as the apparent differences in art styles.

A promising if somewhat unsystematic investigation has already begun of a third cultural option in art style, the option of split- or chain-style depiction. Some examples can be found in ancient Egyptian art, but the style has been most fully developed by the Indians of the Northwest Coast of America (see Fig. 8). Boas (1927), Levi-Strauss (1963), and Werner (1948) all discuss this art style and speculate on its origins at some length. Werner (1965) argued that the style is common not just in primitive people but in children everywhere. Since the data collection was somewhat nonsystematic, this point is certainly debatable, but Deregowski (1969a,b, 1970a,b, 1972) accepted the argument and built a developmental hypothesis around it. He argues that:

> In all societies there is, in children, an aesthetic preference for chain-type drawings and if this preference is not destroyed it persists into adulthood. In most societies this preference is suppressed; this is done because the preferred drawings are worse at conveying information about the depicted objects than are the non-preferred representative drawings. Thus aesthetic preference is sacrificed on the altar of communication efficiency. (1970a, p. 24)

This hypothesis is very interesting but there does not seem to be any data to support it. Hudson (1962b) tested the preferences of South African schoolchildren and one illiterate black sample for the two pictures of elephants shown in Fig. 9. Literate samples generally preferred the legless drawing and the illiterate sample the splay-legged drawing because it depicted four legs. Using the same pictures plus a nonsense drawing, Deregowski (1969a,b) tested adults from rural Zambia and schoolchildren from Lusaka. He found that about half the adults preferred the legless drawing and half the drawing with four legs. These results are difficult to interpret, however, because 37% of the adults preferred the nonsense drawing to the legless drawing. Among the children, 56% preferred the drawing with legs and 43% the legless drawing, but again 32% of the children (40% of the youngest) preferred the nonsense drawing to the legless drawing. Since the legless drawing was presumably generated in accordance with what Deregowski calls "the efficacious conventions of the West," these test results are uninterpretable. Deregowski (1970b) then modified the pictures and presented rural Zambian women of little or no schooling with three new elephant drawings: a front view, a side view, and a chain drawing consisting of a front and side view. He found the front view to be the most preferred and interpretable while the side and chain drawings did not differ in either preference or number of correct identifications, so again his hypothesis received no support.

It is highly regrettable that more systematic work on both aesthetic preference and efficacy of information has not been attempted. Chain-style art is essentially the simultaneous depiction of several points of view or object aspects on the same picture plane, and there is no *a priori* reason of which we are aware for rejecting the possibility of successful information depiction with such a style. Again, the field would greatly benefit from a systematic variation of the pictorial materials which truly does justice to the art styles to be compared. A bird's-eye view of an elephant strikes us as a very odd choice, as does the geometric model of squares in parallel planes tested by Deregowski (1969a,b). The number of choices of nonsense pictures seems to us to be ample proof that the

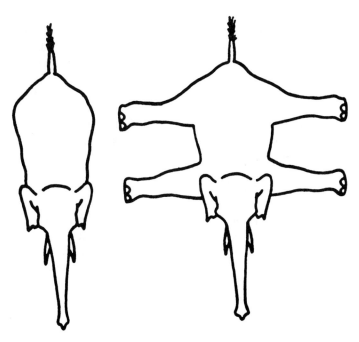

Fig. 9. A Western perspectival and a split-style representation of an elephant. From Hudson (1962b).

subjects shared our opinion of the matter. Holm (1965, 1972) has given the field two excellent analyses of Northwest Coast Indian art from which more adequate pictorial stimuli can certainly be generated.

It should be noted that none of the split- or chain-style work discussed above rests on the explicit assumption that split-style art is indigenous to the cultures tested. On the contrary, Hudson (1962a) writes:

> The black man in Africa has a history of indigenous art, but his culture is non-visual. He expresses himself in the plastic arts such as carving in three dimensions. . . . When he does decorate the walls of his huts or his traditional pottery, he depicts what he knows and not what he sees. His portrayal is always flat . . . when the black man draws he does not make use of the perceptual cues to which we are accustomed and with which we mistakenly assume him to be familiar. (p. 190)

Hudson also says that the African uses a "twisted perspective" in the same way as Ice Age man drew in the Lascaux caves. It is not necessary to go to the caves of France in search of adequate descriptions of African primitive art, however, because in South Africa itself there are over a thousand sites with rock art indigenous to the African culture (Vinnicombe, 1960). Interest in these paintings has greatly accelerated in South Africa since the 1950s and covers a wide variety of areas: ethnology and zoology, history, and archeology (Cooke, 1968). From a perceptual point of view, two aspects of the paintings are of special interest: who made them and what is their content? Who made them is still a subject of some controversy but the weight of the evidence is settling on the Bushmen. Bleek (1930) argues that the Bushmen produced the paintings from internal evidence of the paintings themselves as well as from Bushmen reactions to them recorded as early as 1877. Research by Lee (1972), Sampson (1968), Malan (1965), and Wilcox (1959, 1962, 1966) supports her argument. Dating the paintings is somewhat more difficult than determining authorship. Malan (1965), basing his analysis on the subject matter of the paintings, argues that there are two distinct periods—pre-Bantu and post-Bantu. Similarly, one may often distinguish between paintings rendered before and after the advent of Europeans on the basis of subject matter. Wilcox (1966) writes that it is generally conceded that "all the rock art can be assigned to the Later Stone Age but this lasted from about 10,000 years ago until about a century ago and it is unlikely that any *surviving* paintings or engravings in the conditions of exposure in which they occur could have an age of more than (to stick my neck out) say 2000 years" (p. 9). Wilcox also notes that current research on chemical changes with time which take place in the paint may eventually allow for more precise dating (see Schoonraad, 1971). Bleek (1930) points out that since we know approximately when the Bushmen were killed off or driven out of each painting district, we at least know when the paintings must have stopped. In any case, most of the paintings are not the products of Bantu currently residing in South Africa.

Dating of the paintings is of interest primarily because it arrests our notions of the development of picture making as a recent and "sophisticated" activity and directs attention to the level of sophistication and informational content within the pictures themselves. On the simplest level, the content of the pictures is mainly people and animals in hunting scenes, dancing scenes, etc. For our purposes it is more interesting to consider the nature of the depiction in terms of content of information for both objects and scenes. Figure 10 shows an undated (but presumably early nineteenth-century) painting attributed by Bleek (1930) to Bushmen. It was copied in 1868 by G. W. Stow as were all of the over 70 plates in Bleek's beautiful book. Men, women, and elands are all clearly depicted, albeit in a somewhat stylized manner. Animal bodies are all drawn in profile; human bodies in a variety of attitudes. Woodhouse (1966, 1971, 1972, 1975) in his continuing analysis of rock art reports the presence oi foreshortening, complete profiles, rear views of squatting figures, motion, charging animals, rivers, perspective through grouping, and dozens of variations on the human figure and the relations between men and elands, e.g., man chucking eland under chin (1971). A really complete treatment of the subject would demand dozens of color plates so we suggest both Bleek (1930) and Wil cox (1962) for visual evidence of the richness of the South African paintings We feel that if a more complete analysis of the pictures were undertaken from a perceptual, informational perspective, we would have a far more adequate description of a "primitive" cultural option in artistic style than we are pre

Fig. 10. Early nineteenth-century rock painting attributed to Bushmen. From Bleek (1930).

sently given either by the split-style work or by descriptions such as Hudson's (1962*a*) above. Kennedy (1974, 1975; Kennedy and Ross, 1975) has begun such an analysis, extending his interest to rock art from areas scattered all over the world. He writes:

> It seems that ancient and modern outline artwork present many commonalities. . . . Lines are used to depict similar features of objects, like the edges of their surfaces, often with overlap, and perhaps also patterns marked out by the boundaries of areas of pigment on their surfaces. While modern man would probably have found the parietal artists' language baffling, he would have been able to understand much of his art work without question. (1974, p. 321)

Kennedy suggests that depiction by line is universally understood in an inborn capacity and, as such, will occur everywhere. If Kennedy is right, then the failure of any cultural group to understand such depiction will require very close examination and further investigation. The art of primitive man is stylized, sophisticated, and often even humorous. Characterizations of the "art of the black man" *per se* as flat, twisted, and childlike will not stand up to an analysis of the rock art. Thus, the absence of a representational art style in an existing culture demands explanations beyond those suggested by race or geography. Also, whereas there may be cultural groups who do not and have not ever *produced* two-dimensional depictions, the weight of the current evidence makes it difficult to argue that there are groups who cannot *understand* them.

11. Summary and Future Directions

As is the common fate of such endeavors, this review of the literature of cultural effects on pictorial perception has left us with both tentative conclusions and a myriad of questions. We may conclude fairly confidently that the perception of fully colored and textured pictures is relatively independent of culture and that the black-and-white convention primarily poses problems of attentional deployment. In general, edge information alone in pictures seems to provide an adequate basis for the perception of objects and even on Embedded Figures Tests detection errors are rarely reported. We know that observers of pictorial depth material in conventional minimal outline drawings appear to be either longitudinal, vertical, or flat surface perceivers, and that culture-specific conventions pose great difficulty for groups outside the culture of origin. We also know that artistic, stylistic options outside the Western tradition provide the field of pictorial perception with a relatively untapped fund of information about the complex nature of depiction and the flexibility of human perception.

In our view, the myriad of questions remaining also reduces to a workable subset of problem areas and procedures repeatedly suggested by an overview of the literature. One of the most apparent of these is the problem of attention deployment or capture and the related issue of salience of various informational components. When do observers attend to content and when to surface? When to isolated objects and when to several? Is there sequencing of attention from figure to figure within a picture, or from figures to spatial relations among them? Moreover, which cultural variables, if any, will predict differences in the deployment or selectivity of attention? These and many related questions compose what seems to us to be one of the most fruitful areas of cross-cultural research, although it may indicate a move away from group to individual differences.

The second problem area we see defined by the review of the literature is essentially one of design and procedure. The current nature of the field leaves us with far too many interesting questions about pictorial material unanswered. For instance, are photographs of *scenes* as universally understood as photographs of *objects* seem to be? Are outline drawings more or less difficult to perceive successfully than photographs? When edge information is insufficient for determinate perception, what additional information is needed? What characteristics of the projection surface enhance or depress accurate perception? Are there cross-cultural differences in degree of accuracy of judgment of size, shape, distance, location, etc.? How effective are non-Western artistic styles at depicting objects and surface relations and what are the cultural constraints, if any, on their interpretation? Lastly, but perhaps of greatest importance, how do we trace the continuous modification of information into convention? What are the roots of conventions? Just how conventional are the "hit-or-miss" geometric approximations common to Western free-hand drawing? They are clearly not arbitrary, but they apparently stretch the limits of flexibility of information pickup by naive picture observers. Do these same observers have difficulty with geometrically accurate drawings or with fully colored and detailed pictures? The literature suggests not, but in the absence of systematic variation of stimulus materials, we can reach no firm conclusions.

Cole, Gay, Glick, and Sharp (1971) wrote:

> If experiments are occasions to demonstrate the use of skills, then failure to apply the skills that we assume are used in natural contexts becomes, not an illustration of cultural inferiority, but rather a fact to be explained through study and further experimentation. (p. 217)

These authors stress the need for looking at *patterns* of performance across tasks, materials, and contexts. Further, they suggest that if one begins with a task on which performance of groups to be compared is identical, and then proceeds to systematically vary the nature of the task for both groups, then points of divergence in patterning can be specified and examined. In a similar vein, Price-Williams (1975) has proposed an experimental design which he calls "graduating steps." In such a design, the first level is that of the naturally occurring situation, perhaps real scenes, with a familiar task, context, and material. Then in a series of graduated steps from familiar to unfamiliar the subject is moved from the naturally occurring situation to the unfamiliar formal experiment, perhaps minimal sketch outline drawings.

We feel that these design suggestions are admirably adapted to work in cross-cultural picture perception. They will minimize the apparently inevitable confounding so often due to familiarity, motivational, and language factors and lay the stage for a systematic analysis of informational components so badly needed in the field. If we learn to specify with exactitude the nature of our pictorial materials, then the field of cross-cultural picture perception will be truly illuminating both for theories of pictorial perception and for questions of cultural differences in the perceptual process itself.

ACKNOWLEDGMENTS

We wish to extend our thanks to the following individuals and organizations for permission to reproduce copyrighted materials.

H. F. Duncan, N. Gourlay, Wm. Hudson, and Witwatersrand University Press for Figs. 4 and 5, which are reprinted from *A Study of Pictorial Perception among Bantu and White Primary School Children* (Johanesburg: Witwatersrand University Press, 1973), Figs. B-1, E-2, and H-4.

Wm. Holm and University of Washington Press for Fig. 8, which is reprinted from *Northwest Coast Indian Art* (Seattle: University of Washington Press, 1965), Fig. 58.

Wm. Hudson and the Journal Press for Figs. 1 and 2, which are reprinted from "Pictorial depth perception in sub-cultural groups in Africa," *Journal of Social Psychology,* 1960, *52*, 183–208, Figs. 1 and 3.

Wm. Hudson and the National Institute for Personnel Research for Fig. 9, which is reprinted from "Pictorial perception and educational adaptation in Africa," *Psychologia Africana*, 1962, *9*, 226–239, Fig. 4.

G. Jahoda, H. McGurk, and the International Union of Psychological Science and Dunod Editeur for Fig. 3, which is reprinted from "Pictorial depth perception in Scottish and Ghanaian children," *International Journal of Psychology*, 1974, *9*, 255–267, Fig. 1.

Methuen and Co. Ltd. for Fig. 10, which is reprinted from D. F. Bleek's *Rock Paintings in South Africa* (London: Methuen and Co. Ltd., 1930), Plate 16.

Museum of Fine Arts, Boston, for Fig. 7, *Kibi's Adventures in China* (detail), Japan, Helian period, late 12th century (William Sturgis Bigelow Collection, 32.131).

National Institute for Personnel Research for Fig. 6, which is reprinted from W. Winter's "The perception of safety posters by Bantu industrial workers," *Psychologia Africana,* 1963, *10*, 127–135, Poster D.

The authors gratefully acknowledge the kind assistance of Lloyd Held in the preparation of the manuscript.

12. References

Benson, C., and Yonas, A. Development of sensitivity to static pictorial depth information. *Perception and Psychophysics*, 1973, *13*, 361–366.

Berkeley, G. *An essay towards a new theory of vision*. 1709 (see any modern edition).

Berry, J. W. Temne and Eskimo perceptual skills. *International Journal of Psychology*, 1966, *1*, 207–229.

Beveridge, W. M. Racial differences in phenomenal regression. *British Journal of Psychology*, 1935, *26*, 59–62.

Beveridge, W. M. Some racial differences in perception. *British Journal of Psychology*, 1940, *30*, 57–64.

Bleek, D. F. *Rock paintings in South Africa*. London: Methuen, 1930.

Boaş, F. *Primitive art*. Oslo: Instituttet for Sammenlignende Kulturforskning, 1927.

Bower, T. G. R. *Development in infancy*. San Francisco: Freeman, 1974.

Brimble, A. R. The construction of a non-verbal intelligence test in Northern Rhodesia. *Rhodes-Livingstone Journal*, 1963, *34*, 23–35.

Cole, M., Gay, J., Glick, J., and Sharp, D. *The cultural context of learning and thinking*. New York: Basic Books, 1971.

Cooke, C. K. Interpretation of rock paintings. *South African Journal of Science*, 1968, *64*, 33–36.

Dawson, J. Cultural and physiological influences upon spatial-perceptual processes in West Africa: Part I. *International Journal of Psychology*, 1967a, *2(2)*, 115–128.

Dawson, J. Cultural and physiological influences upon spatial-perceptual process in West Africa: Part II. *International Journal of Psychology*, 1967b, *2(3)*, 171–185.

Deregowski, J. B. Pictorial recognition in subjects from a relatively pictureless environment. *African Social Research*, 1968a, *5*, 356–364.

Deregowski, J. B. Difficulties in pictorial depth perception in Africa. *British Journal of Psychology*, 1968b, *59*, 195–204.

Deregowski, J. B. On perception of depicted orientation. *International Journal of Psychology*, 1968c, *3(3)*, 149–156.

Deregowski, J. B. A pictorial perception paradox. *Acta Psychologica*, 1969a, *31*, 365–374.

Deregowski, J. B. Preference for chain-type drawings in Zambian domestic servants and primary school-children. *Psychologia Africana*, 1969b, *12*, 172–180.

Deregowski, J. B. A note on the possible determinant of "split representation" as an artistic style. *International Journal of Psychology*, 1970a, *5(1)*, 21–26.

Deregowski, J. B. Chain-type drawings: A further note. *Perceptual and Motor Skills*, 1970b, *30*, 102.

Deregowski, J. B. Responses mediating pictorial recognition. *Journal of Social Psychology*, 1971a, *84*, 27–33.

Deregowski, J. B. Orientation and perception of pictorial depth. *International Journal of Psychology*, 1971b, *6(2)*, 111–114.

Deregowski, J. B. Pictorial perception and culture. *Scientific American*, 1972, *227*, 82–88.

Deregowski, J. B. On seeing a picture for the first time. *Leonardo*, 1976, *9*, 19–23.

Deregowski, J. B., and Byth, W. Hudson's pictures in Pandora's box. *Journal of Cross-Cultural Psychology*, 1970, *1(4)*, 315–323.

Deregowski, J. B., and Serpell, R. Performance on a sorting task: A cross-cultural experiment. *International Journal of Psychology*, 1971, *6(4)*, 273–281.

Deregowski, J. B., Muldrow, E. S., and Muldrow, W. F. Pictorial recognition in a remote Ethiopian population. *Perception*, 1972, *1*, 417–425.

Deregowski, J. B., Ellis, H., and Shepherd, J. A cross-cultural study of recognition of pictures of faces and cups. *International Journal of Psychology*, 1973, *8(4)*, 269–273.

Duncan, H. F., Gourlay, H., and Hudson, W. *A study of pictorial perception among Bantu and white primary school children in South Africa.* Johannesburg: Witwatersrand University Press, 1973.

DuToit, B. M. Pictorial depth perception and linguistic relativity. *Psychologia Africana*, 1966, *11*, 51–63.

Ellis, H., Deregowski, J., and Shepherd, J. Descriptions of white and black faces by white and black subjects. *International Journal of Psychology*, 1975, *10(2)*, 119–123.

Gibson, E. J. *Principles of perceptual learning and development.* New York: Appleton-Century-Crofts, 1969.

Gibson, J. J. *The perception of the visual world.* Boston: Houghton Mifflin, 1950.

Gibson, J. J. *The senses considered as perceptual systems.* Boston: Houghton Mifflin, 1966.

Gibson, J. J. The information available in pictures. *Leonardo*, 1971, *4*, 27–35.

Goodman, N. *Languages of art: An approach to a theory of symbols.* Indianapolis: Bobbs-Merrill, 1968.

Gregory, R. L. *Visual illusions.* In B. M. Foss (Ed.), *New horizons in psychology.* Harmondsworth, England: Penguin Books, 1966.

Guthrie, G. M., Sinaiko, H. W., and Brislin, R. Nonverbal abilities of Americans and Vietnamese. *Journal of Social Psychology*, 1971, *84*, 183–190.

Hagen, M. A. Picture perception: Toward a theoretical model. *Psychological Bulletin*, 1974, *81*, 471–497.

Hagen, M. A. The development of sensitivity to cast and attached shadows in pictures as information for the direction of the source of illumination. *Perception and Psychophysics*, 1976, *20*, 25–28.

Hagen, M. A., and Elliott, H. B. An investigation of the relationship between viewing condition and preference for true and modified linear perspective with adults. *Journal of Experimental Psychology*, 1976, *2*, 479–490.

Hagen, M. A., and Johnson, M. M. Hudson pictorial depth perception test: Cultural content and question with a Western sample. *Journal of Social Psychology*, 1977, *101*, 8–11.

Heron, A. Studies of perception and reasoning in Zambian children. *International Journal of Psychology*, 1968, *3(1)*, 23–29.

Hochberg, J., and Brooks, V. Pictorial recognition as an unlearned ability: A study of one child's performance. *American Journal of Psychology*, 1962, *75*, 624–628.

Holm, B. *Northwest Coast Indian art.* Seattle: University of Washington Press, 1965.

Holm, B. *Crooked beak of heaven.* Seattle: University of Washington Press, 1972.

Holmes, A. C. *A study of understanding of visual symbols in Kenya.* London: Overseas Visual Aids Center, Publication No. 10, 1963.

Hudson, W. Pictorial depth perception in sub-cultural groups in Africa. *Journal of Social Psychology*, 1960, *52*, 183–208.

Hudson, W. Cultural problems in pictorial perception. *South African Journal of Science*, 1962a, *58*, 189–195.

Hudson, W. Pictorial perception and educational adaptation in Africa. *Psychologia Africana*, 1962b, *9*, 226–239.

Jahoda, G., and McGurk, H. Pictorial depth perception in Scottish and Ghanaian children: A critique of some findings with the Hudson test. *International Journal of Psychology*, 1974a, *9(4)*, 255–267.

Jahoda, G., and McGurk, H. Pictorial depth perception: A developmental study. *British Journal of Psychology*, 1974b, *65*, 141–149.

Kennedy, J. M. *A psychology of picture perception.* San Francisco: Jossey-Bass, 1974.

Kennedy, J. M. Drawing was discovered, not invented. *New Scientist*, 1975, *67*, 523–525.

Kennedy, J. M., and Ross, A. S. Outline picture perception by the Songe of Papua. *Perception*, 1975, *4*, 391–406.

Kidd, D. *The essential Kafir*. London: Adam and Charles Black, 1904.

Kilbride, P. L., and Robbins, M. C. Linear perspective, pictorial depth perception and education among the Baganda. *Perceptual and Motor Skills*, 1968, *27*, 601–602.

Kilbride, P., Robbins, M., and Freeman, R. Pictorial depth perception and education among Baganda school schildren. *Perceptual and Motor Skills*, 1968, *26*, 1116–1118.

Lee, D. N. Bushman folk-lore and rock paintings. *South African Journal of Science*, 1972, *68*, 195–199.

Levi-Strauss, C. *Structural anthropology*. New York: Basic Books, 1963.

Liddicoat, R., and Koza, C. Language development in African infants. *Psychologia Africana*, 1963, *10*, 108–116.

Littlejohn, J. Temne space. *Anthropological Quarterly*, 1963, *63*, 1–17.

Lloyd, A. B. Acholi country: Part II. *Uganda Notes*, 1904, *5*, 18.

MacArthur, R. Sex differences in field dependence for the Eskimo: Replication of Berry's findings. *International Journal of Psychology*, 1967, *2(2)*, 139–140.

Malan, B. D. The classification and distribution of rock art in South Africa. *South African Journal of Science*, 1965, *61*, 427–430.

McFie, J. The effect of education of African performance on a group of intellectual tests. *British Journal of Educational Psychology*, 1961, *31*, 232, 240.

McGurk, M., and Jahoda, G. The development of pictorial depth perception: The role of figural elevation. *British Journal of Psychology*, 1974, *65*, 367–376.

Miller, R. J. Cross-cultural research in the perception of pictorial materials. *Psychological Bulletin*, 1973, *80*, 135–150.

Mundy-Castle, A. Pictorial depth perception in Ghanaian children. *International Journal of Psychology*, 1966, *1(4)*, 289–300.

Mundy-Castle, A. C., and Nelson, G. K. A neuropsychological study of the Knysna forest workers. *Psychologia Africana*, 1962, *9*, 240–272.

Nadal, S. F. A field experiment in racial psychology. *British Journal of Psychology*, 1937, *28*, 195–211.

Nissen, H. W., Machover, S., and Kinder, E. A study of performance tests given to a group of native African Negro children. *British Journal of Psychology*, 1935, *25*, 308–355.

Omari, I. M., and Cook, H. Differential cognitive cues in pictorial depth perception. *Journal of Cross-Cultural Psychology*, 1972, *3(3)*, 321–325.

Omari, I. M., and MacGinitie, W. H. Some pictorial artifacts in studies of African children's pictorial depth perception. *Child Development*, 1974, *45*, 535–539.

Perkins, D. N. Compensating for distortion in viewing pictures obliquely. *Perception and Psychophysics*, 1973, *14*, 13–19.

Pirenne, M. *Optics, painting, and photography*. Cambridge: Cambridge University Press, 1970.

Price-Williams, D. *Explorations in cross-cultural psychology*. San Francisco: Chandler and Sharp, 1975.

Purdy, W. C. The hypothesis of psychophysical correspondence in space perception. *General Electric Technical Information Series*, 1960, No. R60ELC56.

Ryan, T. A., and Schwartz, C. Speed of perception as a function of mode of representation. *American Journal of Psychology*, 1956, *69*, 60–69.

Sampson, E. W. Styles of rock paintings in the South Western Cape. *South African Journal of Science*, 1968, *64*, 192–195.

Schoonraad, M. Rock paintings of Southern Africa. *South African Journal of Science*, 1971, Special issue No. 2, 1–104.

Schwitzgebel, R. The performance of Dutch and Zulu adults on selected perceptual tasks. *Journal of Social Psychology*, 1962, *57*, 73–77.

Sedgwick, H. A. The visible horizon: A potential source of visual information for the perception of size and distance. Doctoral dissertation, Cornell University, 1973 (University Microfilms No. 73-22; 530).

Segall, M. H., Campbell, D. T., and Herskovits, M. J. *The influence of culture on visual perception.* Indianapolis: Bobbs-Merrill, 1966.

Shapiro, M. B. The rotation of drawings by illiterate Africans. *Journal of Social Psychology*, 1960, *52*, 17–30.

Shepherd, J., Deregowski, J., and Ellis H. A cross-cultural study of recognition memory for faces. *International Journal of Psychology*, 1974, *9(3)*, 205–211.

Sinha, D., and Shukla, P. Deprivation and development of skill for pictorial depth perception. *Journal of Cross-Cultural Psychology*, 1974, *5(4)*, 434–450.

Smith, O. W., Smith, P. C., and Hubbard, D. Perceived distance as a function of the method of representing perspective. *American Journal of Psychology*, 1958, *71*, 662–675.

Thouless, R. H. Phenomenal regression to the real object, I. *British Journal of Psychology*, 1931*a*, *21*, 338–359.

Thouless, R. H. Phenomenal regression to the real object, II. *British Journal of Psychology*, 1931*b*, *22*, 1.

Thouless, R. H. A racial difference in perception. *Journal of Social Psychology*, 1933, *4*, 330–339.

Vinnicombe, P. The recording of rock paintings in the upper reaches of the Umkomaas, Umzimkulu, and Umzimvubu rivers. *South African Journal of Science*, 1960, *56*, 11–14.

Waldron, L. A., and Gallimore, A. J. Pictorial depth perception in Papua New Guinea, Torres Strait, and Australia. *Australian Journal of Psychology*, 1973, *25*, 89–92.

Warburton, F. W. The ability of the Gurkha recruit. *British Journal of Psychology*, 1951, *42*, 123–133.

Werner, H. *Comparative psychology of mental development.* New York: International Universities Press, 1948.

Wilcox, A. R. Hand imprints in rock paintings. *South African Journal of Science*, 1959, *55*, 292–298.

Wilcox, A. R. Marine animals in rock paintings. *South African Journal of Science*, 1962, *58*, 6.

Wilcox, A. R. Who made the rock art of South Africa and when? *South African Journal of Science*, 1966, *62*, 8–12.

Winter, W. The perception of safety posters by Bantu industrial workers. *Psychologia Africana*, 1963, *10*, 127–135.

Witkin, H. A. Cultural influences in the development of cognitive style. In *Cross-cultural studies in mental development.* Symposium 36, XVIIIth International Congress of Psychology, Moscow, 1966, pp. 95–109.

Witkin, H. A., Lewis, H. B., Hartzman, M., Machover, K., Meissner, P., and Wapner, S. *Personality through perception: An experimental and clinical study.* New York: Harper and Brothers, 1954.

Woodhouse, H. C. Prehistoric hunting methods as depicted in the rock paintings of Southern Africa. *South African Journal of Science*, 1966, *62*, 169–171.

Woodhouse, H. C. Strange relationships between men and eland in the rock paintings of South Africa. *South African Journal of Science*, 1971, *67*, 345–348.

Woodhouse, H. C. Some rock paintings of North Western Natal. *South African Journal of Science*, 1972, *68*, 171–176.

Woodhouse, H. C. Enigmatic line feature in the rock paintings of Southern Africa. *South African Journal of Science*, 1975, *71*, 121–125.

Yonas, A., and Hagen, M. A. Effects of static and kinetic depth information on the perception of size in children and adults. *Journal of Experimental Child Psychology*, 1973, *15*, 254–265.

7

Visual Impairment and the Development of Perceptual Ability

EMERSON FOULKE AND EDWARD P. BERLÁ

1. Definition, Prevalence, Etiology

In order to be considered legally blind, a person must have "central visual acuity of 20/200 or less in the better eye, with correcting lenses; or central visual acuity of more than 20/200 if there is a field defect in which the peripheral field has contracted to such an extent that the widest diameter of the visual field represents an angular distance no greater than 20 degrees" (American Foundation for the Blind, 1967). As a consequence of the legal definition, the word "blind" is used as a label that groups together people who are totally without sight and people with a considerable degree of vision. Therefore, it might prove advantageous to use other functional criteria in defining degrees of blindness, such as the ability or inability to read newspaper print, vision that is useful for reading but not for travel, or vision that is useful for travel but not for reading.

For all age groups combined, retinal diseases, cataracts, and glaucoma account for approximately half of all blindness and these causes of blindness increase with age. Approximately 10% of all blind persons are totally blind and an additional 11% have light perception or less. Approximately 7.3% have a restricted visual field. This means that 75–80% of the legally blind population have some vision (Hatfield, 1975). Each year, school-aged, legally blind children across the nation are registered with the American Printing House for the

EMERSON FOULKE • Perceptual Alternatives Laboratory, University of Louisville, Louisville, Kentucky 40208. EDWARD P. BERLÁ, • Special Education Unit. School of Education, University of Louisville, Louisville, Kentucky 40208.

Blind (APH) in Louisville, Kentucky, for the purpose of allocating money under the Federal Quota Act. In 1975, there were 27,320 children registered, with the APH with 6333 reported as reading braille, 12,002 reading large type, 1170 reading both braille and large type, and 7515 reading neither. There were 1168 children classified as deaf-blind. Using a study sample of 3885 students drawn from the 20,216 blind students on the APH registry in 1969, Hatfield (1975) found that the age at onset of blindness was under 1 year for 75% of the sample.

2. Concept Development

It is generally accepted that the experiential deficits caused by blindness interfere with the cognitive development of the blind child (Foulke, 1962; Lowenfeld, 1950) and that the seriousness of this interference depends on the degree of visual impairment and the age of the child at its onset. Lowenfeld (1950, 1973) has concluded that blindness imposes limitations on the range and variety of experiences, on the ability to get about, and on interaction with the environment. Vision gives the sighted infant access to a rich source of informative stimulation. The sighted infant experiences color, brightness, and the movement of objects in an organized pattern at a distance. For the totally blind child, color and brightness are not experienced at all, and he must depend on touch for the learning of many concepts and the identification of many objects. The perceptual organization of the environment, the spatial array, must be acquired through audition and touch. Acoustic energy contains cues that are relevant for some environmental events, but it contains no information about the shapes or surface textures of objects, or about their arrangements in space. Knowledge of these properties must come from direct haptic experience with the environment, or, where this is not possible, careful verbal description.

The totally blind child must learn to associate sounds with the objects to which they refer. However, unless special precautions are taken, the conditions required for the formation of such associations may be met only sporadically. For example, hearing the sound an object makes and feeling that object may be so widely separated in time that the child can form no association between the two experiences. Most objects are not sources of sound, and some objects that make sounds may be completely inaccessible to touch. The child may have no haptic experience with which he can associate the sound made by a bird, a jackhammer, or an airplane. He may be able to associate such sounds with the verbal descriptions he has received from parents, teachers, and other sighted persons, but the verbal descriptions rendered by sighted persons frequently lack meaning for the blind child, because they are given in visual terms. Thus, the blind child may acquire concepts that have no foundation in his own experience and no specific meaning for him. He learns verbal labels for his inadequate concepts, and uses these "verbalisms" in his conversation with others (Do-kecki, 1966). A clear example of verbalism is offered by Cutsforth (1951, p. 52), who quotes a paragraph from an article written by Helen Keller (1930) in which she describes a country scene with such phrases as ". . . glimpsed through a mist of green," ". . . a tide of green advancing upon the silver grey stream," ". . . soft clouds tumbling," and ". . . intensifying the green-ness."

The use of verbalisms has several serious implications for the developing blind child. According to Scott (1969), the blind child whose concept labels are verbalisms does not distinguish adequately between his own experiences and the experiences reported to him by others, and he cannot test the validity of concepts based on the secondhand experience he has received from others, because the validation of concepts often requires replication of the experience from which they were derived, and he cannot replicate secondhand experience (Foulke, 1962). The use of verbalisms also implies an impairment of com-munication that may not be immediately apparent to teachers and others who interact with the blind child. When he uses verbalisms in his conversation with others, they may assume that the words he uses have the same meanings for him as for them. Under these circumstances, the lack of communication may be too remote to be readily associated with their cause.

Even when blind children have direct haptic experience, they often acquire erroneous information about objects and concepts. Deutsch (1940) relates a story about a class of blind children who inspected haptically a stuffed squirrel mounted on a branch of a tree. Subsequently, they were presented with only the branch and called it a squirrel. On numerous occasions, Berlá has observed blind children exploring objects with their hands in an unsystematic and in-complete way, and, when they try to identify the objects they have explored in this manner, the stored information to which they have recourse is inadequate for identification. For instance, when blind children examined geometric forms in a discrimination task (Berlá, 1972b), their judgments of "same" and "dif-ferent" were made without complete exploration of the figures. They would make an erroneous identification of a figure as a square or a triangle after feel-ing only a part of it, and when questioned they would say such things as "It has a corner" or "It has straight lines and corners."

The blind child's conceptual development and his knowledge of his envi-ronment are also impeded by his restricted mobility. At a single glance, a sighted child in a novel environment can acquire information about objects and their spatial relationships. The blind child must acquire this information in a piecemeal fashion by moving about the novel environment and exploring it with his hands. Often, the blind child hesitates to explore novel environments because he apprehends danger. Even if he does explore, he will almost cer-tainly acquire less information than the sighted child because his inspection is less detailed and limited to objects within arm's reach. This analysis is supported by the results of a study reported by Kephart, Kephart, and Schwarz (1974), in which they compared blind and sighted children, between 5 and 7 years of age, with respect to their knowledge of the environment. The blind children had less complete, less detailed, and less accurate information about the environment than the sighted children. They made only one-third as many responses as the sighted children, and 31% of the responses they made were classified as inappropriate: e.g., "trees and buttons are parts of a house." None of the responses of the sighted children was classified as inappropriate.

A number of comparative studies of blind and sighted infants have failed to disclose any developmental differences in the first few months of life (Adelson and Fraiberg, 1974; Fraiberg, 1968; Fraiberg, Siegal, and Gibson, 1966; Freedman and Cannady, 1971; Norris, Spaulding, and Brodie, 1957). The two groups cannot be distinguished by developmental indices such as head, chest, and finger movements, sitting alone, rolling over, or taking steps with hands held. The age at which blind and sighted infants begin to behave differently depends on the behavior that is observed. Sighted infants typically reach for objects at about 3–4 months of age, while blind infants do not reach for objects until they are 9–12 months of age (Adelson and Fraiberg, 1974). Auditory stimuli contain less spatial information than visual stimuli, and hence, it may be that the blind child needs more time to learn the significance of auditory stimuli. Objects whose presence and location are specified by auditory stimuli will not be reached for until this significance is learned. By the time the blind child begins to reach for objects, the sighted child has already had several months of experience in the kind of purposeful reaching behavior that gives him the practice he needs for the coordination of finger, hand, and body movement. Since crawling and walking require the coordination of motor activity and the use of spatial information for the regulation of motor activity, the fact that blind infants reach for objects they hear at a later age than the age at which sighted infants reach for the objects they see is probably a factor of primary importance in explaining the delayed onset of crawling and walking that is generally observed among congenitally blind infants (Adelson and Fraiberg, 1976).

Reaching for objects is a necessary condition for the development of object constancy. For sighted children, object constancy appears to develop at about 2 years of age, but Fraiberg (1968) reports that blind children do not develop object constancy until they are 3–5 years of age. With the exception of objects that make sounds, the blind child can experience only those objects within his reach. If he accidentally puts an object beyond his reach, for instance, by pushing it out of his crib, or if it is placed beyond his reach by another person, the object disappears. There is no remaining evidence of its existence. On the other hand, the sighted child continues to see the object that is placed beyond his reach, and therefore he continues to have evidence of its existence. Furthermore, since the object that is placed beyond his reach on one occasion will, in all likelihood, be placed within his reach again on a subsequent occasion, he has ample opportunity to associate the visual experience and the haptic experience of that object. Some objects are characterized by the sounds they make, and, when this is the case, the blind child will have auditory evidence of the continued existence of an object that has been placed beyond his reach. However, even the objects that make characteristic sounds do not, in most cases, emit sound continuously. The stuffed toy may be identifiable by its squeak, but it does not squeak unless it is squeezed. Since characteristic sounds are usually intermittent, it is difficult for the blind child to learn their predictive significance.

In order to facilitate the attainment of object constancy, those who work with blind children recommend that they be given confined areas in which to play so that toys will always be within reach. Fraiberg, Smith, and Adelson (1969) and Norris et al. (1957) report that when congenitally blind children experience planned, systematic stimulation many of the developmental lags typically observed are substantially reduced, and Fraiberg et al. (1969) have outlined an educational program for congenitally blind children which provides the systematic stimulation they need for proper development.

Legally blind children who have some remaining vision usually do not show the developmental lags that are observed in the behavior of totally blind children. Apparently, very little vision is required to make the developing child aware that there is a world beyond his reach to be explored.

Imitation plays an important role in learning many of the skilled performances acquired by the developing child. Imitation requires observation, and when the imitated activity involves the manipulation of tools, objects, and materials, visual observation is much more informative than haptic observation. For the most part, the information that guides imitation of this kind cannot be acquired by auditory observation. For example, the sound produced by sawing wood contains no information about the tool that is used, the manner of its use, or the result of its use. Of course, verbal descriptions may be used, but verbal description is frequently a poor substitute for direct observation in learning a skilled performance.

Much of the learning accomplished during the developmental years is incidental learning. The child becomes familiar with countless objects that he does not manipulate or use. Many of the objects that furnish the world of the sighted child are accessible by visual observation alone, and they therefore cannot be a part of the blind child's experience. The scale of some objects is inappropriate for haptic observation. The mountain is too large and the details on a coin are too small. In some cases, haptic observation exposes the observer to danger. Consider, for instance, a wasp, or a sewing machine while it is in operation. Some objects, such as snowflakes, are too fragile to withstand haptic observation. Other objects, such as flowers, lack the rigidity that is necessary for haptic observation, and their shapes change when they are touched. Many objects are simply inaccessible. The blind child can never experience clouds or stars. The sighted child becomes familiar with many objects by observing pictures of them, but, since pictures do not exhibit spatial extension in three dimensions, they elude haptic observation. Much of this experiential deficit can be counteracted by providing models that are suitable for haptic observation. But models are often expensive, and, unless particular care is taken, they are apt to lack haptic authenticity.

3. Tangible Graphics

Graphic displays, such as pictures, drawings, diagrams, and maps, constitute an important source of information for those who can see them. However, they are usually intangible, because they are realized in only two dimensions, and they would have to be realized in three dimensions to be discernible by touch. The third dimension can be added by using raised lines, points, and textures. Translations of this sort usually fail to preserve all of the information in visible displays, for several reasons. The haptic perceptual system has much less capacity for pattern resolution than the visual perceptual system. As a result, it is often necessary to enlarge some of the details of visible displays in order for them to be appreciated by touch, and other details must be eliminated to reduce clutter and confusion. Figure-ground relationships are often disturbed, so that what is apparent in the visible display may be obscure in the tangible display. Of course, information that is conveyed by color is lost altogether.

Tangible graphs and maps are used to present information to blind students. As has already been pointed out, the information that can be acquired from such displays is limited by characteristics of the haptic perceptual system. A further limitation is imposed by the experiential deficits that characterize blind children. The blind child cannot interpret schematic representations of aspects of the real world if he has no conception of the aspects that are to be represented schematically. In studies of the geographic knowledge of blind children, Franks and Nolan (1970, 1971) found that they had an inadequate grasp of geographic concepts such as oceans, lakes, beaches, ports, islands, mountains, hills, valleys, and canyons. Of course, tangible maps on which geographic concepts were represented schematically would be uninterpretable by blind children who lacked those concepts. Furthermore, in order for blind children to acquire information from tangible maps and other schematic displays, they must understand that selected features of the tridimensional world can be abstracted and represented by symbols arranged on a bidimensional surface (Berlá and Butterfield, 1975; Wiedel, 1969).

It should be possible, in large measure, to overcome these problems by systematically arranging experiences for the blind child that lead to readiness for the effective use of maps in educational settings, and as sources for some of the information needed for successful mobility. As a beginning, the blind child might be encouraged to make a systematic exploration of a room in which he spends a significant portion of his time, such as a classroom, bedroom, or dining room, in order to acquire an accurate memorial representation of that room. The observing activities in which the blind child must engage in order to acquire the information needed for memorial representations of space are quite different from the observing activities that suffice when vision is used. The sighted child can, at a single glance, become aware of the extension and structure of the space in which he is operating. The blind child must interpret auditory, tactile, and proprioceptive stimulation to become aware of the space in which he is operating. Since the stimulation he can experience is less informative, and since he can observe much less at one time, in order to construct memorial representations of space, he must integrate information about the extension and structure of space that has been acquired serially. He will need more time to construct the memorial representation of space, and the adequacy of that representation cannot be assumed. Therefore, his exploration of the room should be continued until he can demonstrate that he has an accurate memorial representation of its shape and size, of the objects in it, and of their arrangement. When he has achieved an adequate representation, he could be provided with a map of the room that shows its boundaries, the objects in it, and their locations. Then, in order to explicate the relationship between the map and the room, he could be given tasks in which he is required to find objects, both in the room and on the map. This procedure could be repeated for progressively larger spaces, such as the building in which he lives, the building and the yard, the block in which he lives, and his neighborhood.

In constructing a map, the cartographer uses point symbols, linear symbols, and areal symbols. Of course, these symbols must be discriminable, but given the capacity of the visual system for the resolution of pattern, the adequacy of the supply of discriminable symbols is not a serious problem in the construction of visible maps. However, the haptic system has much less capacity for the resolution of pattern, and, as a consequence, the differences that distinguish tangible symbols must often be much larger than the differences that distinguish visible symbols to which meanings can be assigned. Furthermore, those who construct tangible maps have little haptic experience of their own to consult in choosing symbols, and there has been little systematic research concerning the discriminability of tangible symbols.

One approach to the problem of discriminability is to specify a set of tangible symbols for possible use, to determine by experiment the accuracy with which they can be discriminated from each other, and to exclude from the final set those symbols that fail to meet some criterion of discriminability defined in advance of the experiment. Using this approach, Nolan and Morris (1971) identified a set of point symbols, a set of linear symbols, and a set of areal symbols, with high discriminability among the symbols within each set, and Gill and

James (1973) identified a set of highly discriminable point symbols. The practical value of research of this type is obvious. A set of symbols of proven discriminability can be used for map making with reasonable assurance that maps will be legible, as long as no new symbols are introduced into the set, and as long as symbols are always formed in exactly the same way.

An approach that yields results which can be generalized to a variety of situations would be preferable. This objective might be realized by the collection of basic psychophysical data concerning the capacity of the haptic perceptual system in regard to the spatial dimensions of tangible forms. If, for each relevant stimulus dimension, information were available concerning the absolute threshold, the range of usable stimulus values, the size of the just noticeable difference, and the number of absolute identifications of stimulus magnitude that can be made, it should be possible to make a reliable estimate of the internal discriminability of any set of tangible symbols that is proposed for use in a given application, without the necessity of conducting a special discrimination experiment for that purpose. As an example of this approach, Berlá and Murr (1975b) have determined the difference between the widths of two tangible lines that is just noticeable by the preferred index fingertip, the fingertip on which a haptic observer would place considerable reliance in his exploration of a tangible map. For a series of standards ranging from 0.04 inch to 0.25 inch in width, the proportion of change necessary to discriminate a line width as greater than a standard decreased as the standard became larger. The practical implication of this kind of study is that it provides a set of values from which a highly discriminable set of line widths can be determined using the psychophysical functions and these values are not limited to the particular standards used in the experiment.

Even when the symbols used in constructing a tangible map have adequate discriminability, if their density is too high, the result may be a cluttered map surface with reduced legibility. For example, blind children often confuse the lines that denote degrees of longitude and latitude with the lines used to specify political boundaries and denote physical features, such as rivers. Berlá and Butterfield (1975) and some teachers have solved this problem by using removable grids to show the disposition of lines denoting degrees of longitude and latitude. In their studies of the legibility of tangible maps, Wiedel and Groves (1969) have found the compass rose used to indicate compass points on visible maps to be a source of confusion on tangible maps. They therefore omitted this symbol, and provided the cue needed for proper orientation of the tangible map by adding a light texture to its north edge. Schiff, Kaufer, and Mosak (1966), in their study of the legibility of tangible graphs, found that when the symbol used on visible graphs to indicate the direction of an arrow was used on tangible graphs for the same purpose, blind students were frequently unable to make correct determinations of the direction in which the arrow was pointing. Schiff (1966) solved this problem by replacing arrows with raised lines which, like the hair on a dog's back, offer low impedence to stroking in one direction and high impedence to stroking in the other. Thus, a blind student is able to determine the direction of the raised line regardless of where his finger is on the line.

Visual experience is a poor guide in predicting what will be perceived as figure and what as background on a tangible map or graph. As a consequence, the features on a tangible map or graph that ought to be salient are often obscured by background detail. In composing visible graphic displays, differences in color are frequently used to differentiate figure from background, and it is a common assumption that differences in texture can be used for the same purpose in the composition of tangible graphic displays. However, Berlá and Murr (1975a) found that adding a prominent texture to the surface on a tangible map increased the difficulty of finding and identifying point symbols, and decreased the speed with which lines raised above the textured surface could be traced by the fingertip.

It is apparent from the research and experience reviewed so far that we do not yet know how to compose tangible graphic displays which are fully compatible with the perceptual abilities of haptic observers, and that we do not yet know what information to include in those displays. Nevertheless, tangible graphic displays, particularly maps and graphs, are used extensively in the education of blind children. For example, one series of braille textbooks examined by Arampatta (1970) contains 937 tangible maps and representations. Of this number, 837 were raised line representations of the ink print maps. In spite of their uncertain effectiveness, tangible graphic displays are used. Their use is, in part, a consequence of the fact that the braille books with which blind children are provided are transcriptions of printed books, designed for use by sighted children. Also, graphic displays are ideally suited for the communication of some kinds of information. Verbal description is the obvious alternative to graphic display, but in comparison to the graphic explication of relationships verbal explication is often quite cumbersome.

In addition to the perceptual difficulties inherent in tangible graphic displays, their effectiveness is often further limited by serious deficiencies in the observing skills of those who attempt to use them. The blind children observed by Nolan and Morris (1971) lacked even rudimentary skills, such as techniques for ensuring systematic examination of a map surface. It is not surprising that blind schoolchildren lack the skills they need to acquire the information conveyed by graphic displays.

The interpretation of tangible graphic displays is a complex skilled performance, and before it can be taught to haptic observers its component skills must be identified. As a first step in identifying these subskills, Berlá (1972a) questioned a sample of highly educated blind adults, who were skillful map readers, concerning the techniques they used to scan a map. They reported a variety of techniques. Some used both hands. Others used only one. Some scanned from left to right, as if they were reading a braille book, and some scanned from top to bottom or bottom to top. However, regardless of the technique, all of them were systematic in their approach, and scanned the entire map surface.

Berlá (1973) and Berlá and Murr (1974) trained blind students in grades 4–12 to use the scanning techniques reported by the skillful blind adults. One group was trained to scan from top to bottom. Scanning from top to bottom proved to be a more effective way of locating map symbols than scanning from left to right. Those who scanned from top to bottom veered less and covered more map area during each scan than those who scanned from left to right.

In a further effort to identify the subskills involved in map reading, Berlá, Butterfield, and Murr (1976) made video recordings of blind students as they engaged in a task requiring the careful observation of a map. Subjects first examined a cue card on which was displayed the raised outline of one of the American states. They were then given a pseudopolitical map that included the outline displayed on the cue card and asked to find that outline. They were scored for both time and accuracy of identification. Following this, the video tapes were scrutinized in order to identify those observing behaviors that differentiate between good and poor map readers.

The typical good map reader examined the shape outlined on the cue card by picking a starting point, and by tracing the outline in one continuous motion until he returned to the starting point. While examining a shape, he appeared to be searching for distinctive features, such as curves or sharply pointed projections and indentations. The typical poor map reader manifested these behaviors significantly less often. Instead, he skipped around the outline in an unsystematic manner. In his attempt to find on the map the shape outlined on the cue card, the typical good map reader appeared to be searching for the features that impressed him as distinctive during his examination of the cue card. Upon locating a distinctive feature of the target shape, he would trace the entire outline in order to confirm its identification. The typical poor map reader searched for distinctive features significantly less often, and frequently appeared to be attempting the identification of a target shape on the basis of its overall configuration or size. Often, when he appeared to have found the target shape, his behavior suggested that he was distracted in his attempt to trace it by the intersecting lines of adjacent shapes. When he followed an intersecting line, he would become disoriented, and lose the shape he had apparently found. The typical poor map reader was also different from the typical good map reader in terms of the ability to trace lines. He would begin tracing a line with his index finger, stray from the line, and then return to it at a different point than the point of departure.

Guided by these results, Berlá and Butterfield (1977) conducted two additional studies to determine whether the abilities that differentiate between good and poor tangible map readers are responsive to specific training. In each experiment, matched pairs of blind students were divided into an experimental group and a control group. The members of the experimental group were trained in three ½-hr sessions on consecutive days to search for the distinctive features of raised outlines and to trace raised lines. In the first experiment, subjects were administered trials in which they examined the raised outline of a shape and then examined four additional outlines to find one that matched the first outline. The average number of correct recognitions for the experimental group exceeded the average number of correct recognitions for the control group by 32%. In the second experiment, subjects were administered trials in which they examined a cue card displaying the raised outline of a state or country, and they searched for that shape on a pseudopolitical map. The average number of shapes found by the experimental group exceeded the average number of shapes found by the control group by 25%, and the average time spent by the experimental group in finding figures was 41% less than the average time spent by the control group.

4. Mobility

Special educators and rehabilitation specialists have come to recognize the attainment by the blind person of skill in independent travel as a major objective. "Mobility," the term by which this skill is known, can be defined as the ability to travel from one place to another safely, comfortably, gracefully, and independently (Foulke, 1970). Mobility is a composite ability that includes the ability to move through space without disruption because of accidental contact with obstacles, and the ability to maintain the spatial orientation on which purposeful or goal-directed movement depends. The blind person who acquires this skill is released from a life-style characterized by passive reliance on others, and thus the achievement of mobility is a necessary condition for personal independence and vocational success.

Two related approaches can be discerned in the efforts of practitioners and researchers to assist blind persons in the achievement of mobility—the training approach, and the supplementation approach. The objective of the training approach is to improve the ability of the blind pedestrian to acquire and utilize the spatial information on which successful mobility depends. The objective of the supplementation approach is to enrich the supply of spatial information by means of one or more mobility aids.

The training approach has led to the development of orientation and mobility (O&M) programs in which certified O&M specialists provide basic instruction in the skills that underlie orientation and mobility. In general, the approach taken by these specialists begins with an evaluation of each candidate's needs for mobility and his readiness for learning the skills that contribute to mobility. This phase is followed by a period of instruction that is tailored to meet the identified needs of the trainee. However, the training methods and procedures employed by O&M specialists have not been derived from any experimentally validated theory of mobility that defines the mobility task and specifies the sensory, perceptual, cognitive, and motor abilities required for the performance of that task. Rather, they are based on a community of experience and common sense, and there is considerable variety in the methods and procedures used and advocated by O&M specialists (Warren and Kocon, 1974).

The supplementation approach has led to the development of a variety of mobility aids, including the "long cane" (Hoover, 1950), and a number of electronic devices which convert reflected ultrasonic energy or coherent light to auditory or tactile signals, suitable for human reception (Benjamin, 1970; Kay, 1972; Russell, 1971). These aids exhibit considerable diversity with respect to the type and amount of information they display and the sensory channel they address, but they have the common purpose of supplementing the information that is otherwise available to the blind pedestrian.

That blind pedestrians have been helped by training programs and applications of technology is beyond dispute, but in spite of these gains a persistent problem remains. Mobility aids that seemed feasible during development have failed to live up to the expectations of their inventors when judged against the criterion test of acceptance and use by blind pedestrians (Graystone and McLenna, 1968). Likewise, recent observations of the behavior of blind pedestrians indicate that, despite elaborate training programs, the lack of independent mobility continues to be one of the most serious deficiencies of the blind graduates of rehabilitative programs (Cratty, 1971).

The missing factor that may account for the shortcomings of many of the attempted solutions to the mobility problem is an adequate understanding of this complex skill. In the absence of any experimentally verified theory of mobility, practitioners have had no choice but to employ an intuitive and rational approach. In practice, this approach has meant reliance on individual insights, unsupported by objective data, for the elaboration of training methods and the design of sensory aids. Ideally, the development of training methods and the design of mobility aids should be guided by a general theory of mobility, based on research which specifies the sensory, perceptual, cognitive, and motor abilities on which successful performance depends. Such a theory would set the design requirements for mobility aids and provide the clarification of the blind pedestrian's task that is needed in order to increase the effectiveness of mobility instruction.

Two plausible models of the mobility of blind pedestrians have been proposed (Foulke, 1970; Kay, 1974). Both theories propose an internal representation of the blind pedestrian's environment which serves as reference for the evaluation of feedback. Both authors list general properties of the constructs they have proposed, and thus their theories provide testable predictions. However, at present, neither theory can generate the information needed for practical application.

The basic reason for the paucity of the kind of research that tests theories and evaluates training methods and mobility aids has been the lack of suitable methods for measuring the performance of the blind pedestrian. Recently, significant progress has been made in developing methods for measuring the mobility of blind pedestrians that will permit the quantitative assessment of experimental results (Armstrong, 1975; Shingledecker, 1976), and their rigorous employment in well-designed experiments should provide an understanding of the mobility task that can guide the development of training methods and mobility aids.

5. Alternatives to Visual Reading

Because of the way in which they are displayed, the patterns used as symbols in the print code take effective advantage of the ability of the visual system to perceive spatial organization. The relatively high acuity of the visual system enables the discrimination and identification of the relatively small patterns that serve as symbols, and the relatively large field of view of the visual system makes possible the observation, at one time, of a relatively large number of symbols. The information content of individual symbols is low, but with reading experience they can be combined to form spatially extended patterns, such as syllables, words, and phrases, the information content of which is high. Since the spatially extended patterns can be perceived as quickly as their component symbols (Cattell, 1886), the print code can be read at an impressively high rate (Gallo, 1972).

The symbols in the print code are displayed spatially. The visual system is ideally suited for the acquisition of spatially distributed information. This high compatibility between the display and the perceptual system that observes it accounts for the efficiency of visual reading. When visual impairment reduces or eliminates the reader's ability to observe this spatial display, it becomes necessary to alter the display in some manner in order to bring it into a compatible relationship with the remaining perceptual abilities of the visually impaired reader. However, this is not done without a price. If the reader's ability to observe an altered spatial display is reduced, or if a temporal display is substituted for the spatial display, reading performance will suffer. All of the reading alternatives to be considered in this section are inferior to normal visual reading, and in every case this inferiority is explained by the perceptual operations that must be employed by the reader in order to acquire information from the display he is able to observe.

5.1. Reading Large Print

Most of the individuals classified as blind under the legal definition of blindness have some vision, and many of them can see well enough to identify print symbols, if they are made large enough. In fact, a few legally blind per-

sons can read normal print (Sykes, 1971). The requirements of visually impaired readers can be met either by printing larger symbols or by using optical
magnifiers (Sloan, 1972) or electronic magnifiers (Genensky, Barak, Moshin,
and Steingold, 1969) to enlarge conventional symbols. However, the enlarge-
ment of symbols reduces the number of symbols that can be observed at one
time, and this limits the reader's ability to integrate symbols in order to form
spatially extended patterns that specify syllables, words, and phrases. In addition to the loss of acuity that characterizes visual impairment, many visually
impaired readers suffer a restriction of the visual field which also reduces the
number of symbols that can be observed at one time.

The consequence of a reduction in the number of symbols that can be observed at one time should be a reduction in reading rate, and it is. In a project
sponsored by the Education Commission of the States (Gallo, 1972), a median
silent visual reading rate of 195 words per minute (wpm) was found for high
school students who were instructed to read for comprehension, but Nolan,
Morris, Kederis, Fieg, and Smith (1966) found a mean reading rate of 80 wpm
for a representative sample of those students in residential schools for the blind
who read large print.

In addition to letter size, there are other display variables that influence the
performance of the visually impaired reader of large print. These variables
include the color and reflectance of letters, the color and reflectance of the surface on which they are printed, the contrast between letters and the surface on
which they are printed, and the illumination of the field in which they are
viewed. Parametric studies in which these variables have been systematically
manipulated suggest that the reading situation can be optimized for the visually
impaired reader by choosing the proper combination of their values (Eakin and
McFarland, 1960; Eakin, Pratt, and McFarland, 1961; Nolan, 1959, 1961).

In recent years, educators of visually impaired children have been made
increasingly aware of the large differences in visual effectiveness that can be
observed in the performance of visually impaired persons. For example, adults
with serious visual impairments who learned to read before the onset of visual
impairment are often able to read print that cannot be read by persons who did
not learn to read before the onset of visual impairment, because they can take
effective advantage of the reduced cues made available to them by their impaired vision. Visual stimulation has not been an important source of information for many visually impaired persons who could see well enough to acquire
useful information from it, because until recently there was no organized and
systematic effort to teach children with severe visual impairment to interpret visual stimulation. In part, this failure was the consequence of a fairly widely
held belief that the regular use of severely impaired eyes would strain them,
with a further loss of vision as the probable result.

An even more significant factor was the failure to realize the potential visual capability of children with severe visual impairment. As a result, many

visually impaired children with usable vision were taught the coping strategies that would be appropriate for persons without any functional vision. They were taught to be blind. Dr. Natalie Barraga and Dr. Samuel Genensky deserve much of the credit for the current level of awareness of the potential visual capability of children with severe visual impairments. Barraga (1964) has demonstrated that a program of instruction which provides properly selected and sequenced visual experiences can actualize the visual potential of the child with a severe visual impairment. As a result of the heightened awareness of visual potential, many children who would formerly have been taught to read braille are now being taught to read print. Genesky has played a major role in the development of the television reading aid, a device that senses the printed page with a camera and displays the image thus acquired on a television receiver. He has shown (1970) that with the manipulation of display variables afforded by the television reading aid, many children with severe visual impairment can find a combination of display variables that permit them to read ordinary print books.

5.2. Reading Braille

The characters in the braille code are dot patterns to which meanings have been assigned. Included in the code are the 63 dot patterns that can be formed in a matrix with three rows and two columns of possible dot positions. In such a matrix, it is possible to form 64 discrete patterns. Figure 1 shows four exemplary dot patterns. The first dot pattern is the one that results when a dot is placed in each of the six matrix positions. The other three dot patterns are simply examples of the patterns that can be formed in such a matrix. In the parlance of the braille community, the matrix in which dot patterns are formed is called a "cell," and we observe this convention hereafter.

The centers of vertically or horizontally adjacent dots in a cell are separated by 0.090 inch. The centers of dots at corresponding locations in adjacent cells in the line of writing are separated by 0.250 inch. The centers of dots at corresponding locations in adjacent cells that are in adjacent lines of writing are separated by 0.400 inch. The height of a braille dot is between 0.015 and 0.020 inch. Although these spacing values were not determined by the results of formal experiments, subsequent research (Meyers, Ethington, and Ashcroft, 1958) has indicated that they were well chosen.

The meanings assigned to the 63 dot patterns in the braille code include the 26 letters of the alphabet and the punctuation marks. These assignments do

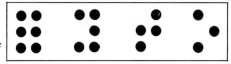

Fig. 1. A filled braille cell and three braille letters.

not exhaust the supply of dot patterns, and frequently recurring letter groups are associated with the remaining dot patterns. Such symbols are called "contractions." Figure 2 affords a comparison of the uncontracted and the contracted form of the word "standing."

The display of braille symbols is, in important ways, analogous to the display of print symbols. Braille symbols are displayed horizontally, in lines that are read from left to right, and lines of symbols are arranged in an ordered sequence from the top of the page to its bottom. Because the two codes are displayed in the same manner, the braille code retains many of the advantages of the print code. The braille reader, like the print reader, can vary his reading rate at will, and retrace at will in order to process ambiguous matter more thoroughly. Furthermore, because braille symbols are displayed spatially, the braille reader, like the print reader, can use such features of the display as paragraph indentations, skipped lines, and centered headings as retrieval cues to guide his search for specific information.

In spite of these advantages, the efficiency of braille reading is limited by a disadvantage of overriding importance, the slow rate at which it is read by most braille readers. Although braille can be read much faster by touch than embossed print, the tactual reading of braille is much slower than the visual reading of print. On the average, the braille reading rate is 60 wpm for junior high school students, 80 wpm for senior high school students (Meyers *et al.*, 1958; Nolan and Kederis, 1969), and 104 wpm for experienced adult braille readers (Foulke, 1964). This reading rate should be compared with the median silent visual reading rate of 195 wpm for high school seniors cited earlier. Just as there are exceptionally able readers of print, there are a few braille readers who can read in the neighborhood of 250 wpm (Grunwald, 1966).

There is considerable variability in the teaching methods employed by

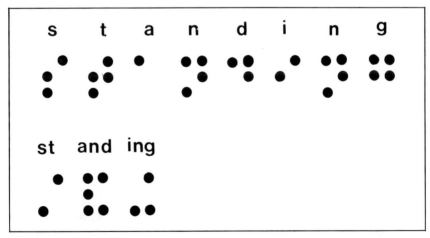

Fig. 2. A word written in contracted and uncontracted form.

those who teach blind children to read braille. Some of these methods are undoubtedly better than others, but there has been little or none of the kind of comparative research in which the conditions of observation are carefully controlled, and the efficacy of any given method is, at present, a matter of opinion, informed or otherwise. In our opinion, even the possibility of formulating a teaching method capable of bringing about a significant improvement in the braille reading rate must await a better understanding than we now have of the basic perceptual processes on which the reading of braille depends.

A review of the research so far conducted discloses three general approaches to the understanding of braille reading. In one of these approaches, an effort is made to obtain a more careful description of the reading behavior of braille readers, and to compare the reading behavior of fast and slow braille readers. A second approach is to measure the legibility of braille symbols and words, and to assess the contribution of legibility to the braille reading rate. In the third approach, variables relating to the display of braille symbols are manipulated in order to observe their effects on braille reading performance. Studies in this category frequently ascertain the effects of the same variables on print reading performance in order to acquire comparative data.

A study reported by Fertsch (1946) is a good example of the first approach. She made motion pictures of the hands of braille readers as they read. By studying these pictures, she found that her subjects used only index fingers for reading and that those who employed two index fingers usually read faster than those who employed only one. When two index fingers were employed, best results were usually obtained by those who divided the reading task between two hands by searching for the beginning of the next line with the index finger of the left hand while reading to the end of the current line with the index finger of the right hand. This strategy permitted the reader to eliminate those periods of time during which no information is acquired that would otherwise be inserted between the finishing of one line and the beginning of the next. Those who employ this method of reading are faster than others not because they can acquire more information from the stimulation provided by braille reading, but because they can make more efficient use of time spent in reading.

Fertsch's movies also provided clear records of the ineffective behaviors of poor braille readers. Poor readers frequently engaged in vertical scrubbing motions. They retraced frequently and often strayed from the line they were reading.

Under the second approach, the objective is to determine the legibility of braille symbols and words by measuring the speed and accuracy with which subjects can identify them absolutely, discriminate them one from another, or reconstruct them from memory. Nolan and Kederis (1969) assessed the legibility of the characters in the braille code by determining their absolute identifiability as a function of time of exposure. If subjects are to make absolute identifications of dot patterns, they must already have learned the dot patterns

Emerson Foulke and Edward P. Berlá

to be identified, the names by which they are identified, and the associations between dot patterns and their names, in order to qualify as experimental subjects. The subjects observed by Nolan and Kederis had years of experience in identifying the dot patterns in the braille code. Consequently, these investigators were able to use the minimum time of exposure at which a pattern is identifiable as the index of its legibility. In their study of legibility, they used the tachistotactometer, a tactual analog of the tachistoscope. The control of the time of exposure afforded by this instrument has made possible fairly accurate estimates of the relative legibilities of the symbols in the braille code. Examples of these measures are shown in Table 1. The symbols in this table are ranked in terms of the threshold times of exposure needed for symbol identification. As threshold increases, legibility decreases.

With legibility measured, it is possible to search for those characteristics of a dot pattern that make it legible or illegible, and Nolan and Kederis found that patterns of many dots were less legible than patterns with few dots, and patterns with dots in the lower one-third of the cell were less legible than patterns with dots in only the upper two-thirds of the cell.

The third approach taken by researchers in their investigation of the per-

Table 1. Legibility Thresholds Obtained with a Tachistotactometer[a]

Symbol	Threshold	Symbol	Threshold	Symbol	Threshold
E	0.02	O	0.04	th	0.07
A	0.02	bb	0.05	F	0.07
I	0.02	ing	0.05	the	0.08
C	0.02	en	0.05	gg	0.08
K	0.02	G	0.05	Y	0.09
st	0.03	H	0.06	P	0.10
B	0.03	ar	0.06	W	0.11
ch	0.04	L	0.06	ed	0.12
in	0.04	S	0.06	T	0.12
D	0.04	N	0.06	ou	0.14
M	0.04	V	0.06	R	0.14
U	0.04	ow	0.07		

[a] From Nolan and Kederis (1969), reprinted by permission.

ceptual factors on which the reading of braille depends has been the manipulation of variables relating to the manner in which braille and/or print symbols are displayed. The print reader can observe more of his display at one time than the braille reader, and, in general, print readers can read print much faster than braille readers can read braille. That the difference in favor of print readers is a consequence of the amount that can be observed at one time by print and braille readers is an obvious hypothesis, and it has been examined in several experiments that varied the number of characters displayed at a time.

In 1886, Cattell reported an experiment in which he demonstrated that the time of exposure needed by his subjects to identify several visual symbols was no greater than the time of exposure needed for the identification of a single symbol. Cattell's results have been confirmed by recent experiments (Doggett and Richards, 1975; Foulke and Wirth, 1973).

In an experiment reported by Troxell (1967), a group of visual readers saw printed text displayed on an oscilloscope under two conditions. In one condition, text was displayed a letter at a time. In the other condition, it was displayed a word at a time. Troxell's instrumentation permitted variation of the rate at which items could be presented, and under each condition the maximum reading rate, in words per minute, was determined. When text was displayed a letter at a time his subjects read 19.5 wpm, and when it was displayed a word at a time they read 108.5 wpm. In another condition of Troxell's experiment, experienced braille readers read text displayed a letter at a time, by sensing, with their fingertips, pins that were raised above the display surface to form braille dot patterns. After brief practice, they achieved a reading rate of 18 wpm, the fastest word rate permitted by his instrumentation. Although we cannot exclude the possibility that the braille reading rate observed under this condition was a function of the limitations imposed by Troxell's instrumentation, unpublished research by Foulke suggests that Troxell's result is a reasonable estimate of the braille reading rate that can be expected when text is displayed in that manner.

Troxell's experiment demonstrates two facts of significance for the present discussion. When text was displayed a letter at a time, the performance of tactual readers was not significantly different from the performance of visual readers, suggesting that when the two perceptual systems function under conditions that equate the amount that can be observed at one time, sequences of symbols can be identified as rapidly by touch as by vision. The finding that visual readers were able to increase their reading rate from 19.5 to 108.5 wpm when given the opportunity to experience whole words suggests that they were able to treat whole words as unitary patterns. They did not read faster because they identified the same units at a faster rate, but because they identified larger units, containing more information, at approximately the same rate.

Troxell's experiment did not include one condition that would have been desirable. It would have been useful to know about the reading rate of braille readers when words are displayed a word at a time, as they were for Troxell's visual readers. If braille readers can observe much less at one time than visual readers, they should not be able to take much advantage of the increased amount that is available for observation when text is displayed a word at a time, and the change from displaying text a letter at a time to a word at a time should not increase their reading rate very much.

Obviously, there is a great deal of research to be done, and our current understanding of the braille reading process is not sufficient to justify final conclusions regarding the manner in which braille is read, or the manner in which it might be read if it were properly displayed to adequately trained readers. However, the picture of the braille reading process that can be supported by the data gathered so far is rather disappointing. Because of the limited sensing area on the fingertips, and because only one fingertip at a time is usually engaged in active perception, not much more than one braille symbol can be observed at a time. Even if this were not the case, the mass of the finger, hand, and arm would prevent the extremely rapid movement from one fixation to the next that the tactual reader would have to accomplish in order to imitate the saccadic movements of the eyes. The efficient perception of braille requires continuous lateral motion of the fingertip that is actively engaged in reading, and as a result of this motion, braille symbols must be encountered and perceived serially.

The serial perception of braille symbols has been demonstrated by Nolan and Kederis (1969), who showed that the time needed for the identification of a word written with braille symbols displayed simultaneously is frequently greater than the sum of the times needed for the identification of the symbols that specify it. Of course, this is not always the case, because readers can often use the cues provided by the initial letters of words to predict their remainders. However, there is a strong suggestion that braille readers often find it necessary to register and store percepts in order to achieve the perception of words.

There are many who dispute this description of the braille reading process (Grunwald, 1966; Lowenfeld, Able, and Hatlen, 1969). They maintain that although the patterns identified by the braille reader are disclosed temporally, there is no reason to believe that he is necessarily limited to their perception one at a time. They believe that the patterns identified by the braille reader can have enough temporal extension to encompass entire words, and they cite the performance of a few exceptionally fast braille readers as proof of their contention. This point of view has merit and it deserves to be investigated. However, there has been very little systematic observation of the behavior of exceptionally fast braille readers, and, as yet, we have no data which could support a detailed description of the process in which such readers engage.

5.3. Reading by Listening

Many of the operations that account for the efficiency with which the visual reader can process his display are not available to the person who reads by listening. The listener must process an acoustic display whose organization and presentation are, for the most part, controlled by another person, the oral reader.

By surrendering control of the display to the oral reader, the person who reads by listening loses the ability to manage his own reading rate. Instead, he reads at a rate that is determined, not by his requirements as a reader, but by those factors which determine the reading rate of the oral reader. The oral reading rate is influenced by such factors as the skill of the oral reader, the average length of the words in the selection being read, the difficulty of the material being read. When professional readers, such as radio and television newscasters, or those who read Talking Books for the Library of Congress, read text of average difficulty, the word rate typically observed is in the neighborhood of 175 wpm (Foulke, 1967; Johnson, Darley, and Spriestersbach, 1963). Although this word rate is below the average rate at which print is read, it is above the average rate at which braille is read, and many braille readers willingly forego the advantages associated with the braille display in order to enjoy the faster reading rate they experience when they read by listening. Of course, only 20% of the blind population read braille, and for those who do not, reading by listening is the only widely available alternative to reading print (Kamisar and Pollet, 1975).

The information in the acoustic signal processed by the listener is displayed temporally. Whereas the visual reader processes a spatial display, the listener processes a display that is revealed to him serially. From the perspective of the listener, the elements of acoustically displayed language are probably the syllables which, either singly or in aggregates, specify the words of a language (van Katwijk and 't Hart, 1970). These elements are presented to the listener sequentially, and he cannot operate upon his display in any way to change this sequence, as can the visual reader. As the listener processes his display, the only information it makes available to him at any given point in time is the information contained in the signal that is present at that point in time. Once an element of the display, in its ineluctable temporal procession, has passed by, it cannot conveniently be recalled by the listener for further consideration. Of course, the listener remembers what he has just heard, and he can, if he needs to, consult his memorial representation of the display. However, because of imperfect initial registration, incomplete storage, and all of the other pitfalls that may beset memory, his memorial representation will often not be an adequate representation of the physically present display to which the visual reader has continuous recourse.

Just as the listener cannot listen ahead, he cannot conveniently listen back. It is true that he can rewind a tape, or set the stylus that is reading a record back a few grooves, but this kind of retracing is very slow and inaccurate when compared to the retracing done almost effortlessly and automatically by the visual reader. As a result, the listener's ability to subject those parts of his display that remain unclear after initial observation to reexamination and further analysis is seriously limited.

It has already been pointed out that when language is displayed on the printed page, sentences are grouped in paragraphs defined by marginal indentations and skipped lines. Paragraphs are grouped under centered or italicized headings, and headings are grouped under chapter titles. This arrangement of the printed matter makes it possible for the visual reader to scan his display rapidly in order to retrieve information he desires. Because this kind of structure cannot be imposed on a temporally ordered display, the operations employed by the visual reader for search and retrieval are not available to the listener. This problem can be solved by storing oral reading matter in computers with ample memory, but such a solution is still too expensive to be practical.

The foregoing analysis of the task of reading by listening clearly implies that increasing the efficiency of reading by listening depends on finding ways to give the listener access to those operations that account for the relative efficiency of visual reading. This can be accomplished most directly by technology that increases the listener's control of the acoustic display. Two kinds of increased control have been investigated—the control needed to vary, at will, the word rate at which recorded speech is reproduced, and the control needed for search and retrieval. Research on the comprehension of time-compressed recorded speech (Foulke, 1968; Foulke and Sticht, 1969) has shown that listening comprehension is not seriously affected until a word rate in the neighborhood of 275 wpm is exceeded, and cassette recorders with facilities for compressing recorded speech are now available. Several methods for retrieving information from recorded cassettes have been investigated (Foulke, 1974, 1975; Nolan, Foulke, Davis, and Murr, 1976), and results obtained with children in several grades at residential schools for the blind indicate that a method which mixes the full text recording and the vocal announcements of indexed text locations in such a way that the announcements of indexed locations are properly reproduced when the cassette recorder is played at the fast forward speed permits accurate and rapid retrieval.

5.4. Machine Translation of the Print Code

Braille reading and reading by listening are examples of an approach in which the reading problem experienced by visually impaired persons is solved by replacing the print code with an equivalent code. A serious disadvantage with this approach is that the existing literature cannot be utilized in its printed form, and must be written again with the characters in the equivalent code. In another approach to the solution of this problem, the print display is sensed by a machine which translates it to a display that can be experienced without vision. Thus, those who can read the machine's display have access to the literature in print.

Machines of two types have been developed. The first and simpler type is the "direct translation machine." This machine is a transducer. The pattern that impinges on the lens of its camera as that camera scans the printed page is transduced to an analogous nonvisual pattern. In order to read with this machine, the nonvisual observer must learn to identify the transduced analogues of the symbols in the print display. The second type of machine is a preprocessor. It examines the pattern that impinges on the lens of its camera as the camera scans the printed page, identifies the symbols displayed on the page, and replaces them with other symbols that can be interpreted more easily by the nonvisual reader.

The best-known example of a direct translation machine is the Optacon (Bliss, Katcher, Rogers, and Shepard, 1970). To read with the Optacon, the reader moves its camera along the line of printed symbols with his left hand, and with the index finger of his right hand in position on the display surface he senses tactual analogues of the print symbols as they flow beneath his fingertip. The Stereotoner (Mauch and Smith, 1974) is a direct translation machine that transduces the symbols in the print code to analogous auditory symbols. The camera's field of view is divided vertically into segments, so that as it is moved along the line of writing it scans a number of horizontal bands extending from the top to the bottom of the space allotted for a line of writing. The presence of ink in a band causes a tone associated with that band to be turned on. Tones with different but harmonious frequencies are assigned to the different bands. As the reader moves the camera from left to right along the line of writing, he hears a procession of tone clusters or chords which specify the print symbols displayed in that line of writing.

Since direct translation machines display the symbols they sense serially, the reading rates achieved by those who use them are fairly low. There has not yet been a study to determine the distribution of Optacon reading rates, but a reading rate in the neighborhood of 50 wpm appears to be typical of good Optacon readers (San Diego Unified School District, 1972; Tobin, James, Mc-Veigh, and Irving, 1973; Weisgerber, Crawford, Everett, Lalush, and Rodebaugh, 1973). Two subjects observed by Craig (personal communication, 1976) have achieved a reading rate of 120 wpm. The distribution of reading rates achieved by experienced Stereotoner readers has not yet been determined, but on the basis of the performance of persons who have just completed an initial training course a reading rate of 30 wpm would be considered good (Weisgerber, Everett, and Smith, 1975).

To date, at least two types of preprocessing machines have received significant development. These machines include computing circuitry which, by analyzing the signal that is generated as a camera is moved along the line of symbols on the printed page, identifies those symbols. In the Kurzweil reading machine (Reading Machine Prototype, 1975) the information thus obtained is subjected to additional analysis in order to determine the phonemes that are specified by the orthographic symbols that have been identified. Phonemic instructions are then used to control a speech synthesizer, the output of which is spoken language. Thus, the Kurzweil reading machine identifies the symbols in the print code and replaces them with the appropriate symbols in the acoustic code. In the Transicom (Bar Lev, 1973), identified symbols in the print code are replaced with the appropriate symbols in the Grade II braille code. This is not simply a matter of replacing each identified print symbol, since the Grade II braille code includes a large number of contractions (contractions are symbols that stand for groups of letters), and, in order to use contractions correctly, a rather complex set of rules must be applied. The braille symbols identified by the Transicom are embossed on paper tape that is read with one or two index fingers as it is transported from right to left across the display surface.

The Kurzweil reading machine is still under development, and, as yet, there has been no study to determine a characteristic distribution of the reading rates of persons who read by listening to the synthetic speech it displays. Synthetic speech is not quite so legible as the speech of a skillful human speaker (Foulke, 1974), but the distribution of the reading rates of persons who read in this manner should not be very different from the distribution of the reading rates of persons who read by listening to human oral readers. The Transicom reader cannot examine his display with as much freedom as the person who reads a brailled page, and the effect of this loss of freedom is not yet known, but the distribution of reading rates for Transicom readers should not be very different from the distribution of reading rates for braille readers in general.

6. Conclusions

In this chapter, we have reviewed the perceptual development of blind children. We have examined the blind child's expanding ability to interpret the signs and symbols afforded by the environment in which he operates, and to use the information thus acquired to manage his interactions with the world in which he lives. According to our analysis, visual stimulation is a rich source of information, and since the blind child cannot experience visual stimulation he cannot acquire the information that mediates many of the behavioral decisions of the sighted child. Much of this information can be replaced with information acquired by interpreting other kinds of stimulation, but the required perceptual learning cannot be assumed to occur without the intervention of parents and teachers who understand the blind child's perceptual problems. To the extent the blind child can learn to exploit perceptual alternatives, he will acquire competence in dealing with the world in which he lives.

7. References

Adelson, E., and Fraiberg, S. Gross motor development in infants blind from birth. *Child Development*, 1974, *45*, 114–126.

Adelson, E., and Fraiberg, S. Sensory deficit and motor development in infants blind from birth. In Z. S. Jastrzembska (Ed.), *The effects of blindness and other impairments on early development*. New York: American Foundation for the Blind, 1976.

American Foundation for the Blind. *Facts and figures about blindness*. New York: American Foundation for the Blind, 1967.

Arampatta, D. Illustrations in social studies textbooks as they affect the visually handicapped. Unpublished specialist in education thesis, George Peabody College for Teachers, 1970.

Armstrong, J. A. Evaluation of man-machine systems in the mobility of the visually handicapped. In R. M. Rickett and T. J. Triggs (Eds.), *Human factors in health care*. Lexington, Mass.: Lexington Books, 1975.

Bar Lev, H. The Transicon. In *Proceedings of the 1973 Carnahan Conference on Electronic Prosthetics*. Lexington, Ky.: College of Engineering, University of Kentucky, 1973.

Barraga, N. C. Increased visual behavior in low vision children. *American Foundation for the Blind, Research Series*, 1964, *13*.

Benjamin, J. M., Jr. The bionic instruments C-4 laser cane. Paper presented at the National Academy of Engineering, Committee on the Interplay of Engineering with Biology and Medicine, Subcommittee on Sensory Aids, Warrenton, Va., 1970.

Berlá, E. P. Behavioral strategies and problems in scanning and interpreting tactual displays. *New Outlook for the Blind*, 1972a, *66*, 272–286.

Berlá, E. P. Effects of physical size and complexity on tactual discrimination performance of primary age blind children. *Exceptional Children,* 1972b, *38*, 120–124.

Berlá, E. P. Strategies in scanning a tactual pseudomap. *Education of the Visually Handicapped*, 1973, *5*, 8–19.

Berlá, E. P., and Butterfield, L. H. Tactual distinctive features analysis: Training blind students in shape recognition and in locating shapes on a map. *Journal of Special Education*, 1977, *11*, 335–346.

Berlá, E. P., and Butterfield, L. H. Teachers' views on tactile maps for blind students: Problems and needs. *Education of the Visually Handicapped*, 1975, *7*, 116–118.

Berlá, E. P., & Murr, M. J. Searching tactual space. *Education of the Visually Handicapped*, 1974, *6*, 49–58.

Berlá, E. P., & Murr, M. J. The effects of tactual noise on locating of point symbols and tracing a line of a tactile pseudomap. *Journal of Special Education*, 1975a, *9*, 183–190.

Berlá, E. P., and Murr, M. J. Psychophysical functions for active tactual discrimination of line width by blind children. *Perception and Psychophysics*, 1975b, *17*, 607–612.

Berlá, E. P., Butterfield, L. H., and Murr, M. J. Tactual reading of political maps by blind students: A videomatic behavioral analysis. *Journal of Special Education*, 1976, *10*, 265–276.

Bliss, J. C., Katcher, M. H., Rogers, C. H., and Shepard, R. P. Optical-to-tactile image conversion for the blind. *IEEE Transactions on Man-Machine Systems*, 1970, *MMS-11(1)*, 58–65.

Cattell, J. M. The time it takes to see and name objects. *Mind*, 1886, *11*, 63–65.

Cratty, B. J. Enhancing perceptual-motor abilities in blind children and youth. Paper presented at the Conference of California State Teachers of the Blind, Palo Alto, Calif., 1971.

Cutsforth, T. D. *The blind in school and society*. New York: American Foundation for the Blind, 1951.

Deutsch, F. The sense of reality in persons born blind. *Journal of Psychology*, 1940, *10*, 121–140.

Doggett, D., and Richards, L. G. A reexamination of the effect of word length on recognition thresholds. *American Journal of Psychology*, 1975, *88(4)*, 583–594.

Dokecki, P. C. Verbalism and the blind.: A critical review of the concept and the literature. *Exceptional Children*, 1966, *32*, 525–530.

Eakin, W. M., and McFarland, T. L. *Type, printing and the partially seeing child*. Pittsburgh: Stanwix House, 1960.

Eakin, W. M., Pratt, R. J. A., and McFarland, T. L. *Type size research for the partially seeing child*. Pittsburgh: Stanwix House, 1961.

Fertsch, P. An analysis of braille reading. *Outlook for the Blind*, 1946, *240*, 128–131.

Foulke, E. The role of experience in the formation of concepts. *International Journal for the Education of the Blind*, 1962, *12*, 1–6.

Foulke, E. Transfer of a complex perceptual skill. *Perceptual and Motor Skills*, 1964, *18*, 733–740.

Foulke, E. *The comprehension of rapid speech by the blind—Part III* (Interim Progress Report Cooperative Research Project No. 2430). Washington, D.C.: United States Department of Health Education, and Welfare, Office of Education, 1967.

Foulke, E. Listening comprehension as a function of word rate. *Journal of Communication*, 1968, *18(3)*, 198–206.

Foulke, E. The perceptual basis for mobility. *American Foundation for the Blind Research Bulletin*, 1970, *23*, 1–8.

Foulke, E. *The Perceptual Alternatives Laboratory: Annual report to the Dean of the Graduate School, 1973–1974*. Louisville, Ky.: Perceptual Alternatives Laboratory, University of Louisville, 1974.

Foulke, E. *The Perceptual Alternatives Laboratory: Annual report to the Dean of the Graduate School, 1974–1975*. Louisville, Ky.: Perceptual Alternatives Laboratory, University of Louisville, 1975.

Foulke, E., and Sticht, T. G. Review of research on the intelligibility and comprehension of accelerated speech. *Psychological Bulletin*, 1969, *72*, 50–62.

Foulke, E., and Wirth, E. M. The role of identification in the reading of braille and print. In E. Foulke (Ed.), *The development of an expanded reading code for the blind: Part II*. Louisville, Ky.: Perceptual Alternatives Laboratory, University of Louisville, 1973.

Fraiberg, S. Parallel and divergent patterns in blind and sighted infants. *Psychoanalytic Study of the Child*, 1968, *23*, 264–300.

Fraiberg, S., Siegal, B., and Gibson, R. The role of sound in the search behavior of a blind infant. *Psychoanalytic Study of the Child*, 1966, *21*, 327–357.

Fraiberg, S., Smith, M., and Adelson, E. An educational program for blind infants. *Journal of Special Education*, 1969, *3*, 121–142.

Franks, F. L., and Nolan, C. Y. Development of geographical concepts in blind children. *Education of the Visually Handicapped*, 1970, *2*, 1–18.

Franks, F. L., and Nolan, C. Y. Measuring geographical concept attainment in visually handicapped students. *Education of the Visually Handicapped*, 1971, *3*, 11–17.

Freedman, D. A., and Cannady, C. Delayed emergence of prone locomotion. *Journal of Nervous and Mental Disease*, 1971, *153*, 108–117.

Gallo, D. R. *National assessment of educational progress: Reading rate and comprehension 1970–71 assessment* (Education Commission of the States No. 02-R-09). Washington, D.C.: U.S. Government Printing Office, 1972.

Genensky, S. M. *Closed circuit TV and the education of the partially sighted*. Santa Monica, Calif.: Rand Corporation, 1970. (P-4343).

Genensky, S. M., Barak, P., Moshin, H. L., and Steingold, H. A closed circuit TV system for the visually handicapped. *American Foundation for the Blind Research Bulletin*, 1969, *19*, 191–204.

Gill, J. M., and James, G. A. A study of the discriminability of tactual point symbols. *American Foundation for the Blind Research Bulletin*, 1973, *26*, 19–34.

Graystone, P., and McLenna, H. Evaluation of an audible mobility aid for the blind. *American Foundation for the Blind Research Bulletin*, 1968, *17*, 173–179.

Grunwald, A. P. A braille-reading machine. *Science,* 1966, *154(3754)*, 144–146.

Hatfield, E. M. Why are they blind? *Sight Saving Review*, 1975, *45*, 3–22.

Hoover, R. E. The cane as a travel aid. In P. A. Zahl (Ed.), *Blindness*. Princeton, N.J.: Princeton University Press, 1950.

Johnson, W., Darley, F., and Spriestersbach, D. C. *Diagnostic methods in speech pathology.* New York: Harper and Row, 1963.

Kamisar, H., and Pollet, D. Those missing readers: The visually and physically handicapped. *Catholic Library World,* 1975, *46(10)*, 426–431.

Kay, L. Evaluation of the ultrasonic binaural sensory aid for the blind. Paper presented at the Conference on Evaluation of Sensory Aids for the Visually Handicapped, National Academy of Sciences, Washington, D.C., 1972.

Kay, L. *Towards a mobility theory for the blind* (Electrical Engineering No. 22). Christchurch, New Zealand: University of Canterbury, 1974.

Keller, H. Holiday in England. *Outlook for the Blind*, 1930, *24*, 14–16.

Kephart, J. G., Kephart, C. P., and Schwarz, G. C. A journey into the world of the blind. *Exceptional Children*, 1974, *40*, 421–427.

Lowenfeld, B. Psychological foundation of special methods in teaching blind children. In P. A. Zahl (Ed.), *Blindness*. Princeton, N.J.: Princeton University Press, 1950.

Lowenfeld, B. Psychological considerations. In B. Lowenfeld (Ed.), *The visually handicapped child in school*. New York: John Day Co., 1973.

Lowenfeld, G., Abel, G. L., and Hatlen, P. H. *Blind children learn to read*. Springfield, Ill.: Charles C Thomas, 1969.

Mauch, H. A., and Smith, G. C. *The development of personal reading machines for the blind.* (VA Bulletin of Prosthetics Research, BPR 10–22). Washington, D.C.: U.S. Government Printing Office, 1974, pp. 427–432.

Meyers, E., Ethington, D., and Ashcroft, S. C. Readability of braille as a function of three spacing variables. *Journal of Applied Psychology*, 1958, *42*, 163–165.

Nolan, C. Y. Readability of large types: A study of type sizes and type styles. *International Journal for the Education of the Blind*, 1959, *9*, 41–44.

Nolan, C. Y. Legibility of ink and paper color combinations for readers of large type. *International Journal for the Education of the Blind*, 1961, *10*, 82–84.

Nolan, C. Y., and Kederis, C. J. Perceptual factors in braille word recognition. *American Foundation for the Blind, Research Series*, 1969, *20*.

Nolan, C. Y., and Morris, J. E. *Improvement of tactual symbols for blind children* (Final Report Grant No. OEG-32-27-0000-1012, Project No. 5-0421). Louisville, Ky.: American Printing House for the Blind, 1971.

Nolan, C. Y., Morris, J. E., Kederis, C. J., Fieg, K. E., and Smith, M. G. *Reading and listening in learning by the blind* (Progress Report PHS Grant No. NB-04870-04). Louisville, Ky.: American Printing House for the Blind, 1966.

Nolan, C. Y., Foulke, E., Davis, K., and Murr, M. J. Comparison of three vocal indexes for tape recordings. In C. Y. Nolan (Ed.), *Facilitating the education of the visually handicapped through research in communication: Part II—Indexes for tape recordings* (Final Report Grant No. OEG-0-73-0624). Louisville, Ky.: American Printing House for the Blind, 1976.

Norris, M., Spaulding, P. J., and Brodie, F. H. *Blindness in children*. Chicago: University of Chicago Press, 1957.

Reading Machine Prototype. *Programs for the Handicapped*, August 11, 1975, p. 9. Publication of the Office for Handicapped Individuals, Washington, D.C.

Russell, L. Evaluation of mobility aids for the blind—Pathsounder Travel Aid evaluation. Paper presented at the National Academy of Engineers, Washington, D.C., 1971.

San Diego Unified School District. *San Diego Optacon Project 1971–72*. San Diego, Calif., 1972.

Schiff, W. *Raised line drawing research project* (Final Report HEW, VRA Grant No. RD-1571-5). New York: Recording for the Blind, Inc., 1966.

Schiff, W., Kaufer, L., and Mosak, S. Informative tactile stimuli in the perception of direction. *Perceptual and Motor Skills*, 1966, *23*, 1315–1335.

Scott, R. A. The socialization of blind children. In D. A. Goslin (Ed.), *Handbook of socialization theory and research*. Chicago: Rand McNally, 1969.

Scott, R. J. Computers for speech time compression. In E. Foulke (Ed.), *Proceedings of the Louisville Conference on Time-Compressed Speech*. Louisville, Ky.: Perceptual Alternatives Laboratory, University of Louisville, 1966.

Shingledecker, C. A. The development of a methodology for the measurement of blind mobility performance. Unpublished doctoral dissertation, University of Louisville, 1976.

Sloan, L. B. Optical magnification for subnormal vision: A historical survey. *Journal of the Optical Society of America*, 1972, *62*, 162–168.

Speech compressors: Actual and imminent. *CRCR Newsletter*, January/February, 1976, pp. 1–4. Publication of the Center for Rate-Controlled Recordings, Perceptual Alternatives Laboratory, University of Louisville, Louisville, Ky.

Sykes, K. C. A comparison of the effectiveness of standard print and large print in facilitating the reading skills of visually impaired students. *Education of the Visually Handicapped*, 1971, *3*, 97–105.

Tobin, M. J., James, W. R., McVeigh, A., and Irving, R. M. *Print reading by the blind: An evaluation of the Optacon and an investigation of some larger learner variables and teaching methods*. Birmingham, England: Research Centre for the Education of the Visually Handicapped, School of Education, University of Birmingham, 1973.

Troxell, D. E. Experiments in tactile and visual reading. *IEEE Transactions on Human Factors in Electronics*, 1967, *HFE 8(4)*, 261–263.

van Katwijk, A., and 't Hart, J. A. A complex unit of intelligibility: The syllable. *Psycholinguistique* (Actes Du Xe Congres International Des Linguistes). Bucarest: Editions de l'Académie de la République Socialiste de Roumanie, 1970.

Warren, D. H., and Kocon, J. A. Factors in the successful mobility of the blind. *American Foundation for the Blind Research Bulletin*, 1974, *28*, 191–218.

Weisgerber, R. A., Crawford, J. J., Everett, B. E., Lalush, S. E., and Rodebaugh, B. J. *Educational evaluation of the Optacon (Optical-to-tactile converter) as a reading aid to blind elementary and secondary students* (Interim Technical Report: Phase I, Contract No. OEG-0-72-5180). Washington, D.C.: Bureau of Education for the Handicapped, U.S. Office of Education, September 1973.

Weisgerber, R. A., Everett, B. E., and Smith, C. A. *Evaluation of an ink print reading aid for the blind: The Stereotoner* (Final Report: Contract No. V101(134)P-163). New York: Research Center for Prosthetics, Veterans Administration, 1975.

Wiedel, J. W. Tactual maps for the visually handicapped: Some developmental problems. *New Outlook for the Blind*, 1969, *63*, 80–88.

Wiedel, J. W., and Groves, P. A. Designing and producing tactual maps for the visually handicapped. *New Outlook for the Blind*, 1969, *63*, 196–201.

8

Perceptual Effects of Deafness

H. N. REYNOLDS

1. Introduction

Deafness imposes a naturally occurring condition of unimodal sensory deprivation, in which information conveyed to the perceptual system is blocked at the
sensory level or disrupted in transmission to the brain. Since spoken language
is a prominent form of auditory information in the human environment, a
primary effect of deafness in humans is that it interferes with communication
through speech. Many of the psychological, social, and educational consequences of deafness can be attributed largely to the individual's lack of exposure to verbal information, and resultant deficiency in comprehension and
expression of spoken and written language (Moores, 1970; Reynolds, 1977).
These effects are most serious when deafness is profound and prelingual—occurring before the acquisition of language, at about the age of 3 years.

Numerous studies of heteromodal sensory deprivation have revealed that
an absolute reduction of sensory input, or a reduced patterning of stimulation,
can produce serious perceptual deficiencies and distortions (Kubzansky and
Leiderman, 1961). If deafness is considered a form of deprivation limited to
one sensory channel, some perceptual deficiencies in other modalities might be
expected. This proposition is sometimes termed the "generalized deficiency
hypothesis" (DiFrancesca, 1969). It is based on the argument that auditory deprivation might interfere with functioning in other perceptual systems through
disruption of normal intersensory relationships, and/or neurological impairment
affecting the other sensory systems.

In opposition to this hypothesis, it might be expected that impairment in
one sensory modality would result in the development of compensatory abilities

H. N. REYNOLDS • Department of Psychology, Gallaudet College, Washington, D.C. 20002.

in other perceptual systems. This "compensation hypothesis" predicts that deaf persons should develop superior capabilities in certain visual, tactual, and other sensory functions, by comparison with people of normal hearing ability. These alternative hypotheses provide a framework for the research results described in this chapter.

2. Visual Perception and Deafness

2.1. Ocular Defects

Since deaf persons must rely heavily on vision for perception of their environment, it is important to know something about the ophthalmological characteristics of this population. Consistent with the deficiency hypothesis, Pollard and Neumaier (1974) have cited a number of studies generally indicating that 40–60% of deaf school-age children have ocular defects, compared with an incidence of 20–30% among hearing students. Their own research showed that refractive errors were more prevalent among deaf students than hearing students. For example, farsightedness was found in 8% of the deaf sample compared with 3% of a hearing sample. Other ocular defects which occurred more frequently in deaf than in hearing subjects were nearsightedness (13.3% vs. about 6.6%), astigmatism (7.3% vs. 1.4%), and anisometropia (5.9% vs. 1.4%). However, the incidence of eye coordination problems (e.g., strabismus, amblyopia) and ocular pathology was about the same for both groups. It is not clear why there should be a higher incidence of refractive ocular defects among deaf children, although a contributing factor may be the visual stress imposed by greater dependence of deaf individuals on their visual system. The higher probability of visual impairment in the deaf population suggests the need for visual screening of hearing-impaired subjects participating in research involving vision, to avoid confounding of results. In addition, considering the extent to which deaf persons must depend on vision, it is obvious that early ophthalmological examination of hearing-impaired children is of great practical importance.

2.2. Visual Test Performance and the Deficiency Hypothesis

A study by Myklebust and Brutten (1953) was among the first of numerous experiments comparing the performance of deaf and hearing children on tests of visual perceptual functioning and visuomotor performance. Their underlying theoretical orientation was consistent with a deficiency hypothesis in stating that deafness should modify visual perception (probably adversely) because of the dynamic interrelationship of all the sensory modalities. Their experiment employed groups of deaf and hearing students (ages 8–11) from residential schools, matched in terms of age, IQ, and other relevant variables. Visuomotor performance tests were selected to avoid test bias against deaf subjects, who were presumed to be characteristically deficient in knowledge of spoken and written language. The test battery included (1) a Marble Board Test (requiring reproduction of a pattern of marbles), (2) the Goodenough Draw-a-Man Test, (3) a Figure-Ground or Embedded Figures Test, (4) a perceptual perseveration test (involving the persistence of a percept with ambiguous figures), and (5) a tachistoscopic pattern recognition test (requiring subjects to reproduce briefly exposed patterns of lines or dots by drawing what they saw). Results showed that the deaf children performed at a lower level than hearing children on the marble board, embedded figures, and pattern recognition tests but did not differ significantly from hearing subjects on other tests in the battery. These findings were interpreted as revealing a deficiency in perceiving abstract stimuli which were difficult to associate with familiar objects or experiences.

Levine (1958) and Suchman (1966) have also reported results consistent with a deficiency hypothesis. Levine reasoned that, because of sensory interaction, visual sensitivity is dependent on both visual and concurrent auditory stimulation. In support of this hypothesis, he compared deaf and hearing subjects on the critical flicker/fusion frequency—the frequency at which a flickering light is just perceived as steady or fused. Results showed that deaf subjects were less sensitive to flicker (perceived fusion at a lower flicker frequency) than hearing subjects. In the Suchman study, deaf and hearing children were compared for color and form preferences in a figure-matching task requiring subjects to identify the two most similar figures from a set of three varying in color and shape (Doehring's test). Hearing children generally preferred to match on the basis of color up to the age of 4–6 years, after which the preference shifted to form. Deaf children generally perseverated in their preference for color up to at least 10 or 12 years. This can be interpreted as a developmental lag in the cognitive growth of deaf children, since the color-to-form shift correlates with other developmental indices. Corresponding to these preferences, Suchman also found that hearing children discriminate more accurately in the form dimension, while deaf children reveal better color discrimination ability. Thus, the "cognitive deficiency" in deaf children is balanced to some extent by a superior sensory capability.

The Myklebust and Brutten study prompted several subsequent attempts at replication, most of which produced results in conflict with those reported in the original article. For example, Hayes (1955) and Larr (1956), using many of the tests employed by Myklebust and Brutten, found the performance of deaf children equal or superior to that of hearing children. However, both Hayes and Larr used deaf students from schools emphasizing oral communication (use of speech for expression, and residual hearing combined with speechreading for reception), while Myklebust and Brutten used deaf students from a school encouraging the use of manual communication (sign language). Hayes and Larr attributed the differences in results between studies to this discrepancy in mode of communication. It is not at all clear, however, why manual communication should be less effective than oral communication in promoting the development of the skills involved in "nonverbal" performance tests.

Other investigators have also reported comparable visual performance in deaf and hearing subjects. An experiment by Rosenstein (1960), for example, using a color and form discrimination task revealed no differences between deaf (orally trained) and hearing children 8 and 10 years of age. Although these results appear to conflict with Suchman's (1966) findings on color-form preference and discrimination, it is possible (but not reported) that Rosenstein's deaf subjects had achieved a higher level of cognitive development resulting in a form over color preference, comparable to that of hearing subjects.

In another study showing subject equivalence, Thompson (1964) compared groups of congenitally deaf children, children with acquired deafness, and hearing children, 6–12 years of age, using three visual discrimination tasks: the Howard-Dolman binocular and monocular depth perception test apparatus, a discrimination test for letterlike forms (after Gibson, Gibson, Pick, and Osser, 1962), and a test of susceptibility to the Müller-Lyer illusion. Results showed no significant differences in performance on any of the perceptual tests among the three subject groups.

The research reviewed here on ocular defects and visual test performance provides only equivocal support for a generalized deficiency hypothesis. Apparently, deafness may involve deficiencies in some visual functions, but research findings are not consistent in identifying these. The following section will review some of the visual research bearing on the compensation hypothesis.

2.3. The Compensation Hypothesis

A deaf person must depend on the remaining perceptual systems, particularly the visual and tactual modalities, to provide as much environmental information as possible. The development of superior sensitivity, discrimination, or other capabilities in these remaining perceptual systems might compensate to some extent for the auditory information lost due to deafness.

A classic example of a learned compensatory ability comes from the study of blindness rather than deafness. Blind persons (and sighted persons given appropriate training) develop a special auditory echolocation ability (sometimes referred to as "facial vision") which enables them to use echos from their own footsteps or other sound sources to detect and avoid obstacles in their vicinity (Ammons, Worchel, and Dallenbach, 1953). This ability compensates to a limited extent for loss of vision, and is acquired gradually with experience in navigating through the environment.

Similarly, a deaf child might become sensitive to subtle changes in visual and tactual stimulation which convey information about environmental events ordinarily detected by the auditory system. Unfortunately, there is very little research to support this hypothesis.

2.4. Visual Memory for Simultaneous and Sequential Stimuli

Perceptual compensation and deficiency are both revealed in studies concerned with visual memory for stimuli presented both simultaneously and successively. For example, an experiment by Blair (1957) employed a matched groups design with deaf and hearing children, ages 7–12. Visual memory tests consisted of the Knox Cube Test, Memory for Designs Test, Object Location Test, and four Memory Span Tests (digit span forward and backward, picture span, dot pattern span). The first three tests involved a number of stimulus elements, presented simultaneously, to be reproduced from memory after exposure. The Memory Span Tests involved rapid sequential presentation of individual stimulus elements, to be reproduced from memory. Deaf children performed better than hearing on the tests involving simultaneous stimulus presentation (Knox Cube, Memory for Designs, and Object Location). However, on the Memory Span Tests, which involved sequential stimulus presentation, hearing children performed better than deaf children. Blair's interpretation was that deaf persons compensate for their hearing loss by developing superior visual ability to organize or integrate holistic or "simultaneously present" information. Ordinarily, this is the kind of information provided by a natural environment for visual exploration. Successive presentation of visual stimuli, involving integration over time, requires a more abstract conceptual process which hearing subjects are better able to accomplish.

A related study was reported by Withrow (1968), who employed a test of immediate recall for silhouettes of a variety of meaningful and random shapes. Stimuli were presented both simultaneously and successively to deaf and hearing children. The recall test consisted of organizing a set of response cards containing the stimulus shapes into the order in which the items were originally presented. With simultaneous presentation, deaf and hearing subjects displayed comparable recall, but, with successive presentation, hearing subjects were superior. Similar findings were obtained in studies by DiFrancesca (1969) and Olsson and Furth (1966). Tervoort (1958) explained this superiority of hearing subjects in terms of transfer from the auditory system, which is better adapted to processing a sequential flow of information, as in speech perception.

The relatively poorer visual memory performance of deaf subjects with sequentially presented stimuli may represent a developmental lag which is eventually overcome. This conclusion is suggested by Furth and Pufall (1966), whose research showed that while deaf children below the age of 10 years were deficient in response learning for sequential stimuli, deaf subjects above the age of 10 performed at about the same level as their hearing peers. These results are consistent with the fact that many studies reporting a deficiency with sequential stimuli were conducted with younger deaf children. Furth and Pufall believe this developmental effect may be due to intensive training in linguistic skills (requiring sequential information processing), which, in the deaf child, is usually not manifested until adolescence. Consistent with this hypothesis, a study by Espeseth (1969) suggested that a training program for visual sequential memory ability can produce significant improvement among deaf children in test performance involving this skill.

The previously described studies of memory for sequentially presented items have used stimuli such as shapes and numbers, usually presented in random order. An interesting experiment by Zakia and Haber (1971) varied this method by presenting letters sequentially to form meaningful words or random letter strings. Letters, composed of illuminated line segments, were presented sequentially in the same location on an electroluminescent display. Three presentation rates were used, corresponding to about 3, 7, and 13 letters per second. Letter sequences consisted of meaningful words, 4, 6, or 8 letters in length, and random letter strings, 4 or 6 letters in length. Deaf, post-secondary school students and hearing college students were shown the letter sequences and asked to write down the letters immediately following each presentation. Surprisingly, results showed that deaf subjects obtained higher percent correct scores for meaningful words than did hearing subjects. By contrast, hearing students performed somewhat better than the deaf with random letter sequences. These results are explained by the authors as due to different visual search strategies employed by deaf and hearing subjects. Most deaf students have considerable familiarity with fingerspelling, which requires the individual to observe a rapid sequence of hand-finger configurations representing alphabetic letters. The deaf individual probably becomes proficient in reading fingerspelling by searching for higher-order units of information, such as spelling patterns or groups of letters which occur together frequently in English orthography. The hearing person, having little or no experience with sequential single-letter presentations, probably attends more to individual letters. In the experimental task, the higher-order search presumably employed by deaf subjects was superior with meaningful word presentations, while the individual-letter search technique possibly used by hearing subjects was superior with random letter sequences.

2.5. Verbal Mediation in Perception and Cognition

Deaf subjects are often used in research concerned with the relationship between language and cognition or perception. The rationale is that deaf persons (especially the prelingually deaf) generally are deficient in comprehension of the grammar and semantics of spoken and written language. Therefore, if language has a determining effect on perceptual/cognitive development, deaf subjects should be deficient, or at least different, by comparison with hearing subjects in cognitive and perceptual abilities (Reynolds, 1977).

Furth (1971) has reviewed a number of recent studies comparing deaf and hearing subjects on various cognitive and perceptual tasks. The research categorized as "perceptual" by Furth produced results ranging from inferior to superior performance by deaf subjects. Specifically, deaf children were found to be inferior in performance on (1) an Embedded Figures (Poppelreuter) Test, (2) drawing of an object from a schematic, three-dimensional sketch, (3) development of form preference over color preference in a figure-matching task (Suchman's results, described previously), and (4) reaction time to paired visual and auditory stimuli. A perceptual lag in deaf children, later overcome with age, was found in (1) ability to make reverse drawings of geometric figures and (2) color-weight associations (e.g., a black object judged heavier than a white object of similar size and shape). Equivalent performance by deaf and hearing subjects was reported for (1) recogniton of objects from schematic drawings, (2) reaction time to visual stimuli, (3) patterns of rapid eye movements (REMs) and finger movements in sleep, and (4) susceptibility to the size-weight illusion, and effects of training to overcome the illusion. Finally, deaf children were found to be superior to hearing children in color discrimination accuracy, reflecting Suchman's finding that a majority of 10-year-old deaf children prefer color over form in a figure-matching task, while a majority of hearing children of the same age prefer form over color.

It is clear from this summary that, in the category of perceptual research, about the same number of studies reported deficiencies among the deaf as reported equivalent performance by deaf and hearing subjects. Nevertheless, from his general review of the literature, Furth concluded that a large number of studies show no substantial differences between deaf and hearing subjects on a variety of cognitive/perceptual tasks. He reasoned that since the vast majority of (prelingually) deaf children have a severe linguistic deficiency, cognitive development (at least through the concrete operational stage) does not require "linguistic support."

This conclusion seems to ignore the fact that there is also a great deal of research showing deficient performance or a developmental lag in deaf subjects. In addition, most studies contrasting the performance of deaf and hearing groups do not really provide evidence that their deaf subjects lacked the language competence to mediate the specific cognitive or perceptual processes (e.g., size-weight illusion) being studied (Bornstein and Roy, 1973; Bonvillian, Charrow and Nelson, 1973). Deaf subjects in these experiments may be "linguistically deficient," but have achieved some level of familiarity with English and often are fluent in sign language. Most studies in this area fail to demonstrate whether or not this linguistic knowledge might have been sufficient to mediate performance in the assigned experimental tasks. For this reason, deaf subjects do not provide an adequate test of hypotheses concerning the relationship between language and cognition or perception, unless their linguistic competence is very carefully assessed.

2.6. Social Perception

Deafness might be expected to alter the socialization process by interfering with the communication of information about societal standards and expectations, emotional states and personality characteristics of interacting persons, and other social or cultural variables. This deprivation can influence the deaf person's perceptual interpretation of social situations, including judgments of emotion from facial expression and judgments of personality characteristics of others. A number of experiments in this area have been reported by Schiff and his colleagues (Schiff and Thayer, 1974).

In one experiment (Schiff and Saxe, 1972), deaf and hearing college students were shown films of two college-age men communicating with each other through speaking and gesturing. Three films were prepared varying in the forcefulness of gestures used, for comparison with a static (no motion) film of the same interactants. Subjects were asked to rate each interactant in the films on 17 traits, such as friendliness, intelligence, and maturity. Generally, for both hearing and deaf subjects, the static film and the motion films differed in subject ratings on 8 of the 17 traits, suggesting that dynamic interactions in the motion films conveyed information used by subjects in forming impressions about characteristics of the interactants. Among other things, differences between the ratings of deaf and hearing subjects were observed as a function of gestural forcefulness. Deaf students tended to rate the forceful film more positively than did hearing students, who were inclined to interpret gestural force as an indication of insincerity or compensation for feelings of inadequacy. Schiff explained this effect as related to differences in the kinds of communication behaviors to which deaf and hearing persons have adapted. Deaf people often use forceful gestures to help convey meaning in a conversation, with the result that observation of emphatic gestures is interpreted in a more positive context.

In another report, Schiff (1973) described an experiment on facial expression labeling by deaf and hearing subjects, ages 12–19 years. Subjects were shown, in random order, each of the schematic faces portrayed in Table 1 for 2 sec. These faces varied only in mouth shape and eyebrow orientation, but conveyed substantial differences in affect. A rating sheet was used by subjects to check the word which best described "how the face feels" for each stimulus presentation. A summarization of Schiff's principal findings is provided in Table 1, which indicates the word label selected by the greatest percentage of hearing and deaf students for each face.

Most of the faces received the same modal label by deaf and hearing groups, although faces 4, 6, and 8 were rated differently. Of these, the differences for faces 6 and 8 will be discussed here. The modal label used by deaf

Table 1. Modal Labels of Emotion Used by Deaf and Hearing Subjects for Schematic Faces[a]

Subject groups	1	2	3	4	5	6	7	8	9	10
Deaf	Happy (84%)	Sad (83%)	Neutral (41%)	Elated (22%)	Sad (19%)	Furious (19%)	Angry (33%)	Angry (23%)	Sad (39%)	Other (75%)
Hearing	Happy (85%)	Sad (83%)	Neutral (78%)	Amused (33%)	Sad (31%) Depressed (31%)	Fiendish (48%)	Angry (52%)	Furious (50%)	Sad (62%)	Other (57%)

[a]See text for explanation. Adapted from Schiff (1973). Reprinted from *Exceptional Children* by permission of The Council for Exceptional Children.

students for face 6 was "furious" (19%) compared with "fiendish" (48%) for hearing subjects. For face 8, the modal labels were "angry" (23%) for deaf and "furious" (50%) for hearing subjects. In both cases, the modal label selected by deaf subjects was less extreme than that selected by the hearing group, a tendency attributed by Schiff to "adaptation resulting from facial grimaces in face to face communication among signing deaf persons." This suggestion follows from Schiff's interpretation of results in the previous experiment. However, these results might also be explained as due to limitations in vocabulary comprehension of deaf subjects, resulting in a preference for more common (and presumably better-understood) words. This interpretation is consistent with data from a current word frequency count (Carroll, Davies, and Richman, 1971) which indicates that "angry" occurs almost 10 times more frequently in written English than "furious" (face 8), while "furious" is about 20 times more frequent than "fiendish" (face 6). Deficiencies in vocabulary comprehension may also be the basis for relatively less consistency among deaf subjects in selecting labels. This tendency is suggested by the results in Table 1 showing that most of the modal labels for the deaf group represent a smaller percentage of subjects than the modal labels for the hearing group.

3. Tactual Perception

Perceptual research with deaf subjects has concentrated on vision as the principal remaining "distance" sense, and therefore the most likely perceptual system to show either deficiencies or compensatory abilities. However, considering the evidence for general sensory interaction effects (London, 1954; Madsen and Mears, 1965), deafness might be expected to have some effect on tactual abilities. A deaf person can employ the tactual system to pick up environmental stimulation (e.g., vibration) which a hearing person would detect auditorily. Perceptual learning might gradually result in a level of tactual sensitivity or "attunement" to certain types of stimulus information greater than that ordinarily developed by hearing persons. Alternatively, tactual sensitivity or discrimination might be either improved by absence of auditory interference or impaired due to loss of intersensory facilitation from audition. Consequently, it is of practical and theoretical interests to review some studies from the smaller body of research literature dealing with tactual abilities of deaf persons.

One of the more systematic studies in this area was reported by Schiff and Dytell (1972), who used tests of vibrotactile sensitivity, two-point threshold, gap (Landolt Ring) detection, roughness discrimination, pattern discrimination, and cross-modal object identification. Subjects consisted of deaf and hearing children, ranging in age from 7½ to 19½ years, selected from schools matched as closely as possible for socioeconomic and racial composition. Results showed that deaf subjects were more sensitive than hearing on the vibrotactile and two-point threshold measures at almost all age levels. However, on most of the other tests in the battery, which involved pattern or shape discrimination, deaf and hearing groups did not differ significantly. Schiff and Dytell explain the superiority of deaf subjects on the vibrotactile sensitivity test in terms of perceptual attunement of deaf children to environmental vibrations. For example, a moving object often can be detected tactually by the vibrations it produces, and deaf individuals probably depend on this information more than hearing persons to perceive events occurring in the peripheral environment. In addition, perceptual learning with vibratory stimulation is probably enhanced by the formal speech training received by most deaf children, which involves tactual perception of vocal vibrations.

The greater sensitivity of deaf children on the two-point threshold measure is more difficult to understand in terms of compensation for deafness. This finding also seems anomalous because other tests which should involve sensitivity to spatial separation (e.g., gap detection, pattern discrimination, object and letter identification) did not yield superior performance by deaf subjects.

A different approach to the study of tactual perception was taken in an experiment by Bishop, Ringel, and House (1972) to determine whether the articulatory deficiencies of deaf children involved deficiencies in oral (orosensory) discrimination of shape. Subjects were deaf and hearing high school students. Small plastic forms were placed in the subjects' mouths for identification of size and shape. Nine forms, consisting of squares, triangles, and parallelograms, with three sizes of each, were presented sequentially, in pairs, for "same-different" judgments. Results showed that deaf students made significantly more errors in paired comparisons judgments (21%) than hearing students (11%). The authors observed that similar oral form discrimination deficiencies had been observed (in another study) in hearing subjects with speech disabilities. Since the deaf subjects in this experiment were selected from a school encouraging the use of manual communication, a follow-up study (Bishop, Ringel, and House, 1973) using the same stimuli and procedure was conducted to compare subjects from the previous experiment with deaf subjects from a school emphasizing oral communication. In this experiment, the orally trained deaf subjects performed at the same level as hearing subjects in the form discrimination task. These results are explained in terms of the training in speech production given to the oral-communication deaf subjects which, the authors suggest, results in improved orosensory discrimination. By comparison, the manual-communication deaf subjects received less training in speech production, and their orosensory discrimination did not improve.

4. Visual and Tactile Displays for Speech Perception

Since interference with the acquisition of spoken language may be the most fundamental and serious consequence of deafness, it is not surprising that numerous attempts have been made to transform speech into coded visual and tactile displays.[1] These devices involve electronic circuits which analyze the speech signal in various ways and present the processed information through a tactile or visual stimulator. Tactile displays have the potential advantage that the skin and the ear show similarities in certain sensory characteristics (Bekesy, 1959). In addition, tactile displays probably do not interfere with visual attention and can be worn inconspicuously under clothing (Pickett, 1975). However, the tactile system is limited because (1) vibratory discrimination diminishes rapidly at frequencies above 200 Hz, (2) rise and decay times for a tactile sensation following stimulation are considerably longer than in the auditory system, and (3) the temporal resolving power of the skin is inferior to that of the ear (Kirman, 1973).

Visual displays have the advantage of utilizing the powerful information-processing capabilities of the visual system and employing a display which is readily portrayed through pictures and diagrams for purposes of training (Pickett, 1975). The visual system, however, is not so effective in processing a temporal flow of sequential information as the auditory system. In addition, a visual display can be a distraction for the observer and interfere with visual attention to other essential information.

Unfortunately, speech aids developed to date have not been very successful, primarily because the visual and tactual systems lack the information-processing characteristics necessary for effective perception of speech.

4.1. Visual Aids for Speech Perception[2]

Visual displays for speech typically employ illuminated matrices of bars or lines, oscilloscope traces, or simply meter readings to represent certain characteristics of speech, such as sound frequency, rhythm, and the occurrence of fricatives and plosions. One example is the Upton Eyeglass Speechreader (Upton, 1968; Pickett, Gengel, and Quinn, 1976). This device, shown in Fig. 1, picks up speech sounds through a microphone, analyzes the sounds into specific speech patterns, and displays these as coded arrangements of illuminated line segments visible through eyeglasses worn by the observer. The display is produced by a small projector mounted on the eyeglass frame which projects an image onto a tiny concave mirror fastened to the eyeglass lens. A virtual image is produced which is viewed in space and can be positioned by the observer close to the mouth of the person speaking. The Upton Speechreader is designed to extract the acoustic features of high-frequency friction (speech sounds such

[1] The term "tactile" will be used to refer to passive reception of information through the skin, as occurs when a cutaneous stimulator is fastened to an area of skin such as the fingertip. By comparison, the term "tactual" is used to refer to information obtained through active touch, as in exploration of an object with the hands and fingers (Gibson, 1962, 1966).
[2] Some of the many visual aids for speech are described by Kirman (1973), Pickett (1968, 1975), and Risberg (1968).

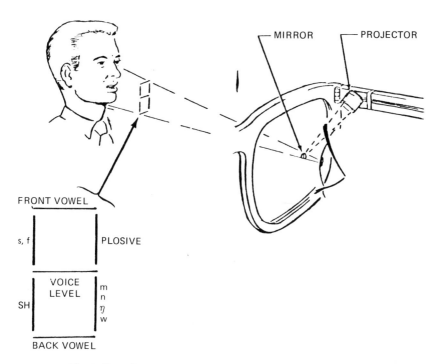

Fig. 1. Upton Eyeglass Speechreader. Courtesy, *Bell Helicopter News.*

as /s/ and /f/), low-frequency friction /sh/, plosion /k, p/, the low-frequency murmur of nasal and glide consonants /m, n, l, w, r/, voice loudness, and the acoustic characteristics of front and back vowels. These features are related to speech patterns that are difficult to read from the lips, and their occurrence is represented by the line segments of the display (Fig. 1). After mastering the code, a deaf person wearing the aid must integrate information from the symbolic display with information from speechreading (i.e., lipreading). Evaluation of the device, currently being conducted by Pickett and his colleagues (1976), suggests some improvement over unaided speechreading ability. However, additional research is necessary to determine its practicality and the audiological characteristics for which it is most effective.

4.2. Tactile Aids for Speech Perception

A number of electromechanical devices have been developed to analyze the speech signal and display certain acoustic features as patterns of vibratory stimulation on the skin.[3] Unfortunately, these tactile speech aids generally have

---

[3] See Kirman (1973) for a review of tactile speech aids.

not been successful in improving speech perception by deaf users under normal conditions of communication. Considering Gibson's (1962, 1966) comments on the perceptual significance of active touch, it is interesting to note that the only cutaneous system which has produced a useful level of speech comprehension is a technique involving at least some tactual exploration by the observer, rather than passive tactile reception of stimulation. This technique, used by the deaf-blind, is called the "Tadoma Method," in which the observer positions his fingers around the lips, nose, cheeks, and throat of the speaker (Kirman, 1973). In addition to the value of active touch, this method may be relatively success-ful because the articulatory movements which are detected in this way probably bear a more invariant relationship to the distinctive features of speech than do the vibrotactile patterns representing characteristics of the acoustic speech sig-nal, as employed by electromechanical aids. In spite of the lack of success with these tactile speech aids, Kirman suggests that their effectiveness might be improved by appropriate structuring of the tactile stimulus to represent various levels of linguistic structure in a spatiotemporal pattern which allows perceptual organization by the tactual system.

5. Conclusions

Most of the studies reviewed in this chapter have been presented in the context of contrasting hypotheses of perceptual deficiency vs. perceptual com-pensation for deafness. The deficiency hypothesis is based on the assumption that all the perceptual systems are interrelated, and auditory impairment might therefore be expected to induce perceptual deficits in the other modalities. Per-ceptual compensation can be interpreted in terms of what Gibson (1966) calls the equivalence of stimulus information for the perceptual systems. That is, equivalent information about the environment can be conveyed to the different perceptual systems by different forms of stimulus energy appropriate for each modality. If deafness limits or precludes the pickup of acoustic information, the visual and tactual systems can still provide equivalent information about envi-ronmental characteristics or events. Through experience, the remaining percep-tual systems may develop improved sensitivity or discrimination for distinctive features of stimulation.

Most of the research reviewed in this chapter is summarized in Table 2, which categorizes studies according to support for perceptual deficiency, equiv-alence, or superiority of deaf compared with hearing subjects. The most obvi-ous conclusion from this table is that very little evidence exists to support the hypothesis of compensatory superiority for deafness. In fact, the only "un-equivocal" support comes from the results on vibrotactile and two-point thresh-olds. The evidence on visual memory for simultaneous stimuli, and recognition of sequentially presented letters forming words, is in at least partial conflict

Table 2. *Summary of Results Showing Perceptual Deficiency, Equivalence, and Superiority of Deaf Compared with Hearing Subjects*

Deficiency	Equivalence	Superiority
Visual memory for sequential stimuli (Blair, 1957; Withrow, 1968)	Visual memory for simultaneous stimuli (Withrow, 1968)	Visual memory for simultaneous stimuli (Blair, 1957)
	Response learning for simultaneous or sequential stimuli, above age 10 (Furth and Pufall, 1966)	
Recognition/recall of sequentially presented random letters (Zakia and Haber, 1971)		Recognition/recall of sequentially presented letters forming words (Zakia and Haber, 1971)
Color over form preference; form discrimination, ages 10–12 (Suchman, 1966)	Color and form discrimination, ages 8–10 (Rosenstein, 1960)	Color discrimination, ages 10–12 (Suchman, 1966)
	Tactile gap detection, roughness discrimination, pattern discrimination, cross-modal object identification (Schiff and Dytell, 1972)	Vibrotactile and two-point thresholds (Schiff and Dytell, 1972)
Marble board pattern reproduction; embedded figures; pattern recognition (Myklebust and Brutten, 1953)	Draw A Man Test; perceptual perseveration (Myklebust and Brutten, 1953)	
	Pattern reproduction and recognition (Hayes, 1955; Larr, 1956)	
Embedded figures; figure reproduction; reaction time to paired auditory-visual stimuli; reverse drawings of geometric figures; color-weight association (Furth, 1971)	Object recognition; reaction time to visual stimuli; size-weight illusion (Furth, 1971)	
	Depth perception; letterlike form discrimination; Müller-Lyer illusion (Thompson, 1964)	
Oral form discrimination (manually trained deaf) (Bishop et al., 1972)	Oral form discrimination (orally trained deaf) (Bishop et al., 1973)	
Intersubject consistency and vocabulary comprehension in facial expression labeling (Schiff, 1973)	Modal response in facial expression labeling (Schiff, 1973)	
Ocular defects (Pollard and Neumaier, 1974)		
Critical flicker frequency (Levine, 1958)		

with results from other studies showing equivalence or deficiency for deaf subjects. Suchman's (1966) research showing superior color discrimination in young deaf children cannot be interpreted as compensation since it corresponds to a color over form preference which is interpreted as a less mature level of cognitive development. The remaining studies are divided between perceptual deficiency and equivalence for deaf compared with hearing subjects. However, some of the results supporting perceptual deficiency probably represent a developmental lag in deaf subjects, which is eventually overcome. Examples are the color over form preference in stimulus matching (Suchman, 1966) and visual memory for sequential stimuli (e.g., Blair, 1957). Developmental factors may explain, in part, why many of the studies listed in Table 2 which show perceptual deficiency are in conflict with other studies showing equivalence between subject groups.

Other reviews of literature on sensory and perceptual functioning in the deaf similarly indicate a paucity of evidence for compensation (Hoemann, 1976; Stark, 1974). To some extent, this may be due to a relative lack of research on perceptual abilities which *might* serve a compensatory function in the deaf. Another possibility, noted by Hoemann (in press), is that compensation might be revealed more clearly in studies providing deaf and hearing subjects with training in specific perceptual abilities. Such training might yield more rapid perceptual learning by deaf subjects, suggesting special potential for the development of abilities which compensate for deafness, given the appropriate learning experiences. However, very few studies of this kind have been conducted. The conflicting results in Table 2 reflect the fact that research on perceptual effects of deafness has been fragmentary, with the result that a coherent picture of perceptual development in the deaf has not yet emerged. Experiments tend to be based on isolated tests of perceptual functioning and lack a theoretical framework. In addition, some of the research in this area suffers from methodological deficiencies, casting doubt on the validity of results or complicating interpretation of findings. Hoemann (in press) has addressed himself to this problem by outlining many of the methodological considerations of importance in designing research on deafness.

Table 2 also suggests further research needed to resolve conflicting results and establish developmental trends in areas such as (1) visual recognition and memory for stimuli presented simultaneously vs. sequentially, (2) cognitive growth as revealed by indices such as color-form preferences in stimulus matching, and (3) tactual discrimination and tactual object or shape perception. Other potentially significant areas for research include peripheral vision, visual imagery, pictorial perception, and the development of reading ability. Peripheral vision may be especially important to deaf persons in maintaining awareness of events occurring in the peripheral visual environment, because such information cannot be detected auditorily. Visual imagery is of theoretical interest because of its probable importance in cognition for deaf children, particularly those who lack a strong linguistic system. Pictorial perception has practical significance in the education of deaf children, which relies heavily on the use of pictures to convey information (Reynolds and Rosen, 1973). This is especially true in elementary reading instruction, which often is taught to deaf children through a process of associating printed words with pictured referents (Reynolds, 1976). Finally, a great deal of new research is needed in the area of reading development in deaf children, a topic not reviewed in this chapter. The lack of research information on reading in relation to deafness is reflected by the dearth of instructional materials designed to teach reading to deaf children, and by the fact that the average reading test performance of 16-year-old deaf students is equivalent to about a fourth grade level by comparison with hearing student norms (Reynolds, 1976).

Future research on perception in relation to deafness will benefit if it is formulated in relation to previous research, as well as practical and theoretical considerations, to form a more coherent structure of research findings. This approach should provide more definitive information about such issues as the developmental sequence of sensory/perceptual abilities in the deaf and the categories of perceptual abilities that are associated in deaf subjects with deficiency, compensatory superiority, or simply equivalence by comparison with hearing subjects.

6. References

Ammons, C. H., Worchel, P., and Dallenbach, K. M. Facial vision: The perception of obstacles out of doors by blindfolded and blindfolded deafened subjects. *American Journal of Psychology,* 1953, *66,* 519–553.

Bekesy, G. V. Similarities between hearing and skin sensations. *Psychological Review,* 1959, *66,* 1–22.

Bishop, M. E., Ringel, R. L., and House, A. S. Orosensory perception in the deaf. *Volta Review,* 1972, *74,* 289–298.

Bishop, M. E., Ringel, R. L., and House, A. S. Orosensory perception, speech production, and deafness. *Journal of Speech and Hearing Research,* 1973, *16,* 257–266.

Blair, F. X. A study of the visual memory of deaf and hearing children. *American Annals of the Deaf,* 1957, *102,* 254–266.

Bonvillian, J. D., Charrow, V. R., and Nelson, K. E. Psycholinguistic and educational implications of deafness. *Human Development,* 1973, *16,* 321–345.

Bornstein, H., and Roy, H. L. Comment on "Linguistic deficiency and thinking: Research with deaf subjects 1964–1969." *Psychological Bulletin,* 1973, *79,* 211–214.

Carroll, J. B., Davies, P., and Richman, B. *Word frequency book.* Boston: Houghton-Mifflin, 1971.

DiFrancesca, K. Recall of visual materials presented sequentially and simultaneously by deaf and hearing children. Unpublished Ph.D. dissertation, St. Louis University, 1969.

Espeseth, V. K. An investigation of visual-sequential memory in deaf children. *American Annals of the Deaf,* 1969, *114,* 786–789.

Furth, H. G. Linguistic deficiency and thinking: Research with deaf subjects. 1964–1969. *Psychological Bulletin,* 1971, *76,* 58–72.

Furth, H. G., and Pufall, P. Visual and auditory sequence learning in hearing impaired children. *Journal of Speech and Hearing Research*, 1966, *9*, 441–449.

Gibson, E. J., Gibson, J. J., Pick, A. D., and Osser, H. A developmental study of the discrimination of letter-like forms. *Journal of Comparative and Physiological Psychology*, 1962, *55*, 897–906.

Gibson, J. J. Observations on active touch. *Psychological Review*, 1962, *69*, 477–491.

Gibson, J. J. *The senses considered as perceptual systems*. Boston: Houghton-Mifflin, 1966.

Hayes, G. A study of the visual perception of orally trained deaf children. Unpublished Master's thesis, University of Massachusetts, 1955.

Hoemann, H. W. Perception by the deaf. In E. C. Carterette and M. P. Friedman (Eds.), *Handbook of perception*. Vol. X: *Perceptual ecology*. New York: Academic Press, in press.

Kirman, J. H. Tactile communication of speech: A review and an analysis. *Psychological Bulletin*, 1973, *80*, 54–74.

Kubzansky, P. E., and Leiderman, H. P. Sensory deprivation: An overview. In P. Solomon, P. Kubzansky *et al.* (Eds.), *Sensory deprivation*. Cambridge, Mass.: Harvard University Press, 1961, pp. 221–238.

Larr, A. L. Perceptual and conceptual abilities of residential school deaf children. *Exceptional Children*, 1956, *23*, 63–66.

Levine, B. Sensory interaction: The joint effects of visual and auditory stimulation on critical flicker fusion frequency. Ph.D. dissertation, Boston University, 1958 (*Dissertation Abstracts*, 1958, *18*, 300).

London, I. D. Research on sensory interaction in the Soviet Union. *Psychological Bulletin*, 1954, *51*, 531–568.

Madsen, C. K., and Mears, W. G. The effect of sound upon the tactile threshold of deaf subjects. *Journal of Music Therapy*, 1965, *23*, 63–66.

Moores, D. Psycholinguistics and deafness. *American Annals of the Deaf*, 1970, *115*, 37–48.

Myklebust, H., and Brutten, M. A study of the visual perception of deaf children. *Acta Oto-Laryngologica*, 1953, Supplement 105.

Olsson, J. E., and Furth, H. G. Visual memory-span in the deaf. *American Journal of Psychology*, 1966, *79*, 480–484.

Pickett, J. M. (Ed.) Proceedings of the conference on speech-analysing aids for the deaf. *American Annals of the Deaf*, 1968, *113*, 116–330.

Pickett, J. M. Speech-processing aids for communication handicaps: Some research problems. In D. Tower (Ed.), *The nervous system*. Vol. 3: *Human communication and its disorders*. New York: Raven Press, 1975, pp. 299–304.

Pickett, J. M., Gengel, R. W., and Quinn, R. Research with the Upton eyeglass speechreader. In G. Fant (Ed.), *Proceedings of the Stokholm Speech and Communication Seminar, 1974*. Vol. 4. New York: Wiley, 1976.

Pollard, G., and Neumaier, R. Vision characteristics of deaf students. *American Annals of the Deaf*, 1974, *119*, 740–745.

Reynolds, H. N. Development of reading ability in relation to deafness. *Proceedings, VIIth World Congress of the World Federation of the Deaf, 1975*. Washington, D.C.: National Association of the Deaf, 1976.

Reynolds, H. N. Psycholinguistic effects of deafness. In B. B. Wolman (Eds.), *International encyclopedia of psychiatry, psychology, psychoanalysis and neurology*. Vol. 9. New York: Aesculapius Publishers (Van Nostrand Reinhold), 1977, pp. 252–256.

Reynolds, H. N., and Rosen R. F. The effectiveness of textbook, individualized, and pictorial instructional formats for hearing impaired college students. Paper presented at the annual meeting, American Education Research Association, New Orleans, 1973. *Research in Education*, No. ED 075 968, 1973.

Risberg, A. Visual aids for speech correction. *American Annals of the Deaf*, 1968, *113*, 178–194.

Rosenstein, J. Cognitive abilities of deaf children. *Journal of Speech and Hearing Research*, 1960, *3*, 108–119.

Schiff, W. Social perception in deaf and hearing adolescents. *Exceptional Children*, 1973, *39*, 289–297.

Schiff, W., and Dytell, R. S. Deaf and hearing children's performance on a tactual perception battery. *Perceptual and Motor Skills*, 1972, *35*, 683–706.

Schiff, W., and Saxe, E. Person perceptions of deaf and hearing observers viewing filmed interactions. *Perceptual and Motor Skills*, 1972, *35*, 219–234.

Schiff, W., and Thayer, S. An eye for an ear? Social perception, nonverbal communication, and deafness. *Rehabilitation Psychology*, 1974, *21*, 50–70.

Stark, R. E. *Sensory capabilities of hearing-impaired children.* Baltimore: University Park Press, 1974.

Suchman, R. G. Color-form preference, discriminative accuracy and learning of deaf and hearing children. *Child Development*, 1966, *37*, 439–451.

Tervoort, B. T. Acoustic and visual language communicating systems. *Volta Review*, 1958, *60*, 374–380.

Thompson, R. E. The development of visual perception in deaf children. Ph.D. dissertation, Boston University, 1964.

Upton, H. W. Wearable eyeglass speechreading aid. *American Annals of the Deaf*, 1968, *113*, 222–229.

Withrow, R. Immediate memory span of deaf and normally hearing children. *Exceptional Children*, 1968, *35*, 33–41.

Zakia, R. D., and Haber, R. N. Sequential letter and word recognition in deaf and hearing subjects. *Perception and Psychophysics*, 1971, *9*, 110–114.

PART III

Effects of Short-Term Experience on Human Perception

Introduction

The perceptual rearrangement or distortion experiment was one of the earliest designed to show the effects of experience on perception. One aim of such studies was the resolution of the nativism-empiricism controversy. The contention was that if mature perceivers could adapt to a radical optical rearrangement such as the "reinversion" of the retinal image it was likely that normal spatial perception and perceptual-motor coordination developed through experience in the first place. This rationale seems to be misguided. Even if mature perceivers were able to adapt, it is possible that they would do so by a completely different mechanism than that by which perception developed. Clever adults can bring a variety of strategies to bear in such abnormal situations. Conversely, if mature perceivers cannot adapt, it may not be that the system was preformed to begin with. Perhaps an originally malleable system had become fixed through overlearning or some critical period had been passed. Nevertheless, interest in implications of the distortion experiment by itself for nativism-empiricism persisted at least into the 1950s (Snyder and Pronko, 1952).

An elaborated approach to the distortion experiment which makes its implications for perceptual development clearer was carried out by Held and his colleagues in the late 1950s and 1960s (e.g., Held and Freedman, 1963). Here the distortion experiment is carried out in parallel with animal-rearing experiments. In this approach, an attempt is made to establish an isomorphism between the effects of particular kinds of rearrangements in adults and particular kinds of early and prolonged experience in the developing organism. Held and his colleagues attempted to implicate active, self-produced movement as an important factor in both adaptation to perceptual-motor rearrangements and in normal development of perceptual-motor coordination. The approach led to a fascinating series of experiments on the development of perceptual-motor coordination in the cat (for example, Hein, 1972). However, the particular relation between development and adaptation turned out to be more complex than expected.

Besides this one primary example of the rearrangement experiment as a tool for understanding perceptual development, the rearrangement experiment can serve as a technique for studying the structure and organization of perception and perceptual-motor coordination. Where is a perceptual or perceptual-motor system flexible and where it is rigid? What inferences can be made about mechanisms underlying any flexibility? How do the various sense modalities interact when the input from one modality does not match the information provided by another? Is there a hierarchy, or are they all equal? These are the questions that are most readily investigated by the distortion experiment, and Howard's chapter on the effects of exposure to spatially distorted stimuli addresses such issues.[1] Howard is also sensitive to the distinction between changes of perception as a consequence of exposure to distortion and changes of perceptual-motor coordination. The early experiments using distortion were typically focused on changes in perception and relied heavily on introspective reports. Later on, under the influence of the behaviorists, primary emphasis was given to perceptual-motor behavior. Recently, interest in perceptual changes has again become fashionable, but the questions are being asked in more sophisticated psychophysical terms (e.g., Fiorentini, Ghez, and Maffei, 1972; Hay, Pick, and Rosser, 1963).

The discrimination learning situation is a second experimental paradigm used to investigate the effects of experience on perception. For this paradigm a subject is typically presented repeatedly with a pair of stimuli over a series of trials. The relative positions of the two stimuli are irregularly varied. This technique was originally developed in animal psychology and had more use in research on the associative aspects of learning than on its perceptual aspects. The concepts of acquired equivalence and acquired distinctiveness of cues (e.g., Miller, 1948; Hake and Eriksen, 1955) were attempts to approach the perceptual aspects of discrimination learning from a behaviorist point of view. Essentially that view was that if one learned to make the same response to two different stimuli they would become perceptually more equivalent and if one learned to make a different response to two similar stimuli they would become perceptually more distinctive. The rationale for this view was that similar or distinctive proprioceptive feedback from the responses was added to the original stimuli to make the total configuration more or less distinctive. This approach was questioned by the Gibsons (1955), in part because two similar stimuli would have to be discriminable to begin with in order to associate

[1] This summary ignores the classical recombination studies of Weiss, Sperry, and others (e.g., Weiss, 1941; Sperry, 1941). In these studies, muscles and nerves were transplanted and/or reconnected. The kinds of recovery observed and kinds of failure of recovery provided elegant information about the organization of sensorimotor coordination.

distinctive responses with them. Nevertheless, under appropriate conditions the discrimination learning paradigm can be used to assess the changes in perception as a function of experience. Conversely, the improvement in discrimination in such learning can sometimes he attributed to changes in perception. These two connotations of perceptual learning serve as the starting point for the chapter by Tighe and Tighe.

A central issue in the Tighes' chapter is whether the stimuli in a discrimination learning situation are perceived as overall configurations (gestalts or wholes) or in terms of stimulus dimensions. Young children and animals tend to perceive in terms of configurations while older human subjects tend to be more analytic and perceive in terms of stimulus dimensions. However, these tendencies are not all-or-nothing; they can be biased by the setting and by training. One of the most interesting results reported by the Tighes is that *perceptual* pretraining of subjects can result in an increased tendency to perceive on the basis of stimulus dimensions. However, this pretraining must provide experience with a minimum of three values along the relevant stimulus dimensions. The Tighes suggested that three values elicit an ordering principle or concept while only two values do not.

A final point we wish to emphasize in the Tighes' discussion is the character of the change in perception brought about by experience. The Tighes contend that the perceptual learning they discuss is not of the classical sort conceived by the empiricists—the adding of meaning to raw sensations through some sort of association. Rather, following the Gibsons (1955) they argue that the perceptual learning involves becoming sensitive to new variables or features of stimulation. The evidence adduced to this point is quite convincing. Relevant to the nature of the perceptual learning is the question of whether verbal mediators can account for what appears to be dimensional perception. Verbal mediation is a recent counterpart to the proprioceptive mediators of acquired equivalence and distinctiveness of cues, which in turn is a neoempiricist doctrine in perception. The Tighes argue on the basis of their data that verbal mediation cannot account for development of attention to stimulus dimensions.

The perceptual distortion experiments discussed by Howard typically involve modifications of experience of minutes, hours, or days in duration. The perceptual learning experiments discussed by the Tighes typically involve experimental sessions of 15–30 min, sometimes with repeated sessions on successive days. These are short-term modifications of experience compared to the life-span experience discussed in part II. However, there are a number of phenomena demonstrating the effects on perception of *very* short durations of experience ranging from milliseconds to seconds to minutes. The sensory effects demonstrating temporal integration are probably the most basic or primitive examples of very-short-term experiential effects on perception. Bloch's law that *intensity* times *time* is a constant is one manifestation of such temporal integration. A less intense stimulus presented for a longer time will produce the same effect, i.e., reach threshold, as a more intense stimulus presented for a shorter time. A classical example of a phenomenon perhaps more perceptual in nature which illustrates the effects of experience on perception is the figural aftereffect. The figural aftereffect is a perceived spatial displacement which occurs when a contour is projected to the eye so as to fall near a recently stimulated area. In such a case the perceived locus of the new contour is displaced from its actual position in a direction away from the original stimulation. That is, the prior stimulation seems perceptually to repel the later stimulus. This phenomenon was taken to support the gestalt physiological field theory of brain function (Köhler and Wallach, 1944). This physiological theory has been more or less discredited but the phenomenon of figural aftereffects remains, never completely satisfactorily explained.

Helson's concept of adaptation level implicates short-term experience in perception. According to this concept, preceding stimuli in a series of psychophysical judgments help establish an adaptation level which in turn modulates the perception of a current stimulus. Bevan and Gaylord explicate this concept and the theory developed around it. The theory considers that all relevant prior experience has an effect on the current adaptation level, but immediately preceding experience and stimuli have a greater effect than more temporally distant stimuli. Most of the experiments demonstrating the effects of prior experience are concerned with preceding stimuli in a series of psychophysical judgments. These experiments include the traditional studies of anchor effects and time order errors. However, as Bevan and Gaylord point out, there have been studies of individual differences in life experience which would lead to generally different adaptation levels. Thus, they explain that watchmakers consistently judge laboratory weights to be heavier than weightlifters do.

An interesting aspect of adaptation-level theory is the relation between prior and concurrent stimulation as they effect perception. Background stimulation affects the adaptation level in the same way that prior stimulation does. And any particular stimulus is judged in relation to the adaptation level. Thus, adaptation-level theory unites the effects of prior and concurrent background stimulation.

About 45 years ago, Gibson (1933) discovered an aftereffect which he explained in terms much like the concept of adaptation level. He noted that if an observer stared at a curved line for several minutes it would appear less curved and a subsequently presented straight line would appear curved in the opposite direction. He conceptualized what was going on to be a shift in the neutral point of a dimension of curvature. A new norm of straight was established in the direction of the fixated stimulus so stimuli less curved than that norm or neutral point, e.g., straight, would appear to be curved in the opposite direction. This curvature normalization phenomenon and an analogous tilted-line phenomenon (Gibson, 1937) were investigated intermittently over a 30-year period but seemed to be curious isolated phenomena. After Hubel and Wiesel discovered neural detectors in the cortex sensitive to features such as orientation of lines and direction of motion, Gibson's technique of exposure to a very specific type of form stimulus seemed to offer the possibility for investigating detectorlike mechanisms in the human. If such a mechanism existed it might show properties of fatigue and aftereffect. McCullough (1965) with her color-orientation-contingent aftereffects was the first one to exploit this paradigm. Since then there has been almost an explosion in use of the technique. Eimas and Miller in their chapter review this research, showing how it has been combined with linear systems analysis in visual form perception and how it has been extended from vision to the speech-relevant aspects of auditory perception.

Not only is the selective adaptation experiment of interest as it pertains to the role of experience in perception, but also, as Eimas and Miller point out in their introduction and emphasize throughout their chapter, this paradigm provides information about the normal functioning of a perceptual system. Of particular interest in this regard is the question of what unit is being adapted. In the speech-relevant research reviewed by Eimas and Miller, this takes the form of trying to decide whether adaptation operates at the level of distinctive features or that of phonemes. Obviously such issues have direct implication for understanding the units of perception.

The adaptation-level and selective adaptation paradigms involve the modification of a current percept by prior experience. In contrast, the topic of the chapter by Uhlarik and Johnson concerns the buildup over time of the percept itself. This is the so-called repetition effect wherein a stimulus is presented for so brief a duration that it is imperceptible. However, if the presentation is repeated again and again, it gradually becomes more perceptible on a single presentation. The interstimulus interval is long enough so that the increased perceptibility is not a matter of temporal integration of the type described by Bloch's law. Uhlarik and Johnson relate the repetition effect to the general issue of the buildup of perception over time. This general problem, often called the "microgenesis of perception," concerns the way percepts develop over very short time intervals. That is, what happens immediately after the lights come on? Uhlarik and Johnson suggest that the repetition effect procedure may be a way of slowing down the normal buildup of perception and examining it in detail.

In this context the repetition effect represents a modern example of a long tradition of investigation of the microgenesis of perception. Interest in the problem and the term itself, as Uhlarik and Johnson point out, can be traced back to Heinz Werner. The research on visual masking arose originally out of this tradition with interest in what happens to a target stimulus when it is preceded or followed by a second stimulus. This interest, of course, led to the discovery of the paradoxical backward masking phenomenon: a later stimulus masks an earlier one. Indeed, one root of the current information-processing approach is probably Werner and his interest in the microgenesis of perception. Uhlarik and Johnson relate the repetition effect not only to the microgenesis of perception but also to the breakdown of perception, i.e., the fragmentation which occurs under stabilized retinal images. Ideally both these phenomena as well as the selective adaptation phenomenon would converge in identifying similar units of perception. One wonders whether another kind of repetition-adaptation would also provide converging evidence on the units of perception—this is Richard Warren's verbal transformation effect (Obusek and Warren, 1972). Warren has discovered that if a word is presented rapidly over and over again at normal listening levels, perception will be normal and correct at first but soon will become distorted and different, although related words are heard. For example, "ring, ring, ring, ring, . . ." might be heard as "ring, . . . , ring, sing, ling, ..."

Finally we would like to comment on two general issues which cut across several chapters in this part of the book. One is the question of the persistence of these effects of short-term experience on perception. This arises most vividly with the selective adaptation experiments discussed by Eimas and Miller. Some motion aftereffects are reported to last as long as 24 hr, and some color-contingent aftereffects have been found to last for days or weeks. Why do some aftereffects last and others dissipate quickly? One could imagine two different types of mechanisms. One could simply be fatigued by overstimulation to the adapting stimulus. This fatigue would simply wear off in the absence of the fatiguing stimulus. The other might be a mechanism which was set to a new value by the adapting stimulus. For this latter mechanism to be reset would require a counteradapting stimulus. Given the specific nature of some of the adaptation stimuli, such counteradapting stimuli might be relatively rare in a person's normal environment and hence aftereffects would be very persistent. Ainsworth (1977) proposes a model for a similar distinction (see also MacKay and MacKay, 1975). Relatively long persistence also occurs with some of the other phenomena discussed in this section. The persistence of adaptation effects in some of the perceptual and perceptual-motor distortion experiments is quite long, occasionally lasting days and weeks. However, in these cases the exposure to distortion is considerably longer than in the case of selective adaptation experiments. Systematic work on readaptation from the effects of distorted visual input has only recently been undertaken (Redding and Wallace, 1976; Choe and Welch, 1974). The conditions which facilitate and retard readaptation are simply not known. Bevan and Gaylord mention adaptation-level effects lasting up to a week, but again there is very little systematic work on persistence of adaptation-level effects. The same lack of research on persistence is true for Uhlarik and Johnson's repetition effect. One would expect the perceptual learning described by the Tighes to be relatively longlasting, but again little systematic work has been done. The question of persistence is relevant to whether the phenomena discussed in this section are related to the perceptual effects of early and/or prolonged experience discussed in the other parts of the book. For example, could the speech-relevant selective adaptation experiments discussed by Eimas and Miller elucidate the mechanism underlying the cultural differences in categorical perceptual judgments discussed by Strange and Jenkins?

The second general issue derives from the empiricist interpretation that treats perception more or less as a cognitive act. One of the earliest examples of this view was Helmholtz's "unconsious inference." The possibility that the effects of experience occur in this inferential mode is raised explicitly in two of the chapters in this section. Uhlarik and Johnson describe a Bayesian statistical decision model from the literature to account for the increasing perceptibility in the repetition effect—a very sophisticated form of an inferential model. They themselves subscribe to a more neutral associationistic empiricist model involving integration of memory with present stimulation. Bevan and Gaylord convincingly argue in a whole section of their chapter that the effects of adaptation level are perceptual and not judgmental in nature. And Howard in his own work has taken pains to demonstrate that adaptation to distortion can occur without conscious awareness of a distortion. He has introduced prismatic distortion in stages so small that subjects were not aware of any optical displacement. They adapted to each increment before he introduced the next one. The weight of the evidence from these three chapters is that the effect of experience on perception is not a matter of a conscious inferential process. The evidence leaves open the possibility that an unconscious inferential model is an adequate description of such effects of experience on perception.

References

Ainsworth, W. A. Mechanism of selective feature adaptation. *Perception and Psychophysics*, 1977, *21*, 365–370.

Choe, C., and Welch, R. B. Variables affecting the intermanual transfer and decay of prism adaptation. *Journal of Experimental Psychology*, 1974, *102*, 1076–1084.

Fiorentini, A., Ghez, C., and Maffei, L. Physiological correlates of adaptation to a rotated visual field. *Journal of Physiology*, 1972, *227*, 313–322.

Gibson, J. J. Adaptation, aftereffect, and contrast in the perception of curved lines. *Journal of Experimental Psychology*, 1933, *16*, 1–31.

Gibson, J. J. Adaptation and negative aftereffect. *Psychological Review*, 1937, *44*, 222–244.

Gibson, J. J., and Gibson, E. J. Perceptual learning: Differentiation or enrichment? *Psychological Review*, 1955, *62*, 32–41.

Hake, H. W., and Eriksen, C. W. Effect of number of permissible response categories on learning of a constant number of visual stimuli. *Journal of Experimental Psychology*, 1955, *50*, 161–167.

Hay, J. C., Pick, H. L., Jr., and Rosser, E. Adaptation to chromatic aberration by the human visual system. *Science*, 1963, *141*, 167–169.

Hein, A. Acquiring components of visually guided behavior. In Pick, A. D. (ed.), *Minnesota symposia on child psychology*. Vol. 6. Minneapolis: University of Minnesota Press, 1972, pp. 53–68.

Held, R., and Freedman, S. J. Plasticity in human sensimotor control. *Science*, 1963, *142*, 455–462.

Köhler, W., and Wallach, H. Figural aftereffects: An investigation of visual processes. *Proceedings of the American Philosophical Society*, 1944, *88*, 269–357.

MacKay, D. M., and MacKay, V. What causes decay of pattern contingent chromatic aftereffects? *Vision Research*, 1975, *15*, 462–464.

McCullough, C. Color adaptation of edge-detectors in the human visual system. *Science*, 1965, *149*, 1115–1116.

Miller, N. E. Theory and experiment relating psychoanalytic displacement to stimulus response generalization. *Journal of Abnormal and Social Psychology*, 1948, *43*, 155–177.

Obusek, C. J., and Warren, R. M. Relation of the verbal transformation and the phonemic restoration effects. *Cognitive Psychology*, 1972, 97–107.

Redding, G. M., and Wallace, B. Components of displacement adaptation in acquisition and decay as a function of hand and hall exposure. *Perception and Psychophysics*, 1976, *20*, 453–459.

Synder, F. W., and Pronko, N. H. *Vision with spatial inversion*. Wichita, Ks.: University of Wichita Press, 1952.

Sperry, R. W. The effect of crossing nerves to antagonistic muscles in the hind limb of the rat. *Journal of Comparative Neurology*, 1941, *75*, 1–19.

Weiss, P. Self differentiation of the basic patterns of coordination. *Comparative Psychology Monographs*, 1941, *17*, No. 4.

9

Effects of Exposure to Spatially Distorted Stimuli

I. P. HOWARD

1. Introduction

The successful execution of most pieces of behavior requires that the animal correctly perceive the positions and movements of its own body parts and the positions and movements of external objects. Many spatial skills are so vital that they are innately determined, or require very little experience for their development. For instance, the wildebeest is able to run after its mother within hours of being born, and most mammals avoid the edges of cliffs that they can see, even when they encounter them for the first time. Nevertheless, whether particular spatial perceptual mechanisms are innate or not, they possess a degree of flexibility; i.e., they may be temporarily, or permanently, modified by experience. Such flexibility is required to correct for the changes that occur when an animal grows, is injured, or encounters unusual types of stimulation. It is also required to correct for the tendency of any complex system to drift from its peak performance.

There are several ways of studying the flexibility of the spatial aspects of perception. One way is to alter radically the normal anatomical connections, another is to rear young animals in severely anomalous sensory environments. The results of such studies are reviewed in earlier chapters of this volume. Such methods cannot normally be applied to humans, although useful data may be gathered by studying the effects of radical surgery or naturally occurring sensory deformities in man. The flexibility of spatial perception in humans may, however, be studied by distorting temporarily the input to one or other sense

I. P. HOWARD • Department of Psychology, York University, Toronto, Ontario, Canada.

organ and measuring the adaptive changes that occur in selected perceptual and perceptual-motor tasks. The results gained from this kind of study will be reviewed in this chapter.

The classic study of sensory distortion in man was conducted by Stratton in 1897, who wore, continuously, for several days spectacles which inverted and reversed the visual scene. Stratton gave himself no systematic tests, but recorded his experiences in the context of his normal routine of life. He found that his actions gradually became more smoothly coordinated, although each action had to be separately mastered. Similar studies were done by Erisman and Kohler in Innsbruck (see Kottenhoff, 1957, for an English summary of this work). Like Stratton, they also found that there was little transfer of learning from one action to another. Apart from this rather general conclusion, these experiments revealed very little about the nature of visuomotor adaptation to distorted vision. This was because the exposure and testing procedures were unsystematic and because wearing reversing and/or inverting spectacles disturbed many aspects of behavior simultaneously, so that it was difficult to isolate particular effects. These difficulties were particularly apparent when these investigators asked whether the inverted scene appeared to right itself and come to look "normal." Later in this chapter, I hope to show why this apparently simple question can be so confusing.

In recent years, more clearly formulated questions about the flexibility of spatial behavior have been studied by quantitatively assessing the effects of simpler types of distortion on the performance of defined tasks. The rest of this chapter will describe what these questions are and the main findings and areas of active controversy.

There are three main ways of spatially distorting a sensory input. The first way is to expose the sense organ to asymmetrical stimulation. Sensory dimensions in which there is a central point of symmetry are referred to as "normative dimensions," and the point of symmetry is referred to as the "norm." For instance, the visual straight ahead is the norm for visual direction, and the vertical is the norm for tilt. In each case, one can study the effects of exposing the sense organ to stimuli which are asymmetrical with respect to the norm.

The second way of distorting sensory inputs is to present particular stimulus objects in an unusual spatial disposition. Many stimulus objects tend to occur with certain constant spatial properties or in particular orientations. For instance, the walls of a room tend to be vertical, the surface of water is horizontal, and mountains do not move. Objects which possess familiar constant features such as these act as frames of reference. One may study the effects of exposing a person to frames of reference in unusual orientations.

The third way of distorting sensory inputs is to alter the normal relationship between two stimulus dimensions (defined later as stimulus covariance functions). For instance, one may introduce an anomalous relationship between the seen and felt position of the arm by viewing the arm through a prism which

Table 1. Stimulus Structures in the Spatial Domain

			Stimulus covariances					
			Vantage-point-dependent covariance				Vantage-point-independent covariance	
			Exafferent; passive movement of observer or movement of object		Reafferent; motorsensory covariance			
Stimulus symmetries or norms	Stimulus constants or frames of reference	Contamination (no information) covariance	Intrasensory	Intersensory	Self-observation reafference	Locomotory reafference	Taxonomic properties	Causally related properties
The visual vertical; straight ahead	Familiar vertical objects; large stationary objects	e.g., Chromatic aberration of eye's lens; contingent aftereffects	Size-distance invariance; shape of image and tilt of object	Sight and sound of bell; seen size and felt size of an object	Sight of moving hand	Image motion due to eye movements; feeling objects with mobile hand	Shape and sound of a bee; color and shape of a suit of playing cards	Tipping of glass and pouring of liquid; hitting of billiard ball and direction of travel

displaces the visual scene to one side. I introduced the term "discordance" to refer to such distortions (Howard, 1968), a term which has been generally adopted.

These three types of sensory distortion will be discussed in turn. For the purpose of exposition, I have further subdivided them as shown in Table 1. The meaning of the subdivisions will be made clear in the course of the chapter.

2. Effects of Asymmetrical Stimulation

2.1. The Tilt Aftereffect

The tilt aftereffect is a typical phenomenon resulting from asymmetrical stimulation. A luminous line seen in the dark, tilted in the frontal plane by about 10° from the vertical, appears progressively less tilted during prolonged viewing and a vertical line seen subsequently in the same location appears tilted in the opposite direction. The progressive change in the tilt of the inspected line is referred to as "normalization," and the apparent tilt in the vertical test line is the tilt aftereffect. Both effects are typically about 2° in magnitude. Similar effects occur with inspection of a line tilted with respect to the horizontal. The balance of evidence suggests that tilt normalization and the tilt aftereffect are confined to lines which are imaged on the same region of the retina as that occupied by the tilted inspection line (Campbell and Maffei, 1971; Coltheart and Cooper, 1972).

The neurophysiological studies of Hubel and Wiesel (1962) on the visual cortex of the cat have revealed that there are certain neurons in the visual cortex, each of which responds maximally when the image of a line has a specific orientation within a particular region of the retina. The response rate of each neuron or unit declines as the orientation of the image on the retina departs from the "preferred" orientation up to a limit of about 20° either way. The response ranges of different units overlap, and it is assumed that some measure of central tendency in the overall response pattern determines the perceived orientation of the stimulus. To explain the tilt aftereffect, one need only assume that during prolonged viewing of an inspection line, the cortical units which respond to that line become less sensitive, so that when a test line of a slightly different orientation is viewed the central tendency of the response pattern which it evokes, and hence its perceived tilt, is shifted away from the orientation of the adapting stimulus (Coltheart, 1971).

Although this theory accounts for the tilt aftereffect, it does not account for the fact that a tilted line comes to appear more vertical (normalization). This and other perceptual phenomena suggest that the vertical and horizontal detectors have special properties (see Appelle, 1972). For instance, acuity for vertical and horizontal lines is greater than for oblique lines. This effect is known as "meridional astigmatism" to distinguish it from astigmatism due to defects in the optics of the eye.

There is some evidence that the superiority of the main meridia is innate. For instance, Leventhal and Hirsch (1975) found that the development of cortical units which respond to diagonal lines requires a more specific visual input than does the development of vertical or horizontal units. Furthermore, Leehey, Moskowitz-Cook, Brill, and Held (1975) found that very young infants spend more time looking at horizontal and vertical lines than at oblique lines. On the other hand, there is considerable electrophysiological evidence that experience also contributes to the superiority of the vertical and horizontal units. For instance, it has been found that cats reared in environments consisting of only vertical stripes do not develop cortical units that respond to horizontal lines (Blakemore and Cooper, 1970), and Mitchell, Freeman, Millodot, and Haegerstrom (1973) have produced evidence that uncorrected optical astigmatism can cause meridional astigmatism in humans. Even more striking evidence that experience can affect meridional astigmatism in humans was reported by Annis and Frost (1973). They found that a sample of Cree Indians who live in conical-shaped tents did not exhibit the higher resolution for vertical and horizontal gratings that was shown by a sample of city-dwelling Canadians of European descent. However, the conclusion that this difference was due to experience has been questioned by Timney and Muir (1976), who found that there are racial differences in meridional astigmatism, when the factor of experience is held constant. The results of a study by Fiorentini, Ghez, and Maffei (1972) show that even short-term experience can modify meridional astigmatism. In this study subjects wore Dove prisms, which rotated the visual field by 30°, for periods of up to 7 days. The differences in contrast threshold between vertical and oblique targets decreased or disappeared, but reappeared within 2 hr after the prisms were removed.

In accounting for meridional astigmatism, it has been suggested that vertical and horizontal units, compared with oblique units, may be (1) more sensitive, (2) more finely tuned to a particular orientation, (3) more numerous, and (4) less readily adapted. However, the electrophysiological evidence for these differences is contradictory, and this question is far from being finally resolved (for more details about this issue, see Barlow, 1975; Lewis, 1975; Mitchell, this volume).

We can certainly conclude that there is something special about the perception of vertical and horizontal lines, and we can be reasonably certain that the neural organization of the visual system, although primed by innately determined processes, has a degree of flexibility. The existence of experience-dependent changes in neural organization should not be taken as evidence that basic sensory functions can be improved by training in an adult living in a normal environment; the demands of a normal environment are probably sufficient to keep sensory systems functioning at a level of efficiency close to their theoretical limit.

The tilt aftereffect is only one of many effects of asymmetrical visual stimulation. If one views a moving pattern for some time, the movement appears to slow down and a stationary pattern seen subsequently appears to move in the opposite direction. This effect is known as the "movement aftereffect." If the left edge of a square is viewed for some time, it appears to become more centrally placed and a square subsequently placed in the center of the visual field appears to be displaced toward the left (see Howard and Templeton, 1966, p. 281). If two objects in a similar direction but at different distances from the observer are inspected for a few minutes, they appear to become more equidistant, and objectively equidistant objects seen subsequently in the same direction seem to be separated in depth in reversed order (Howard and Templeton, 1964).

2.2. Kinesthetic Asymmetry

If a blindfolded person holds his extended arm out about 45° to the median plane of the body for a few minutes, he typically misplaces it about 6° in the direction of previous asymmetry when he attempts to bring his hand into the median plane. This type of effect has been called "postural persistence." Similar effects are produced by holding the eyes or the head in an asymmetrical posture. A related effect is the kinesthetic figural aftereffect produced by stroking a tapered or tilted bar.

Postural persistence could be due either to adaptation of receptors in the joint capsule or to "muscular" factors such as changes in motor innervation or adaptation in muscle spindles and tendon organs. Attempts have been made to isolate the "muscular" component from the "joint" component in kinesthetic aftereffects. However, Collins (1971) has convincingly argued that the results of such studies are irrelevant to this issue because of the complexity of the tasks used.

Howard and Anstis (1974) attempted to resolve this issue. They found a 6° shift in the apparent position of the head after holding it turned 24° to one side, but no aftereffect of holding the head straight while straining against a torque. Aftereffects in the felt position of the head were also assessed by asking the subject to point with unseen hand to straight ahead of his nose with the head in various positions. The aftereffect was reduced but still present when the head was tested at 24° to the opposite side to that in which it had been held. The most reasonable interpretation of these findings is that postural persistence is due to selective adaptation in joint receptors with fairly broad response characteristics within the joint's angular range. The presence of joint receptors with a response range averaging 73° is confirmed by physiological evidence (Mountcastle, Poggio, and Werner, 1963). McCall, Farias, Williams, and BeMent (1974) recorded from the receptors in the knee joint of the cat and plotted the response curves for various static positions of the joint, first in the direction of extension and then in the direction of flexion. They found that the two curves were out of phase by about 6°. This hysteresis effect is the same magnitude as postural persistence in human limbs.

3. Effects of Distorting Frames of Reference

The tilt aftereffect is normally about 2° or 3° in magnitude, and it has been assumed that it is due to a direct effect of tilted lines on slant-detecting units occurring at any early stage in perceptual processing. However, under certain conditions, the apparent visual vertical can be displaced through much larger angles than 3°. For instance, a person in an airplane will perceive the inside of the plane to be vertical even when it is tilted through a considerable angle. A pilot, flying in a cloud, may not even be aware that his plane is upside down. Wertheimer in 1912 noticed how a room seen in a tilted mirror soon came to appear upright. Observers in this type of situation take the walls of the room as their standard of verticality, or frame of reference, even though the walls may not be normally oriented. The frame of reference for motion is illustrated by the experience we have when we sit in a train and accept the train next to our own as our frame of reference for motion. When that train moves, we ascribe the motion to the train in which we are sitting in spite of contradictory information from the vestibular senses. In a similar way a plumb line hanging in the cabin of a ship seems to sway from side to side, whereas, in fact, it is the cabin which is swaying. A pervasive visual frame of reference that is often overlooked is the nose and orbital ridges. An image of these structures projects far into the visual field of each eye and provides a reference against which object motion and visual direction may be assessed (see Bower, 1974, for an elaboration of this idea). A frame of reference may thus be defined *as an attribute of a certain stimulus object which does not normally vary, and in terms of which variations of the same attribute in other objects perceived at the same time may be judged*.

A quantitative study of the effects of disturbing the frame of reference for verticality was conducted by Asch and Witkin (1948). The subject sat inside a room which was tilted 22° and set a rod, seen in the tilted room, to appear vertical. The rod was displaced on average 15° in the direction of the tilted room. In a second condition, the subject stood outside the tilted room so that he saw it in the context of the normal room. Now the rod was displaced only 8.5° on average. These large displacements of the visual vertical, found when the visual field is filled with a tilted scene containing objects which are known to be normally vertical, are known as "visual frame effects." They differ from the smaller tilt aftereffect in at least two other respects.

In the first place, the tilt aftereffect is limited to the retinal location of the induction line and can thus produce an apparent shift in the orientation of a line imaged in one part of the retina relative to lines imaged in other, unaffected parts. This is not so in the case of the frame effect, which is defined as due to the fact that the subject refers to the orientation of certain objects when judging the orientation of other objects; relative orientations of objects are not affected. The frame effect is like changing the zero point on a measurement scale, which leaves all relative values unaffected, while the tilt aftereffect is like compressing one part of a scale relative to the rest. The best way to get a pure measure of the tilt aftereffect is to ask the subject to set a test line, in the region of the previously inspected tilted line, to be parallel with a line imaged in an unaffected region of the retina.

The second difference between the tilt aftereffect and the frame effect is that the evidence we have suggests that the frame effect shows little, if at all, as an aftereffect. In a study by Fiorentini *et al.* (1972), subjects wore prisms for 7 days that tilted the visual scene 45°. The tilt aftereffects revealed by setting an isolated luminous line to the apparent vertical were on average between 5° and 10°. However, after the fifth day, familiar objects no longer appeared tilted; i.e., there had been a visual frame shift of 45°. It is a pity that the parallel-line test was not used in these studies, for then we would be able to distinguish between the two effects more clearly.

4. Perceptual Polarity: Effects of Reversed Frame of Reference

The effects to be considered in this section are due to reversing frames of reference with respect to their normal disposition in the sense organ.

Ever since the seventeenth century, when Kepler revealed that the retinal image is inverted and reversed relative to the scene, scientists and philosophers have puzzled about why the world appears erect. It was this same puzzle that stimulated Stratton to conduct his famous experiments in which he wore lenses which inverted and reversed the visual scene. He wanted to know whether the world would come to appear erect again. This is a very ambiguous question and attempts to answer it have led to confusion.

Most objects and features of the visual world have a top and a bottom because they and we maintain a consistent orientation to gravity. Such objects are referred to as "mono-oriented" and may be difficult to recognize when upside down. Only a few objects, such as shoes, clocks, and books have a left side which is distinguishable from the right side.

One behavioral consequence of the up-down polarity of the world is the development of terms like "upright," "wrong-way round," and "upside down." But these terms are often ambiguous and are best avoided in investigations of the effects of reversed vision. The best way to study the effects of reversed vision on perception is to measure speed and correctness in the performance of discrimination or recognition tasks. For instance, the following measures may be used:

1. The speed and accuracy of recognition of mono-oriented objects in various orientations. A particularly good measure of this kind is the time it takes to recognize a person from an upside-down picture. It is not difficult to recognize that the picture is of a person, but the difficulty is being able to say which person it is.
2. The correctness and speed of identification of mono-oriented objects, in various orientations, hidden in a background of distracting lines.
3. The speed of reading upside-down or reversed print. The study by Kolers and Perkins (1969) is a good example of a study using this measure, although the results are not relevant here.
4. The first figure to be recognized in a composite ambiguous figure in which the alternative figures are separated by a specified angle (for details, see Howard and Templeton, 1966, p. 323; Rock, 1973).

There are three possible reasons why familiar objects are difficult to recognize when upside down. The first is that the salient features that we may normally use to recognize an object are not where we expect them to be, and we thus waste time looking for them. Adaptation to inverted vision would consist of relearning where things are to be found. The second reason why upside-down objects are difficult to recognize is that the descriptions which we have stored and which we evoke when trying to recognize something may be coded in terms of the relative orientation of parts of the object. For instance, part of the description of "eye" which we use when recognizing an eye may be that it occurs above the nose. An eye seen below the nose may evoke the descriptive schema for "mouth," in which case the eyelids will be seen as if they were lips. Adaptation to inverted vision would consist in this case of "rewriting" our descriptive schemata. The third reason why upside-down objects are difficult to recognize may be that we store a pictorial template of the object in a particular orientation. It seems unlikely for several reasons that we use simple templates for recognizing things. For instance, we recognize an object when it projects different-sized images, and it is difficult to see how we could have a template for each size. Metzler and Shepard (1974) and, more recently, Cooper (1976) have shown that a process analogous to the rotation of a mental image underlies our ability to recognize whether two abstract objects in different orientations are the same or are mirror images. However, the property of being a mirror image is not an intrinsic property of a shape, so that in the task of discriminating an object from its mirror image the subject cannot make use of intrinsic orientation-free features. In this case, the subject has no option but to mentally rotate one object with respect to the other in order to decide about their similarity.

It is only the intrinsic properties of objects that allow us to form orientation-free descriptions. For instance, an eye may be described as a dark disk with an oval-shaped lighter surround, and this description holds, no matter which way round the face is. Furthermore, most familiar objects have many salient local features which allow us to bypass the problem of orientation. For instance, the sight of an earlobe may suffice to tell us that there is a face there, no matter which way round the face is. The fact that recognizability is disturbed by disorientation suggests that not all our descriptive schemata are orientation free, but many of them must be, or else we would be more disturbed by disorientation than we are. When we have learned to recognize upside-down things, such as upside-down writing, it is unlikely that we rotate mental images, as the work of Shepard might suggest. We might do this initially, to some extent, but in the long run we probably construct new descriptive schemata that are orientation free or that are relevant to the new orientation of things.

Let us now take a look at the question of whether the world appears to look right side up after a period of wearing inverting spectacles. Ivo Kohler reported that, when inverting spectacles have been worn for some time, objects which have been handled appear to be erect, but objects which have not been handled appear to be inverted. For instance, it was reported that the contents of a room may look erect while the scene outside the window looks inverted. Several commentators, such as Taylor (1962), have maintained that this report implies that if the subject is asked to draw what he sees, he will draw the room erect and the objects seen out of the window upside down. But this confuses the geometric arrangement of images with visual polarity. The distinction between the inside and outside of the room is that only for objects inside the room has the subject's polarity behavior become adapted. He will recognize objects in the room quickly, identify their tops and bottoms, predict their direction of fall, etc., whereas objects outside the window, having been seen less and handled less, will elicit the old inappropriate, polarity habits. The subject cannot depict his change of polarity behavior in a drawing, for no geometric change is involved.

Kohler himself may be partly responsible for this widespread misunderstanding because, in an attempt to illustrate the experiences of his subjects, he produced a film in which some parts of a scene were shown erect and other parts inverted. In his writings, however, he does not make this mistake. For instance, in describing his own experiences while wearing left-right reversing spectacles he wrote, "but this isn't a sudden reversal; it remains the same picture experienced differently." He went on to describe how inscriptions on buildings or advertisements were still seen in mirror-writing, but the objects containing them were seen the right way round and how vehicles seen as driving on the right (in Austria this is correct) nevertheless carried license numbers in mirror-writing. Again Kohler commented that "the purely pictorial impression remains reversed" (Kohler, 1955). One of Kohler's subjects (Kottenhoff, 1961) reported that things sometimes looked upright but that this did not mean that things appeared to turn around; he wrote, "I see always the same, but the interpretation is different."

Consider what would happen if you were allowed to see only upside-down print for a month or so. At first your reading would be slow and the book would look upside down. But after a while your reading speed would return to normal and the book would lose that upside-down look. It would no longer look strange—but it would not geometrically right itself so as to look like an ordinary book. Suppose you learned to read upside-down words well but were never shown upside-down numbers. Is it not reasonable to suppose that when shown both together the letters would have lost their upside-down appearance, but the numbers would still look upside down? What had changed for the subjects wearing inverting spectacles was not the apparent geometric arrangement of parts of the visual field but merely the sense of strangeness or upside downness which the parts evoked.

I come now to the third way of distorting sensory inputs, namely that of introducing a discordance between related stimulus dimensions.

5. Effects of Discordant Sensory Stimulation

The visual world is not chaotic. Similar configurations of stimuli recur in patterns and predictable sequences, which I shall refer to by the general term "stimulus covariance functions." Perceptual learning is in part a question of constructing internal schemata or maps of these functions so that behavior can be more effectively controlled.

Stimulus covariance functions fall into three main classes (see Table 1). In the first class are those that convey no useful information to the perceiver. An example is provided by the chromatic fringes produced by the lens of the eye. Although these fringes can be shown to exist optically, we are not aware of them. This suggests that we have a neural mechanism for canceling out the perceptual effects of these color fringes. The physical function that relates the order of colors in the fringes to the direction of the contrast gradient must somehow be nulled by an inverse function somewhere in the visual system. If this is so, it should be possible to adapt to color fringes produced by looking through lenses which are not corrected for chromatic aberration. Hay, Pick, and Roser (1963) found that such artificially produced chromatic fringes are no longer perceived after about 2 days of continuous wearing of chromatically aberrant lenses. Perhaps the mechanism responsible for adaptation to color fringes is related to the contingent color aftereffect discovered by McCollough (see Skowbo, Timney, Gentry, and Morant, 1975; Eimas and Miller, this volume). Here, too, as in the case of chromatic aberration, a covariance between color and contours generates the inverse function in the nervous system.

The two remaining classes of covariance functions (see Table 1) convey useful information to the perceiver and are therefore not canceled out, but rather coded in such a way that the information they contain is accurately extracted. In one class are those that depend on the observer's vantage point, and in the other class are those that are independent of the observer's vantage point. An example of a vantage-point-dependent function is that which relates the size of the retinal image of an object to the distance of the object from the observer. Examples of vantage-point-independent functions are the relationship between the shape of a bee and the buzzing sound that it makes, and the relationship between the suit of a playing card and its color. Relationships of this type between features or properties of objects are referred to in Table 1 as "taxonomic" properties. Other vantage-point-independent functions are included under the heading of "causally related stimuli." Included here are such things as the causal relationship between the act of tipping a glass of water and the sight of pouring water. The possibility of studying taxonomic and causal perceptual schemata by the procedure of introducing discordances has been discussed in Howard (1975). In the present chapter further discussion will be limited to the topic of vantage-point-dependent covariance.

A person must be able to allow for the effects of changes in his vantage point if he is to perceive the objective properties of objects. For instance, the shape of the retinal image of an object changes as the observer moves about. But a similar change in image shape can be produced by a movement of the object relative to the stationary observer or by a plastic deformation of the object. This type of ambiguity may be resolved in two ways. The first way involves the use of a covariance schema, the second way involves the use of a frame of reference. The distinction between the two should become clear in what follows.

When a person moves, there are velocity signals from the vestibular system, velocity and position signals from the joint receptors in the limbs, and, if the movement is self-generated, correlated motor-nerve discharges. The function that relates these body motion signals to the resulting changes in the retinal image is the stimulus covariance function for this situation. The term "invariant" is often used to denote these constant relationships between stimuli, but the term is not always consistently applied. A perceiver may be born with, or may acquire by experience, an internal representation of the stimulus covariance function which I shall refer to as a "stimulus covariance schema" or simply "covariance schema." A perceiver with a schema for the task we are considering "knows" what image changes to expect as he moves in a certain way relative to a fixed object at a given distance from him. If the image changes differ from this standard, he will perceive the object as moving or deforming in such a way that will account for that difference. Needless to say, this is not normally a conscious process. This type of mechanism has been called a "cancelation process" (Gregory, 1966), but the term "cancelation" is a little misleading, for it suggests that perceived changes in the retinal image are canceled by the body motion signals. They are not canceled by the body motion signals but rather assessed with respect to those signals (MacKay, 1972). The image changes are still perceived, but they are perceived as due to body motion and not as due to object motion.

This servosystem model of perceptual constancies, in which the way one stimulus varies with another is compared with a covariance schema, has inspired most experiments on the effects of sensory discordance. The idea is that by artificially changing the way in which two related stimuli covary, we can study the way in which the system recalibrates its covariance schemata. This is a useful idea, but in *normal environments, covariance schemata may not be required for perceptual constancies.* Frames of reference often provide a simpler mechanism. Consider the example of body and object motion that we used before. When we move about in a normal room we assume that the room is not moving, and therefore any image motion may be ascribed to head or body motion without further ado. We do not need to appeal to covariance schemata, and we do not require information about head or body motion.

To study covariance schemata, we introduce a physical distortion or discordance into the covariance function. For intance, one may have a subject view his arm through a prism which physically distorts the relationship between distal and proximal visual stimuli, and this has the effect of physically distorting the covariance function between the felt and seen position of the arm. In such studies, either frames of reference should be minimized by using highly abstract displays, or their effects should be assessed by controls.

Studies of the effects of sensory discordance fall into three classes. In the first class, there are those studies concerned with the perceptual effects of discordance between stimuli in the same modality, or *intrasensory discordance*. Second, there are the studies concerned with the perceptual effects of discordance between stimuli in different modalities or *intersensory discordance*. Third, there are studies of the perceptual effects of *motorsensory discordance*. The perceptual effects of these three types of discordance will now be considered under separate headings before their effects on sensorimotor coordination are considered (see Table 1).

5.1. Effects of Intrasensory Discordance on Spatial Judgments

The discussion of intrasensory discordance will be confined to three examples. The first example is provided by the studies of Rock on the effects of minification (see Rock, 1966, for details). Rock had his subjects play cards and draw pictures while looking into a curved mirror that reduced all images by half. This procedure introduced a discordance between the image size of any object in view and its distance from the subject. It is important to note that subjects could see their own hands, which would be a particularly strong indication of the presence of the mirror and which introduced an added discordance between the seen and felt sizes of things. Before looking through the mirror, subjects were shown a standard 12-inch line. After the subjects had been exposed to the mirror for about half an hour, they were presented with a luminous line and asked to adjust its length to equal the remembered length of the standard line. On average, the line was set shorter than the remembered standard by 1.35 inches, which was about one-fourth of the amount that would have represented full adaptation to the minified world. Rock also found similar evidence of adaptation when subjects viewed playing cards and other familiar objects that were not reduced in size by a mirror but were actually half their normal size. In this case, subjects did not handle the objects because, had they done so, they would have seen their normal-sized hands. It is not clear in these studies just what instigated the adaptive change. In the experiment with the mirror, it may have been the discordance between the visual sizes and the felt sizes of the objects, but in the experiment with small objects, there was no discordance, and the effect in this case must have been due to contrast between the expected and actual size of familiar objects seen at particular distances—a sort of frame of reference effect.

The second example of intrasensory discordance involved a discordance between various visual cues to distance. A discordance of this kind is produced by wearing, in front of one eye, a cylindrical lens with its axis vertical. Such a meridional lens magnifies horizontal dimensions in one eye relative to those in the other eye, an effect known as "aniseikonia." This introduces anomalous horizontal disparities between the two images. Horizontal binocular disparities are normally produced by objects which lie outside the plane of fixation, and such disparities indicate differences in depth; i.e., they are the basis of stereoscopic vision. Aniseikonia thus causes surfaces in the frontal plane to appear to slant away in a direction which depends on the nature and placement of the cylindrical lens.

Aniseikonia may also occur when a person wears spectacles with differential correction for astigmatism. It is a common experience that, when such spectacles are worn for the first time, surfaces, such as walls, and floors, seem to slant away in one direction. After a few days these distortions disappear. However, they reappear in unfamiliar surroundings in which there is a paucity of cues to depth. The question arises therefore to what extent such adaptation is due to the rescaling of binocular disparities and to what extent it is due to the increased reliance on other cues to depth that are not disturbed by the aniseikonia.

In order to investigate this question, Ogle had three subjects wear a 6% horizontal magnification lens in front of the right eye for periods of 8–10 days.

During the last few days before the lens was removed, the subjects usually found it impossible to detect the distortion in ordinary surroundings. However, when Ogle (1964) applied a test of depth perception that involved only the cue of binocular disparity he found that by the fourth day only about a third of the initial distortion due to the artificially induced aniseikonia had been compensated for. No further adaptation occurred after that.

Ogle's results are complicated by the fact that he found no evidence of compensation when he allowed the subject to move his gaze over the stereoscopic test array, and he was reluctant to draw any firm conclusion about whether any part of the adaptation was due to a recalibration of binocular disparity, or whether it was all due to an increased reliance on other cues to depth. The effect of adaptation on the frontal plane test still showed 24 hr after the lens was removed, showing that it was not merely a temporary contrast effect.

In a series of recent studies, using a test similar to that used by Ogle, Epstein found evidence of adaptation to quite short periods (30 min or less) of artificially induced aniseikonia (see Epstein and Morgan-Paap, 1974). Epstein interpreted his results thus: "the continuous pairing of disparity with discrepant monocular determinants of depth causes the relationship between disparity and perceived depth to be modified congruent with the depth specified by the discrepant monocular inputs." However, Epstein makes no mention of the fact that simply inspecting a slanting surface for a few minutes induces a temporary shift in the apparent position of the frontal parallel plane. This effect occurs when there is no discrepancy between monocular and binocular cues, and is simply the result of asymmetrical stimulation. In other words, the effect that Epstein reports may be a conventional depth contrast effect and not an effect due to discordance.

This is a general problem in studies of the effects of discordance, because any discordance necessarily produces an asymmetry in one or other of the stimulus dimensions that are discordant. A control for the effects of this asymmetry must always be done if one wishes to draw any conclusions about the effects of the discordance. It is unfortunate that controls of this kind have been omitted more often than they have been included.

The third example of intersensory discordance is provided by a study by Wallach and Frey (1972). They measured the effects on depth perception of wearing lenses which altered the normal relationship between accommodation and convergence and other cues to distance. One set of spectacles that was used was called "near glasses" because, when they were worn, the oculomotor adjustments of accommodation and convergence were appropriate to an object nearer than the actual distance of the object viewed. Subjects wore them for 15 min during which time they handled wooden blocks. Note that there was a discordance between accommodation-convergence on the one hand and other cues to distance, such as perspective, sizes of familiar objects, and the felt size of the objects, on the other hand. A size-distance estimation test, in which all cues to size apart from accommodation and convergence were eliminated, was given before and after adaptation. Changes in the apparent sizes of test objects in the expected direction were found and interpreted by the authors as being primarily due to changes in apparent distance induced by the discordance between accommodation-convergence and other cues to distance. It seems that this effect too may have been due, not to any discordance between depth cues, but merely to a size-contrast effect, or, more probably still, to the simple aftereffect of maintaining an unusual degree of convergence. This latter effect would be a case of postural persistence that has been mentioned already. This interpretation of Wallach and Frey's results is supported by the results of a study by Ebenholtz and Wolfson (1975) in which they found that maintaining a particular convergence angle of the eyes leads to aftereffects like those found by Wallach and Frey. Wallach and Frey needed a control in which miniature, but otherwise concordant objects were viewed and a second control in which convergence was held at a point nearer than, and also further away than, the test objects.

These examples of intravisual discordance involved altering the normal relationship between two or more stimulus dimensions, and were therefore concerned with the adaptability of spatial constancy mechanisms, but they should have included controls for the effects of contrast and stimulus asymmetry.

5.2. Effects of Intersensory Discordance on Spatial Judgments

The direction of an object may be judged simultaneously by sight, by touch-kinesthesis, and by ear if it makes a noise. The stimuli which indicate direction in each modality covary in a characteristic way as the position of the object is changed relative to the observer. It is reasonable to suppose that these intersensory covariance functions are represented by corresponding covariance schemata. The presence of such a schema would be revealed if a person noticed when the normal relationship between two cues to direction in two modalities was artificially disturbed. However, people do not notice such discrepancies. For instance, if a person looks at a ringing bell through prisms which displace the image to one side, he does not notice the discordance between visual and auditory cues—the sound appears to come from where the bell is seen.

Stratton made some observations on intersensory discordances while wearing his reversing and inverting spectacles. He reported that sounds of objects out of sight, e.g., the sounds made by stones thrown to one side so that they landed out of sight, seemed to come from the opposite direction to where they had been seen to pass out of sight. However, when the source of sound was in sight, the sound seemed to originate in the visible object responsible for the sound. In this case, therefore, vision dominated.

Jackson (1953) conducted quantitative experiments in which subjects were required to make judgments about the position of a steaming kettle when visual and auditory stimuli were made to conflict by the use of silent steam kettles and hidden compressed-air whistles. The whistling sound appeared to originate from the kettles until the steaming kettles and the whistles were presented at angular separations exceeding 30°. Witkin, Wapner, and Leventhal (1952) conducted a similar experiment and obtained similar results. Separations of this order indicate clearly that we are concerned not with a simple problem of poor spatial acuity, but rather with a mechanism, or mechanisms, in which spatial information in one modality is partly or wholly discarded in favor of that in the other. This phenomenon, which has been called the ''stimulus dominance effect,'' operates when we watch the cinema and remain unaware of the fact the loudspeakers and the screen are separate, or when a ventriloquist makes it appear that his doll is speaking. The dominance of vision over audition is also referred to as the ''ventriloquist effect.''

When two pieces of spatial information are discordant it is reasonable to suppose that that which is normally least precisely perceived will be discarded. Fisher (1962) carried out a series of experiments to test this idea. Subjects were told that two stimuli in two different modalities originated in the same object on a horizontal semicircular arc in front of them and at arm's length. In fact, their relative locations were varied and the subject had to indicate by pointing where they judged the object to be. Visual, auditory, and tactile-kinesthetic stimuli were used. Visual stimuli were completely dominant over both tactile-kinesthetic and auditory stimuli, and tactile-kinesthetic stimuli tended to be dominant over auditory stimuli. This is the order of dominance which Fisher predicted from the order of precision of localization of individual stimuli within each of the modalities.

Rock and Victor (1964) confirmed that vision is dominant over touch-kinesthesis. In this experiment subjects handled a square object seen through a lens which caused it to appear rectangular. They were asked to select a matching object from among a set of objects that they could feel but not see and from a set of objects that they could see but not feel. The use of two types of judgment to measure the effect of the discordance controlled for the possible contaminating effects of a response bias. Subjects were also asked to draw the standard object that they had seen and felt. In all conditions, for most subjects, the visual impression was dominant and very few subjects were aware of any conflict. Hay, Pick, and Ikeda (1965) also confirmed that vision dominates kinesthesis. They asked subjects to point with their hidden right hand to the apparent position of their left hand seen through 10° displacing prisms. Subjects pointed very close to the seen position of the displaced left hand. Over (1966) also confirmed that vision dominates touch-kinesthesis. Subjects were asked to set a bar to the horizontal while feeling the bar and viewing it through prisms which apparently rotated it to 15°. For larger discordances, compromise settings were made.

The dominance of touch-kinesthesis over audition has been confirmed by

Pick, Warren, and Hay (1969). Blindfolded subjects were asked to point with their right hand to the apparent position of their left hand, while the left hand was touching a loudspeaker which was emitting clicks. The two hands were not allowed to touch. At the same time, the subjects wore a pseudophone which displaced the apparent source of the clicks by 11° to one side. Subjects pointed to the true position of the left hand and ignored the discordant auditory information. Willott (1973) confirmed this finding using a testing procedure that did not involve pointing, showing that the results of Pick *et al.* were not due to the biasing effect of their kinesthetic testing procedure.

Thus, there seems to be general agreement that vision dominates audition. However, this unanimity in the findings of several investigators must be treated with caution, because there are several factors which must be taken into account when interpreting the results of experiments of this kind:

1. The test used to reveal the way that the subject has resolved the conflicting spatial information must not bias the outcome. It has already been mentioned that Rock and Victor controlled for this source of bias by giving two types of test, but not all investigators have taken this precaution.

2. The synchrony of the two discordant stimuli must be controlled. Several investigators have added controls in which nonsynchronous discordant stimuli were presented. Subjects tended to localize the source of stimulation accurately in each modality when this was done. However, synchrony alone is not sufficient to produce ventriloquism effects, as we shall see.

3. The subject must be made to believe that the discordant stimuli arise from the same object. Thurlow and Jack (1973) showed that vision is dominant over audition only when subjects are convinced that the two stimuli come from the same object. Miller (1972) obtained a greater degree of visual dominance when subjects were told that the visual and discordant tactile stimuli originated from the same object than when they were led to believe that there were two objects.

4. The results must not be generalized beyond the type of display used in the experiment. For instance, in many of the studies in which it was found that vision dominates audition, the visual stimulus was set in a full field of view containing other objects, while the auditory stimulus was the sound from a single source. It is to be expected, under these circumstances, that more reliance will be placed on visual information than on auditory information. Radeau and Bertelson (1976) found a greater degree of visual dominance over discordant auditory stimulation when a full field of objects was visible than when the visual stimulus was a luminous point in a dark surround.

5. The duration of exposure to the discordant stimuli should be controlled. If the experiment is designed to explore how people resolve conflicting spatial information in two modalities, the stimuli should be presented for only a short period and ideally only once to each subject. Rock and Victor took these precautions in their study of visual-kinesthetic discordance. Other investigators have

not always been so careful. The simplest explanation of the way in which one modality tends to be dominant under these circumstances is that the subject localizes on the basis of one stimulus dimension and ignores the other. There is no need to assume that one modality has modified the other, and there is no need to suppose that there will be any aftereffects of brief exposure to intersensory discordance.

On the other hand, if the stimuli are presented repeatedly or for long periods of time, the discordance may begin to induce a change in one or other modality. Such a change is best measured as an aftereffect in localization tests applied after the discordant stimuli have been removed, because an aftereffect provides convincing evidence that there has been a change in the way spatial information is coded. Experiments of this kind, which are reviewed later, have typically revealed that discordance gradually modifies the way in which spatial information is coded by each modality in such a way as to nullify the effects of the discordance. This suggests that we do indeed possess intersensory covariance schemata which are subject to modification through experience.

5.3. Effects of Motorsensory Discordance on Spatial Judgments

When we move a part of the body we receive stimulation which is a consequence of that motion. For instance, when we move our eyes, the retinal image of stationary external objects moves over the retina. Von Holst (1954) introduced the term "reafference" to refer to such sensory consequences of self-produced movement. He contrasted it with "exafference," or stimulation resulting from events in the environment that are not due to self-produced movements of the perceiver.

In order to orient themselves, animals must be capable of distinguishing between reafferent and exafferent stimulation. According to von Holst, the changes in the stimulation of the sense organs which a given pattern of muscular innervation normally produces is "allowed for" in processing the information from the surroundings. This is another instance of what has been referred to here as a covariance schema. In this section, I shall review some studies of artificially disrupting normal motorsensory covariance functions. But some important distinctions must first be made.

In the first place, there are two types of reafference (see Table 1). There is the type involved when a person observes a moving part of his body. In this case the stimulus moves and the sense organ is stationary. This type of reafference may be called "self-observation reafference." On the other hand, there is the reafferent stimulation involved when a person observes a stationary object with a moving sense organ. For example, one may observe the world while walking or feel an object with a moving hand. This type of reafference may be called "locomotory reafference."

The distinction between self-produced movement involving reafferent stimulation and passive movement involving exafferent stimulation is not always clear. For instance, the left arm may be moved by the right arm, or the whole body may be moved by pushing the wheels of a wheelchair. In an extreme case the subject may have his limbs supported in a machine and control their movement by giving verbal commands to the operator of the machine. If one asks what role reafference plays in sensorimotor learning, one must define one's concept of reafference more carefully than has been usual in this area. Most studies of reafference have been concerned with the visual consequences of movements of the eye or the head. Some of the issues involved in such studies will now be discussed.

When spectacles which reverse the visual scene from left to right are worn, a sideways motion of the head causes the retinal image to move across the retina in a direction opposite to that in which it normally moves. This anomalous image motion is interpreted by the viewer as a rotation of the scene in the opposite direction to the head motion and at twice the speed. Stratton found by the third day of wearing his reversing spectacles that head movements were still accompanied by a slight swinging of the scene. By the sixth day, he wrote, "Movements of the head or of the body, which shifted the field of view, seemed now to be in entire keeping with the visual changes thus produced; the motion seemed to be towards that side on which objects entered the visual field, and not towards the opposite side, as the pre-experimental representation of the movement would have required. And when, with closed eyes, I rocked in my chair, the merely represented changes in the visual field persisted with the same rhythmic variation of direction which they would have shown had I opened my eyes" (Stratton, 1897, p. 249).

This experience suggests that a new head-movement to image-movement covariance schema was acquired by Stratton. However, a study by Hay (1968) suggests that image motion was not involved. In this study, the subject was asked to nod his head up and down while following the movement of a point of light on an oscilloscope. The movement of the light was coupled to the head movement in such a way that, as the head moved up and down, the spot moved from left to right. Thus the subject's eyes had to move diagonally in order to keep the image of the light centered on the fovea. After exposure to this discordant situation, the subject was asked to judge whether a stationary point of light appeared to move as he continued to nod his head. After as little as 1 min of exposure, the subject reported that the stationary object moved left and right in synchrony with his head, but with directions reversed with respect to the exposure condition. Controls showed that a movement of head alone or of the light alone did not produce the aftereffect. What was learned here was a new coupling between head movement and eye movement. Retinal image motion was not involved, because the point of light was always fixated. It is a pity that Hay did not measure the movements of the eyes in the aftereffect, but the implication is that they were moving in an anomalous way (see Wallach, Stanton, and Becker, 1974; Wallach and Flaherty, 1974, for other studies of this type).

In a more recent study by Gauthier and Robinson (1975), eye-movement recordings were made before and after a subject wore telescopic lenses for 5 days. A subject wearing such lenses must learn to move his eyes faster than normal for a given speed of head motion in order to keep the image of a stationary object on the fovea. Gauthier and Robinson found that this experience produced a change in the vestibulo-ocular reflex, i.e., in the way the eyes move reflexly under the control of stimuli from the semicircular canals when the eyes are closed. Recent investigations have revealed the mechanism depicted in Fig. 1. There is a nervous pathway running from the semicircular canals to the vestibular nuclei and eye-muscle nuclei via the vestibular nerve and medial longitudinal fasciculus. It is now known that the flocculus in the cerebellum can both facilitate and inhibit the response of the vestibular nuclei and hence control the strength of vestibular reflexes and, in particular, vestibular nystagmus. There is also a pathway from the retina via the inferior olive to the flocculus. The flocculus is thus in a position to compare the impulses generating reflex eye movements with the consequent movements of the retinal image. It is reasonable to suppose that any discrepancy between these signals will induce the flocculus to control the vestibular outflow so as to restore the adequacy of the pursuit phase of the nystagmic eye movements. This supposition is supported by the fact that the removal of the flocculus in cats and rabbits prevents those

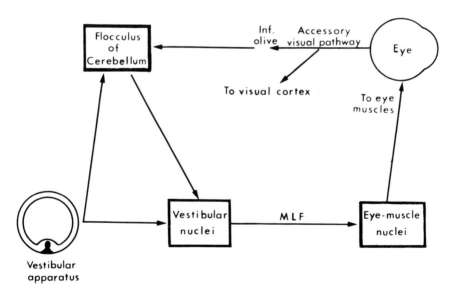

Fig. 1. Components and pathways that could be involved in the adaptation of vestibulo-optic reflexes.

animals from habituating to anomalous image movements when their heads are rotated. The flocculus may thus be the site of vestibulo-ocular habituation—but that is not to say that other and higher centers may not have access to this control system (for further details, see Chapters IV and VII of Kornhuber, 1974).

Looking back at Stratton's experiences, it can be seen that what he learned may also have been a new coupling between head movements and eye movements rather than a new coupling between head movements and retinal-image movements as Stratton thought.

5.4. Sensorimotor Consequences of Discordant Stimulation

Experiments in which the prime concern is with the effects of discordance on sensorimotor coordination will be considered in this section.

Stratton and Ivo Kohler examined the effects of wearing inverting spectacles on visuomotor coordination. However, with this technique, the effects of the distortion on visuomotor coordination are contaminated by intrasensory effects, such as the upside-down appearance of things, and by intersensory effects, such as the discordance between visual and auditory space. For this reason, the favored procedure now is to have the subject wear prisms, which simply displace the visual scene horizontally, and study the effects that this has on his ability to point to visual targets.

Several elementary precautions must be taken in using this technique. A displacing prism causes symmetrically placed visual targets to appear asymmetrical. This contaminating factor may be easily eliminated by offsetting the visual display so that it is centered in the field of view seen through the prism. However, there will now be an asymmetry in the movement of the arm after the subject has learned to point to the objectively asymmetrical target. The effects of one or other of these asymmetries must be assessed by an appropriate control experiment. A prism displaces one side of the field of view more than the other and causes all vertical and horizontal lines, except the midhorizontal line or horizon, to appear curved. Therefore, if possible, the visual display should consist of single points of light arranged along the horizon in otherwise dark surroundings.

The task that all investigators have used for measuring the degree of visuomotor adaptation to visual displacement is that of pointing the unseen finger at a visual target at arm's length, although it has usually been supplemented by a variety of other tests. However, several procedures have been used for the training or exposure condition. I previously reviewed these procedures and suggested the following terminology, which is now generally adopted (Howard, 1968).

Held introduced the procedure in which the subject moves his arm from side to side as he views it through the prism. The subject is not asked to point at targets. This procedure is referred to as "concurrent display with no target" or simply as "Held's procedure." Other investigators allow the subject to see his own arm while aiming at a visual target. This is referred to as "concurrent display with target." In another procedure, the subject aims at a target and is allowed to see his fingertip only at the termination of his aiming movement. This is referred to as "terminal display." In all these procedures the displacement of the scene is typically 15° and the subject is initially aware that his arm is not where it appears to be visually.

This awareness may lead the subject merely to correct consciously for this discrepancy when tested. To overcome this difficulty, I suggested a technique in which the prismatic displacement is progressively introduced in steps of about ½°, while the subject makes repeated attempts to hit the target with terminal display of his error. One's normal accuracy is such that an occasional ½° step is not noticed, especially if the visual targets are moved so that they are always centered in the subject's field of view. This technique is referred to as "prismatic shaping."

Several studies have been done showing that the terminal display procedure leads to a larger degree of adaptation to prismatic displacement than the other procedures (Welch, 1969; Uhlarik and Canon, 1971). This is not surprising, because in that procedure the subject is presented with the most precise information about his error of pointing, which is given by the sight of his finger in relation to the target. In all these procedures, the subject will be convinced that the hand he sees is his own. Nielsen (1963) introduced the novel procedure of using mirrors to project another person's hand into the region where the subject expected his own hand to be. Welch (1972) used this technique in a prism adaptation study and showed that some adaptation occurred in the direction of the false finger, even with subjects who knew that it was not their own finger that they were seeing.

A closed-circuit TV system, rather than a prism, can be used to displace the image of the hands. Smith and Smith (1962) introduced this technique and Howard and Templeton (1966, p. 374) suggested an improved arrangement. The hand as seen by the subject on the TV minitor may be distorted, rotated, or displaced in any way that the experimenter wishes. Pick, Warren, McIntyre, and Appel (1972) used this procedure in a study on the extent to which adaptation to various types of distortion transfers from one part of the body to other parts.

Experiments in this field have been directed towards two issues: the discovery of the site and nature of the processes underlying adaptive changes in performance and the elucidation of the conditions under which adaptation occurs. I shall deal with these in turn.

5.5. Site of the Recalibration Involved in Visuomotor Adaptation

A person can bring his unseen finger to within about 1° of a visual target. This skill depends on the correct integration of several pieces of spatial information. The first is the position of the image of the target on the retina. In almost all studies, the subject was allowed to fixate the visual target, so that the retinal location of the target has not been a variable factor in such experiments. The second piece of spatial information is that regarding the position of the eye in the head. There are thought to be no sense organs which indicate eye position. However, the eye is unique among mobile parts of the body in that its movements are never subjected to varying loads. This means that each position of the eye is associated with a unique pattern of motor innervation to the three pairs of extraocular muscles that hold the eye in position. It is the registration of this pattern of motor innervation that is thought to serve the sense of eye position. It is assumed that a central copy of this pattern of motor innervation is received by those centers in the brain that coordinate spatial behavior. This is often referred to as the "efference copy" or "corollary discharge." The third piece of information is the position of the head on the body. This is signaled by joint receptors in the neck. Finally, the ability to point to a visual target requires information about the position of the various joints of the arm, which is signaled by receptors in the ligaments and tendons of those joints. For the sake of simplicity it will be assumed that the arm has only one joint, at the shoulder.

The whole sequence of sense organs and joints forms a control loop. If there is no error feedback provided, the loop is said to be open, and if the subject is informed about his error in pointing, the loop is said to be closed. Only in the latter case can the discordance produced by a prism be detected and adaptation occur. In the Held training procedure, where the subject does not point at a target, there is no explicit error, but the subject can see his hand, so that the control loop is closed. There have been several claims that adaptation can occur when the loop is open, but in these cases the "adaptation" must be the result of uncontrolled sources of asymmetrical stimulation, or of undetected sources of feedback.

A change in the spatial coding of information from any one sense organ in the eye-hand control loop will disturb the whole system, because each component is "in series" with every other component. The system is like a chain, the strength of which depends on the integrity of every link. Thus, in theory, the recalibration of the system responsible for the adaptation of pointing to a displaced visual target could be a recalibration of information from any or all of the sense organs we have considered, or of the motor command system that directs movements of the arm.

Figure 2 is a schematic representation of the sensory and motor components involved in pointing to a visual target with unseen hand. The structural components and sense organs are shown in solid black lines. The hypothetical processes in the central nervous system that code the spatial information are shown connected by dotted lines.

Nobody has suggested that the signals generated by the sense organs change during adaptation to displaced vision; the change is surely in the way

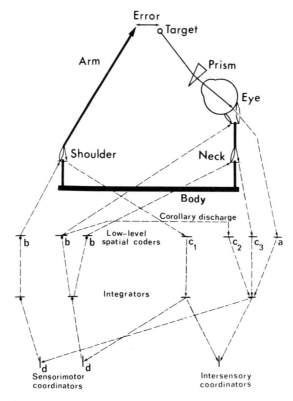

Fig. 2. Flow chart for the visuomotor system. Basic structural components of the eye-hand coordination system are drawn in lines of medium thickness (the instantaneous position of the hand and the light ray from target to eye and retina are also considered to be structural components—lighter lines). The body (extra thick line) is considered to be fixed to the ground. Components are linked by articulations; the following symbols are used: ⌐⌐, position-sensitive receptors; ⌐⌐, muscular elements. Neural elements are drawn in interrupted lines; junctions represent neural coding processes; arrows depict inputs to sensory elements; and filled circles depict inputs to motor elements. The letters a, b, c, and d indicate possible sites of recalibration which are discussed in the text. Adapted from Howard (1971, p. 249).

these signals are coded or interpreted in the central nervous system. The various possible sites of the recalibration are indicated by letters in Fig. 2. Two of the possibilities may be readily dismissed. The change cannot be in the coding of the retinal location of the visual target (site a) because the target is always imaged on the fovea, and this is a very distinctive landmark. Perhaps such a change could occur if the target were imaged in the periphery of the retina. Futhermore, it is evident that the change is not in the motor command system of the arm, eye, or neck (site b), because adaptation is shown when the muscles used during exposure are not the same as those used when the effect is measured after training. We are thus left with sites c and d. Site c_1 codes the felt position of the arm, c_2 the felt position of the eye (by means of the corollary discharge), and c_3 the felt position of the head.

Harris (1965) championed the view that adaptation to displaced vision involves a change in the felt position of the arm. He reported that, after adaptation, subjects misplaced the arm in the adaptive direction when asked to point straight ahead with eyes closed. They similarly misplaced the arm when asked to point to a sound source, or to the other, nonadapted arm. Furthermore, Harris claimed that the effects of training one arm did not transfer to the other arm. Harris argued that these and similar findings only fit the assumption that the felt position of the arm has changed. However, other investigators (e.g., Hamilton, 1964) have reported that under certain circumstances there is some intermanual transfer of training, and some investigators have found that the apparent straight-ahead position of the eyes is altered by adaptation (Craske, 1967). Harris has accommodated these findings by broadening his theory to include changes in the felt position of the eyes in the head or of the head on the body.

In contrast to Harris's general "felt-position" theory, Held has championed the view that adaptation involves a change at a higher level of processing—at a level where the felt position and potential movements of the arm (or other adapted organ) are assessed in relation to the sensed direction of an external target or of a target consisting of some other part of the body. Such a theory predicts, as did the felt-position theory, that adaptation transfers to other modalities or shows in a test in which the trained arm points to the hand of the untrained arm. However, Held claimed that, unlike the felt-position hypothesis, the sensorimotor hypothesis predicts no effect of adaptation on a test in which the subject is asked to relocate his unseen arm into a position into which he was trained to put it before exposure to the prism. Held interpreted this task as a pure measure of a change in felt position, because the arm is not being directed to a target and is therefore not affected by a sensorimotor change. Using this and other tests, Hardt, Held, and Steinbach (1971) obtained results which they claimed supported the sensorimotor hypothesis.

In terms of the scheme depicted in Fig. 2 the site of the adaptive changes suggested by Held would be at the level of the sites marked d, i.e., at the level of what I have called coordinators. Held suggested that what is adapted is a very general coordinator that controls directed movements of a particular limb with respect to all targets. This does not have the specificity of the coordinators depicted in Fig. 2. However, these are meant to indicate only the logical status of coordinators in the total system. The scheme sets no limit on the types or complexity of coordinators.

Figure 2 clearly brings out the main logical point underlying the debate between theorists like Harris, who emphasize changes at a low level in the spatial coding process, and theorists like Held, who emphasize changes at a higher level of processing. The important point is that in a hierarchical system higher-level processors receive their information from the lower-level processors. Therefore, any change at a low level affects all tasks involving that level of processing and all tasks involving related higher levels of processing, but any change in a higher-level processor affects only those tasks that involve that level of processing.

To resolve the issue, we need a set of tasks that diagnose specific changes at the various levels of the system. Held proposed that his task, in which the arm is relocated to a remembered position, is such a specific task for diagnosing low-level changes in the system. However, it is not clear just what sort of task this is, because it assumes that the system which remembers limb position is immune to the effects of training. In any case, Kennedy (1969) found that the relocated position of the arm was affected by training, so that the evidence resulting from the use of this test is equivocal.

Templeton, Howard, and Wilkinson (1974) attempted to resolve this issue by applying, both during and after training, a series of tests which were designed to diagnose changes at each level of the system. A test of pointing at the unseen toe measured changes in the felt position of the arm, and a test of looking at the unseen toe measured changes in the felt position of the neck or eye. If felt-position changes alone account for adaptation of pointing behavior, then changes in these two subtests should add to the total adaptive shift as measured by the error in pointing to visual targets with unseen hand. If the total adaptive shift exceeds the sum of the shifts on the subtests, this would be evidence of a shift in a higher part of the control hierarchy. The two felt-position shifts were found to add to the total shift in pointing at a visual target in trials given when the prism was at its maximum displacement of 15°. However, tests given during training, while the prism displacement was increasing, revealed that the shift in pointing to visual targets exceeded the sum of the felt-position shifts. This suggests that a higher-level system intervenes while learning is proceeding, but that the effects of training consolidate at lower levels of the system when adaptation is complete. This result was not in any obvious way due to conscious intervention, because the gradual shaping procedure was used and subjects were not aware that the visual targets had been displaced.

It would thus seem that changes in the felt position of parts of the system are mainly responsible for visuomotor adaptation, but that changes higher in the system may also occur. This experiment, like all others, was conducted with certain arbitrary stimulus constraints and demand characteristics. It may be that the relative importance of felt-position changes and changes at higher levels will be reversed under other circumstances. No experiment in psychology reveals which mechanism *must* operate, but only which mechanism may operate under certain circumstances. The human central nervous system is very flexible, and works more like a programmable computer than like a machine with a single fixed way of doing things. Basic mechanisms of behavior which experimenters claim to have "discovered" often turn out to be the result of hidden assumptions, arbitrary stimulus configurations, or particular demand characteristics. Several arbitrary constraints of these kinds are evident in studies of prism adaptation. For instance, all investigators have allowed the subject to fixate the visual target, thus constraining him to use his fovea rather than the periphery of the retina, and it may be only because of this procedural "accident" that changes in retinal local sign have not been revealed. Another example of a hidden constraint is the fact that most investigators have used a training procedure in which the subject moves his arm, rather than other parts of the body, and perhaps this procedural "accident" has also biased the results.

This thought prompted Howard, Anstis, and Lucia (1974) to compare the amount of intermanual transfer of prism adaptation produced by two types of training. In one type of training the subject looked through a prism in the dark and repeatedly ran his finger along a track until he judged it to be in front of his stationary nose. In the second type of training, the subject repeatedly aimed his nose toward his stationary finger. In both cases, the subject was allowed to see his error at the end of each movement. It was found that there was less intermanual transfer; i.e., the adaptation was more specifically related to the trained arm when the head was mobile than when the arm was mobile during training. Thus, the position sense of a stationary joint adapts more than that of a mobile joint. This result makes sense when considered in conjunction with the well-known fact that we are less certain about the felt position of a stationary limb than about the position of a moving limb and the fact that adaptation tends to be associated with that part of the system about which there is most position uncertainty (Wilkinson, 1971). It is the "weakest" part of the system that adapts.

The locus of attention has also been shown to be a factor determining the site of adaptation to displaced vision. In a study by Canon (1970) subjects were exposed to conflicting visual and auditory cues regarding the direction of a sound-emitting visible object. It was found that adaptation occurred in the modality which was not attended to during exposure to intersensory discordance. This finding has been confirmed in a study using a conflict between vision and proprioception (Kelso, Cook, Olson, and Epstein, 1975).

Thus, the question about the site of the adaptive shift underlying adaptation to displaced vision is one that does not have a single answer. All systems beyond the most peripheral processes in sense organs are probably capable of adapting to unusual circumstances, given the correct set of constraints and demands.

5.6. Conditions for Visuomotor Adaptation

The second question that has engaged the attention of investigators in this field is that concerning the conditions under which adaptation occurs. Held proposed that active movement is necessary for visuomotor adaptation to displaced vision. This hypothesis has inspired most of the subsequent work in this area. Held derived his idea from the theoretical analysis by von Holst which has already been discussed.

Held applied this idea to the case of human visuomotor adaptation to displaced vision. The schematized process which he proposed is shown in Fig. 3. It is similar to the one proposed by von Holst except for the addition of the "Correlation storage." In Held's words, "the reafferent visual signal is compared (in the Comparator) with a signal selected from the Correlation Storage by the monitored efferent signal. The Correlation Storage acts as a kind of memory which retains traces of previous combinations of concurrent efferent and reafferent signals. The currently monitored efferent signal is presumed to select the trace combination containing the identical efferent part and to activate the reafferent trace combined with it. The resulting revived afferent signal is sent to the Comparator for comparison with the current reafferent signal. The outcome of this comparison determines further performance" (Held, 1961, p. 30). From this model, Held predicted that self-produced movement of some part of the body is essential for adaptation to displaced vision, because the calibration of the system depends on the covariance between efferent, or motor, signals and the resulting afference, and therefore a detected change in this covariance function is required in order for the calibration to change. Held and Hein (1958) tested this prediction by allowing the subject to see his own arm through a prism under three training conditions: with the hand motionless, with the hand moved passively from side to side by the experimenter, and with the hand moved in the same way but actively by the subject. In conformity with the prediction, only the self-produced-movement condition gave rise to any adaptation as revealed in a test in which the subject pointed to visual targets with unseen hand.

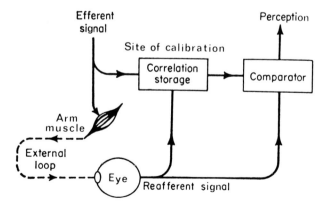

Fig. 3. Schematized process assumed by Held to underlie the adaptation of the visuomotor system to discordant reafference. From Held (1961).

There is a theoretical difficulty in the way Held and Hein applied von Holst's model to their data. The difficulty is that the motor outflow to a limb does not determine its position; it determines only the amplitude, direction, and speed of movement of the limb for a given load. In order to account for Held's result, one must assume that self-produced movement somehow accentuates arm-position sense or that it induces the subject to pay attention to what is happening. Moreover, several studies have demonstrated that self-produced movement is not necessary for visuomotor adaptation (Pick and Hay, 1965; Templeton, Howard, and Lowman, 1966). In these studies, the subject had to estimate when his passively moved, hidden finger was under a visual target seen through prisms. He was shown his error after making his estimation. This discordance between passive arm-position sense and the sight of the arm generated some adaptation, as was revealed in an active pointing task. It is to be noted that in this procedure the subject's attention is directed to the discordance, and when this is done he adapts.

Further evidence against Held's interpretation of his data is provided by Moulden (1971), who found that adaptation occurred when the subject was allowed only momentary glimpses of his actively moved arm, which prevented him from seeing the arm in motion. According to Held's reafference theory, adaptation should not occur if the subject does not see his arm in motion.

Finally, evidence against Held's hypothesis comes from several studies in which it has been shown that adaptation of pointing to displaced visual targets occurs after exposure to discordant exafferent stimulation. For instance, Howard, Craske, and Templeton (1965) obtained shifts in pointing to visual targets after subjects were exposed to the experience of a rod, seen through prisms, coming toward them and hitting them at an unexpected place on the forehead. Although Halper-Smith (1971) failed to replicate this effect, a similar effect was reported by Radeau and Bertelson (1969), who exposed passive subjects to a conflict between visual and auditory cues to the direction of an object and found evidence of an adaptive shift in a task of pointing to visual targets (see also Radeau, 1973).

Held has also claimed that self-produced movement is necessary for the initial development of spatially organized behavior in the neonate. This assertion was based on his well-known experiment with kittens in a carousel (Held and Hein, 1963). In these experiments, in which an actively walking kitten caused a second kitten to be moved passively inside the same visual surroundings, only the active kitten developed certain visuomotor responses. I have previously (Howard and Templeton, 1966) criticized the conclusions from this study on the grounds that only two sources of exafferent stimulation (a visually moving scene and vestibular stimulation) were tried. To establish their thesis, Held and Hein should have exposed the passive kitten to all possible correlated exafferent inputs. For instance, possibilities which were not tried are to allow visual objects to hit against the passive kitten and to have visible objects emit sounds.

More recent experiments from Held's laboratory may be subjected to a similar criticism. In these experiments kittens and young monkeys wore ruffs around their necks from birth which prevented them from seeing their own limbs. This interference with the normal reafferent signals inhibited the development of visuomotor coordination of the limbs (Hein, Gower, and Diamond, 1970; Hein, Held, and Gower, 1970). However, we do not know whether the animals would have developed visuomotor coordination if they had been allowed to see their passively moved limbs, and without this information we still cannot conclude that self-produced movement is necessary for visuomotor development.

Howard and Templeton (1966) argued that adaptation occurs in response to many forms of discordant information and that the important thing is that salient information regarding the discordance (not necessarily consciously perceived) should be available to the subject. The discordance is the mismatch between the unusual stimulus covariance function and the subject's inappropriate covariance schema. According to this view, adaptation is enhanced by anything which increases the saliency and amount of information about the discordance in covariant stimulation. There are four important factors which determine the effectiveness of information about discordance:

1. The first factor is the extent to which the subject is convinced that the discordant stimuli arise from the same object or part of the body. In the typical prism adaptation study, this is the degree to which the subject relates his seen hand with his felt hand. Several studies have shown the importance of this factor. For instance, Welch (1972) showed that subjects who believed that the finger they saw was their own adapted more readily than subjects who did not believe this.

2. The second factor which determines the effectiveness of information about discordance is the vividness of the display of the discordance itself. Evidence on this point has been provided by Van Laer, Swartz, and Van Laer (1970), who showed that the amount of adaptation is a function of the amount of error feedback during training, and also by Coren (1966), who showed that there is more adaptation when the subject is allowed to correct his errors of pointing compared with when the finger is guided to the target by the experimenter. Welch and Abel (1970) also showed that the opportunity for error correction is an important factor in prism adaptation. Furthermore, Dewar (1971) found that a suddenly introduced visual displacement is more effective than a gradually introduced displacement. The error feedback need not be visual. For instance, Lackner (1974) found that tactile feedback provided by contact between the hand and visual target is sufficient, and Radeau (1974) found that a buzzing sound emitted from the actual location of the visual target is sufficient. Uhlarik (1973) obtained adaptation by informing subjects verbally about the extent of their pointing error.

3. The third factor which determines the effectiveness of information about discordance is the precision of the sense of position of the various joints

involved in the task being studied. There is abundant evidence that, in the Held training procedure, anything which enhances the sense of position of the arm leads to a greater degree of adaptation. For instance, Kravitz and Wallach (1966) showed that adaptation occurred after a subject inspected his immobile arm which was passively vibrated. The vibration presumably enhanced the sense of position of the arm. Melamed, Haley, and Gildow (1973) found that adaptation occurred in a passive-movement training condition when visible contours were provided on the background against which the arm was passively moved. These contours presumably enhanced the visual impression of the position of the arm. It is reasonable to suppose that, when the position sense of the arm is accentuated in the Held training procedure, adaptation occurs more readily because the discordance is more easily detected. If the sense of position of any one component were very poor, even a large discordance would go unnoticed in the Held training procedure and adaptation would not occur. However, it has already been described how, with a target-training procedure in which the discordance is vividly displayed, adaptation is more likely to be associated with that part of the system about which there is most uncertainty. Thus when discordance is vividly displayed, increasing the precision of the system should make it more resistant to adaptation. If we were as certain about the position of each component as we are about the retinal position of the image of a fixated object, the system would hardly adapt at all. Thus the effect that an increase in the precision of position sense will have depends on what training procedure is used.

4.   The fourth factor that might determine the effectiveness of information about discordance is the similarity between the training procedure and the procedure used to test the extent of the adaptation. In the original experiments by Held and Hein, the active testing procedure resembled the active training procedure more than it resembled the passive training procedure, and this may have been part of the reason why active training gave a greater measure of adaptation. However, Pick and Hay (1965) replicated Held and Hein's experiment, but added a passive test of the degree of adaptation, and found that the degree of similarity between the training and test procedures did not affect the amount of adaptation. However, other differences between training and testing procedures have been found to have an effect. For instance, Wallace (1974) found that there was more adaptation when the visual targets used for training (by the terminal display or concurrent display procedure) were the same as the targets used in the test procedure, compared with when the targets were not the same. Baily (1972) found that the effect of training on pointing to targets with rapid or ballistic arm movements revealed itself with both rapid and slow test movements, but that the effect of training with slow arm movements revealed itself only with slow test movements. Thus differences between training and test procedures can be important, as one might have thought.

The safest conclusion at the moment is to suppose that animals seek out covariance functions within modalities, and between different modalities, as well as between corollary motor discharges and reafference. The perceptual-motor system will surely correlate what it can in order to reduce uncertainty, to economize on coding, and to coordinate action. Once such covariance functions have been detected and stored by the animal, any persistent discrepancy in current stimulation will be discordant with respect to these stored schemata, and the system will adjust itself accordingly.

6. References

Annis, R. C., and Frost, B. Human visual ecology and orientation anisotropies in acuity. *Science*, 1973, *182*, 729–731.

Appelle, S. Perception and discrimination as a function of stimulus orientation. *Psychological Bulletin*, 1972, *78*, 266–278.

Asch, S. E., and Witkin, H. A. Studies in space orientation. II. Perception of the upright with displaced visual fields and with body tilted. *Journal of experimental Psychology*, 1948, *38*, 455–477.

Baily, J. S. Arm-body adaptation with passive arm movements. *Perception and Psychophysics*, 1972, *12*, 39–44.

Barlow, H. B. Visual experience and cortical development. *Nature*, 1975, *258*, 199–204.

Blakemore, C., and Cooper, G. Development of the brain depends on the visual environment. *Nature*, 1970, *228*, 477–478.

Bower, T. G. R. *Development in infancy*. San Francisco: Freeman, 1974.

Campbell, F. W., and Maffei, L. The tilt after-effect: A fresh look. *Vision Research*, 1971, *11*, 833–840.

Canon, L. K. Intermodality inconsistency of input and directed attention as determinants of the nature of adaptation. *Journal of Experimental Psychology*, 1970, *84*, 141–147.

Collins, J. K. Isolation of the muscular component in a proprioceptive spatial aftereffect. *Journal of Experimental Psychology*, 1971, *90*, 297–299.

Coltheart, M. Visual feature-analyzers and aftereffects of tilt and curvature. *Psychological Review*, 1971, *78*, 114–121.

Coltheart, M., and Cooper, C. M. The retinal reference of the tilt aftereffect. *Perception and Psychophysics*, 1972, *11*, 321–324.

Cooper, L. A. Demonstration of a mental analog of an external rotation. *Perception and Psychophysics*, 1976, *19*, 296–302.

Coren, S. Adaptation to prismatic displacement as a function of the amount of available information. *Psychonomic Science*, 1966, *4*, 407–408.

Craske, B. Adaptation to prisms: Change in internally registered eye-position. *British Journal of Psychology*, 1967, *58*, 329–335.

Dewar, R. Adaptation to displaced vision: Variations on the "prismatic-shaping" technique. *Perception and Psychophysics*, 1971, *9*, 155–157.

Ebenholtz, S. M., and Wolfson, D. M. Perceptual effects of sustained convergence. *Perception and Psychophysics*, 1975, *17*, 485–491.

Epstein, W., and Morgan-Paap, C. A. The effect of level of depth processing and degree of informational discrepancy on adaptation to uniocular image magnification. *Journal of Experimental Psychology*, 1974, *102*, 585–594.

Fiorentini, A., Ghez, C., and Maffei, L. Physiological correlates of adaptation to a rotated visual field. *Journal of Physiology*, 1972, *227*, 313–322.

Fisher, G. H. Resolution of spatial conflict. *Bulletin of the British Psychological Society*, 1962, *46*, 3A.

Gauthier, G. M., and Robinson, D. A. Adaptation of the human vestibuloocular reflex to magnifying lenses. *Brain Research*, 1975, *92*, 331–335.

Gregory, R. L. *Eye and brain*. New York: McGraw-Hill, 1966.

Halper-Smith, C. Unpublished doctoral thesis, Stanford University, 1971.

Hamilton, C. R. Intermanual transfer of adaptation to prisms. *American Journal of Psychology*, 1964, *77*, 457–462.

Hardt, M. E., Held, R., and Steinbach, M. J. Adaptation to displaced vision: A change in the central control of sensorimotor coordination. *Journal of Experimental Psychology*, 1971, *89*, 229–239.

Harris, C. S. Perceptual adaptation to inverted, reversed, and displaced vision. *Psychological Review*, 1965, *72*, 419–444.

Hay, J. C. Visual adaptation to an altered correlation between eye movement and head movement. *Science*, 1968, *160*, 429–430.

Hay, J. C., Pick, H. L., and Roser, E. Adaptation to chromatic aberration by the human visual system. *Science*, 1963, *141*, 167–169.

Hay, J. C., Pick, H. L., and Ikeda, K. Visual capture produced by prism spectacles. *Psychonomic Science*, 1965, *2*, 215–216.

Hein, A., and Held, R. A neural model for labile sensorimotor coordinations. In *Biological prototypes and synthetic systems*. Vol. I. New York: Plenum Press, 1962.

Hein, A., Gower, E. C., and Diamond, R. H. Exposure requirements for developing the triggered component of the visual-placing response. *Journal of Comparative and Physiological Psychology*, 1970a, *73*, 188–192.

Hein, A., Held, R., and Gower, E. C. Development and segmentation of visually controlled movement by selective exposure during rearing. *Journal of Comparative and Physiological Psychology*, 1970b, *73*, 181–187.

Held, R. Exposure history as a factor in maintaining stability of perception and coordination. *Journal of Nervous and Mental Diseases*, 1961, *132*, 26–32.

Held, R., and Hein, A. Adaptation of disarranged hand-eye coordination contingent upon re-afferent stimulation. *Perceptual and Motor Skills*, 1958, *8*, 87–90.

Held, R., and Hein, A. Movement-produced stimulation in the development of visually guided behaviour. *Journal of Comparative and Physiological Psychology*, 1963, *56*, 872–876.

Howard, I. P. Displacing the optical array. In S. J. Freedman (Ed.), *The neuropsychology of spatially oriented behavior*. Homewood Ill.: Dorsey, 1968, pp. 19–36.

Howard, I. P. Perceptual learning and adaptation. *British Medical Bulletin*, 1971, *27*, 248–252.

Howard, I. P. Proposals for the study of adaptation to anomalous schemata. *Perception*, 1975, *3*, 497–513.

Howard, I. P., and Anstis, T. Muscular and joint-receptor components in postural persistence. *Journal of Experimental Psychology*, 1974, *103*, 167–170.

Howard, I. P., and Templeton, W. B. The effect of fixation on the judgment of relative depth. *Quarterly Journal of Experimental Psychology*, 1964, *16*, 193–203.

Howard, I. P., and Templeton, W. B. *Human spatial orientation*. London: Wiley, 1966.

Howard, I. P., Craske, B., and Templeton, W. B. Visuo-motor adaptation to discordant ex-afferent stimulation. *Journal of Experimental Psychology*, 1965, *70*, 189–191.

Howard, I. P., Anstis, T., and Lucia, H. C. The relative lability of mobile and stationary components in a visual-motor adaptation task. *Quarterly Journal of Experimental Psychology*, 1974, *26*, 293–300.

Hubel, D. H., and Wiesel, T. N. Receptive fields, binocular interaction and functional architecture in the cat's visual cortex. *Journal of Physiology*, 1962, *160*, 106–154.

Jackson, C. V. Visual factors in auditory localization. *Quarterly Journal of experimental Psychology*, 1953, *5*, 52–65.

Kelso, J. A., Cook, E., Olson, M. E., and Epstein, W. Allocation of attention and the locus of adaptation to displaced vision. *Journal of experimental Psychology: Human Perception and Performance*, 1975, *104*, 237–245.

Kennedy, J. M. Prismatic displacement and the remembered location of targets. *Perception and Psychophysics*, 1969, *5*, 218–220.

Kohler, I. Experiments with prolonged optical distortions. *Acta Psychologica*, 1955, *11*, 176–178.

Kolers, P. A., and Perkins, D. N. Orientation of letters and errors in their recognition. *Perception and Psychophysics*, 1969, *5*, 265–269.

Kornhuber, H. H. (Ed.) *Handbook of sensory physiology*. Vol. VI, Part 1: *Vestibular system*. New York: Springer, 1974.

Kottenhoff, H. Situational and personal influences on space perception with experimental spectacles. 1. Prolonged experiments with inverting glasses. *Acta Psychologica, 1957*, *13*, 79–97, 370–405.

Kottenhoff, H. *Was ist richtiges Sehen mit Umkehrbrillen und in welchem Sinne stellt sich das Sehen um?* Meisenheim am Glan, Germany: Anton Hain, 1961.

Kravitz, J. H., and Wallach, H. Adaptation to displaced vision contingent upon vibrating stimulation. *Psychonomic Science*, 1966, *6*, 465–466.

Lackner, J. R. Adaptation to displaced vision: Role of proprioception. *Perceptual and Motor Skills*, 1974, *38*, 1251–1256.

Leehey, S. C., Moskowitz-Cook, A., Brill, S., and Held, R. Orientational anistropy in infant vision. *Science*, 1975, *190*, 900–901.

Leventhal, A. G., and Hirsch, H. V. Cortical effect of early selective exposure to diagonal lines. *Science*, 1975, *190*, 902–904.

Lewis, R. Cat's brains are controversial. *New Scientist*, 1975, *20*, 457–458.

MacKay, D. M. Voluntary eye movements as questions. In J. Dichgans and E. Bizzi (Eds.), *Cerebral control of eye movements and motion perception*. Basel: Karger, 1972, pp. 369–376.

McCall, W. D., Farias, M. C. Williams, W. J., and BeMent, S. L. Static and dynamic responses of slowly adapting joint receptors. *Brain Research*, 1974, *70*, 221–243.

Melamed, L. E., Haley, M., and Gildow, J. W. Effect of external target presence on visual adaptation with active and passive movement. *Journal of Experimental Psychology*, 1973, *98*, 125–130.

Metzler, J., and Shepard, R. N. Transformational studies of the internal representation of three-dimensional objects. In R. Solso (Ed.), *Theories of cognitive psychology*. Potomac, Md.: Erlbaum, 1974.

Miller, E. A. Interaction of vision and touch in conflict and nonconflict form perception tasks. *Journal of Experimental Psychology*, 1972, *96*, 114–123.

Mitchell, D. E., Freeman, R. D., Millodot, M., and Haegerstrom, G. Meridional amblyopia: Evidence for modification of the human visual system by early experience. *Visual Research*, 1973, *13*, 535–558.

Moulden, B. Adaptation to displaced vision: Reafference is a special case of the cue-discrepancy hypothesis. *Quarterly Journal of Experimental Psychology*, 1971, *23*, 113–117.

Mountcastle, V. B., Poggio, G. F., and Werner, G. The relation of thalamic cell response to peripheral stimuli varied over an intensive continuum. *Journal of Neurophysiology*, 1963, *26*, 807–834.

Nielsen, T. I. Volition: A new experimental approach. *Scandinavian Journal of Psychology*, 1963, *4*, 225–230.

Ogle, K. N. *Binocular vision*. New York: Hafner, 1964.

Over, R. An experimentally induced conflict between vision and proprioception. *British Journal of Psychology*, 1966, *57*, 335–341.

Pick, H. L., and Hay, J. C. A passive test of the Held reafference hypothesis. *Perceptual and Motor Skills*, 1965, *20*, 1070–1072.

Pick, H. L., Warren, D. H., and Hay, J. C. Sensory conflicts in judgments of spatial direction. *Perception and Psychophysics*, 1969, *6*, 203–205.

Pick, H. L., Jr., Warren, D. H., McIntyre, C., and Appel, L. Transfer and the organization of perceptual-motor space. *Psycholgische Forschung*, 1972, *35*, 163–177.

Radeau, M. The locus of adaptation to auditory-visual conflict. *Perception*, 1973, *2*, 327–332.

Radeau, M. Differences in visual and auditory adaptation to prismatic displacement. *Année Psychologique*, 1974, *74*, 23–33.

Radeau, M., and Bertelson, P. Adaptation à un déplacement prismatique sur la base de stimulations exafférentes en conflit. *Psychologica Belgica*, 1969, *9*, 133–140.

Radeau, M., and Bertelson, P. The effects of a textured visual field on modality dominance in a ventriloquism situation. *Perception and Psychophysics*, 1976, *20*, 227–235.

Rock, I. *The nature of perceptual adaptation.* New York: Basic Books, 1966.

Rock, I. *Orientation and form.* New York: Academic Press, 1973.

Rock, I., and Victor, J. Vision and touch: An experimentally created conflict between the two senses. *Science*, 1964, *143*, 594–596.

Skowbo, D., Timney, B. N., Gentry, T. A., and Morant, R. B. McCollough effects: Experimental findings and theoretical accounts. *Psychological Bulletin*, 1975, *82*, 497–510.

Smith, K. U., and Smith, W. M. *Perception and motion.* Philadelphia: Saunders, 1962.

Stratton, G. M. Vision without inversion of the retinal image. *Psychological Review*, 1897, *4*, 341–363, 363–481.

Taylor, J. G. *The behavioral basis of perception.* New York: Yale University Press, 1962.

Templeton, W. B., Howard, I. P., and Lowman, A. E. Passively generated adaptation to prismatic distortion. *Perceptual and Motor Skills*, 1966, *22*, 140–142.

Templeton, W. B., Howard, I. P., and Wilkinson, D. A. Additivity of components of prismatic adaptation. *Perception and Psychophysics*, 1974, *15*, 249–257.

Thurlow, W. R., and Jack, C. E. Certain determinants of the "ventriloquism effect." *Perceptual and Motor Skills*, 1973, *36*, 1171–1184.

Timney, B. N., and Muir, D. W. Orientation anisotrophy: Incidence and magnitude in Caucasian and Chinese subjects. *Science*, 1976, *193*, 699–71.

Uhlarik, J. J. Role of cognitive factors on adaptation to prismatic displacement. *Journal of Experimental Psychology*, 1973, *98*, 223–232.

Uhlarik, J. J., and Canon, L. K. Influence of concurrent and terminal exposure conditions on the nature of perceptual adaptation. *Journal of Experimental Psychology*, 1971, *91*, 233–239.

Van Laer, E. S., Swartz, A., and Van Laer, J. Adaptation to prismatically displaced vision as a function of degree of displacement and amount of feedback. *Perceptual and Motor Skills*, 1970, *30*, 723–728.

von Holst, E. Relations between the central nervous system and the peripheral organs. *British Journal of Animal Behaviour*, 1954, *2*, 89–94.

Wallace, B. Preexposure pointing frequency effects on adaptation to prismatic viewing. *Perception and Psychophysics*, 1974, *15*, 26–30.

Wallach, H., and Flaherty, E. W. Covariance as a principle in perceptual adaptation. *Psychologia*, 1974, *17*, 159–165.

Wallach, H., and Frey, K. J. Adaptation in distance perception based on oculomotor cues. *Perception and Psychophysics*, 1972, *11*, 77–83.

Wallach, H., Stanton, L., and Becker, D. The compensation for movement-produced changes of object orientation. *Perception and Psychophysics*, 1974, *15*, 339–343.

Welch, R. B. Adaptation to prism-displaced vision: The importance of target-pointing. *Perception and Psychophysics*, 1969, *5*, 305–309.

Welch, R. B. The effect of experienced limb identity upon adaptation to simulated displacement of the visual field. *Perception and Psychophysics*, 1972, *12*, 453–456.

Welch, R. B., and Abel, M. R. The generality of the "target-pointing effect" in prism adaptation. *Psychonomic Science*, 1970, *20*, 226–227.

Wilkinson, D. A. The visual-motor control loops: A linear system? *Journal of Experimental Psychology*, 1971, *89*, 250–257.

Willott, J. F. Perceptual judgments with discrepant information from audition and proprioception. *Perception and Psychophysics*, 1973, *14*, 577–580.

Witkin, H. A., Wapner, S., and Leventhal, T. Sound localization with conflicting visual and auditory cues. *Journal of Experimental Psychology*, 1952, *43*, 58–67.

10

Effects of Selective Adaptation on the Perception of Speech and Visual Patterns: Evidence for Feature Detectors

PETER D. EIMAS AND JOANNE L. MILLER

1. Introduction

A trend in modern psychology is to assume that during perception complex stimulus events are first analyzed by neuronal structures or feature detectors into their component properties or features. The final percept is assumed to be a result of the recoding of these features according to the rules of operation of some higher, integrative level of processing. This type of perceptual model has had wide application in modern psychology, having been proffered in a variety of forms to explain such phenomena as the perception of visual patterns, including geometric shapes, letters, and words (e.g., Neisser, 1966), and the perception of the segmental units of speech (e.g., Abbs and Sussman, 1971).

The strongest evidence for feature detectors and the analysis of stimulus events into component parts comes from neurophysiology, in particular from electrophysiological recordings from individual neurons in the perceptual systems of infrahuman organisms (e.g., Hubel and Wiesel, 1962, 1965, 1968). As

PETER D. EIMAS • Walter S. Hunter Laboratory of Psychology, Brown University, Providence, Rhode Island 02912.   JOANNE L. MILLER • Department of Psychology, Northeastern University, Boston, Massachusetts 02115. Preparation of this chapter and the authors' research reported herein were supported by Grant HD 05331 from the National Institute of Child Health and Human Development and Grant NS 00143 from the National Institute of Neurological and Communicative Disorders and Stroke.

we shall attempt to demonstrate in this chapter, there is also strong inferential evidence for the existence of feature detectors in human sensory systems that serve to analyze complex events into component features. Most of the studies with human observers that have been concerned with the featural analysis of stimulus events have used a selective adaptation procedure. The rationale for this procedure is that if neural structures exist for the analysis of stimulus patterns, then the repeated stimulation of one of these structures by an adequate stimulus should fatigue this mechanism and alter its manner of functioning, making it, for example, less efficient or sensitive. The operation of any detector not tuned to the adapting information should remain unaffected, unless the adapted and unadapted detectors are linked by inhibitory connections, in which case the unadapted channel should be more sensitive after adaptation. Thus, the assumption has been that by distorting the perceptual system knowledge may be acquired about its normal operating characteristics.

In the present chapter, we have reviewed the selective adaptation literature in the areas of speech perception and pattern vision from the viewpoint of feature detector theories of perception, citing when appropriate relevant electrophysiological studies with animal observers. Our selection of these particular modalities was guided not only by our own interests (and competencies) but also by our belief, based on similar reviews in other areas of perception, that the conclusions permitted by the selective adaptation studies on speech and pattern vision apply at least in principle to other modalities.

2. Selective Adaptation and the Perception of Speech

Although the selective adaptation procedure has only recently been applied to the study of speech perception, a large number of studies using this experimental paradigm have already been reported. The primary reason for the wide acceptance of this procedure is that results from these studies were able to provide a data base for theories of speech perception based on feature detectors, which by the 1970s had begun to acquire considerable support (Abbs and Sussman, 1971; Stevens, 1973; for related discussions, see Lieberman, 1970, and Stevens, 1972). One factor contributing to the emergence of these feature detector models, and thus indirectly to the growth of selective adaptation experiments, was the publication of a series of studies on the ability of the human infant to perceive speech (e.g., Eimas, 1975; Eimas, Siqueland, Jusczyk, and Vigorito, 1971; Lasky, Syrdal-Lasky, and Klein, 1975). These studies provided strong inferential evidence for the existence of feature detectors, in that the infant listener, like the adult listener, was found to perceive the distinctive features of speech categorically. That is, evidence for the discrimination of two speech patterns was obtained when the two sounds signaled different phonetic feature values and not when they signaled acoustic variations of the same phonetic feature value. This occurred despite the fact that the acoustic difference between the sounds was very nearly the same in the two instances. Moreover, this form of perception appears before the infant is able to articulate the perceived distinctions (e.g., Port and Preston, 1974) and it occurs without specific linguistic experience: infants were able to make categorical distinctions even when the phonetic distinction did not occur in the immediate linguistic environment (Eimas, 1975; Lasky *et al.*, 1975).

Another factor influencing the development of feature detector models of speech perception was the considerable neurophysiological evidence for the existence of feature detectors in the visual and auditory systems of lower organisms (e.g., Capranica, 1965; Hubel and Wiesel, 1962, 1965; Lettvin, Maturana, McColloch, and Pitts, 1959; Winter and Funkenstein, 1973; Wollberg and Newman, 1972) and the considerable psychophysical data favoring the existence of feature detectors in the human visual system (e.g., Anstis, 1975; Blakemore and Campbell, 1969; McCollough, 1965; and the present review of this literature). The influence of these converging lines of evidence helped to establish a *Zeitgeist* that was favorably disposed toward research and theory concerned with the role of feature detectors in the perception of speech—an undertaking for which the selective adaptation paradigm was especially well suited.[1]

2.1. Analysis of Voicing and Place of Articulation

The majority of studies that have assessed the effects of selective adaptation on the perception of speech have used procedures similar to those introduced by Eimas and Corbit (1973). In essence, listeners are required to assign phonetic labels to the members of one or more series of synthetic speech patterns that vary along a single, albeit often complex, acoustic dimension. The variation in the acoustic continuum is always sufficient to signal a change in a phonetic feature value, and hence in the final percept. Identification functions are obtained when listeners are in a normal, unadapted state and after they have been selectively adapted with a member of the identification series or with a stimulus that shares some acoustic and/or phonetic information with the identification series. The effects of selective adaptation are assessed by comparing the locus of the phonetic boundary (the stimulus value that is assigned equally often to both phonetic categories) obtained before selective adaptation with the locus that is obtained after adaptation. According to the rationale offered by Eimas and Corbit (1973), "repeated presentation of the feature . . . to which a

---

[1] There are many masking studies using speech stimuli (including dichotic listening experiments) that can be considered instances of very brief selective adaptation. However, because of space limitations we have not reviewed this literature and will only note in passing that a number of the masking studies permit the inference that the speech signal is analyzed into features similar to those that can be inferred from the studies that are reviewed (*cf.* Studdert-Kennedy and Shankweiler, 1970; Wolf, 1976).

given detector is sensitive should fatigue the detector and reduce its sensitivity. As a consequence, the manner in which stimuli are assigned to phonetic categories would be altered, especially for those stimuli near the phonetic boundary where both detectors may be somewhat sensitive to the same values'' (pp. 101–102). More specifically, the expectation is that stimuli near the boundary that were assigned to the adapted feature category before adaptation will be assigned to the unadapted feature category after adaptation. In other words, after adaptation, the locus of the phonetic boundary should shift toward the category that was selectively adapted.

In the Eimas and Corbit (1973) study, the stimuli were two series of synthetic speech sounds that varied in voice onset time (VOT). The two series differed from each other only in the perceived place of articulation, i.e., in the place of the greatest constriction of the vocal tract during production. In one series, the acoustic parameters signaled a major constriction at the region of the lips and the stimuli were perceived as the voiced or voiceless bilabial stop consonants, [b] or [p], respectively. In the second series, the acoustic parameters signaled a major constriction at the alveolar ridge and the members of the series were perceived as the voiced or voiceless alveolar [d] or [t]. After obtaining the unadapted identification functions for the two series, three listeners were selectively adapted with [b], [d], [p], and [t] and identification functions were again obtained for both series of stimuli.

The results for a representative listener are shown in Fig. 1. For each of the eight adaptation-identification conditions there was a marked shift in the locus of the phonetic boundary toward the category of the adapted feature value, indicating that a greater number of the identification responses were assigned to the unadapted mode of voicing. It is of particular importance to note that the effects of adaptation were present even when the adapting stimulus and identification stimuli were from different series and thus spectrally different, a finding that rules out adaptation at the level of the phonetic segment or syllable, and also rules out explanations of the boundary shift in terms of simple contrast effect or response bias at the level of the syllable or phonetic segment. (We will consider the issue of response bias vs. sensory fatigue in greater detail below.) Eimas and Corbit (1973) also found that the peak in the discrimination function, indicative of the categorical manner in which listeners perceived these stimuli, likewise shifted after selective adaptation. Moreover, the shift in the discrimination peak corresponded almost perfectly with the shift in the phonetic boundary—evidence consistent with the hypothesis that the identification and discrimination of speech sounds are served by the same channels of analysis.

Cooper (1974a) found evidence for a feature detector system underlying the analysis of the information for perception of the three major feature values for place of articulation: bilabial, alveolar and velar.[2] Each of the three places

---

[2] The major constriction for the velar stop consonants occurs at the region of the velum (soft palate).

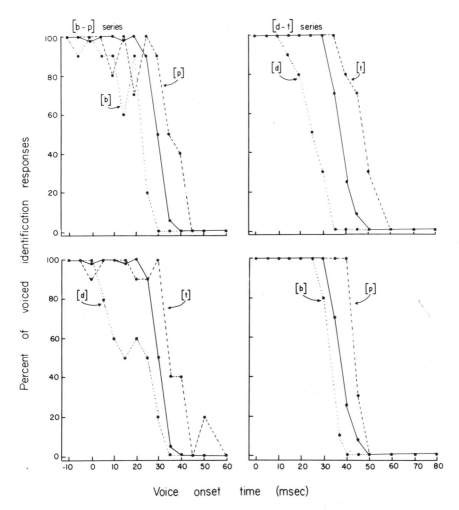

Fig. 1. Percentages of voiced identification responses ([b] or [d]) obtained with and without adaptation for a single subject. The functions of the [b,p] series are on the left and those for the [d,t] series are on the right. The solid lines indicate the unadapted identification functions, and the dotted and dashed lines indicate the identification functions after adaptation. The phonetic symbols indicate the adapting stimulus. From Eimas and Corbit (1973).

of articulation has associated with it a number of acoustic properties that specify the particular place value. One of these properties is the direction and extent of the second- and third-formant transitions,[3] which when varied systematically is sufficient to change the perceived value of place from bilabial to alveolar to

[3] Formant transitions are rapid changes in the center frequencies of the intense energy bands or formants that correspond to the resonant frequencies of the vocal tract.

velar (e.g., Liberman, Harris, Hoffman, and Griffith, 1957). Using a continuum of synthetic speech stimuli that varied continuously along this property,
Cooper obtained a significant shift in the bilabial-alveolar ([b–d]) boundary
after adaptation with [b] and a significant shift in the alveolar-velar ([d–g])
boundary after adaptation with [g]. Adaptation with the alveolar stop [d] produced reliable boundary shifts in both the [b–d] and [d–g] boundaries. In all instances, the direction of the boundary shift was in accord with a model that
posits three detectors for the analysis of place information. These detectors
were further assumed by Cooper to be organized along a single complex dimension and arranged in the order bilabial–alveolar–velar such that there was overlap only between adjacent detectors, i.e., between the bilabial and alveolar
analyzers and between the alveolar and velar analyzers. Cooper (1974a) also
found that adaptation with [b] and with [g] produced noticeable shifts in the
discrimination peaks and that these shifts matched the shifts in the phonetic
boundaries in both direction and magnitude. Finally, Cooper showed that adaptation with a bilabial stop consonant that differed from the identification series
in voicing (i.e., [p]) or in the following vowel ([i] rather than [æ]) produced
reliably smaller adaptation effects. These latter effects indicate that the detectors for the analysis of place of articulation are also selectively tuned for voicing and vowel information. By selective tuning we actually mean two things:
(1) that a detector is responsive to only a limited range of the values associated
with a feature (place of articulation in this instance), and (2) that a detector
varies in its responsivity to this range of values as the context in which the subset of place values is embedded varies (in this instance, the contextual variation
in voicing and vowel quality).

In a second series of studies, Eimas, Cooper, and Corbit (1973) found that
presenting the adapting stimulus to one ear and the identification series to the
other ear yielded a shift in the phonetic boundary not appreciably smaller than
that obtained after binaural adaptation and testing, i.e., when the adapting stimulus and test stimuli were presented to both ears. Ades (1974a) on the other
hand found a considerably smaller interaural transfer, 55% compared with the
95% transfer obtained by Eimas et al. (1973). The source of this difference is
not known, although it may be attributable to the fact that Eimas et al. used
stimuli that differed in voicing, whereas Ades used stimuli that differed in place
of articulation. Ades (1974a) also presented even more convincing evidence for
a central locus in that greater adaptation effects were obtained when the components of the adapting stimulus were presented in a manner that permitted binaural fusion than when fusion was not possible.

2.2. Manner of Articulation

Several recent studies have investigated the mechanisms responsible for
the analysis of the acoustic information underlying the phonetic distinctions

based on manner of articulation.[4] Manner of articulation refers to the type of constriction in the vocal tract during production and distinguishes such classes of speech sounds as stops, nasals, fricatives, and glides or liquids. Cooper, Ebert, and Cole (1976), using synthetic speech patterns, have shown that the distinction between stop consonants and glides, [ba] vs. [wa] and [ga] vs. [ya], may be mediated by detectors that are sensitive to the duration of formant transitions (cf. Diehl, 1976). Furthermore, these duration detectors may be selectively tuned for information concerning place of articulation. Using a selective adaptation procedure with carefully modified natural speech, Cole, Cooper, Singer, and Allard (1975) and Cole and Cooper (1976) have investigated several other manner distinctions. For example, by systematically reducing the duration of the nasal resonance in the syllable [ma], they were able to produce a series that was perceived as [ma] or [ba]. Adaptation with the endpoint stimuli produced reliable alterations in the phonetic boundary in the expected direction, as did adaptation with the alveolar nasal consonant [na] and with a 150-msec segment of nasal resonance alone (cf. Miller and Eimas, 1977; Samuels, 1975). Cole et al. (1975) and Cole and Cooper (1976) also constructed a series of stimuli that were perceived as either the voiced affricate [ǰ] (the initial sound in Java or jump) or the voiced stop [d] plus the vowel [a] by reducing the initial burst of [ǰ] in equal steps. Adaptation with [ǰa], [da], [ǰi], and [di] all produced significant adaptation effects in the anticipated direction. A third series, which was perceived as the voiceless fricative [f] or the voiced stop [b], plus the vowel [a] also yielded significant boundary shifts after adaptation with [ba] and with [va], the voiced counterpart of [fa], but surprisingly there was no shift in the boundary after adaptation with [fa].

2.3. Contingent Adaptation Effects

A number of studies (Cooper, 1974b; Miller and Eimas, 1976; Pisoni, Sawusch, and Adams, 1975; and see Ades, 1976, for a review of the literature) have reported the occurrence of contingent adaptation effects that are analogous to the contingent adaptation effects found in vision (e.g., McCollough, 1965, to be discussed below). Contingent adaptation effects are evidenced by changes in the perception of the information for a particular feature after selective adaptation that are at least in part governed by the context in which the critical feature information is embedded. The implication of contingent aftereffects is that

---

[4] There are two selective adaptation studies that do not fit into our outline but which deserve mention. In the first study, Verbrugge and Liberman (1975) found that the distinction between the liquids [r] and [l] might be subserved by a feature detector system and, in the second study, Morse, Kass, and Turkienicz (1976) investigated the effects of selective adaptation on the perception of a vowel series. Their results support, in general, a feature detector model, although the exact nature of the detectors cannot be specified, given the complexity of their findings.

there is not a single structure (i.e., detector) for the analysis of the feature information under question, but rather that there exist many such structures that are tuned not only to the critical feature information but also to restricted ranges of information arising from contextual variables. In the first contingent adaptation study, Cooper (1974b) adapted listeners with an alternating sequence of [da] and [ti]. The effects of adaptation were measured by comparing the locus of the phonetic boundary of a [ba–pa] series with the locus of a [bi–pi] series, both before and after adaptation. If voicing information is extracted independently of the vowel environment, than no adaptation effects should occur, inasmuch as the effects of simultaneously fatiguing the voiced and voiceless detectors should cancel each other. If, however, the analysis of voicing information is dependent on the vowel environment, then both series should show alterations in the locus of the phonetic boundary, but in opposite directions: the boundary for the [ba–pa] series should shift toward the voiced end of the continuum whereas the boundary for the [bi–pi] series should shift toward the voiceless end. The data were clearly in accord with a vowel-dependent analysis of voicing information.

Miller and Eimas (1976) replicated this effect and further demonstrated as did Pisoni et al. (1975) that the information for place of articulation is analyzed in terms of the following vowel. Thus, for example, adaptation with an alternating sequence of [bæ] and [di] shifted the locus of the phonetic boundary of a [bæ–dæ] series toward the [b] category and at the same time shifted the boundary of a [bi–di] series toward the [d] category. In addition, Miller and Eimas (1976) showed that the information for place of articulation in initial syllabic position is analyzed independently of the information for place in final syllabic position (cf. Ades, 1974b; Tartter, personal communication).[5] That is, adaptation with an alternating series of [bæb] and [dæd] did not differentially alter the phonetic boundaries for the initial consonant of the two test series [bæb-dæb] and [bæd-dæd]. In fact, there was no significant change in either of the boundaries, indicating a cancelation of the effects of adaptation with the syllable-initial [b] and the syllable-initial [d]. Finally, Ades (1976) has summarized a number of other contingent effects that have recently been reported for place of articulation: (1) the ear of origin[6] (Ades, 1974a; Lackner and Goldstein, 1975) (2) fundamental frequency (pitch) (Ades, 1976, and compare

[5] As a consequence, we would expect contingent-adaptation effects if we adapted listeners simultaneously with [bæ] and [æd] and tested them on a [bæ-dæ] series and on a [æb-æd] series. That is, the boundary of the [bæ-dæ] series should shift toward the [b] category and the boundary of the [æb-æd] series should shift toward the [d] category.
[6] The experiments of Lackner and Goldstein (1975; Goldstein and Lackner, 1974; Lackner, Tuller, and Goldstein, 1976) used a different procedure for adaptation, one based on Warren's (1968) methodology for investigating the verbal transformation effect. In general, their findings can be interpreted within the context of a feature detector model (but see Lackner et al., 1976, for a discussion of this contention).

Lackner, Tuller, and Goldstein, 1976), and (3) intensity (Ganong, personal communication).

2.4. Auditory vs. Phonetic Loci of the Adaptation Effects [7]

Eimas *et al.* (1973) found that adaptation with the initial 50 msec of voiced stop consonant, which is not perceived as speech by most listeners, did not produce a reliable adaptation effect. A similar finding has been reported by Tartter and Eimas (1975), although in only one of many conditions, and by Verbrugge and Liberman (1975). Eimas *et al.* concluded from this and the nearly complete adaptation effects when the adapting and test stimuli were from different series that the detector systems underlying the perception of speech are phonetic in nature and are not a part of the more general auditory system. Further evidence for this conclusion has come from studies by Diehl (1975) and Ganong (1975). Both investigators reported reliable adaptation effects when the adapting stimulus and test series shared phonetic information but very little in the way of common acoustic information. For example, in the Diehl study adaptation effects were obtained when the place of articulation of the adapting stimulus was signaled by the information in the initial burst (there being no formant transitions), whereas the information for place of articulation in the test series was signaled by formant transitions (there being no initial bursts). Diehl (1975) also found that it was the perceived phonetic value of the adapting signal (the actual phonetic segment that was heard by the listener), and not the acoustic structure *per se* (the actual physical parameters of the adapting signal) that determined the direction of the adaptation effect (*cf.* Ades, 1974 *b*, experiment 2; Cooper *et al.*, 1976).

Although these studies are in accord with a phonetic locus of the adaptation effects, it has been possible to explain these findings on the basis of auditory detectors alone (Ades, 1976; Ganong, 1975). In addition, there are a number of findings that seriously question the existence of a phonetic level of adaptation. First, Blumstein and Stevens (1975), contrary to Diehl (1975), have shown that the acoustic structure and not the listener's perception of the segmental quality of adapting stimulus determines the direction of the adaptation effects. Second, as mentioned earlier, a large number of studies have demonstrated marked reductions in the magnitude of the adaptation effect when the spectral composition of the adapting and test stimuli differed (e.g., Cooper, 1974*a*), and Ades (1974*b*) and Tartter and Eimas (1975) have found small, but

---

[7] A number of studies, using a variety of experimental paradigms other than selective adaptation, have yielded considerable evidence for at least two levels of processing: a general auditory level and a phonetic level (e.g., Fujisaki and Kawashima, 1969; Pisoni, 1973; Pisoni and Tash. 1974). However, more specific descriptions of these levels of processing are not permitted by the data, e.g., whether detector systems exist at both levels.

reliable, shifts in the phonetic boundary after adaptation with components of
the speech signal. Finally, Ades (1974a) and Tartter (personal communication)
failed to find a shift in the locus of the phonetic boundary along a [bæ–dæ]
series of synthetic speech after adaptation with [æb] or [æd]. Nor did adaptation with [bæ] or [dæ] alter the perception of a vowel-consonant series
[æb–æd].

As a consequence of these findings, and the fact that much of the evidence
favoring a phonetic level of adaptation can be explained by detectors that are
auditory in nature (cf. Ades, 1976), we believe that it is valid, and certainly
more parsimonious, to assume a single site of the adaptation effects—the auditory level. We will consider the tuning of these detectors and the manner in
which they map onto higher levels of processing in greater detail below.

2.5. Response Bias vs. Sensory Explanations

It was noted by Eimas and Corbit (1973) that the selective adaptation effect might simply be a consequence of response bias. There are, however, a
number of arguments to be made against this proposition, without denying that
a portion of these effects may be attributable to processes that operate during
some relatively late, decision stage (cf. Miller and Eimas, 1976). First, there
are cross-series effects, i.e., shifts in the location of the phonetic boundary
after adaptation with stimuli that differ in phonetic quality from the identification series (Anderson, 1975; Cole et al., 1975; Cooper and Blumstein, 1974;
Cooper et al., 1976; Eimas and Corbit, 1973; Miller and Eimas, 1976). Findings of this nature certainly exclude attributing the entire selective adaptation
effect to response bias factors at the segmental or syllabic levels. Second,
Sawusch and Pisoni (1973) and Sawusch, Pisoni, and Cutting (1974) have presented evidence that identification functions for stop consonants are virtually
unaffected by stimulus frequency manipulations that would be expected to
produce marked changes in phonetic assignments according to the assumptions
of signal detection theory or adaptation level theory. However, in that these
findings were not obtained with the selective adaptation paradigm, the evidence
is at best weakly supportive of a sensory interpretation of selective adaptation.
Third, there are several demonstrations to the effect that selective adaptation
with portions of the speech signal, which themselves are not perceived as
speech, produces shifts in the phonetic boundary (Ades, 1974a; Tartter and
Eimas, 1975). These effects are difficult to accommodate within a response
bias model that operates on the segmental or syllabic level. Fourth, there are
data that indicate that the magnitude of the adaptation effect is related to the extent to which the adapting stimulus is in acoustic terms, a good exemplar of the
feature category (Anderson, 1975; Miller, 1976). Both Anderson and Miller
found less adaptation effects with stimuli closer to the phonetic boundary,
despite the fact that all of the adapting stimuli were consistently perceived as

good exemplars of the adapted feature category—findings obviously not in accord with a response bias explanation. Finally, Cole *et al.* (1975) and Cooper *et al.* (1976) have performed a d′ analysis of the identification data before and after adaptation. This analysis permitted an assessment of the extent to which the alterations in perception after adaptation could be attributed to changes in sensitivity over and above changes in response bias. Although all of these analyses were not fully consistent with a sensory interpretation of the selective adaptation effect, the weight of evidence from the d′ analyses and the arguments presented above support a sensory, as opposed to response bias, interpretation.

2.6. Nature of Feature Detectors for Speech

Given the evidence, we believe that the detector systems underlying speech perception are auditory in nature (*cf.* Ades, 1976; Pisoni and Tash, 1975) and that the individual detectors are selectively tuned to a number of acoustic characteristics of the speech signal. The actual inputs to these detectors are the neural transforms of the acoustic signals for speech, perhaps a syllable in length (*cf.* Studdert-Kennedy, 1974). The outputs of these detectors provide sufficient information for the assignment of distinctive phonetic values by some higher, more abstract level of processing. Given the multiple tuning of these channels of analysis and hence the large number of detectors signaling a particular feature value, a many-to-one mapping is required; i.e., many auditory analyzers provide equivalent input information to a single higher-order mechanism that yields a context-independent phonetic feature value. The tuning of these detectors and the manner in which they map onto higher values are most likely determined by both genetic and experiential factors (e.g., Eimas, 1975; Lasky *et al.*, 1975; Stevens, 1973).

With respect to the tuning characteristics of these detectors, it is necessary to distinguish two forms of selective tuning. The first pertains to the acoustic information directly relevant to the phonetic feature under consideration and the second pertains to the acoustic context in which the feature information is embedded. Thus, for example, a detector for the analysis of place information is sensitive to a relatively restricted range of initial burst and formant transition information, which signals a place value, as well as to parameters of the speech signal which specify the vowel environment, syllabic position, fundamental frequency, intensity, voicing, manner of articulation, and perhaps other dimensions that derive from the consequences of coarticulation and within- and between-speaker variability.

There are several reasons for assuming this form of feature analyzer as opposed, for example, to integrative analyzers (*cf.* Cooper, 1974c) which are activated by the weighted outputs of lower-order detectors. First, the results of the contingent adaptation studies and the many studies showing smaller adaptation effects when the adapting and test stimuli differ in their acoustic structure argue for feature detectors that are tuned along a number of dimensions. Second, there is now substantial evidence (*cf.* Blakemore, 1975) to argue against a hierarchical system of analysis of the form proposed by Hubel and Wiesel (1962, 1965) for the visual system. Although considerably less is known about the auditory system, it also appears that a convincing case cannot be made for a hierarchical system of analysis in this modality (*cf.* Abbs and Sussman, 1971; Stevens, 1973). Finally, there are electrophysiological data from studies of infrahuman auditory systems that indicate the existence of analyzers that are tuned to quite complex aspects of acoustic signals (e.g., Evans and Whitfield, 1964; Nelson, Eruklar, and Bryan, 1966) as well as analyzers that are tuned to complex species-specific vocalizations (Capranica, 1965; Capranica, Frishkopf, and Nevo, 1973; Hoy and Paul, 1973; Winter and Funkenstein, 1973; Wollberg and Newman, 1972). Analyzers for comparable levels of complexity in the human auditory system would not seem to be impossible.

2.7. Operating Characteristics of Feature Detectors for Speech

Eimas and Corbit (1973) offered a number of assumptions that were intended to describe the manner in which feature detectors analyze speech and yield the identification functions obtained with and without selective adaptation. These assumptions, modified and expanded, are as follows: (1) There exist multiply tuned feature detectors, each of which is sensitive to a restricted range of complex acoustic information that is sufficient to signal a single phonetic feature value. (2) The greatest sensitivity of a detector occurs at some set of acoustic values that correspond to the modal acoustic consequences of articulating that feature value under a particular set of conditions with sensitivity declining as the input signal departs from modal values. (3) Some acoustic signals, those near the phonetic boundary, excite more than one detector and the graded outputs of both detectors are available to higher-order mechanisms for decisions regarding the phonetic feature value in the signal (*cf.* Miller, 1975). (4) All other factors being equal, the phonetic boundary lies at the stimulus value that excites the two detectors signaling different feature values equally. (5) Adaptation reduces the sensitivity and consequently the output signal of a detector for all stimulus values to which the detector is sensitive. For purposes of simplicity the reduction in sensitivity is assumed to be equal for all of these stimulus values. It follows from this that selective adaptation alters the phonetic boundary by shifting the point of equilibrium. (6) The degree to which a detector is fatigued by adaptation is proportional to the proximity of the adapting stimulus to the detector's modal values (*cf.* Miller, 1976). Figure 2 shows, in schematic form, how feature detectors are assumed to determine the locus of the phonetic boundary before and after adaptation.

A comparison of the assumptions offered here with those presented by Eimas and Corbit (1973) reveals two significant changes. First, rather than as-

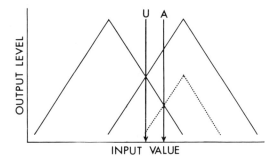

Fig. 2. Model of a feature detector system. Output level is given as a function of input value prior to adaptation (solid lines) and following adaptation (dotted lines) with a modal stimulus from one phonetic category. Line U indicates the location of the unadapted boundary, and line A indicates the location of the adapted boundary. Adapted from Miller (1975).

suming that when two detectors are excited by the same signal "only the output signal with the greater strength reaches higher centers of processing and integration" (Eimas and Corbit, 1973, p. 108), we have assumed that the graded signals of both detectors are available for further processing (assumption 3). This revision was necessitated by a number of findings. Using a dichotic listening paradigm, Miller (1976) showed that the effectiveness of an attended-to stimulus in competing for processing with an unattended-to stimulus (in the other ear) was a function of the extent to which each of the stimuli approached the modal value of its feature category. Furthermore, Miller (1975, 1976) and Sawusch (1975) found that adaptation affected the processing of nonboundary as well as boundary exemplars of a phonetic category. Finally, several studies (Anderson, 1975; Pisoni and Tash, 1974) have found marked increments in category decision times for stimuli at or near the phonetic boundary. This effect can be accommodated by assumption 3, provided that the time to make a phonetic decision is inversely related to the difference in strength of the competing output signals.

The second change in the model is the addition of the assumption that a detector is fatigued in proportion to the extent that it is activated by the adapting stimulus. This assumption was included to accommodate the finding, recently obtained with a variety of response measures, that adaptation with stimuli near the modal value produces a larger effect than adaptation with stimuli near the phonetic boundary (Anderson, 1975; McNabb, 1975; Miller, 1976).[8]

---

[8] Hillenbrand (1975) has shown that the magnitude of the adaptation effect also increases with increases in intensity and number of presentations of the adapting stimulus. It is certainly not unreasonable to expect that more intense stimuli (up to some limit) and more repetitions of a given stimulus (again up to some limit) will produce greater fatigue and hence a greater shift in the phonetic boundary.

Furthermore, Miller (1976) reported that, although the magnitude of the adaptation effect was a function of the value of the adapting stimulus, a given adapting stimulus produced an approximately equal effect for all values of the test stimuli as would be expected by assumption 5.

2.8. Summary

Studies on the effects of selective adaptation on the perception of speech have yielded evidence for a process of analysis and at least a partial list of defining features for the segmental units. Although most of the effects of adaptation can be explained by multiply tuned feature detectors, detectors of this nature present a serious problem regarding the extent to which a detector shows invariance in its responsivity (cf. Blakemore, 1975; Lettvin, Maturana, Pitts, and McColloch, 1961). One of the guiding principles of feature detector theories of perception is that there exist trigger features in the world, relatively few in number, to which detectors always respond, regardless of the context in which the feature information is embedded. In essence, by assuming that detectors respond in an invariant manner to trigger features, the outputs of feature detectors can be considered to provide the invariant information to higher centers that is necessary for perceptual constancy. However, the greater the number of dimensions to which a detector is tuned, the greater is the loss of invariance. Indeed, carried to the extreme, a detector that is tuned to all of the relevant dimensions exhibits no invariance in its responsivity and in fact can be classified as an object detector rather than a feature detector—it responds only when an appropriate value is present along each of the n dimensions that specify an object in the world. Obviously, a theory of this nature not only is without explanatory value because of the vast number of detectors that are required but also is absurd.

It is possible to escape the theoretical bind of object detectors by assuming some limit on the number of contextual dimensions to which any single detector for speech is tuned. However, even if evidence for a limitation were obtained, thereby eliminating the possibility of object detectors, the number of detectors would still be large. The reason for this is that different sets of detectors must be available, each of which analyzes the same phonetic information in conjunction with one or more (but not all) of the contextual attributes. As our discussion of the feature detector systems for vision will indicate, problems related to the number of detectors are not unique to speech.

3. Selective Adaptation and Visual Perception

As in the study of speech perception, the use of selective adaptation to determine the channels of analysis of visual information has increased greatly in the past decade. The general experimental paradigm, like that used for speech, measures some aspect of perception along the dimension of interest before and after exposure to an adapting stimulus that has some value along this dimension. In the visual studies that we have considered, there are two major variations in the way in which the adapting stimulus is presented. First, there is the direct analogue of the speech adaptation studies in which the adapting visual information is presented for relatively long periods of time, i.e., from seconds to hours, and in which the adapting information always precedes the test stimuli. The second paradigm, which has been called "visual masking," presents the adapting information for very brief periods of time, usually measured in milliseconds, and in some variants of this procedure the adapting stimulus is actually presented after the test stimulus (backward masking) or the two stimuli are presented simultaneously. The visual adaptation studies have measured the effects of selective adaptation on the perception of suprathreshold stimuli (the visual aftereffects) and on the detection and recognition of near threshold stimuli (the threshold elevation effects).

The impetus for much of the visual adaptation work has come from the discovery of orientation-contingent color aftereffects by McCollough (1965) and from recent developments in neurophysiology (e.g., Campbell, Cooper, and Enroth-Cugell, 1969; DeValois, 1965; Hubel and Wiesel, 1962, 1965, 1968). Our discussion of the evidence for channels of analysis in the human visual system will consider first a number of features in isolation (orientation, spatial frequency, and motion) and then consider these features in combination, especially the combinations involving color. (For a summary of the analysis of color information, see DeValois, 1965, and Graham and Brown, 1965.)

3.1. Orientation

Hubel and Wiesel (1962, 1965, 1968), Pettigrew, Nikara, and Bishop (1968), and Campbell, Cleland, Cooper, and Enroth-Cugell (1968) have found single neurons in the visual cortex of the cat and monkey that are selectively sensitive to orientation. Although these detectors respond to a wide range of orientations, there is usually a marked decrement in responsivity as the orientation of the pattern deviates 15–20° from the neuron's preferred orientation (Hubel and Wiesel, 1965). The evidence to be presented permits similar conclusions about the human visual system.

Campbell and Maffei (1970) reported a marked decrement in the cortical evoked response when the adapting and test gratings had the same orientation. The magnitude of the evoked response increased with an increase in the angular disparity between the two gratings, with full recovery of the evoked response occurring at 15–20° of difference. Presumably, the weaker-adapted channels were not contributing to the evoked response beyond this angular difference. Campbell and Kulikowski (1966) found that the contrast threshold for vertical and oblique gratings was markedly increased by a simultaneously presented masking grating and that the magnitude of this effect declined as the difference in orientation between the adapting and test gratings increased. The halfwidth of the inferred detectors at half amplitude (i.e., the angular discrepancy that produces half of the maximal effect) was 12° and 15° for vertical and oblique gratings, respectively, findings in close accord with those derived from electrophysiological procedures. However, other procedures have yielded finer estimates of tuning (Kulikowski, Abadi, and King-Smith, 1973; Movshon and Blakemore, 1973). Further evidence for orientation detectors is found in the masking studies of Gilinsky (1967, 1968), Gilinsky and Mayo (1971), Houlihan and Sekuler (1968), and Sekuler (1965). Moreover, Gilinsky and Doherty (1969) found nearly complete interocular transfer of masking effects for orientation, indicating a central locus for these effects.[9]

The perceived displacement in the orientation of lines and gratings after exposure to similar stimuli of different orientations, the tilt aftereffect extensively studied by Gibson (1933, 1937; Gibson and Radner, 1937; see also Howard, this volume), provides another measure of the effects of adaptation. The tilt aftereffect is evidenced, for example, by a vertical grating perceived as being tilted counterclockwise after adaptation with a line tilted in a clockwise manner.[10] Tilt aftereffects have also been obtained for curved lines (e.g., Gibson, 1937), but whether curvature detectors exist apart from orientation detectors is a matter of debate (e.g., Blakemore and Over, 1974; Riggs, 1974; Stromeyer, 1974a). In a series of studies Campbell and Maffei (1971) found that there was no tilt aftereffect when the adapting and test stimuli had the same orientation, but there was an increasing aftereffect as the angular difference between the adapting and test gratings increased up to 10°, after which it declined to very nearly zero at 40°. The finding that the maximal effect does not occur at zero angular differences has been termed the "distance paradox." An explanation of this paradox in terms of feature detectors has been offered by Coltheart (1971) and will be considered below.

It is of interest to note that the resolving power of the human visual system

---

[9] There are other data to support the contention that the analyses of spatial orientation occur at or beyond the point of binocular cortical cells in the human visual system (e.g., Campbell and Maffei, 1970; Felton, Richards, and Smith, 1972; Julesz and Miller, 1975; Tyler, 1975), as well as evidence that these effects occur before the level of binocular interaction (Blake and Fox, 1974). It may of course be the case that the analysis of spatial information occurs at more than one level, and that different procedures necessitate the use of information at different levels (cf. Andrews, 1972).

[10] There is also an indirect tilt aftereffect. An adapting grating of +10° will not only cause a vertical grating to be perceived as being tilted in a counterclockwise manner but also cause a horizontal grating to be tilted in a similar manner, although to a lesser extent. Coltheart (1971) has explained this effect in terms of hypercomplex cells, which have two preferred orientations 90° apart. This explanation, while possible, does not explain the smaller magnitude of the indirect effect or why such cells are not activated under all conditions.

is considerably more acute for horizontal and vertical information than for oblique information (see Appelle, 1972, and also Mitchell, this volume, for a review of this literature, and Maffei and Campbell, 1970, for electrophysiological evidence for this effect in humans). Findings from neurophysiological studies with animals, indicating a predominance of neurons maximally sensitive to horizontal and vertical orientations (Mansfield, 1974; Pettigrew *et al.*, 1968; but see Hubel and Wiesel, 1962, 1965, for contradictory evidence), provide a plausible, but perhaps untestable, explanation of the oblique effect in human observers.

In summary, the evidence clearly supports the existence of detectors or channels of analysis for orientational information in the human visual system that have rather narrow tuning characteristics and a central location. These detectors can be fatigued or made less sensitive by adaptation procedures, yielding elevations in the contrast threshold and apparent tilts in the perceived orientation of similar gratings.

3.2. Spatial Frequency

In recent years, Fourier theory (Goldman, 1967) has been applied to the analysis of visual forms and has been extended to serve as the basis of a model for the analysis of spatial information by the visual system. According to Fourier theory, any complex waveform can be analyzed into a number of component waveforms each with a given frequency and conversely a complex waveform can be synthesized from appropriate component waveforms. In extending Fourier theory to serve as a model of the visual system, it has been assumed that a complex visual pattern can be represented by a complex waveform that is composed of a number of individual waveforms. Each of these component waveforms has a spatial frequency, which is defined as the number of light-dark cycles per degree of visual angle (cycles/deg). It has been further assumed, in the multiple-channel model, that the visual system possesses a number of independent channels, each of which is sensitive to a restricted range of spatial frequencies.

Evidence supportive of this model has come from a number of sources. Individual neurons have been found in the visual cortex of cats and monkeys that are responsive to limited bands of spatial frequencies (Campbell *et al.*, 1969*a*; Campbell, Cooper, Robson, and Sachs, 1969; Maffei and Fiorentini, 1973). In addition, Maffei, Fiorentini, and Bisti (1973) demonstrated that these neurons are fatigued by prolonged exposure to spatial frequency information within the tuning characteristic of the neuron and that this effect transfers interocularly. Using the evoked potential in response to gratings that alternated 180° in phase, Campbell and Maffei (1970) found, in human observers, that the evoked response increased linearly with the logarithm of the contrast of the grating. In addition, the slope of the function increased with an increase in the number of simultaneously presented gratings, each of which had a different spatial frequency. The latter finding presumably was a result of the activation of more channels of analysis.

Psychophysical studies with human observers likewise permit the inference of detectors for the analysis of spatial frequency information. Campbell and Robson (1968) found that the contrast thresholds for a number of different waveforms can be related by Fourier theory and that over a wide range of spatial frequencies the threshold of a complex waveform is determined by the amplitude of the fundamental. In addition, they found that a grating with a complex waveform cannot be distinguished from a sinewave grating with a frequency equal to the fundamental until the amplitude of any of the higher harmonics reaches its independent threshold—the first evidence for a system of independent channels. Blakemore and Campbell (1969), using a selective adaptation method, found that the contrast threshold for a grating of the same frequency as the adapting grating increased manyfold (cf. Stromeyer and Julesz, 1972) and the bandwidth at half amplitude was one octave. These findings held for the middle range of spatial frequencies; for higher spatial frequencies the bandwidth was smaller, and for spatial frequencies less than 3 cycles/deg the maximal effect always occurred at 3 cycles/deg. On the basis of similar threshold elevation effects with squarewave gratings, Pantle and Sekuler (1968a) concluded that channels sensitive to spatial frequency may underlie the analysis of bars of a given width, but their conclusion has been challenged by Sullivan, Georgeson, and Oatley (1972), who observed that "the effects of adaptation to single bars of a given width and to gratings of a given frequency are quite different" (p. 391; cf. Weisstein, 1973).

Blakemore and Sutton (1969) have shown that the perceived spatial frequency of gratings is altered by adaptation to gratings of similar spatial frequencies: gratings of a higher spatial frequency than the adapting grating appear even higher and gratings with lower spatial frequencies than the adapting grating appear even lower. This aftereffect is analogous to the tilt aftereffect discussed above, in that there is no perceived spatial frequency shift when the spatial frequencies of the adapting and test gratings are equal and when the two gratings differ greatly, i.e., by two octaves or more (Blakemore, Nachmias, and Sutton, 1970b). Blakemore et al. (1970b) also found that with spatial frequencies less than 3 cycles/deg the effect remains centered at 3 cycles/deg (cf. Blakemore and Campbell, 1969) and that the magnitude of the perceived shift increases with increases in the contrast and presentation duration of the adapting grating.

The ability to discriminate one spatial frequency from another has been found to obey Weber's law over a wide range of spatial frequencies, the Weber fraction being approximately 0.06 (Campbell, Nachmias, and Jukes, 1970). Moreover, given the absence of local irregularities in the discriminability function or in the contrast threshold curve for spatial frequency (Blakemore and Campbell, 1969), the spacing of the central frequencies of these analyzers is probably small compared to their bandwidths (Campbell *et al.*, 1970). Although there is evidence that these channels operate independently of one another at threshold levels of contrast (Campbell and Robson, 1968; Graham and Nachmias, 1971; Sachs, Nachmias, and Robson, 1971; but see Stecher, Sigel, and Lange, 1973*a*,*b*), at suprathreshold levels of contrast there is evidence for an interaction between channels (Campbell and Howell, 1972; Tolhurst, 1972). This latter finding questions the validity of using Fourier theory as a model for the analysis of spatial information by the visual system (*cf.* Sekuler, 1974).

One further finding deserves consideration. Maffei and Fiorentini (1972) have demonstrated that the brain is capable of synthesizing the components of a squarewave to yield the percept of a squarewave, as would be expected if the brain were capable of functioning in accord with Fourier theory. Observers who were presented the fundamental and third harmonic dichoptically observed the best approximation to a squarewave when the third harmonic had an amplitude equal to one-third that of the fundamental—a result exactly in accord with Fourier theory.

Although the evidence indicates that the analysis of spatial patterns provides information about spatial frequency and orientation, it is unlikely that the detectors for these two forms of information constitute independent detector systems. Several studies have demonstrated that the channels for orientation are selectively tuned for spatial frequency and similarly the channels for spatial frequency are tuned for orientation (Blakemore and Nachmias, 1971; Blakemore, Muncey, and Ridley, 1973; Movshon and Blakemore, 1973).[11] Given these dependencies, it is not unreasonable to assume that the analysis of orientation and spatial frequency has a common detector system, centrally located.

3.3. Motion

As is true for the analysis of orientation and spatial frequency, there are single units in the cat's visual cortex that respond to a single preferred direction of movement (Hubel and Wiesel, 1959). Moreover, different neurons respond optimally to different velocities (Hubel and Wiesel, 1965). The response of ganglion cells in the rabbit to continuous movement in an appropriate direction shows an initial increase in activity and then a marked decline. With the cessation of movement there is a further decrease in activity below normal baseline level that recovers slowly (Barlow and Hill, 1963), a pattern of neural activity that could explain adaptation effects in psychophysical studies of motion.

After adaptation with a pattern moving in one direction, the largest thresh-

---

[11] Early reports (Campbell and Maffei, 1971; Parker, 1972) indicated that the tilt aftereffect was independent of the spatial frequencies of the adapting and test gratings. However, more recently Georgeson (1973) and Ware and Mitchell (1974) have indicated that this is most likely not the case (*cf.* Wyatt, 1974).

old elevation effect was found for a test pattern moving in the same direction, with progressively smaller effects occurring as the angular difference in direction increased (Sekuler and Ganz, 1963; Sekuler, Rubin, and Cushman, 1968). In fact, adaptation with a grating moving in one direction produces a threshold elevation for a grating moving in the opposite direction (Pantle and Sekuler, 1969; Sekuler and Ganz, 1963; Sekuler et al., 1968). However, Pantle and Sekuler (1969) have argued that this may in fact be the result of a threshold elevation for the analysis of orientation and not for motion. An implication of this argument is that the channels of analysis for motion are direction specific, which has been quite convincingly demonstrated by Levinson and Sekuler (1975). In a study comparing the tuning of motion detectors for direction with the tuning of spatial frequency detectors for orientation, Sekuler et al. (1968) found a markedly smaller bandwidth for orientation. Motion detectors are also tuned for velocity, although Pantle and Sekuler (1968b) found that the maximal threshold elevation did not occur when the adapting and test patterns moved with the same velocity, but rather occurred when the adapting pattern had a slightly greater velocity than the test pattern. With increasing differences between the velocities of the adapting and test stimuli, the magnitude of the threshold elevation effect declined.

In human observers, Sekuler and Pantle (1967) showed that the duration of the motion aftereffect (the apparent movement of a stationary pattern in a direction opposite to the direction of movement of the adapting pattern) was related to the velocity and exposure duration of the adapting pattern. The actual relation between the adapting velocity and the duration of the aftereffect was shown by Sekuler and Ganz (1963) to be curvilinear. In addition, Masland (1969) reported that motion aftereffects may last for as long as 24 hr, which is considerably longer than the 3 or 4 hr estimated to be the duration of the spatial frequency aftereffect (Blakemore et al., 1970b; Blakemore and Sutton, 1969).

Further evidence for the multiple tuning of channels of analysis for motion comes from contingent aftereffects, whereby two different aftereffects are produced along one dimension each dependent on a different value along a second dimension. For example, Mayhew and Anstis (1972) established a contingent motion aftereffect by pairing two directions of motion with two different spatial frequencies. During adaptation, subjects were alternately presented with broad stripes (e.g., 2 cycles/deg) moving upward and narrow stripes (e.g., 4 cycles/deg) moving downward. Subsequently, stationary broad stripes appeared to move downward and narrow stripes appeared to move upward. The direction of apparent motion can also be made contingent on the brightness or orientation of the pattern (Mayhew and Anstis, 1972), the texture of the pattern (Walker, 1972), the spatial frequency or orientation of a stationary surround (Potts and Harris, 1975), and the direction of gaze (Mayhew, 1973a). Finally, Anstis and Harris (1974) report that a motion aftereffect contingent on binocular disparity (perceived depth) can be generated. It should be noted that there is probably not a single system of motion detectors underlying all of these effects. Evidence for this has been reported by Mayhew (1974) who found pattern-specific and pattern-nonspecific motion analyzers and by Anstis and Moulden (1970) who demonstrated a peripheral and central location for motion aftereffects. In addition, other studies have indicated that the detection of movement and the detection of pattern information may be mediated by different analyzers (Kulikowski and Tolhurst, 1973; Sharpe and Tolhurst, 1973; Tolhurst, 1973).[12]

3.4. Orientation and Color

We have argued that the selective adaptation paradigm has provided evidence for the existence of channels of analysis that are selectively tuned along such visual dimensions as orientation, spatial frequency, and direction of motion and that these channels show multiple tuning, or dependencies, responding maximally to a stimulus with a particular combination of feature values. There are data to indicate that at least some of these detectors are also tuned for wavelength.

McCollough (1965) was the first to demonstrate that the color of an aftereffect can be made contingent on the orientation of the test grating. During the adaptation phase of her experiment, subjects were presented with a vertical black and orange grating alternating every few seconds with a horizontal black and blue grating. They were shown vertical and horizontal achromatic test gratings and were asked to report any color seen. The gratings appeared tinged with the complement of the adapting color: the vertical stripes appeared bluish and the horizontal stripes appeared orange. When the test pattern was rotated 45° so that all the lines were oblique, no color was seen. That the effect is dependent on retinal orientation was demonstrated by the finding that when the subjects tilted their heads 45° the effect disappeared and a reverse effect appeared with a tilt of 90° (*cf.* Ellis, 1976 but also Mikaelian, 1976, for evidence that the perceived orientation of the adapting pattern can be critical). Finally, two recent studies have shown that the orientation-contingent aftereffect is most likely mediated by units that are sensitive to the orientation of the spatial frequency components of the patterns rather than to the orientation of the edges (Green, Corwin, and Zemon, 1976; May and Matteson, 1976).

Estimates of orientation tuning for the inferred detectors vary. In a study using vertical and horizontal adapting gratings, Teft and Clark (1968) found that the test gratings could be rotated only about 26° from the adapting orienta-

---

[12] Just what information motion detectors respond to is not known, although Beck and Stevens (1972) have argued that motion analyzers are sensitive to sequential changes in position. They found that adaptation to apparent movement in one direction produced the perception of a more rapid apparent movement in the opposite direction than was really the case and that adaptation to the successive presentation of lights produced an analogous aftereffect in the speed of perceived succession.

tion before the color aftereffects disappeared. Fidell (1970) showed that the magnitude of the effect was not dependent on the absolute orientation of the adapting gratings as long as they differed by 90°. However, the magnitude of the effect decreased as the difference between adapting orientations decreased, with angular differences less than 22° yielding no effect, although an effect can be obtained with adapting gratings separated by less than 22° if the orientations of the test patterns are separated by a greater amount (Stromeyer, 1974a). Related studies in which adapting patterns of only one orientation were used provide somewhat broader estimates of tuning, indicating that the narrower tuning found in the contingent studies may be due in part to an interaction of two independent effects, each due to one of the two adapting patterns (cf. Ellis and Castellan, 1975). However, even these estimates vary considerably, ranging from no orientation selectivity (Leppmann, 1973) to a half bandwidth (at half amplitude) of 45° (Ellis and Castellan, 1975). Given the variety of procedures and the diversity in the obtained values, an exact estimate of the degree of tuning for orientation is not possible, although there is usually little or no effect when the adapting and test patterns differ by 45°, which agrees with the tuning estimate for the tilt aftereffect (e.g., Campbell and Maffei, 1971).

Patterns of curves and angles, as well as those of straight lines, can also elicit contingent aftereffects of color (Crassini and Over, 1975; MacKay and MacKay, 1974; Riggs, 1973, 1974; Sigel and Nachmias, 1975; Stromeyer, 1974a; White and Riggs, 1974). The mechanism underlying this aftereffect, however, is in some dispute. Riggs (1973) and White and Riggs (1974) have argued that orientation detectors cannot account for the curvature or angle effects and that detectors responsive to the rate of change of slope are necessary. However, based on the results of studies that systematically manipulated the manner in which the adapting and/or test patterns were inspected, MacKay and MacKay (1974), Sigel and Nachmias (1975), and Stromeyer (1974a) have all concluded that the aftereffect can be explained by the adaptation of orientation detectors (cf. Crassini and Over, 1975).

A number of additional parameters of the orientation-contingent color aftereffect have been examined. Harris and Gibson (1968) demonstrated that the aftereffect is not simply due to negative afterimages, although the effects can be induced by afterimages (Murch and Hirsch, 1972). Piggins and Leppmann (1973) further showed that retinal image motion is necessary for the establishment of the effect, although it is not necessary during the testing of the effect. Moreover, these aftereffects have been shown to be specific to retinal area (Harris, 1969; Stromeyer, 1972a), although Murch (1969) did report that test patterns that are larger than the adapting patterns appear colored all over and not just at the location corresponding to the adapting pattern. This spread of color may result from eye movements or the judgment procedure (cf. Stromeyer, 1972a).

Hue and luminance parameters have also been investigated. Stromeyer

(1969) found that the strongest aftereffects are obtained with red and green adapting colors, although colors other than red and green can produce strong effects if the appropriate spatial frequencies are used (Stromeyer, 1972b). A number of factors can influence the color of the aftereffect, including exposure to homogeneous colored fields during the adapting procedure (Hirsch and Murch, 1972) and the contrast parameters of the test pattern (Stromeyer, 1971). White (1976) found that the magnitude of the effect increased as the luminance of the adapting pattern increased and decreased as the luminance of the test pattern increased (cf. Skowbo, Timney, Gentry, and Morant, 1975). The magnitude of the effect also varies as a function of the contrast of the adapting grating (Ellis and Castellan, 1975; Harris and Barkow, 1969).

Finally, certain temporal factors have been considered. One of the most striking characteristics of contingent aftereffects is that they are very persistent, often lasting for days or weeks (e.g., Jones and Holding, 1975; Mayhew and Anstis, 1972; McCollough, 1965). The decay function is complex (Riggs, White, and Eimas, 1974; but see MacKay and MacKay, 1973a) and depends on the initial strength of the aftereffect (Riggs et al., 1974), the testing procedure (Jones and Holding, 1975), and the type of visual stimulation presented between adaptation and testing (MacKay and MacKay, 1975a; Skowbo et al., 1975). Finally, whereas the initial strength of the effect is a function of the duration of the total inspection time of the alternating adapting patterns (Riggs et al., 1974), it does not differ over a wide range of rates of alternation (White and Ellis, 1975).

The studies reviewed so far involved the establishment of a color aftereffect that is contingent on orientation. If these effects are mediated by neural units that are tuned to both orientation and wavelength, then it should be possible to obtain the reverse effect, namely, an orientation aftereffect that is contingent on color. Held and Shattuck (1971) have reported such an effect. After viewing red gratings tilted clockwise off vertical alternating with green gratings tilted counterclockwise off vertical, red vertical gratings appeared tilted counterclockwise and green vertical gratings appeared tilted clockwise. In addition, the magnitude of the aftereffect increased as the orientation of the adapting stimuli increased up to about 15° off vertical and then dropped to zero at about 40° (cf. Broerse, Over, and Lovegrove, 1975; Campbell and Maffei, 1971; Lovegrove and Over, 1973).

Although the aftereffect data reviewed above clearly indicate that at least some of the detectors sensitive to orientation are tuned to wavelength, related electrophysiological and threshold elevation studies provide conflicting data on the color selectivity of orientation detectors. On the one hand, May, Leftwich, and Aptaker (1974) found that the visual evoked response to a colored grating is diminished by prior exposure to an adapting grating with the same orientation and wavelength but not to a grating that differs in either of these parameters, and May (1972) and Lovegrove and Over (1973) reported similar results for threshold elevation effects. On the other hand Timney, Gentry, Skowbo, and Morant (1976) failed to find a color-sensitive threshold elevation effect for orientation. In the same study, however, they did find an orientation-contingent color aftereffect, yielding the possibility that these two effects are actually mediated by different neural mechanisms (cf. Kulikowski and Tolhurst, 1973).

3.5. Spatial Frequency and Color

May (1972) and Maudarbocus and Ruddock (1974) have observed threshold elevation effects for spatial frequency that are color selective. In addition, many studies have reported color aftereffects that are contingent on the spatial frequency of gratings (Breitmeyer and Cooper, 1972; Harris, 1970, 1971; Leppmann, 1973; Lovegrove and Over, 1972; Stromeyer, 1972a,b; Uhlarik and Osgood, 1974). Breitmeyer and Cooper (1972) found that the strength of the color aftereffect increased as the difference in spatial frequency between the adapting patterns increased, with all subjects reporting an effect when the separation was two octaves. In a similar vein, Lovegrove and Over (1972) found that to establish the effect it was necessary for the two inspection gratings to differ by at least one octave and that the largest effects occurred when the adapting and test gratings matched. These results agree quite well with the estimates of spatial frequency tuning based on individual aftereffects (cf. Blakemore and Campbell, 1969). Furthermore, the magnitude of the aftereffect is a function of the absolute spatial frequency of the gratings, with the strongest effects in the frequency region of 5 cycles/deg (Stromeyer, 1972a). In fact, it is typically quite difficult to obtain contingent aftereffects with frequencies below about 3 cycles/deg (Lovegrove and Over, 1972; Stromeyer, 1972a), although Stromeyer (1974b) has reported obtaining these effects under scotopic viewing conditions. Finally, the color aftereffect was found to be dependent on retinal, rather than perceived, spatial frequency (Harris, 1970), although color aftereffects have been made contingent on apparent spatial frequency (Stromeyer, 1972a; Wyatt, 1974).

Further evidence for color-selective spatial frequency channels was obtained by Virsu and Haapasalo (1973), who demonstrated a spatial frequency aftereffect contingent on color, analogous to the color-contingent tilt aftereffect found by Held and Shattuck (1971). In a related study, Wyatt (1974) found a triple contingency between orientation, spatial frequency, and wavelength, implicating detectors that are tuned to all three dimensions. Finally, there are a number of related contingent aftereffects that presumably also involve detectors selective to parameters of spatial frequency and wavelength: e.g., a color aftereffect can be made contingent on the size of contours (Harris, 1972; MacKay and MacKay, 1975b) and on the phase relation between frequency components in complex gratings with identical spectra (Stromeyer, Lange, and Ganz, 1973).

3.6. Motion and Color

Hepler (1968) was the first to demonstrate a motion-contingent color after-effect. She adapted subjects with an alternating sequence of green stripes moving upward and red stripes moving downward. Following adaptation, upward-moving stripes appeared pinkish and downward-moving stripes appeared greenish. Stromeyer and Mansfield (1970) and Favreau, Emerson, and Corbalis (1972) reported similar findings with rotating spirals. Stromeyer and Mansfield (1970) also found that the color aftereffect is specific to retinal area (cf. Masland, 1969; Sekuler and Pantle, 1967) and dependent on the orientation and the velocity of stripes on the retina. Furthermore, since the aftereffect can be elicited by sweeping the eye over stationary stripes, the underlying neural unit must be responsive to the direction of movement across the retina, and not perceived direction (Stromeyer and Mansfield, 1970).

A number of studies have reported motion aftereffects that are contingent on color (e.g., Favreau et al., 1972; Mayhew, 1972, 1975; Mayhew and Anstis, 1972). For example, Favreau et al. (1972) adapted subjects with a rotating spiral that alternated in direction and in color. After adaptation, a colored stationary spiral appeared to move in a direction opposite to the direction it moved during adaptation and the apparent motion faded quickly during each test trial (cf. Mayhew and Anstis, 1972; Stromeyer and Mansfield, 1970). In accord with these motion aftereffects, Mayhew (1973b) found a threshold elevation effect for motion that was color selective: after subjects had been adapted to a red pattern moving clockwise alternating with a green pattern moving counterclockwise, the threshold for clockwise motion was greater than that for counterclockwise motion when the pattern was red, and conversely when the pattern was green (cf. Lovegrove, Over, and Broerse, 1972).

3.7. Monocularity of Color-Selective Units

Unlike the channels of analysis sensitive only to spatial information, the channels that are selective to both spatial and wavelength information are probably all monocular (cf. Coltheart, 1973; Over and Wenderoth, 1974). A number of studies have failed to find a color aftereffect contingent on orientation when the adapting stimuli were presented to one eye and the test pattern was viewed with the other eye (e.g., McCollough, 1965; Murch, 1972) and two opposite contingent aftereffects can be simultaneously established, one in each eye (McCollough, 1965). Lovegrove and Over (1973) found that the tilt aftereffect was color selective only when the adapting and test gratings were presented to the same eye, and Broerse et al. (1975) found a lack of color selectivity when the color and spatial information for inducing a tilt aftereffect was presented to different eyes. Furthermore, the color sensitivity for orientation-specific threshold elevation is not maintained either when the test stimuli are shown to one eye and the inspection stimuli to the other eye (Maudarbocus and Ruddock, 1973) or when the contour and color information is presented separately to the two eyes during inspection (Broerse *et al.*, 1975). Similar to the findings for orientation and color, no interocular transfer was obtained for effects involving color and spatial frequency (e.g., Stromeyer, 1972*b*) or color and motion (e.g., Murch, 1974; Stromeyer and Mansfield, 1970). Finally, consistent with the lack of interocular transfer is the inability to produce a color aftereffect that is contingent on stereoscopic depth (Over, Long, and Lovegrove, 1973; *cf.* Lu and Fender, 1972; Ramachandran and Sririam, 1972).

Both the lack of interocular transfer of aftereffects involving color and the inability to produce color effects contingent on disparity information are consistent with the claim that these effects are mediated by monocular channels. However, there are certain findings in the literature suggesting that there is some interaction for color-coded information between the two eyes (MacKay and MacKay, 1973*b*, 1975*b*; Shattuck and Held, 1975; White and Riggs, 1974). For example, White and Riggs (1974) report that color aftereffects contingent on angle can be generated when half of the angle is presented to one eye and half to the other eye during inspection. Furthermore, MacKay and MacKay (1973*b*, 1975*b*) claim to have established pattern-contingent color aftereffects by presenting the pattern information to one eye and the color information to the other eye, although Over *et al.* (1973) have failed to replicate these findings under similar conditions. At present, no satisfactory resolution of the discrepant findings is available.

3.8. Nature and Operation of Detectors for Visual Information

A model based on the adaptation of feature detectors, similar to the one posited by Coltheart (1971; and see Anstis, 1975) to explain the tilt aftereffect, can accommodate most of the visual threshold and aftereffect data. According to this model, the analysis of visual information is subserved by detectors that are multiply tuned and thus maximally sensitive to a particular combination of stimulus values. The responsivity of a detector declines as the stimulus departs from the preferred value of the analyzer along any of the dimensions of tuning. For any single dimension, the ranges of sensitivity of the detectors overlap, so that a particular value along this dimension will excite a number of detectors. The overall pattern of excitation determines the percept, with the perceived dimensional value given by the central tendency of the population of neurons that are excited. Furthermore, it is assumed that exposure to a stimulus decreases the responsivity of the detectors excited by that stimulus. The magnitude of decrease is related to the sensitivity of the unit to the stimulus and, for a given unit, the decline in sensitivity is equal for all stimulus values to which the unit responds.[13]

---

[13] Although we have not discussed the issue of mapping the outputs of populations of detectors for
    visual information onto higher mechanisms, it is apparent that such a process is required for

Consider first how this model can account for threshold elevation effects along a single dimension. Since a unit is fatigued in proportion to its responsivity to a particular stimulus, the greatest loss in responsivity will occur for the unit tuned to the adapting value, with progressively less decrement occurring as the preferred value differs from the adapting value. Given the assumption that the threshold value is inversely related to the responsivity of an analyzer, two predictions can be made: (1) the greatest threshold elevation will occur for the test stimulus that has the same value as the adapting stimulus, and (2) the magnitude of the effect will decline in an orderly manner as the two stimuli differ in value. It is important to note that the first prediction will be confirmed only if there is a detector with a preferred value equal to that of the two stimuli—and if this is true for all values, then there must be a potentially infinite number of detectors along the dimension—obviously a problem for a detector model. With two exceptions, the available evidence for orientation, spatial frequency, and direction and velocity of motion confirms both predictions. One exception is that the maximal effect for velocity occurs when the test stimulus has a slightly lower value than the adapting stimulus, perhaps indicating an asymmetry in the tuning characteristic of velocity detectors (Pantle and Sekuler, 1968b). The second is that at low contrast the greatest threshold elevation effect for spatial frequency can occur when the adapting and test frequencies differ (Stecher *et al.*, 1973b).

Consider next the aftereffects of orientation and spatial frequency. First, since exposure to a stimulus along the dimension is assumed to produce a symmetrical decrease in sensitivity, no shift in the perceived value of the test stimulus should occur when the adapting and test stimuli have the same value. Second, a shift in the perceived value of the test stimulus should occur when the adapting and test stimuli have somewhat different values, reflecting the shift in the central tendency of the population of detectors responsive to the test pattern. Finally, when the difference between adapting and test stimuli is so large that different populations of analyzers are involved in their analysis, no change should occur in the perceived value of the test stimulus. The aftereffect data agree with these predictions. The maximal effect occurs at a value near the adapting value (the "distance paradox") and no apparent shift occurs when the adapting and test stimuli have either the same value or very different values. Figure 3 demonstrates in schematic form the manner in which orientation (or spatial frequency) aftereffects can be predicted from the model.

The aftereffects of both color and direction of motion, unlike the aftereffects of orientation and spatial frequency, are the complementary values of the adapting stimulus. For this model to accommodate these aftereffects, it must be

---

vision as well as for speech. The evidence indicates that there are often different detector systems signaling the same visual information, the systems being differentiated by the contextual dimensions to which they are tuned. Consequently, it is necessary to have some mechanism that yields the same percept despite contextual variations.

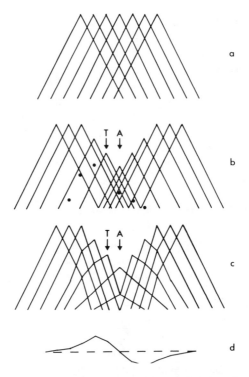

Fig. 3. Tuning curves model. (a) Schematic diagram of hypothetical channels tuned to orientations (or spatial frequencies, etc.). Tuning curves are arbitrarily assumed to be Λ-shaped. (b) Adapting orientation (A) produces a V-shaped depression in the population of tuning curves. Subsequent response of adapted population to a test orientation (T) is shown by the spots. The horizontal position of the spot indicates the channel to which the spot refers; the height of the spot indicates the sensitivity of that channel after adaptation. (c) Adapted *population* curves are plotted for various orientations. The adapted population curve for the test orientation (T) is simply a function connecting the spots in (b). The other population curves were obtained in the same manner. (Note these are not tuning curves of individual channels.) Adaptation has skewed the curves, shifting their central tendency, hence (it is argued) the apparent orientation of the test stimuli. (d) Perceived orientation shifts ("tilt aftereffect") plotted as a function of test orientation. Notice the distance effect. From Anstis (1975) with some modification of the text.

further assumed that the detectors sensitive to color and those sensitive to direction of motion each form an opponent-process-like system. In a system of this nature, there are two interconnected channels that analyze opposing (complementary) information along a single dimension. The percept of a stimulus that lies along this dimension is determined by the relative contributions of each of these channels of analysis. In the unadapted state, the two opposing analyzers are balanced and a test stimulus appears "neutral"—e.g., an achromatic grating appears white and a stationary pattern does not appear to move. After adaptation, however, the unadapted channel will be more responsive than the adapted channel, with the result that the test stimulus will appear to have the value of the unadapted channel.

Contingent aftereffects are also explicable within the framework of a model that assumes the adaptation of multiply tuned feature detectors. As will be recalled, contingent aftereffects are two different aftereffects produced along a single dimension, each of which is dependent on a different value along a second dimension. Consider, for example, the orientation-contingent color aftereffect. Adaptation with a red vertical grating will reduce the relative responsivity of the population of detectors tuned to red and vertical, and adaptation with a green horizontal grating will similarly reduce the relative responsivity of detectors tuned to green and horizontal. There will be an imbalance in the red-green system tuned to vertical favoring green and an analogous imbalance in the red-green system tuned to horizontal favoring red. Thus, vertical achromatic gratings will appear greenish and horizontal achromatic gratings will appear pinkish. Similar analyses will explain the complement of this contingent aftereffect, namely, the color-contingent orientation aftereffect, as well as the remaining contingent aftereffects that have been reported.

Although a model based on the fatiguing of multiply tuned detectors is capable of explaining many of the effects of selective adaptation in vision, there are certain findings that are not consistent with this model. Two of these findings are most noteworthy in that they have resulted in serious attempts to construct alternative theoretical descriptions of the adaptation effects. The first is the persistent nature of the contingent aftereffects (e.g., Mayhew and Anstis, 1972; Riggs et al., 1974). While such extended rates of decay are clearly incompatible with notions of sensory fatigue, it is doubtful whether the alternative models based on principles of associative learning that have been proposed will be any more successful in explaining the nature and duration of these effects (see Skowbo et al., 1975, and Stromeyer, in press, for discussions of learning models as they apply to contingent aftereffects). The second finding concerns the nonrandom "hallucinations" or apparent patterns seen on a blank screen after prolonged exposure to gratings (Georgeson, 1976). Georgeson has attempted to explain these effects in terms of an inhibition model (cf. Blakemore, Carpenter, and Georgeson, 1970a; Over, 1971). However, inhibition models also encounter difficulties. For example, since the adaptation of a detector is assumed to cause disinhibition, i.e., a reduction of the inhibition on neighboring channels, the sensitivity of neighboring channels should show increased sensitivity—a finding not reported in the literature. Whether or not a model based on the fatiguing of feature detectors will eventually be able to explain these findings remains a matter for conjecture at present and should not detract from the model's capacity to accommodate much of the selective adaptation effects in visual perception.[14]

---

[14] For additional discussions of the role of feature detectors in perception, the reader is referred to Erickson (1974), Gregory (1975), Uttal (1971), and Werner (1974).

4. Final Comments

The evidence from the selective adaptation studies strongly supports the proposition that there is an initial process of analysis by multiply tuned feature detectors during the perception of speech and visual patterns. In addition, the results of these studies have provided at least the beginning of a list of features that compose the segmental units of speech and the spatial patterns of vision. Of particular interest for theories of speech and visual perception is the fact that the number of features on each list is relatively small, thereby making it feasible to define the stimulus events in terms of these features and their relations to one another. Although the number of features will undoubtedly grow in time, given the present rate of discovery, it is doubtful whether the number will become so large that stimulus definitions in terms of features will become impossible or even unwieldy.

Our theoretical descriptions of the feature detectors for speech and vision,[15] although capable of accommodating many of the effects of adaptation with quite similar sets of assumptions, have encountered two serious difficulties. First, the available data indicate the possibility that it will be necessary to assume the existence of a very large and perhaps infinite number of detectors either because the analysis of certain features of the visual and auditory world requires a very large (or infinite) number of analyzers or because analyzers for certain dimensions, especially those for speech, are selectively tuned to numerous dimensions, and a detector must exist for every combination of stimulus values.

Second, as the number of attributes to which a feature detector is tuned becomes increasingly large, feature detectors begin to take on the characteristics of object detectors, and, as has been repeatedly noted, theoretical descriptions of perception based on the existence of a different object detector for every recognizable stimulus are untenable. Whether or not these issues are ultimately resolved in a manner compatible with the metatheoretical assumptions of a feature detector theory of perception, the evidence for an analytic process during perception as well as for a limited list of features will remain, and consequently must be accounted for by theories of perception, regardless of their form.

5. References

Abbs, J. H., and Sussman, H. M. Neurophysiological feature detectors and speech perception: A discussion of theoretical implications. *Journal of Speech and Hearing Research*, 1971, *14*, 23–36.

---

[15] It should be noted that the models for speech and vision differ in one critical respect. Each visual dimension is assumed to be analyzed by a very large, potentially infinite, number of detectors. In speech, however, information signaling a phonetic feature is analyzed by very few detectors, precisely one for each phonetic feature value.

Ades, A. E. Bilateral component in speech perception? *Journal of the Acoustical Society of America, 1974a, 56*, 610–617.

Ades, A. E. How phonetic is selective adaptation? Experiments on syllable position and vowel environment. *Perception and Psychophysics, 1974b, 16*, 61–67.

Ades, A. E. Adapting the property detectors for speech perception. In R. Wales and E. Walker (Eds.), *New approaches to language mechanisms*. Amsterdam: North Holland, 1976.

Anderson, F. Some implications for the operation of feature detectors in speech perception: Use of identification response time as a converging operation. Unpublished doctoral dissertation, Brown University, 1975.

Andrews, D. P. The site of the adaptation shown in figural after effects. *Vision Research, 1972, 12*, 1065–1067.

Anstis, S. M. What does visual perception tell us about visual coding? In M. S. Gazzaniga and C. Blakemore (Eds.), *Handbook of psychobiology*. New York: Academic Press, 1975, pp. 269–333.

Anstis, S. M., and Harris, J. P. Movement aftereffects contingent on binocular disparity. *Perception, 1974, 3*, 153–168.

Anstis, S. M., and Moulden, B. P. Aftereffect of seen movement: Evidence for peripheral and central components. *Quarterly Journal of Experimental Psychology, 1970, 22,* 222–229.

Appelle, S. Perception and discrimination as a function of stimulus orientation: The "oblique effect" in man and animals. *Psychological Bulletin, 1972, 78*, 266–278.

Bailey, P. Perceptual adaptation for acoustical features in speech. In *Speech perception: Report on research in progress in the department of psychology*. Vol. 2.2. Belfast: The Queen's University of Belfast, 1973, pp. 29–34.

Bailey, P. J. Perceptual adaptation of speech: Some properties of detectors for acoustical cues to phonetic descriptions. Unpublished doctoral dissertation, Cambridge University, 1975.

Barlow, H. B., and Hill, R. M. Selective sensitivity to directional movement in ganglion cells of the rabbit retina. *Science, 1963, 139*, 412–414.

Beck, J., and Stevens, A. An aftereffect to discrete stimuli producing apparent movement and succession. *Perception and Psychophysics, 1972, 12*, 482–486.

Blake, R., and Fox, R. Adaptation to invisible gratings and the site of binocular rivalry suppression. *Nature, 1974, 249*, 488–490.

Blakemore, C. Central visual processing. In M. S. Gazzaniga and C. Blakemore (Eds.), *Handbook of psychobiology*. New York: Academic Press, 1975, pp. 241–268.

Blakemore, C., and Campbell, F. W. On the existence of neurones in the human visual system selectively sensitive to the orientation and size of retinal images. *Journal of Physiology, 1969, 203*, 237–260.

Blakemore, C., and Nachmias, J. The orientation specificity of two visual after-effects. *Journal of Physiology, 1971, 213*, 157–174.

Blakemore, C., and Over, R. Curvature detectors in human vision. *Perception, 1974, 3*, 3–7.

Blakemore, C., and Sutton, P. Size adaptation: A new aftereffect. *Science, 1969, 166*, 245–247.

Blakemore, C., Carpenter, R. H. S., and Georgeson, M. A. Lateral inhibition between orientation detectors in the human visual system. *Nature, 1970a, 228*, 37–39.

Blakemore, C., Nachmias, J., and Sutton, P. The perceived spatial frequency shift: Evidence for frequency selective neurones in the human brain. *Journal of Physiology, 1970b, 210*, 727–750.

Blakemore, C., Muncey, J. P. J., and Ridley, R. M. Stimulus specificity in the human visual system. *Vision Research, 1973, 13*, 1915–1931.

Blumstein, S. E., and Stevens, K. N. Property detectors for bursts and transitions in speech perception. *Journal of the Acoustical Society of America, 1975, 57*, S52:Y10.

Breitmeyer, B. G., and Cooper, L. A. Frequency-specific color adaptation in the human visual system. *Perception and Psychophysics, 1972, 11*, 95–96.

Broerse, J., Over, R., and Lovegrove, W. Loss of wavelength selectivity and contour masking and aftereffect following dichoptic adaptation. *Perception and Psychophysics, 1975, 17*, 333–336.

Campbell, F. W., and Howell, E. R. Monocular alternation: A method for the investigation of pattern vision. *Journal of Physiology*, 1972, *225*, 19P–21P.

Campbell, F. W., and Kulikowski, J. J. Orientational selectivity of the human visual system. *Journal of Physiology*, 1966, *187*, 437–445.

Campbell, F. W., and Maffei, L. Electrophysiological evidence for the existence of orientation and size detectors in the human visual system. *Journal of Physiology*, 1970, *207*, 635–652.

Campbell, F. W., and Maffei, L. The tilt aftereffect: A fresh look. *Vision Research*, 1971, *11*, 833–840.

Campbell, F. W., and Robson, J. G. Application of Fourier analysis to the visibility of gratings. *Journal of Physiology*, 1968, *197*, 551–566.

Campbell, F. W., Cleland, B. C., Cooper, G. F., and Enroth-Cugell, C. The angular sensitivity of the visual cortical cells to moving gratings. *Journal of Physiology*, 1968, *198*, 237–250.

Campbell, F. W., Cooper, G. F., and Enroth-Cugell, C. The spatial selectivity of the visual cells of the cat. *Journal of Physiology*, 1969a, *203*, 223–235.

Campbell, F. W., Cooper, G. F., Robson, J. G., and Sachs, M. B. The spatial selectivity of visual cells of the cat and the squirrel monkey. *Journal of Physiology*, 1969b, *204*, 120P–121P.

Campbell, F. W., Nachmias, J., and Jukes, J. Spatial frequency discrimination in human vision. *Journal of the Optical Society of America*, 1970, *60*, 555–559.

Capranica, R. R. *The evoked vocal response of the bullfrog*. Research Monograph 33. Cambridge, Mass.: MIT Press, 1965.

Capranica, R. R., Frishkopf, L. S., and Nevo, E. Encoding of geographical dialects in the auditory system of the cricket frog. *Science*, 1973, *182*, 1272–1274.

Cole, R. A., and Cooper, W. E. Sensory and response models of speech adaptation. Unpublished manuscript, 1976.

Cole, R. A., Cooper, W. E., Singer, J., and Allard, F. Selective adaptation of English consonants using real speech. *Perception and Psychophysics*, 1975, *18*, 227–244.

Coltheart, M. Visual feature-analyzers and aftereffects of tilt and curvature. *Psychological Review*, 1971, *78*, 114–121.

Coltheart, M. Colour specificity and monocularity in the visual cortex. *Vision Research*, 1973, *13*, 2595–2598.

Cooper, W. E. Adaptation of phonetic feature analyzers for place of articulation. *Journal of the Acoustical Society of America*, 1974a, *56*, 617–627.

Cooper, W. E. Contingent feature analysis in speech perception. *Perception and Psychophysics*, 1974b, *16*, 201–204.

Cooper, W. E. Selective adaptation for acoustic cues of voicing in initial stops. *Journal of Phonetics*, 1974c, *2*, 303–313.

Cooper, W. E., and Blumstein, S. E. A labial feature analyzer in speech perception. *Perception and Psychophysics*, 1974, *15*, 591–600.

Cooper, W. E., Ebert, R. R., and Cole, R. A. Perceptual analysis of stop consonants and glides. *Journal of Experimental Psychology: Human Perception and Performance*, 1976, *2*, 92–104.

Crassini, B., and Over, R. Curvature-specific color aftereffects. *Perception and Psychophysics*, 1975, *17*, 398–404.

DeValois, R. L. Analysis and coding of color vision in the primate visual system. *Cold Spring Harbor Symposia on Quantitative Biology*, 1965, *30*, 567–579.

Diehl, R. H. The effect of selective adaptation on the identification of speech sounds. *Perception and Psychophysics*, 1975, *17*, 48–52.

Diehl, R. H. Feature analyzers for the phonetic dimension *stop vs. continuant*. *Perception and Psychophysics*, 1976, *19*, 267–272.

Eimas, P. D. Speech perception in early infancy. In L. B. Cohen and P. Salapatek (Eds.), *Infant perception*. Vol. 2. New York: Academic Press, 1975, pp. 193–231.

Eimas, P. D., and Corbit, J. D. Selective adaptation of linguistic feature detectors. *Cognitive Psychology*, 1973, *4*, 99–109.

Eimas, P. D., Siqueland, E. R., Jusczyk, P., and Vigorito, J. Speech perception in infants. *Science*, 1971, *171*, 303–306.

Eimas, P. D., Cooper, W. E., and Corbit, J. D. Some properties of linguistic feature detectors. *Perception and Psychophysics*, 1973, *13*, 247–252.

Ellis, S. R. Orientation constancy of the McCollough effect. *Perception and Psychophysics*, 1976, *19*, 183–192.

Ellis, S. R., and Castellan, K. Orientation specificity of the McCollough effect: An equivalent contrast transformation. Paper presented to the meeting of the Association for Research in Vision and Ophthalmology, Sarasota, Fla., 1975.

Erikson, R. P. Parallel "population" neural coding in feature extraction. In F. O. Schmitt and F. G. Worden (Eds.), *The neurosciences: Third study program*. Cambridge, Mass.: MIT Press, 1974, pp. 155–169.

Evans, E. F., and Whitfield, I. C. Classification of unit responses in the auditory cortex of the unanesthetized and unrestrained cat. *Journal of Physiology*, 1964, *171*, 476–493.

Favreau, O. E., Emerson, V. F., and Corbalis, J. C. Motion perception: A colorcontingent aftereffect. *Science*, 1972, *176*, 78–79.

Felton, T. B., Richards, W., and Smith, R. A., Jr. Disparity processing of spatial frequencies in man. *Journal of Physiology*, 1972, *225*, 349–362.

Fidell, L. S. Orientation specificity in chromatic adaptation of human "edge-detectors." *Perception and Psychophysics*, 1970, *8*, 235–237.

Fujisaki, H., and Kawashima, T. On the modes and mechanisms of speech perception. In *Annual report of the Engineering Research Institute*. Vol. 28. Tokyo: Faculty of Engineering, University of Tokyo, 1969, pp. 67–73.

Ganong, W. F. An experiment of "phonetic adaptation." In *Quarterly progress report Research Laboratory of Electronics*. No. 116 Cambridge, Mass.: MIT, 1975, pp. 206–210.

Georgeson, M. A. Spatial frequency of a visual tilt illusion. *Nature*, 1973, *245*, 43–45.

Georgeson, M. A. Psychophysical hallucinations of orientation and spatial frequency. *Perception*, 1976, *5*, 99–111.

Gibson, J. J. Adaptation aftereffect and contrast in the perception of curved lines. *Journal of Experimental Psychology*, 1933, *16*, 1–31.

Gibson, J. J. Adaptation and negative aftereffect. *Psychological Review*, 1937, *44*, 222–244.

Gibson, J. J., and Radner, M. Adaptation, aftereffect and contrast in the perception of tilted lines. I. Quantitative studies. *Journal of Experimental Psychology*, 1937, *20*, 453–467.

Gilinsky, A. S. Masking of contour-detectors in the human visual system. *Psychonomic Science*, 1967, *8*, 395–396.

Gilinsky, A. S. Orientation-specific effects of patterns of adapting light on visual acuity. *Journal of the Optical Society of America*, 1968, *58*, 13–18.

Gilinsky, A. S., and Doherty, R. S. Interocular transfer of orientational effects. *Science*, 1969, *164*, 454–455.

Gilinsky, A. S., and Mayo, T. H. Inhibitory effects of orientational adaptation. *Journal of the Optical Society of America*, 1971, *61*, 1710–1714.

Goldman, S. *Frequency analysis, modulation and noise*. New York: Dover Publications, 1967.

Goldstein, L. M., and Lackner, J. R. Alterations of the phonetic coding of speech sounds during repetition. *Cognition*, 1974, *2*, 279–297.

Graham, C. H., and Brown, J. L. Color contrast and color appearances: Brightness constancy and color constancy. In C. H. Graham (Ed.), *Vision and visual perception*. New York: Wiley, 1965, pp. 452–478.

Graham, N., and Nachmias, J. Detection of grating patterns containing two spatial frequencies: A comparison of single-channel and multiple-channel models. *Vision Research*, 1971, *11*, 251–259.

Green, M., Corwin, T., and Zemon, V. A comparison of Fourier analysis and feature analysis in pattern-specific color aftereffects. *Science*, 1976, *192*, 147–148.

Gregory, R. L. Do we need cognitive concepts? In M. S. Gazzaniga and C. Blakemore (Eds.), *Handbook of psychobiology*. New York: Academic Press, 1975, pp. 607–628.

Harris, C. S. Retinal localization of orientation-specific color aftereffects. Paper presented to the meeting of the Optical Society of America, San Diego, 1969.

Harris, C. S. Effect of viewing distance on a color aftereffect specific to spatial frequency. Paper presented to the meeting of the Psychonomic Society, San Antonio, 1970.

Harris, C. S. Orientation-specific color aftereffects dependent on retinal spatial frequency, rather than on stripe width. Paper presented to the meeting of the Optical Society of America, Tucson, 1971.

Harris, C. S. Color adaptation dependent on contours but not on orientation. Paper presented to the meeting of the Association for Research in Vision and Ophthalmology, Sarasota, Fla., 1972.

Harris, C. S., and Barkow, B. Color/white grids produce weaker orientation-specific color aftereffects than do color/black grids. Paper presented to the meeting of the Psychonomomic Society, St. Louis, 1969.

Harris, C. S., and Gibson, A. R. Is orientation-specific color adaptation in human vision due to edge detectors, afterimages, or "dipoles"? *Science*, 1968, *162*, 1506–1507.

Held, R., and Shattuck, S. R. Color and edge-sensitive channels in the human visual system: Tuning for orientation. *Science*, 1971, *174*, 314–316.

Hepler, N. Color: A motion-contingent aftereffect. *Science*, 1968, *162*, 376–377.

Hillenbrand, J. M. Intensity and repetition effects on selective adaptation to speech. In *Research on speech perception, progress report, No. 2*. Bloomington, Ind.: Department of Psychology, Indiana University, 1975, pp. 57–137.

Hirsch, J., and Murch, G. M. Variation in hue of a contour-contingent aftereffect due to color adaptation during inspection of the stimulus patterns. *Perception and Psychophysics*, 1972, *11*, 406–408.

Houlihan, K., and Sekuler, R. W. Contour interactions in visual masking. *Journal of Experimental Psychology*, 1968, *77*, 281–285.

Hoy, R. R., and Paul, R. C. Genetic control of song specificity in crickets. *Science*, 1973, *180*, 82–83.

Hubel, D. H., and Wiesel, T. N. Receptive fields of single neurones in the cat's striate cortex. *Journal of Physiology*, 1959, *148*, 574–591.

Hubel, D. H., and Wiesel, T. N. Receptive fields, binocular interaction and functional architecture in the cat's visual cortex. *Journal of Physiology*, 1962, *160*, 106–154.

Hubel, D. H., and Wiesel, T. N. Receptive fields and functional architecture in two non-striate visual areas (18 and 19) of the cat. *Journal of Neurophysiology*, 1965, *28*, 229–289.

Hubel, D. H., and Wiesel, T. N. Receptive fields and functional architecture of monkey striate cortex. *Journal of Physiology*, 1968, *195*, 215–243.

Jones, P. D., and Holding, D. H. Extremely long-term persistence of the McCollough effect. *Journal of Experimental Psychology: Human Perception and Performance*, 1975, *1*, 323–327.

Julesz, B., and Miller, J. E. Independent spatial-frequency-tuned channels in binocular fusion and rivalry. *Perception*, 1975, *4*, 125–143.

Kulikowski, J. J., and Tolhurst, D. J. Psychophysical evidence for sustained and transient detectors in human vision. *Journal of Physiology*, 1973, *232*, 149–162.

Kulikowski, J. J., Abadi, R., and King-Smith, P. E. Orientational selectivity of grating and line detectors in human vision. *Vision Research*, 1973, *13*, 1479–1486.

Lackner, J. R., and Goldstein, L. M. The psychological representation of speech sounds. *Quarterly Journal of Experimental Psychology*, 1975, *27*, 173–185.

Lackner, J. R., Tuller, B., and Goldstein, L. M. Further observations on the psychological reality of speech sounds. Unpublished manuscript, 1976.

Lasky, R. E., Syrdal-Lasky, A., and Klein, R. E. VOT discrimination by four to six and a half month old infants from Spanish environments. *Journal of Experimental Child Psychology*, 1975, *20*, 215–225.

Leppmann, P. K. Spatial frequency dependent chromatic after-effects. *Nature,* 1973, *242,* 411–412.

Lettvin, J. Y., Maturana, H. R., McColloch, W. S., and Pitts, W. H. What the frog's eye tells the frog's brain. *Proceedings of the Institute of Radio Engineers (N.Y.),* 1959, *47,* 1940–1951.

Lettvin, J. Y., Maturana, H. R., Pitts, W. H., and McColloch, W. S. Two remarks on the visual system of the frog. In W. A. Rosenblith (Ed.), *Sensory communication.* Cambridge, Mass.: MIT Press, 1961.

Levinson, E., and Sekuler, R. The independence of channels in human vision selective for direction of movement. *Journal of Physiology,* 1975, *250,* 347–366.

Liberman, A. M., Harris, K.S., Hoffman, H. S., and Griffith, B. C. The discrimination of speech sounds within and across phoneme boundaries. *Journal of Experimental Psychology,* 1957, *54,* 358–368.

Lieberman, P. Towards a unified phonetic theory. *Linguistic Inquiry,* 1970, *1,* 307–322.

Lovegrove, W. J., and Over, R. Color adaptation of spatial frequency detectors in the human visual system. *Science,* 1972, *176,* 541–543.

Lovegrove, W. J., and Over, R. Colour selectivity in orientation masking and aftereffect. *Vision Research,* 1973, *13,* 895–902.

Lovegrove, W. J., Over, R., and Broerse, J. Colour selectivity in motion after-effect. *Nature,* 1972, *238,* 334–335.

Lu, C., and Fender, D. H. The interaction of color and luminance in stereoscopic vision. *Investigative Ophthalmology,* 1972, *11,* 482–490.

MacKay, D. M., and MacKay, V. The time course of the McCollough effect and its physiological implications. *Journal of Physiology,* 1973a, *237,* 38–39P.

MacKay, D.M.., and MacKay, V. Orientation-sensitive after-effects of dichoptically presented colour and form. *Nature,* 1973b, *242,* 477–479.

MacKay, D. M., and MacKay, V. Do curvature-contingent chromatic aftereffects require "detectors for curvature"? *Vision Research,* 1974, *14,* 1285–1287.

MacKay, D. M., and MacKay, V. What causes decay of pattern-continent chromatic aftereffects? Vision Research, 1975a, *15,* 462–464.

MacKay, D. M., and MacKay, V. Dichoptic induction of McCollough-type effects. *Quarterly Journal of Experimental Psychology,* 1975b, *27,* 225–233.

Maffei, L., and Campbell, F. W. Neurophysiological localization of the vertical and horizontal visual coordinates in man. *Science,* 1970, *167,* 386–387.

Maffei, L., and Fiorentini, A. Processes of synthesis in visual perception. *Nature,* 1972, *240,* 479–481.

Maffei, L., and Fiorentini, A. The visual cortex as a spatial frequency analyzer. *Vision Research,* 1973, *13,* 1255–1267.

Maffei, L., Fiorentini, A., and Bisti, S. Neural correlate of perceptual adaptation to gratings. *Science,* 1973, *182,* 1036–1038.

Mansfield, R. J. W. Neural basis of orientation perception in primate vision. *Science,* 1974, *186,* 1133–1135.

Masland, R. H., Visual motion perception: Experimental modification. *Science,* 1969, *165,* 819–821.

Maudarbocus, A. Y., and Ruddock, K. H. The influence of wavelength on visual adaptation to spatially periodic stimuli. *Vision Research,* 1973, *13,* 993–998.

Maudarbocus, A. Y., and Ruddock, K. H. Comments on "Adaptation to pairs of coloured gratings: Inhibition between color-specific spatial detectors in the human visual system?" by C. R. Sharpe. *Vision Research,* 1974, *14,* 1485–1487.

May, J. G. Chromatic adaptation of orientation- and size-specific visual processes in man. *Vision Research,* 1972, *12,* 1509–1517.

May, J. G., and Matteson, H. H. Spatial frequency-contingent color aftereffects. *Science,* 1976, *192,* 145–147.

May, J. G., Leftwich, D. A., and Aptaker, P. Evoked potential correlates of adaptation to wavelength and orientation. *Vision Research*, 1974, *14*, 143–146.

Mayhew, J. E. W. Directional asymmetry in the duration of simple movement aftereffects produced by movement aftereffects contingent on colour. *Perception*, 1972, *1*, 453–457.

Mayhew, J. E. W. After-effects of movement contingent on direction of gaze. *Vision Research*, 1973a, *13*, 877–880.

Mayhew, J. E. W. Luminance thresholds for motion contingent on colour. *Perception*, 1973b, *2*, 41–51.

Mayhew, J. E. W. Nulling the movement aftereffect: Evidence for pattern specificity. *Perception*, 1974, *3*, 267–274.

Mayhew, J. E. W. The effect of stationary patterns on adaptation for movement: Evidence for inhibitory interaction. *Perception*, 1975, *4*, 311–329.

Mayhew, J. E. W., and Anstis, S. M. Movement aftereffects contingent on color, intensity, and pattern. *Perception and Psychophysics*, 1972, *12*, 77–85.

McCollough, C. Color adaptation of edge-detectors in the human visual system. *Science*, 1965, *149*, 1115–1116.

McNabb, S. D. Must the output of the phonetic detector be binary? In *Research on speech perception, progress report, No. 2*. Bloomington, Ind.: Department of Psychology, Indiana University, 1975, pp. 166–179.

Mikaelian, H. H. Plasticity of orientation specific chomatic aftereffects. *Vision Research*, 1976, *16*, 459–462.

Miller, J. L. Properties of feature detectors for speech: Evidence from the effects of selective adaptation on dichotic listening. *Perception and Psychophysics*, 1975, *18*, 389–397.

Miller, J. L. Properties of feature detectors for VOT. Paper presented to the meeting of the Acoustical Society of America, Washington, D.C., 1976.

Miller, J. L., and Eimas, P. D. Studies on the selective tuning of feature detectors for speech. *Journal of Phonetics*, 1976, *4*, 119–127.

Miller, J. L., and Eimas, P. D. Studies on the perception of place and manner of articulation: A comparison of the labial-alveolar and nasal-stop distinctions. *Journal of the Acoustical Society of America*, 1977, *61*, 835–845.

Morse, P. A., Kass, J. E., and Turkienicz, R. Selective adaptation of vowels. *Perception and Psychophysics*, 1976, *19*, 137–143.

Movshon, J. A., and Blakemore, C. Orientation specificity and spatial selectivity in human vision. *Perception*, 1973, *2*, 53–60.

Murch, G. M. Size judgments of McCollough afterimages. *Journal of Experimental Psychology*, 1969, *81*, 44–48.

Murch, G. M. Binocular relationships in a size and color orientation specific aftereffect. *Journal of Experimental Psychology*, 1972, *93*, 30–34.

Murch, G. M. Color contingent motion aftereffects: Single or multiple levels of processing? *Vision Research*, 1974, *14*, 1181–1184.

Murch, G. M., and Hirsch, J. The McCollough effect created by complementary afterimages. *American Journal of Psychology*, 1972, *85*, 241–247.

Neisser, U. *Cognitive psychology*. New York: Appleton-Century-Crofts, 1966.

Nelson, P. G., Eruklar, S. D., and Bryan, S. S. Responses of units of the inferior colliculus to time-varying acoustic stimuli. *Journal of Neurophysiology*, 1966, *29*, 834–860.

Over, R. Comparison of normalization theory and neural enhancement of negative aftereffects. *Psychological Bulletin*, 1971, *75*, 225–243.

Over, R., and Wenderoth, P. Is spatial masking selective to wavelength? *Vision Research*, 1974, *14*, 157–158.

Over, R., Long, N., and Lovegrove, W. Absence of binocular interaction between spatial and color attributes of visual stimuli. *Perception and Psychophysics*, 1973, *13*, 534–540.

Pantle, A., and Sekuler, R. Size detecting mechanisms in human vision. *Science*, 1968a, *162*, 1146–1148.

Pantle, A. J., and Sekuler, R. W. Velocity-sensitive elements in human vision: Initial psychophysical evidence. *Vision Research*, 1968b, 7, 445–450.

Pantle, A., and Sekuler, R. Contrast response of human visual mechanisms sensitive to orientation and direction of motion. *Vision Research*, 1969, 9, 397–406.

Parker, D. M. Contrast and size variables and the tilt aftereffect. *Quarterly Journal of Experimental Psychology*, 1972, 24, 1–7.

Pettigrew, J. D., Nikara, T., and Bishop, P. O. Responses to moving slits of single lines in the striate cortex. *Experimental Brain Research*, 1968, 6, 373–390.

Piggins, D. J., and Leppmann, P. K. Role of retinal image motion in evoking the McCollough effect. *Nature New Biology*, 1973, 245, 255–256.

Pisoni, D. B. Auditory and phonetic memory codes in the discrimination of consonants and vowels. *Perception and Psychophysics*, 1973, 13, 253–260.

Pisoni, D. B., and Tash, J. Reaction times to comparisons within and across phonetic categories. *Perception and Psychophysics*, 1974, 15, 285–290.

Pisoni, D. B., and Tash, J. Auditory property detectors and processing place features in stop consonants. *Perception and Psychophysics*, 1975, 18, 401–408.

Pisoni, D. B., Sawusch, J. R., and Adams, F. T. Simple and contingent adaptation effects in speech perception. In *Research on speech perception, progress report, No. 2*. Bloomington, Ind.: Department of Psychology, Indiana University, 1975; pp. 22–55.

Port, D. K., and Preston, M. Early apical stop production: A voice onset time analysis. *Journal of Phonetics*, 1974, 2, 195–210.

Potts, M. J., and Harris, J. P. Movement aftereffects contingent on the colour or pattern of a stationary surround. *Vision Research*, 1975, 15, 1225–1230.

Ramachandran, V. S., and Sriram, S. Stereopsis generated with Julesz patterns in spite of rivalry imposed by colour filters. *Nature*, 1972, 237, 347–348.

Riggs, L. A. Curvature as a feature of pattern vision. *Science*, 1973, 181, 1070–1072.

Riggs, L. A. Curvature detectors in human vison? *Science*, 1974, 184, 1199–1201.

Riggs, L. A., White, K. D., and Eimas, P.D. Establishment and decay of orientation-contingent aftereffects of color. *Vision Research*, 1974, 16, 535–542.

Sachs, M. B., Nachmias, J., and Robson, J. G., Spatial-frequency channels in human vision. *Journal of the Optical Society of America*, 1971, 61, 1176–1186.

Samuels, A. G. Nasality: A selective adaptation study. Unpublished manuscript, 1975.

Sawusch, J. R. Selective adaptation effects on end-point stimuli. In *Research on speech perception, progress report, No. 2*. Bloomington, Ind.: Department of Psychology, Indiana University, 1975, pp. 139–155.

Sawusch, J. R., and Pisoni, D. B. Category boundaries in speech and nonspeech sounds. Paper presented at the 86th meeting of the Acoustical Society of America, Los Angeles, 1973.

Sawusch, J. R., Pisoni, D. B., and Cutting, J. C. Category boundaries for linguistic and nonlinguistic dimensions of the same stimuli. Paper presented at the 87th meeting of the Acoustical Society of America, New York, 1974.

Sekuler, R. W., Spatial and temporal determinants of visual backward masking. *Journal of Experimental Psychology*, 1965, 70, 401–406.

Sekuler, R. Spatial vision. In M. R. Rosezweig and L. W. Porter (Eds.), *Annual review of psychology*. Palo Alto, Calif.: Annual Reviews, 1974, pp. 195–232.

Sekuler, R. W., and Ganz, L. Aftereffect of seen motion with a stabilized retinal image. *Science*, 1963, 139, 419–420.

Sekuler, R., and Pantle, A. A model for aftereffects of seen movement. *Vision Research*, 1967, 7, 427–439.

Sekuler, R. W., Rubin, E. L., and Cushman, W. H. Selectivities of human visual mechanisms for direction of movement and contour orientation. *Journal of the Optical Society of America*, 1968, 58, 1146–1150.

Sharpe, C. R., and Tolhurst, D. J. The effects of temporal modulation on the orientation channels of the human visual system. *Perception*, 1973, 2, 23–29.

Shattuck, S., and Held, R. Color and edge sensitive channels converge on stereo depth analyzers. *Vision Research*, 1975, *15*, 309–311.

Sigel, C., and Nachmias, J. A re-evaluation of curvature-specific chromatic aftereffects. *Vision Research*, 1975, *15*, 829–836.

Skowbo, D., Timney, B. N., Gentry, T. A., and Morant, R. B. McCollough effects: Experimental findings and theoretical accounts. *Psychological Bulletin* 1975, *82*, 497–510.

Stecher, S., Sigel, C., and Lange, R. V. Composite adaptation and spatial frequency interactions. *Vision Research*, 1973a, *13*, 2527–2531.

Stecher, S., Sigel, C., and Lange, R. V. Spatial frequency channels in human vision and the threshold for adaptation. *Vision Research*, 1973b, *13*, 1691–1700.

Stevens, K. N. The quantal nature of speech: Evidence from articulatory-acoustic data. In E. E. David, Jr., and P. B. Denes (Eds.), *Human communication: A unified view*. New York: McGraw-Hill, 1972, pp. 51–66.

Stevens, K. N. The potential role of property detectors in the perception of consonants. Paper presented at Symposium on Auditory Analysis and Perception of Speech, Leningrad, USSR, 1973.

Stromeyer, C. F., III. Further studies of the McCollough effect. *Perception and Psychophysics*, 1969, *6*, 105–110.

Stromeyer, C. F., III. McCollough effect analogs of two-color projections. *Vision Research*, 1971, *11*, 969–978.

Stromeyer, C. F., III. Contour-contingent color aftereffects: Retinal area specificity. *American Journal of Psychology*, 1972a, *85*, 227–234.

Stromeyer, C. F., III. Edge-contingent color after-effects: Spatial frequency specificity. *Vision Research*, 1972b, *12*, 717–733.

Stromeyer, C. F., III. Curvature detectors in human vision? *Science*, 1974a, *184*, 1199–1201.

Stromeyer, C. F., III. Form-specific colour after-effects in scoptic illumination. *Nature*, 1974b, *250*, 266–268.

Stromeyer, C. F., III. Form-color aftereffects in human vision. In R. Held, H. Leibowitz, and H. L. Teuber, (Eds.), *Handbook of sensory physiology: perception*. Berlin: Springer-Verlag, in press.

Stromeyer, C. F., and Julesz, B. Spatial-frequency masking in vision: Critical bands and spread of masking. *Journal of the Optical Society of America*, 1972, *62*, 1221–1232.

Stromeyer, C. F., III, and Mansfield, J. W. Colored aftereffects produced with moving edges. *Perception and Psychophysics*, 1970, *7*, 108–114.

Stromeyer, C. F., III, Lange, A. F., and Ganz, L. Spatial frequency phase effects in human vision. *Vision Research*, 1973, *13*, 2345–2360.

Studdert-Kennedy, M. The perception of speech. In T. A. Sebeok (Ed.), *Current trends in linguistics*. The Hague: Mouton, 1974.

Studdert-Kennedy, M., and Shankweiler, D. Hemispheric specialization for speech perception. *Journal of the Acoustical Society of America*, 1970, *48*, 579–594.

Sullivan, G. D., Georgeson, M. A., and Oatley, K. Channels for spatial frequency and the detection of single bars by the human visual system. *Vision Research*, 1972, *12*, 383–394.

Tartter, V. C., and Eimas, P. D. The role of auditory feature detectors in the perception of speech. *Perception and Psychophysics*, 1975, *18*, 293–298.

Teft, L. W., and Clark, F. T. The effects of stimulus density on orientation specific aftereffects of color adaptation. *Psychonomic Science*, 1968, *11*, 265–266.

Timney, B. N., Gentry, T. A., Skowbo, D., and Morant, R. B. Threshold elevation following adaptation to coloured gratings. *Vision Research*, 1976, *16*, 601–607.

Tolhurst, D. J. Adaptation to square-wave gratings: Inhibition between spatial frequency channels in the human visual system. *Journal of Physiology*, 1972, *226*, 231–248.

Tolhurst, D. J. Separate channels for the analysis of shape and the movement of a moving visual stimulus. *Journal of Physiology*, 1973, *231*, 385–402.

Tyler, C. W. Stereoscopic tilt and size aftereffects. *Perception*, 1975, *4*, 187–192.

Uhlarik, J. J., and Osgood, A. G. The role of some spatial parameters of gratings on the Mc-Collough effect. *Perception and Psychophysics*, 1974, *15*, 524–528.

Uttal, W. B. The psychobiological silly season—or—what happens when neurophysiological data become psychological theories. *Journal of General Psychology*, 1971, *84*, 151–166.

Verbrugge, R. R., and Liberman, A. M. Context-conditioned adaptation of liquids and their third-formant components. Paper presented at the meetings of the Acoustical Society of America, Austin, Tex., April 1975.

Virsu, V., and Haapasalo, S. Relationships between channels for colour and spatial frequency in human vision. *Perception*, 1973, *2*, 31–40.

Walker, J. T. A texture-contingent visual motion aftereffect. *Psychonomic Science*, 1972, *28*, 333–335.

Ware, C., and Mitchell, D. E. The spatial selectivity of the tilt aftereffect. *Vision Research*, 1974, *14*, 735–737.

Warren, R. M. Verbal transformation effect and auditory perceptual mechanisms. *Psychological Bulletin*, 1968, *70*, 261–270.

Weisstein, N. Beyond the yellow-volkswagen detector and the grandmother cell: A general strategy for the exploration of operations in human pattern recognition. In R. L. Solso (Ed.), *Contemporary issues in cognitive psychology: The Loyola symposium*. Washington, D.C.: V. H. Winston, 1973, pp. 17–51.

Werner, G. Neural information processing with stimulus feature extractors. In F. O. Schmitt and F. G. Worden (Eds.), *The neurosciences: Third study program*. Cambridge, Mass.: MIT Press, 1974, pp. 171–183.

White, K. D. Luminance as a parameter in establishment and testing of the McCollough effect. *Vision Research*, 1976, *16*, 297–302.

White, K. D., and Ellis, S. R. McCollough effect: Pattern alternation rate influences establishment. Paper presented to the meeting of the Optical Society of America, Boston, 1975.

White, K. D., and Riggs, L. A. Angle-contingent color aftereffects. *Vision Research*, 1974, *14*, 1147–1154.

Winter, P., and Funkenstein, H. H. The effect of species-specific vocalization on the discharge of auditory cortical cells in the awake squirrel monkey (*Saimiri sciureus*). *Experimental Brain Research*, 1973, *18*, 489–504.

Wolf, C. G. A recognition masking study of consonant processing. *Perception and Psychophysics*, 1976, *19*, 35–46.

Wollberg, Z., and Newman, J. D. Auditory cortex of squirrel monkey: Response patterns of single cells to species-specific vocalizations. *Science*, 1972, *175*, 212–214.

Wyatt, H. J. Singly and doubly contingent after-effects involving color, orientation and spatial frequency. *Vision Research*, 1974, *14*, 1185–1193.

11

Development of Form Perception in Repeated Brief Exposures to Visual Stimuli

JOHN UHLARIK AND RICHARD JOHNSON

1. Introduction

Many contemporary accounts of visual pattern perception hold that visual form is analyzed in terms of processes whereby specific features are extracted and compared to representations of previously experienced visual forms stored in memory. Two issues arising from this kind of information processing approach are (1) the nature of the features of the visual forms stored or encoded in memory and (2) the nature of the processes by which the stored information interacts with incoming information.

A number of different methodologies produce a class of experimental results known as "fragmentation effects" which may prove useful in understanding these two issues. Fragmentation effects occur under certain experimental conditions when a visual form is seen to break up into smaller elements or components of the original stimulus. Viewing a stabilized retinal image is an example of an experimental technique which results in fragmentation effects. A stabilized image involves the presentation of a visual form in a manner whereby eye movements can play no role regarding the retinal position of the image of the form. In addition to the scanning and fixating functions of eye movements,

JOHN UHLARIK • Department of Psychology, Kansas State University, Manhattan, Kansas 66502.   RICHARD JOHNSON • U.S. Army Research Institute for the Behavioral and Social Sciences, Alexandria, Virginia 22333.

very small eye movements provide a continuously changing pattern of stimulation on retinal receptors. This changing pattern of stimulation is necessary for normal vision, as demonstrated by the disappearance of visual forms presented as stabilized retinal images (e.g., Pritchard, 1961). Furthermore, it is typically found that a stabilized image fades and regenerates in a nonrandom fashion (e.g., Pritchard, 1961). These fragmentation effects have been observed using a variety of procedures which produce stabilized retinal images such as scleral contact lenses, prolonged afterimages, and steady fixation of low-luminance figures (e.g., MacKinnon, Forde, and Piggins, 1969). Although the processes responsible for fragmentation are not agreed upon, interpretation of such results by many investigators centers around the notion that the orderly manner in which forms fragment reveals some hierarchical processing mechanism for visual forms (cf. Heckenmueller, 1965).

Cheatham (1952) noticed a similar type of fragmentation of visual forms while studying masking of visual forms by light flashes. In general, masking is the reduction in effectiveness of a visual stimulus (target) by the presentation of another stimulus (mask) which either precedes or follows the presentation of the target stimulus. As the mask became less effective with increases in the interval between the target and mask, his subjects typically reported parts of the target figures (e.g., square or triangle) before the complete figure was reported. Sides of the figures appeared before any angle between the lines developed. Cheatham did not give a detailed analysis of the fragments reported by his subjects since he was primarily concerned with masking effects. However, his description of fragments reported by his subjects is generally consistent with those reported for viewing stabilized retinal images.

More recently, Evans (1968) and Johnson and Uhlarik (1974) have utilized a somewhat different technique which also yields fragmentation effects similar to those described above. Basically, this effect obtains when a visual stimulus is repeatedly presented for brief exposures at a constant duration. The duration is typically selected such that on the initial exposure the observer is unaware of any aspect of the stimulus. With well-spaced repeated presentations, parts of the stimulus are reported. Gradually these fragments become more complex. Eventually the entire stimulus is recognized on every trial even though the luminance and exposure duration are the same as for the initial trials when nothing was reported. Thus the repetition effect consists of improvement in the identification of the same visual stimulus as the result of repeated observations.

The sequential construction of the pattern of fragments in the studies conducted by Evans and by Johnson and Uhlarik were quite similar in many respects to the fragmentation effects obtained using other techniques. However, it should be noted that the pattern of fragmentation is generally in the opposite direction for the repetition effect relative to the pattern obtained using stabilized retinal images, viewing of prolonged afterimages, and conditions of steady fixation. Thus, the sequence of fragments in the repetition effect might be more appropriately referred to as "construction" rather than fragmentation since even though the stimulus is always present, only parts are perceived prior to correct identification. For the other kinds of conditions the percept of the initial form is clear and complete and then "breaks up" or fragments into smaller parts of the original form and eventually disappears completely. However, the overall qualitative and quantitative similarity of the results produced by these various experimental techniques suggests a pattern of feature extraction which shows systematic organization. It is to be hoped that this organization is indicative of processes that underlie the perception of form.

2. Theoretical Background

2.1. Microgenetic Theory

Microgenetic theory represents an early interest in sequential processes in perception and cognition. The term "microgenesis" was introduced by Werner (1956) as an approximate translation of the German word *Aktualgenese*. Gestalt psychologist Friedrich Sander initially used *Aktualgenese* to refer to the fact that "the transition from maximally unfavorable to normal circumstances give[s] rise to a whole series of sense experiences, whereby the evolution of configurations is exhibited in logical order" (1930, p. 193). Sander's translation of *Aktualgenese* was "genetic realization" and he further stated that perceptual constructs during the configurative process are "by no means mere imperfect or vague versions of the final figure which appear under maximally favorable conditions, but characteristic metamorphoses with qualitative individuality, 'preformulations' (*Vorgestalten*)" (p. 193).

The microgenetic paradigm consisted of successive presentations of a stimulus under conditions of increasing objective clarity. This is different from procedures employed in contemporary research on the repetition effect, in which factors affecting objective clarity are typically held constant on successive exposures. In the microgenetic approach objective clarity was manipulated by presenting visual stimuli, for example, very briefly, under low levels of illumination, or in periphereal vision. Gradually, one of these parameters was altered to produce conditions of increasing (or decreasing) objective clarity on successive exposures. This was considered to be the experimental homologue of the near-instantaneous processes involved in normal perception and also of the ontogenetic stages involved in the initial organization of perceptual development. A large body of research conducted in both Germany and the United States found evidence that the perceptual responses to repeated presentations of the same stimulus consisted of a series of conceptually distinct stages (see

Flavell and Draguns, 1957, for an extensive review of this literature). These studies typically report that initially the percept is diffuse and undifferentiated. In the next stage, figure-ground relationships merge. In the next stage, contour and inner contents of the stimulus are differentiated; however, the configurations of this *Vorgestalt,* or *Pregestalt,* are still tentative and labile. In the final stage, the processes of gestalt formulation become complete. The reverse order of the sequence of stages obtains when the stimulus is presented under conditions of decreasing objective clarity.

According to Werner's (1961) theory of perceptual learning and development, the fundamental law of development was the increase of differentiation and hierarchical integration. It should be noted that although the microgenetic findings are discussed in terms of stages, they are usually interpreted as implying continuous processes of growth rather than qualitatively different discrete operations being performed on the percept. It is also interesting to note that the microgenetic studies report that perception begins with *whole* percepts which gradually become sharpened and internally differentiated, whereas incomplete percepts, or fragments of the complete stimulus, are initially reported with the repetition effect discussed previously. There could be several reasons for this apparent disparity of empirical findings. For example, the operations for measuring and evaluating the perceptual response were typically informal in microgenetic research. Often the phenomenal verbal (anecdotal) descriptions by the observers were the only data. In addition, the kinds of stimuli employed in the microgenetic investigations were typically much more complex than the relatively simple geometric form, Landolt rings, and graphemes used in the more recent research. Also, microgenetic studies were usually based on a small number of observers who were not experimentally naive, and hence the general pattern of results could have been in part due to experimenter and/or subject expectations. This last issue will be dealt with in greater detail in subsequent sections.

Flavell and Draguns (1957) have criticized microgenetic theory on theoretical grounds. Specifically they state that "the abstractness, looseness of logical structure, and general semantic impression which characterizes present-day microgenetic theory may be in part responsible for the ease with which it seems to subsume so many diverse cognitive phenomena" (p. 212). Thus, it seems that the major contribution of this approach was early interest in temporal processes which later combined with other orientations to provide the foundation and impetus for what is currently referred to as information-processing approaches to visual perception (see Haber, 1969, for further discussion of the characteristics of this approach). In the following sections, research concerned with the repetition effect will be reviewed with an emphasis on how the development of percepts from repeated brief exposures to stimulation provides insight regarding the nature of information processing underlying visual form perception.

2.2. Clarity Hypothesis and Hebbian Cell Assemblies

Haber and his associates have reported several studies over the last 10 years which indicate that repeated exposures of word stimuli increase the clarity of the percept of the word presented. Haber and Hershenson (1965) presented subjects with English words for 25 exposures while holding duration and luminance constant. The observer's task was to report letters of the words presented. On the first few trials only parts or letters of the words were seen. However, after several presentations the entire word was correctly reported. According to Haber and Hershenson (1965), "repeated exposures of a word at constant duration does contribute to the growth of the phenomenal experience of the word" (p. 45). Haber reported that the percept of the word that developed after repeated exposures was not hazy, fuzzy, or a guess, but assumed a very clear status. Hence, he proposed that the phenomenal clarity of the percept increases as a function of repetition. Haber presented his data in terms of a growth function that plotted the probability of reporting the entire word as a function of repeated exposures. The probability rose quite sharply over the first five exposures, and then gradually tapered off to an asymptotic level representing less than perfect performance. Haber concluded on an empirical basis that continued exposures after the asymptote was reached were unlikely to produce further increases in identifiability.

In order to evaluate the possibility that his subjects were making better guesses as to what word was being presented from letters previously reported, subjects in a second study (Haber, 1965) were given prior knowledge of the words to be presented. In addition, sets of rare and frequent words were used as stimuli. Haber found a small but significant difference in the probability of perception of frequent and rare words with no prior knowledge. The high-frequency words had a slightly greater overall probability of identification than the rare words. However, the difference between rare and frequent words disappeared with prior knowledge. The shape of the growth function remained the same as in the no prior knowledge condition, although the initial probabilities of reporting the words presented were somewhat higher than was the case when subjects were not given prior knowledge. Haber concluded that response processes, or biases, may affect the initial probability of perceiving a word, but that these factors do not affect the *rate* in growth of clarity over repeated exposures. Haber felt that these findings were consistent with an Hebbian cell assembly interpretation. A cell assembly, described by Hebb (1949), is the mechanism of form integration and is a collection of interconnected neurons which respond to a given pattern of visual stimulation. These cell assemblies grow by lowering synaptic resistance between cells and were postulated to be formed as a function of repeated experience with objects in the visual world. If one assumes that the effect of repeated exposures is the formation of new cell assemblies and/or the activation of previously existing cell assemblies, the cell assemblies for frequent words would be a priori better established than those for rare words in the no knowledge condition. However, in the prior knowledge condition, the cell assemblies for both rare and frequent words would be expected to be equally salient. Thus, the initial activation of the appropriate cell assembly could account for the initial differences in recognition probability of rare and frequent words. Haber also assumed that the activation of the cell assembly as a result of repeated exposures takes place at a constant rate, and thus accounted for the relative constancy of the shape of the growth function for all conditions.

Haber, Standing, and Boss (1970) investigated the possibility that "sensory enhancement" could be a factor accounting for the repetition effect. They presented single letters that varied from exposure to exposure in typeface style, size, and retinal position. No effect of repeated exposures would be expected if sensory enhancement were responsible for the effect of repetitions, since sensory summation would require the same stimulus to be repeatedly presented in the same retinal position. In addition, it is unlikely that luminance summation is responsible for the repetition effect. Sensory facilitation due to luminance summation is the addition of stimulus energy on successive exposures which produces the net effect of a higher energy stimulus. The interexposure interval in studies producing the repetition effect is on the order of 5–10 sec, which is far longer than the 100 msec over which luminance summation occurs. Haber *et al.* found the repetition effect for all conditions of their study and concluded that these findings also were consistent with a cell assembly interpretation, since cell assemblies are assumed to be responsive to transformations of a similar visual form (i.e., the upper- and lowercase letters) and different retinal location (Hebb, 1949).

In order to ascertain whether phenomenal clarity increases over repeated exposures, Standing, Sell, Boss, and Haber (1970) obtained subjective ratings of clarity for five exposures of single letters. In addition, the observers were asked to subvocalize (or visualize) either the same or a different letter than the one to be presented. It was found that subvocalizing a different letter retarded the rated clarity of the exposures, as compared to subvocalizing the same letter as the one presented. However, in all cases the rated clarity increased over the five exposures. Standing *et al.* argued that the imagery conditions affected the salience of the appropriate cell assembly but not its growth in clarity.

In summary, Haber and his co-workers feel that a sensory facilitation effect cannot account for the repetition effect. Rather, they maintain that the percept of stimuli presented for repeated exposures grows in phenomenal clarity as a result of a process analogous to the development and activation of Hebbian cell assemblies. It should be noted that Haber (1969) is cautious to point out that although his data are consistent with a Hebbian interpretation, they do not confirm the cell assembly account of the repetition effect.

2.3. Decision-Making Models

Doherty and Keeley (1972) took issue with Haber's clarity interpretation of the repetition effect. While not questioning the validity of the repetition effect, Doherty and Keeley felt that increases in phenomenal clarity were not responsible for the effect. Rather, they maintained that the subjects in Haber's studies were highly susceptible to committing the "stimulus error" in that they may have been trying to report what was "out there" rather than the contents of their own immediate experience. According to Doherty and Keeley, this would lead to the development of a problem-solving set on the part of the subjects. Doherty and Keeley hold that the subjects in a repeated exposures situation aggregate or combine information obtained on successive observations which are perceptually independent. Hence, they maintain that a direct measure of clarity would show no systematic change as a function of repeated observations. On the other hand, Haber would maintain that clarity increases as a function of number of repetitions. Standing, Sell, Boss, and Haber (1970) showed that *rated* clarity did, in fact, increase as a function of repetitions. However, Doherty and Keeley argue that rated clarity is inextricably confounded with increasing certainty in this situation. Doherty, Keeley, and Norton (1971) presented observers with multiple presentations of Landolt rings and required them to draw what they saw on each exposure. A second set of subjects was then asked to identify the gap position from the drawings of the first group of subjects. Doherty *et al.* were attempting to determine if the decisions of the second group of subjects were more accurate based on four-exposure drawings than one-exposure drawings. If the four-exposure drawings were "clearer" than the one-exposure drawings, the accuracy of the judgments of the second set of subjects should have increased as a function of the exposure order of the drawings. Doherty and his co-workers found this not to be the case and considered this evidence to be sufficient to reject the clarity hypothesis.

In another attempt to get directly at the issue regarding the growth of phenomenal clarity, Weintraub and McNulty (1973) had observers independently rate clarity and identifiability of nonsense figures. Nonsense figures were used to preclude the possibility that expectancies could influence clarity ratings for familiar or meaningful figures in that subjects might be reluctant to give a high clarity rating if they saw only a fragment of a familiar figure. Weintraub and McNulty found that both identifiability and rated clarity increased with increasing *objective* clarity and/or stimulus duration. However, repetitions of a pattern of fixed objective clarity and exposure duration produced increases in identifiability but not rated clarity. It was concluded that since there was no concomitant improvement in rated clarity as stimulus identification improved across repetitions, the former could not be the cause of the improvement in the latter.

As an alternative to the clarity interpretation, Keeley and Doherty (1968) discussed several decision-making approaches which they ultimately considered to be inadequate descriptions of the repetition effect. However, Doherty and Keeley (1969) suggested a decision model based on Bayes' rule for the aggregation of independent events. In general, Bayes' rule concerns the effect of gathering evidence (e.g., observations, information) concerning hypotheses of the "true state of nature" in ambiguous situations. A probability is associated with each hypothesis. In addition, these hypotheses can be modified on the basis of experience. Bayes' rule concerns the manner in which these data allow modification of the original (prior) probabilities to new (posterior) probabilities (*cf.* Lee, 1971). Doherty and Keeley presented experimental evidence consistent with the Bayesian model when the stimuli were Landolt rings or graphemes presented for four exposures using a forced choice response (Doherty and Keeley, 1969; Keeley and Doherty, 1971; Keeley, Doherty, and Bachman, 1970).

The studies of Doherty and Keeley differed in several methodological aspects from the studies conducted by Haber and his co-workers and Johnson and Uhlarik (1974). The appropriate set of responses was clearly defined for subjects via the forced choice procedure used by Doherty and Keeley. This procedure required that subjects have, *a priori*, an exhaustively defined response set. This was accomplished by using subjects that were highly practiced in the identification of the alternative Landolt rings. Haber typically used a verbal or written response to letter stimuli. Johnson and Uhlarik obtained an open-ended response by instructing subjects to "draw whatever you saw." No pre-training was given with either procedure. In addition, in the latter procedure subjects were not provided with information that the same stimulus would always be presented. In fact, observers often expressed surprise at the end of the experiment when informed that the same stimulus had been presented on each exposure. Thus, it is doubtful that an exhaustive response set could be defined for this situation, nor was there any way for the subject to determine the size of the alternative set of responses. Furthermore, a great deal of information regarding the nature of the stimulus must be extracted *ad hoc* from the repeated exposures. It appears then that the methodology employed by Doherty and Keeley would enhance the tendency to utilize a decision-making strategy, and would therefore be described by a Bayesian decision-making model.

It should be noted that a clear-cut effect of repetitions obtained in Doherty and Keeley's studies. It is possible, however, that Doherty and Keeley's procedure effectively bypassed some components of the repetition effect. These components may include such factors as "growth in clarity" and/or other processes by which the information provided *a priori* to their subjects must be extracted *ad hoc* in the procedures utilized by Haber and Johnson and Uhlarik. Further research is called for whereby the free response tasks and the forced choice response procedures can be directly compared. Such a procedure would help determine the degree to which the effect of repetitions can be attributed to differences in response requirements which may reflect different levels of information processing.

2.4. Other Accounts of the Repetition Effect

The studies of Haber and Doherty and Keeley have dealt with the repetition effect in the most detail. Three other investigators (Neisser, 1967; Weintraub and McNulty, 1973; Dodwell, 1971) have also been concerned with the effects of repeated exposures. All three accounts have a common feature in that they all conceive of the repetition effect as resulting from the combination or integration of information obtained on previous exposures with incoming information on subsequent exposures. The integration of information takes place in some unspecified memory store. In Neisser's (1967) terms, "a letter or fragment synthesized on an earlier trial can easily be reconstructed on the next one, freeing most of Ss capacities for figural synthesis to work on a different fragment" (p. 125). Weintraub and McNulty's (1973) position is essentially the same as that of Neisser.

Dodwell (1971) has proposed an autocorrelation model of the repetition effect. An autocorrelation is a two-dimensional correlation of spatial overlap of a pattern with respect to itself, over time. Because of eye movements, a retinal image is constantly changing its position on the retina. The spatial overlap or redundancy in this sequence provides correlated information, and perceptual clarity is determined by the degree to which this autocorrelation function is specified. According to Dodwell, brief tachistoscopic exposures do not allow sufficient time for the autocorrelation function to be completed. Partial information for the autocorrelation function is stored and summated on subsequent exposures to account for the increased detectability of stimuli in the repetition effect. Dodwell also states that the autocorrelation function is performed predominantly on the horizontal and vertical dimensions of a pattern, which is consistent with orientation effects which have been reported by Johnson and Uhlarik (1974). Dodwell based his reasoning on the extensive literature showing superiority of horizontally and vertically oriented stimuli in various visual tasks as well as on the existence of orientation specific cortical cells (*cf.* Appelle, 1972). Dodwell's model predicts an asymptotic growth function for the effect of repetitions since the model states that the less completely the autocorrelation function can be specified on the first exposure, the less well it can ever be specified. Indeed, the repetition effect does appear to reach asymptotic levels at recognition performance probabilities of less than unity (e.g., Haber, 1965; Johnson and Uhlarik, 1974), depending on the exposure duration and luminance.

An information starvation hypothesis has been proposed by Evans (1968). Evans argued that, in stabilized image studies, compensation for eye movements retards the flow of information necessary for continuous activation of the recognition system and its perceptual units, but does allow for the formation of percepts of subunits or features of the pattern presented. The tachistoscopic presentation of patterns also reduces the opportunity to extract information from a stimulus form. Johnson and Uhlarik (1974) suggested that this may in part be due to the lack of opportunities to make use of systematic eye movements in the tachistoscopic task, and could therefore also account for the fragments reported by subjects observing repeated brief presentations of visual stimuli. Evans's discussion of the repetition effect is qualitative in nature and does not deal with how information is accumulated over repeated exposures.

More recently, Johnson and Uhlarik (1974) and Johnson (1975) have conducted a series of experiments which led to a model that specifies in some detail how incoming information may be combined with previously stored form information. The subjects in these studies were presented with repeated exposures to random sequences of different stimuli. Although the stimuli were different, they were components of a common figure (*viz.*, an equilateral triangle). Thus, the seven different stimuli consisted of the three line elements of the triangle presented separately, in pairs (the three angles), or as the complete triangle; an eighth stimulus was a blank presentation or "catch trial."

One important question concerned the rate of growth in identifiability when several stimuli were presented, since in previous work only one stimulus was presented in any given sequence. The repetition effect for any individual stimulus was of the same form as was found when a single stimulus was presented on all exposures. That is, the greatest increase in correct identifications occurring over the first 10–12 exposures, with little gain thereafter. Thus, information concerning several different stimuli can be accumulated without altering the growth of the repetition function.

A second aspect of the Johnson and Uhlarik studies concerned the types of error responses (incorrect identifications) reported by the observers. For example, subjects sometimes reported only a single line or angle when the complete triangle was presented. On the other hand, if a single line was presented, observers would sometimes report an angle or the complete triangle. A systematic analysis of these types of error responses resulted in a model of the effect of repetitions that specified a mechanism for the combination of newly extracted and previously stored stimulus information.

A wide range of both traditional and contemporary theories of perceptual learning and development consider that "something" is added to preliminary registration of the environmentally produced stimulation, itself an elementary, meaningless, even punctate affair (see Gibson, 1969, for a review of these theories). For example, the nineteenth-century structuralists had a perceptual theory based on meaningless sensations and the compounding of complex perceptions by some sort of accretion process. Various other theories have espoused the concept that the contribution of the perceiver lies in a variety of mediating processes such as unconscious inferences, hypotheses, probabilistic weighting of cues, attitudes, affect, and response-produced cues. In order to eliminate confusion when discussing the development of form perception, it is necessary to make certain distinctions between concepts such as perception, recognition, and identification. All of these aspects are present in our immediate phenomenal awareness or "perception" of an object, but these different aspects of our experience often are not explicitly differentiated by various theoretical treatments of the development of form perception. According to Rock (1975),

> one must distinguish between the content of phenomenal experience and the functional events that give rise to such experience. Therefore, although we simultaneously perceive a familiar and meaningful object of a given shape, still as regards the origin of these several components of our experience, logical considerations compel us to make certain distinctions. The familiarity of an object, i.e., whether we recognize it or not, is by definition a matter of past experience. Similarly, identification is an outcome of prior learning. But phenomenal shape of an object is not necessarily based on past experience. (p. 335)

Information-processing approaches to perception typically make these distinctions in terms of various stages of processing that are associated with the various functional events. The main component of such a model of the repetition effect proposed by Johnson (1975) and Johnson and Uhlarik (1974) is designated the "integrator," which compares and combines incoming stimulus information which has been extracted from a short-term sensory (iconic) store, with information from previous presentations which has been accumulated in a longer-term secondary store. This kind of model of the repetition effect is conceptually related to the issue of perceptual learning and development in that it involves the integration of newly extracted information from an external stimulus with information that has been previously stored. The integration of this new and stored information can be accomplished in two different ways and determines the phenomenal percept experienced by the observer.

One integration process involves the combination of only those stimulus elements that are common to both the newly extracted and previously stored information. In the case of the components of the equilateral triangle, for example, if the two line elements forming the left oblique angle were in the secondary store and a left oblique line were extracted from the stimulus, the left oblique line would be common to both the stored and incoming information, resulting in the phenomenal perception of a left oblique line. A second integration process involves the formation of a percept by combining all of the newly extracted stimulus elements with all of those previously stored. Using the same example described above for the integration of common elements, the second kind of integration would result in the percept of a left oblique angle. Of course, when there is no information contained in the secondary store the percept would depend exclusively on the incoming information, and hence this second type of integration could account for the first-time perception of novel forms or fragments thereof. In set-theoretical terms the two integrative functions are called "intersection" and "union," respectively, and were used to derive quantitative predictions which fit the data from the Johnson (1975) and Johnson and Uhlarik (1974) studies quite well.

A subsequent masking study (Uhlarik and Johnson, 1976) also obtained results that were consistent with the qualitative properties of the proposed model. This experiment involved backward masking by visual noise. A stimulus is said to be a backward mask if it reduces the effectiveness of a previously presented target stimulus. Backward masking with visual noise is an extremely effective method of reducing form recognition. The reason for this is generally assumed to be that (1) the mask eliminates (or degrades) the representation of the target in the sensory (iconic) store, and/or (2) the mask interrupts the transfer of information from the sensory store to a more permanent (secondary) store. If the proposed integration model is correct, a backward mask should eliminate the repetition effect. The results of the Uhlarik and Johnson (1976) study showed this to be the case. Specifically, a backward mask was most effective in interfering with recognition when the interstimulus interval between the target and mask was between 0 and 25 msec (relative to conditions in which the interstimulus interval was either 50, 100, 150, 200, or 500 msec, and a no mask condition). In addition, the pattern of fragmentation typically found for the repetition effect did not obtain with interstimulus intervals of 0 or 25 msec, whereas a repetition effect did obtain for the other conditions. This finding suggests that the elimination of the repetition effect with a backward mask might be due to the fact that the information usually available in the sensory store is not integrated with that in the secondary store.

3. Summary and Conclusions

In general, the experimental findings regarding the effects of repetitions on the development of a percept indicate that when an initially subthreshold stimulus is presented for repeated observations while exposure parameters are held constant, identifiability of the stimulus increases. In cases where geometric forms are presented, fragments of the pattern are perceived and gradually the entire form is constructed. There is little controversy concerning the validity of the repetition effect; however, there are considerable differences regarding the interpretation of the processes responsible for the effect. It is appropriate to consider the relevance that these different interpretations have concerning the development, or genesis, of form perception. The research reviewed has been mainly concerned with the genesis of form perception in terms of what Flavell and Draguns called "microgenesis." Under normal viewing conditions we might think of our perceptions as immediate. However, when we do not have an adequate stimulus (e.g., very brief duration or low luminance), the complete formation of the percept is blocked. When the adequacy of the stimulus is experimentally manipulated, the nonimmediacy of perception is revealed through the perception of pattern fragments, and hazy or unclear percepts which we do not normally encounter with an adequate stimulus. Thus, in a developmental sense, the repetition effect is dealing with how a percept "develops" from the time the stimulus is presented through the brief period of time which ensues before a complete percept is experienced. The research strategy is to present inadequate stimuli in an attempt to reveal stages of the processing of visual form information as it leads to the development of a well formed percept. Haber (1971) noted that some critics of this approach suggest that the reliance on inadequate stimuli, particularly the extensive use of brief tachistoscopic displays, results in perceptual theories relevant only to viewing the world during a lightning storm! However, these procedures are of fundamental importance for revealing the stages of processing associated with the formation of a percept, and provide an experimental paradigm for examining the processes mediating sensation and perception.

4. References

Appelle, S. Perception and discrimination as a function of stimulus orientation: The "oblique effect" in man and animals. *Psychological Bulletin*, 1972, *78*, 266–278.

Cheatham, P. G. Visual perceptual latency as a function of stimulus brightness and contour shape. *Journal of Experimental Psychology*, 1952, *43*, 369–379.

Dodwell, P. C. On perceptual clarity. *Psychological Review*, 1971, *78*, 275–289.

Doherty, M. E., and Keeley, S. M. A Bayesian prediction of four-look recognition performance from one-look data. *Perception and Psychophysics*, 1969, *5*, 362–364.

Doherty, M. E., and Keeley, S. M. On the identification of repeatedly presented brief visual forms. *Psychological Bulletin*, 1972, *78*, 142–154.

Doherty, M. E., Keeley, S. M., and Norton, G. K. A test of the clarity interpretation of the repetition effect. *Cognitive Psychology*, 1971, *2*, 386–399.

Gibson, E. J. *Principles of perceptual learning and development*. New York: Appleton-Century-Crofts, 1967.

Evans, C. R. Fragmentation of patterns occurring with tachistoscopic presentation. Proceedings IEE/NPL conference on Pattern Recognition, July 1968, pp. 250–263.

Flavell, J. H., and Draguns, J. A microgenetic approach to perception and thought. *Psychological Bulletin*, 1957, *54*, 197–217.

Haber, R. N. Effect of prior knowledge of the stimulus on word recognition processes. *Journal of Experimentalk Psychology*, 1965, *69*, 282–286.

Haber, R. N. Repetition as a determinant of perceptual recognition processes. In R. N. Haber (Ed.), *Information processing approaches to visual perception*. New York: Holt, Rinehart and Winston, 1969.

Haber, R. N. Where are the visions in visual perception? In J. J. Segal (Ed.), *Imagery: Current cognitive approaches*. New York: Academic Press, 1971.

Haber, R. N., and Hershenson, M. Effects of repeated brief exposures on the growth of a percept. *Journal of Experimental Psychology*, 1965, *69*, 40–46.

Haber, R. N., Standing, L., and Boss, J. Effect of position and typeface variation on perceptual clarity. *Psychonomic Science*, 1970, *18*, 91–92.

Hebb, D. O. *The organization of behavior*. New York: Wiley, 1949.

Heckenmueller, E. G. Stabilization of the retinal image: A review of method, effects, and theory. *Psychological Bulletin*, 1965, *63*, 157–169.

Johnson, R. M. The processing of visual form information as a function of repeated brief exposures to visual stimuli. Doctoral dissertation, Kansas State University, 1975. *Dissertation Abstracts International*, 1976, *36*, 4732-B (University Microfilms No. 76-5868).

Johnson, R. M., and Uhlarik, J. J. Fragmentation and identifiability of repeatedly presented brief visual stimuli. *Perception and Psychophysics*, 1974, *15*, 533–538.

Keeley, S. M., and Doherty, M. E. Simultaneous and successive presentations of single-features and multi-featured visual forms: Implications for the parallel processing hypothesis. *Perception and Psychophysics*, 1968, *4*, 296–298.

Keeley, S. M., and Doherty, M. E. A Bayesian aggregation of independent successive visual inputs. *Journal of Experimental Psychology*, 1971, *90*, 300–305.

Keeley, S. M., Doherty, M. E., and Bachman, S. P. A Bayesian prediction of four-look recognition performance from one-look data. II. *Perception and Psychophysics*, 1970, *7*, 218–220.

Lee, W. *Decision theory and human behavior*. New York: Wiley, 1971.

MacKinnon, G. E., Forde, J., and Piggins, D. J. Stabilized images, steadily fixated figures, and prolonged afterimages. *Canadian Journal of Psychology*, 1969, *23*, 184–195.

Neisser, U. *Cognitive psychology*. New York: Appleton-Century-Crofts, 1967.

Pritchard, R. M. Stabilized images on the retina. *Scientific American*, 1961, *204*, 72–78.

Rock, I. *An introduction to perception*. New York: Macmillan, 1975.

Sander, F. Structures, totality of experience, and gestalt. In C. Murchison (Ed.), *Psychologies of 1930*. Worcester, Mass.: Clark University Press, 1930, pp. 188–204.

Standing, L. G., Sales, D., and Haber, R. N. Repetition versus luminance as a determinant of recognition. *Canadian Journal of Psychology*, 1968, *22*, 442–448.

Standing, L., Sell, C., Boss, J., and Haber, R. N. Effect of visualization and subvocalization on perceptual clarity. *Psychonomic Science*, 1970, *18*, 89–90.

Uhlarik, J. J., and Johnson, R. M. *Masking the repetition effect*. Manhattan, Ks.: Kansas State University Psychology Series, HIPI Report No. 76–10, 1976.

Weintraub, D. J., and McNulty, J. A. Clarity versus identifiability of repeatedly flashed patterns. *Journal of Experimental Psychology*, 1973, *99*, 293–305.

Werner, H. Microgenesis and aphasia. *Journal of Abnormal and Social Psychology*, 1956, *52*, 347–353.

Werner, H. *Comparative psychology of mental development* (Rev. ed.). New York: Science Editions, 1961.

12

Stimuli, the Perceiver, and Perception

WILLIAM BEVAN AND SUSAN GAYLORD

1. Introduction

Virtually every boy who has grown up in a cold climate has had the experience of warming his hands after making snowballs by holding them in water from the cold water tap. Nearly everyone who has been ill with a high fever has noted how cool the hand of the examining physician or nurse feels. And certainly everybody has observed that a flashlight which shines brightly at night will appear dim during daylight, if indeed it is seen at all. These experiences are examples of successive thermal contrast and simultaneous brightness contrast, two of the phenomena with which this chapter is concerned. They illustrate the very important fact that the appearance of a stimulus (the water, the hand, the light) depends not only on its physical intensity but also on the intensity of its immediately surrounding area as well as on that of stimuli immediately previously experienced. As the cold hand approaches the temperature of the tap water, the tap water will cease to feel warm. When it equals that of the tap water no temperature sensation will be experienced at all. And if the hand is further warmed by being placed in water from the hot water tap, water from the cold water tap will then feel cold. These changes in experience illustrate two important psychological principles, namely that perception is relative and depends on some psychological referent or base line and that these psychological base lines change with experience over time.

    The purpose of this chapter is to demonstrate how the present or focal stimulus, its background, and the past experience of the observer interact in perception and to do so through the idiom of adaptation-level theory. "Adapta-

WILLIAM BEVAN AND SUSAN GAYLORD • Department of Psychology, Duke University, Durham, North Carolina 27706.

tion level" is Helson's name for the shifting psychological base line and his adaptation-level theory deals with the perceived properties of stimuli as a reflection of the discrepancy between the stimulus and its context, both present and past. In the years since its inception, adaptation-level theory has been widely influential not only in the understanding of perceptual phenomena such as constancy, assimilation, and contrast but also in dealing with phenomena as widely different as reinforcement effects (Bevan and Adamson, 1962), motivation (McClelland, Atkinson, Clark, and Lowell, 1953), and personality and psychopathology (Goldstone and Goldfarb, 1964; Haertzen and Hooks, 1971).

2. A Case of Serendipity

The observation that ultimately eventuated in the formulation of the principle of adaptation level occurred by accident in the 1920s. Professor Harry Helson, smoking while doing darkroom work with the usual ruby-red illuminant, noticed that the tip of his cigarette glowed a highly saturated green (Helson, 1972, pp. 101–102). There was no known physical reason for the glow to appear the complement of its natural color and nothing available in the color literature provided a clue to the experience. Excited by his finding, Helson's next step was to demonstrate its reproducibility. This he did at a meeting of the Optical Society of America with a large box, its front face matte white and containing a small aperture. The inside of the box was illuminated by an incandescent bulb, yielding an aperture color that approximated white. However, when the face of the box was flooded with red light, the aperture glowed a deep green. This demonstration was next succeeded by a series of experiments (Helson, 1964a, pp. 260–270) utilizing the full range of reflectances and a variety of monochromatic as well as complex sources, the results of which are summarized in the principle of color conversion.

3. The Principle of Color Conversion

The principle of color conversion (Helson and Michels, 1948, p. 1031) states that when achromatic (gray) stimuli are bathed in a chromatic illuminant a neutral zone (adaptation level) exists for the viewer such that stimuli with reflectances above this level appear to have the hue of the illuminant, those below have the hue of its complement, while those at or near the zone appear achromatic or weakly saturated. Thus, a gray square or patch with a reflectance of 27% on a white background bathed in red light will appear gray, on a gray background will appear yellowish red, and on a black background will appear red. However, a gray square with a reflectance of 10% on the same three backgrounds will appear blue green, gray, and red, respectively. Helson (1938) devised an empirical equation based on Fechner's law which treats the achromatic zone (adaptation level) as a weighted geometric mean of the reflectances of stimulus patches and of the background in which the influence of the background is estimated to be 3 times that of the stimuli. From these experiments, two important conclusions emerged. The color of an object does not stand in invariant relationship to the light it reflects and its appearance cannot be characterized in terms of a single physical variable but depends on the interaction of two variables, the reflectance of the object and that of its surrounding area.

4. On the General Nature of Adaptation-Level Theory

In describing the principle of color conversion we have presented the concept of adaptation level in descriptive terms and have illustrated the two significant psychological principles on which it is based: the notions of the relativity of response and of pooling. Judgments change as viewing conditions change and the standard of judgment (adaptation level) derives from the combination (i.e., pooling) of several properties of the viewing situation.

Stated in the general case, the adaptation level principle holds that a judgment—and the perception it reflects—depends on the relationship of the stimulus being judged to the adaptation level momentarily prevailing for the stimulus dimension under consideration. The response is defined as the product of three classes of variable, the stimulus being judged (the focal stimulus), its background, and the residual, e.g., determinants that reflect the status of the organism—its past experience, motivation, bodily condition—at the time that judgment occurs. In some instances such as the simplified setting of the lifted weight experiment, the residual consists of the sequential patterns of prior stimulus input (past experience within the experiment) as they related to subsequent judgments (cf., e.g., Di Lollo, 1964); in others, notably the complex circumstances of social judgment, the residual is essentially equated with the unassessed variance among the observations (cf., e.g., Helson, 1964a, p. 244). Because the residual reflects the condition of the organism and is admittedly at present an obscure composite, the successful analysis of its components and their interrelationships is potentially the condition on which adaptation-level theory as a general theory will stand or fall.

A-L theory is an outgrowth of gestalt psychology. It represents a marriage between Helson's early interest in the organizational concepts of gestalt psychology and his long standing interest in objectifying and quantifying psychological data. In its basic formulation it embodies a formal in contrast to a physiological model. Although Helson has coupled it with homeostasis in certain of his discussions (cf., e.g., 1957, pp. 571–572) and others (e.g., Wilson and Wilson, 1967, p. 71) have classified it, along with Hebb's notion of the cell assembly, as a coded representation of the physiological programming mechanism for partitioning stimuli, it in itself provides no obvious clue as to how in specific physiological terms the brain works in such matters. Indeed, if a physical analogy is at all appropriate it is that of the analog computer which generates outputs through the integration of inputs over time. A-L theory is molar and it is descriptive. It is defined by a set of expressions (equations) that indicate the relative contribution of the three general classes of variable described above—two stimulus and one organismic—to the production of particular responses. In addition to the assumptions of relativity of judgment and pooling, it requires the assumption that all response dimensions accommodated by the theory are bipolar in nature. This latter assumption is obviously valid in the case of sensory dimensions. Whether or not it can be shown to hold for all other kinds of situational variable is another consideration crucial to the status of AL as a general in contrast to a specialized theory. And although Helson and others (e.g., Ross and Thibaut, 1974) have used A-L theory in the study of cognitive variables, and others have found it useful in the study of such problems as recognition (e.g., Parducci and Sandusky, 1970) and detection processes (Durlach and Braida, 1969), adaptation-level theory as it is formulated at present is not a cognitive theory. It does not represent judgment as an intellectual process of selecting response alternatives, despite the fact that Swets (1971) has spoken of the response criterion of signal detection theory as an A L of probability expectation. When viewed in the context of current response-oriented theories of perception, adaptation-level theory is seen to be part of the long tradition of perceptual theories that have conceptualized the processes of perception as automatic and the perceiver as passive viewer, and it will remain in this tradition at least until experimenters succeed in refining our understanding of what takes place within the residual. Greeno (1973, p. 155) correctly recognizes that the central concern of A-L theory is to understand the appearances of stimuli. Accordingly, it has implicitly assumed an isomorphic correspondence between the properties of judgment which it measures and the underlying properties of perception which are its ultimate concern. This assumption has been variously challenged, mainly on methodological grounds, but no challenge has succeeded in disposing of perceptual relativity as a well-established general principle.

In the course of the present chapter we shall examine the concept of adaptation level in relation to the following perceptual problems: anchor effects, time-order errors, contrast and assimilation, perceptual constancy, transposition and stimulus generalization, illusions, and stimulus detection and vigilance. We shall also deal with the issue of whether the response shifts described in the AL literature represent changes in perception or, more simply, changes in judgment, the questions of which inputs combine to influence the AL, and the matter of the relation of adaptation-level theory to the tradition of psychophysics.

5. Anchor Effects, Contrast, and Assimilation

The concept of the "anchor" has been in the repertoire of experimental psychologists for a considerable period. The term is most frequently used to refer to any stimulus that influences judgment of other stimuli that occur with it because of its striking difference in magnitude, frequency, or duration of presentation, or because of instructions or other reinforcers that accompany it. Helson's 1947 experiment with lifted weights provides a convenient illustration of anchor effects. When the presentation of an anchor weight of strikingly larger magnitude preceded the presentation of each stimulus in a series of weights, the series stimuli were more frequently judged to be lighter than when they were presented without the anchor. Conversely, a lightweight anchor increased the heaviness judgments. As a general rule, the greater the difference in magnitude between anchor and series stimuli, the greater the induced change in judgment. However, there are limits beyond which anchors are diminished in their effectiveness. Indeed, weights exceedingly large or small in comparison to their series stimuli may have no effect at all on the perceived weight of the series members (Helson and Nash, 1960).

In adaptation-level terms the anchor constitutes the background, while the series members are focal stimuli and a change in judgment can be effected by an alteration in either focal stimulus or background. For example, Künnapas (1955) found that subjects' judgments of length of lines could be modified by either changing the size of a square that formed their background or changing the length of the lines themselves. When an anchor of comparatively large magnitude is interpolated into a stimulus series, there is a decrease in the number of responses in the categories nearest the anchor and an increase in the categories farther away. Thus the average scale values of the series stimuli are lowered and the anchor appears to repel the series members, the effect being greatest for the series members closest to the anchor. This shift in scale values is called "contrast." However, if the anchor is very similar or identical to the heaviest series member, it may be judged as belonging to the same category, with the result that average scale values will increase and the anchor will appear to attract the series members (Sherif, Taub, and Hovland, 1958). These effects, which are called "assimilation," have been observed less frequently than contrast effects and will be discussed later in this section.

When two objectively equal stimuli are experienced one after the other, the second usually appears greater in magnitude than the first when interstimulus intervals are longer than about 3 sec. This phenomenon was referred to as the "negative time-order error" by early psychophysicists, who attributed it to the fading stimulus trace and set about finding ways to eliminate it. However, when Pratt (1933) showed that by first judging a series of loud tones and then a series of comparatively soft tones both negative and positive time-order errors could be produced the time-order error became an object of study in its own right. Helson (1964*a*, pp. 203*ff*) has explained time-order errors in terms of the fact that the adaptation level, because it is a weighted average, will be "decentered," i.e., correspond to some value other than the midpoint between the two stimulus magnitudes.

In work by Bevan, Barker, and Pritchard (1963*a*) the upward or downward bowing found in ratio scales (what Stevens has called "hysteresis") was shown to be due to temporal and spatial orders of presentation of stimuli. Markers representing a series of weights were equally spaced along the baseline of a matrix. Subjects were then presented the series in either ascending or descending order and asked to adjust the markers to a height that represented the heaviness of each weight relative to the one just previously lifted. Upward-bowing curves were obtained when judgments were made in light-to-heavy order, and downward-bowing curves were obtained when judgments were made in heavy-to-light order. Stimuli judged in left to right spatial order yielded psychological functions with greater curvature than when judged right to left. Bowing therefore cannot be attributed to poorer discriminability at the upper end of the stimulus series, as Stevens (1958) has suggested, but depends rather on whether or not the greater stimulus is presented before or after the lesser in the temporal-spatial order of trials.

Simultaneous as well as successive contrast effects are accommodated within the AL descriptive framework. Helson's demonstration of color conversion is, of course, an example of simultaneous contrast. Another example is found in the classical demonstrations of lightness contrast, in which gray areas are lightened by a dark background and darkened by a light background. In a series of experiments using vertical white lines of various widths and spacing on backgrounds of different reflectance, Helson and his co-workers (Helson and Rohles, 1959; Helson and Joy, 1962; Helson, 1963; Steger, 1968, 1969) discovered a continuum of contrast and assimilation (the lightening of gray areas by a light background and the darkening by a dark background) and thus demonstrated the complementarity of these two processes. For example, with a background of 36% reflectance, assimilation effects occurred with generally narrow lines spaced wide apart, while contrast effects were obtained with generally wider lines. Whether one obtains contrast or assimilation depends on the mutual relation of line width, width of intervening space, and background reflectance, for near-white (80%) and near-black (14%) backgrounds yield only assimilation. Helson explains the occurrence of contrast and assimilation as follows: Contrast will occur when AL has a value that falls between that of the reflectance of the focal stimulus and that of its background; assimilation will occur when the value of AL is either above or below that of the contiguous areas.

As the above findings indicate, anchor effects, contrast, and assimilation may all be brought together within the framework of adaptation-level theory and accommodated by a single set of rules governing the relationships of stimuli to their context, both past and present.

6. Constancy, Transposition, and Stimulus Generalization

The phenomenon of perceptual constancy is perhaps the most obscure and at the same time most challenging among those perennial challenges to perceptual theory, for it requires that the theorist explain how the organism acquires and maintains a stable and veridical perception of its immediate surroundings in the face of constant and marked changes in the nature of the proximal stimulus, i.e., the pattern of stimulation at the sense organ. The answer of gestalt psychology is found in the principle of the invariant relationship: perceived size is always size at a perceived distance; perceived shape is always shape in perceived orientation; and perceived brightness is always relative reflectance at a given ambient illumination (Koffka, 1935, Chapter 6). Following the strategy of David Katz, it has been customary to measure constancy by matching the shape, size, or lightness of a target against that of a standard under two conditions of observation (open observation when both the stimuli and their surroundings are open to view and observation through apertures when only the stimuli themselves are seen) and comparing the matches. Various investigators (e.g., Brunswik, Thouless) have devised formulas for expressing degree of constancy. Lightness constancy may be taken as the illustrative case: Thouless's widely cited formula is

$$C = \frac{\log s - \log p}{\log w - \log p}$$

where s represents the degree of target whiteness that matches a shadowed standard in open observation, p is the degree of target whiteness that yields a match with observation through the apertures, and w is the degree of whiteness of the shadowed standard. But s and p will change when the depth of shadow or the reflectance of the background changes, and, as Helson and his colleagues (Helson, 1964a, pp. 278–282) have empirically shown, generalizations regarding reflectance of the target and the depth of shadow cannot be made without reference to background reflectance as well as the level of illuminance on both lighted and shadowed stimuli.

A-L theory approaches constancy through the problem of stimulus equivalence and its definition in terms of the several classes of variable that determine the stability of the adaptation level. Because stimulation is pooled in the establishment of particular AL's, it is possible to produce *equivalent AL's* with different patterns of stimulus input as long as their *average effect* is the same.

For example, examination of Helson's formula for predicting judged heaviness reveals the *reciprocity* between stimulus frequency and stimulus magnitude in the generation of A-L values. Thus, if one holds constant both the relative frequency and the physical magnitudes of a set of series stimuli, one should be able to add any number of different anchor magnitudes without causing the AL to shift as long as the relative frequency of presentation is maintained at the appropriate level. Bevan and Darby (1955) did such an experiment and found that AL could be held constant over a wide range of combinations of anchor magnitude and frequency—at one extreme an anchor of 312.1 g presented 200 times for each presentation of the series of 220, 260, 300, and 340 g weights; at the other, 1231 g presented once for each presentation of the series—and as long as the adaptation level remained constant the mean heaviness judgments of the individual series stimuli also remained the same.

The fact that laboratory weights are judged consistently heavier by watchmakers than by weightlifters (Anderson, 1975, p. 94) and individuals consistently taller by short people than by tall and consistently older by young people than by old (Hinckley and Rethlingshafer, 1951; Rethlingshafer and Hinckley, 1963) constitutes a kind of constancy that can result only from a very powerful and stable residual.

Anderson (1975, p. 57) has pointed out the relation of the transposition phenomenon to constancy. A familiar example involves the transposition of a lightness relation by animals in the discrimination-learning situation. A white rat, for example, can be taught to select the lighter of two patches in order to receive food. If the test situation is then arranged so that the lighter stimulus of the training pair becomes the darker of a test pair, the animal will no longer select the patch on which it was rewarded during training, but instead the new and lighter one. The earliest experiment on transposition done from the perspective of A-L theory is an unpublished study of Helson and Kaplan (1950). Human subjects were presented a selection of gray patches in random order on a black background, with the middlemost member of the series being reinforced as the "correct" stimulus. When the criterion of ten consecutive correct choices had been made, the series was presented on a white background, with the result that 61% chose a patch of higher reflectance as the correct stimulus. James (1953) was the first to formulate an explanation of transposition in the quantitative terms of adaptation-level theory. In this formulation, an analogue of the AL is established through consistent reinforcement. When this value lies between the stimulus value of the pair to be discriminated, successful transfer may be expected. However, if the value of the discriminanda fall on the same side with reference to the transfer AL, choice will be harder until a new AL has been appropriately established. With this model, James was able to handle quite neatly the results of a number of studies of intradimensional transfer. However, he was unable, as he recognized, to account for transposition involving intermediate magnitudes. Zeiler (1963a,b) has accommodated this problem in a further adaptation of A-L theory. In the intermediate-magnitude problem the three discriminanda represent a stimulus series to be integrated, with the AL a weighted average of the three. Initial learning involves selecting a stimulus that corresponds most closely to this average. In the test situation, the original AL will shift with the integration of the new stimuli of the test series. Early in the test period, transposition will fail since the intermediate magnitude of the test series will not constitute a good match with the cumulative AL. However, with continued presentation of the test stimuli, the AL will eventually reach a level that will allow a successful match with the intermediate magnitude.

Closely related to transposition is the phenomenon of stimulus generalization. Investigations of this latter phenomenon within the context of A-L theory are principally identified with Thomas and with Capehart and their respective co-workers. A convenient example is found in a 1962 study of Thomas and Jones in which human subjects were asked to remember a green of a particular wavelength (the training stimulus), and then were presented in random order a set of greens (the test stimuli) from which to select the previously presented training stimulus. These experimenters found that the generalization gradient peaked at values either above or below that of the training stimulus, when the position of the training stimulus fell, respectively, below or above the center of the series. In interpreting these results, they conceptualized the role of the test series as generating AL's against which the training stimulus is compared. When the test stimuli are asymmetrical about the original training stimuli, the position of the AL will differ from that of a symmetrical series with a corresponding change in the memory of the training stimulus. While it had initially been assumed (cf., e.g., Capehart, Tempone, and Hébert, 1969) that the AL was first set by the value of the training stimulus, later studies (cf. Thomas, Strub, and Dickson, 1974) have shown that this is not necessarily the case, since the AL may be influenced by a strong residual—long-term memories of, for example, the "best green." Similarly, an overrepresentation of one member of the test series may produce a generalization gradient that is biased toward the overrepresented stimulus (Hébert, Bullock, Levitt, Woodward, and McGuirk, 1974), an effect reminiscent of assimilation.

7. Illusions

In recent years a small literature has begun to appear that links A-L theory to the explanation of visual illusions, in particular, illusions of extent. Restle has been the major systematist. In a typical experiment, Restle and Merryman (1969) had subjects judge lines of varying length connecting two boxes of varying size. Lines, regardless of length, connecting larger boxes were judged to be shorter, while line lengths connecting small boxes, in contrast, were judged to be longer than they actually were. Their explanation: The pair of boxes serves as a frame of reference, its influence depending on the relation of box size to length of line judged. Particular line lengths, as they are placed in fields having different AL's, are thus necessarily judged differently. Similarly, work by Avant and his students (Avant, 1971a; Avant and Kent, 1970; Wagner and Avant, 1970) indicates that spatially contiguous anchors influence the magnitude of the Müller-Lyer and Titchener illusions. Finally, Gilinsky (1971) has proposed an AL explanation of that most perplexing of illusions, the moon illusion, based on the notion of Ptolemy that a filled extent appears greater than the same extent of empty space and the concept of an internal referent (the "memory moon" of "true" size) located in space where normal viewing distance and normal viewing elevation of the moon coincide. The larger the value of this internal referent (A) the more expanded the visual world and the farther away the horizon and thus the more closely objects will approximate their "true" size and the more likely perceived distance will resist foreshortening and correspond to true distance. Neither the actual size nor distance of the moon changes with angle of elevation. Thus, its projective (retinal) size is constant, and apparent size and distance will depend on where it intersects the visual distance scale relative to the position of A. As angle of elevation decreases, A recedes from the position of the viewer with the result that the moon appears closer and larger.

8. Vigilance

Studies of the properties of vigilance from the perspective of A-L theory were carried out by Bevan and his students during the middle 1960s. Their work rests on a model in which both expectancy and arousal are treated as the product of focal, background, and residual stimulation. Except for one study on arousal (Bevan, Avant, and Lankford, 1967), the vigilance experiments were all directed toward the properties of expectation, and a single experimental paradigm, a modification of one first used by Mowrer, Rayman, and Bliss (1940), was employed throughout the series. This experimental strategy involves presenting the subject a series of conditioning signals at some constant time interval followed without notice by a test signal introduced under some condition of change.

The initial study by Hardesty and Bevan (1965) will serve to illustrate this work. In the first of three experiments subjects were presented a brief visual signal at one or another of three fixed intervals and were told to press a key as soon as it was seen. There were 20 such signals followed by a 21st (test signal) at the same interval or one or the other of two shorter or two longer intervals. When the series and test intervals were the same, the difference in average response latency between series and test trials (ΔRL) was essentially zero. As the discrepancy between series and test intervals increased, so did the ΔRL. In the second experiment the fixed-interval conditioning series was replaced by variable-interval series with average interval equal to one or the other of the fixed series. Again, ΔRL was zero when *average* series and test intervals coincided and increased as the discrepancy in intervals became larger. The third experiment employed a variable-interval conditioning series, with test interval set at either the mean, the mode, or the midrange of the conditioning series. Based on the AL assumption of pooling, expectation was for RL to be minimal when the test interval coincided with the mean of the conditioning series. This expectation was confirmed.

9. Adaptation-Level Shifts: Changes in Judgment or Perception?

An early criticism of A-L theory was voiced by Stevens (1958). It took the form of a methodological attack in which the AL experiments were faulted because subjects had expressed their judgments in terms of ordinal values. But almost certainly Stevens' rejection of the A-L work reflected a metaphysical bias, for while he had rejected the Fechner law in favor of his power law, like Fechner, he was still committed to the assumption that the psychophysical relationship could be fully defined on the psychological side in focal stimulus terms alone. Adaptation-level shifts, he contended, were explainable in terms of what he called "semantic relativity"; i.e., the introduction of an anchor into a stimulus series resulted in an increase in the range of stimuli to be ordered and thus caused a rearrangement of category labels. It thus would follow that A-L shifts reflected changes in judgmental response rather than in perception. This is a perfectly plausible argument, and, indeed, quite probably accounts for a number of anchor effects. But it does not explain away all such shifts. Vourinen (1970, pp. 10 and 15), an otherwise severe critic of AL, acknowledges the authenticity of perceptual changes following the introduction of an anchor as a result of his own experimental work. Indeed, Ellis (1972) has reviewed the several studies directed toward testing Stevens's notion of semantic adjustment and other related experiments and finds that none have successfully established the Stevens hypothesis.

Support for the perceptual character of response changes associated with A-L theory comes from a variety of sources.

First, there is the testimony of personal observation. Some effects are so clearly and directly observable as to establish their basis in experience. Two obvious examples, both already described earlier, are Helson's demonstrations of color conversion and the widely familiar phenomenon of successive thermal contrast that has provoked scholarly attention for at least the past almost 300 years (Berkeley, 1713; Locke, 1690). Anyone who has participated in these demonstrations knows that perceptions do change with changes in context.

Second, there are data that have been obtained with methods that preclude verbal mediation or are otherwise immune to the criticisms applied to the rating-scale method. Campbell and various colleagues, for example, have demonstrated perceptual contrast in experiments using what Campbell calls "absolute, extensive, and extraexperimentally anchored response language" (cf., e.g., Harvey and Campbell, 1963). These have variously been numerical codes for particular auditory frequencies (e.g., E-flat above middle C is "43"), inches, and ounces. While the contrast effects obtained with the absolute, physical language were less pronounced than those with category ratings, they did occur and indicate that judgmental responses may reflect the properties both of perception and of the response language. More recently, Helson and Kozaki (1968a) have reported anchor shifts in judgments of the size of clusters of up to 18 dots when the response language of the experiment was a limited range of cardinal numbers. Finally, Murray (1970) has shown that reaction time varies with apparent loudness in contrast to physical loudness, the former having been conditioned by the intensity of prior stimuli.

Contextually produced perceptual shifts have been reported in experiments employing the method of adjustment, the method of reproduction, and the method of comparative judgment. Von Wright and Mikkonen (1964) and Mikkonen (1969) presented subjects a target stimulus (a weight) for memorization and then required them to reproduce this magnitude using a special apparatus that made possible rapid response. When the judgment of a series of stimuli was interpolated between the initial stimulus presentation and response, the result was perceptual contrast relatable to the AL of the interpolated series. In two experiments, one involving the comparative judgment for similarity of pairs of achromatic chips against white, gray, and black backgrounds and the other the adjustment of scale position for members of a set of seven chips on each of three backgrounds, Egeth, Avant, and Bevan (1968) found the nature of the perceptual scales obtained to vary markedly, depending on the reflectance of the particular background with which the scaling responses were made.

Related are several studies dealing with the influence of incidental stimuli. In one, Dinnerstein (1965) obtained a context effect when subjects made comparative judgments of weights with the right hand while the left hand simultaneously lifted but did not judge other weights. These results she interpreted as genuine perceptual changes associated with shifts in the judgmental norm. In a similar study, Turner and Bevan (1964b) presented subjects a series of constant-intensity tones at equal intervals along with synchronized brief increases in ambient illumination, varying in intensity. Although only a few subjects reported being aware of the changes in illumination, seven-eighths of the subjects described auditory rhythms that matched the patterning of the illumination shifts.

Third, there are supportive data from the study of subliminal anchors. In the earliest study, Black and Bevan (1960) conducted a Helsonian anchor experiment with mild electric shocks to the right wrist as stimuli and with subliminal anchors interpolated between successive series presentations without the subject's knowledge. They found that the judged intensity of the series stimuli was enhanced in the group receiving the subliminal anchor, with the greatest enhancement occurring, consistent with A-L theory, in the region of the series closest to the anchor. Interrogation of the subjects failed to reveal any awareness of the presence of subliminal stimuli. Furthermore, no galvanic skin responses recorded during testing could be linked with any confidence to the presentation of these anchors. Similar results have been found for shock stimuli by Goldstone, Goldfarb, Strong, and Russell (1962), for size by Boardman and Goldstone (1962), and for the loudness of tones by Bevan and Pritchard (1963a). Dixon (1971, pp. 31–38) has made a careful examination of these experiments and has concluded, as has Kakizaki (1967), that these subliminal anchor effects are real. Accepting this view, it is impossible to interpret the related judgmental shifts in other than perceptual terms. Certainly they cannot be reduced to questions of semantic adjustment, verbal mediation, or response bias.

A fourth set of data supporting the perceptual nature of adaptation-level phenomena is drawn from the literature on reinforcement and learning, particularly that obtained from the study of animals. In an early study, Campbell and Kral (1958) showed that parakeets will transpose a lightness discrimination response from the rewarded stimulus to a nonrewarded one when background reflectance is shifted. In the first experiments designed to test their pooling model of reinforcement, Bevan and Adamson (1960) preadapted human subjects to shocks of either high or low average intensity and then charted their learning of a maze with reinforcement shocks of intermediate magnitude for errors. They found that the performance of those adapted to relatively strong average stimulation was poorer than that of a control group while those adapted to weak average shock did clearly better than the control subjects. If reinforcement is accepted to be as effective as it is pleasant or unpleasant, then the differences in quality of learning must obviously reflect the results of sensory contrast. Similar results have been reported for the speed of rats running a straightaway (Black, Adamson, and Bevan, 1961) and bar-pressing for light (Hurwitz, 1960), and for rate of self-stimulation of the brain (MacDougall and Bevan, 1968). A summary of the work relating to the pooling model of reinforcement can be found in Bevan (1966).

Finally, the relation of anchors to two additional perceptual phenomena, spatial orientation and perceptual grouping, is relevant for the present discussion. In a series of three experiments Turner and Bevan (1964a) used a mixing tachistoscope to present cubes in outline varying from an unambiguously left-oriented cube to one that was unambiguously right-oriented. The center of the series was occupied by the maximally ambiguous Necker cube. During a pretest series presented to each subject, the cubes were varied in ambiguity in one orientation while kept unambiguous in the opposite orientation; were varied in the relative frequency with which the ambiguous cubes occurred in one orientation as contrasted to the other; or were varied in the frequency with which cubes in one orientation, as contrasted to the other, were verbally reinforced. Three presentations of the maximally ambiguous Necker cube constituted the test. In the case of every pretest procedure, this test cube was reported on the predominant number of test trials to be oriented in the direction opposite that favored in the pretest conditioning series. Perceived orientation is an elemental response. If it is right, it cannot be left. And if it is shown to reflect the processes of perceptual contrast, as it was in the above experiment, this fact cannot be explained away as the product of semantic relativity.

A 1964 experiment of Rock and Brosgole revealed anchor effects in perceptual grouping when a columnar matrix of dots was rotated out of the frontal-parallel plane, with the judgment of columnar grouping persisting beyond the point justified by the angular separation of the dots. In a 1968 study, Bell and Bevan applied the anchor paradigm to the study of four gestalt organizing principles: proximity, similarity, good continuation, and closure. In the case of proximity, an anchor consisting of a matrix of dots unambiguously organized as rows (or columns) increased the frequency with which the more ambiguous patterns were perceived as columns (or rows). In the case of similarity, an anchor matrix of alternating black and white rows (or columns) increased the frequency with which more ambiguous patterns of gray patches were perceived as columns (or rows). In the case of good continuation, the anchor, which consisted of a discontinuous linear pattern, increased the frequency with which other similar patterns were judged to be continuous. And in the case of closure, an anchor-circle containing a wide gap increased the frequency with which circles containing smaller gaps were judged to be complete. Perceptual grouping, like perceptual orientation, is an either-or phenomenon, and the demonstration that it is susceptible to influence by the perceiver's pattern of prior experience is the demonstration of a perceptual effect.

10. Conditions for Pooling

The organism is constantly presented with a countless array of stimuli of which only a relatively limited number can conceivably arouse and shape its perception and its judgment. The fundamental question for all students of perception—as for all students of behavior, whatever its form—is which do and which do not. This question has been variously phrased by those with interests in adaptation level as the problem of limits and the problem of relevance. Within what range of time and of intensity will stimuli pool (i.e., integrate) to produce shifts in AL? What are the relationships among stimuli that lead to their being pooled? Within what psychophysical context are such relationships defined—dimensional, interdimensional, topological, functional? The question of relevance, taken at face value, encompasses, as Helson has noted (1971, p. 13), a certain tautology. If a stimulus influences AL it is relevant, and if it does not, it is not and almost all stimuli may be made to influence another and thus become relevant, else classical conditioning, for example, would not be possible.

Perhaps the most straightforward way to summarize the conditions that make for pooling is to attempt to identify those associated with the focal stimulus, with the background, and with the residual, respectively. However, if one attempts to do this, one is immediately confronted by the fact of *interaction* and finds that the matter is reduced, on the one hand, to those variables that are best defined in situational terms and, on the other, to those most easily described in terms of the organism. And in this perspective, the question of limits becomes identified with situational determinants, while relevance is associated with organismic variables. Looked at in this way, it is important to note, as Dinnerstein (1971, p. 90) already has, that the sharp distinction between perception, on the one hand, and memory, on the other, disappears. Indeed, to look at the interaction of focal, background, and residual determinants of behavior is to analyze the relationship between perception and memory.

A particularly interesting and important aspect of the question of limits is whether or not change in a stimulus from anchor to nonanchor status occurs abruptly or gradually. The Pritchard and Bevan (1966) study of the influence of changes in the size of anchors involved in the judgment of shape suggests that the shift in status is essentially an all-or-nothing matter. Similarly, the response latency data of Bevan, Bell, and Taylor (1966) appear to include a "terminal threshold of relevance." (The notion of terminal threshold comes from a 1963 suggestion by Swets that irrelevant signals may become relevant with a change in response strategies.) At the same time, the drop from maximal anchor effectiveness to zero, while rapid, was to some degree gradual. Bevan, Bell, and Taylor attributed this to individual differences in threshold level, with increasingly fewer persons within the experimental groups being sensitive to anchors as their distance from the series increased. The gradual change thus was viewed as a by-product of grouped data.

The effectiveness of pooled anchors increases within limits with the duration of their presentation (Helson and Kozaki, 1968*b*), their relative frequency of presentation (*cf.*, e.g., Harvey and Campbell, 1963), their distance from the series stimuli (Helson, 1947), and the recency of their presentation. While stimulus interactions in the psychophysical setting are typically confined to individual test sessions (*cf.*, e.g., Bevan and Saugstad, 1955), Helson and Steger (Helson, 1964*b*, pp. 29–30) have found anchor effects that persist for as long as a week.

Whether or not a stimulus assumes the anchor role will depend, as we have noted, on the *interaction* of such variables as relative frequency of presentation, magnitude, duration, and recency. The Bevan and Darby (1955) experiment referred to earlier was planned as a test of the limits of A-L theory, recognizing the reciprocity between frequency and intensity long known to physiologists and implicit in Helson's quantitative formulation of the AL principle. This study has the value of emphasizing the importance of conceptualizing anchors in terms of sets of interacting conditions rather than in terms of stimuli with special properties.

Anchors exert their influence across dimensions (shape and orientation, Bevan and Pritchard, 1963b; shape and size, Pritchard and Bevan, 1966; color and size, Helson and Kozaki, cited by Avant and Helson, 1973, p. 442; and duration and intensity, Adamson and Everett, 1969), intermanually (Dinnerstein, 1971), and across modalities (cf., e.g., Behar and Bevan, 1961).

The Behar and Bevan experiment is illustrative of this general class of study. Subjects judged the durations of tones or lights. Anchors, which were judged along with the series stimuli, were presented to the same or to the alternate modality. The resulting data revealed both intra- and intermodal anchor effects. While the effects across modalities were of significantly less magnitude than those produced by a comparable anchor within the same modality, the important thing is that they occurred reliably. That these effects across dimensions and across modalities are not simply a matter of relative similarity is indicated by a 1966 study by Helson, Bevan, and Masters. Subjects were asked to judge the size of circles. The anchors consisted of sets of smaller circles and smaller circles containing angles which were correlated with the size of the circles. While the smaller circle anchors induced changes in judgment of the series stimuli, this effect was greatest for the anchor circles which contained angles, possibly because these latter anchors accentuated the anchor property of smallness.

Anchors are more effective if they are judged than if they are not judged. Brown's 1953 experiment with lifted weights is a useful example. Both weights and trays on which the series weights could be placed were used as anchors. Weights as anchors had a more potent influence than did trays as anchors. However, both kinds of anchors were more effective when they were judged than when they were not judged. The fact that the trays had no effect on judgment when they were not identified as anchors suggests that they were not perceived as part of the relevant context.

The changes in function of the trays with instructions are suggestive of the distinction between figure and ground. The influence of such a change in status was investigated by Bevan, Maier, and Helson (1963b) in an experiment in which subjects were asked to judge the number of beans in each of two types (large and small) of jar. Two sets of instructions were used to effect the shift from figure to ground status or vice versa. Under figure instructions the judges were asked to regard the jars as integral with their contents; under ground instructions they were told to think of the beans and the jars as two distinctly separate things. Under figure instructions, the estimates of number were consistently largest for the large jars and consistently smallest for the small jars. Under ground instructions, the size of the container had apparently no effect on the estimates of number.

The results of the two studies just described were achieved through the differential effect of instructions and thus through the directive role of set. Similar mechanisms undoubtedly underlie the demonstration of simultaneously induced multiple anchor effects by Turner and Bevan (1962) and Steger and O'Reilly (1970). In the Turner and Bevan experiment, for example, subjects were asked to make judgments of shape, size, and lightness when rectangular stimulus figures were simultaneously varied on these three attributes. Several sets of anchors were used: large dark rectangles, large elongated rectangles, and elongated dark rectangles. Two distinctly separate anchor effects occurred simultaneously with every possible combination of two stimulus attributes in the anchor, even when the direction of shift for one stimulus attribute was the opposite of that for another (e.g., size or shape vs. lightness). These results suggest that the presentation of the task was so structured as to set the judges to conceive of the attributes to be judged as separate and distinct and the judgmental task to consist in fact of several separate and distinct tasks. In contrast, in cross-modal anchor experiments such as that of Behar and Bevan the task would appear to have been perceived as involving a *single* underlying dimension of magnitude.

The nature of the literature on relevance from the Brown study forward inclines us to put strong emphasis on the role of the assumptions made by the judge when confronted by the judgmental task. These assumptions in turn appear to relate to the perceived relationship between series and anchor stimuli (effective anchors must possess the *critical* attributes of the stimuli, the judgment of which they influence) or the perceived nature of the task (there is a single or there are several judgmental tasks to perform). This takes us beyond the literal view of the physical nature of stimuli and responses and their correlation to an examination of how they represent and reflect the underlying perceptual-judgmental system. A major virtue of the perspective of adaptation-level theory, as both Brown and Reich (1971, p. 219) and Dinnerstein (1971, p. 82) point out, is that it highlights the property of system flexibility: the flexible responsiveness of the organism in the face of the stimulus field which encompasses it and its capacity to extract appropriate information and make it useful.

11. Adaptation-Level Theory and Psychophysics

Helson's general quantitative statement of the concept of Adaptation Level is contained in the following expression:

$$A = K(\overline{S}^p \, B^q \, R^r)$$

where A is the origin of the response dimension (adaptation level) expressed in stimulus terms, K is an empirical constant, S is the mean of the stimuli toward which the responses are focused, B is the ambient background stimulation, and R is the residual, a composite of past experience and all else that the organism brings to the response situation. Adaptations of the general expression to accommodate individual response settings have involved empirically determining the value of the exponents and adding constants to reflect the special requirements of the particular situation.

In first formulating the adaptation-level principle quantitatively, Helson committed himself to the metaphysical proposition, drawn from Fechnerian psychophysics, that the relationship between physical properties and those of experience is expressed in logarithmic terms and that Weber's law identifies psychological interval size and is constant. Thus AL was first spoken of as a weighted geometric mean of all the stimuli that affect the organism (cf., e.g., Helson, 1964a, Chapter 4).

At the same time the approach of A-L theory represents a radical departure from Fechnerian psychophysics in two respects. Psychological dimensions are conceived to be bipolar, with the neutral point of these dimensions, rather than the absolute threshold, constituting the scalar origin and with this value changing across time as the product of the interaction of focal (series) stimuli with background and residuals. This reformulation of Fechner's law (Michels and Helson, 1949) was derived from assumptions embodied in the rating-scale technique used in early A-L experiments. And these assumptions became an early basis for criticism.

In fact, the types of criticism leveled against A-L theory have taken three forms: those concerning the ontological basis of Fechner's law, those involving the limitations of the rating- or category-scale method, and those related to the empirical outcomes of certain experiments.

The underlying philosophical concerns have also been of several sorts. First, the Fechnerian assumption that corresponding psychological and physical properties stand in a linear/logarithmic relationship has been questioned. Stevens (1961) has replaced Fechner's law with the power law. However, Stevens did not at the same time abandon Fechner in the matter of the parameters of the law. These are solely physical magnitudes, on the one hand, and response magnitudes, on the other. Context consequently constitutes a source of error and its influence must be minimized. Helson, meanwhile, has not over the years been compulsively wed to the weighted geometric mean as the single best estimate of AL. He has recognized the versatility of the power mean and has even introduced AL into the formulation of the power law (1964a, pp. 222–225). In addition, he has recognized (1964a, p. 60) situations in which the power mean (Behar and Bevan, 1961) and other measures of central tendency like the median (Parducci, Calfee, Marshall, and Davidson, 1960) and the arithmetic mean (Podell, 1961; Bevan et al., 1963b) provide the most useful estimate of AL. In point of fact, Helson has not used the weighted geometric mean for *prediction* for several decades (Avant, 1971*b*, p. 21), and if one examines the general expression for AL one recognizes that by writing $K\overline{S^p}$ Helson has taken the mean of the powers of the stimuli as one determining factor of AL. Indeed, by a little logical exercise one can quickly show that Stevens's power law is a special case of the adaptation-level principle applying to situations in which the contributions of the B and R variables to AL are so small as to be insignificant. The power law, written for the general case to a first approximation, is

$$\text{perceived intensity} = KS_i^{\,n}$$

Stevens assumes that scalar magnitude is referenced to what he calls the "effective threshold" (S_0), which he identifies with the absolute threshold. Thus

$$\text{perceived intensity} = K\,(S_i - S_0)^n$$

Now, if we assume that the effective threshold is identified with the subjective neutral point of a bipolar dimension rather than the absolute threshold, then

$$S_0 = \text{AL}$$

and

$$\text{perceived intensity} = K\,(S_i - \text{AL})^n$$

Another metascientific concern, one voiced by Vourinen (1973), perhaps the most insistent critic of A-L theory since Stevens, concerns the contention that AL is a descriptive theory. Moreover, he points out that it is in a certain sense a black-box theory (the residual remains unanalyzed) with no ready access to underlying physiological mechanisms or hypothesized physiological mechanisms. This must be recognized as the statement of a legitimate bias concerning the ultimate role of theory but also one that has its alternatives among working scientists, for it views the role of theory as one of providing a glimpse of the ultimate nature of reality, not of constituting a heuristic tool that produces empirical strategies for acquiring new information. There are some within the scientific community who contend that the heuristic approach is the only economical one in the early stages of the development of a science like psychology.

Still a third general concern of this sort applied to A-L theory—this one also voiced by Vourinen (1973)—derives from the assumption that general theories are highly unlikely outcomes for psychology. While metaphysical in nature, it is partly methodological in its derivation, for it relates to the fact that different psychophysical methods yield different versions of the psychophysical function and little progress has been made in clarifying with precision the nature of the several measures—relative to each other—that are derived from these different methods. This, in effect, says to Stevens and to Helson a plague on both your houses.

There are two answers to such a proposition. First, A-L theory, in its most general sense, does not stand on or fall with the goodness of fit of particular types of psychophysical curves. As we have pointed out above and in other parts of this discussion, AL effects have been obtained with the constant-stimulus method, with the method of paired comparisons, with the method of magnitude estimation, and with the method of adjustment, as well as with absolute, physical language. Second, if AL is, as it contends, a theory of *perceptual relativity,* then it cannot constitute a universal and invariate psychophysical law but rather must stand as a formal description of interacting variables as they relate to a specific class of responses.

The second type of criticism of A-L theory centers about the fact that much of the early work associated with the adaptation-level approach employed the category method and the argument that data obtained with this method confuse perceptual and judgmental processes. First, this position was phrased in terms of semantic set and more recently in terms of equal-frequency response bias. Neither allegation has been firmly established. Furthermore, as we have just noted, anticipated AL effects have been obtained with stronger methods. At best, given the concept of response relativity, such criticism should represent a challenge to tease out the separate entities and relationships that make up the residual. Indeed, at this stage in the development of A-L theory, the nature of the residual must now be brought under more precise analytical scrutiny. Sarris (1967) has presented his similarity-classification model to account for the loss in potency of distant anchors. However, his numerical corrections are purely empirical, and whether his approach is sufficiently parsimonious remains yet to be seen. Parducci and Marshall (1962) have developed the range-frequency model to accommodate empirically the nature of the AL obtained with certain skewed stimulus distributions, but Calfee (1975, pp. 150–163) has suggested that while the averaging model (AL) is aimed at a formal description of input-output relationships, the range-frequency model is aimed at characterizing the underlying cognitive processes. Similarly, Broadbent (1971, pp. 230–236), following Parducci, proposes what he calls a simple modification of A-L theory to make it compatible with decision theory. Indeed, these latter formulations are in a domain different from A-L theory and it is hard to see how they in fact could conflict with it.

The third class of criticism concerns the relationship of A-L theory to the outcomes of particular experiments. For example, Vourinen (1973) suggested that A-L theory can predict only contrast. However, Helson (1964a), Parducci and Marshall (1962), and Broadbent (1971) have all described how assimilation can also be accommodated. In 1959 Morikiyo stressed the need to accommodate certain time parameters within A-L theory, particularly as they relate to time-order effects. But sequence effects, including time order error, have long since been rather adequately handled by means of the principle of pooling, and the work of Helson and Kozaki (1968*b*) represents a beginning toward the accommodation of duration.

12. Conclusion

As a conceptual approach to psychology, adaptation-level theory has proved to be exceedingly robust. Presented first in 1938, after 10 years of experimental work, as a mechanism for solving certain fundamental problems in color vision (Helson, 1938) and again, after a decade, as a general approach to perception (Helson, 1948), it is now 38 years later still attracting wide attention as a tool for empirical investigation. In the past 5 years at least 100 articles relating to adaptation level have appeared, with an increasing number coming from laboratories outside the United States. Over the years, it has been subjected to criticisms, centered largely about its methodology and psychophysical assumptions, but none has nullified its value as a fundamental descriptive principle.

Still, many readers of this chapter will share Vourinen's dissatisfaction with A-L theory because it does not identify underlying physiological mechanisms. But given our still relatively limited psychological knowledge of perception and the cognitive processes, one can hardly expect to identify specific physiological mechanisms in the immediate future. The great value of theories like AL is that they put known facts in perspective and lead to the acquisition of others. When a science is young, the characteristic view of the relation of fact to theory is that the role of facts is to confirm or confute theory. In the more mature disciplines, theories are more likely to be viewed as tools—often with a very short useful life—the major functions of which are the discovery and elaboration of new facts.

13. References

Adamson, R., and Everett, K. Response modification by "irrelevant" stimulus attributes. *Psychonomic Science,* 1969, *14*, 81, 83.

Anderson, B. F. *Cognitive psychology.* New York: Academic Press, 1975.

Avant, L. L. Contrast and assimilation effects in judgments of line configurations containing the Mueller-Lyer figure. *Perception and Psychophysics,* 1971*a*, *10*, 437–440.

Avant, L. L. Psychophysics and scaling. In M. H. Appley (Ed.), *Adaptation-level theory.* New York: Academic Press, 1971*b*, pp. 19–25.

Avant, L. L., and Helson, H. Theories of perception. In B. B. Wolman (Ed.), *Handbook of general psychology.* Englewood Cliffs, N.J.: Prentice-Hall, 1973, pp. 419–448.

Avant, L. L., and Kent, M. Anchoring lines and the Mueller-Lyer illusion. U.S. Army Human Engineering Laboratories Technical Note No. 6–70, 1970.

Behar, I., and Bevan, W. The perceived duration of auditory and visual intervals: Cross-modal comparison and interaction *American Journal of Psychology,* 1961, *74*, 17–26.

Bell, R. A., and Bevan, W. Influence of anchors upon the operation of certain gestalt organizing principles. *Journal of Experimental Psychology,* 1968, *78*, 670–678.

Berkeley, G. *Three dialogues between Hylas and Philonous.* London: 1713. Reprint ed. Chicago: Open Court Publishing Company, 1927.

Bevan, W. An adaptation-level interpretation of reinforcement. *Perceptual and Motor Skills,* Monograph Supplement 3-V23, 1966.

Bevan, W., and Adamson, R. Reinforcers and reinforcement: Their relation to maze performance. *Journal of Experimental Psychology,* 1960, *59*, 226–232.

Bevan, W., and Adamson, R. E. Internal referents and the concept of reinforcement. In N. F. Washburne (Ed.), *Decisions, values, and groups.* Vol. 2. New York: Pergamon Press, 1962, pp. 453–472.

Bevan, W., and Darby, C. L. Patterns of experience and the constancy of an indifference point for perceived weight. *American Journal of Psychology,* 1955, *68*, 575–584.

Bevan, W., and Pritchard, J. F. Effect of "subliminal" tones upon the judgment of loudness. *Journal of Experimental Psychology,* 1963a, *66*, 23–29.

Bevan, W., and Pritchard, J. F. The anchor effect and the problem of relevance in the judgment of shape. *Journal of General Psychology,* 1963b, *69*, 147–161.

Bevan, W., and Saugstad, P. Experience, discrimination, and generalization efficiency, *British Journal of Psychology,* 1955, *46*, 13–19.

Beven, W., Barker, H., and Pritchard, J. F. The Newhall scaling method, psychophysical bowing, and adaptation level. *Journal of General Psychology,* 1963a, *69*, 95–111.

Bevan, W., Maier, R. A., and Helson, H. The influence of context upon the estimation of number. *American Journal of Psychology,* 1963b, *78*, 464–469.

Bevan, W., Bell, R. A., and Taylor, C. Changes in response latency following shifts in the pitch of a signal. *Journal of Experimental Psychology,* 1966, *72*, 864–868.

Bevan, W., Avant, L. L., and Lankford, H. G. Influence of interpolated periods of activity and inactivity upon the vigilance decrement. *Journal of Applied Psychology,* 1967, *51*, 352–356.

Black, R. W., and Bevan, W. The effect of subliminal shock upon the judged intensity of weak shock *American Journal of Psychology,* 1960, *73*, 262–267.

Black, R., Adamson, R., and Bevan, W. Runway behavior as a function of apparent intensity of shock. *Journal of Comparative and Physiological Psychology,* 1961, *54*, 270–274.

Boardman, W. K., and Goldstone, S. Effects of subliminal anchors upon judgments of size. *Perceptual and Motor Skills,* 1962, *14*, 475–482.

Broadbent, D. E. *Decision and stress.* London: Academic Press, 1971.

Brown, D. R. Stimulus-similarity and the anchoring of subjective scales. *American Journal of Psychology,* 1953, *66*, 199–214.

Brown, D. R., and Reich, C. M. Individual differences and adaptation-level theory. In M. H. Appley (Ed.), *Adaptation-level theory.* New York: Academic Press, 1971, pp. 215–231.

Calfee, R. C. *Human experimental psychology.* New York: Holt, Rinehart and Winston, 1975.

Campbell, D. T., and Kral, T. P. Transposition away from a rewarded stimulus card to a nonrewarded one as a function of a shift in background. *Journal of Comparative and Physiological Psychology,* 1958, *51*, 592–595.

Capehart, J., Tempone, V. J., and Hébert, J. A theory of stimulus equivalence. *Psychological Review,* 1969, *76*, 405–418.

Di Lollo, V. Contrast effects in judgment of lifted weights. *Journal of Experimental Psychology,* 1964, *68*, 383–387.

Dinnerstein, D. Intermanual effects of anchors on zones of maximal sensitivity in weight discrimination. *American Journal of Psychology,* 1965, *78*, 66–74.

Dinnerstein, D. Adaptation level and structural interaction: Alternative or complementary concepts? In M. H. Appley (Ed.), *Adaptation-level theory.* New York: Academic Press, 1971, pp. 81–93.

Dixon, N. F. *Subliminal perception: The nature of a controversy.* London: McGraw-Hill, 1971.

Durlach, N. I., and Braida, L. D. Intensity perception. I. Preliminary theory of intensity resolution. *Journal of the Acoustical Society of America*, 1969, *46*, 372–383.

Egeth, H., Avant, L. L., and Bevan, W. Does context influence the shape of a perceptual scale? *Perception and Psychophysics*, 1968, *4*, 54–56.

Ellis, H. D. Adaptation level theory and context effects on sensory judgments: Perception or response? *Perception*, 1972, *1*, 101–109.

Gilinsky, A. S. Comment: Adaptation level, contrast, and the moon illusion. In M. H. Appley (Ed.), *Adaptation-level theory*. New York: Academic Press, 1971, pp. 71–79.

Goldstone, S., and Goldfarb, J. L. Adaptation level, personality theory, and psychopathology. *Psychological Bulletin*, 1964, *61*, 176–187.

Goldstone, S., Goldfarb, J., Strong, J., and Russell, J. Replication: Effect of subliminal shock upon judged intensity of weak shock. *Perceptual and Motor Skills*, 1962, *14*, 222.

Greeno, J. G. A survey of mathematical models in experimental psychology. In B. B. Wolman (Ed.), *Handbook of general psychology*. Englewood Cliffs, N.J.: Prentice-Hall, 1973, pp. 123–162.

Haertzen, C. A., and Hooks, N. T. Contrast effects from simulation of subjective experiences: A possible standard for behavioral modification. *British Journal of Addiction*, 1971, *66*, 225–227.

Hardesty, D., and Bevan, W. Response latency as a function of the temporal pattern of stimulation. *Psychological Record*, 1965, *15*, 385–392.

Harvey, O. J., and Campbell, D. T. Judgments of weight as affected by adaptation range, adaptation duration, magnitude of unlabeled anchor, and judgmental language. *Journal of Experimental Psychology*, 1963, *65*, 12–21.

Hébert, J. A., Bullock, M., Levitt, L., Woodward, K. G., and McGuirk, F. D. Context and frequency effects in the generalization of a human voluntary response. *Journal of Experimental Psychology*, 1974, *102*, 456–462.

Helson, H. Fundamental problems in color vision. I. The principle governing changes in hue, saturation, and lightness of non-selective samples in chromatic illumination. *Journal of Experimental Psychology*, 1938, *23*, 439–476.

Helson, H. Adaptation-level as a frame of reference for prediction of psychophysical data. *American Journal of Psychology*, 1947, *60*, 1–29.

Helson, H. Adaptation-level as a basis for a quantitative theory of frames of reference. *Psychological Review*, 1948, *55*, 297–313.

Helson, H. Adaptation level theory. In S. Koch (Ed.), *Psychology: A study of a science*. Vol. 1. New York: McGraw-Hill, 1957, pp. 565–621.

Helson, H. Studies of anomalous contrast and assimilation. *Journal of the Optical Society of America*, 1963, *53*, 179–184.

Helson, H. *Adaptation-level theory*. New York: Harper and Row, 1964a.

Helson, H. Current trends and issues in adaptation-level theory. *American Psychologist*, 1964b, *19*, 26–38.

Helson, H. Adaptation-level theory: 1970 and after. In M. H. Appley (Ed.), *Adaptation-level theory*. New York: Academic Press, 1971, pp. 5–17.

Helson, H. Some highlights of an intellectual journey. In T. S. Krawiec (Ed.), *The psychologists*. Vol. 1. New York: Oxford University Press, 1972, pp. 91–111.

Helson, H., and Joy, V. L. Domains of lightness assimilation and contrast. *Psychologische Beiträge*, 1962,*6*, 405–415.

Helson, H., and Kaplan, S. Effects of background reflectance on transposition of lightness discrimination. Unpublished study, 1950. Cited in H. Helson, *Adaptation-level theory*. New York: Harper and Row, 1964, pp. 413–414.

Helson, H., and Kozaki, A. Anchor effects using numerical estimates of simple dot patterns. *Perception and Psychophysics*, 1968a, *4*, 163–164.

Helson, H., and Kozaki, T. Effects of duration of series and anchor-stimuli on judgments of perceived size. *American Journal of Psychology*, 1968b, *81*, 291–302.

Helson, H., and Michels, W. C. The effect of adaptation on achromaticity. *Journal of the Optical Society of America*, 1948, *38*, 1025–1032.

Helson, H., and Nash, M. C. Anchor, contrast, and paradoxical distance effects. *Journal of Experimental Psychology*, 1960, *59*, 113–121.

Helson, H., and Rohles, F. H., Jr. A quantitative study of reversal of classical lightness-contrast. *American Journal of Psychology*, 1959, *72*, 530–538.

Helson, H., Bevan, W., and Masters, H. G. A quantitative study of relevance in the formation of adaptation levels. *Perceptual and Motor Skills*, 1966, *22*, 743–749.

Hinckley, E. D., and Rethlingshafer, D. Value judgments of heights of men by college students. *Journal of Psychology*, 1951, *31*, 257–262.

Hurwitz, H. M. B. The effect of illumination conditions on the effectiveness of light-onset as a reinforcer: A test of the Bevan-Adamson reinforcement theory. *British Journal of Psychology*, 1960, *51*, 341–346.

James, H. An application of Helson's theory of adaptation level to the problem of transposition. *Psychological Review*, 1953, *60*, 345–352.

Kakizaki, S. Semantic effects in perceptual judgments. *Psychologia*, 1967, *10*, 187–196.

Koffka, K. *Principles of gestalt psychology*. New York: Harcourt Brace, 1935.

Künnapas, T. M. Influence of frame size on apparent length of a line. *Journal of Experimental Psychology*, 1955, *50*, 168–170.

Locke, J. *An essay concerning human understanding*. Book 2, Sect. 21. London: 1690. A later edition, New York: Valentine Seaman, 1824.

MacDougall, J., and Bevan, W. Influence of pretest shock upon rate of electrical self-stimulation of the brain. *Journal of Comparative and Physiological Psychology*, 1968, *65*, 261–264.

McClelland, D. C., Atkinson, J. W., Clark, R. A., and Lowell, E. L. *The achievement motive*. New York: Appleton Century, 1953.

Michels, W. C., and Helson, H. A reformulation of the Fechner law in terms of adaptation-level applied to rating-scale data. *American Journal of Psychology*, 1949, *62*, 355–368.

Mikkonen, V. On the retention of perceptual quantities. *Commentationes Humanarum Litterarum, Societas Scientiarum Fennica*, 1969, *44(3)*, 92.

Morikiyo, Y. Time-order error in the successive comparison of tones: An examination of adaptation-level theory. *Japanese Journal of Psychology*, 1959, *30*, 198–207.

Mowrer, O. H., Rayman, N., and Bliss, E. L. Preparatory set (expectancy): An experimental demonstration of its central locus. *Journal of Experimental Psychology*, 1940, *26*, 357–372.

Murray, H. G. Stimulus intensity and reaction time: Evaluation of a decision-theory model. *Journal of Experimental Psychology*, 1970, *84*, 383–391.

Parducci, A., and Marshall, L. M. Assimilation vs. contrast in the anchoring of perceptual judgments of weight. *Journal of Experimental Psychology*, 1962, *63*, 426–437.

Parducci, A., and Sandusky, A. J. Limits and the applicability of signal detection theories. *Perception and Psychophysics*, 1970, *7*, 63–64.

Parducci, A., Calfee, R. C., Marshall, L. M., and Davidson, L. P. Context effects in judgment: Adaptation level as a function of mean, midpoint, and median of the stimuli. *Journal of Experimental Psychology*, 1960, *60*, 65–77.

Podell, J. E. A comparison of generalization and adaptation-level as theories of connotation. *Journal of Abnormal and Social Psychology*, 1961, *62*, 593–597.

Pratt, C. C. Time-errors in the method of single stimuli. *Journal of Experimental Psychology*, 1933, *16*, 798–814.

Pritchard, J. F., and Bevan, W. Anchor effectiveness as a function of stimulus variation on an incidental dimension. *Journal of General Psychology*, 1966, *74*, 245–251.

Restle, F., and Merryman, C. Distance and an illusion of length of line. *Journal of Experimental Psychology*, 1969, *81*, 297–302.

Rethlingshafer, D., and Hinckley, E. D. Influence of judges' characteristics upon adaptation level. *American Journal of Psychology*, 1963, *76*, 116–119.

Rock, I., and Brosgole, L. Grouping based on phenomenal proximity. *Journal of Experimental Psychology*, 1964, *67*, 531–538.

Ross, M., and Thibaut, J. Determinants of standards of judgment. *Journal of Personality*, 1974, *42*, 383–398.

Sarris, V. Adaptation-level theory: Two critical experiments on Helson's weighted-average model. *American Journal of Psychology*, 1967, *80*, 331–334.

Sherif, M., Taub, D., and Hovland, C. I. Assimilation and contrast effects of anchoring stimuli on judgments. *Journal of Experimental Psychology*, 1958, *55*, 150–155.

Steger, J. A. Reversal of simultaneous lightness-contrast. *Psychological Bulletin*, 1968, *70*, 774–781.

Steger, J. A. Visual lightness assimilation and contrast as a function of differential stimulation. *American Journal of Psychology*, 1969, *82*, 56–72.

Steger, J. A., and O'Reilly, E. Simultaneously contrasting anchors. *Perception and Psychophysics*, 1970, *7*, 281–283.

Stevens, S. S. Adaptation-level vs. the relativity of judgment. *American Journal of Psychology*, 1958, *71*, 633–646.

Stevens, S. S. To honor Fechner and to repeal his law. *Science*, 1961, *133*, 80–86.

Swets, J. A. Central factors in auditory frequency selectivity. *Psychological Bulletin*, 1963, *60*, 429–440.

Swets, J. A. Comment: Adaptation-level theory and signal-detection theory and their relation to vigilance experiments. In M. H. Appley (Ed.), *Adaptation-level theory*. New York: Academic Press, 1971, pp. 49–53.

Thomas, D. R., and Jones, C. G. Stimulus generalization as a function of the frame of reference. *Journal of Experimental Psychology*, 1962, *64*, 77–80.

Thomas, D. R., Strub, H., and Dickson, J. F., Jr. Adaptation level and the central tendency effect in stimulus generalization. *Journal of Experimental Psychology*, 1974, *103*, 466–474.

Turner, E. D., and Bevan, W. Simultaneous induction of multiple anchor effects in the judgment of form. *Journal of Experimental Psychology*, 1962, *64*, 589—592.

Turner, E. D., and Bevan, W. Patterns of experience and the perceived rotation of the Necker cube. *Journal of General Psychology*, 1964a, *70*, 345–352.

Turner, E. D., and Bevan, W. The perception of auditory patterns as a function of incidental visual stimulation. *Psychonomic Science*, 1964b, *1*, 135–136.

von Wright, J. M., and Mikkonen, V. Changes in repeated reproduction of weight as a function of adaptation level. *Scandinavian Journal of Psychology*, 1964, *5*, 239–248.

Vourinen, R. Effects of series and anchor weights on adaptation-level. *Reports from the Institute of Psychology, University of Helsinki*, No. 2, 1970.

Vourinen, R. The concept of adaptation-level in psychological research. *Scandinavian Journal of Psychology*, 1973, *14*, 228–240.

Wagner, K., and Avant, L. L. Anchoring stimuli and Titchener's illusion. U.S. Army Human Engineering Laboratories Technical Note No. 7–70, 1970.

Wilson, W. A., Jr., and Wilson, M. Physiological psychology: Neuropsychology. In H. Helson and W. Bevan (Eds.), *Contemporary approaches to psychology*. Princeton, N. J.: Van Nostrand, 1967, pp. 35–89.

Zeiler, M. D. The ratio theory of intermediate size discrimination. *Psychological Review*, 1963a, *70*, 516–533.

Zeiler, M. D. New dimensions of the intermediate size problem: Neither absolute nor relational response. *Journal of Experimental Psychology*, 1963b, *66*, 588–595.

13

A Perceptual View of Conceptual Development

THOMAS J. TIGHE AND LOUISE S. TIGHE

1. Introduction

Our theoretical and research interests have focused on the interface between perception and learning. This interface poses two fundamental questions: To what extent is learning a matter of perception? and To what extent is perception a matter of learning? Each of these questions requires a consideration of the possible modification of perception through experience, the first because the issue is whether the changes observed in traditional learning paradigms can be attributed to changes in perception, and the second because the issue is whether experience does work enduring change in perception. In approaching either of these issues, then, the starting point must be a consideration of what is perceived in a given situation at the outset of a given experience and what are the possibilities for change in perception. The premise of this chapter, and of much of our work, is that in addressing these questions those working within the learning orientation have underestimated the perceptual possibilities of the typical laboratory task, with the consequence that important contributions of perception to learning and of learning to perception have been overlooked.

In dealing with this matter, the first problem is to establish a plausible case that there *is* a problem. Let us begin by analyzing the stimulus side of a relatively simple form of learning. Consider a simultaneous discrimination task involving stimulus objects varying in size and brightness. The objects are presented in pairs, each pair presentation constituting a discrete trial on which the

THOMAS J. TIGHE AND LOUISE S. TIGHE • Department of Psychology, Dartmouth College, Hanover, New Hampshire 03755.

subject must choose one member of the pair. Figure 1 shows the four settings possible within this task, i.e., the four pairings that exhaust the possible combinations of the size, brightness, and position features. Choice of an object containing a given stimulus aspect (e.g., "black") is rewarded in each pair, while choice of the stimulus object containing the opposing aspect is never rewarded. Over trials the stimulus aspects that determine reward and nonreward are combined with the remaining stimulus aspects equally often but in a random order. Training continues until the subject consistently chooses the rewarded stimulus object.

What are the perceptual possibilities in this situation? If this question is to be meaningfully pursued in relation to the discrimination paradigm, it must first be rephrased in terms appropriate to test of its answer. With respect to the paradigm of Fig. 1, to assert that an organism perceives the learning situation in such and such a manner is to say that the given specification of the stimulus can be shown to be in correspondence with discriminative response. To rephrase the question, then, we can say: What are the possible controlling stimuli for the subject's choice?

We approach this question from the premise that virtually any learning situation affords alternative bases for a response. This circumstance is recognized in the common distinction between *potential* stimuli, defined as all situational aspects which might become related to the behavior in question, and *effective* stimuli, or those aspects which in fact come to control behavior. Even in the simplest learning tasks, there are apt to be different ways of apprehending the stimulus-reward relationship. When there exist specifiable alternative perceptual modes that are equally adequate to the demands of the task, then one may properly question which alternative is utilized by the organism. Thus, in the task schematized in Fig. 1, a successful choice could be based on either single or combined aspects of the stimulus objects. For example, a subject rewarded as in Fig. 1 could accomplish the task by learning to approach "large black" and "small black," or other stimulus aspects in combination with "black," or, alternatively, by learning to approach "black." To say that these are alternative bases for solution is simply to say that they are stimulus aspects that stand in constant relation to presence/absence of reward and therefore are logically possible controlling stimuli.

Must we seriously entertain the possibility of such seemingly inefficient solutions as an approach to stimuli composed of relevant and irrelevant stimulus aspects? If we have recourse to current discrimination learning theories, it is clear that the answer is no. These theories assume that learning is a highly selective process whereby a restricted portion of the stimulus complex is abstracted in association with the learned response (e.g., Trabasso and Bower, 1968; Sutherland and Mackintosh, 1971; Zeaman and House, 1963). While it is generally recognized that stimulus selection is a more or less matter, i.e., that it may involve one or more component dimensions or cues, it is clear that the

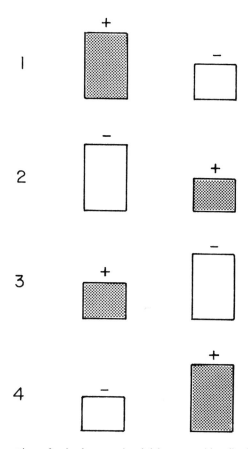

Fig. 1. The four settings of a simultaneous size, brightness, position discrimination task.

eventual learned association is viewed as being restricted to the relevant cues. In essence, reinforced training as in Fig. 1 is seen as strengthening attention to the relevant cues ("black-white") and simultaneously extinguishing attention to the other stimulus aspects, with the result that by the end of training the organism chooses on the basis of a single aspect ("black"). Under this view, the compound solution modes suggested above are not viable alternatives.

2. Subproblem Analysis of Discrimination Learning

A simple test of this issue is possible. Suppose that after the subject has achieved solution of the task set in Fig. 1, the stimulus-reward relations are shifted so that only choice of the large stimulus objects is rewarded (as in Fig.

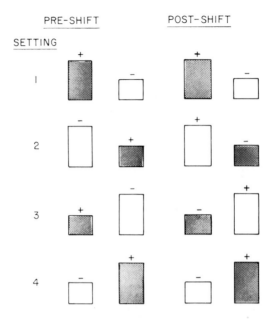

Fig. 2. An extradimensional shift from brightness relevant to size relevant.

2) and training is continued until the subject again attains a solution. In the language of the discrimination theorists, this change in reinforcement contingencies would constitute an extradimensional shift, and would be conceptualized as change in the relevance of the task *dimensions*. While this operation can be described at such a relatively abstract level, i.e., in terms of the changed reward status of stimulus classes or dimensions, it also can be described in terms of its specific effects within particular settings of the task. Note that the reward shift affects only two of the four task settings. Specifically, it changes (reverses) the stimulus-reward relations within settings 2 and 3 but leaves unchanged the stimulus-reward relations within settings 1 and 4 (see Fig. 2). This circumstance makes it possible to secure evidence on the nature of the controlling stimulus. If a choice of "black" is the basis of the solution in the preshift phase, then the extradimensional shift should disrupt performance on all task settings since the shift invalidates the "black"-reward relationship which obtains within all settings. On the other hand, if the subject perceives two stimulus-reward relations in the preshift problem, "large black"-reward and "small black"-reward, and chooses on these bases, then the shift should disrupt performance only within settings 2 and 3 since the shift invalidates only the "small black"-reward relation.

Figure 3 depicts the pattern of results obtained when the setting (subproblem) analysis is performed with lower organisms. The figure shows the group

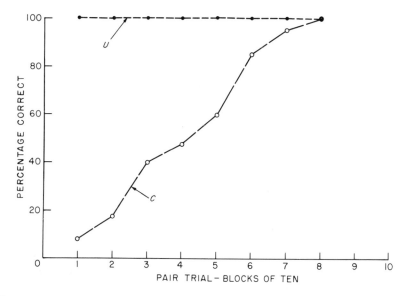

Fig. 3. Percentage correct choice as a function of trials for the changed (C) and unchanged (U) set-tings of an extradimensional shift from brightness to hue. The data of this analysis are from Graf and Tighe (1971).

learning functions of animals on the unchanged and changed settings of an ex-tradimensional shift carried out within a simultaneous hue and brightness dis-crimination in the manner shown in Fig. 2. Specifically, the task involved two stimulus pairs, a bright red light vs. a dim orange light and a dim red light vs. a bright orange light. The shift depicted in Fig. 3 involved a change from bright-ness relevant to hue relevant, and the function labeled U (unchanged) shows the mean percent correct choice on the pair that maintained the stimulus-reward relations of the preshift phase, while C (changed) shows the mean performance on the pair which underwent reversal of stimulus-reward relations. As seen in Fig. 3, there was no decrement whatsoever in performance on the unchanged settings; all subjects continued at 100% correct choice on these settings throughout the shift phase even though one of the components of the previously correct stimulus compound was undergoing extinction on the changed settings. In contrast, performance on the changed settings begins near zero correct and improves gradually over trials. These differing functions on the changed and unchanged settings clearly indicate the operation of different controlling stimuli on the different settings.

Analyses of performance on the changed and unchanged settings of ex-tradimensional shifts have been carried out with a variety of infrahuman spe-cies, including rats, pigeons, turtles (T. J. Tighe, 1973), and monkeys (Medin, 1973), with results approximating those seen in Fig. 3. In fact, an experiment of this type that included analysis of choice times (Kulig and Tighe, 1976) found that the subjects were learning to make a *more* rapid choice of the correct compound in the unchanged setting at the same time that they were relearning (reversing) their choice to the compounds in the changed setting! Taken together, the findings indicate that in such tasks learning may proceed, at least at the infrahuman level, on the basis of what may be termed lower-order perceptions of stimulus compound-reward relations, as an alternative to a solution based on isolated component-reward relations. For a detailed discussion of the inadequacy of current dimension-attention theories in relation to data like that of Fig. 3, see Medin (1973) and T. J. Tighe (1973).

Turning now to the ontogeny of human learning, which is a focus of this chapter, we have conducted similar analyses of extradimensional shift performance by children of different ages. One analysis compared 4- and 10-year-old children who had been trained in a simultaneous size-brightness discrimination in precisely the manner shown in Fig. 2 (T.J. Tighe, Glick, and Cole, 1971). Half of the children at each age shifted from size to brightness and the other half shifted from brightness to size. Figure 4 shows the trial-by-trial group learning functions for each age level on changed and unchanged settings of the shift problem. Considering the performance of the 4-year-olds, a marked difference in performance on the two types of setting is apparent with subjects exhibiting a relatively high proportion of correct choices on unchanged settings throughout shift, but a slow learning of correct choices on the changed settings. In contrast, in the curves of the 10-year-olds, we see the first evidence that task solution is based on an abstraction of the single cue-reward relation. Choice performance of the 10-year-old children is disrupted on *both* changed and

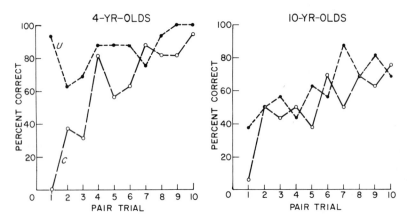

Fig. 4. Group learning functions of 4- and 10-year-old children on changed (*C*) and unchanged (*U*) settings of an extradimensional shift within a three-dimensional task. From T. J. Tighe *et al.* (1971).

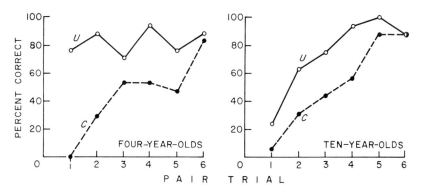

Fig. 5. Group learning functions of 4- and 10-year-old children on changed (*C*) and unchanged (*U*) settings of an extradimensional shift within a two-dimensional task, collapsed across dimensions. From T. J. Tighe (1973).

unchanged settings, and the learning functions on the two types of settings overlap throughout shift. Some further indicators of an age difference in the nature of the controlling stimulus are worthy of note. Ten of the 16 older children in this experiment reversed their choice on their first postshift exposure to an unchanged setting after nonreward on a changed setting. That is, nonreinforcement on the changed setting caused these subjects to change their response on the unchanged setting even though they had never experienced nonreward on this setting. In comparison, only one of the sixteen 4-year-olds showed such spontaneous reversal of choice on unchanged settings. In fact, seven of the 4-year-olds never made an error on the unchanged settings throughout the shift learning. All of the older children made at least one error on unchanged settings during relearning.

T. J. Tighe (1973, experiment VI) also tested 4- and 10-year-old children in a task of low complexity involving an across-modality (vision, position) shift, but with training conditions otherwise similar to those of the preceding experiment. The choice stimuli varied only in brightness and position, and at each age level 17 children shifted from brightness to position and another 17 shifted from position to brightness. As seen in Fig. 5, an age difference in learning on the unchanged settings is again manifest, with 4-year-olds showing a higher proportion correct on the initial shift trials than the 10-year-olds. Also, the older children again showed significantly more spontaneous reversal behavior than the younger subjects. Nine of the younger children solved the shift problem without making an error on unchanged settings, while all of the older children made one or more errors on unchanged settings.

Additional data in the vein of Fig. 4 and 5 could be cited. For example, Cole (1973) has obtained similar age effects within shift learning by rural Mexican children aged 4 to 10. However, the data above, in conjunction with the subproblem data from infrahuman subjects, should be sufficient to establish (1) that solution of a discrimination task may be based on differing perceptions of the stimulus-reward relations, differing perceptions as defined by differences in the stimuli shown to control choices, and (2) that there are reliable age and species differences in stimulus control. The data of the 10-year-old children are fully consistent with the view that choices by these subjects are based on a single stimulus property, or cue, that is common to, but functionally independent of, the particular stimulus settings of the task. The infrahuman data indicate that choices by these subjects are based on combined properties unique to each stimulus setting; such dependence of response will hereafter be referred to as "setting control." The choice behavior of the younger children appears to be intermediate in these respects between that of older children and that of infrahumans. We will discuss these data later. The point we wish to make now is that the answer to the question posed at the outset of this section (must we seriously entertain the possibility of solution based on stimulus *compounds* as well as on *components*?) is yes.

Next we will consider some experiments that extend these observations of age differences while providing information on the mechanisms involved.

3. Performance on Successively Learned Instances of a Concept

Caron (1968) also found evidence of strong contextual or setting control of young children's choice behavior in a study that required 3-year-olds to discriminate in succession five pairs of geometric figures comprising a common angularity-curvature discrimination. The children were rewarded for choice of the same stimulus value (angularity) in all pairs, but were trained on each pair to a criterion of three correct choices on four consecutive trials (i.e., presentations of the pair) *before* progressing to the next instance (pair) of the angularity-curvature dimension. The stimulus pairs consisted of black outline drawings on a white background (see Fig. 6A), and varied from trial to trial in left-right position of the pair members. Note that within the pairs the stimuli are equated on features other than angularity-curvature; i.e., pair members are equivalent in height, width, brightness, area, and general pattern. Under these conditions, it might be expected that the subjects would quite readily learn to choose the angular stimulus and achieve errorless learning on the latter pairs of the series. But Caron found that choices on the first presentation of each pair generally remained at chance level through the five pairs. Specifically, on the first trial of the fifth stimulus pair, only 12 of the 28 children chose correctly. The failure to find positive transfer across pairs is more remarkable in view of the fact that as subjects achieved criterion on each pair, they received additional training on that pair interspersed with the previously learned pairs. For example, after the

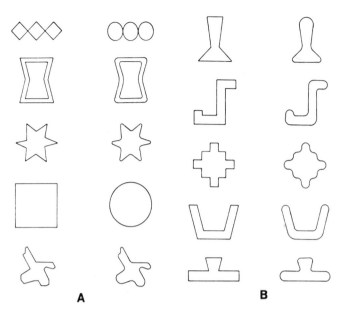

Fig. 6. A: The five stimulus pairs used by Caron. B: The five additional stimulus pairs used by
L. S. Tighe and Nagy.

subject had attained criterion on stimulus pair 2 in the series he received four
trials involving the already learned pairs 1 and 2 in random order before going
to the first trial of pair 3. The children have little difficulty in producing correct
response on these review trials. Thus, even though the children had learned and
were correct on temporally adjacent successive instances of the concept, each
newly introduced instance was treated by the group as an independent, to-be-
learned discrimination. In short, the subjects apparently discriminated each pair
in isolation.

Caron (1968) showed in other experimental treatments that the failure to
learn the stimulus pairs in unitary fashion was not due to inability to discriminate the angularity-curvature feature. In our view, the independent learning of
successive concept instances that Caron observed constitutes strong evidence of
setting control of choice behavior, i.e., control by stimulus properties unique to
each stimulus presentation array. We adopted Caron's task to study this phenomenon further. One experiment carried out by L. S. Tighe and J. Nagy sought
a fuller definition of the phenomenon by applying the task at different age
levels with the number of concept instances increased from five to ten. The five
additional stimulus pairs were taken from the pre- and posttraining phases of
Caron's study (1968), and are shown in Fig. 6B. The apparatus and procedure
were identical in all respects to those employed in the control condition of
Caron's experiment, and hence need not be detailed here. The major procedural

features were as follows: subjects were trained on one stimulus pair at a time; subjects had to achieve a criterion of three correct choices on four consecutive trials before progressing to the next pair; and beginning with the second stimulus pair, four review trials followed attainment of criterion on each stimulus pair. The review trials consisted of one presentation of the pair just learned interspersed with three presentations of previously learned instances (randomly selected after training on the fifth pair). The task was given to kindergarten, second, fourth-, and sixth-grade children. While the instructions at all ages were those Caron had devised for nursery school children, the use of these instructions and other simple aspects of procedure was rationalized for the upper three grades by adding that "we want to see how older and younger children will do when the game is played in exactly the same way."

There was clear evidence of a developmental difference in the method of solution. The proportions of kindergartners, second-, fourth-, and sixth-graders who chose the correct stimulus on the first presentation of the ninth and tenth stimulus pairs were 0.56, 0.68, 0.96, and 0.96, respectively. The kindergartners and second-graders did not differ, but both were significantly less likely to choose correctly as compared to the upper grades. Thus it appears that a sizable proportion of the kindergarten and second-grade children discriminated the stimulus pairs in isolation while nearly all of the fourth- and sixth-grade children discriminated on the basis of the *relation* common to the stimulus pairs. The use of ten stimulus pairs allows a rigorous statistical definition of the solution mode for the individual subject. Since five consecutive correct choices is an outcome beyond chance expectations, correct first choices on pairs 6–10 would indicate solution on the basis of the common relation. The proportions of subjects who displayed this choice pattern, from the lowest to highest grades, were 0.30, 0.56, 0.91, and 0.88. The proportions in each of the two lower grades were significantly smaller than those in the two upper grades, while the differences within these two groupings were not significant.

These data, then, extend Caron's in providing evidence of setting control of choices in second-graders and in showing the loss of such control by the fourth-grade level. It should also be noted that some individual subjects at all age levels solved on the conceptual basis.

In another part of their study, L. S. Tighe and Nagy sought evidence for the process underlying the developmental shift from independent to unitary learning of the task instances. They hypothesized that independent learning predominates in the young child in this situation not because he is unable to abstract the concept (angularity-curvature) but because he has difficulty discriminating the dimension-reward relation as it obtains across settings. If so, mere juxtaposition of the task instances might be expected to increase the more abstract solution. To test this, second-grade children (experimental group) were trained on the ten-pair task with a slightly modified procedure. When experimental subjects reached the learning criterion on the first stimulus pair, the experimenter placed a distinctive tag on the correct member and left the pair in view. On the first presentation of the next pair, the experimenter directed the child to look at the previously learned pair, pointed out the correct member of that pair, and asked the child to try to pick the correct member of the newly introduced pair, noting that it would be like the one that had the tag on it. This procedure was followed *on the first trial only of each pair*; on all other training trials, previously learned pairs were not present to view. An additional group of second-graders (control group) was trained in the manner described for the previous successive instance experiments.

The results indicated that the modified procedure facilitated the more abstract solution. Specifically, 0.88 of the experimental subjects chose correctly on the first presentation of pairs 6–10, while only 0.56 of the controls did so. Experimental subjects rarely made an error on trials following the initial presentation of each instance.

Overall, then, the successive instance experiments provide further evidence of an age difference in the relative strength of specific instance as compared to stimulus dimension control of choices, and suggest that one reason the young child exhibits more learning of individual instances is because he has difficulty isolating the dimension-reward relation across different settings of the task.

Let us now turn to a line of research that deals in a different fashion with the question of specific instance vs. more abstract dimensional control of choices.

4. Studies of Perceptual Pretraining

The observations in this area are drawn primarily from studies of discrimination- or concept-shift learning in children. The defining feature of the shift experiment is a sudden, unannounced change in stimulus-reward relations such that an initially learned solution is rendered inappropriate and a new problem posed. A major interest in this research has been to compare the ease with which organisms accomplish a reversal shift, which requires reversal of the choice of stimulus values on the relevant dimension, as opposed to an extradimensional shift, which requires the choice of stimulus values on a previously irrelevant dimension. Figure 7 illustrates the comparison. Note that extradimensional shift procedure is the same as that employed in the subproblem analyses of discrimination learning discussed earlier (Fig. 2). Considerable interest in the reversal-extradimensional comparison has been generated by the contention (Kendler and Kendler, 1962) that young children find reversal shift to be the more difficult problem while older subjects find reversal shift relatively easy. L. S. Tighe (1965) has detailed how a developmental trend in this direction could be expected from the assumption of an age difference in the

FIRST   SECOND
DISCRIMINATION   DISCRIMINATION

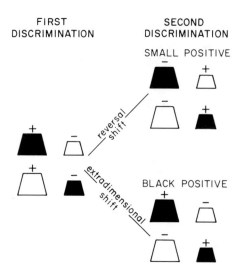

Fig. 7. Example of the reversal-extradimensional shift comparison. The two pairs of test stimuli and the rewarded stimulus are shown for each phase of the experiment.

type of stimulus control of choice behavior. Briefly, to the degree that the subject discriminates on the basis of the object-reward relationships of the task, a reversal shift should be relatively difficult since all of those relationships are changed in reversal shift while only half are changed in extradimensional shift (see Fig. 7). In contrast, when the subject learns primarily on the basis of stimulus dimension-reward relations, there is a basis for positive transfer in a reversal shift in the form of attention to the relevant feature-reward relation, while such attention should hinder extradimensional learning. In formulating this hypothesis, L. S. Tighe was guided by the differentiation theory of perceptual development (Gibson, 1969), which posits that sensitivity to stimulation is not static but rather changes significantly with perceptual experience. Particularly important to performance in standard discrimination problems is the assumption that organisms differ both individually and developmentally in their ability to detect and use distinguishing features of stimuli to respond to differences among objects and events.

Thus young children's shift learning might be altered toward reversal shift by training that is designed to facilitate abstraction of the stimulus dimensions of the task. To test this hypothesis, L. S. Tighe (1965) gave 5- and 6-year-old children perceptual pretraining with stimuli (tumblers varying in height and brightness) similar to those to be used in later tests of shift learning. In pretraining, subjects viewed a standard tumbler of a given height and brightness and then gave nonreinforced same-different judgments on a series of successively presented comparison stimuli, some of which differed from the standard only in height (four values), others only in brightness (four values), and others simultaneously in height and brightness. Subjects had two such judgment series with each of four different standard stimuli. Thus, subjects had relatively brief but concentrated practice in discriminating the objects along each of the task dimensions independently of the other and in the context of covariation of dimensions. Consistent with the hypothesis, the perceptually pretrained children learned a reversal shift faster than an extradimensional shift while children in the control group, who had been pretrained in tasks unrelated to the shifts, did not differ in speed of learning reversal and extradimensional shifts.

The perceptual pretraining procedure described above was subsequently applied in several related experiments, all based on the assumption of an age difference in the degree of control exerted by task instances as opposed to task (stimulus) dimensions. The first of these (L. S. Tighe and T. J. Tighe, 1969) tested the hypothesis that the beneficial effects of perceptual pretraining should become increasingly evident with increase in the number of task dimensions. First-grade children learned a reversal shift with one relevant dimension and either zero, one, or two irrelevant dimensions after receiving either the perceptual pretraining or control pretraining. The number of stimulus pairs necessary to represent the possible dimensional variations with these degrees of task complexity are one, two, and four, respectively (excluding consideration of position cues). The major finding was that perceptually pretrained and control subjects did not differ in speed of reversal learning with zero dimensions irrelevant, but with an increasing number of irrelevant dimensions the reversal shift performance of the controls deteriorated markedly in a linear manner while the performance of perceptually pretrained children did not change. This indicates that perceptual pretraining brought the choice behavior under the control of the relevant dimension.

Another experiment tested the hypothesis that transposition behavior[1] and reversal shift in young children would be facilitated by the same perceptual pretraining procedure (T. J. Tighe and L. S. Tighe, 1969a). The guiding assumption was that both transposition and ease of reversal shift reflect control by the dimensional properties of the task stimuli rather than by their absolute or object properties. The experiment also included a comparison of the effectiveness of perceptual training and training in verbal labeling, since failure to apply verbal mediators to the task stimuli has been held to underlie reported age difference in transposition and reversal shift (Kuenne, 1946; Kendler and Kendler, 1962). Specifically, first-grade children received one of three pretraining treatments on

---

[1] The transposition experiment allows the subject to transfer from one set of stimuli to another on the basis of either their absolute or their relational properties. Thus, after being consistently rewarded for choosing a 4-inch square over a 2-inch square, the subject might be presented with an 8-inch square and a 4-inch square and rewarded for either choice. Continued choice of the 4-inch square would indicate response to absolute stimulus properties, while choice of the 8-inch square would indicate response to relational properties, or transposition.

size and brightness dimensions: (1) perceptual pretraining as described above, (2) perceptual plus verbal training in which subjects received training identical to that given perceptually pretrained subjects but with added training in applying appropriate verbal labels to the stimuli, and (3) control pretraining involving tasks unrelated to the subsequent discrimination problems. One-half of each pretraining treatment group then learned a reversal shift and the other half received tests of transposition in a simultaneous size and brightness discrimination. As predicted, subjects in the perceptual pretraining and perceptual plus verbal pretraining groups were significantly and *equally* facilitated on *both* reversal and transposition tests as compared to the controls.

Another series of experiments sought to specify more precisely the conditions of perceptual pretraining that facilitate discrimination learning in children (L. S. Tighe and T. J. Tighe, 1968; T. J. Tighe and L. S. Tighe, 1968, 1969b). These experiments tested either reversal shift or transposition in first-grade children with a number of variations of the perceptual pretraining procedure. Conditions of pretraining investigated included manner of stimulus presentation (simultaneous vs. successive presentation of the standard and comparison stimuli), type of response (same-different judgment vs. passive observation of the stimuli), number of stimulus values appearing on each dimension, amount of pretraining (4, 8, or 12 experiences per stimulus), and presence or absence of information about correctness of judgment. It was found that effective perceptual pretraining required that subjects make same-different judgments (i.e., as opposed to passive observation of the stimuli), that more than two stimulus values appear on each dimension, and that there be at least eight experiences per stimulus. Transfer from pretraining did not vary with information about the correctness of judgment in pretraining, nor did transfer vary with manner of stimulus presentation (simultaneous or successive).

To recapitulate briefly, a set of nonassociative pretraining conditions has been isolated which facilitates young children's performance in reversal and transposition tasks. The major feature of the pretraining is that subjects make same-different judgments to stimulus objects varying along the dimensions appearing in the subsequent discrimination problems. Transfer from such perceptual pretraining does not vary with the presence or absence of reinforcement (in the sense of external confirmation), nor does it vary with added training in applying verbal mediators, but transfer does vary significantly with conditions that affect the nature and extent of the subject's perceptual experience with the task dimensions. Data corroborative of these general findings have been reported by several investigators. Vance and Siegel (1971) found that the perceptual pretraining procedure facilitated a reversal shift on pictorial stimuli in first-grade children while passive observational pretraining was without effect. Silleroy and Johnson (1973) report that the perceptual pretraining procedure facilitated the performance of 5-year-old children on a concept identification task with a nonpreferred relevant dimension. Seitz (1968) provided evidence that nonreinforced similarity judgments on the task stimuli facilitate a later optional reversal shift in 6-year-olds, and Caron (1969) found reversal learning in 3-year-olds facilitated by pretraining that required the subjects to match stimulus values along the task dimensions.

Our general interpretation of perceptual pretraining is that it is a more efficient and effective means of making young children learn about stimulus dimensions rather than about objects, the same effect normally produced by extended discrimination training, whether laboratory training or the training that occurs in natural life situations. Our hypothesis as to the specific mechanism underlying effective perceptual pretraining will be discussed in a later section.

5. Memory for Instances and Categories

The final research operation to be described is derived from the foregoing paradigms. The logic of the approach is that if there is an age-difference in what is learned in simple concept tasks, then evidence for that difference should appear in a memory task. If children do tend to learn more about task instances than about task categories as compared to adults, they can be expected to remember the specific instance of the task better than adults; adults, on the other hand, would be expected to show good memory for the task categories but relatively poor memory for the particular instances that specified those categories. It should be noted that the predictions are assumed to hold for tasks involving categories that younger subjects are capable of using appropriately.

T. J. Tighe, L. S. Tighe, and Schechter (1975) tested these propositions with 7-year-olds and college students. The subjects were first trained in making an instrumental response to one-half of a list of randomly ordered words and a different instrumental response to the remaining half. The two response-defined word sets also comprised two familiar conceptual categories (animals and parts of the body), and thus subjects could discriminate on the basis of the specific properties of the words, their categorical meanings, or both (cf. Underwood, 1969). The subjects were told only to learn which response was correct for each word, and were not told there was a conceptual basis for the responses. To assess whether the children were capable of categorizing the stimuli appropriately, an independent sample of 7-year-olds was asked to classify the items as either "animals" or "parts of the body" as they were presented one at a time. Classification was virtually perfect throughout this sample.

Either immediately following discrimination training or after a 3- to 4-week delay, the subjects received a recognition test that assessed memory for the instance vs. categorical properties of the task stimuli by embedding words from the original list with confusion items from either the same or different categories. The subject was presented a series of word triads with instructions to choose the one word in each triad that had appeared on the learning task. There were several triad types (randomly ordered), each defined by the nature of the confusion items. In type A triads the two new items were from different categories than those on the original list, e.g., *bear-apple-door*. On this triad type, knowledge of the task categories is sufficient to enable choice of the target item, and hence adults were predicted to perform as well as or better than children. In type B triads the two new words were from the same category as the "old" word, i.e., as the word from the learning task, e.g., *chin-ankle-chest*. Since all items on these triads are from the learning task categories, retention of the specific instance is required for correct identification of the target items, and hence children were predicted to perform better than adults. In type C, one of the new items was from the same category as the old word and one was from a different category than those on the original list, e.g., *dog-car-cat*. The interest was in how erroneous choices at each age level would be distributed over the same and different category confusion items. Type D triads were the same as type C except that the different category word was acoustically similar to the old item, e.g., *arm-farm-nose*. The interest was in whether the younger subjects' recognition behavior would be influenced by the irrelevant instance property of word sound, as suggested by some observations by Bach and Underwood (1970). Finally, type E triads consisted of a *new* word from categories on the original list and two words from different categories, e.g., *neck-peach-belt*.

When the memory test was administered immediately following training, there were few recognition errors by either age group, regardless of triad type. This outcome, in particular the failure to find errors on type B triads, indicates that the task instances had been learned by both adults and children.

However, the recognition performance of both adults and children deteriorated markedly on the delayed (3–4 week) memory test. Of major interest to the hypothesis was the fact that while adults and children did not differ in overall errors, they differed significantly in their distribution of errors by triad type. Three aspects of performance on the delayed test indicated that adults responded primarily by identifying the task categories while children sought to identify the task instances. (1) On A triads, where knowledge of task categories is sufficient to enable choice of the target item, adults never made an error, but on B triads, where retention of specific instances is necessary to correctly identify the target item, adults exhibited their highest error rate for any triad. In contrast, children's performance did not vary significantly over A and B triads, and they made significantly *fewer* errors than adults on B triads. The predictions for type A and B triads were thus confirmed. (2) Recognition errors by adults on C and D triads were invariably choices of confusion items from the same category as the target word, whereas children's errors were equally likely to involve choice of same and new category items. (The acoustic similarity aspects of the D triads had no effect on the recognition behavior of either children or adults.) (3) The adults' error rate varied directly with the degree of categorical competition with the target item, being minimal in A triads, maximal on B triads, and at an equal and intermediate level in C and D triads, while the children's error rate showed little variation over the triad types. In this respect, the children appeared to treat all triads as simply presentations of three specific instances.

These aspects of performance comprise strong evidence that adults' choices on the delayed test were controlled primarily by categorical properties of the test items and children's choices by specific instance properties. In this light it is not surprising that on E triads, which did not contain a task instance, adults chose the word from the learning task categories virtually without exception. But, surprisingly, the children also showed a high degree of categorical control on E triads, selecting words from learning task categories at a rate well beyond chance expectations in both immediate and delayed memory tests.

The children's data thus require that a sharp distinction be drawn between knowledge and utilization of the categorical attributes. On the one hand, there was clear evidence that the children could readily group the task instances into the appropriate categories, as seen in the classification behavior of the independent sample, and that they were sensitive to the categories as features of the task throughout discrimination training, as shown in their E triad performance. On the other hand, the children did not appear to utilize the task categories to assist learning and memory performance, as evidenced by their performance on triads A-D. In short, children's utilization of the task categories did not match their knowledge of them.

The nature of the age difference in categorical vs. instance control in this situation was given more precise definition in a recently completed experiment by L. S. Tighe and G. Potts, which sought evidence for categorical control of children's memory on the *immediate* test. Given the proximity of this test to the learning phase, it seemed possible that children's choices on A-D triads may have been influenced by categorical properties of the test items but that this influence was masked by the near-perfect performance on this test. To test this possibility, Tighe and Potts studied response latencies to the recognition triads as a presumably more sensitive measure of categorical control than error scores. They reasoned that if subjects have knowledge of the categorical organization of the task items, this knowledge could be used to rapidly narrow recognition search only to items from the task categories, and in consequence response latencies would vary with the number of task category items in the triad. In the absence of such knowledge, all items in any recognition triad must be regarded as potential target instances, and latencies would not be expected to vary across A-D triads.

The L. S. Tighe and G. Potts study replicated in major respects the training and immediate memory test phases of T. J. Tighe *et al*, (1975), except that (1) the D triads (with the acoustic similarity cue) were dropped from the memory test since they had proven noninformative, and (2) on the memory test the subjects were instructed to choose as quickly as possible consistent with choosing correctly every time.

L. S. Tighe and G. Potts again found virtually errorless recognition performance on the part of both adults and children. Considering the adults' latency data first, latencies on A triads were significantly faster than on all other triad types. This outcome is clear evidence that their recognition memory was influenced by categorical properties of the test items. Comparison of latencies on B and C triads did not approach significance. This is somewhat surprising since B triads contain two confusion items from the task categories while C triads contain one such confusion item. However, the advantage (to response speed) of having task categories to guide search might not be appreciable when more than a single triad item is from the task categories. Finally, latencies on E triads were significantly slower than on all other triad types.

The most surprising outcome in the context of the T. J. Tighe et al. (1975) study is that the children's latency pattern was virtually identical to that of adults. Children's A latencies were significantly faster than B latencies and tended to be faster than C latencies ($p = 0.07$). Like adults, children's latencies on B and C triads did not differ and their latencies on E triads were far slower than on all other triad types. The latency data, then, indicate that recognition search on the immediate test proceeded in the same way in adults and children and that both age groups had acquired some organized knowledge of the categorical structure of the learning task. In contrast, the children's error pattern on the delayed memory test in the study of T. J. Tighe et al. had provided little, if any, evidence of learning and usage of the categorical organization of the task items.

These outcomes can be accounted for by an assumption that the children did learn the categorical organization of the task items but only to a degree sufficient to enable use of this information on the immediate test. Under this view the children's learning of the item-category relationships was inferior to that of adults and consequently these relationships were not available to the children on the delayed test. The important feature of this interpretation is that it maintains that the difference between categorical control of learning and memory as manifested by adults and children in this situation is one of *degree*. Note that the children's latency data do not require an assumption that they had acquired complete knowledge of the categorical organization of the task; faster response to A triads could result from such incomplete knowledge as "there are a lot of animal and body words on this task." These general considerations, in turn, suggest that while children may process the task categories at a relatively low level, it should nevertheless be possible to eliminate or significantly reduce the age differences in delayed memory by special training. Specifically, if children can be induced to augment their processing of the task categories during learning, then we can expect an adultlike error pattern on the delayed test. The similarity between this line of reasoning and the rationale of the perceptual pretraining experiments is apparent.

6. Overview

The four research areas reviewed here attest strongly in various ways to an age difference in learning of the stimulus aspects of discrimination-concept tasks. Three of the paradigms, the subproblem, successive instance, and memory paradigms, produced clear evidence that choice behavior of young children is controlled to a greater degree by the specific stimulus objects or instances of the task than by the task dimensions, and that the opposite is true for the more mature subject. This age difference appears to have generality, since it was found under several different training procedures, in tasks of varying complexity, and with a variety of stimulus categories, including verbal stimuli as well as visual dimensions. Further, the stimulus dimensions in these tasks were familiar ones and included features that by independent measures the young children were capable of responding to selectively. Data from the successive instance paradigm indicated that instance vs. dimensional control varies not only developmentally but also among individuals at the age levels studied, and both the subproblem and memory paradigms indicated that the age difference in instance vs. dimensional control is a matter of degree rather than an "either-or" matter. Finally, there was evidence from the successive instance paradigm that young children's relatively weak learning of task dimensions is linked to their difficulty in detecting these features as they obtain across task settings, and there was abundant evidence from the perceptual pretraining paradigm that transition from instance to dimensional learning in several traditional discrimination tasks can be effected by manipulating the subjects' perceptual experience with the task dimensions.

7. Theoretical Treatment

7.1. Proposition: A Perceptual Basis of Conceptual Development

Let us begin by again considering Fig. 1 as an exemplar of traditional learning tasks. As successive trials unfold, certain objects are regularly followed by reward or by nonreward, and certain components of dimensions are regularly related to reward or to nonreward. The object-reward regularities can be isolated or known within settings, i.e., within the presentation arrays (cf. Fig. 1), but the dimension or component-reward relations can be isolated or known only across settings. As previously discussed, the subject can meet the primary task demand ("choose correctly every time") either by responding on the basis of the object-reward relations or by responding on the basis of the dimension-reward relations. Both object-reward and dimension-reward relations are *facts* of the learning environment, and therefore both are potential discriminations of any subject.

Our basic assumptions are that organisms differ in their likelihood of discriminating object-reward relations vs. dimension-reward relations and that this difference is at base a matter of a difference in perception. We assume that this difference in stimulus processing underlies the species and developmental differences in stimulus control as observed in the four paradigms reviewed above. Specifically, and focusing on the developmental differences, we maintain that the younger subject is less likely to abstract the dimensions and dimension-reward relations *as they obtain across settings* of the task. In this regard, we believe that a clear distinction should be made between an organism's sensitivity to stimulus dimensions *per se* and sensitivity to dimensions as they appear over different task settings and in relation to reward/nonreward outcomes. Our position is that even though a subject may be able to abstract and utilize a given dimension to distinguish objects in a given array or setting, at the same time he may not abstract and utilize that dimension to classify over successive arrays into aspects related to reward and aspects unrelated to reward, a classification which, as noted above, can be made and validated only over settings. We wish to emphasize that discrimination of object-reward relations and discrimination of dimension-reward relations are *not* mutually exclusive bases of solution. Rather, we assume that these two basic aspects of the stimulus input are normally processed concurrently. Given this view, choice behavior may be guided both by knowledge of object-reward relations and by knowledge of dimension-reward relations, but the degree of control associated with each can be expected to vary with a number of conditions working to favor or hinder abstraction of the task dimensions, e.g., salience of the dimensions.

In further elaboration of our basic assumptions, it should be noted that the terms "object-reward relations" and "dimension-reward relations" each indicate a class of possible discriminations. That is, both object-reward learning and dimension-reward learning can proceed at different levels of differentiation; the stimulus compounding that marks object-reward learning may not involve all possible stimulus values, and subjects may learn some but not all dimensions and cue-reward relationships within a task. The typical learning task, then, affords mutiple levels of abstraction, but these are classed most significantly into those which relate objects or combined properties of an object to reward within settings and those which relate dimensions or components of dimensions to reward across settings. (Incidentally, it might be noted in this connection that the subproblem analysis provides a technique for empirically determining what aspects of the test objects have been related to reward by the subject. That is, by applying the subproblem analysis to the possible extradimensional transfer sequences of a multidimensional task, it is possible to isolate the compounded and noncompounded cues, as T. J. Tighe, 1973, has shown in a series of experiments with infrahuman subjects.)

Next, let us consider several basic questions that can be directed to the analysis advanced here.

7.2. Is the Facilitative Pretraining Perceptual in Nature?

We have argued that the age shift in degree of object vs. dimensional control, as observed in the four paradigms reviewed here, is perceptually mediated. The evidence for this proposition comes primarily from research on the effects of perceptual pretraining on young children's learning. As reviewed above, these experiments have repeatedly found increased dimensional control, as indexed by transposition and shift performance, from pretraining designed to assist abstraction of the task dimensions. A fundamental question here is whether we are justified in characterizing the pretraining in these experiments as being perceptual in nature, rather than assuming that the pretraining works through some traditional learning mechanism. Several factors indicate that the perceptual conception is warranted. First, the pretraining operations were explicitly designed to promote stimulus differentiation while minimizing opportunities for other types of change (L. S. Tighe, 1965; L. S. Tighe and T. J. Tighe, 1966). Thus the pretraining does not manipulate conditions which, by principles of learning or mediation theory, differentially influence instrumental or mediational response strength to the task cues and dimensions. The pretraining is nonassociative and nonreinforced, the responses required of the subject are purely perceptual in nature (same-different judgments), and the stimulus presentation and judgment sequences were designed to provide practice in utilizing the dimensions independently of one another in the context of covariation of dimensions, thereby acting against the tendency to compound stimuli that is presumed for subjects of this age. Of course, it is possible that changes other than stimulus differentiation might still occur implicitly during the pretraining. We have attempted to check on this possibility in several ways. First, by means of a word association test we showed that children who undergo perceptual pretraining are no more likely to use task-relevant words than are nonpretrained children (L. S. Tighe, 1965). Second, pretraining identical to perceptual pretraining but with added explicit training in applying relevant verbal labels was found to be no more effective than perceptual pretraining alone in facilitating either transposition or reversal behavior (T. J. Tighe and L. S. Tighe, 1969a, 1970). Third, the perceptual pretraining procedure does not change children's preference for the stimulus dimensions involved (Silleroy and Johnson, 1973), and thus by strong implication does not change probabilities of attending to the several stimulus dimensions. In this regard it should also be noted that in all of the perceptual pretraining experiments children received equal training on each of the task dimensions, whether relevant or irrelevant, and therefore the facilitative effect of pretraining on transposition and reversal shifting cannot be accounted for on the basis of increased attention selective to the relevant task dimension.

Another consideration favoring a perceptual interpretation is that the parameters of effective pretraining are not predicted in any clear fashion by traditional learning theories, but rather appear to be conditions affecting the subject's perceptual experience with the task dimensions. For example, as noted earlier, effective perceptual pretraining requires that more than two stimulus values appear on each dimension in pretraining (L. S. Tighe and T. J. Tighe, 1968; T. J. Tighe and L. S. Tighe, 1968). In the section below we attempt to account for this finding in terms of a perceptual mechanism, but it is not apparent how it would be explained by learning theories. Similarly, it has been found that the effectiveness of pretraining does not vary with the presence vs. absence of reinforcement, in the sense of external confirmation of correct/incorrect response (T. J. Tighe and L. S. Tighe, 1968; Buss and Rabinowitz, 1973). This outcome is consistent with a perceptual learning interpretation of pretraining (L. S. Tighe and T. J. Tighe, 1966) but is not a normal expectation from traditional learning theory.

A final consideration is that subproblem analysis provides evidence that perceptual pretraining does mediate transition from within-setting to across-setting control in the manner claimed by the perceptual interpretation. The analysis was carried out on data from a study of perceptual pretraining and reversal shifting as a function of number of task dimensions (L. S. Tighe and T. J. Tighe, 1969), a study that had been reported only in terms of overall trials and errors during learning. The individual setting performances of children trained with the condition of greatest complexity—three dimensions represented in four stimulus pairs—were examined for evidence of spontaneous reversal. In reversal shift, 62% of the pretrained children reached the solution without making an error on all four stimulus pairs, while only 7% of the nonpretrained children did. By the spontaneous reversal measure, then, independence in performance on the task settings was significantly greater in nonpretrained children than in perceptually pretrained children. In this connection, it might be noted that Caron (1968) found that 3-year-olds trained in the successive instance paradigm no longer learned the angularity-curvature pairs in isolation when discrimination was accompanied by procedures that highlighted the stimulus dimensions.

It might be argued that while the considerations advanced to this point support a perceptual interpretation of pretraining in general terms, they do not speak to the question of the specific way in which the pretraining might alter perception of the task stimuli to mediate the observed transfer effects. To speak to this question, we think there are now considerable data that suggest the critical ingredient in pretraining is a kind of stimulus ordering or seriation experience. We have noted that pretraining with only two values per dimension has no effect on learning in the transfer task while identical pretraining with three or more values per dimension facilitates both transposition and reversal learning. In various experiments we have established that this cannot be attributed to differential discriminability of the values presented in pretraining or to differences in amount of pretraining (L. S. Tighe and T. J. Tighe, 1968; T. J. Tighe and L. S. Tighe, 1968, 1969b). In attempting to account for these observations, we noted that it is only when three or more stimulus values appear on each dimension that stimulus ordering by the subject is likely to be brought into play (T. J. Tighe and L. S. Tighe, 1960b). That is, only when at least three values appear would correct judgment, i.e., the same-different pretraining judgments, be appreciably facilitated by location (coding) of the position of each object presented within an ordered series. When only two stimulus values specify the dimensions, the subject can readily judge the pretraining stimuli in absolute terms, e.g., "the big one," "the dark one." But with the addition of even a single intermediate value, errors are likely to be made unless the subject is sensitive to the *degree* of the stimulus property presented, and ordering the stimuli on their dimensional attributes would be an efficacious means of accomplishing such discriminations of degree. Stimulus ordering during pretraining should, in turn, increase the likelihood that the subject responds to the dimensional properties of the stimuli rather than to their instance properties. In the subsequent transfer task, then, the subject would be more likely to detect the dimensions and dimension-reward relations in the face of the irrelevant setting contexts. Note that an ordering explanation of the effects of perceptual pretraining would be consistent with the previously noted failures to find effects from either reinforcement or verbalization in pretraining. That is, the ordering hypothesis indicates that it is the *way* subjects process the stimulus instances that is important rather than whether they label them or receive feedback for their judgments about them.

The suggestion that stimulus ordering is the critical variable in the perceptual pretraining is supported by several lines of research. Riley, McKee, and Hadley (1964) observed that considerable transposition obtains in young children when the stimuli involved are ones which these subjects find easy to place in order along a dimensional attribute (e.g., auditory intensities), but little transposition obtains when the stimuli are relatively difficult to order (e.g., auditory frequencies). Johnson and White (1967, 1968) have demonstrated a positive relation between children's ability to order a set of stimuli and both speed of mandatory reversal shift and frequency of optional reversal shift on these stimuli. Buss and Rabinowitz (1973) found that explicit ordering pretraining increased tranposition in first- and second-grade children, and far more than did same-different pretraining. Moreover, in agreement with outcomes of our perceptual pretraining research, they also found that seriation pretraining did not affect rate of learning in the initial discrimination preceding the transposition tests, and that the effectiveness of the ordering pretraining did not vary with presence vs. absence of reinforcement during pretraining. Finally, Timmons and Smothergill (1975) tested the prediction from the ordering hypothesis that perceptually pretrained children should be found superior to nonpretrained children in performance on ordering the stimulus dimensions of pretraining. Their subjects were kindergarten children who evidenced little correct ordering within height and brightness dimensions prior to the training. Training consisted of nonreinforced same-different judgments to wooden dowels varying in height, or in brightness, or simultaneously in height and brightness. Consistent with the ordering hypothesis, it was found that perceptual training did facilitate ordering, particularly if both the height and brightness dimensions varied simultaneously in training.

Taken together the foregoing observations provide substantial support for the hypothesis that perceptual pretraining works in significant part by inducing a stimulus ordering that fosters attention to the dimensional rather than the absolute properties of the task stimuli. While we argue that stimulus ordering is critical to effective perceptual pretraining, it is clear that other forms of training can also assist isolation of the task dimensions (e.g., Caron, 1968, 1969). In particular, the L. S. Tighe and Nagy experiment described in an earlier section found that dimensional learning could be markedly increased within the successive instance paradigm primarily by juxtaposing the task instances. It is worth noting, however, that in the L. S. Tighe and Nagy and Caron experiments the effective training procedures manipulated only the subject's perceptual responses to the task stimuli.

7.3. Are the Age Differences in Object vs. Dimensional Control a Matter of Ability or of Performance?

Is it the case that the young child can utilize dimension-reward relations but does not for reasons unrelated to abstracting skill *per se*? Or is the young child basically less skillful in abstracting such stimulus relations? This is a complex issue in the vein of the classic issues of learning vs. performance and production vs. mediation, and no simple, conclusive answer can be given. Here we will simply briefly indicate our position.

It should first be underscored that the age difference at issue is probably seldom, if ever, an all or nothing affair. Rather, as we have stressed, it is a matter of the relative weighting of two types of differentiation in the problem-solving process, and moreover a relative weighting that can be shown to vary, sometimes quite dramatically, with specific conditions of testing. For example, selection of optional reversal shift, a generally accepted index of the operation of dimensional control, may range from 0 to 100% among 3-year-olds depending on whether the relevant dimension is of low or high relative salience (T. J. Tighe and L. S. Tighe, 1966). Similarly, Cole (1976) has recently shown that the degree of specific instance vs. dimensional learning in young children may vary even between the original learning and transfer phases of a shift experiment. Nevertheless, while the age difference in object vs. dimensional learning is of a conditional nature, it is certainly not of a limited nature. In fact, as indicated by our review of the four research paradigms presented here, the difference appears quite pervasive, and we take this pervasiveness, coupled with the relative inefficiency of an object-reward solution, as presumptive evidence that the younger subject is in some fundamental sense less able to abstract the dimension-reward relations.

Of course, younger subjects might exhibit a broadly generalized tendency toward the less efficient object-reward learning not because they are less able to abstract the dimension-reward relations but because such abstraction is not a clear demand of the task. However, there is evidence from other research areas that the age difference persists even when dimension abstraction is demanded. For example, in several experiments Pick and her co-workers have shown that second-graders are less able than sixth-graders to focus exclusively on one of several simultaneously varying dimensions even when given foreknowledge of the relevant task dimension and explicitly instructed to respond to it (Pick, Christy, and Frankel, 1972; Pick and Frankel, 1973). Note that the skill at issue in these experiments, that of abstracting a relevant feature from an irrelevant stimulus context, is essentially the skill at issue in the four paradigms reviewed here. In the studies of Pick *et al.* the age difference in this skill was not decreased by giving subjects knowledge of the relevant dimension, as might be expected if the difference were a performance difference, but rather was actually increased. Some experiments by Kemler, Shepp, and Foote (1976) are also pertinent here. They made use of an incidental learning paradigm whereby, first, subjects are trained to solution on a multidimensional discrimination problem in which only one dimension is relevant and then, in further training trials, one of the previously irrelevant dimensions is made additionally relevant, i.e., redundant with the original relevant dimension. The interest in this experiment was in the degree of postsolution learning of the added relevant dimension as a function of whether or not that dimension had been sampled and rejected as irrelevant during the initial task. Kemler *et al.* found that while children between the ages of 5 and 10 did not differ in their learning about dimensions they had not previously sampled, the amount of postsolution learning about dimensions previously rejected as irrelevant was markedly age dependent; 10-year-olds gave no evidence of learning anything about these attributes but 5- and 7-year-olds exhibited significant learning of them. These data indicate that even when the uselessness of a task dimension has been clearly demonstrated, learning to ignore such dimensions proceeds more slowly in younger than in older children.

Taking, now, a broader perspective on the issue of ability vs. performance, we feel that there has been a tendency to overrate the evidence of abstraction skills in young children. Evidence frequently cited in this regard comes from the comparison of transfer of discrimination to *new* stimulus values on a previously relevant dimension (an intradimensional shift) with transfer to *new* values on a previously irrelevant dimension (an extradimensional shift). The fact that all subjects, regardless of age, learn an intradimensional shift faster than an extradimensional shift has been used to argue that stimulus dimension learning always predominates in the discrimination and transfer learning of young children. But since transfer of object control is eliminated in the intradimensional-extradimensional shift comparison, this paradigm should be considered as an unusually sensitive test of whether stimulus dimensions have been abstracted. As we have seen, when there is opportunity for transfer of stimulus dimension *and* object learning, as in comparison of reversal and extradimensional shifts involving stimulus objects identical to those in the preshift stage, a somewhat different picture of dimensional control emerges (Cole, 1973; T. J. Tighe, 1973).

Another paradigm frequently cited in relation to young children's abstraction skill is Levine's (1966) blank trial procedure, as applied to children's learning by a number of investigators (e.g., Eimas, 1969; Gholson, Levine, and Phillips, 1972). The critical feature of this procedure is the insertion during multiple problem discrimination training of a run of nonreinforced trials so structured that the subject's choice pattern on these blank trials defines the rule underlying his choices. A salient finding in these experiments is that young children's response patterns on blank trials indicate that their learning proceeds by systematic selective testing of dimension- and cue-reward relations, much in the manner observed with human adults in similar tests. But the blank trial experiment involves quite special training whereby the children are given explicit instruction in use of the relevant set of hypotheses during preliminary practice problems. Also, in research of this type typically only 15–30% of the problems learned by the subjects qualify for use in the hypotheses systems analysis (Gholson and Danziger, 1975). These considerations surely question the representativeness of the selective dimensional choices seen in these experiments.

7.4. Is Dimensional Learning a Function of Maturation or of Experience?

In our view the increased tendency toward dimensionally based learning comes about primarily through experience. To the degree that abstraction is assisted by language, an underlying maturational variable may be involved. However, we regard language as a secondary factor in the process in the sense that features must be perceptually isolated before they can be labeled. We assume, then, that primarily through cumulative perceptual experience the organism becomes better able to isolate the distinguishing features of objects, events, and sequences in its environment. A particularly important aspect of this experiential development is the improved differentiation of features (dimensions) as they obtain over different settings and over stimulus sequences. The improved differentiation of features, in turn, facilitates their utilization in differentiating stimulus relations across instances. In terms of the discrimination tasks we have been discussing here, the organism becomes better able to process the sequence of presentation arrays into dimension-reward relationships. In more general terms, it is a matter of perceptual experience working a change in the organism's usual mode of perceptual processing, a shift to more abstract, integrative, and informative units of processing.

This account stresses that the inexperienced organism's perception is more context bound, that abstraction of features and stimulus relations over settings is a relatively difficult matter for them, as indicated, for example, by young children's failure to transfer across instances of the simple discrimination employed in the successive instance paradigm. The stronger influence of setting context in young children's performance could reflect a general tendency to process stimulus sequences into segments determined by structural boundaries or breaking points (*cf.* Fodor, Bever, and Garrett, 1974). With reference to the discrimination learning situation, perhaps the choice and consequence on each trial constitute a salient breaking point in children's processing. If so, forms of experience or training that minimize such boundaries while inducing processing of dimensional properties (e.g., perceptual pretraining) may be particularly effective in assisting abstraction of features.

7.5. Relation of Present Theory to Others

Finally, a word might be said about the relation of the present formulation to two major theories of the development of discrimination, those of Kendler and Kendler (1962, 1968) and Zeaman and House (1963, 1974). For nearly a decade these formulations were sharply divided on the issue of the presence vs. absence of dimensional mediation in young children's discrimination learning. The Kendlers held that young children solve discrimination problems by forming only single-unit associations between choices and the task stimuli, while older subjects make use of mediating responses that represent the task dimensions. Zeaman and House, on the other hand, contended that mediation, in the form of attention to specific dimensions, obtains in the learning of all subjects, regardless of age. It can now be argued that each of these formulations was correct in its emphasis. From the viewpoint of the present analysis, single-unit learning, or what we have termed "object-reward learning," *is* relatively strong in young children's problem solving, but, at the same time, these subjects are not incapable of dimensionally based learning. By hindsight, it appears that each of these theoretical positions emphasized paradigms that favored the operation of the form of learning postulated, e.g., the intradimensional-extradimensional vs. the reversal-nonreversal shift comparisons.

Both theories have undergone significant modification. The Kendlers have moved from their initial strong assumption of an age transition from nonmediated to mediated learning and now hold that dimensional mediation becomes increasingly likely with increasing age (Kendler and Kendler, 1968). Zeaman and House (1974) accommodate the data from subproblem experiments and other evidence of "object learning" in young children by incorporating into their otherwise monistic attentional theory the notion of a compound dimension. The essential feature of this modification is that subjects are no longer assumed to attend only to the individual dimensions of the task but may also attend to and learn about the stimulus compounds or objects as such. Thus, both theories have come to make explicit provision for the possibility of varying degrees of both object and dimensionally based learning in young children, and in this regard they now resemble the position reviewed here. There appears to be an important area of agreement emerging among the three formulations, then, in the notion that with increasing age there will be a significant increase in stimulus dimension control of learning and a significant decrease in object control of learning. But the three theories differ, of course, in the mechanisms assumed to underlie the change in stimulus control. As we have pointed out elsewhere (T. J. Tighe and L. S. Tighe, 1972), these mechanisms, although fundamentally different, are not necessarily incompatible.

8. References

Bach, M. J., and Underwood, B. J. Developmental changes in memory attributes. *Journal of Educational Psychology*, 1970, *61*, 292–296.

Buss, J. L., and Rabinowitz, F. M. The intermediate-hue transposition of children after same-different and seriation pretraining. *Journal of Experimental Child Psychology*, 1973, *15*, 30–46.

Caron, A. J. Conceptual transfer in preverbal children as a consequence of dimensional training. *Journal of Experimental Child Psychology* 1968, *6* 522–542.

Caron, A. J. Discrimination shifts in three-year olds as a function of dimensional salience. *Developmental Psychology*, 1969, *1*, 333–339.

Cole, M. A developmental study of factors influencing discrimination transfer. *Journal of Experimental Child Psychology* 1973, *16*, 126–147.

Cole, M. A probe trial procedure for the study of children's discrimination learning and transfer. *Journal of Experimental Child Psychology*, 1976, *22*, 499–510.

Eimas, P. D. A developmental study of hypothesis behavior and focusing. *Journal of Experimental Child Psychology*, 1969, *8*, 160–172.

Fodor, J., Bever, T., and Garrett, M. *The psychology of language*. New York: McGraw-Hill, 1974.

Gholson, B., and Danziger, S. Effects of two levels of stimulus complexity upon hypothesis sampling systems among second and sixth grade children. *Journal of Experimental Child Psychology*, 1975, *20*, 105–118.

Gholson, B., Levine, M., and Phillips, S. Hypotheses, strategies, and stereotypes in discrimination learning. *Journal of Experimental Child Psychology*, 1972, *13* 423–446.

Gibson, E. J. *Principles of perceptual learning and development*. New York: Appleton, 1969.

Graf, V., and Tighe, T. Subproblem analysis of discrimination shift learning in the turtle (*Chrysemys picta picta*). *Psychonomic Science,* 1971, *25*, 257–259.

Johnson, P. J., and White, R. M., Jr. Concept of dimensionality and reversal shift performance in children. *Journal of Experimental Child Psychology*, 1967, *5*, 223–227.

Kemler, D. G., Shepp, B. E., and Foote, K. E. The sources of developmental differences in children's incidental processing during discrimination trials. *Journal of Experimental Child Psychology*, 1976, *21*, 226–240.

Kendler, H. H., and Kendler, T. S. Vertical and horizontal processes in problem-solving. *Psychological Review*, 1962, *69*, 1–16.

Kendler, H. H., and Kendler, T. S. Mediation and conceptual behavior. In K. W. Spence and J. T. Spence (Eds.), *The psychology of learning and motivation*. Vol. 2, New York: Academic Press, 1968, pp. 197–224.

Kuenne, M. R. Experimental investigation of the relation of language to transposition behavior in young children. *Journal of Experimental Psychology*, 1946, *36*, 471–490.

Kulig, J. W., and Tighe, T. J. Subproblem analysis of discrimination learning: Stimulus choice and response latency. *Bulletin of the Psychonomic Society*, 1976, *7*, 377–380.

Levine, M. Hypothesis behavior by humans during discrimination learning. *Journal of Experimental Psychology*, 1966, *71*, 331–338.

Medin, D. L. Subproblem analysis of discrimination shift learning. *Behavior Research Methods and Instrumentation*, 1973, *5*, 332–336.

Pick, A. D., and Frankel, G. W. A study of strategies of visual attention in children. *Developmental Psychology*, 1973, *9*, 348–357.

Pick, A. D., Christy, M. D., and Frankel, G. W. A developmental study of visual selective attention. *Journal of Experimental Child Psychology*, 1972, *14*, 165–176.

Riley, D. A., McKee, J. P., and Hadley, R. W. Prediction of auditory discrimination learning and transposition from children's auditory ordering ability. *Journal of Experimental Psychology*, 1964, *67*, 324–329.

Seitz, V. R. The measurement of dimensional dominance and its role in a concept-shift learning task. Unpublished doctoral dissertation, University of Illinois, 1968.

Silleroy, R. S., and Johnson, P. J. The effects of perceptual pretraining on concept identification and preference. *Journal of Experimental Child Psychology*, 1973, *15*, 462–472.

Sutherland, N. S., and Mackintosh, N. J. *Mechanisms of animal discrimination learning*. New York: Academic Press, 1971.

Tighe, L. S. Effect of perceptual pretraining on reversal and nonreversal shifts. *Journal of Experimental Psychology*, 1965, *70*, 379–385.

Tighe, L. S., and Tighe, T. J. Discrimination learning: Two views in historical perspective. *Psychological Bulletin*, 1966, *66*, 353–370.

Tighe, L. S., and Tighe, T. J. Transfer from perceptual pretraining as a function of number of stimulus values per dimension. *Psychonomic Science*, 1968, *12*, 135–136.

Tighe, L. S., and Tighe, T. J. Transfer from perceptual pretraining as a function of number of task dimensions. *Journal of Experimental Child Psychology*, 1969, *8*, 494–502.

Tighe, T. J. Subproblem analysis of discrimination learning. In G. H. Bower (Ed.), *The psychology of learning and motivation*. Vol. 7. New York: Academic Press, 1973, pp. 183–226.

Tighe, T. J., and Tighe, L. S. Overtraining and optional shift behavior in rats and children. *Journal of Comparative and Physiological Psychology*, 1966, *262*, 39–54.

Tighe, T. J., and Tighe, L. S. Perceptual learning in the discrimination processes of children: An analysis of five variables in perceptual pretraining. *Journal of Experimental Psychology*, 1968, *77*. 125–134.

Tighe, T. J., and Tighe, L. S. Facilitation of transposition and reversal learning in children by prior perceptual training. *Journal of Experimental Child Psychology*, 1969a, *8*, 366–374.

Tighe, T. J., and Tighe, L. S. Perceptual variables in the transposition behavior of children. *Journal of Experimental Child Psychology*, 1969b, *7*, 566–577.

Tighe, T. J., and Tighe, L. S. Optional shift behavior of children as a function of age, type of pretraining, and stimulus salience. *Journal of Experimental Child Psychology*, 1970, *9*, 272–285.

Tighe, T. J., and Tighe, L. S. Stimulus control in children's learning. In A. D. Pick (Ed.), *Minnesota symposia on child psychology*. Vol. 6. Minneapolis: University of Minnesota Press, 1972, pp. 128–157.

Tighe, T. J., Glick, J., and Cole, M. Subproblem analysis of discrimination-shift learning. *Psychonomic Science*, 1971, *24*, 159–160.

Tighe, T. J., Tighe L. S., and Schechter, J. Memory for instances and categories in children and adults. *Journal of Experimental Child Psychology*, 1975, *20*, 22–37.

Timmons, S. A., and Smothergill, D. W. Perceptual training of height and brightness seriation in kindergarten children. *Child Development*, 1975, *46*, 1030–1034.

Trabasso, T., and Bower, G. H. *Attention in learning: Theory and research*. New York: Wiley, 1968.

Underwood, B. J. Attributes of memory. *Psychological Review*, 1969, *76*, 559–573.

Vance, B. J., and Siegel, A. W. The relative effectiveness of observing response vs. predifferentiation pretraining on children's discrimination learning. *Psychonomic Science*, 1971, *24*, 183–185.

White, R. M., Jr., and Johnson, P. J. Concept of dimensionality and optional shift performance in nursery school children. *Journal of Experimental Child Psychology*, 1968, *6*, 113–119.

Zeaman, D., and House, B. J. The role of attention in retardate discrimination learning. In N. R. Ellis (Ed.), *Handbook of mental deficiency*. New York: McGraw-Hill, 1963, pp. 159–223.

Zeaman, D., and House, B. J. Interpretations of developmental trends in discriminative transfer effects. In A. D. Pick (Ed.), *Minnesota symposia on child psychology*. Vol. 8. Minneapolis: University of Minnesota Press, 1974, pp. 144–186.

Author Index

417

Subject Index

Acoustic
  cues and birdsongs, 110–112
  isolation and birdsongs, 108, 114, 116
Action and perception, 120
  perception and production of speech,
    159–160
Adaptation level
  definition, 361–363
  persistence of effects, 266
  theory, 264
Aerial perspective, 172, 196
Alternating monocular occlusion, 23–26,
    30–31, 42, 48, 50
Altricial species
  depth perception, 82–84
Amblyopia, 53–54, 59, 60
Anchor effects
  adaptation level theory, 365–367
  pooling or integration of stimulation,
    375–377
  response bias, 372–373
Aniseikonia, 282–283
Anistropy, 59
Anomalous
  early visual input, 47, 69
Assimilation and adaptation level theory,
    365
Association theories
  of discrimination learning, 388
Astigmatism, 1, 53–55, 59–60, 62–64, 273
Audiospectogram
  of birdsongs, 106, 107, 109, 111, 114
Auditory
  deprivation, 2
  development, 1
  experience and birdsongs, 113
  feedback, 113-116

Autocorrelation model
  and repetition effect, 355

Bayes's theorem
  and repetition effect, 267, 354
Bilinguals
  children, 156–158
  speech perception, 146–147
Binocular deprivation (kittens) 10, 11,
    15–17, 20, 22, 23, 30
Birdsongs, 107–117
  as related to visual depth perception, 100
Blank trial procedure, Levine, 412
Blind
  early and late blind and reading, 226
  legal definition, 213
  perceptual development, 119
Bloch's law, 263–265
Braille, 221, 227–231
  good and poor readers, 229
  legibility thresholds, 230
Bushmen paintings, 204–205

"Carpentered" visual environment, 4, 123
Cataract removal, 38
Categorical perception, 122, 267
  basic phenomenon, 130–137
  definition, 130–132
Cell assembly
  and repetition effect, 351–352
Chain or split style in pictures, 202–204, 206
Chromatic aberration
  adaptation to, 279–280
Clarity hypothesis
  and repetition effect, 351–352